I0767001

ROBERT MUGABE, KCB

ROBERT MUGABE, KCB

ROBERT MUGABE, KCB

Black Supremacist

Esau Ncube

Copyright © 2020 by Esau Ncube.

Library of Congress Control Number:		2019917130
ISBN:	Hardcover	978-1-7960-6726-2
	Softcover	978-1-7960-6725-5
	eBook	978-1-7960-6724-8

All rights reserved. No part of this book may be reproduced or transmitted in any form or by any means, electronic or mechanical, including photocopying, recording, or by any information storage and retrieval system, without permission in writing from the copyright owner.

Any people depicted in stock imagery provided by Getty Images are models, and such images are being used for illustrative purposes only.
Certain stock imagery © Getty Images.

Print information available on the last page.

Rev. date: 02/12/2020

To order additional copies of this book, contact:
Xlibris
1-888-795-4274
www.Xlibris.com
Orders@Xlibris.com
804208

CONTENTS

"There is a certain people scattered abroad.... Their laws are diverse from those of every people, neither keep they the king's laws, therefore it is not for the king's profit to suffer them".

Dedication

This book is dedicated to the memory of my father George Gray Ncube, my brother Phikelela Moyo and the other one hundred thousand Matabele victims of the 5th Brigade genocide, who were killed by the Zimbabwe government's security forces between 1983 and 1987.

Chapter I

Introduction

The world was watching, the region bore witness, as the new find in the league of statesmen, even before the drums of his inauguration ceremony had subsided, turned against his colleagues like a demented lioness that devours the soft flesh of her own cubs with chisel sharp fangs and iron claws. Thirty - nine years later, today, the devouring orgy continues as human suffering falls short of appeasing ravenous and congenitally angry tribalist demi gods.

The victims, the affected, the foot soldiers and architects of Gukurahundi, both living and dead have a right to know, to be known, to be remembered and to be judged. The perpetrators have an obligation to account. The country and the world must know. The need for resolution and closure keeps getting stronger as the years go by and evidence gets eroded and eaten away by the passage of time.

Tyranny, genocide, crimes against humanity, political violence, vote rigging, elite capture of the state, tribalism, racism, nepotism, corruption, economic incompetence are but a few of the maladies bedeviling Zimbabwe's polity. The strongmen whose policies militated such an unimaginable and unprecedented collapse of the country's body politics, social fabric, ethos and economy, hold on unrelentingly to power with an iron and death grip.

The victims and survivors have never had a conducive truth – telling platform to speak about their experiences, fears, wishes and dreams. They still harbour trauma, anxiety, stress, psychosomatic disorders, nightmares, physical disabilities, morbid anger, distrust, fear, hate and contempt.

The masterminds and perpetrators of the Gukurahundi genocide have never been brought to account, may be in need of psychological therapy, may need an opportunity to own up and clear their consciences before their own inevitable rendezvous with their ultimate destiny.

Then came the sequel to the Gukurahundi genocide: gukurahundism and its ever – in - attendance compatriots; zanuism and mugabeism, sucking in everyone. The survivors of Gukurahundi could only go so far. The wider net of gukurahundism caught up with them together with those that thought they were safe from Gukurahundi. The lucky few who slipped through the openings of the net, battered, bruised and traumatized but hopeful, joined the rest of Zimbabwe that had never experienced Gukurahundi and gukurahundism in a dark jamboree snare of zanuism and mugabeism. Like a plague, the quadrominium trap settled on and swept across Matabeleland and Midlands before encroaching ever so stealthily onto the rest of the country. There is no survivor after the fourth trap door.

No Zimbabwean dead or alive can claim neutrality about the quadrominium trap. None is immune to it, irrespective of age, sex, tribe, race, religion, political affiliation, creed, socio economic status or whatever distinguishing mark they have or think they have. Every Zimbabwean is a involved. Consciously or subconsciously, they are villains, beneficiaries or victims or any of the three in whatever combination. By design, some chose or choose to be villains in the real life tragi - drama. Some opt to be beneficiaries, while some have beneficence and or victimhood thrust upon them. The inclination to claim innocence by many Zimbabweans due to absence or the 'i was not there' fallacy is natural and understandable, yet not good enough, since today they are thrust in the quadrominium trap by virtue of citizenship / residence.

There are some who opted to trudge along the quiet diplomacy route but unwittingly found themselves lumbering down the villains' path. At times the insidious position of quiet diplomacy made them bystanders and therefore inexorably, accomplices to crimes against humanity. Some thought they could hide behind religion and claimed to be blind to the matters of the 'world'. Unwittingly they became accomplices as they became the watchmen that failed to warn the city dwellers of impending danger or the witness that looked the other way.

Gukurahundi, gukurahundism, zanuism and mugabeism, the four demons of Zimbabwe politics are like a cicatrix on a beautiful face of a woman. A scar on a granite rock surface that can only be removed by defacing the rock. The scar has since convoluted into a festering and gangrene infected and cancerous wound that keeps decaying and eating deep into the flesh, while reproducing and replicating itself cancerously over the anatomy that is Zimbabwe. Urgent surgery is now an imperative to peace, stability and development.

The grisly memories and wounds of those who perished in the genocide which was sadistic by its nature and callous by its execution, some of whom were buried dead, some mained and buried alive in shallow graves, others warehoused in mine shafts, some mass - dumped in makeshift graves, some left to rot in the sun and rain, some devoured by scavenging birds and animals of prey and those who were mass-burnt and their ashes blown away by winds or washed away by storm waters over almost four decades, still cry for justice. The sordid quantum impact of the Gukurahundi genocide in terms of deaths, disappearances, injuries, disabilities, trauma, displacement, property loss, missed opportunities, denial of family and social support due to forced separation, is yet to be officially established.

Millions of Zimbabweans scattered around the world as economic and political refugees due to Gukurahundi, gukurahundism, zanuism and mugabeism which are responsible for marginalization, tribal discrimination and domination, the collapse of the economy and political persecution, are suffering daily due to separation from loved ones, loss of a familiar environment, lack of social support systems, as they have to forego many rights as a consequence of living in foreign lands. While the country bleeds, not only the blood of its citizens but its brains too, other countries flourish at Zimbabwe's expense by employing her professionals and her hardworking menial labourers. Zimbabwe's teachers, nurses, doctors, engineers, social workers, economists, athletes, security personnel, waiters, cooks, bankers etc have littered the diaspora for four decades, yet they would rather be in Zimbabwe than contributing to growing foreign economies. All are victims of the quadrominium trap.

A toxic cocktail of ethnic tension and tribal discrimination has taken deep root on the Zimbabwean soil. The sons and daughters of the soil are traversing foreign lands. At home some have degenerated into a hotch - potch of marauding self aggrandizing, tribal, power, rumor and money mongering mafia – style mob.

Should Zimbabweans persist as victims, perpetrators of and or profiteers from the quadrominium trap, they risk a lifetime of continued polarization between Ndebele and Shona. For another hundred years they might be caught up in the clutches of the quadrominium trap like mummified flies trapped in a spider's web: entangled, lifeless, terrified, confused and turning against each other like a troop of baboons under a leopard scare. Until they brace themselves and grab the buffalo bull by the horns, confront their horrific past with renewed resolve, they will bestow on the future generations nothing but a debilitating curse. That is not an abdicable responsibility. If Zimbabweans keep procrastinating and succumbing to the seduction of ZANU PF politics, they will continue to confront their demons apart and therefore stay perennial economic under achievers, political foes and tribally hostile.

While the Ndebele had good reason for saying *'zonelwa mvunye'*, (a crime by one is a crime by all), the belief that the sins of the fathers must be judged on them and not on their sons is more prudent. That creed may vanish or get blurred in the detail of the lines and pages of this book but it will always be there as a sobering reminder and must never be discarded or forgotten, for it is the hinges upon which socio - political sobriety as well as genuine and lasting peace can be founded.

While reading through this book, it is essential to be consistently aware of the following:

a)   One must avoid the simplistic and inaccurate perception of all Shona people as villains, perpetrators and beneficiaries of the quadrominium trap (gukurahundi genocide, gukurahundism, zanuism and mugabeism) and that all Ndebele people are the victims.

b)   Not all Ndebeles were and are dissidents as much as not all of them disapproved of dissidents and dissidentry.

c)   Not all Shonas were and are Gukurahundists and not all of them practice gukurahundism, zanuism and mugabeism, yet not all of them disapproved of Gukurahundi as much as not all of them disapprove of gukurahundism, zanuism and mugabeism today.

d)   Not all Shona people are guilty of the Gukurahundi genocide and the other three evils but many are.

e)   It is the ponderous duty of all Zimbabweans to condemn the quadrominium trap or its individual facets wherever and whenever it occurs but it is also their right to be silent about it.

f)   The quadrominium trap narrative is not about Ndebele and Shona only, as there are other tribes and even countries involved.

The terms Matabele and Ndebele may be used interchangeably, yet Matabele in this book is used (by no means in a bid to undermine the existence of, or ignore the individuality of any distinct and sovereign tribe) to refer to all the tribes of Matabeleland namely, Ndebele, Kalanga, Tonga, Xhosa, Sotho, San, Nambya, Dombe, Venda, Nyanja, Lozwi etc. Ndebele refers to the descendents of people that followed King Mzilikazi from Zululand, those that were assimilated from the Transvaal (South Africa), Barotseland (Zambia), Bechuanaland (Botswana) and Mthwakazi (the land bordered by the Zambezi river, the Limpopo river, the Shashi river and the Jameson Line which ran along the Sanyati and Tokwe rivers) to form a nation which spoke the Ndebele language, used or adopted Ndebele names and symbols and practiced the Ndebele culture and identified themselves as amaNdebele.

Chapter II

Power Maddens

"Rejected by mankind, the condemned do not go so far as to reject it in turn. Their faith in history remains unshaken...They do not despair. The proof: they persist in surviving not only to survive, but to testify. The victims elect to become witnesses"

Elie Wiesel (1928 -). Romanian - born U.S. writer.

Oftentimes in the path of men of clout and influence, there comes a point when they accord themselves or are invariably endowed by their ardent followers the power to deprive others of their rights and the liberty to sanction life and death. They get contemptuous of human life and blind to the agony they inflict. Pleas for mercy only serve to drive them deeper into the sadistic resolve to author suffering and exterminate fellow humans. They elevate themselves to a semi celestial pedestal where other people can only grovel below them and survive on their mercy and patronage. The powerless get reduced to sub - human levels and can therefore be treated with impunity and be deprived of anything from daily basic essentials to life itself with random spite. The whims and caprices of the elite, the rich, the well connected and the powerful, fast blend into reality and even the law. The quest for political capital results in a crescendo of economic looting and lurking. The indispensible distinguishing line between the law of the land and the machinations of the distinguished, quickly gets consumed by the ferocious tide of human greed and malice.

There is something in human nature that causes her to turn against her own self, tearing at her own kind like an angry and ravaging whirlwind intent on extinguishing itself to extinction. Like a tornado that starts in the Sahara desert, rages against the Egyptian pyramids, settles in the shores of Equatorial Guinea, rushes past the streets of Uganda, ravages the Congo forests, threatens to fizzle out years ahead in the Burundi and Rwandan mountains, yet gathers momentum menacingly in Zimbabwe. Something shockingly intolerant, that will not take any prisoners, that preys on even the most insignificant line of diversity. Differences that normally unite people, get exploited in the corridors of power.

Perpetrators of crimes against humanity take to the tumultuous stage as if it were an act in a play. Lives have been wasted at the behest of men in authority for a multiplicity of feeble reasons. At times to assert their authority, to announce their advent or merely because the victims belong to a different race, tribe, religion, region, creed or political party. People get killed on account of an act or omission because it was done or not done by another with something in common with them. Deeds or misdeeds which are at times perceived and never authenticated, provide the death knell to hundreds of thousands of innocents. In Africa too many times mankind has proven to be a danger to herself.

Is it a consequence of absolute power or an inclination for self preservation and survival by the powerful? Is it an inherent desire to agonize and distress or a nurtured habit? Maybe it is an overwhelming sense of self or a hatred of independent life. It can be incapacity to reconcile differences or a basic desire for the punitive and sadistic. Probably it is intolerance of diversity and a detestation of the lesser, the weaker and the few. Is it a loathing of challenge or contempt for dissent? Is it a vociferous appetite for political agendas, social domination, economic marginalization, cultural imperialism or a means to personal aggrandizement or self deitification? Is it vindictiveness for past wrongs or fear of future reprisal? Is it a madness or a malady that preys on the elite and the powerful?

Whatever it is, humankind needs to fast find an antidote, especially in Africa where God has always planted abundant meat but the devil somehow always managed to send the cooks. The cure will rid Africa of such strongmen and despots like Francisco Macias Nguema of Equatorial Guinea, 1968, Col. Obiang Nguema of Equatorial Guinea, 1979, Jean Bedel Bokassa of Central African Republic, 1965, General Joseph Desire Mobuto of Zaire, 1965, Gen Idi Amin Dada of Uganda 1971, Major Mengistu Haile Mariam of Ethiopia, 1974, Hastings Kamuzu Banda, Malawi 1966. A serum needs to be urgently identified for the contemporary crisis in Zimbabwe precipitated by the most sly, oldest and longest serving tyrant of them all, Robert Gabriel Mugabe and his successor and coup plotter Emmerson Dambudzo Mnangagwa.

It was indeed the force that drove Stalin into the most bizarre extension and refinement of his predecessor Lenin's rule. Joseph Vissarionovich Djugashvili popularly known as Stalin commissioned a jaggernaught of mass terror from 1928 until his demise in 1953 (Payne 1965). He presided over the terror apparatus that exhibited utter disregard for empathy, with uncommon proficiency and was devoid of all forms of compunction. Stalin's *"tiger"* mentality during the great chistka of 1937 to 1938 exterminated no less than eight million *"enemies of the people"* (Payne 1965).

The affliction manifested itself again in 1945 at the end of the World War II. The Germany Nazi political party under the marshaldom of the Fuhrer, Adolf Hitler, methodically executed an estimated six million Jews in a demented perennial orgy of gas chambers, firing squads and imprisonment without trial. Thousands of non-Jewish people were killed in pursuit of Hitler's dream of the perfect human race or in retribution for imaginary crimes omitted or committed against his person, his race, his party and his regime. Hitler's fiendish concoction, which was the first to qualify for and to be termed the holocaust was as brutishly vindictive as it was historically unprecedented.

The Khmer Rouge regime's ascent to power in Cambodia (Kampuchea) in 1975 kick - started a ruthless mechanism of murder, torture and psychological abuse of dire corollary. The despotic regime targeted urban dwellers whom they ejected from their town houses and coerced into rural areas where they were forced into menial hard labour. They were made to toil in less than human settings and they died in droves. Four years of harrowing ordeals were like a lifetime in hell for the ordinary Cambodian. When the regime was eventually dethroned in 1979 by the Vietnamese army, three million people had already been killed or had died of sub human treatment in prisons, hospitals and even in the streets and at their homes. By the fall of the regime, Cambodians had been reduced to a people afraid of their own children, spouses, neighbors, themselves and even their own shadows.

After seizing power from Milton Obote through a coup, Ugandan president General Idi Amin Dada CBE (Conqueror of the British Empire) and the self anointed *"King of Scotland"* as he used to affectionately refer to himself, from 1971 to 1978 presided over a period which he and his henchmen shaped with an indelible chisel of cold terror. He turned Uganda into a land of desolation and blood - letting. Initially, thousands of political figures, both opponents and allies perished at his whim. Displaying an atypically inhuman determination to purge all mankind, he on inklings, allegations or trumped - up and malevolent charges ordered the deaths of thousands of Ugandan politicians. Senior government officials and the clergy were not spared either. Condemned with equal reprisal were Obote's Lango and the Acholi tribes people who were killed en masse. By the time he was removed through a coup, the face of Uganda was scarred undyingly from the forehead to the chin by such an atrocious condescension for fundamental human rights. Never before had such distinctive suffering been visited upon a people by their own kind or by any force, natural or otherwise in Africa. By 1978 his victims included two of his cabinet ministers, a chief justice, an archbishop, a university of Makerere vice chancellor and a former reserve bank governor. According to Amnesty International half a million people had died (BBC). Ugandans still pray that they never again witness such dimensions of total anguish and absolute civilian vulnerability.

On 04 April 1994 the Rwandan president Juvenal Habyarimana of the majority Hutu ethnic origin died when his plane was shot down and crashed. He was coming from a meeting with members of the Rwandan Patriotic Front (FPR), a political organization with strong minority Tutsi backing. The death ignited one of the most gory and inhuman events in the history of mankind. An absolute and reckless disregard for human life unprecedented in the entire African continent and the world was unfolding. The world for the first time was to witness a most chilling epoch in the history of tribal conflict. Two days after the death of the president, the macabre killings began. The government army composed of largely Hutu tribesman and a Hutu extremist militant group termed Interahamwe, spearheaded a campaign of unparalleled human slaughter. It lasted a hundred days with an average of eight thousand human deaths per day. The target were the minority Tutsi people and the Rwandan Patriotic Front. By the lapse of one hundred days no less than eight hundred thousand people had perished.

As if not to be out done, Zimbabwe in 1980 gave birth to an independent state whose advent turned out to be a tragedy of undreamt of magnitudes to the people in the west and south west of the country. Matabeleland and Midlands. In a weird scenario of reconciliation, the Robert Mugabe and ZANU PF party - led government, buried the hatchet with former white minority Rhodesian Front regime Prime Minister Ian Smith, his party and security forces personnel. Some of those former Smith regime security personnel were retained in the new government formation. Yet Mugabe condemned 100 000 civilians from Matabeleland and the Midlands provinces to a bitter death and the entire Ndebele nation to an existence of uncertainty and fear. The only - just crowned government failed to accept ZAPU and the Matabeleland tribes who had opposed minority rule with them with equivalent veracity and resolve for twenty years and waged a revolutionary war against a common enemy with them for more than ten years.

The basis for such a calamitous feat are still locked away in a mystery cabinet. The masterminds and schemers are still lurking, dangerous behind a grey veil of confidentiality, political muscle and ethnic hegemony. The damage committed and the suffering experienced are yet to be explored and the quantum determined, thirty - seven years since the onset of the onslaught against civilians whose sin or crime was belonging to a different tribe, speaking a different language, being a minority and supporting the political party of their choice. The Mugabe regime made sure that there was no written record of the genocide, by pulling an iron curtain of secrecy and silence around the killings. Some politicians only referred to the atrocities as a convenient campaign stratagem. Thereafter the issue was allowed to conveniently recline into the subconscious only to be recollected at the next poll-canvassing period.

At the helm of supremacy during the genocide were such Mugabe die hard and hard core loyalists like Emmerson Mnangagwa, Sydney Sekeramayi, Perence Shiri and Rex Nhongo (Solomon Mujuru). The first three, according to Enos Nkala in an interview with VOA Africa radio were the sons of Belial. Strutting and prancing the length and breadth of the corridors of power in Harare, the men wielded immense power and influence. They exhibited a monolithic and mammoth presence. Under their gigantic strides the beleaguered tribes of Matabeleland could only grovel and beg haplessly at their feet. They defended the slaughter of thousands religiously and vigorously with uncanny zealotry and vitriol. Their political and military whims immediately assumed command status and sent shivers into the arid desert - like sands of the entire Matabeleland and Midlands region. Even the casual mention of their names, conjured a portentous resonating cord of terror in the hearts and minds of most Ndebeles, Kalangas, Sothos, Vendas, Xhosas etc. Children in rural areas would scurry and scamper into the bush at the mere sound of an approaching car, afraid it was the government soldiers coming to terrorize everyone.

Mnangagwa, Shiri, Sekeramayi and Mujuru, the firemen, who with staggering mechanical resolve, stridently fed the colossal boiler with human coals. They kept the fires of terror blazing and blistering, with the men, women and children of the Ndebele and Kalanga forfeited as firewood. Religiously, as if under the command of minuscule and invisible demons frantic on their shoulders, they issued orders to weed the land and rid it of the Ndebele and Kalanga as if mowing grass and burning chuff. They were the iron – clad talons that reached out, grabbing former ZPRA soldiers, ZAPU supporters, Kalangas and Ndebeles of all ages and both sexes and shuttered them like dry twigs.

Their claws were the ten security instruments, namely the newly created Zimbabwe National Army (ZNA), the Presidential Guard, the Support Unit, the Zimbabwe Republic Police (ZRP), the Central Intelligence Organization (CIO), the Criminal Investigation Department (CID), Police Internal Security and Intelligence unit (PISI), the Gukurahundi battalion (CCJP and LRF 1997) as well as the ZANU PF Youth Brigade Artillery Regiment and the Zimbabwe People's Militia (Ndlovu – Gatsheni 2002)

The army comprised mostly of former ZANLA combatants and remnants of ZPRA and the Rhodesia army. The commanders of the army were mainly former Rhodisian army and ZANLA, despite the latter's known inferior training. Within no time those that were at divergent views with ZANU ideology which was always profoundly predisposed by ZANLA, were compelled to tow the line or merely cowed into servitude. Hundreds of former ZPRA were surreptitiously eliminated.

Surprisingly, while the former ZPRA guerrillas were treated with suspicion and palpable contempt, to the former Rhodesian Defense Forces (RDF) elements, was extended an olive branch that fooled the world including the Queen of England, Elizabeth II, into endorsing the autocratic regime as a democracy. The former Rhodesian security personnel were incorporated into the army and the CIO.

The dreaded CIO which was as fierce as it was mysterious in its operations and could only be paralleled by Hitler's Gestapo, was referred to as The President's Office, because it was accountable to the President directly. The Gukurahundi also operated outside the army chain of command and it reported directly to the president. The proverbial long arm of the law transmuted into a grotesque and ghastly caricature with ten horrific state security fingers that crafted an unnaturally malevolent, powerful and demonic hand that was employed to torture, maim and crush the people of Matabeleland and the Ndebele speaking parts of Midlands. Such tough security muscle had never been flexed even by Mugabe's predecessor, the kingpin of white minority rule, Ian Smith. For a population of ten million, such a rigorous security regimen could only be a toxic and insidious recipe for high- handedness and barefaced tyranny.

Although the North Korean trained and equipped battalion was called Gukurahundi by Mugabe in 1981, that was not the first time the concept, principle and experience of Gukurahundi had occurred in Zimbabwe. According to Sithole and Makumbe (1997), Mugabe had in 1979 declared that year *"gore reGukurahundi"*, meaning the year of the storm that would *"annihilate"* everything in its wake. They further asserted that indeed the *"momentum of Gukurahundi swept Mugabe and his party to power in the independence election in 1980"* with ZANLA being the implementing arm of the annihilating storm. Sithole and Mukombe were talking about the raw terror that ZANLA unleashed on the Shona supporters of ZAPU just before the 1980 elections and the intra party purges that resulted in the death of the legendary ZANLA commander Josiah Tongogara in 1979.

In celebrating the victory of the 5th brigade (Gukurahundi) a multi storey building was constructed in the central business district of the capital. It was named *Karigamombe* in praise of Robert Mugabe. *Karigamombe* is a Shona term meaning one who has slaughtered the bull. The bull was ever a symbol of power, prosperity and wealth within Ndebele society since the days of Zululand, Shaka, Mzilikazi and Lobhengula. The black bull was revered as a spiritual being, representing *amadlozi*, the ancestral spirits who communicated with God on behalf of the Ndebele people. Once ensconced with the status of *inkomo yamadlozi* (the cow of the ancestors) the bull became sacrosanct and would not be yoked, whipped or even kraaled, if he opted not to go into the byre. He would not be slaughtered and would die of old age or other natural causes. If on the rare occasion, there was need to slaughter it, a ritual would be done in order to transfer the *amadlozi* onto another before it was put down.

The black charging bull was the symbol of ZAPU. When celebrating their electoral victory in 1985, despite losing all seats in Matabeleland, ZANU supporters provocatively slaughtered many black bulls in the region and ate the meat in victory rallies. Symbolically, by felling the black bull, the ZANU government had accomplished a feat of unprecedented and unimaginable dimension. They had not only destroyed ZAPU and the spirit of resistance and dissipated the power, confidence, prosperity and wealth of Matabeleland but had killed the representative of the ancestral spirits. The spirits would turn their back on the Ndebele nation. It was beyond political victory but a social, economic and cultural conquest. ZAPU, Matabeleland and parts of the Midlands were set to experience the full meaning of the loss. That initial loss symbolized the marginalization the region was subjected to for decades to come.

A hundred years earlier the Anglo-Ndebele war had shattered Ndebele pride by decimating the king's royal regiment and captured the King's cattle including *inkomo yamadlozi*. This time around, in the absence of war, a black authority had shattered the very spirit of the nation, thereby epitomizing and personifying its goal, the end of the Matabele nation as a factor in the socio-economic-politico and cultural landscape.

The transition from minority rule to majority rule paradoxically turned out to be a curse, an albatross, gruesome, fratricidal, heavy and deadly around the neck of

Matabeleland. Ironically, 'freedom' hauled the region's people down the depths of poverty, deprivation, domination and marginalization. It became a transition from white minority racism to black apartheid and tribalism championed by ZANU despotism under the indomitable guise of democracy and majority rule. Independence became a bizarre 'upgrade' from repression by the minority to subjugation by the majority, like jumping into the sea to run from the rain. Unbelievably, in Matabeleland, independence dragged the educated and the illiterate and inumerate, the professional and the novice, the city dweller and the villager, the saint and the sinful, the politician and the pious, the freedom fighter and the collaborator, all in one fell swoop, down an abyss of hopelessness and despair. Robert Mugabe and ZANU became to Matabeleland a horrified mirror image of Ian Smith and the Rhodesian Front.

While Mashonaland was ecstatic about independence, Tsholotsho, Gwayi, Lupane, Binga, Beitbridge, Zhombe, Silobela, Insiza, Nyamandlovu, Gwanda, Mbembesi, Bubi, Filabusi, Matobo, Plumtree, Gokwe, Hwange, etc were being consumed by the raging flames and choking smoke of ZANU nationalism in a new colonialism. As observed by Barber (2017), *"Matabeleland was inherited by Zimbabwe as a colonil gift. This irresponsible decolonization process placed Matabeleland under another, more ruthless ethnic domination. The people of Matabeleland found themselves silently sleep - walking their way to eventual extinction".*

The spectre of black subduing fellow black was not feasible from a distance, therefore not so worrisome an idea after all, more so since the Africans had fought white minority rule claiming to be one and seemingly homogenous in identity and purpose. However unbeknown to most, just before *uhuru* in 1980 the 'sons and daughters of the soil' realized they did not spring forth from the same ground and soil after all. They went their separate ways. While some of the Shona population was abidingly innocent and viewed their Matabeleland compatriots as equals, the political leadership and the ZANU activists harboured rancorous discrimination for their western countrymen and women.

Although constitutionally, the Zimbabwe state after independence embodied nationalist aspirations, the practice was something else. The Matabele were excluded from mainstream economics and political decision making of the land. The police, the army, the public service, the courts, the attorney general's department and even parliament were designed to entrench and pioneer the interests of the majority Shona at the expense of the minority ethnic Matabele.

Albert Camus must have had Mugabe and his aristocrats in mind when he postulated that *"every revolutionary ends up becoming either an oppressor or a heretic*", or both, he could have added. Those men that had so ardently and passionately preached multi party ism, democracy, freedom, human rights and the equality of all men irrespective of tribe, colour or creed, outlandishly mutated and metamorphosed into gods, spewing and spitting fire, brimstone and all the curses in the book, on ethnic minorities. Their speeches were punctuated by comparisons of their leader with God or God - like prowess. Their fury swept across Matabeleland furtively and indiscriminately washed away all, the good, the bad and the ugly, like an aggrieved tidal wave that drowns fishing vessels, men, fish and debris in one ferocious gust.

According to the Chronicle (5 April 1983), Emmerson Mnangagwa when addressing residents in Matabeleland North decided to done a godly cloak and delivered a tendentious sermon, albeit devoid of all Godliness when he threatened, *"blessed are they who will follow the path of government laws, for their days on earth shall be increased. But woe unto those who will choose the path of collaboration with dissidents for they will certainly shorten their stay on earth".* As if usurping the holy scriptures was not enough, Mnangagwa was to later directly assume the role of life giver more specifically when he avowed, *"I will shorten on earth the stay of any cockroaches that oppose Mugabe".* This became Mnangagwa's admission that as far as ZANU was concerned, opposing Mugabe reduced one to cockroach status. That status spelt death by some kind of fumigation or other.

That was at a time when all Matabeleland and the Ndebele speaking parts of Midlands were anti Mugabe and ZANU. That meant that to them, Matabeleland and Midlands were home to the dirty pest, or simply that the Matabele were cockroaches and Mnangagwa was going to shorten their stay on 'his' earth. When Mugabe described ZAPU and Nkomo as a *"cobra"* that had to be dismembered, he too was agreeing with his lieutenant and giving a more than tacit permission to anyone who could, to hunt ZAPU down and kill them like they would a venomous viper.

Indeed, Mugabe and ZANU had amassed so much potency they could play God, by giving and taking life at their whim. By their word of mouth and not even by the famous stroke of a pen, thousands would soon perish at their behest. Fellow citizens who only yesterday had been preaching adherence to the tenets of the American Declaration of Independence, the United Nations Charter on Human and People's Rights and the International Convention against Torture, had turned killers of the Matabele. ZAPU, in shock witnessed their former comrades readily tossing through the window, those world and time treasured manuscripts of the UN and USA. They shuddered to see ZANU and the State arming their foot soldiers with the entire arsenal of torture instruments left behind by the retreating Smith regime and setting them upon civilians.

The people of both Matabeleland and Mashonaland cringed as Mugabe and his tribal retinue unabashedly collapsed the new state into a fiefdom, a private and exclusive conservarotarium, owned by a deified despot, run by vicious bull terriers - like hatchet men and tribal gate keepers. Atypical of cultism, national resources were surrogated into personal asserts for auctioning as trophies for personal aggrandizement. The elite got fat and a few crumbs fell from the rich feeding trough for Mashonaland to pick. As for Matabeleland she had naught but memories of a bitter but better colonial past of being called kaffir on a full stomach and probably being arrested and be issued with a detention order by a minority government. Now they were called comrade by one corner of the mouth and dissident by the other corner, incarcerated without due process, tortured in detention and murdered like rabid dogs by a majority government.

The ZAPU leadership sounded the Corte Devorean, Houp' Pouet Boigny's alarm, *"it is not the shell of independence that counts, it is the contents that count, the economic contents, the social contents, the human contents"* (Meredith 2005). No one heard the alarm.

Independence became an empty dry shell and a poisoned chalice for Matabeleland. For the Matabele, independence surprisingly turned into a nightmarish apparition symbolizing a gonzo transition from white colonialism to Shona nationalism, marshaled by an aloof magisterial autocrat, presiding over a majoritarian regime. Mhlanga (2009) decried that sorry condition when he observed that, *"little did we know that the political and socio - cultural descriptors of 'independence' and 'freedom' which we had embraced, would not apply universally to all Zimbabweans. The mistaken assumption of most Zimbabweans was that independence meant freedom and vice versa.... Independence and liberation were, for the Ndebele people, synonymous with suffering. We had been turned into beasts of burden and we understood the true yearning for freedom"*. Irrefutably, it was a case of *vae victis*, for Matabeleland.

Dr. Obert Mpofu (ZANU PF Secretary for Administration) agreed with Mhlanga that independence resulted in *"suffering"* for Matabeleland when he wrote in the Sunday News weekly of 14 July 2019 that, *"the independence of many African states in the continent signaled the gradual end of a century of oppressive white colonial rule...Although this came with real joy for Africa....some of these African countries unfortunately plunged into ethnic and tribal conflicts....the end of suffering as a result of the end of colonial rule, but also the beginning of suffering as a result of ethnic and political divisions....Like the fate of many African countries, the independence (of Zimbabwe) quickly resulted in a sharp ethnic and political division. The hallmark of this was the escalation of this deep rooted ethnical and political division into a sharp crisis which became known as Gukurahundi".*

Joshua Nkomo echoed that predicament of the Matabele, when he wrote; *"I have learnt this late in life, that a people can gain independence and still remain not free"* (Nkomo 1999). Matabeleland was beleaguered, not free. Those countries like the UK, that could make a difference claimed to be focussing on helping establish what they termed a stable government in Zimbabwe. However, they soon found themselves abetting a blood thirsty dictatorship in the name of the majority. Matabeleland was once more destined for another eon of oppression, this time at the injunction of the majority fellow black people and not the minority white people. As they discarded the yoke of colonialism, the Matabele assumed the burden of freedomless independence and adorned it like the tunic of Nessus (the poisoned gift shirt given by Nessus to Hercules which caused the latter's death)

Chapter III

FOUNDATIONS OF CONFLICT

"on 24 March 1896 'the Ndebele abandoned soft words . . . and came to Bulawayo with assegais in their hands'. By the evening of 30 March, not a white man was left alive in the outlying districts of Matabeleland, and by mid-April, Bulawayo was almost entirely surrounded".

Austin (1975:25)

Matabeleland is the region in the southwest of present day Zimbabwe, stretching from the Zambezi River in the north west for hundreds of kilometres up to the Limpopo river to the south. Matabeleland is inhabited mainly by the Bantu-speaking Ndebele, Xhosa, Sotho, Kalanga, Venda, Tonga, Nambya, San, Lozwi, Lubale, Nyanja/Chewa and Dombe peoples. The region includes the southwestern part of the country's High and Middle velds and it is a plateau area that ranges in elevation from 3,000 to 5,000 feet (900 to 1,500 m). Matabeleland is a largely savanna or tropical grassland region with wooded savanna areas as well (American Heritage Dictionary 2000).

It boasts of the Beitbridge border post, the gateway to the exceedingly rich Republic of South Africa and also the busiest inland port of entry and exit south of the Sahara. It is also home to the Plumtree and Victoria Falls ports of entry which are the second and third busiest in the country. The region measuring approximately 181 605 square kilometres is endowed with an amazing assortment of mineral deposits that include gold, coal, tin, limestone, quartz and methane gas. It is also home to dense forests of world class hardwood timber, rivers including the mighty Zambezi on which is the world's largest waterfalls, the Victoria Falls. It has the country's biggest game reserve, the Hwange National Park with a wildlife population that includes the famous big five (elephant, rhino, buffalo, lion and leopard).

Present day Zimbabwe is home to a heterogeneity of tribes. There are over 20 tribes which include, Chewa, Dombe, Kalanga, Karanga, Korekore, Lozwi, Lubale, Manyika, Nambya, Ndau, Ndebele, San (abaThwa), Sotho, Shangani, Tonga, Venda, Xhosa and Zezuru. Due to cultural and linguistic similarities, geographic locations and ethnic sympathies as well as historiographical dimensions, these tribes can be classified into two major groupings. The Matabele (Ndebele, Xhosa, Tonga, Shangani, Kalanga, Nambya, Venda, Sotho, Dombe, Lozwi, Lubale, San) and Shona (Zezuru, Karanga, Manyika, Korekore). The Ndau who were more Ndebele than Shona were usually classified as Shona due geographical and political factors. The Nyanja / Chewa are not easily classifiable since they are very recent and mostly economic immigrants from Zambia and Malawi. They migrated in small family or individual groups and tended to settle anywhere in the country. They normally identified themselves with the dominant ethnic group in the area of their residence and therefore some are Matabele and some are Shona.

While the tribes under the Matabele kraal are distinct individual entities with dissimilar languages, cultures and histories and most of them were components of the Mthwakazi state (Maphenduka 2015), the Shona groups (Karanga, Zezuru, Manyika and Korekore) are dialects of the same people sharing a common history and a largely similar language.

There is debate on where the Shona came from and when they arrived in present day Mashonaland. Other historians say they arrived during the 1700s while some like Berlyn (1978), say they are descendents of a people that migrated southwards from the area of Lake Tanganyika between the 8th and 14th centuries in small numbers. According to Maphenduka (2015) the Shona are made of groups that migrated from Malawi and Tanzania. Nyathi (2005) concurred that the Shona migrated from Tanzania. It is said by some that by the 11th century, the Shona had fully settled in present day Mashonaland. On arrival they displaced the Khoisan / San people who had inhabited the territory for thousands of years. It is alleged that the name 'Shona' was given to the peoples of the Mwene Mutapa (Monomotapa / Munhu Mutapa) confederacy to the east and the Rozvi confederacy to the west of 1890 Mashonaland, by the Nguni. Some say the name was given to them by some white traders.

History has it that the Tonga were already occupying the Zambezi plateau while the Kalanga, Nambya and Venda peoples were already settled in present day

Matabeleland, parts of Midlands and Masvingo as the Mambo Dynasty, when the Shona peoples arrived and settled to the east.

By the time of the arrival of the Ndebele in 1839, the two Shona empires had been broken by the first Zulus that came and went (Thomas 1996). The Rozvi empire had been shattered and their last Mambo (King) had been killed by Zwangendaba, another of King Shaka's generals who was fleeing northwards. (Austin 1975, Mabhena 2014).

Mitchell (1960:178) held that the Shona were a *"patrilineal, cattle-keeping, weak chieftancy, rain cults"*. They were a deeply religious people to whom spirit mediums occupied a very senior stratum in society. The Shona were ardent cultivators of the land, traders, with metal working and stone building skills and to a lesser extent, pastoralists. They traded with the Indians and Portuguese in the coast of Mozambique. From 1830 they started to experience a string of raids from as far afield as Zululand. Their grain, cattle and women constituted the bulk of the booty for the invaders. They suffered raids from the Ndebele under King Lobhengula more than under his father and predecessor King Mzilkazi (Maphenduka 2015).

The remnants of the Rozvi confederacy could hardly be organized into resisting the Ndebele from establishing their kingdom in the territory (Alexander, McGregor and Ranger 2000). The adept nation builder King Mzilikazi quickly assimilated some of the Shona groups and together with other tribes built a powerful and flourishing military kingdom (Beach 1986).

The Ndebele are a nation built by King Mzilikazi in the 19th century. Mzilikazi Khumalo (1792 /1790 - 1868) was born in Nquthu / Ndinaneni in Zululand. He rose to the rank of *induna* (chief) of the Khumalo clan in 1816 after the death of his father Matshobana. He soon saught refuge from the King of the Ndwandwe, Zwide Nxumalo who had gruesomely killed Matshobana, by submitting himself and his people under the reign of King Shaka Gumede of the Zulu. He became a gallant warrior and influential leader under King Shaka. King Shaka promoted Mzilikazi to *induna yempi* (major general equivalent in modern terms).

King Shaka however soon distrusted Mzilikazi and endeavoured to have him killed in battle (Nyathi 2005). In the face of a strained relationship, in 1821 Mzilikazi rebelled against his mentor and master. Mzilikazi had opted to break away from the custom of surrendering all war booty to the king by keeping a head of beautiful cattle for himself. That being an offence punisheable by death, King Shaka dispatched a regiment to reposess the cattle and deal with Mzilikazi. After the battle, Mzilikazi who could not wait for another attack by Shaka, was impelled to flee. Taking with him an army of two to three hundred trusted warriors (Sagay and Wilson 1978, Ndlovu, Ndlovu and Ncube 1995), Mzilikazi left his kraal at the Ngome forest north east of modern day Durban heading northwards in a frantic bid to distance himself as much as possible from the wrath of King Shaka. Mzilikazi was installed as king in the Transvaal and by the time his people crossed the Limpompo, he was a fully fledged monarch.

That became a period of conquest and nation building for King Mzilikazi and his warriors. They fought, defeated and subdued the tribes they found on their way. The defeated who included the Sotho, Tswana, Xhosa, Fengu, Kololo, the Venda and later the Kalanga, Tonga, Nambya (Mambo dynasty), San, Lozwi and the Karanga (Rozvi confederacy) were assimilated into the new nation. However, King Mzilikazi did not only use conquest to expand his group to a large nation, but negotiation and persuasion with those groups that were amenable to peaceful conciliation. That technique of nation building had been used by King Shaka when he was founding the Zulu kingdom. Having learnt at Shaka's feet the art of arbitration by the assegai as well as the skill of negotiation, Mzilikazi horned the two to perfection as he enlarged his group.

With the dreaded assegais, the knobkerries, the massive shields, the fierce war cry "*ngadla*" and war dances, they vanquished and scattered their victims. Mzilikazi went past present day Pretoria and the Transvaal where they were given the name Matebele (long shields) by the Sotho. In January 1837, Mzilikazi and his growing nation left the Transvaal after a surprise attack by a band of Boers which left them depleted and demoralised. They headed into Bechuanaland (Botswana), through the Makgadikgadi pan and the Okavango Delta. They crossed the Chobe river into Barotseland (Zambia) before turning back into present day Victoria Falls and headed in a south easterly course towards what was to be the all time capital of Matabeleland, Bulawayo. The area was inhabited by the BaKalanga, many of whom were assimilated into King Mzilikazi's nation.

In search of a good pastoral land with plenty grass and water for the cattle, they went past the Gwayi catchment area until they set up the capital at Mzingwane and called it Gibixhegu in 1839. The King's capital changed a number of times until King Lobhengula set his capital in Bulawayo in present day Matabeleland, Zimbabwe. The place still bears the name Bulawayo to this day. The territory to the east was called *izwe lamaTshona* (Mashonaland) because it was inhabited by the Shona (Karanga, Korekore, Zezuru, Manyika). By that time Mzilikazi's band of warriors had grown to a nation and his head of cattle had become a national asset and a source of great pride. He called his new state *uMthwakazi*. The people of the new nation were called Matebele by the Sotho but Mzilikazi and his people corrupted the name Matebele into Ndebele in line with their lingual rhyme and rhythm.

The Ndebele state was a large, ethically diverse yet centralized kingdom with a military set up of garrisons (eg. Nyamayendlovu which is still there in Matabeleland North province) stationed far away from the capital, in all directions. Each garrison was under the command of *induna yebutho* (modern day colonel). The *induna yebutho* had a regiment (eg, *uZwangendaba, iNsukamini, amaBhukudwane, aMhlophe* etc) made up of 800 to 1000 soldiers who protected the community in the garrison. The regiment was the equivalent of modern day infantry battalion. There was strict discipline within the regiments. In addition to guard duties the soldiers performed ceremonial parades, police duties as well as tax collection. That was the social and military arrangement that King Mzilikazi brought into Mthwakazi.

There are different versions as to the origins of the name *Mthwakazi*. According to Maphenduka (2015), it was in honour of the local queen Muthwa of the San people who inhabited the area. Some say the name was derived from the Ndebele term *umbuthwa* which means a collection. Then the term *kazi* which means massive, was added to mean a massive collection of peoples as u*Mbuthwakazi*. Gradually the term was shortened to *Mthwakazi*.

According to Nyathi (2005), when Mzilikazi arrived in present day Matabeleland he found Queen Nyamazana Dlamini (who had brocken ranks with Zwangendaba Jele on his northward march away from King Shaka) already presiding over a state called *Mthwakazi*. As a negotiation strategy, Mzilikazi married Queen Nyamazana and maintained the name *Mthwakazi*. What is not in dispute however is that the Ndebele and *uMthwakazi* were both pacific and aggressive. The nation was clearly an amalgam of various ethnic groups bonded together by a combination of conquest, compromise, convenience, negotiation and consent.

Upon sojournaying in Mthwakazi, the new nation amassed more potency and confidence as they carried out frequent raids into the surrounding regions. The *impis* (warriors) under King Mzilikazi's son King Lobhengula, at times marched and conquered the neigboring lands and tribes and captured cattle, grain, young men for integration into the army and ordinary people for assimilation and nation building. At times in their trail the *impis* left desolation, devastation and misery amid the scanty remains. Once assimilated these people were taught the language, culture, customs and traditions of Mzilikazi and his people. Some tribes that were too far away to be vanquished and incorporated, paid periodic tribute to the King through cattle, grain, metal, iron products etc.

In 1829 at Mosega, king Mzilikazi had accepted as a friend, the missionary Robert Moffat (Mtshede), the founder of the London Missionary Society (LMS) which was later known as the United Congregational Church of Southern Africa (UCCSA). The missionary was to subsequently establish the first Christian mission station in the kingdom in 1859. In 1889 the first missionary school (present day Inyathi High School) was founded at the then Ndebele capital some 68 km to the north of present day Bulawayo. Despite the king's warm attitude towards Moffat, the kingdom discouraged the Ndebele from converting to Christianity and attending the white men's school. However, that stance was not law and those that wanted could be part of the new religious and educational set-up.

Some historians claim that some of the assimilated were eager to be converted to Christianity and be educated by the white men since they were in search of a new life. They therefore sought solace, succour and strength in a superior than human deity, probably in line with Karl Marx's observation that religion was the opium of the masses. The Ndebele were more of warriors than a religious society and converting them to any religion was always going to be a toll order, therefore the majority of initial converts to Christianity were the assimilated that were recent recruits / arrivals into the Ndebele nation.

The Ndebele in their might and valour saw little if any benefit from the white men's education. It was that early that the Ndebele proved to be less accommodative to the way of life of the westerners. It was also at that initial stage that the colonialists showed preference for the people of the neighboring state of Mashonaland who were more keen to accept the whitemen's religion and their way of life.

Mzilikazi, a most stern warrior who could only be equated to his former master and military guru King Shaka of Zululand, died of natural causes on 09 September 1868. By the time of his death his sons included Mangwana begotten by MaDlodlo, Muntu begotten by MaSiwela, Qalingana begotten by Masuku, Lopila begotten by MaFuyane and Nkulumana whose mother was Mwaka Zwide Nxumalo (Nyathi 2005). Mzilikazi was succeeded by his son Lobhengula whose mother was Fulatha Tshabalala. Lobhengula turned out to prefer diplomacy than military aggression in his relations with whitemen.

Lobhengula ascended to the thrown in 1870 after a bitter civil war with one of his father's valiant chiefs, Mbiko Masuku. The heroic Masuku had preferred Lobhengula's half and elder brother Nkulumana Khumalo to succeed Mzilikazi but when the former could not be found in Zululand where his father had banished him, Masuku decided to wrestle the throne from Lobhengula. Masuku's primary objection to Lobhengula's ascendency as he put it, was that Lobhengula was a half breed and not pure Nguni since his mother was Swazi from the house of King Sobhuza I (Sibanda 1981, Nyathi 2005). Two years after King Mzilkazi's death, Lobhengula became King in 1870.

In 1885 King Lobhengula signed a Peace Treaty with Paul Kruger of the Boer Republic in the Transvaal. In July 1887 the Ndebele king signed yet another treaty with Pieter Grobbler a representative of Paul Kruger. The treaty established the Limpompo river as the boundary between Mthwakazi and the Transvaal to the south of Bulawayo. That boundary still stands to this day.

On 11 February 1888 the King signed another treaty of *"Peace and Unity"* with John Moffat who represented the British government. The treaty was ratified on 25 June 1888 by Sir Hercules Robinson, governor of the Cape Colony on behalf of Lord Salisbury the then Prime Minister of Britain. The treaty recognised the boundary between the Mthwakazi Kingdom and the British protectorate of Bechuanaland (Botswana) as the Shashi river to the west and south west of Bulawayo. That boundary still stands to this day.

The boundary with the British Barotseland (Zambia) to the north of the Ndebele Kingdom was set as the Zambezi river, hence the arrangement between King Lobhengula and Charles Dunell Rudd who represented the British government in the Rudd Concession of 1888 to position a steam boat with guns for defence of Mthwakazi for the King, on the Zambezi river (Thomas 1996). That boundary still stands to this day.

On 30 October 1888 King Lobhengula appended his signature to a document called The Rudd Concession. Charles Dunell Rudd affixed his signature on behalf of the B.S.A Company. The concession granted the company *"complete and exclusive charge over all metals and minerals situated and contained in my kingdom, principalities and dominions, together with full power to do all things that they deem necessary to win and procure the same.."* Since the king could not read, he relied on the interpretation by the settlers. Unknowingly, yet in good faith, the king was inveigled into granting sweeping powers to the concessionaires for them to do whatever was in their power to achieve their mining objectives.

In return the King was to receive 1000 Martini – Henry rifles, 100 000 rounds of ammunition, a steam boat with guns for defensive purposes on the Zambezi river and £100 per month. The £100 stipend was soon termed *"blood money"* by the King when he was repudiating the Rudd Concession a few months later. Cecil John Rhodes used the concession document to obtain a Royal Charter from the British government in October 1889. The charter gave his company permission to govern the area of the Rudd Concession while developing the area at no cost to the British government. Verbal guarantees during the Rudd Concession negotiations had been given to the king that only ten or less white men would come into his territory (Thomas 1996). There clearly was absent a *consensus ad idem* and little did the King realise that he was dealing with unscrupulous and dishonest men whose thrust was conquest and plunder. Shortly they would march on the king's lands with some 652 heavily armed whitemen and 652 Shona batmen. So much for the promise of not more than ten whitemen.

When the Pioneer Column marched into present day Zimbabwe, the corps, police and the Bechuanaland contingents deliberately steered clear of Matabele territories. They made sure that the closest they came to a Matebele Kraal was 100 miles. On 13 September 1890 the British South Africa Company (BSAC), a company owned by Cecil John Rhodes, raised the Union Jack flag at Fort Salisbury to mark the occupation of Mashonaland. The column established forts at Victoria (Masvingo), Charter and Salisbury (Harare). Celebrating his achievement, Rhodes stated, *"(w)ithout firing a single shot we have occupied probably the richest gold –field in the world, with the acquiescence of the natives…"* (Thomas 1996:220). In May 1891 Britain declared a protectorate over Mashonaland (Austin 1975).

In the process of colonizing Mashonaland, Rhodes and the B.S.A. Company pretended and misrepresented that the Rudd Concession gave them the authority to occupy the territory, yet they knew that King Lobhengula's kingdom did not include the area they occupied. The King had also not given them a mandate to set up a government in Mashonaland or within his lands for that matter. Still King Lobhengula did not militarily resist the occupation of Mashonaland because it was not part of his kingdom, although he did wield influence on those Mashonaland chieftaincies within the reach of his *impis* and considered them as his subjects. Those beyond the reach of the *impis* did not consider themselves his subjects either (Vambe 1972).

On 15 June 1891, King Lobhengula signed the last of his peace treaties with Leander Starr Jameson representing the British government. The treaty recognized and reaffirmed the boundary to the east of the Mthwakazi state with the Mashonaland protectorate as what became known as the Jameson Line. The Jameson Line ran along the Sanyati river, the Tokwe river and the Shashi river (Maphenduka 2015). Thomas (1996) confirms the existence of the Mthwakazi boundary along the Shashi and Tokwe rivers and that it passed through Fort Victoria [Fort Victoria

(Masvingo) was, as intimated by Thomas, positioned along the boundary between Matabeleland and Mashonaland so it could be used as a pretext for invading King Lobhengula's kingdom later]. That boundary was deliberately violated by the B.S.A. Company on 3 November 1893 when they raided Mthwakazi. Thenceforth all successive British and Zimbabwe governments took turns to continue violating the boundary by pretending it never existed and by erasing it from their books of history.

From 1890 until the second Ndebele - Anglo war of 1896, the British had cordial and harmonious relations with the various Shona communities. The Shona were found to be very acquiescent as observed by Thomas (1996) who summerised them as the *"gentle Shona"* while the Ndebele he described as *"one of the most formidable warrior nations on the continent"*. Faced with those two contrasting nation characters, the British opted to befriend the amenable Shona.

Many of the Shona readily converted to Christianity and embraced a western life style much to the censure and mortification of their spirit mediums Sekuru Kaguvi and Mbuya Nehanda. Some argued that part of the reasons for their conversion was that they felt the white men would be a lesser evil compared to the Ndebele who constantly raided them for tribute, cattle and grain. As a result, most first black policemen, servants, converts, porters, teachers etc were of Shona origion.

Tindall (1968:161) observed that when the Ndebele - Anglo war of 1893 broke out, both parties had been agitating for it for a while. On the part of the Ndebele it was the *amajaha*, the young warriors that were itching to wield the devastating assegai against the 'arrogant' whitemen who were after their land. On the part of the British, it was the entire senior structure of the BSAC, B.S.A. Police, lords and lieutenants. As noted by Thomas (1996), in a correspondence to Lord Rothschild, Cecil John Rhodes stated, *"the Matabele King is the block to Central Africa... once we have his territory, the rest is easy...if we get Matabeleland we shall get the balance of Africa"*.

In reference to the Ndebele, John Moffat (son of Robert Moffat, the whiteman most trusted by King Mzilikazi) who was the assistant commissioner of the Bechuanaland protectorate, in 1888 weighed in with his indictment, *"until there has been a breaking up of the Matabele power....it will be a blessing to the world when they are broken up...I am sure their days are numbered"*. Not to be outdone was Sidney Shippard, the Commissioner of Bechuanaland who aired his dream in the most eeirie of terms when he avowed, *"..it would offer me sincere and lasting satisfaction if I could see the Matabele...cut down by our rifles and machine guns like a cornfield by a reaping machine".* It was very hard to reconcile such speech with men that claimed to be conduits of christianity and civilization.

Maphenduka (2015) in turn posited that, spoiling for war, Leander Starr Jameson ordered the assassination of Prince Mgandane (King Lobhengula's brother in – law) and 600 of his soldiers as they inspected the royal head of cattle at the Nuanetsi Royal Ranch near Fort Victoria on the border with the British Mashonaland Protectorate. Thomas (1996) asserted that a Captain Lendy, an ever trigger happy officer of the BSAP, with 38 mounted men gunned Prince Mgandane Dlodlo down together with 60 warriors in cold blood.

On 3 November 1893, the Ndebele Mthwakazi state was invaded by her neighbor, the British Mashonaland protectorate. The Ndebele nation fought and lost the war against the pioneer column force of the British South Africa Company (BSAC) under the command of Leander Starr Jameson, an employee of Cecil John Rhodes and a representative of the British government and Queen of England. The king's personal body guards, the crack Imbizo regiment (6255 strong) led four other battalions at the Battle of Mbembesi known as eGadade in Mbembesi, some 32 kilometers out of Bulawayo along present day Harare road. The Imbizo, Ingubo and three other regiments succumbed to superior weapons of war that included five Maxim machine guns (used for the first time against the Ndebele *impis*), three other machine guns, two 7 – pound field pieces and the Martini-Henry rifles. 6000 *amabutho* were killed in the four months - long battle while the BSAC soldiers suffered fewer casualties. Superior weaponry carried the day in a war where the BSAC mercenaries were bolstered by 652 Shona batmen. (Maphenduka 2015).

A depiction of the 1893 war at the Bulawayo museum shows the B.S.A. Company columns in the laager, which was a defensive arrangement of the wagons in a rectangular format so that the British soldiers were shooting at their targets from behind them. The columns comprised the V, S and N columns for Victoria, Salisbury and *"Mashona camp followers"* in that order.

Under Allan Wilson who promised each of his recruits 6000 acres of land anywhere in Matabeleland, 20 gold claims and a share of the loot, and Major Forbes, the invaders marched to Bulawayo in the most barbaric bloodletting. They burnt everything in their wake, raped women and executed the elderly. They crushed all resistance they encountered from the remnants of the king's armies and executed prisoners of war and the injured. When they got to the Royal palace in Bulwayo, only the King and his personnal bodyguards were missing. The King had fled south westerly. The ordinary day to day resident population of 25 000 to 30 000 was still there and every structure was intact. Major Forbes' soldiers razed the capital to the ground. They burnt all the food reserves and gunned down many cattle. Almost half of the capital's population were killed by the British soldiers. Those they did not burn or bludgeon to death, they shot.

Many were scattered far and wide from Bulawayo but most could not get away. Three massive squatter camps of thousands desperate, hungry, sick, injured and scared residents of Bulawayo, emerged some few kilometres around the King's palace. Within days, there was a food crisis. Many died of starvation and disease. All in all, approximately 12 000 elderly men, women and children were sacrificed to the god of British imperial interests to mark the great fall of the Ndebele Kingdom.

Bulawayo was burnt down by the B.S.A. Company army to conceal evidence of the most horric and barbaric slaughter in colonial times, orchestrated in the name of the Queen of England by a 'civilized' army of men claiming to be followers of God. King Lobhengula was pursued by Allan Wilson up to the Lupane area. Wilson was killed by the King's bodyguards commanded by *induna* Mtshana Khumalo as he closed in on them on the banks of the Tshangane river at the battle of ePupu. The King died presumably in 1893/94 at an unknown location and the site of his grave and remains were kept permanently secret. Some Ndebele traditionalists claimed that King Lobhengula disappeared upon crossing the Tshangane river.

It is probable that the King died at the ePupu battle and the story of him disappearing was created in order to preserve the dignity of the monarchy and not to demoralize the nation and *amabutho* (regiments). Since that story was agreed upon by the King's surviving body guards who were sworn to confidentiality regarding the King's affairs, it was perpetuated successfully. Nobody could tell a different story because the only possible source of controversy could be the Briton Allan Wilson and his army but they were all killed by the King's army. Not even one of them survived to tell any tales.

According to Ndebele and former ZAPU historian Mr. Saul Gwakuba Ndlovu, King Lobhengula, upon crossing the Tshangane river travelled on to present day Pashu in Binga and was hosted hospitably by Chief Pashu of the Tonga people. Chief Pashu also facilitated the crossing of the Zambezi river on canoes into present day Zambia by the king and his party of one queen and bodyguards. In Zambia the king went on to stay with his cousin King Mpezeni Jele of the Angoni people in the eastern region. According to Ndlovu, King Lobhengula died among the Angoni in Zambia in 1920.

The war of 1893 was embedded in the memories of the Ndebele nation as symbolized by the song,

Kudala kwakungenje
Umhlab' uyaphenduka
Kwakubus' uMambo loMzilikazi
Sawela kuTshangane
Saguqa ngamadolo:
INkos' uLobhengula
Yasinyamalala
Kwasekusin' izulu,
Yasinyamalala.....
(Ndlovu T.M. and Ndlovu D.N. 1995)

(The world is changing; things were not like this in the olden days.
The reigning kings were Mambo and Mzilikazi.
But when we fought at Tshangane River
And we fell on our knees,
King Lobengula then disappeared) (Ndlovu – Gatsheni 2008)

Until the early 1990s every primary school pupil in Matabeleland sang that song and internalized it as part of their proud history and heritage. However, the ZANU PF government who viewed Ndebele history as divisive and dangerous memory, made sure that the teaching and singing of the song was surreptitiously scrapped from being a consistent educational practice.

On 4 November 1893 the B.S.A. Company flag was hoisted above the King's tree of justice in Bulawayo, three years after Mashonaland had been occupied, to mark the demise of the Ndebele Kingdom and the beginning of a new administration under the Crown of the British empire as a colony. Maphenduka (2015) observeed the paradox of the B.A.S. Company army raisng and saluting the union jack flag and imploring God to save the Queen as they sang the British national anthem while standing knee deep in the cold blood of 18000 of their Matabele victims. History has it on record that the next day being a Sunday the raiders who were in the company of a bishop held a church service.

Rhodes built his cottage on the spot where King Lobhengula's palace had stood. Today the site is home to an unkempt statehouse which the head of state never uses. Such was the arrogance of the victorious as they always wanted to make a statement that they had ushered in a new and better dispensation. The site of the King's palace became an ignored relic from the past and a symbol of defeat, demolition and replacement of Ndebele might. It was meant to remind them of the discomfiting retreat of their king and the crushing of ZAPU.

The white members of the invading army were rewarded for their gallant slaughter in Bulawayo by a bountiful share of the King's cattle from Nuanetsi and large tracts of prime land from Mthwakazi while their Shona colleagues were given a smaller share of the cattle as gratitude for their services.

On 18 July 1894 the British Privy Council passed into law the Matabeleland Order in Council, giving the Chartered Company jurisdiction over Matabeleland (Thomas 1996, Berlyn 1978). The Order in Council published in the B.S.A. Company Government Gazette of 5 October 1894 authorized the company to rule Mthwakazi by conquest to ensure she never rose again. Consequently, in November 1894 The B.S.A. Company then called Mthwakazi Matabeleland and subsequently Leander Starr Jameson was appointed governor therein in 1894 with Archibald R. Colquhoun having been appointed governor for Mashonaland in 1890.

There was never any love lost between the Ndebele and the colonialists, therefore it was not a surprise when the Ndebele rebelled against the Company administration in March 1896. However, due to their perceptions, accurate or misguided the settler government was shocked when they learnt that their former allies the Shona had also revolted in June 1896. They presumed that the Shona were inherently civil by nature and habit and that they were content with the rulership of the white men, therefore were incapable of armed resistance, moreso considering the way they had not resisted the initial invasion and perversion of their land in 1893. While the Ndebele were perceived to be warlike and rebellious the Shona were regarded as cooperative and subservient therefore the BSAC was taken aback when the Shona rebelled.

Due to that perception the B.S.A Company administration and the subsequent governments by whites exhibited and extended a friendly demeanour to the Shona and Mashonaland while they regarded the Ndebele with suspicion levels that varied from vacillating to resolute. Mistrust of the Ndebele saw the white administration recruit Shona labourers for industries in Bulawayo from as early as the 1920s. The divisive recruitment policy led to a twelve day riot between the Ndebele residents of Bulawayo and Shona workers in 1929. That conniving attitude by the British was to play a very critical influence on the behind the scenes caucus at Lancaster in 1979, to determine the eventual successor to the colonial government in 1980 as Mugabe. It also laid the foundations of economic marginalization which was flagrantly pursued by ZANU from independence day.

In 1896 the Ndebele rebelled against their new rulers in what was called *Impi yehloka elibomvu* (war of the red axe) *or impi yomvukela* (war of rebellion) which historians say was started by *Indlovukazi* (Queen) Lozikeyi Dlodlo who went into battle wielding a red axe and prince Nyamande Khumalo. The Ndebele were once more defeated and the last remnants of their great *impis* were laid to rest.

The Ndebele. A nation begotten from the wrath of Africa's most legendary, luminous and prominent King, Shaka Zulu and an offspring of the most vivacious yet fiercest of kingdoms, the Zulu. Descendents of a mighty people and products of the assegai. After seventy fours years of out - maneuvering, negotiating, vanquishing, dominating and overshadowing all around them, succumbed to advanced weapons of war. With the fall they lost not only their independence but worse their land and sovereignty, which they still are yet to recover.

According to Maphenduka (2015), in 1918 the Matabeleland Royal Council dispatched a delegation led by Prince Nyamande (King Lobhengula's son) to Britain to pertition the Queen to grant Mthwakazi a revocation of the Matabeleland Order in Council of 1894. That, it was envisaged would automatically abrogate the Rule by Conquest provision therein and Mthwakazi would regain her sovereignty. The request was denied by the British Privy Council who argued that the Mthwakazi state had been vanquished and replaced by a *"better"* order.

It is noteworthy that that was not the first time the Ndebele had attempted to safeguard their sovereignty. On 6 February 1889, King Lobhengula's two chiefs, Mtshede and Babayane had sailed off from Cape Town on a mission to England to tell the queen that the King had not given away his land and kingdom to the British through the Rudd Concession. After delays in Cape Town, deliberately orchestrated by Cecil John Rhodes, the chiefs did eventually arrive in England and delivered the King's missive.

It was a contradiction in terms that Her Majesty, Queen Victoria assured the King in writing that Rhodes, Rudd and all whites pestering the King for mining and hunting rights were doing so illegally, yet her government would within four months, in July 1889 grant Cecil John Rhodes his much - sought - after Royal Charter. The Charter which read very much like a rape certificate authorizing the holder to savage and pillage, provided the B.S.A. Company to, inter alia have *"all powers necessary for the purpose of government...cultivate and improve the land...to preserve peace and order....and for that objective to obtain a force of police and have its own flag"* (Thomas 1996:211). That marked the first in a series of double standards and denials by the British government to grant Mthwakazi/ Matabeleland her sovereignty.

In 1923, instead of granting Mthwakazi her sovereignty, the British government ended the tenure of the B.S.A. Company as a government and accorded the territory the status of a self - governing British colony. In honour of his pay master, Cecil John Rhodes' imperialistic acrobatics, Leander Starr Jameson had called the territory Southern Rhodesia in 1895. The two distinct and sovereign kingdoms of the Ndebele known to its people as uMthwakazi with Bulawayo as the capital (*isigodlo*) and that of the Shona (present day eastern Zimbabwe, a coalition of numerous chieftainces including the Zezuru, Manyika, Karanga, Korekore and Ndau ethnic groups) were merged for imperial, political, economic as well as administrative convinience to form one country under a unitary system of government in 1923. A volitional mistake which the people of Matabeleland have rued ever since.

The leadership and the general populace of uMthwakazi or Matabeleland were never consulted on the amalgamation, neither were the people of Zimbabwe or Mashonaland. The Ndebele state and the people of Mashonaland were summarily annexed into a country as if they were sugar beans put into a pot full of water and then set on fire. When the water started to boil they were tossed around the pot and knocked violently against each other. Knocking against each other is what characterized the relations between Ndebele and Shona ever since.

The policy of amalgamating disparate and divergent people into one country was as habitual and calculated to the British as it was inopportune and egregious to the various British colonies. Ignoring the Jameson Line (boundary between Mthwakazi and Mashonaland), political, cultural and tribal dynamics between the Ndebele and the Shona, predictably saved the insidious purpose tantamount to enclosing two stranger bulls in the same byre. By the time they eventually strike some form of understanding, very little of the byre and the bulls themselves will be identifiable. That political gimmick became a master stroke for the colonialists as more than a century and two decades later, the two bulls would still be goring at each other, with lack of housing, employment, food, education, health-care and a plethora of other social, economic, cultural and political ills still topping the list of threats to the very fabric and soul of the country.

For the next almost one hundred years the colonialists would pit one tribe against the other in some way, e.g. they would use police officers from Mashonaland to drastically administer and enforce harsh laws on Matabeleland, provide semi education to Mashonaland and even less to Matabeleland, employ one and pay them a pittance yet starving the other. At the end of the day none of the two really benefited from the system although they felt one was favoured and therefore better than the other. The system worked perfectly to its design specifications so much so that even after independence from Britain and the minority regime, the ruling majority tribe leadership relentlessly endeavoured to maintain the status accorded them by the colonists. They adopted the colonial system hook line and sinker before perfecting it.

The boundaries of African countries were drawn by Western European states in the 19th century. Today the multiple African nations within those many countries are failing to achieve cohesion and solidity. England, France, Germany, Portugal, Italy, Belgium etc met at the Berlin Conference to draw the map of Africa in 1884. Those same colonists set up a precedent with long term catastrophic ramifications for their colonial subjects. In Zimbabwe they lumped together more than twenty tribes and disorganized two major states and several minor states into one country. In Zambia more than twenty 25 tribes were congregated into an imaginary one nation. In Nigeria they grouped two hundred and fifty tribes into the largest, most populous, most ethnic and religiously conflicted country in the continent.

The Berlin Act of 1885 which was sponsored by Prince Otto Von Bismark, galvanized European states into the scramble for Africa. Among other provisions, it provided, according to Ndabaningi Sithole (1959), for, *"freedom of trade for all nations, suppression of the slave trade, the civilising of the natives of Africa as well as their evangelization, protection of religions.... and the preservation of law, order and peace"*. Far from it, there was nothing legal, orderly and peacefull in the colonization of Africa. The conduct of European imperialism in Africa had very little to do with civilization. To the African, it was the zenith of barbarism. Ironically the same 'civilizing' European states laid the foundations for civil wars and ethnic conflicts in Africa after independence from colonialism.

With utter disregard to local political, ethnic and demographic dynamics, the colonialists ignored pre colonial boundaries and used geographic landmarks such as rivers and mountains as boundaries between countries. The Zambezi river was used as a boundary between Zimbabwe and Zambia. That act split the Tonga nation which was settled on either side of the river between two countries, with members of the same clan becoming citizens of two different countries, needing to travel hundreds of kilometers to visit each other while previously they needed a canoe to cross a few metres of river water with no immigration and customs formalities.

Very disparate and even antipathetic kingdoms were forced into one country. The rationale for that calamitous policy which later resulted in civil wars and genocides, was convenience for the colonialists. Besides, the Africans were subject to conquest and had no say on their future and therefore citizenship could be allocated to them by the conquerors. The settlers wanted to establish a new order which had no room for pre colonial arrangements which would give Africans confidence to regroup and resist European domination. Where possible African nations and states had to be distributed into a number of countries so they could be disunited and therefore governable. Africans were regarded as disorganized and their boundaries were not 'clear anyway' so the whitemen had to 'civilize' the boundaries. There was also a need to have as much land in terms of size as possible for the imperial country and therefore it did not matter who was on the land.

As noted by Bailey in Cocodia (2008), *"(t)he political map of Africa is a western colonial creation, drawn by western powers with little regard to the boundaries of historic ethnic homelands or the ethnic compositions of the subject population, and today these artificial or multi-ethnic nations lack the internal political cohesion necessary for survival as nations"*. The territory called Rhodesia by the British and later Zimbabwe when it gained independence, was created out of that avaricious and twisted reasoning and domineering spirit of European imperialism. The aim was to crush potential African (especially Ndebele) resistance, establish their so called order, civilization and government, emancipate the Shona from Ndebele dominance and demarcate as much land for the British crown as possible in order to exploit the vast mineral and other natural wealth therein.

Consequently, two kingdoms / states were collapsed into one Rhodesian country. The Mthwakazi State which comprised the Ndebele, Kalanga, Xhosa, Shangani, Sotho, San, Venda, Nambya, Tonga and some Karanga and Mashonaland, home to the Zezuru, Korekore, Manyika, Ndau and Karanga. Two very distinct kingdoms that were to prove inexorably incompatible nation - states were merged in the most dissolute of manners. Two naturally dissimilar sovereignties were bungled together in intransigent defiance of the Jameson Treaty of 1891.

The Jameson Treaty was signed by King Lobhengula of Mthwakazi and Leander Starr Jameson of Mashonaland on behalf of the British crown. It provided for and spelt out the boundary between the two kingdoms. When the Mthwakazi state and Mashonaland were amalgamated into one country, that was in brazen violation of existing boundaries and the Jameson Treaty. The deliberate and malignant dismissal of existing institutions was typical of British colonialism. It was a recipe for disaster and Zimbabwe is yet to disentangle herself from that botch-up, which the African nationalists either failed to understand or for some reason could not prioritise and correct when they reclaimed independence from Britain at Lancaster in 1979.

The African nationalists had to admit that, while it was rational that if the West had to colonize Africa and create new countries, they could not create a country for every nation or tribe on the continent, but it is equally sensible that they had to respect existing treaties and boundaries. Where no such boundaries existed, conventional wisdom dictated that they had to consult the locals and strike a balance between respect for diversity and administrative efficiency by coming up with a dermacation model and or government system that did not attempt to crush the individuality of the various nations. However, expecting settlers to have colonized Africa in an orderly, logical and democratic manner was probably tantamount to expecting a bandit to be civil and respectful while raping and plundering his victim.

The colonists were outlaws and their conduct was in line with the twisted and warped reasoning of criminals. Therefore, the nationalists should have demanded a rescission of the agreement made by criminals simply because such contract was illegal and therefore could not continue binding Africans. The unitary and centralist system of government adopted by the minority settler governments were suitable for the colonialists in the short term but transmuted into an albatross on the neck of the sovereign African states soon after independence from colonialism. Tragically the nationalist governments would later inherit that system and seemed to enjoy the exploitive nature of centralist unitary states.

In 1924 the first legislative assembly elections were held. Only white people participated in the plebiscite as was going to be the trend for the next fifty - six years. Sir Charles Coghlan was elected and he became the first Prime Minister of Rhodesia.

In December 1959 Joshua Mqabuko Nkomo and Michael Mawema formed the National Democratic party. Mawema was the president but was soon replaced by Nkomo after some discrepancies in party funds were noticed. In November 1961 the party was banned. In September 1961 the Zimbabwe African People's Union (ZAPU) a revolutionary party calling for black majority rule on a *"One Man One Vote"* basis was formed under the leadership of Joshua Nkomo. Revolutionary propaganda and ideology gathered momentum among the black people, especially in the shanty townships of Makhokhoba in Bulawayo and Mbare in Salisbury. At the forefront of nationalism were the oppressed black workers who were prone to racist and inequitable treatment in the factories.

In 1962 the Rhodesian Front government was elected into office. The new right wing government tightened security laws and a lot of black Africans were incarcerated in an apartheid like set - up. The Law and Order Maintenance Act (LOMA) and the Emergency Powers Act were passed into law in 1960. Those became the most repressive pieces of legislation in the history of contemporary politics. Many cases of abuse of human rights and freedoms were perpetrated under their auspices. The laws were to remain in place long after independence until Mugabe gazetted the sequel to LOMA, the Public Order Security Act (POSA) in 2002.

In August 1963 after Joshua Nkomo was accused of indecisiveness by his lieutenants, ZAPU split. The rebels formed a new political party the Zimbabwe African National Union (ZANU). In 1964 at the first ZANU congress in Gwelo, Reverend Ndabaningi Sithole was elected party president. Sithole then appointed Robert Mugabe to be the secretary general. The real reason for the split however was outright raw tribalism which fed power mongering on the part of the leaders of the splinter faction.

The founders of ZANU were, Ndabaningi Sithole, Enos Nkala, Herbert Chitepo, Leopold Takawira and Edgar Tekere. ZANU was enmeshed in rabid tribalism and corrosive regionalism on the anvil. Washington Malianga and Leopold Takawira were the arch tribalists, that according to Nkomo (1984) influenced the young politicians like Mugabe towards the split. Tribalism was the bedrock from which ZANU sprang and tribalism is what split the party into two in 1976. That was corroborated by Ndlovu - Gatsheni (2008;45) who posited that, *"since that time, the history of ZAPU and ZANU had become a tale of ethnic politics and tribalism, bringing more division than unity to the Ndebele and the Shona".*

After the 1963 split, ZAPU still maintained a national character although the tribal division lines were easily discernible. Msindo and Sibanda in Muzondidya and Ndlovu - Gatsheni (2007:282) argued that, following the 1963 fragmentation, ZAPU strove to maintain tribal balance in its leadership elite but failed to arrest *"ethnic politics and ethnic - induced crises whereby 1971 witnessed tribal clashes which pitted Ndebele/Kalanga-speaking politicians, such as Jason Moyo, Edward Ndlovu, Jane Ngwenya and George Silundika, against their Shona-speaking counterparts, James Chikerema and George Nyandoro. They culminated in the second split of ZAPU in exile".*

In 1964 Sithole, Mugabe, Tekere and Maurice Nyagumbo were arrested by the Smith government. They were kept in detention for ten years. While in detention, Sithole appointed Herbert Chitepo to lead the party.

After breaking away from ZAPU, ZANU who thought they had freed themselves from the Ndebele / Kalanga dominance, embraced new deadly intra tribal feuds. They went on to split in 1975. One faction, ZANU Ndonga was led by the Rev. Ndabaningi Sithole from the Ndau tribe and the other, ZANU by Robert Mugabe a Zezuru. After the split, ethnic schisms persisted to the point of suspected assassinations within ZANU. Bhebe (1999:58) espoused that Hebert Chitepo (Manyika), the ZANU leader during the time when Robert Mugabe (Zezuru) was incarcerated by the Smith regime was assassinated in Zambia on 18 March 1975 as a result of territorial tensions between the Manyika and the Karanga ethnic groups while there were *"some unscrupulous Zezuru trying to fish in troubled waters…(r)egionalism or tribalism for Zimbabwe is their Heel of Achilles and was even more so during the liberation struggle"*.

The view on ethnic violence was corroborated by Grundy (2008) who stated that James Chikerema used to talk of a *"Karanga mafia in ZANU"*. He asserted that Chikerema was convinced Chitepo was murdered by Josiah Tongogara (Karanga) so much that Chikerema drew a pistol at Tongogara on the morning of the assassination. Chikerema had to be restrained by the Zambian police. Tongogara himself died in a mysterious car accident on the eve of Zimbabwe's independence. Speculation was rife that he was 'eaten up' by the revolution, meaning that he was killed by his colleagues.

Mutizwa (2010) weighed in by arguing that at Chitombo Camp, *"Tongogara supported by Manyika used Gukurahundism to overrun rebels who had studied Lennism and Marxism…. Mugabe applied Gukurahundism to deal with the Veshindi Karanga group who had resisted his leadership"*. Indeed, there were deadly tribal plots within tribal plots.

Mutizwa (2010) went on to state that Tongogara who died on 26 December 1979 was eventually consumed by his own *magnum opus,* since he was party to the architecture of the liquidation system. Maphenduka (2015) noted that ultimately Zezuru hegemonic machinations won the day as they managed to keep the other Shona groups under check in ZANU while maintaining a choking grip on the country. That strangle – hold was finally undone by the Karanga in 2017 when Mnangagwa ousted Mugabe in a coup d' etat.

That was the classic yet bizarre manifestation of the vile and homicidal ethnicism that foxed ZANU from the anvil and by extension, Zimbabwean politics parties to this day. Tribalism inspired the formation of ZANU, then possessed the founders, propelling them to unheard - of hights of hate. Tribalism characterized their policies and practice day and night. It hovered over them imperturbably and preyed on their actions for seventeen years (1963 – 1980). It was tribalism gone berserk that gorged vulture - like on the blood of one hundred thousand Matabeles from 1980 to 1987. Inspite of so much blood – letting, the beast of ZANU's tribal hate would not be sated. It incessantly asked for more blood year in and year out, as the leaders and the supporters kept chanting the mantra, *"ZANU ndeyeropa"*, which either meant ZANU feeds on blood, ZANU is made of blood or ZANU is founded on blood.

The last one was the more comprehensible of the three blood mantras. However, one wondered whose blood they were referring to. Was it the blood of their enemies, their victims, their members or their countrymen. Strangely, ZANU historians over the years failed to recognize the value of the blood of the all those that died during the war of liberation, be they black or white, ZAPU or ZANU, especially if they are Ndebele. ZANU trashed the founding values of the nationalists and the struggle for self determination by their insatiable craving for more blood.

The ZANU obsession with blood saw the Mugabe government going for the Matabele jagular as he entered the office of Prime Minister in 1980. ZANU historians pretended that they had ran out of paper and ink when it came to that chapter. To them Matabele blood had less value than Shona blood.

For example, due to their participation in the 1896 rebellion war, the ZANU historians later called that war, the 1st *Chimurenga*. *Chimurenga* was a Shona term, meaning an uprising or a revolt (Wohlers 2010). That act of recognizing the 1896 war as the mother of all wars displayed the exclusive and discriminative nature of ZANU ideology. It showed that *chimurenga* was not a national term, referring to a national legacy, memory, symbols, heritage or events, although ZANU patricians and historians would want the world to believe it so. They made it an exclusivist locution, referring to Shona heritage and resistance against white rule and domination. If it was a part of national nomenclature, then what is called the 1st *Chimurenga* of 1896 should actually be called the 2nd *Chimurenga*. That is because the first war was the Anglo - Ndebele war of 1893 where the Ndebele had fiercely faught against the same colonial army and lost more than 18 000 lives in addition to property, land and sovereignty. That was a very significant and symbolic war in view of the heavy human costs as well as in its being the first act of armed resistance to colonialism and forced foreign rule within the borders of present day Zimbabwe.

The war of 1893 deserved as much, if not more recognition than the war of 1896, but the reversal was true for one simple reason. Ndebele blood was shed in that war and to ZANU PF, Ndebele blood was less valuable. The Shona did not participate in that war, instead 652 people from British Mashonaland fought on the side of the white invaders (Maphenduka 2015). That fact was a constant source of embarrassment for present day ZANU historians. It was the same historians who always conveniently forget to mention that it was the Ndebele who started the so called 1st *Chimurenga* war on 20 March 1896 and the Shona joined the war three months later on 14 June 1896. That was probably the reason behind the same historians' attempt to delete ZAPU and ZPRA's role in what they term the 2nd *Chimurenga* (liberation war of the 1970s) because *chimurenga* was all about Shona exploits and not a national narrative. Instead of *chimurenga* being a monument that inspired nationalistic ideals and invoked national pride, it remained a tribal construct that conjured only among the Shona, memories of a heroic past.

For their role in dismembering history, the troop of ZANU scholars, whose concocted and choreographed version of events was as unscholarly as it was unethical, reduced themselves to atavistic scribes, scribbling for their supper.

From the time he wrestled the leadership of ZANU from Rev. Sithole in 1976/77 under very opaque and arcane circumstances, Mugabe's life became supremely and principally devoted to the quest for Shona hegemony and Zezuru aristocratic supremacy. With rare zeal and iron tenacity, he made those a life - time pursuit. That became his food and drink, sleep and dreams. The national interest and wellbeing of other ethnic groups were reduced to second fiddle and were rendered subservient to his personal and sub ethnic group interests. His quest for Zezuru laterality over the rest could only be matched by his hatred for the Ndebele and ZAPU.

Under the intense pressure of the 1963 ZAPU split and the subsequent minor (by comparison) splits, the revolution suffered, reeled and almost veered off course. As if that was not enough, the state of the revolution was further dealt a heavy blow in 1965 when the Rhodesian Front won the elections and Ian Douglas Smith became the Prime Minister. Having campaigned for white supremacy by promising independence from Britain, no majority rule in a thousand years, no franchise for blacks, suppression of the socio-political and economic progression of black people and the wide-ranging fortification of white minority rights which guaranteed the superior status of whites while protecting their properties and interests, the Rhodesian Front and Ian Douglas Smith won all the A roll seats. Buoyed by the triumph, in November of the same year, Ian Smith with a free reign, announced the Unilateral Declaration of Independence (UDI) from Great Britain.

That marked the escalation of repressive policies and practices by the regime on the majority black people in general and the nationalists in particular.

Meanwhile, the volatile leopard and dog relationship between ZAPU and ZANU from 1963 was another setback for the revolution. The leopard would not change his spots nor would the dog give away his bone. The parties were embroiled in mutual exploits of violence against each other. Reciprocated suspicions, allegations of counter revolutioneryhood, contempt for each other and negative propagandism towards each other, retarded the potential gains of the liberation struggle. It became patent, although ZAPU always had more than 50% of their Politburo (highest policy making organ) being people of Shona stock and ZANU had only one Ndebele (Enos Nkala) in their Politburo from 1963 to 1987, that the former was a Ndebele party while the latter was a Shona party. Various attempts at unifying the two always crumbled dismayingly like a house of cards.

Sithole in Muzondidya and Ndlovu – Gatsheni (2007) contended that, particular attention was taken to guarantee that ZANU's leadership positions were a reflection of ethnic balancing among the major Shona groups of the Manyika, Karanga and Zezuru. The Matabele were not a factor there. He also argued that in ZAPU the leadership positions were also an ethnic balancing exercise with the Ndebele, Kalanga and Shona taking senior roles. Those were early indicators that Ndebele / Kalanga people were not (and now with the benefit of hindsight would never be) welcome in ZANU, while ZAPU treated Ndebeles and Shonas with equity.

While the discord between ZAPU and ZANU was demonstrably tribal and historical, it was also attributable to a number of other factors. The Rhodesian security agents would set up one against the other by the employment of multifarious schemata, resulting in the two turning their guns on each other with the animosity and ferocity of direct foes. That resulted in more than noticeable attrition, much to the satisfaction and benefit of the RDF and the Smith government. Secondly, while ZAPU and ZPRA were funded, advised and trained by the Soviet Union, ZANU and ZANLA were sponsored by China. During the Cold War era those guarantors, the Russians and Chinese, were protagonists on the international scene and their rivalry was extended and inherited by their protégés.

Thirdly the ZPRA forces were charged from Lusaka in Zambia and were accommodated in neighbouring Botswana. They were moulded into a disciplined guerilla and conventional army which had no shortage of the requisite military hardware. ZPRA was trained in various countries including Russia, Romania and Czechoslovakia while ZANLA was trained from Mozambique and waged a

Maoist type of campaign which relied more on numbers than military skill. At independence ZPRA had a modern military, stationed in Zambia and Angola, with Soviet-manufactured airforce Mikoyan fighters, tanks and armoured personnel carriers on standby in the Soviet Union, as well as well trained artillery units. According to Nyathi (2017) *"...the Soviets were arming ZPRA with sophisticated military arsenal including Surface – to – Air Missiles (SAM 7). Among the liberation movements backed by the Soviets and their allies, ZPRA was the best equipped militarily"*. The Soviet Union gave military support to SWAPO in Namibia, MPLA in Angola, ANC in South Africa and ZAPU in Southern Rhodesia.

Moorcraft (1979:164) described ZANLA as having, *"attempted to wage a Maoist – style campaign in the countryside. Unlike the disciplined ZPRA guerillas, many of Mugabe's troops were merely teenage ruffians. As Van Der Byl said of ZAPU's superiority over ZANU, they were 'men with cleaner guns and more of the hearts and minds staff'"*. Clearly their tactics were worlds apart. ZANLA was evidently an awkward squad while ZPRA was made up of hardened soldiers.

ZPRA superiority is further confirmed by Alexander et al (2000) who commented that ZANU at independence was distrustful of ZPRA's capacity for conventional warfare and feared ZAPU would use her forces against her. While ZPRA would deploy a hundred hard trained men into combat, ZANLA deployed thousands militia style recruits with instructions for mobilizing, drilling and politicization of villagers in all night mini rallies termed *"pungwe"*, the Shona word meaning till sunrise or all night vigil.

That impression of ZANLA being a rag tag and bobtail, amateurish, para - military outfit, was bolstered by Sidney Sekeramayi in 1982, who as minister of defense was caught on video by BBC Panorama admonishing former ZANLA combatants during ZNA training by British instructors for trembling as they held guns as if for the first time. A hugely and obviously discomfited Sekeramayi, in a mortified bid to shut out the British military trainers from the communication, upbraided in Shona *"musabvunde, musabvunde"* (do not tremble, do not tremble).

Kumbirai Kangai A ZANU PF stalwart and cabinet minister agreed with the impression of ZANLA as a sorry and amateurish semi military outfit. In the Sunday Mail of October 18 – 24, 2012 he stated that ZANU was very disorganised and had a haphazard military stratagem. He revealed that ZANLA would send poorly trained militia, armed with nothing but pistols or at times without ammunition to the war front. It is such military cruelty, importunity and half baked military tactics that lamentably contributed to the loss of young lives as they were deployed to face the well armed and trained Rhodesian Defense Forces with nothing but their lives.

The *musabvunde* episode gave plausibility to the allegations that ZANLA mustered *mujibhas* (war errand boys) who had never even seen the inside of guerilla training camps in Mozambique, into the Assemly Points. The *mujibhas* were eventually covertly sneaked into the ZNA as ZANLA combatants. That was done to beef up ZANLA numbers, crowd and shut ZPRA out as well as to provide jobs for tribemen, cronies, relatives, party supporters etc. The *mujibhas* were however very conspicuous in APs due to their failure to complete elementary military assignments like identifying gun characteristics, disassembling and assembling a gun.

Lamentably for the country, that initial *mujibhas* scandal gave rise to the most economically debilitating and corrupt practices withing the civil service. Many years later it was revealed that the government salary bill was fraught with what was termed 'ghost workers' or non existant workers. The ghosts were ZANU PF members, friends, girl / boy friends, relatives etc of party big wigs, who were incorporated into the civil service pay roll. They were then paid monthly salaries as teachers, nurses, soldiers, clerks etc, without even setting foot into their allocated work place. The tax payer was swindled of millions in United States dollars by the ruling party and the government.

Fourthly, as a consequence of the differing recruitment drives and regions, ZANLA always had tens of thousands cadres in her camps in Mozambique and in the districts of eastern Rhodesia. That, rendered ZANLA a more amenable to attack and easier target for Rhodesian security forces than ZPRA who had fewer recruits. The appalling massacre of approximately 1300 ZANLA combatants at the Nyadzonya camp in Mozambique in 1976 by the Rhodesian Airforce (RAF) indicated that ZANLA had thousands of personnel in their camps at any given time. On the other hand when the Rhodesians attacked ZPRA's Freedom Camp in Zambia, less than a hundred combatants were killed. While human life holds the same intrinsic worth, the larger numbers of casualties incurred by ZANLA were more dismaying and more heart-rending than ZPRA's casualties. Meanwhile ZPRA was suffering fewer losses and due to that they were suspected by ZANLA of being given the kid gloves treatment by the enemy. While numbers could be a liability, no war can be won without a large pool of human resources and ZPRA could not help but envy ZANLA's limitless reserves.

Fifth, ZPRA boasted of the best military hardware in terms of both quality and quantity, including tanks and MIG fighter planes that were on standby in the Soviet Union with personnel trained to use them. Yet ZANLA longed for efficient and enough rifles. It is said that one ZANU official once confessed that, *"we needed rifles, they (ZAPU) wanted tanks"* (Moorcraft 1979:168). Those jealousies ate deep into the troubled souls of the nationalist organisations and their differences became insurmountable and irreconcilable. One of the reasons why ZPRA had better weaponry was that they would put the weapons supplied by the Soviets to good use. The Soviets supplied both ZPRA and ZANLA with weapons. Nonetheless, they had an intricate information gathering system that gave them data, even from inside the RDF. That data included how ZPRA and ZANLA used their weapons. The better use their guns were put to, the more they supplied the user. Hence ZPRA got more and better guns than ZANLA.

After a ten - year period of an internecine revolutionary war, waged from two fronts by ZAPU and ZANU against the Rhodesian government but produced no winner (although ZANU was to claim military victory in their 1980 election manifesto), the warring parties concurred to a negotiated settlement at Lancaster in England. Grumbling Mugabe, never amenable to negotiations, was dragged to Lancaster by Zambia's Kenneth Kaunda, Botswana's Seretse Khama, Tanzania's Julius Nyerere and Mozambique's Samora Machel. Strangely, despite inadequate funding and leading a structurally weak and poorly equipped ZANLA against a well drilled, fed and equipped Rhodesian army, Mugabe argued that he was on the verge of a military victory and saw no logic in negotiations. He wanted to pursue his internal military terrorism strategy of offering unarmed young ZANLA guerillas to the Rhodesians in droves. He was prepared to send the 40 000 strong ZANLA to their graves than negotiate a peaceful settlement.

Some analysts say that Mugabe was naturally averse to negotiations, but nothing could be further from the truth. Mugabe did not favour negotiations during that period because Joshua Nkomo preferred negotiations. Nkomo was an experienced negotiator, having cut his teeth as a leader of labour unions in addition to being more experienced and travelled a politician. Mugabe, recently freed from prison after ten years, was afraid that the negotiation table would usher his rival as the new leader of the country. However, he must have fancied his chances in the battlefield where his army out numbered Nkomo's ZPRA two to one. He thought war would gain him the presidency, while Nkomo thought the negotiation table would catapault him to state house. Both men did not know what a surprise awaited them in England.

ZAPU and ZANU attended the Lancaster House Constituitional conference in December 1979 as one entity under the banner of the Patriotic Front. They negotiated as one (Mabhena 2014), on the advice of the Frontline States that argued that negotiating as one and contesting the impending elections as one would give the organisations some sort of formidable impact. What they lost and won at Lancaster, they did as one. However, the merger which ZAPU and Nkomo took seriously was just a smokescreen which ZANU, Mugabe and Margaret Thatcher used for convenience, as events would shortly reveal. Despite the negotiations and conscious deliberate attempts by Kaunda, Khama, Machel and Nyerere to unite the two, ZAPU and ZANU were as far apart as north is from south by the end of the conference. It was all pretentions and grand - standing to convince the world that the two major nationalist parties were united, yet in reality ZAPU and ZANU had never been further apart.

Due to the Lancaster talks, on 11 December 1979 the Rhodesian Front government under Ian Douglas Smith gave up their independence and the country reverted to its former status of British Colony under the governorship of Lord Soames. On 21 December 1979 the freedom pact was signed by Nkomo, Mugabe, Muzorewa and Lord Carrington (British Foreign Secretary 1979 - 1982) who was chairing the talks. In his concluding remarks Carrington promised that, *"we should give you all the support in developing a spirit of reconciliation in Zimbabwe and throughout all Southern Africa and ensuring the next decade there, will be one of peace and prosperity"*.

Lord Carrington's closing statement shortly proved to be merely a play for the gallery, hollow and devoid of all forms of sincerity. When Mugabe exhibited zero reconciliation with ZAPU and the Matabele, the good Lord Carrington and his government were unflustered and placid. Instead, they covertly and overtly supported the slaughter in Matabeleland and the Midlands. A few months later, Mugabe displayed servile obedience to Lord Carrington by unreseverdly 'reconciling' with the Rhodesian whites. The reasons for the obsequious compliance were neither natural nor holy. As would soon unfold, an unholy deal had been struck between Mugabe and the British establishment.

In essence the Lancaster House Agreement was more of a rigging concordat than a freedom pact because it set the foundation for Mugabe to blaze the trail for an election fraud system. It is well known that the concord was largely a British imposition on the nationalists as well as on the Rhodesian Front government. The British were under great pressure from the international community as well as from ZAPU and ZANU to force the Smith regime to accept majority rule. They realized that independence was inevitable and they wanted a Brexit deal from Rhodesia that provided them with a soft landing. They wanted the fastest and softest means out of the Rhodesian headache. Their hands were tied and they had to sacrifice the government of their kith and kin in Rhodesia. Still, they could not surrender the future of white Rhodesians and British economic interests to unpredictable democracy. Democracy could easily land them on the lap of the Soviets. They needed to salvage the situation by identifying and opting for the better devil. They settled for Mugabe.

They then through Lancaster, dictated arbitrarily that there should be twenty uncontested seats for white people, twenty seats for Matabeleland and sixty seats for Mashonaland in the next parliament of a total hundred seats. By that stage it was crystal clear that ZAPU was Matabeleland and ZANU was Mashonaland based, therefore Nkomo would win only in Matabeleland and Mugabe would emerge victorious courtesy of superior tribal statistics if he paled the ethnic card well.

The number of parliamentary seats per region were not based on population statistics, otherwise it would imply that there were as many whites in the country as there were Ndebeles, Kalangas, Vendas, Sothos, Tongas, Xhosas, Nambyas, Dombes etc put together. For the record, in 1980 there were about 250 000 whites and about two million Matabele. The seats were not based on geographic size either because Matabeleland was by far more than a third of general Mashonaland. The number of seats were based on the notion that ZANU had to win the 1980 elections at all cost, therefore Mashonaland was given sixty seats arbitrarily and Mugabe was instructed to go to Zimbabwe and use his tribal majority to win the elections and not harm the whites, their businesses and their property in the country. The deal was presumably silent on how he would treat his fellow blacks because the British could not have instructed Mugabe to butcher the Matabele, but they gave him free rein and promised to support him through and through.

The election rigging jaggernaught was therefore commissioned at Lancaster by the Margaret Thatcher British administration when they threw out the window democracratic ethos and the policy of equal representation between Matabeleland and Mashonaland.

Nkomo could not have missed the seats arithmatics but he accepted it for two reasons. First he was under the illusion that the elections would be contested by one party called the Patriotic Front (comprising ZAPU and ZANU) against the rest. On 22 December 1979, Nkomo was still at Lancaster waiting for Mugabe to show up as appointed, for a meeting of the two. The meeting was to prepare and tighten the nuts and bolts of the Patriotic Front party modalities before going back to their country where they woud meet their delegates to finalise on such issues as party symbol, candidature details etc. Unbeknown to Nkomo was that a lot of hurried behind the scene caucusing, conniving and plotting against him and ZAPU had been ongoing since their arrival at Lancaster. That is why Mugabe was a no – show at their meeting of 22 December 1979. He had boarded a British chartered plane to Tanzania. Nkomo was completely taken off guard and shocked to hear Mugabe announce on radio from Tanzania that he was going to contest the elections as ZANU. What is yet to be known was the role played by Tanzania's Julius Nyerere if any, in Mugabe's somersault, but Nkomo had just bought himself a big dummy from the conference and Mugabe.

Meanwhile, the ZPRA commanders who had as per Patriotic Front arrangement travelled to Salisbury (Harare) ahead of the political leadership of both ZAPU and ZANU for a rendezvous with their ZANLA counterparts, also hit a stone wall. The commanders were supposed to arrive first and declare a cease - fire to their respective armies, create assembly camps and inform the armies that they were going to form one national army. Then the politicians would come to tell the country that ZAPU and ZANU had merged into the Patriotic Front (Dabengwa interview 17 March 2017, Bulawayo). While Masuku, Dabengwa and others waited in Salisbury the delayed ZANLA delegation did not show up. Tragically their commander and the man who was alleged to be pro the Patriotic Front and anti Mugabe, Josiah Tongogara was reported to have died in a car accident en route to Salisbury in December 1979.

According to Mufuka (2019) at Lancaster, *"General Josiah Tongogara, Dabengwa and Solomon Mujuru were in general agreement. Mujuru was younger, 28, and was conned to abandon this path by promises of a high position. Tongogara's life was forefeited.."*

The suspicious fatal car accident and the death of Tongogara at that critical moment remained a mystery and is yet to be told in accuracy and in full. The enigma surrounding Tongogara's death was partially unveiled by Dumiso Dabengwa when he was interviewed by CITE in 2019. He mentioned that Tongogara's greatest mistake was that at Lncaster he had unequivocally displayed his preference for the Patriotic Front. He had also indicated that he preferred Nkomo to lead the Patriotic Front ahead of his party's Mugabe. That revelation, coming from the commander of his army must have been a very bitter pill for Mugabe to swallow as well as for the British government who preferred Mugabe. According to Nkomo (1983), *"Josiah Tongogara had been the great revelation at the Lancaster house Conference...he was a true patriot, dedicated to the unity of Zimbabwe....I was confident that within ZANU, Tongogara would be a powerful voice for unity".*

It would appear like some very powerful forces did not share Nkomo's confidence in Tongogara. As commander of ZANLA, he was the one to influence the army into supporting the Patriotic Front party. As a result of Tongogara's death, the commanders' meeting was cancelled and was not rescheduled. With Tongogara's remains from the suspicious car accident, was interred all hope of a Patriotic Front party.

When the politicians finally arrived, Nkomo according to Dabengwa was still hopeful that the Patriotic Front arrangement would still stand. ZAPU pursued the issue and called for meetings with ZANU but the latter were very slippery and elusive. The governor Lord Christopher Soames was not very helpful either although he could, with the powers bestowed on him at Lancaster, whip Mugabe back into the Patriotic Front line. Why Lord Soames was unwilling to pull the leash on Mugabe would soon unravel. ZANU dilly dallied and procrastinated until the day of the nomination court.

The Front Line States who had conceived the idea of the Patriotic Front (PF) did not come in to get Mugabe and ZANU to keep their word either. Obviously they were reluctant to be seen to be meddling and rocking the boat at such a delicate and critical stage. Besides there were grey areas around Tanzania's influence over Mugabe. Nyerere most probably did not subscribe to the Patriotic Front party arrangement.

When Nkomo heard that Mugabe had registered to contest the elections as ZANU, he instructed his lieutenants, Joseph Msika and others, to register ZAPU to contest the election as the Patriotic Front. That was how ZAPU contested the 1980 elections as the Patriotic Front. Nkomo could not divorce from the illusion of the Patriotic Front party despite bright and glaring indicators showing that it was nothing but a still birth. He could not accept that the idea was just a drifting cloud because after Lancaster, he knew that his hopes of winning lay in the PF and nowhere but the PF.

Through the radio announcement from Tanzania, Mugabe unilaterally dissolved the Patriotic Front party idea. Indeed, the Patriotic Front had never been more than a *"paper alliance"* (Berlyn 1978:115) One did not need divine revelation to realize that Mugabe, just like the British was very scared that the Patriotic Front was going to usher in Nkomo as the leader of a combined ZAPU and ZANU coalition against the Rhodesian Front and the other smaller parties. Mugabe could not countenance a government whereby Nkomo was the leader and him as something else but leader. In like manner the British were not prepared to allow Nkomo to win the elections for several reasons including that it meant the strengthening of Soviet influence in the region. That common fear concretized their already existing friendship.

Secondly, Nkomo accepted the skewed parliamentary constituency arrangement because he genuinely believed himself to be a national leader and not a regional or tribal leader. Yet another miscalculation emanating from a weakness which he himself admitted to possessing. He had too much trust and faith in other people's inclination for honesty. Little did he realize that, who one is, is not entirely a determinant of their effort but a result of what other people think of and say about him / her. What other people think and say are factors way out of one's control, no matter how honest and clean hearted one is. Nkomo knew people in Mashonaland supported him and called him 'Father Zimbabwe', not father Matabeleland. They had given him the Shona name *'Chibwechitedza'*, the slippery rock, in awe of his ability to avoid arrest by the Rhodesian government. He thought they would vote for him just as they had supported ZAPU through the years. But times had suddenly changed and someone would petition their tribal loyalty and consciousness against him while alleging a lot of other flaws in him and ZAPU.

Misihayirambwi – Mushonga (2010) answered the question, why the British opted for Mugabe and not Nkomo. She contended that it was the *"principle of collusion"* that from time to time in various African countries was employed by the West. She stated that *"In Zimbabwe, that collusion started in the pre-colonial era, in particular during the Lancaster House negotiations when white capital forces' self-interest meant that between a Ndebele leader and a Shona, they stood to benefit more by a transition from Ian Smith to a Shona leader. This is explained by the support that Mugabe received in spite of earlier demonization -- a terrorist became the darling of the West. It is that collusion which explains the silence of the same white capital forces during the Gukurahundi era. Is it not surprising that given the arrests of many political activists during that era, with some of them dying in prison, there wasn't a single draft UN Security Council Resolution against the ZANU regime?*

According to Moorcraft (1979), ZPRA's shooting down of the Viscount aircraft just before the Lancaster talks did not do Nkomo any favours. Joshua Nkomo's reaction and unrepentant comments after the shooting did not win him friends either. Instead, the British liked Mugabe's speeches. One diplomat is said to have noted, *"(h)e doesn't say things to please people. Frankly I think we can work with him"* Moorcraft (1979:170). At that stage the British and Americans were said to have been wooing Mugabe for some time. Moorcraft further revealed that the Americans theorized that the Kenyan experiment where a tribal majority of Kikuyus had been used to preside over a pro western administration could be repeated in Zimbabwe by enthroning a Shona tribal dominance under Mugabe. Tribalism ruled the day. The British government noticed that Mugabe came from a tribal majority and rigging the elections in his favour would not be very difficult nor arouse suspicions.

Another factor that worked in Mugabe's favour was the fact that he had left no doubt in anyone's mind that a ZANU electoral loss would result in the resumption of war. He had said too many times that he and his party would not accept the election result if it was not in their favour. Not prepared to call his bluff, the British believed his threat and endeavoured to avoid that from happening. Besides, they knew Mugabe was a very intense and serious personage, who even while in detention in 1974 had been apathetical to negotiations that involved Nkomo and ZAPU. The British further knew that Lancaster had been forced down his throat by the Front Line states presidents. He had indicated unequivocal hostility to a peaceful solution too often for them not to take his threats of war seriously. They knew Mugabe would accept one outcome and one outcome only. A win by himself.

They were caught in a dilemma. Their main man Ian Smith would never win a free and fair election in Rhodesia. That is why he was stripped of his position as Prime Minister of Rhodesia at Lancaster and he and his party did not contest the elections. Their second preference, Bishop Abel Muzorewa was out of contention as their surveys must have revealed to them that he was far from popular among the black people. Therefore, whatever outcome of the election, the next Prime minister would be one of the black nationalists, Nkomo and Mugabe.

The British headache was securing their interests i.e. the security of their nationals in Rhodesia and their business interests. Mugabe was threatening both their concerns by threatening war if he lost the elections. Therefore, a win by Nkomo, Sithole, Ndiweni, Muzorewa, Chikerema etc would bring about a civil war, they could not doubt that. What the British did not desire in their scramble from Africa was to leave behind them a legacy of civil war(s). That would not augur well for their image, their nationals in the former colony and their economic interests. They therefore figured that the best way out of Southern Rhodesia would be to ensure Mugabe won the elections with their help as a bribe for his cooperation in order to leave behind a 'peaceful' country. It was that twisted concoction of conflicting interests that saw the British government bribe the very person that was blackmailing them.

Therefore, all the stakes were against Nkomo. In addition to coming from a minority tribe, Nkomo was a known advocate for land redistribution. One of the reasons why ZAPU was calling for a one - man - one vote system was that there was need for equitable distribution of land. The white commercial farmers in the country, by then owned vast tracts of land and immense wealth while the majority blacks were crowded in arid and barren Native Reserves. It was clear that should Nkomo win the 1980 election, that White monopoly privilege could be under threat. Although that fear later proved to be a false alarm, at Lancaster it was real and it undid Nkomo. That was another reason why from the British point of view, Nkomo had to loose at all costs.

Dabengwa (interview, 17 March 2017) postulated that, both the British and Americans had strongly detested the ZAPU 1977 Turning Point strategy. The Turning Point strategy was the brain child of Nkomo when he came from Gonakudzingwa prison. It was meant to push the war suddenly to a point where the Smith government would be forced to capitulate. It wass the plan that saw ZPRA recruit and train a conventional army of regular battalions. The battalions were supposed to consolidate and occupy those areas in the country including, according to Dabengwa, Guruve, Hurungwe, Zvimba, Zvishavane and most of Matabeleland. Those areas had been taken by the ZPRA guerilla units and declared no go zones for the RDF. Once the regular battalion units had occupied those areas, the guerilla units would push further into the the country gunning for the towns.

The ZPRA airforce would have taken the Victoria Falls airport, the Wankie Safari Lodge (Dete) air strip and the Kariba airport whence they would timeously fly in to defend the regular units against the RAF. {The plan of taking over the three airports was however described as suicidal by Moorcraft (1979)}. The strategy was already underway with two regular battalions already in the country to take over the Victoria Falls airport when Margaret Thatcher called for the Lancaster Constitutional Conference talks. The Turning Point strategy was then called off pending the results of the talks.

The British government had noticed that if ZPRA had employed the strategy and brought in their MIG fighter planes, apartheid South Africa which had a military pact with Southern Rhodesia would have brought in her airforce to assist the RDF. They were also convinced that the Soviet Union would have been forced to fly in and bail out ZPRA. The war would have escalated into a carnage and many white people would have died while the Soviets would probably have won the war for ZAPU, thereby gaining prominence. That prospect made the Turning Point strategy and ZAPU very unpopular with the British and Americans. Its architects who happened to be the descendents of the assegai wielding Matabele *impis* that had killed many a Briton including Allan Wilson in 1894, became their number one enemies of all times in colonial Africa. King Lobhengula's descendents had to lose the elections.

The British were later to rue the day they helped Mugabe assume power in 1980. The admission was written in 2016 by David Owens, the former British Foreign Affairs Secretary when he lamented, " ....*for all his crookedness and indecision Nkomo would be a better leader initially of Zimbabwe"*, (The Zimbabwe Independent 6 – 12 April 2018).

Mugabe knew as he appended his mark to the freedom pact at Lancaster that he was going to ditch Nkomo and renege on the Patriotic Front arrangement the very next day. He was also resolved that he was going back home and would hit the ground running along the majoritarian and ethnic line, waving his tribal trump card. He would appeal for his Shona tribe not to vote for "*zimuNdewere*" (the biggish Ndebele) as Leopold Takawira the then ZANU vice president and one of Nkomo's main critics would put it. His multitudes of ZANLA soldiers that had not gone into the designated Assembly Points and militia who became armed election agents, would use violence to coerce those Shonas who were 'foolish' enough to ignore tribal politics and campaign for Nkomo in Mashonaland.

No one summed up the tribal nature of Mugabe and ZANU in 1978/1980, than Ken Mufuka, a Shona. Writing in 2019 after the death of Dumiso Dabengwa, Mufuka argued that, "*..we were shocked when....Mugabe separated ZANU from the Patriotic Front. We felt betrayed and shocked. The dream which I had shared with Dabengwa in Jamaica, that tribal fissures were a thing of the past, had been betrayed. We in ZAPU were true nationalists as Dabengwa had explained to me. Zimbabweans were free to adopt different identities, while the supra organization, Zimbabwe was representative of all nationalities. We know for certain that there was opposition within ZANU to this direction*"

Despite Mugabe's devious treachery, Nkomo instilled in his supporters the ideal of unity as evidenced by the LMG (a group of former ZPRA) choir song, "*sasuka le emakhaya saqonda eChina*" (we abandoned our homes and headed to China for weapons). While ZPRA did obtain weapons from China, the bulk of their hardware came from Russia. ZANLA got the bulk from China. That song showed that, ZPRA after independence wanted the people to see no distinction between them and ZANLA. On the other hand, ZANU gentry and supporters saw ZAPU and ZPRA as the enemy, hence their songs "*Nkomo arembera pamuchinjikwa*" (Nkomo is hanging on the cross) and *"maruza imi"* (you Ndebeles, ZAPU and Nkomo have have lost the elections). The songs were demeaning, chiding and scornful to ZAPU and the Matabele.

If thus far nothing had awakened ZAPU and the Matabele to the painful reality of freedomless independence, then those songs must have suddenly rekindled memories of Ian Smith singing *"Bobbejaan klim die berg"* on 03 April 1970. They realized that they had undertaken a more than two decades long and tortuous journey to nowhere. Ian Smith had called them baboons and now Mugabe and his executives were about to call them snakes and cockroaches. No matter how optimistic Nkomo, ZAPU and the Matabele were, they were bound to accept that freedom was an expensive product, so expensive that the war and all the blood that had been shed were not enough to buy it for them.

On 26 February 1980 the British governor and supervisor of the elections, Lord Soames held a cloak – and - dagger meeting with Mugabe for two hours in Salisbury (Harare). Maphenduka (2015) questioned the motive and agenda of the secret meeting held on the eve of the elections by Lord Soames and Mugabe. After promising to preside over a free and fair election, there was nothing fair in the governor and presiding officer convening a private, hush – hush, eleventh hour meeting with one of the candidates. The suspicious nature of that engagement was further exacerbated by the fact that the governor himself had admitted at a meeting attended by all political parties a few days earlier, that ZANU was guilty of electioneering violence. He had stated that a fair election was going to be impossible in those areas in Mashonaland where ZANU / ZANLA had unleashed terror on ZAPU supporters.

Sometime between September 1979 and 26 February 1980, the British government and Mugabe must have struck an unholy concord. On 26 February 1980 at Government House in Salisbury the pact was sealed. What the world knows about the discussions during the meeting is what the two 'friends' chose to tell the world. One certainty however is that they did not disclose all their resolutions. According to Meredith (2007) the meeting was a trust building exercise between the two men who prior to the meeting, the world is made to believe, haboured severe mutual distrust. He stated that at the meeting, Lord Soames, who had been advised by all, including his closest advisors to either ban ZANU from the election completely or in those areas where they were guilty of intimidation, informed a relieved Mugabe that he would not ban Mugabe and ZANU anywhere.

It was also said that the two discussed the post – election period which was a concern to Lord Soames. Mugabe then assured Soames that there would be no reprisals, discrimination or disenfranchisement of the white population in his country. At the same meeting Mugabe invited Soames to help him run his government since he and his team had no experience of state craft. Mugabe lastly invited Soames to stay on in the country for as long as he liked, as part of Mugabe's government (Meredith 2007). It would appear as if that was all that was discussed in that meeting.

On 26 February 1980 at night, a few hours before the commencement of the elections, at the insistence of Lord Soames, Mugabe had yet another hugger – mugger engagement, this time with General Peter Walls. In that meeting Mugabe, offered Walls the position of Commander of the Armed Forces in the impending new dispensation. Walls accepted, albeit without much keenness and conviction as events that would soon unfold suggested (he also resigned from the position within four months of the appointment).

The two under wraps meetings pointed to nothing but a conspiracy by the British to rig the elections in Mugabe's favour. If not, then the following concerns needed answers: first, why did Lord Soames not invite Nkomo, Sithole, Ndiweni, Chirau and other candidates to the same meeting or to similar engagements? Probably he did not bother engaging them because he knew they would not win the elections. According to Meredith (2007), Somaes refused to ban ZANU and Mugabe despite indisputable evidence of voter intimidation by them because he had concluded that Mugabe would win anyway. Therefore, he argued that a ban would be pointless and would jeopardize any chances of working with Mugabe to achieve an *"orderly transition"*. The question screaming for an answer was, how could he have known that Mugabe was going to win? Such a conclusion from an envoy meant to supervise a free and fair election was most irresponsible and ourageous to say the list.

Even if Soames had gotten somekind of revelational insight on the election outcome and was convinced that Mugabe would win the elections, his role as presiding officer precluded him from undertaking any action that betrayed or confirmed that conviction. In addition to being incompetent for the job (Meredith 2007), Lord Soames was unbelieveably biased and compromised. The only logical explanation to Soames' bungling could be that, he was an interested party and therefore incapable of objectivity.

The most possibly ludicrous assertion by a presiding officer is to predict that a particular candidate would win the election, yet Lord Soames predicted that Mugabe would win, days before the voting had started. As if that was not enough electoral thuggery, he used his powers of prophesy to inform his decision making. Soames clearly conducted himself like a high ranking member of the ZANU commissariat. One needs to read Meredith's (2007) account of Soame's description of Nkomo immediately after the latter had lost the election, to know that the former was in a celebratory mood. Soames and the British wanted to have a good relationship with Mugabe and what better way to achieve that than to help him win the elections?

Secondly, if the meeting of 26 February 1980 during the day was the first friendly private engagement between the British and Mugabe, then judging by its accomplishments, it was the most progressive meeting in that year under the sun. Political negotiations the world over are characterized by shuffling to and fro party headquarters as negotiators consult their principals, especially if there is mutual distrust. Actually, the world thought there was more than animosity between Mugabe and the British since sixteen days earlier an assassination attempt had been made on the former's life in Fort Victoria (Masvingo) and he had not minced his words as he unequivocally laid the blame on the British door step. According to Meredith (2007), after that assassination attempt on 10 February 1980, *"their exchanges became increasingly acrimonious"*. One then wondered how a single meeting between the two men, in the absence of their advisors created such camaraderie and 'love' in a single stroke? The answer was obvious: that was not the first and only engagement between Mugabe and the British government and there is no reward for guessing what they had discussed and agreed upon on previous encounters.

Thirdly, if the appointment of Peter Walls as commander of the armed forces had been proposed to Mugabe by Soames in the afternoon of 26 February 1980, how was it possible that Mugabe accepted the arrangement during the meeting and effected it by the night of the same day? Given that there had been no time between the two meetings for Mugabe to convene a ZANLA war council or a ZANU politburo meeting, there was no doubt that the issue had been dealt with before. Besides, too many commanders and heavy weights within ZANLA and ZANU were eying the position of commander of the armed forces for Mugabe to unilaterally impose Walls on them. There was no doubt that Wall's appointment had been agreed upon, way before 26 February 1980. It was a *quid pro quo* affair whereby Mugabe had to accept Walls as army commander while the British delivered him electoral victory the next day. The night meeting was meant for Mugabe to prove his commitment and deliver his end of the bargain before the elections. It was critical for the British that Walls be the commander of the armed forces because they wanted a guarantee that their nationals in the country would not be harassed and butchered by the new army under the charge of a black Maoist commander like Tongogara. Most probably one of the reasons why Tongogara died was to create a vacancy of commander of the army, because ZANLA had no substantive commander by February 1980. There was no doubt that if Tongogara had been alive, he would not have accepted the appointment of Walls ahead of himself.

Therefore, the two meetings of the 26 February 1980 were for the governor on behalf of the British government, to cash in on the favours they had done for

ZANU and Mugabe at Lancaster and for ignoring Nkomo's complaints of voter intimidation by ZANU. Ergo, Mugabe had to show final commitment to matters previously agreed upon, namely that if the British won him the election, he would protect not only their economic interests in the country but the white community as well, by appointing Peter Walls as commander of the armed forces and some white Rhodesians into cabinet as agriculture and transport ministers.

Maphenduka (2015) was probably in the right by contending that it was in that clandestine meeting that concessions and compromises were reached and a mutually gratified friendship was struck between Soames and Mugabe. He observed that it was at that meeting that probably they agreed that Mugabe would not be penalized for the violence unleashed on ZAPU supporters in Mashonaland that resulted in the deaths of two ZAPU candidates and eighteen supporters. That being the case, Mugabe won the first supposedly democratic elections held on 27 February 1980 on 26 February 1980, courtesy of the British labour government under Mrs Margaret Thatcher.

The speculation that the British rigged the elections for Mugabe, was further explored by Prof. Scarnecchia's assertion in the Zimbabwe Independent of 5 September 2013 article titled, 'how Zimbabwe assisted apartheid South Africa'. He noted that, *"(t)here are at least four periods in the transition from Rhodesia to Zimbabwe during which the US and the UK offered opportunities to Mugabe and his allies to attain power and then consolidate it...The third was during the elections after the Lancaster House Agreement when the British under American pressure, rushed an election and peace settlement in order to pre – empt further Soviet and Cuban involvement in Zimbabwe, which resulted in a victory for Mugabe"*.

Who can be blamed, based on the conniving and surreptitious character of the engagement between Soames and Mugabe, for assuming that it was at this meeting that the idea of a sham government of national unity with ZAPU and the idea of Gukurahundi were hatched or refined. It was not surprising that on 18 April 1980 Mugabe confessed to *"implicitly trusting ... fondly loving"* Soames. Definitely, something fishy was afoot because given the rigorous nature of holding elections and campaigning, there was precious little socializing, hobnobbing and relationship building the two men could have made in such a short period of time for the two of them to develop such a compelling romance. Obviously the romance was born or blossomed in that clock and dagger, mother of all meetings of 26 February 1980. After winning the elections Mugabe simply could not hold back his elation and gratitude to Soames, hence his unwitting declaration of love.

From the 27th February 1980, the elections were held for three days in the presence of a Commonwealth Peace Keeping mission commanded by a Briton. Many international observer missions and journalists were also present. The election results announced on 4 March 1980 by the Commonwealth Secretary General Sir Shridath Ramphal, showed that ZAPU had won all the 20 seats in the western part of the country (Matabeleland) while ZANU won 57 seats to the east (Mashonaland) and Bishop Abel Muzorewa's UANC won the remaining 3 seats in Mashonaland. The outcome indicated unequivocally that the voting trend was (not weirdly but distressingly so) aligned to ethnicism. It became apparent despite vehement refutation from both protagonists that ZAPU was a Matebele while ZANU was a Shona party. Pundits correctly observed that that first election and the 1985 plebiscite were nothing but ethnic censuses.

The election results could not, by any stretch of the imagination be taken to reflect a democratic majority. Instead the results suggested the horrific existence of a tribal majority. A tribal majority whereby political power rested in the hands of a particular tribe by virtue of their superior numbers, before their elite went on to repress the minority groups simply because they were fewer and belonged to a different tribe. The events that unravelled in the next few months confirmed the dreadful fears of a tribal majority and the possibility of tyranny by the elite in the name of the majority.

Peter Walls had fears too, although he was more afraid of a Marxist type of government. He was appalled by the unblushing rigging and was seemingly not too keen to work for Mugabe in fulfillment of the 26 February 1980 secret meetings. In a top secret letter to Margaret Thatcher on 01 March 1980, after pronouncing his complete lack of confidence in Lord Soames' *"moral courage"* and capacity to be equal to the onerous task of supervising the elections, a defiant Walls implored the British Prime Minister to declare the elections null and void in the event of an impending Mugabe win. He proferred his reasons as "... *intimidation, breeches of the ceasefire and sheer terror accepted pathetically by your representative.......especially as reports from all around the country indicate that massive intimidation makes a victory by Mugabe the most likely if not inevitable result of the election".*

Walls further indicated his preparedness to unconstitutionally (militarily) intervene to avert an impending rigged outcome and a Marxist take over. An unpublicised response to his correspondence was dispatched from number 10 Downing Street on 03 March 1980. Since Thatcher did not declare the elections null and void, since Walls did not stage a coup d' etat after the win by Mugabe was announced, since Mugabe by his conduct and in his victory speech assured the British government, the white Zimbabwe Rhodesians and Walls, that there would be no leftist - Marxist government and the white establishment would be held sacrosanct, the gist of Thatcher's reply is easily fathomable.

Peter Walls was obviously told to back off and suspend whatever ideas of military adventure he was entertaining. Maybe he was mollified by the offer of the 26 February 1980 tete a tete between himself and Mugabe. Maybe he was reminded of the bigger picture whereby his looming appointment to a senior position in Mugabe's army would work for the general good since he would monitor the latter to make double assurance that the white people's interests were preserved. Maybe he was bluntly told to lump it, if he did not like it. Whatever Thatcher said, what is crystal clear is that Walls was told the election results would be upheld, that there would be no military coup d' etat by him and that Britain would uphold the results despite the hundreds of signed affidavits telling about ZANU / ZANLA electioneering violence.

It was not Walls alone that had to bite the bullet. In the face of having protested to Lord Soames the British High Commissioner prior to the elections, in spite of the latter's concurrence that there was terrorism and mass intimidation of the electorate in the eastern provinces and after a team of election supervisors from Britain had affirmed that 50% of the voters were living in a milieu where a free and fair plebiscite was impracticable, Joshua Nkomo and ZAPU accepted the outcome. Their consolation lay in the illusionary notion that African nationalism had triumphed over white minority rule. Deep down his heart Nkomo should have known that tribal nationalism, Zezuru hegemony and British imperialism had triumphed over African nationalism. Ndabaningi Sithole, the ZANU Ndonga leader whose supporters in Manicaland had been terrorized by ZANLA campaigners as well, must have had that insight.

Nkomo should have realized that the problem with Ian Smith and his government and all successive governments since 1924, was not the rule by white minorities but entrenched discrimination, segregation and oppression of black people. Nkomo and ZAPU should have realized that only the white face of the Prime minister had changed to a black face and the rule by a minority hand changed to rule by the majority. Those changes alone were meaningless, empty and deceptive like a castle in the air. In their hunger for freedom ZAPU and Nkomo refused to accept, despite the abundant evidence, that the discrimination, segregation and oppression of the Matabele had just taken a more acute and sinister turn.

By 1984, Joshua Nkomo had acknowledged that Zimbabaweans had been taken down the hell path. He lamented that, as part of their electioneering strategy

ZANU had adopted such slogans as *"down with ZAPU....down with Nkomo"*. That hate speech became, over the years a persistent motif that rallied ZANU supporters in an orgy of intolerance and violence to the point of death. The Shona language word for down (*pasi*) also meant ground or earth. The meaning of the slogan was to put ZAPU and Nkomo to the ground, a euphemism for 'kill ZAPU or kill Nkomo'. That crude and callous mantra was so compelling an intonation to some voters in the Mashonaland provinces that they were caught on camera by panorama screaming obscenities at Joshua Nkomo. Some said that he must be hanged. The reason for the death sentence given by one woman was that Nkomo was "silly". Such was the compelling power of political rallying cries, once taken literally, people could be hanged for being 'silly'.

According to Joshua Nkomo, who was ever moderate, liberal and mild in his assessment of Mugabe inspite of repeated slaps to his face by the latter, speeking at the funeral of Lookout Masuku on 12 April 1986, the term *"pasi"* meant to oppress. That meant that when ZANU sloganeers repeatedly chanted the slogan, they were calling for the oppression of the subject of the slogan. Clearly there was something askew with their politics. How could a president of a country call for the oppression of a section of the country, no matter how different or politically misguided they were. Not even Ian Smith had the effrontery to publicly instruct white people to oppress black people.

Slogans such as *"pasi nemadissident"* (down with dissidents) at a time when all Ndebeles were perceived and classified as dissidents, did not help some of the Shona people view the Ndebele people as equals. To some, the slogan meant that Ndebeles should be killed while to some it probably meant they should be oppressed. The ZANU elite wanted the the Shona to feel superior and separate from the Ndebele. That was achieved with some Shona people particularly after the 1985 elections when they started getting all the police, army, immigration, customs, teaching, nursing etc, jobs everywhere in Matabeleland while the Matabele went jobless. The people were antagonised, with the majority firmly behind Mugabe and his ZANU party. The ground was level for Mugabe to do as he pleased. 'Divide and conquer' had worked perfectly. It was hunting season for Mugabe and his huntsmen.

Conversely, the election results hinted it and Mugabe set about accomplishing the dichotomization of Zimbabwe into two politically antagonistic camps, Matabeleland and Mashonaland. Nkomo must have seen it coming when Mugabe told him to his face to, *" ..go and campaign in your country Matabeleland.."* Nkomo and 'his country' Matabeleland would be shocked out of their wits in the next months when they gazed at triumphant tribal nationalism in the face while their decades - old dream of democratic black majority rule went up in flames.

On the 18th April 1980, Zimbabwe declared independence from Britain and minority rule by white settlers after the first 'democratic' elections conducted under the maxim *"one man one vote"* ushered in Mugabe as Prime Minister and ZANU as the new ruling party. An election victory for Mugabe and ZANU, that according to Scarnecchia (2013), was not without the assistance of the UK and the USA. Dabengwa (interview, 17 March 2017) agreed with Scarnecchia when he observed that, *"the elections were a mere formality, the elections were determined by the time we finished Lancaster. Mugabe had been taken aside and he knew he would win"*.

Soon after using the tribal card to win the 1980 elections, the ZANU government religiously pursued the demonization and demolition of everything and everyone that was not ZANU and ZANLA. In the name of the people, [eg such catch phrases as *"gore remasimba evanhu"* (the year of the power of the people) were popularized on national radio and televion] the country was divided up along a narrow ethnic and partisan line so that ZANU could have absolute power.

They used the majority to oppress and subjugate the minority, although not much but piecemeal structural development accrued to the majority in Mashonaland. Only education and health received substantial attention in the eastern districts. The elite benefited immensely, while the masses enjoyed preferential treatment in the fields of education, health, job creation and recruitment bias in employment at the expense of Matabeleland. What mostly caused Mashonaland to feel like they were a class above Matabeleland was the euphoric notion of triumphalism. That feeling was further buoyed by such taunting songs as *"maruza imi"* (you have lost) and *"wuyayi mowone Nkomo arembera pamuchinjikwa"* (come and see Nkomo hanging on the cross).

Notwithstanding, it must be noted that the Mugabe that surfaced in 1980 was not a British creation from Lancaster. The british government merely egged him on, refined him and gave him the wings of wax before instructing him to fly as high as he wanted. From 1976 to 2013 Mugabe was consistent in his quest for absolute and unshared power attained by all means fair or foul.

In 1976 when the guns of war were blazing and all were intoxicated with the euphoria of the revolution, many did not notice any anormally in his avowal that, *"our votes must go together with our guns; after all, any vote we shall have, shall have been the product of the gun. The gun, which produces the votes, should remain its security officer, its guarantor. The people's vote and the people's guns are always inseparable twins*". That was a dangerous creed and years later when the wax in his wings started to melt because he flew too high, he would regret it. From that Machiavellian attitude stemmed the root of all the political violence. Mugabe accorded himself *carte blanche* and in the name of the people he was to commit the most atrocious evils in the land. That statement was a future declaration of war on anyone who would attempt to out vote him within and outside ZANU. He went on to employ the gun as a tool to win not only the first but eight more elections. Violence prior to, during and post voting were his means of power retention and regime security. Indeed, the gun and the vote became the siamese twins he had intimated.

Mugabe was to celebrate the twin – some (the gun and the vote) until 2017 when the guns were turned against him. Then he lamented, *"...we will not allow the gun to lead politics. Our philosophy is, politics leads the gun"*. Mugabe was then begging the African Union (AU) commission chairperson Mr. Moussa Faki Mahamat on 19 February 2018, to intervene after he had been forced to resign from the office of president at gun point. Suddenly, yet sadly too late for him, Mugabe realised the gun should not have been given twin status with the vote. No one took heed or pitied him because it was his own poisoned arrow that was sticking out of his bowels.

In 1979 Mugabe had declared that if ZANU lost the election they would go back to the bush and resume the war. That was a pronouncement of ZANU nationalism and not African nationalism. It meant that only ZANU could win the elections. Many celebrated his decree without realizing the full implications therein. ZANU nationalism quickly transformed to majoritarian nationalism. A win by ZAPU, UANC, NDP, NDU or UNFP would be considered a precursor to war. He repeated that intransigent stance when he categorically threatened in 1985 that voting for ZAPU was tantamount to voting for war. In 2011 his securocrats led by Brigadier Douglas Nyikayaramba and semi permanent loyalist Didymus Mutasa, amid a chorus by their like minded apparatchiks repeatedly lambasted the opposition for being in opposition and made it clear that the army would not allow anyone else but Mugabe to be president of the country.

Influencing his bootlickers in no small way, Mugabe exhibited the sanctimonious attitude of *aut Caesar aut nullus* (either Caesar or nobody) before he had even won the elections in 1980. He was prepared to pull and raze everything to the ground until he had his way. The evil demon of craving for absolute power and never brooking any thought of another person taking over had already inhabited his soul long before the Lancaster House negotiations in 1979. It never let him free through the turn of the millennium all the way to the coup in 2017. Unlike Joshua Nkomo, Mugabe instead of the team, believed in himself and himself alone. He replaced leadership with rulership especially in Matabeleland where he was perceived as a ruthless, remorseless and absolute tyrant emperor.

By employing the invidious tactics of murder, impositions, intimidation, coercion, violence and patronage, Robert Mugabe became the grand master of equivocation, prevarication, propaganda and deception. He would retain power, poll after poll in 1980, 1985, 1990, 1996, 2000, 2002, 2005, 2008 and 2013. The 2008 elections were held at the height of his unpopularity. It was for the first time since 1896 that Mashonaland concurred with Matabeleland on the need for political change and the how part of it but he still maintained a death-grip on the throne as if his very life depended on it.

After the 1980 elections, amid the euphoria of independence, none in the domestic, regional or international arena bothered to analyse deeper, the circumstances of his victory, Mugabe's personality, his assertions and his conduct. If anyone did, they opted to be politically correct by holding their peace. Otherwise someone would have questioned the coincidence of a man (and his wife) educated by the generosity of the Ariel Foundation, a supposedly private philanthropic institution, yet in reality owned by the British, Secret Intelligence Service, winning an election against an extremely popular icon in the country.

An icon who however had a penchant of singing out of tune by calling for land redistribution to accommodate the landless black masses. The bulk of the land which was owned by the minority white farmers of British origin. An icon whose forefathers belonged to a state that had violently resisted British colonialism from 1893 to 1897 in a war described by Austin (1975) as *"by far the strongest and bloodiest in the history of early African resistance to nineteenth-century colonialism"*. An icon who unfortunately for him was sponsored by the Soviet Union who were much dreaded by the British. The elections which were supervised by the British, who soon after the plebiscite flew the ballot papers by British helicopter to Britain making sure there was no record for the future.

On 18 April 1980 Robert Gabriel Mugabe (1924 – 2019) was sworn in as the Prime Minister of Zimbabwe and head of government. On 17 April 1980 he had, in his inaugural speech exhibited singular and infrequent magnanimity. He delivered what turned out to be a *locus classicus* to many columnists in the world when he stated that, *"if yesterday I fought you as an enemy, today you have become a friend and ally with the same national interest, loyalty, rights and duties as myself. If yesterday you hated me, you cannot avoid the love that binds you to me and me to you…… The wrongs of the past must now stand forgiven and forgotten. If ever we look to the past, let us do so for the lesson the past has taught us, namely that oppression and racism are inequalities that must never find scope in our political and social system. An evil remains as evil whether practiced by white against black or black against white".*

Two factors were noteworthy about that celebrated speech. Mugabe was lying when he declared that the past must be forgotten because he of all people knew that it was impossible to deliberately forget that past. He was never prepared to and he never did forget the past. That was proven by his numerous dictions by the turn of the century which had turned much distasteful to the British. His rants against the British proved beyond words that he was hopelessly shackled to the past. Secondly he was merely dancing to Lord Carrington's plea for reconciliation. That is why he reconciled, although temporarily with the British because he was indepted to them for their helping him to rig the elections.

Mugabe in reality extended the proverbial olive branch to the former Rhodesian Front, Ian Smith and his former colleagues in the previous government and white people in general and ostensibly to everybody else. He was talking of white against black and black against white. He was not talking about black against black or Shona against Ndebele. He was declaring a truce and an end to racial discrimination. Evidence which was to be laid bare on the ground soon after his much acclaimed pontification suggested that, excluded from his conciliatory stance was tribal discrimination. It soon was discovered by the Matabeleland peoples that that demagogic speech was not mere triumphant rhetoric but a carefully chosen, rehearsed and masked diatribe, meant to conceal a swooping axe. When the axe landed, the Ndebele would soon realize that the hope of arriving was better than arriving.

To the cheers of the democratic world, on freedom day Mugabe went on to aver that, *"it could never be correct justification that because the whites oppressed us yesterday when they had power, that the blacks must oppress them today because they have power"*. That must have been the sweetest music even to the most thoroughbred dyed - in – the - wool white Rhodesian pessimist. Yet it soon proved to be the most acidulate music for the Matabele. Mugabe failed dismally on the tribal front. The editor of the Zimbabwe Independent (February 19 to 25, 2016) summerised it quite appositely when he noted that, *"while at independence some African leaders were eager to denounce tribalism, Mugabe not only failed to tackle it, but in fact institutionalized and entrenched the scourge, hence crude slogans like "Zezurus unconquerable!".* Mugabe nailed his colours to the mast on day one in office but no one saw them for what they were.

Stuart Doran germanely analysed Mugabe's victory speech when he observed that, *"while overtures to the whites were unambiguous, the signals given to ZAPU and other minority black parties were more equivocal and complex. This was a theatre whose language was poorly understood by Western observers, most of whom were impressed and distracted by Mugabe's temperance towards the white community and its insitutions"* (The Zimbabwe Independent 6 – 12 April 2018)

The white establishment could be criticized for jumping off their seats in jubilation and failing to notice the snear at the other corner of the smiling mouth, but there was no way they could have known that 20 years on, their new knight in shinning armour would defy those very vocalizations in the most tragic and dramatic of fashions. After 2000, Mugabe contradicted his independence day speech word for word. The whites were aghast when on numerous occasions in justification of his land expropriation policy, he stated that yesterday the whites had grabbed land from blacks because they had vanquished the latter, today the blacks now in power were taking back what was stolen from them by whites. In 1980 they had celebrated him, in 2000, they had to just grin and bear him.

It was too late when the whites to realized that Mugabe's independence day speech had been a cheap veneer of window dressing cosmetics disguised in diplomatic rhetoric. Mugabe did not repossess land from white commercial farmers in order to right a historical injustice (although he made many believe that that was the case). He repossessed the farms because he had the power and wanted to retain the power. The war veterans were threatening to jump the ZANU PF ship and vote for the opposition MDC should he not redistribute the land. They arm – twisted him and when he complied, even they were shocked at how far he could go.

The 18 April 1980 speech endeared Mugabe to the international community including the American, Canadian and Australian governments as well as Margaret Thatcher the British Prime Minister and even the Queen of England, Queen Elizabeth II. Overnight he became much acclaimed. Bouquets were thrown at him from all over. He was accorded, somewhat hastily the status of a true African statesman.

In his generosity of spirit, by way of an amnesty, the new Prime Minister extended a long olive branch to the Rhodesian Front party, the Rhodesian army, Selous Scouts, Secret Service agents and mercenaries. He pardoned the executors of human rights abuses and their handlers that had relentlessly oppressed black people. Some of them were security agents who had been responsible for his incarceration for ten years and torture. That was unprecedented, the epitome of reconciliation, or so many thought.

The obvious yet ignored paradox was that every institution promoting democracy and sound governance, peace and reconciliation, including international aid agences, churches, NGOs, neighboring states then referred to as Frontline States and the AU were consumed with the race question and paid no care to the ethnic dynamic, while there were contemporary pointers to conflict as much as there was an abundance of historical warning signs.

The whole world was expectant, not sure if the new African government was going to choose the West, communist China or worse the Soviet Union. That was an epoch when colonial masters like Britain, France, Portugal and Belgium were anxiously desirous of maintaining relations with new independent former colonial territories while Russia and China wanted to establish new relations. In his soon – to - be - discarded safari suits, Mugabe embraced his new found admirer and benefactor, Margaret Thatcher and Britain but did not spurn the Chinese, his wartime benefactors. He shelved the Chinese in his bottom drawer where he was to retrieve them decades later when Anglo - Zimbabwe ties were severed.

The lackadaisical attention to tribal relations encouraged Mugabe's long held repressive presumption that Zimbabwe was or should be a nation - state. A Shona nation - state. That presumption furtively and conveniently swept a heterogeneity of tribes under the poignant rug of nationalism, thereby creating a regional conundrum that was to haunt social justice and the political discourse for decades to come. Mugabe and his ZANU regime noticed that they could do as they pleased with fellow black people as long as they did not rock the whitemen's boat.

Dementedly blinded by an inopportune and temporary desire to reconcile and appease the British and crush completely, ZAPU, ZPRA, Nkomo and the Ndebele, Mugabe bent over backwards to accommodate and appease the former enemies of the revolution. He appointed Ken Flower who had presided over the Central Intelligence Organization (CIO) from 1963 under then Prime Minister Winston Field and through Ian Smith's tenure to continue as head of the (CIO) under him. Ken Flower a vicious master-spy who had not only marshaled the arrest, torture and the deaths of many a freedom fighter, but was suspected of having links with RENAMO in Mozambique, British MI6, Rusian KGB, American CIA as well as the South African Bureau of State Security (BOSS).

Years later after the Mugabe – British romance had soured, Flower revealed that Mugabe *"saw practical advantages in continuing the association* (with Pretoria) *via a white like myself."* Flower was writing about the period soon after independence. Obviously Mugabe had assigned him, being white, to be the link between apartheid Pretoria and Harare because he would be inconspicuous and his activities unobtrusive, while Pretoria would be warm towards him.

The ugly question could not be avoided. What links did Mugabe need with Pretoria when South Africa was under UN sanctions for practising apartheid. Besides, that was at a time when Mugabe used to lambast Pretoria for attempting to destabilize his new government. That implied that there was hypocrisy and a clandestine night - time flirting relationship between the apartheid administration and the ZANU regime. Worse still, that was at a time when Super ZAPU dissidents were sponsored by Pretoria to tarnish Matabeleland's image as home to rebels and during the sabotage of ANC properties and killings of their personnel in Zimbabwe by South Africa's BOSS intelligence operatives. The possible nature and quantum of coopearation and information exchange between Harare and Pretoria through Flower's liaison was too ghastly to contemplate.

Dumisani Muleya in 2019 exposed the egregious and shameful nature of that relationship. It was in defence of Dumiso Dabengwa who was under fire from ZANU PF and the Mnangagwa government's apologists. Dabengwa was being criticised for telling a South African ANC conference that ZANU / ZANLA had never been an ally of ANC / UMkhonto Wesizwe. He revealed the horrendous and nauseous nature of the Harare - Pretoria romance. Muleya stated that, *"When Mugabe took over, Oliver Thambo, the ANC leader came to see him with Thabo Mbeki and in meetings, Mugabe with Mnangagwa refused to allow them to open bases in Zimbabwe....Mugabe offered them symbolic support. That is why no senior ANC guy lived in Zimbabwe except Joe Gqabi who was killed at the ANC house in Avondale in Harare. Even then ANC guys are convinced that Mugabe and ZANU sold out Gqabi...... A lot of ANC guys were targeted in Zimbabwe in raids and bombs which they think the Mugabe regime was part of. .... Mugabe was afraid of apartheid in a big way, so he made an agreement with them. He would not house the ANC and MK as they wanted to shift their headquarters from Lusaka to Harare. This fear was fueled by apartheid's raids on Southern Africa during it's Total Strategy campaign. So Mugabe secretly sent Mnangagwa to Pretoria to negotiate a clandestine cooperation deal with apartheid South Africa at the expense of ZAPU / ZPRA and ANC / MK. This became part of the Gukurahundi campaign. Mugabe wanted to destroy ZAPU / ZPRA structures, while Botha and later De Klerk wanted to destroy ANC / MK structures, so a marriage of convenience arose".*

That was one reason why Mugabe retained former white minority regime security operatives and why he chose to fraternize with apartheid Pretoria. That political amorous affair between independent Zimbabwe and apartheid South Africa gave rise to a lot of incurable diseases like the Gukurahundi genocide and the assassinations of uMkhonto weSizwe cadres in Zimbabwe, yet strangely some ANC luminaries like Thabo Mbeki and Cyril Ramaphosa could not remember that, even after Dabengwa had reminded them in 2019.

Kevin Woods, another white CIO operative was also retained from the previous regime. Just before his adoption by Mugabe, Woods, the founder of Renamo in Mozambique, handed over his files and custody of the rebel group to the South African security apparatus. He obviously wanted the Mozambicans to continue with the civil war. That act proved that despite working for a majority nationalist government, Woods was still pushing the agenda of the former oppressive regime. He was to latter write a book, *"Under the Shadow of Mugabe's gallows"*, chronicling his role in the CIO during the Gukurahindi genocide and his relationship with Mugabe during the same period.

Mugabe also employed as head of a security branch, Matt Calloway from the previous Ian Smith government. Calloway defected to South Africa and became a saboteur a few years later. Lieutenant General George Peter Walls (G.L.M.; D.C.D.; M.B.E.) whose military prowess was as definitive as his reputation for callousness was monolithic, was accorded by Mugabe the office of Commander of the Combined Operations Headquarters of the Military of Zimbabwe or commander of the armed forces, until his retirement on 29 July 1980. That was the same Lt. Gen. Walls who in 1977 with the Prime Minister Ian Smith's consent, had announced his infamous credo, *"from contain and hold, to search and destroy"*. In furtherance of that myopic and sadistic ideology, Walls in May of that year attacked ZANLA in Mozambique hammer and tongs. He inflicted irreparable human damage in the process by use of the Rhodesian Air Force and paratroopers. In September 1978 he announced that on a daily basis the Rhodesian forces would be carrying out incursions into Zambia, Angola and Mozambique to flash out ZPRA and ZANLA.

So disreputable was Lt. Gen. Walls that ZPRA had attempted to eliminate him on 12 February 1979. ZPRA shot and destroyed The Umniati, a Vickers Viscount airplane, with a SAM-7 missile in a bid to assassinate him. The General and his wife were however not on board the beleaguered flight, but had boarded another Viscount that had taken off from Victoria Falls airport 15 minutes later. The 59 passengers, including Lieutenant Spike Powell all died in the attack. Joshua

Nkomo said Walls was responsible for the passengers' deaths because he was the *"biggest military target."*

According to Nkomo, also retained from the previous regime were operatives, Fraser Arnold (CIO) and DSO Kaurayi who later incarcerated, interrogated and tortured former ZPRA army commander, Lookout Masuku and former ZPRA intelligence chief and secretary of the War Council, Dumiso Dabengwa soon after independence.

The former Smith regime agents whose colleagues could not stomach integration into the new combined Zimbabwe army but preferred to join the racist apartheid South African Defense Forces, became double agents. They became Robert Mugabe's intelligence of misinformation. One of their early missions on behalf of Pretoria, while running errands for Mugabe, was to drive a wedge between the historically antagonized ZAPU and ZANU so that they stayed apart. That mission they accomplished with glee and infrequent distinction.

Those were the men Robert Mugabe preferred to put in charge of the security apparatus of the new state and to be responsible for integrating ZPRA, ZANLA, and the Rhodesian Defense Forces. While there was nothing inherently wrong, considering the spirit of conciliation in the air by then, with accepting Lt. Gen. Walls and the entire suspicious assemblage of former Rhodisians, there was something conspicuously sinister in Mugabe shunning Akim Ndlovu the first ZPRA commander, Intelligence Chief Dumiso Dabengwa, Charles Grey and other ZPRA military luminaries. Freedom fighters who had sacrificed limb and life in defence of an ideology that had ushered him into power. Lt. Gen Lookout Masuku who was commander of ZPRA's 15 000 strong army was appointed deputy commander of the ZNA but was soon arrested on treason charges and later died in prison.

It was as certain as night follows day, that Ndlovu, Masuku, Dabengwa and the entire ZPRA command could not be accommodated because they were Ndebele and ZPRA. It was a paradox that the western media houses unwittingly praised Mugabe incessantly for statesmanship, unconditional reconciliation and altruism while he was bathing his hands in the blood of his fellow blacks. So lucid was Mugabe, that he did not dummy Ronald Reagan the US President alone, but Margaret Thatcher, the British establishment and the West were so elated, they lost all rationale and got blinded to all the sins and crimes the man was to soon commit in Matabeleland and Midlands provinces. To them the olive branch extended to the whites was enough and the Matabele could go to waste.

Mugabe was terrified of an imaginery ZAPU / ZPRA military *coup d' etat* and therefore sought to disenfranchise them from security operations. The Catholic Commission for Justice and Peace (CCJP) and the Legal Resources Foundation (LRF) in their research study report, Breaking the Silence, Building True Peace, noted that despite the fact that ZPRA had a *"well established intelligence unit"*, she was not invited to avail her services to the new regime. In addition to the ground force, ZPRA had a well grilled air force and tank regiments with enough hardware to storm and inflict real damage to the RDF. Unlike ZPRA, ZANLA had no conventional battalions and did not possess tanks and aircraft units. That was part source of Mugabe's apprehension.

One would have been correct to assume Mugabe would at independence trust ZPRA and not the Selous Scouts with the security of the state, government and the country. On the contrary it appeared as if ZPRA's well oiled machinery earned ZAPU a lot of distrust from the new government. According to Alexander et al (2000:181) in Mashingaidze (2005), *"ZPRA's capacity for conventional warefare was also a source of friction. Following ZANU's victory in the February 1980 elections, the possibility that the clearly surprised and disappointed ZAPU would use these forces which were still based outside the country to obtain victory by other means was a source of concern for ZANU. These seeds of distrust and division fell on fertile ground in the early 1980s"*. Still it would have made peaceful sense for him to have trusted both ZAPU and the Rhodesian Front. Instead he trusted the latter and spurned ZAPU. Little did he know that trusted Peter Walls had been within a whisker of staging the coup he was so perturbed about soon after his electoral victory.

Mugabe's consciously high-minded speech at independence, coined to deceive, ushered in a singularly curious relationship which was as convenient as it was historical. It was a bizarre and macabre repeat of that shameful occassion the government prefers to omit from their official history books, when in 1893 the British colonialist Leander Starr Jameson enlisted the services of 652 Shona warriors as porters and amateur marksmen to attack the Mthwakazi state, the Ndebele capital Bulawayo and King Lobhengula. Reminiscent of that sad month when the British and the 652 in cahoots, invaded Mthwakazi and burnt to the ground King Lobhengula's capital, the new ZANU government in 1983 recruited the former settlers as they maimed, tortured and butchered the descendents of Kings Mzilikazi and Lobhengula.

The recruits and some former ZANLA, in an unholy consortium, like a jaggernaught of death oiled by human blood, cruised through Matabeleland and parts of Midlands. Like a carnivorous dinosaur through a calves' byre, it was devilishly powered by state granted immunity.

Robert Mugabe had learnt a lot from the previous administration, including one strategy from the desk of former governor Lord Christopher Soames. He granted immunity to state security agents for any activities carried out in the name of securing the country from both foreign and domestic threats. With the immunity, the 5th Brigade, ZNA, Support Unit, CIO, PISI, ZRP, Prisons, CID and even the youth militias, transformed into tough talons of ruthlessness that dealt with real and imagined threats to law and order with a sinister and ominous knack, that only institutionalised impunity could guarantee.

When quizzed about the romping in of Smith's CIO operatives, the Mugabe regime said that they needed their intelligence experience since ZANLA had had no intelligence wing (CCJP and LRF 1997). Events that followed the appointments answered the question of why the ZPRA intelligence department under Dumiso Dabengwa was shunned. Why Mugabe trusted Ian Smith's Ken Flower and not Joshua Nkomo's Dumiso Dabengwa. The unbearable and devastating answer was that Mugabe had plans that he did not desire known by ZAPU. Plans that he could only afford to let the former government establishment and not the Matabele know. Plans of the Gukurahundi genocide. Again, apperantly Mugabe was paying back the favours extended to him by the Lords, Lord Carrington at Lancaster and Lord Soames in Salisbury just before the 1980 elections. Appointing a Soviet trained intelligence supremo (Dabengwa) would be against British Cold War interests. Besides Mugabe was having too many sleepless nights in fear of a ZAPU / ZPRA coup.

Robert Mugabe's lionized discourse and carriage on 18 April 1980 coupled with the 1979 Amnesty Ordinance 3 by British Governor Lord Soames,' rendered the former torturers and security operatives, free men. Free enough to join the new government as *"integral"* components to the security forces, according to Emmerson Mnangagwa, Mugabe's strongman and former personal aide and next president. They were given freedom to assume new identities but pursue the age old schema of kidnapping, detaining indefinitely without trial, ignoring due process, torturing detainees and shooting suspects through the back of the head. They trained, propped up and beefed up the uniformed forces and the secret service of the new regime. Such reconciliation, absolution and exoneration were novel and famous to some and yet dangerous in its uninterrogated opaque motives, to ZAPU and ZPRA.

The sad enigma was that Mugabe unilaterally declared that there would be no retribution, punitive justice or truth and reconciliation exercise in the mould of the South African experience of 1996 and was still celebrated as a statesman par excellence. He made it his sole responsibility not to consult other players in politics, government and the general public that had borne the brunt of colonialism, UDI and the war of liberation. He singularly pardoned all, the good, the bad and the ugly, yet amnesty was supposed to be a collective decision, resulting from broad based consultations.

Coltart (2016) argued that "...*the absence of a truth commission at independence had locked us all in the past. Whites had not had to confront their complicity in historical injustice and black politicians were wont to dig up that past to further partisan ends*". Mugabe indeed later developed a penchant for digging up that smelly past and dangling the evils of colonialism before the whites as a reminder of their sins, contrary to his 18 April 1980 exhortation to all, to forget. The amnesty became to ZANU a locking vault where they stored some stinking skeletons which they at convenient times unlocked and displayed for political mileage. The spectre of colonialism which was not exorcised through a truth commission in 1980 would be resurrected by Mugabe daily after 2000, to cow the British into a guilty self deprecating silence.

Most were fooled by the superficial nobility in Mugabe's speech and were blinded to the amoral hypocrisy lurking underneath. Worse still on that fateful day, by granting blanket amnesty, Mugabe sawed the enmeshing seed of unilateralism which would ensnare most players in the Zimbabwe body politic, including the opposition as far ahead as 2018. For example, years later in June 2013 he rebuffed his partners in the GNU, Professor Welshman Ncube and Morgan Tsvangirai, by unilaterally decreeing that elections were to be held on 31 July 2013. Prior to that decree, in the preceding four years Mugabe had been notorious for autarchically appointing high and supreme court judges, traditional chiefs, military service chiefs, commissioners etc in violation of state policy.

Robert Mugabe duped the world and eluded the proverbial king's men and horses in their might and flight. By revealing his bright side as he took the first steps in his ascent to the throne, he dazzled so much his brightness hid the zenith of his hatred for the Ndebele people, Joshua Nkomo and ZAPU.

Gatsheni - Ndlovu (2008) captured it appositely when he pointed out that, "*it took a long time for scholars to abandon celebratory analysis of the liberation struggle that included hagiographies and the popular studies of peasant consciousness. Even in the midst of ethnic cleansing orchestrated by ZANU-PF and Mugabe in the 1980s, scholars and the international community remained silent and continued to pile praises on the Zimbabwe government as a successful transition story".*

The wise and astute political scientists and think tank institutions were fooled by his eloquence and mastery of the English language, a tool that he would use for the next almost four decades to confuse, confound, convince and diffuse with equal measure. That talent was part inborn and part a present bequeathed on him by Ian Smith's prison policy which enabled him to study and acquire degrees while incercarated. Ironically during his tenure, it became very difficult financially for a gifted youth outside prison with both parents working, to graduate with a degree from the University of Zimbabwe built by the previous regime. It even became virtually impossible in independent Zimbabwe for prisoners to have one decent meal a day and to save six months in prison and emerge without a sickness due to the inhuman treament and the squalid conditions of the holding cells and jails, let alone to study.

Mugabe refined his demagoguery and over the years he became a demagogue par excellence. If election numbers were anything to go by, he was literally worshipped by the majority in Mashonaland except for the Ndau who kept faith with Rev. Ndabaningi Sithole, leader of ZANU Ndonga for many years. As Mugabe became the equivalent of a deity to the majority and a top - shelf statesman to the British government, very few in the entire international political community outside Matabeleland and parts of Midlands spoke in criticism of him. Very few realized that on the other side of that paragon of reconciliation was a dark portentous personna and countenance. As most of Zimbabweans and Magaret Thatcher's government viewed him as the salt of the earth, he succeeded in showing the rest of the world a façade, and Matabeleland the reality. A very dark, sinister and bitter reality.

Underneath the articulacy, was brewing and simmering a fetid concoction of hate, vengeance and a bloated and bruised ego. A boiling cauldron of historical and tribal tension rising from a fatherless childhood and fermented in the too dark depths of nationalism and the revolution. As poignantly discussed by the Zimbabwe Independent (2016) commentary, Mugabe's dark side was informed by the "*..childhood that made him: the early years defined by a lonely, bitter and angry existence; an absentee father who deserted the family; and a troubled psyche that never lets go of grudges*". Too grey to be noticeable to most at independence, when it eventually did float to the surface, the spectre and stench of his complex was so mordant it could choke the dead.

As he took the oath of office of Prime Minister, Mugabe was still a multi – dimensional slave. A slave of his childhood past, a slave of the rigours of liberation war, a slave of his fears of ZAPU / ZPRA but worse, a slave of his own hate driven ambition.

Little did the world leaders and champions of democracy notice that they had just propped up a monocracy presided over by a killer despot who would in the long term be another of Africa's gerontocracy. That fatal error in judgement was confirmed by former British Foreign Secretary David Owens who conceded too late in 2016. Owens wrote, *"initially I was attracted by his seriousness, his careful use of words and apparent integrity: reluctance to lie, and high personal standards with no evidence of corruption.... From 1980 to 1982 I felt embarrassed that I had misjudged Mugabe's personality....he...remains to this day a deeply conflicted zealot, the sort of person who should never be president of any country"* (The Zimbabwe Independent, 16 – 12 April 2018).

Indeed, the entire British establishment should have been embarrassed at their school boy blunder of falling in love at first sight with Mugabe. As early as 1980, Mugabe was exhibiting evidence of raw and unbridled habitual lies, infectious corruption and infidelity. His speeches were contrived, his integrity phony and his words learnt. There was virtually nothing genuine in him to justify Owen's initial assessment of him except for his seriousness even when he was lying and cooking up stories, fantasy and horrors.

It was not uncommon in the 20th Century for the USA and western governments as well as some African states to abet the setting up and sustenance of oppressive regimes and tyrants. They did that, at times advertently and in some other times they fell to the deception of ambitious and evil machinations of political tricksters. Similarly the conservative government of the iron lady, Margaret Thatcher, set up the Mugabe regime, nurtured and nourished it. They managed to install a dictatorship and destroyed a potential democracy in a single move. Initially they hoped to prop up a puppet regime but when they realized it was a tyranny, they thought that there was more to gain than to lose in letting Mugabe be.

The habit of propping up despots was not novel to Mugabe. Buoying and nursing Congolese Mobutu Sese Seko's greed, financial exigencies, moral depravations and general vicissitudes, was the USA in the 1980s. Mobutu boasted of being friends with George Bush Snr. Throughout his tenure as director of CIA, Vice President and latter President of the USA, Bush spoke highly of Mobutu. Mobutu was the first African head of state to pay Bush a visit after his inauguration as President in 1989. It was sad that such a mature democracy as the USA could endorse such despotism and describe it as *"dedication to fairness and reason"* (Meredith 2005). That was said in the face of the arbitrary arrest of opposition politician Tshisekedi among a litany of other human rights violations including abductions, murders and massive corruption.

Even the most vile of would - be despots always managed to flatter to deceive, so did Africa's number one autocrat before Mugabe, General Idi Amin Dada. The Ugandan secretary to the cabinet, Henry Kyemba said of him after his first cabinet meeting in 1971, *"a model of decorum and generosity"* (Meredith 2005). Amin did give a red herring to the world and all went after it helter skelter. Initially he projected an assuaging fascia for official and public consumption yet privately he orchestrated death hit squads to eliminate real and created former president Milton Obote loyalists and supporters in the uniformed forces. None noticed at independence that Mugabe was singing directly from Idi Amin's book of Friday the thirteenth night songs.

When leaders of ZAPU, especially Mr. Sydney Malunga the first Member of Parliament for Makhokhoba in Bulawayo and ZAPU chief wip, criticised Mugabe, they were labelled obdurate tribalists. ZAPU leaders either died mysteriously (Malunga who became a fervent critic of Mugabe's policies was to die with his driver in a mysterious car accident on 28 August1994) or were imprisoned, blackmailed or bribed into ominous silence. The Westminster adopted whipping system ensured compliance of a few ZANU MPs who might have thought differently. Parliament was dominated by ZANU and therefore in essence a domain of Mugabe's crew boys who dared not criticise him. He was untouchable while successive British administrations continued to feed his hunger and stroke his ego for twenty years until the monster of their creation turned against their kith and kin in the Zimbabwe farms.

In 1987, thanks to the lawyer Dr Eddison Zvobgo, parliament gazetted amendment number 7 of the constitution which became the chief nail on the coffin of answerability by Mugabe. The amendment repealed the office of Prime Minister and created a de-facto regal cum executive president. Executive President Mugabe became supreme to the House of Assembly and did not have to seat in the parliament. He became immune to calls for accountability. He could no longer be called upon to respond to questions by members of the house. Any potential criticism was quashed one way or the other.

For more than two decades in imposing numbers, most in Mashonaland would rally behind Mugabe, ignoring the complaints of marginalization, stories of atrocious killings and other reports of human rights abuses from Matabeleland

and parts of Midlands. For nineteen years their loyalty was absolute, hard, fast, thick and almost blind until 1999. In that year the town folk finally lost constancy and ultimately acknowledged that the ZANU PF administration had failed the country's economy. Eventually, confidence in Mugabe fractured and waned in his stronghold of Mashonaland. Still, he remained popular among many. It was not until March 2008 that Mashonaland inevitably agreed with Matabeleland that Mugabe was a liability. The last time that the two regions had taken such collective decisive action was on 15 June 1896 when the Shona joined the Ndebele in rebellion against the settler government by the B.S.A. Company.

At the combined, presidential and parliamentary elections of 2008, the strongman of Zimbabwe politics accepted that his people preferred another and that his throttlehold was flagging. Still, that was a little too late because Mugabe had entrenched himself deep over a twenty - eight year period and would not check - out of office. He would not heed the very people that were cheering and routing for him over the years, because despite disapproval by most, he still enjoyed the support of many and he was a megalomanic that was guilty of too many crimes and would not risk prosecution by vacating the office of president.

Amid mounting unpopularity, Mugabe was still feared as the devil incarnate in Matabeleland and revered as a demigod in some parts of Mashonaland. He countered his fast declining unpopularity by tightening his death grip on ZANU PF and the armed forces. ZANU PF had long become a monolith personality cult. He employed patronage to keep his cult largely intact and many still trusted his ruinous managent style. Surrounded by zealot praise singers from his tribe, and some patronage - seeking foot soldiers from Matabeleland, he professed to have a seventh degree in violence and more than twenty tricks to win elections. By 2008 he had barely employed half of those tricks he claimed. At 89 he claimed to have the strength of a youth and even challenged opposition leader Morgan Tsvangirai who was in his late fifties to a boxing bout. Many that had been hoping and praying either for his death due to old age and sickness, both of which were patently abundant in him or his departure from office somehow, despaired.

As his star was fading, he seemed to defy his destiny each time rumours about his death were proved false. The miasmic adulation accorded him, permeated the fabric of the country politics and corrupted most of the players. A monstrous miscreant and malformation born of the conflict between colonialism and nationalism, Mugabe, despite his advanced age and poor health was still embittered by historical legacy. The past was both his friend and foe. He was tormented by an unbridled ambition for the future and rendered spurious by a constant apprehension for the present while his personal and political past held him hostage by the throat. Other people upon getting to that stage in life shade off most vices due to the wisdom in the grey hair. But not Mugabe. At 89 he was the same man that he had been in 1977 (53 years old) when he espoused that Zimbabwe was a natural Shona nation with deep precolonial roots. He, according to Mlambo (2013) failed throughout his tenure to see Zimbabwe beyond his Shona ethnic group. There was no room for other nations like the Ndebele, in Mugabe's Zimbabwe.

It was probable that when he envisioned Zimbabwe as a natural Shona state, Mugabe could have been speaking of the pre colonial Shona kingdom outside Matabeleland. A Shona kingdom which was never monolithic since it had many sub tribal groups bound together by an almost similar language and a common history but with varied political economies, values, ideological inclinations and cultural practices. If he envisioned Zimbabwe as a natural Shona state next to the Mthwakazi state he was correct but he should have insisted on the return to the two precolonial states at the decolonization Lancaster House talks in 1979. Assuming, as he indeed did, that the Ndebele and all Matabeleland tribes would succumb and be part of that Shona nation state was a calculated, tribalistic and deliberate mischief. Upon realsing that a Shona state was not possible with the Matabele around, he resolved to force it by breaking them. According to Matikiti (2012), in order to achieve a *"nation state"* the government unleashed Gukurahundi, confiscated ZAPU assets, fired Nkomo and other ZAPU ministers from the government, cleansed the army of ZPRA, arrested Masuku, Dabengewa and others from the ZPRA high command.

In February 1982 the highest ranking ZPRA personnel, Lieutenant General Lookout Masuku and Dumiso Dabengwa, the ZPRA Commander in Chief and Chief of Intelligence respectively and Dr. Isaac Nyathi, were arrested for plotting to depose the government. Five others (Mr. Sydney Malunga, the firebrand and vocal MP, Mr. Edward Ndlovu MP, Mr Vote Moyo and brigadiers Tshila Nleya and Kindness Ndlovu) were arrested with them. Mugabe alleged that Dabengwa, also known as the 'Black Russian' because of his fluency in the Russian language and due to his KGB training, had written a letter to the USSR president Mr. Michael Gorbachev appealing for help in toppling his government. The Russians dismissed that allegation which turned out to be either a figment of Mugabe's spooky imagination or an outrightly malicious work of fiction.

If only Mugabe could read the future, he would have known that indeed a coup would come his way but not from the direction of ZAPU and ZPRA. It would hit him hard, from within the very bowels of ZANU and ZANLA that begot him and probably assisted by the UK that had perfected him. Strangely, in spite of repeated warnings from a Ndebele, he would fail to arrest the real coupists until the end. What an irony.

Some of the reasons for the treason charges were the arms caches found in two farms owned by Nitram. According to Dabengwa (interview on 17 March 2017, Bulawayo), Nitram whose managing director was Dr. Isaac Nyathi had been formed for the sole purpose of acquiring properties for the benefit of and rehabilitation of lower ranks former ZPRA guerillas, some of whom were disabled, disoriented, destitute, widowed, stranded and excluded from the ZDF. The biggest of the farms was in Gweru along the Shangani river with an initial 4000 heard of cattle and land for many homes.

Dabengwa revealed that ZPRA, just like ZANLA was caching weapons at the time, but the commanders were not aware of the size and quantities of the weapons. The observation that both armies were guilty of arms caches was corroborated by non other than the ZANU PF Secretary for Administration, Obert Mpofu in the Sunday news of 14 july 2019 when he asserted that, *"it is alleged that ZANLA was involved in armed conflicts in Mutoko, Mt. Darwin and Gutu. Both sides were involved in the concealing of weapons outside the APs"*.

At Matopo, ZPRA commanders had ordered that weapons belonging to the ANC's uMkhonto weSizwe (MK) be cached. Dabengwa said those were reserved for MK soldiers who were still active in the Kezi and Zezani areas. The arms could not be surrendered to the Zimbabwean government because they did not belong to ZPRA. Nonetheless, the weapons that were discovered in the two farms were neither for MK nor for ZPRA sanctioned. Both armies were shocked by the quantities. It was discovered in court that the regime CIO in a hoodwinking exercise, had pursueded ZPRA junior soldiers, unbeknown to the commanders, to cache arms as security against an 'impending ZANLA onslaught'. The Gwayi case whereby ZPRA's Soneni Moyo had instructed soldiers under him to cache weapons and keep that secret from Masuku and Dabengwa whom he said were selling out to ZANU was submitted in court as evidence of the involvement of the CIO. The suspects were thus exonerated, in the face of evidence that the arms caches were planted by the state CIO.

During the trial, the judge remarked that Dabengwa was the most credible witness to take the witness stand. The judge also observed that the ZPRA commanders were *"the antithesis of people scheming to overthrow the government"*. They were acquitted of all the charges due to lack of evidence, by the High Court judge Justice Hilary Squires in April 1983 and were released. The then Minister of Home Affairs, Dr. Herbert Ushewonkunze embittered by the judgement, in a script that would be repeated for years to come, rancorously lambasted the judge by retorting, *"(l)et it be stated that the acquittal of Dabengwa and others proves once more that the judiciary we inherited from Smith is not in tune with the present government"*.

That pregnant comment by Ushewokunze indicated his desire to have a bench that churned out partisan and not justiciable verdicts. To arm twist the judiciary into servitude and hammer them into line, the entire bench of white judges were repeatedly derided and denigrated by Mugabe and his cabinet for reputedly upholding minority white interests. They were labelled white supremacists before they were wiped off the bench and replaced by black judges. Needless to dwell on where the loyalty of the new crop of judges was invested and where their bread was buttered. Justice Hilary Squires went on to serve diligently as a judge in South Africa until he died there in July 2019.

In a bizzare twist of justice that rendered the just ended court process and acquittal a non event, Dabengwa, Masuku and the rest were re-arrested soon after their high court acquittal. They were incarcerated without trial for four years under the Law and Order Maintenance Act (LOMA) of 1960 which empowered the state to detain a suspect indefinitely without going to trial. Dabengwa saved a total of four years and ten months in prison after having been found not guilty by the high court. The four years he and Masuku spent in detention after the high court ruling indicated that their imprisonment in the first place was for political reasons. The court process was merely to legitimize ZANU tomfoolery, otherwise they were arrested because they were ZAPU, ZPRA and Ndebele.

Soon afterwards, the government embarked on a siege of all the arms of the state including the judiciary by pounding them into a system of zanuism. ZANU became synonymous with the legislature, malevolently coining statutes and laws solely for the preservation of the regime and vanquishment of the opposition. The executive became ZANU *in toto* for all intents and purposes. The judiciary became ZANU, failing to defend the innocent, dishing out cruel and vindictive punishment to those the ruling party wanted punished. The prisons became ZANU hell – holes where inmates were abused, killed, physically beaten, denied food, company, visits, reading material, hygiene and basic decency.

Lieutenant General Lookout Masuku (April 7, 1940 – April 5, 1986) died of torture complications (others believe he was poisoned at Chikurubi prison) on 5 April 1986 after having been transferred under heavy guard on a sick bed from Chikurubi maximum security prison to Harare's Pararinyatwa hospital less than a month earlier on 11 March 1986. Whatever angle one looked at it and however much they stretch their liberal imagination, Masuku died in detention although the government media (ZIANA) was fond of stating that he was released and died soon afterwards. It is no secret that he was transferred from maximum security prison to intensive care. He was in a terrible shape and he was dying. There was a sentry at his hospital door. He was a prisoner in hospital. The death in prison led the Matabeleland Freedom Party's David Magagula in 2009 to announce that his party intended to focus awareness on, *"the almost certain murder of Lookout Masuku"*.

The official version of the cause of his death as per government autopsy, was that he died of cryptococcus meningitis (an inflammation of the brain membrane). He was initially buried at Lady Stanley cemetery in Bulawayo, a clear sign that he was a *persona non grata* to the Harare government which buried the priviledged ones at the shrine in Harare. With him died some of Mugabe's fears of a coup d'etat by ZAPU / ZPRA. Masuku's remains were years later exhumed for reburial at the Heroes Acre in Harare obviously for political capital.

Earlier in January 1980 Masuku (40) had been interviewed by Time Magazine's editor, William McWhirter about the significance of the just ended revolutionary war. He had replied, *"We wanted to vote and to be able to choose our own destiny. Instead, parties were banned, people were arrested and killed, and there was nothing left but to wage an armed struggle......... We have been fighting so that the people could express their will. That is what the country has won."*

Little did Masuku realise how wrong he was about people choosing their own destiny and not being arrested and killed. He himself was shortly arrested and killed and the will of the people would be suppressed for decades. If only he had known that the fruits of the revolution would go stale and sour within a year and he would be incarcerated, tortured and killed in prison like a mad rabid hound, he probably would have authored that letter to Gobachev of the USSR. General Lookout Khalisabantu Vumindaba Masuku, very much a student of Joshua Nkomo, accepted the victory by ZANU and Mugabe as a victory for 'all the black people', a victory for the country, a victory for ZAPU and a victory for himself as well. He could not be further from reality. Masuku obviously realized too little too late that what he termed winning was nothing but Pyrrhic victory, a victory for others to celebrate and his to rue and lament.

Mugabe's intelligence machinery must have read the Time Magazine interview and the security chiefs must have briefed him about it. They knew Masuku's position but they preferred to heed their naïve and paranoid fears of a coup d'etat orchestrated by him and Dabengwa.

Four other former ZPRA personnel, colonel J.Z Dube, Kembo Mohadi (minister of home affairs, minister of State Security under Mugabe and Mnangagwa's Vice President in 2018), colonel Edward Sigogi and brigadier Charles Grey, were later arrested and charged with treason as well. They were detained without trial and tortured senseless. All were eventually released after the state failed to have them convicted of any wrong doing. For those men, independence proved to be a nine days wonder and they could swear that if Ian Smith was Herod, then Mugabe had out Heroded Herod.

Dumiso Dabengwa (06 December 1939 to 24 May 2019) was released from prison in December 1986 some eight months after Masuku's death. He lived to tell the tale about the harrowing ordeals of torture and the dehumanising humiliation he suffered during the imprisonment.

Mugabe's new allies the Rhodesian Defence Forces (RDF), personified by General Walls were in charge of the Assembly Points and supervised the integration of the three armies (ZPRA, ZANLA and RDF). The first two armies were warehoused at Assembly Points (APs) in Entumbane in Buawayo, Ntabazinduna, a few kilometers outside Bulawayo, Gwayi, some 180km from Victoria Falls along the Bulawayo road, Glenville and Connemara in Gweru, Tongogara in Mutare as well as Silobela in the Midlands among others.

With the traditional and expected distrust of the Smith regime by ZPRA and ZANLA armies, it is comprehensible why they both cached weapons of war in the bushes. Some of them did not declare all their hardware in case there was an outbreak of hostilities and there was need for defending themselves. The two armies had been fighting the RDF for more than a decade and there was no way the armies could just kiss and make up immediately after the cease fire. By taking long, the intergration and demobilization processes did not help matters either.

The distrust was not confined to the RDF but it was mutual between ZPRA and ZANLA as well. ZPRA thought ZANLA was waiting for an opportunity to gun her down and vice versa. The animosity was so thick that the ZNA commander Solomon Mujuru who was then using the *nom de guerre* Rex Nhongo, according to Panorama wanted the entire ZPRA army demobilized so that the new Zimbabwe National Army (ZNA) could be made up of ZANLA and RDF armies only. The acrimony was also revealed by Edgar Tekere the ZANU secretary general when he said, *"we did not need his (Nkomo) army in the war, so why are they making a nuisance of themselves now?"* (Ndlovu – Gatsheni 2011).

There is no ideal recipe for military attrition and calamity than incubating two hostile armies with a history of shooting at each other on sight, in a military camp under the supervision of an authority both inmates spent a decade embroiled in an internecine guerrilla war against. That was a set up best analogized by the cat and the rat housed together in a cell under a sentinel, the dog. War was the only possible outcome and Mugabe wanted it badly, so that ZAPU / ZPRA could be blamed as sore losers, rebels and sabotauers. Once that happened he could conveniently wipe them out using his recently acquired state military might.

That Molotov cocktail of the bottle, the petrol and the fire was designed to inevitably fail to hold and explode. The three armies were the bottle, the petrol and the fire. It should have been envisaged that that tripartite marriage would culminate in a highly explosive detonation. Mugabe was intent on making a fire in a petrol room.

When the explosion came, it was first in November 1980 after Enos Nkala minister of national supplies gave an inflammatory speech at a rally at the White City stadium in Bulawayo. He castigated ZAPU as the enemy of the state. That speech epitomized the disdain with which ZAPU was held. It instantly atrophied whatever little tolerance had been achieved in the preceding months. It also announced that the intergration of the three armies had failed as per the ZANU plan.

At the same rally Nkala refered to Nkomo as a *"self appointed Ndebele King"* in the mould of *"Ojukwu of Biafra, Tshombe of Congo, Harry Nkumbula of Zambia and Odinga Odinga of Kenya who tried to appoint themselves as tribal leaders"*. Nkala further said that Nkomo and ZAPU had contributed to the liberation of the country in a *"small way"* (Ndlovu – Gatsheni and Willems 2010). How ZAPU had transformed itself into an enemy of the state at that early juncture of the celebrations was not only implausible but also esoteric to Nkala and his masters in Harare.

The Nkala speech provided the impetus for the uprising at Entumbane (a high density suburb, home to thousands in Bulawayo) Assembly point. Two days of heavy fighting between ZPRA and ZANLA armies ensued before it was quelled by senior commanders from both camps. The fighting re – ignited in February 1981 early in the morning at Entumbane again.

Why such an unstable and potentially capricious military concoction was put up within a residential area defeated reason through and through. It was merely by the grace of God that not many civilian lives were lost at the Entumbane debacle since bullets were flying over houses. For years afterwards, bullets could be found embedded in the tree trunks along the roads and pathways around the assembly point and the township. The second Entumbane uprising spread to Ntabazinduna, Silobela, Silalabuhwa, Chitungwiza, Glenville and Connemara camps, although the magnitude of the fighting was lesser in those assembly points. Some 300 soldiers, mostly ZPRA died before the units of the RDF were enlisted to intervene and stop the fighting.

After the first breakout of violence at Entumbane, according to the CCJP and LRF, some 500 more ZANLA combatants were deployed there while ZAPU officials were arrested. That deployment implied that ZPRA was to blame for the outbreak of the inter army fighting. It could not be doubted that the government opted to reinforce ZANLA presence in Bulawayo in anticipation of further planned armed shenanigans. What other reason could there be for increasing ZANLA numbers and reducing ZPRA. That act alone put to shame and doubt the government's commitment to integration of the armies and unity in government. ZPRA soldiers could not help it but accept that ZANU was spoiling for civil war and they were targeted for elimination. Thereafter massive defections ensued.

After Entumbane in 1981, Prime Minister Robert Mugabe appointed a high court judge, Enock Dumbutshena to head a commission of inquiry. The commission was mandated to investigate what happened at Entumbane, Ntabazinduna, Connemara and Glenville between November 1980 and March 1981. The commission's report and findings are to this day a top – of - the - order secret, locked away in a massive cast iron master safe in Mugabe / Mnangagwa's office. The government, even after the Government of National Unity (GNU) of 2008, still claimed that the report was meant for its sole use and was neither duty nor legally bound to publicise the report. In an obvious cover – up, in 2000, Mnangagwa representing Mugabe infomed the Supreme court that the commission report together with the Chihambakwe Commission report had been lost. Probably if the Dumbutshena commission report had been made public, negative future events would have avoided.

Within a short period of operations, the former ZPRA soldiers that had been intergrated into the ZNA became very aggrieved. Their discomfort which ranged from welfare issues to disappearances of colleagues, soon turned into full scale desertions. Former ZPRA soldiers thought that there was an assortment of differential treatments, which included severe punishment for minor offences while their erstwhile ZANLA compatriots often went unreprimanded for similar or even worse conduct. They also realized that while in camp they were not allowed to carry arms while some of the former ZANLA comrades always had guns. Also the numbers of former ZANLA soldiers kept swelling up while the ZPRAs were dwindling. Lastly, their complaints on these and an array of grievances fell on deaf ears and in most instances seemed to result in further stringent conditions.

The disappearances of their colleagues was the major concern to former ZPRA. To be in the ZNA, became for them, the most perilous predicarment in the post – independence era. In short, ZPRA noticed that they were disintegrating due to the integration process and appealed to Joshua Nkomo for an end to the integration. That did not help them much since Joshua Nkomo went to the Gwayi Assembly Point, where he declared that there would be no stopping the integration and that there would be no pulling out of ZNA. Nkomo's intervention did not quell the apprehension. The soldier's grievances went unaddressed. They were in a quandary in the middle of a raging storm.

Tensions kept escalating between ZPRA and ZANLA. The situation turned dire as tens of former ZPRA soldiers started disappearing mysteriously on a daily basis. One morning they would wake up to observe that some of their comrades had gone missing during the night and would not come back. Some would go on a short leave days and that would be the last they would hear from them. Soon the news crept back that some of their colleagues never got home on their leave days but their decomposed bodies were found far from their destinations with bullet holes. They would hear that some were languishing in the notorious Khami or Chikurubi prisons without trial. They realised they were all in the line of fire and decided to jump ship. This time they did not seek audience with Nkomo, they fled for their lives. Many former ZPRA soldiers deserted the ZNA because they felt they were in danger of dying (CCJP and LFR 1997)

Individually and in small bands, independent of instruction from Nkomo, Masuku, Dabengwa or anyone in the ZPRA command structure, the ZPRA soldiers deserted from the ZNA. They were convinced by the treatment they got from the ZNA that the ZANU government was not committed to full equity and fair integration. They also suspected a civil war would break out and what better position for them than to revert to their pre cease fire positions, safe behind their guns of war and the forests of Matabeleland. Still, many of them that had been intergrated into the ZNA, oblivious to the danger around them or due to procrastination or out of some sense of security or blind trust, justified or not, stayed behind. Some of them also deserted later after the formation of the 5th Brigade. Some were discharged from the army without due process or cause. In total about 500 ex ZPRA soldiers deserted the army and Assembly Points.

According to the CCJP and LRF (1997), after witnessing the arrest of their leaders and the disappearances of colleagues, some former ZPRA soldiers started deserting the Zimbabwe National Army. Nkomo (1984) also said that due to discriminatory treatment at Assembly points and the selective investigations, interrogations, torture and disappearances of their colleagues, some ZPRA soldiers were compelled to run for their lives.

The desertions were halted by the deployment of the ZNA to Mozambique in November 1982 to combat Renamo rebels. For ten years, thousands of ex ZPRA soldiers were deployed to help fortify security in Mozambique. Once focused on an enemy and in a distant geographical location it became difficult to desert. Once in Mozambique it became easier to be killed by friendly fire. Many a ZPRA soldier were killed by 'friendly' fire.

The Catholic Commission for Justice and Peace and Legal Resources Foundation (1997), asserted that the dissidents were used as a pretext for setting the Gukurahundi battalion on Matabeleland and parts of Midlands. They were loyal to ZPRA ideology but were so few they did not number as much as four hundred. Some human rights organisations said that more than 30 000, while some said as much as five hundred thousand civilians were murdered by security forces, buried in mass graves, deposited in mine shafts like Antelope Mine and Bhalabwe. Some were mass burnt after being force marched into grass thatched houses while some were buried alive. Thousands simply disappeared without trace after they were abducted by government security forces who were purpotedly hunting for the dissidents.

Whoever they were and whoever was their principal(s) the dissidents did not possess the military hardware, the financial means and the political will to inflict much damage to the government, to warrant unleashing Gukurahundi on Matabeleland and the Ndebele speaking parts of the Midlands civilian population.

While ZPRA was accorded the respect of a snake in the house, such personnel as Ken Flower, Gen. Peter Walls, Kevin Woods, Lt Colonel Lionel Dyke and Matt Calloway were offered the red carpet. The former Prime Minister, Ian Douglas Smith was allowed the proper decency of retirement to his farm in Selukwe (a Ndebele name meaning let the nation be knit together but later Shonalised to Shurugwi which was meaningless). Smith later criticized Mugabe for breaching the Lancaster House agreement and unleashing Gukurahundi. He said, *"they broke the promises with Nkomo and ZAPU after Lancaster.... they have driven the Matabele into a corner. What do you expect the Matabele to do?.... they (government) provoke it and then throw up their hands in horror and say look what they are doing to us*" (BBC Panorama 1983). He also said that the Matabeleland problem was a creation of the government's policies ever since Nkomo had indicated that he was opposed to the one party state position just like Smith himself because that would militate against economic investment. Smith eventually died of natural causes on 20 November 2007 at the age of 88.

There was validity in Smith's theory that Nkomo's refusal of the one party state precipitated the Gukurahundi genocide and that Mugabe was determined that if he could not get the one party state by consensus then he would get it by whatever means necessary (BBC Panorama 1983). However, that alone could not have been reason enough, otherwise Mugabe should have deployed Gukurahundi against the whites since Ian Smith also opposed the one party Marxist state system and had informed Mugabe just like Nkomo. The reason why the Gukurahundi Brigade was let loose on the Matabele had to do with Mugabe's one party state plans as much as it had to do with their being Matabele, ZAPU and ZPRA.

A phony and withered olive branch was offered to ZAPU when Joshua Nkomo, Josiah Chinamano, and Jimmy Ntuta, in a postiche maneuver to give an impression of a government of national unity, were appointed cabinet ministers of the state. They were offered cabinet posts by Mugabe but were summarily discharged on allegations of attempting to overthrow the regime. That way they could be blamed for the failure of the government of national unity. As Nkomo aptly put it to Mugabe, *"It is clear you wanted us to pull out of your government at that time so as to destabilize the army and the police, create dissidents out of the deserting ZPRA men and then call us plotters against your government"*.

The allegations of overthrowing the government were never proved. Joshua Nkomo the icon of the revolution was hounded out of his high density home in Phelandaba in Bulawayo day and night like a mongrel, until he escaped the country to Britain in 1983. The long and short of it was that the proverbial olive branch of reconciliation which was generously offered to the racist Rhodesian Front party and government and the white community, was denied to African nationalists Joshua Nkomo, Rev. Ndabaningi Sithole, Ndebele paramount Chief Khayisa Ndiweni, Bishop Abel Muzorewa and the minority Matabele. At that stage no one noticed the incongruity, not even most of the would-be victims.

To prove that the government of national unity was but a shameless parody, was the fact that UANC and Bishop Abel Muzorewa, a signatory to the Lancaster House agreement that ushered Mugabe into office and winner of three parliamentary seats in the 1980 elections, was left out of the government. Mufuka (2019) agreed that the government of national unity was indeed a *"charade"* because in October

1980, Mugabe was already negotiating with the North Koreans for the training of the 5th Brigade. Also left out of the government was Rev Ndabaningi Sithole the founder and first president of ZANU. The two were demonized and vilified by ZANU historians and politicians as murderous sellouts who betrayed the revolution. While it is beyond the scope of this discourse to attempt to dispute or confirm that historical narrative, it is true that those two Zimbabweans could not have been worse than the linchpin of Southern Rhodesian apartheid, Ian Smith, the Rhodesian Front party and Peter Walls and their ancestors who were responsible, from 1893 to 1979 for the deaths of not less than 80 000 blacks including ZPRA and ZANLA soldiers and civilians during the war but were part of the 1980 inclusive government. If Ian Smith could be accepted as a *"friend and ally"* by Mugabe, what stopped Mugabe from extending the same *"love"* to Sithole and Muzorewa? Both current and dated history, testified that Nkomo was Mugabe's nemesis and more of a threat than Sithole and Muzorewa put together.

Therefore, the only reason ZAPU and Nkomo were included in Mugabe's first government was that they were a food item on the 'independence' celebrations dinner menu. They were being set up for failure. Mugabe had plans to give them a bad name and then hang them, as events did prove shortly. Indeed, Mugabe managed to paint to the international community, a picture of his government as victims of a security threat from ZAPU and ZPRA. That manuevre was pointed out by the New York Times of 28 April 1980 which reported on the trial of Dabengwa, Masuku and others. The publication reported of the ZANU *"government's determination to go on branding Mr. Nkomo's party, ZAPU as subversive"*. No one in New York and elsewhere listened.

Joshua Nkomo, probably assuming there was still present in his former colleague, the human element that should have been in charge of him at some point in the past, attempted to plead and even beg Mugabe to reconsider, but the latter was single – minded and obdurately angling towards genocide. It took time for Nkomo to accept that Mugabe was hell bent on building a case against him and ZAPU. Like a train, nothing short of an accident would remove him from that track.

After a marathon of meetings with Mugabe, a series of turned down appointments and unkept promises by the same, Nkomo ever patient and hopeful, on the 6th June 1983 authored a 116 points letter to Mugabe, appealing to both the Prime Minister's reason and emotions. At some point in the letter he stated that, *"It is a well known fact that in Zimbabwe today, there are more people detained without trial than in fascist South Africa............These people are not enemies of Zimbabwe, but patriots ....caught, in a conflict the government itself created............The double tragedy of Zimbabwe today is, firstly, that the routine and administrative use of detention, torture and arbitrary repression has been adopted by an independent government, and secondly, that this government uses the very same mercenaries and torturers as the former regime used against the struggling people. In fact, the situation today is in some respects even worse, as our government has abandoned even those standards of bourgeois legality which the Smith regime generally attempted to hide their repression behind............. we have taken the methods and men used to oppress, torture and kill our people and tried to use them to consolidate our 'independence'.........They must smile to themselves when they are ordered to continue their torture of patriots by an independent government"*

Such a statement coming from Mugabe's former leader and party president, telling him his government was fast degenerating into something worse than the monster they had fought against, should have sounded in him the early wake - up call. Regrettably, Nkomo might as well have been kicking against the goads. The leader in Mugabe, just like the teacher, the academic, the brother, the comrade, the husband and the parent in him, was too drunk with partisan triumphalism, too consumed with self preservation, too obsessed with a one party state ideology and too possessed with tribal hate to heed Nkomo's pleas. Mugabe became selectively deaf and impervious to pleas for a return to sanity. He gathered around himself a cabal of mostly fellow Zezuru tribesmen, preoccupied with singing his favourite praises day and night.

Only the combatant soldier (which he never really was since he had received no military training) responded to Nkomo's appeal. He dismissed Nkomo from his government and arrested his generals. Mugabe hoped they would emulate Jonas Savimbi and MPLA in Angola and Alfonso Dlakama and RENAMO in Mozambique by resorting to civil war. However, Nkomo was too full of Shakespeare's *"milk of human kindness"* and peace to adopt that route, much to Mugabe's frustration.

From the outset, ZANU fervidly and violently sought to establish a one party and a one tribe nation state. That alone rendered Mugabe unfit for service in the tribally diverse country as head of state. That must have been observed in the early processes of forming the first black majority government and should have been corrected during his first term. Muage failed dismally and his services should have been terminated at the 1985 elections.

Mugabe wanted the spoils of the revolution for himself and ZANU and to no other. He wanted to be the sole victor. Anyone who came to the victory party was supposed to be undeserving and doing so at his benevolent invitation, as losers. As a founding nationalist, Nkomo and ZAPU were deserving and under normal circumstances were expected to be part of the new dispensation. Nkomo and

ZAPU chose to view independence as a win for all people including themselves. Ian Smith on the other hand could not do that. The whole wide world knew Smith's and the RF's racist ideology of white supremacy had lost and their presence in his government was nothing but proof of Mugabe's acumen and reconciliation. He took credit for Smith's presence in his government.

When Nkomo and ZAPU refused to be losers by saying his victory was a triumph for Black Nationalism which was what they actually wanted, it irked Mugabe. He wanted them to be sore losers so that they would erase their credibility and contribution to the triumph of nationalism over minority rule. He wanted them to go down in history as those that attempted to circumvent democracy and not as fighters for independence. That way ZANU would get all the credit for winning the war and ushering in independence. When they refused that role, he labelled them dissidents. When they refused to be dissidents he nonetheless called them rebels and butchered their Matabele tribe. When they refused to fight back, his historians set about writing a version of history about the liberation struggle that did not acknowledge the critical role played by ZAPU, ZPRA and Nkomo.

It was upon such a tribally discordant, socially alienated, militarily tense and politically polarized foundation that independent Zimbabwe was built. It was a concoction of electoral fraud and violence, historical tribal hostilities and recent ethnic detestation, partisan misgivings and contestations, individual contempt and overwhelming ambition, institutional insecurities and personal vendettas born during and soon after the protracted revolutionary war, that set the climate and agenda from which the country is yet to recover thirty - nine years on.

As Zimbabweans from all walks of life including the losers from ZAPU and Matabeleland, celebrated the demise of the almost ninety - year epoch of white minority rule, while congratulatory messages poured in, some even from Africa's former colonisers, nobody could have noticed the covert cataclysmic advance of a dark ominous cloud in the distant horizon. Nobody could have guessed that tears of joy and embraces would, within a couple of months translate into tears of horror strangles and strangulation of freedom. Little did everybody realise that the red wine and champagne glasses would be discarded for bayonets dripping with blood. Nobody was liable for failing to guess that the attainment of independence could be a precursor of genocide never even imagined under the recently ousted Ian Smith regime. Not even the most saintly of prophets or the most precise traditional diviners could have guessed that black would turn on black in such a confounding mode within so impromptu an interlude.

✧ ✧ ✧ ✧

From almost the cradle of nationalist politics, Joshua Nkomo had been the face of the movement for the freedom of Rhodesia's majority blacks. He was admired and almost revered across the diverse ethnic spectrum. He was known as *Umdala Wethu* (our old man, a sage and source of wisdom and inspiration) *uMqabuko* (the rare first fruit), *Chibwechitedza* (the slippery rock that eluded his persecutors), *Ramatsatsi (the one that astonished us)*. The first two titles were Ndebele, the third was Shona and the fourth was Sotho / Tswana. That collection of names was not merely an appreciation of his massive reputation and colossal political stature, but a statement that his stride straddled across ethnic divides.

Joshua Nkomo had a massive heart. He was accommodative to all and was in turn accepted and respected as a leader by all the tribes of present day Zimbabwe. It was cultural practice for a leader among the Ndebele to have *izibongo* (praises) and an *imbongi* (praise singer / poet) who eulogized his prowess and exploits, told his history while reminding him of his weaknesses and even mistakes. That helped the leader maintain touch with reality, earn respect and trust by the people, scare his enemies away, boost his confidence while he remained within the limits of humanity and humility. Below is an extract from Nkomo's praises as echoed at Chinotimba stadium in 1985 by *imbongi* Cainos Moyo;

Inkunzi emnyama kaNyongolo.
Inzima esikhumb' esehlula abatshuki
Abayivalel' eGonakudingwa yafohla.
Bangayivaleli yavuk' ikhona.

Indlov' enkulu eyawel' uGwembe,
Kwahlehl' ingwenya lamagagasi.
ELusaka bayethes' ubukhosi,
Yona yathi inkosi yinkosi ngabantu.

Inyez' ethethel' izizwe
Yakhalel' amabhunu emandlebeni
Kwaze kwasa bebandwa ngamakhanda
UMqabuko owaqabukw' eNjelele
Kwakhulum' izintaba

Ingqungqul' emnyama
Emadolwabomvu
Ngokuguq' engazini zabafo....

(The black bull son of Nyongolo.
The black bull whose hide could not be tanned.
They imprisoned him at Gonakudzingwa and he broke out,
When they forgot to close the prison gates he did not escape.

The great elephant who crossed the Zambezi,
The crocodiles and the waves gave way.
In Lusaka they crowned him King
But he said kingship is derived from the people

The cricket that speaks for the nations,
He complained to the whitemen.
By morning their heads were still aching
Mqabuko who visited Njelele
And the mountains spoke

The black eagle with red knees,
Due to kneeling of the blood of his enemies).

One would have to be conversant with Nkomo's history and understand Ndebele culture to understand his *izibongo* clearly. However, simple practical analysis revealed comparisons with the majestic black bull, a symbol of authority, wealth and confidence, the elephant which personified enormous capacity, might and valour, the eagle with unparalled eyesight / foresight and a minute (by comparison to the bull and elephant) cricket which represented a trouble maker. The *izibongo* were a narration of Nkomo's past which portrayed him as a prisoner, a respected and humble foreigner with respect for democratic principle, the voice of the various tribes, the all seeing eye gazing into the future and a noise making irritant as far as the white government was concerned.

Still, the praises and titles did not breed in Nkomo a big man. His reputation and stature were big but he did not attempt to be the big man of nationalist politics. He accepted the title of Father Zimbabwe as a symbol of his founding and guiding role in nationalist politics and not as a prerogative and entitlement to being worshipped or a weapon to be used in the domination of others. He remained a player within the party and within the nationalist movement, allowing others to grow into integral players too. His critics and contemporary competitors misinterpreted that as cowardice and being indecisive. They wanted an autocrat and a bully and not a democrat. They wanted a ruler not a leader. Probably that is what cost him the ultimate imperial throne which Mugabe grabbed with zest.

Mugabe on the other hand, fast became a big man as observed by Kofi Annan, the United Nations Secrtary General (1997 - 2006) who noted, *"(t)he support for the Big Man system (Robert Mugabe an example) created a political culture that simply encourages autocrats and dictatorships"*. Due to the big man mentality which ZANU nurtured during the liberation war and cultivated soon after independence, Big Man Mugabe started writing the epitaph for democracy and accountability to the electorate, years before his first day in the office of independent Zimbabwe's Prime Minister.

Mugabe's lack of *izibongo* was a cultural ommission but it could also be a hint at his lack of social virtues. While his treatment of ZAPU and the Ndebele betrayed his personal hatred and lack of social finesse and humane acumen, his handling of the economy proved his masters degree in economics was a piece of paper that denied to prove that he was a master of much in that field. By the turn of its first decade, his fragile administration started having economic challenges. The need for external aid was apparent after Mugabe had managed to crush the economic train and drained all the reserves from the Reserve Bank left behind by Ian Smith.

On the recommendation of the World Bank, Zimbabwe implemented the Economic Structural Adjustment Program (ESAP) in 1990. US$125 million was acquired from the African Development Bank (ADB) to facilitate the program, while other forms of aid were proffered by other international bodies. Nevertheless, the program was a failure and the expected outcomes were not realised. Ojo and Ajayi (1997), reasoned that the envisaged economic efficiency and restoration of macro - economic equilibrium as well as Gross Domestic Product (GDP) growth were not realized. Instead ESAP achieved the opposite. The economy shrunk, exports dwindled while imports of even basic commodities escalated. The confidence index in Mugabe and ZANU was plummeting rapidly.

By the early 1990s the developmental growth inconsistencies among regions that were beginning to be discernible by the mid - 1980s, were getting rudely manifest. Matabeleland was increasingly getting agitated by the obviously skewed development bias for the general benefit of Mashonaland but mostly concentrated in Harare. Infrastructural development projects in Matabeleland would lie stagnant due to lack of funding for too long while the people there thought Mashonaland was enjoying the development cake. On the ground however there was evidence that other provinces like Masvingo, Manicaland and Midlands were lagging behind too as was noted by Hill (2003). He stated that Masvingo was the largest province but it was mainly bushes devoid of meaningful commercial farming which could be witnessed only in the areas around Harare. In spite of that, probably due to ethnic ties between Manicaland, Masvingo, the Shona inhabited parts of the Midlands and Mashonaland, those provinces were not as perturbed by the discrimination as much as Matabeleland was.

For Matabeleland, hope was the only respite. When John Moffat, probably in a rare moment of contrition, considering his earlier dream to see the Ndebele might shattered, prophetically monished that, *"Rhodes is prancing around....there will be a crash some day...and men will suddenly recollect that there is still such a thing as justice, even to niggers"* (Thomas 1996), it rang hollow and shrimpy to the defeated Matabele. That prophecy was meant to be fulfilled in 1980. Be that as it may, the fulfillment was hijacked and it turned out to be a phony justice to the Matabele who still had to wait for justice.

Now it was Mugabe that was *"strutting and fretting his hour upon the stage"*, riding roughshod and trampling at will on the rights of both the Matabele and the Shona too. Just as Rhodes realized from his grave in the Matopos, seventy - eight years after his death, Mugabe, Mnangagwa, Sekeramayi, Shiri and their huntsmen will also realize, probably after their demise too, that there can be justice for Matabeleland and the Midlands.

Chapter IV

GUKURAHUNDI GENOCIDE

"when men and women provide food for dissidents, when we get there we eradicate them. We don't differentiate when we fight, because we can't tell who is a dissident and who is not"

Robert Mugabe April 1983 (Financial Times, Telegraph and The Times, 15.4.83).

The Convention on Prevention of the Crime of Genocide defined genocide as *"the crime of destroying, or conspiring to destroy a national, ethnic, racial or religious group"*. That definition became a binding aspect of international law when it was adopted by the United Nations (UN) General Assembly on the 9th December 1948.

Until 2019, well after Mugabe had been ousted from power, the prevailing environment in Zimbabwe had been such that any discussion or interrogation of the massacre in Matabeleland and Midlands was done in hushed tones, privately or in moderate terms at police sanctioned and monitored gatherings. That condition precipitated misinformation, half backed definitions and absence of consensus on what transpired, let alone whether it was genocide, civil war, murder, disturbances or a mere law enforcement exercise characterized by excessive force here and there.

The questions that mattered, such as who ordered the genocide and when they would face justice in court for their actions, continued to be proscribed and off limits even after 2019 under Emmerson Mnangagwa who made an attempt to open up the space for debate on the genocide. Under Mnangagwa the National Peace and Reconciliation Commission (NPRC) allowed at public meetings, people to unreservedly express their feelings on the genocide. Notwithstanding, the mere fact that the commission was appointed by Mnangagwa, one of the founding fathers of the genocide was a restriction on its own.

At a poorly orgarnised and attended meeting of the NPRC held in Lupane in 2019 and chaired by former judge Selo Nare, it was manifest that the people were still afraid of the government, hence the poor attendance. The fear was not without reason either because there were plain clothes security agents in that already small audience. The commissioner Mr Lesley Ncube (son of ZANU PF stalwart Mr. Abednico Ncube) took it upon himself to threaten participants with arrest and imprisonment should they lie about their experiences during the genocide. The presence of a judge as chairperson of the commission which would portend well in a Western country, achieved the opposite in rural Matabeleland where judges were more feared than appreciated as they were associated with harsh laws, prisons and prison sentences. The commissioner's threat and the judge's presence coupled with Mnangagwa's presidency could only drive terror into the small group of participants. None could freely speak their mind, let alone call for criminal justice processes for the genocide.

As recent as 2019, the people of Matabeleland and parts of the Midlands were still very terrified of the possible revisitation of the past by the government and were very apprehensive of the future because of what happened in the past.

It is simplistic folly for people to judge the future through the events of the past, yet it is only a simpleton that trashes the lessons in the events of the past. While the Matabele must not judge the future from their sufferings of the past, Gukurahundi can never be forgotten, if not for the sack of justice and history, then for the lessons therein. It is true that retribution belongs to God but memories belong to men and women. Mankind will always cringe at memories and tell their children tales of the horrific experiences of past generations.

One of the lessons that students of history are entitled to know is the simple chronology of events leading to the deployment of Gukurahundi into Matabeleland and the Ndebele speaking parts of the Midlands.

In August 1980, according to the Chronicle of the 12th, Mugabe claimed that there was need for a militia to deal with *"malcontents"* in Matabeleland.

Consequently, in October 1980, Mugabe concluded the Kim II Sung pact with the North Korean president. The agreement provided for the training of former ZANLA combatants by the North Koreans.

In November 1980, Enos Nkala gave a speech claiming that ZAPU was the enemy of the state. Nkala declared in Bulawayo at a rally that, *"as of today ZAPU has become the enemy of ZANU PF. The time has come for ZANU PF to flex its muscles. Our supporters must now form vigilante committees for those who want to challenge us. .... Organize yourselves into small groups in readiness to challenge ZAPU in its own home ground. If it means a few blows, we shall deliver them"*.

In November 1980 following Nkala's speech, ZAPU and ZANU supporters fought running battles in the streets of Bulawayo. On account of that speech, the first Entumbane battle between ZPRA and ZANLA took place. For two days the armies were at war.

In February 1981 the second entumbane battle happened and it left 300 people dead.

After the second Entumbane battle the first defections from the ZNA by ZPRA soldiers started.

In August 1981 a crack team of one hundred and six instructors from North Korea landed at Harare airport, armed to the teeth with their training kit. They immediately started training thousands of former ZANLA soldiers in the art of mass murder without compunction.

In February 1982, a week after ZAPU had refused to be frog marched into a unity with ZANU (Shaw 1986), arms caches were discovered at two farms owned by Nitram (a private company owned by some former ZPRA soldiers).

In February 1982 after the discovery, ZPRA commanders were arrested and Nkomo and other ZAPU leaders were dismissed from the government by Mugabe.

It was evident from the above chronology of events that Mugabe had either to be some kind of prophet or oracle. Otherwise how else could he have known in October 1980 that he would need a special brigade *"to combat dissidents"* when the first army defectors (assuming they became dissidents) defected from his army after February 1981? Therefore, since it was well known that Mugabe was neither obscurely prophetic nor did he possess any oracular powers, there could only be one explanation to his 'divining' the future. The malcontents, the dissidents just like the special brigade, were a result of his planning. The dissidents could only have been a product from a laboratory and the benefit of hindsight helped to locate the laboratories in Harare and Pretoria.

ZANU knew they would need a pretext for a military crackdown and an onslaught in Matabeleland and the Midlands, so they manufactured dissidents. They became adept at manufacturing events, events that would be a pretext for justifying future repressive action.

That is a history that Matabeleland and Midlands genocide victims should pass on for posterity.

At the start of independent Zimbabwe in 1980, the Commander in Chief of the defence forces was the newly elected Prime Minister Robert G. Mugabe. The Zimbabwe National Army (ZNA) was under the command of Lt. Gen. Alistair Maclean (1980 – 1981), ex – RDF. Rex Nhongo, ex – ZANLA was to take over the ZNA from 1981 to 1992. Vitalis Zvinavashe (1992 – 1994) and Constantine Chiwenga (1994 – 2003) both ex – ZANLA were to assume the command of the ZNA. Chiwenga was elevated to ZDF commander until 2017 when he was appointed Vice President after a coup. The Airforce of Zimbabwe (AFZ) was under Air Chief Marshall Norman Walsh (1981 – 1983) ex – RAF. Azim Daulpota who was on loan from Pakistan was Air Chief Marshall from 1983 to 1986. Then Josiah Tungamirai, ex – ZANLA took over from 1986 to 1992 before Perence Shiri assumed command of the airforce.

The Central Intelligence Organisation (CIO) was under Ken Flower, ex – Rhodesian intelligence. Flower was succeeded by another ex – Rhodesian, Danny Stannard before Happyton Bonyongwe ex – ZANLA took over the reins. The Zimbabwe Republic Police was led by Commissioner General Wiridzayi Nguruve who was succeeded by Henry Mukurazhizha then Augustine Chihuri (who was removed in 2017 after the Mnangagwa coup), all ex - ZANLA. The administration made sure that there was no ex – ZPRA in the military high command structure.

The fact that the senior commanders of the ZDF were either ex Rhodesian Defense Forces or ex ZANLA should have sounded the early alarm bells for ZAPU and Matabeleland. Clearly a poison was brewing in the barracks. If not, the command of ZNA, AFZ, CIO and ZRP could have been shared among the three armies. The Zimbabwe Defense Forces command structure, especially at independence and for the next few years thereafter, was supposed to reflect participation of the three armies. Since ZANLA had had no intelligence and airforce branches they could have headed the army and police, while ZPRA got the CIO and Prisons and the RDF Army got the airforce. However, any other arrangement would have been acceptable as long as the three armies would have shared the five security brances. Common sense presupposes that the senior command of the integrated uniformed forces would reflect the integration so that all could derive confidence and a sense of security if not for fairness and equity.

That was not be the case nevertheless, as the presence of ZPRA was only barely detectable at the lower ranks. Such a military power sharing arrangement could not be tenable because it was incompatible with the genocidic planning by Mugabe and ZANU.

The only Matabele and the only ex – ZPRA to ever command a branch of the Zimbabwe Defense Forces (ZDF) was Lt. General Philip Valerio Sibanda who was ZNA commander from 2004 to 2018 when he was elevated to commander ZDF after the coup by Mnangagwa. Lt. General Lookout Masuku was appointed Rex Nhongo's deputy as ZNA commander for a short while in 1981 before he was arrested and charged with treason.

The events in Matabeleland put it beyond the need for intelligence to ascertain why all the top brass of the armed forces were either former ZANLA or ex RDF. They were loyal to and could be trusted to do Mugabe's personal bidding because they were his paid tribesmen. The senior ZPRA luminaires and commanders like Lookout Masuku, Dumiso Dabengwa, Akim Ndlovu (the first ZPRA commander), Charles Grey, Richard Dube, Thomas Ngwenya, Ambrose Mutinhiri, Sigogo Mlotshwa, Jevan Maseko, Phillip Valerio Sibanda and others, could not be trusted and were left out of the army senior command.

Most of those that were accommodated were soon compelled to retire when the ZANU sniff dog machine started hunting them down in the early 1980s. Some of them were quickly arrested and charged with treason or kept incommunicado in detention without trial. Many other ex – ZPRAs were murdered during operations or in detention while some escaped into exile.

As per design, the ZDF senior command became exclusively ZANLA with elements of the RDF. No doubt the new regime knew they would soon embark on a military operation that could never be feasible with former ZPRA personnel in charge of any section of the uniformed forces.

When the ceasefire was declared in 1979 the liberation armies of ZPRA, ZANLA and the RDF were supposed to be integrated into the Zimbabwe National Army (ZNA). Some 65 000 ex ZPRA and ZANLA guerrillas were warehoused in Assembly Points. Assembly Points were massive camps, eg Entumbane in Bulawayo, Ntabazinduna, Gwayi in Matabeleland North, Connemara in Gweru, Chitungwiza in Harare and many others. From the Assembly Points, some were intergrated into the new ZNA, while some were demobilized. By the end of 1980 a mere 15 000 had been integrated, much to the frustration of many ex combatants. That did not help in reducing the escalation of tensions within the three armies.

In May 1980 Brigadier Shute, Col Des Fountain, Peter Walls, all former Rhodesian Defense Forces, Rex Nhongo, former ZANLA, Dumiso Dabengwa and Charles Grey, former ZPRA led a military delegation of the integration committee to Gwayi River Assembly Point, some 240 km from Bulawayo on the Victoria Falls road in Matabeleland North province. Gwayi River was a camp for the former ZPRA regular brigade who had come from Zambia and were awaiting to be integrated into the new Zimbabwe National Army (ZNA) where they would serve alongside their erstwhile foes from the Rhodesian Defense Forces as well former comrades in arms today and would - be killers tomorrow, ZANLA. The regular brigade was made of well drilled, disciplined, hardened, properly psyched up and well armed soldiers. It could be the pride of any army and was indeed the jewel on the ZPRA crown.

Upon inspecting the ZPRA Regular Brigade in parade at Gwayi Assembly Point, the World War II veteran Peter Walls observed that, *"given the ZPRA force I saw today and the South African Airforce, I can conquer Africa"*. While the evident discipline and training exhibited by the ZPRA battalions impressed Walls, it left the senior ZANLA commanders seeing red and it miffed Robert Mugabe who immediately redoubled efforts to neutralise them. To that end, by August 1981, Gwayi River base station was disarmed. Weapons including artillery guns, defence weapons and small arms were taken by the government. The ZPRA Regular Brigade was completely integrated into the ZNA. In the ZNA they were hunted down and killed or somehow haunted and hounded out of the army. That marked the end of ZPRA pride and supremacy and the birth of dissidents.

The visit and the whole integration exercise revealed to ZANLA a fact that made the government want to bury all memories of and rewrite the history of the liberation war. They starred ZPRA military superiority in the face. The fears of the ZANLA delegation were aroused and confirmed. What they saw at Gwayi made them hate ZPRA even more and they endeavoured to wholly quash it.

Due to her being and her refinement, ZPRA courted the ire from two fronts and both set out to liquidate her. ZANLA wanted ZPRA out of the way due to old rivalries. Having come face to face with an evidently militarily superior former rival, their hatred was rekindled and became palpable and almost tangible. Mugabe also feared a coup d' etat orchestrated by ZPRA. Besides, the continued existence of ZPRA would be a rallying point for any possible offensive and a pillar of resistance to his planned one party state. In an interview with Harry Kreiser in 2001, Shari Eppel a Bulawayo psychologist and civic rights activist corroborated the existence of Mugabe's fear of ZAPU when she noted that, *"Mugabe, coming from a tiny Marxist framework, had set his heart on a one-party state. And so his desire was to cut Zapu as soon as he came into power in 1980. Zapu was the only hindrance to a one party state"*.

To the neighboring South Africa, intelligence supplied by some of the former Rhodesian spies like Ken Flower whom Mugabe had retained, showed that ZPRA was powerful and organized enough to be a threat to their interests and an inspiration and support source for the ANC and Umkhonto WeSizwe. They also feared that ZPRA could influence the Soviet Union to sopply arms and funds to the ANC and their army. Therefore, ZPRA had to be uprooted like a poisonous weed in the fields. Apartheid Pretoria shared a common burning desire with ZANU / ZANLA / Harare, to see the urgent demise of ZPRA, albeit for different reasons.

The minority regime in South Africa like the majority regime in Zimbabwe strongly detested the historically and culturally inspired relationship between the Ndebele in Zimbabwe and the Zulu in South Africa, ZAPU and ANC, ZPRA and Umkhonto Wesizwe, the ANC military wing. In august 1967 ZPRA and Umkhonto WeSizwe had launched a guerilla invasion in the northwest of Sourthern Rhodesia as a first in a military relationship where officers and soldiers from both armies fought many a battle against the Rhodesian and South African armies especially in the Wankie region of Matabeleland. (Mandela 1994, Austin 1975). The Wankie and Sipolilo battles saw ZPRA's Dumiso Dabengwa and MK's Chris Hani and Joe Modise side by side, shooting it out againt the RDF and SADF armies.

After the combined operations, the ANC soldiers would proceed to carry out sabotage missions in South Africa. If ZPRA was given free rein to self – perpetuate even within the ZNA, then Umkhonto Wesizwe would be inspired and be resourced to persist as a threat to the South African government. The termination of ZPRA in Zimbabwe was therefore the weakening of the ANC and Umkhonto WeSizwe in South Africa. Hence, the fear of the two guerilla armies by the two governments became the magnet that brought apartheid Pretoria and independent Harare into a strange marriage.

As if the Gwayi Assembly Point expose' was not enough intimidation for ZANLA, more lay in store. At its formation, the ZNA comprised four brigades, namely, 1 Brigade in Matabeleland, 2 Brigade in Mashonaland, 3 Brigade in Manicaland and 4 Brigade in Masvingo. The brigades were made up of 29 battalions. ZPRA superiority to ZANLA was proven soon after independence when twelve senior personnel from each former liberation army were co-opted to form the senior command of the battalions of the new army. Before being deployed and before some were assigned the command of various battalions the twenty - four were taken to Gweru for a month long training and assessment for suitability exercise. The envisaged command structure was that the best performing candidates would be battalion commanders. In order to maintain balance between the two liberation armies, it was arranged that if the battalion commander was ZPRA, his / her second in command would be ZANLA and vice versa. The exercise proved to be a disaster for the government because it exposed ZANLA's deficiencies. ZPRA officers simply proved to be more knowledgeable and adept at military concepts than their ZANLA counterparrts.

At the end of the training the government was embarrassed by the spectre of having to appoint mostly ex ZPRAs as battalion commanders. For example Smile Madubeko (ZPRA) was appointed commander of 2 : 1 infantry battalion in Mt. Darwin and Todd Mpala (ZPRA) became commander of 2 : 2 battalion in Mudzi. Before they could appoint another ZPRA commander, they had to save ZANLA the embarrassment. A compromise was reached and Happyton Bonyongwe (future Director General of CIO) was appointed commander of 2 : 3 battalion in Mutoko but not necessarily on merit. Had they not done that, the three 2 Brigade battalions would have been commanded by former ZPRA soldiers.

The government had to accept that ZANLA was in need of further training if they were to be at par with ZPRA. To make up for that glaringly discomposing deficiency in military acumen, sixty ZANLA officer cadets were sent for counter training in Nigeria. One of the trainees was Mike Nyambuya, who later became Minister of Energy and Governor of Manicaland province (interview with retired Col. Lazarus Ray Ncube, Harare 2010).

The practice of appointing battalion commanders on merit was quickly abandoned because it could have resulted in an entirely ZPRA command structure. By early 1981 commanders were being appointed politically and the structure fast became mostly ZANLA. The concept of maintaining a balance of the armies was furtively discarded.

The argument that ZANLA lacked adequate training and that by independence their senior officers still could not tell how many beans made five, was bolstered by a former British Military Advisory and Training Team (BMATT) instructor, a Mr Freath. Freath told the Sunday Times newspaper that in 1982, Constantine Chiwenga (Vice President after the coup in 2017) who was already a Brigadier by then had shot himself twice in the chest after he was caught cheating by Freath during a military examination. The penalty for cheating was dismissal from the ZNA. However, Freath had protected Chiwenga by not reporting him to the ZNA.

What ZANU lacked in the military barracks, they made up for in the political arena. Mugabe gave his ZANLA army the upper hand. In April 1983 Prime Minister Robert Mugabe declared that,*"when men and women provide food for dissidents, when we get there we eradicate them. We don't differentiate when we fight, because we can't tell who is a dissident and who is not"* (Financial Times, Telegraph and The Times, 15 April 1983). The Prime Minister was describing his actions in Matabeleland and Midlands as eradication of the people there.

Eradicate was a term used to mean, to exterminate, wipe out, annihilate, massacre or completely get rid of something. It was only by the most reckless stretch of the imagination that one could imagine a prime minister of any state using such egregious, flagrant and rank terminology in reference to civilians or citizens of his / her country. The Prime Minister of Zimbabwe, Robert Mugabe unashemadely told the British press and therefore Her Majesty the Queen of England, that his government was going to *"eradicate"* the Ndebele people. It is not unimaginable that the British government smiled at him in encouragement since he went on to effect his threat and they did nothing to stop him. Instead a few months later they showered him with praises and awarded him the highest honour even for a British citizen. The Queen of England conferred him the knighthood in the Order of the Bath.

In justifying his planned annihilation of the people of Matabeleland, Mugabe impishly claimed incapacity to distinguish between dissident and non – dissident. It was mind - boggling to assume that any government with all its financial and human resources could claim such deficiency to the hearing of the whole world. That claim was grossly and unimaginably criminal but it was employed to justify genocide to the world. Mugabe had the temerity to stand on a pedestal and announce that he intended to wipe off the face of the earth, the Matabele for habouring what he called dissidents. Maybe he was mad, as he claimed years later, but how about the UN, AU, UK and USA, the world prefects? How about the Frontline Line states? Why did they not censure Mugabe?

It was most horrifying that Mugabe said he and his hatchet men would *"eradicate"* those who provided food to dissidents because they could not tell who was a dissident and who was not. Yet they could tell who provided food to dissidents. If they could tell that someone had provided food to a dissident, then they knew that the provider of food was not a dissident. Then why eradicate them if it was not for the sake of eradicating them out of spite, hate and maybe some vengeful spirit? That the government, army, police and the intelligence departments could not distinguish between an outlaw dissident and a frail old woman, a heavily pregnant woman, an infant or a primary school student was outrageously outlandish.

The distinction between a dissident and a pregnant woman was supposed to be obvious to a man of Mugabe's intellectual faculties. For him to claim failure to discern between those prototypes was the most sheepish yet bellicose and malevolent excuse for genocide ever. The ways of a dissident and those of a grade 6 pupil were supposed to be worlds apart even to a man drunk with the intoxication of victory and power. Due to that claimed odd incapacity, Mugabe's army went on to butcher old women, pregnant women, infants, primary school children and other such obviously innocent citizens in Matabeleland and Midlands before branding them as dissidents.

According to CCJP and LRF (1997:54) "...*government ministers continued to make statements that indicated little desire to distinguish innocent from guilty, and indeed displayed a tendancy to see all communal dwellers as potential dissidents deserving of punishment*". There simply was absent the will to differentiate between dissidents and non dissidents in order to protect civilians because that would defeat the government's purpose for deploying the Gukurahundi brigade to Matabeleland and parts of the Midlands. Besides, an attempt to tell apart between dissidents and non dissidents would defeat the government's purpose for creating dissidents in the first place. Thus, in order to justify their extremist approach, they claimed that everyone they killed was a dissident.

Mugabe's attitude towards the Matabele gave birth to the seeds of scorn that he went on to sow on the minds of ordinary citizens. That mentality was attested as early as 1984 during a daily early morning promotional program on the state owned national radio station called Radio 2. An innocent sounding Shona woman in a grocery shop was asked what a dissident was. She inanely blurted her response, to the chagrin and mortification of many in Matabeleland, "*muNdewere*", her Shonalised version of the term Ndebele. In her unwitting innocence she knew and said a dissident was a Ndebele. The radio station was very popular, being the only vernacular station at a time when the independence euphoria was still young, what with the ZANLA liberation songs ever in the air. It had a massive audience not only among the majority Shona but the Ndebele listened to the programs and news in their language although the Ndebele news played a translational role every hour. The woman's response therefore reverberated in all the urban streets and was discussed with both appreciation and disdain in restaurants, churches, buses, schools, bars and stadia. It was also echoed in the gorges of Victioria Falls, the mountains of Vumba, the curves of Chinhoyi, the fields of Mazoe, the sands of Gwanda, the hills of Matopo and the forests of Lupane. The entire country had been informed by a State radio station that Ndebeles were dissidents

That identity distortion and assassination was not corrected by the programme host, the producer, the ZBC director nor the ministry of information. The woman's response was accepted by the powers that be. Therefore, the fallacy that Ndebele was synonymous with dissident was perpetuated with the blessing and sanction of the government. The term dissident assumed a new form. It meant Ndebele and Ndebele meant dissident. The eccentric, uninformed and dangerous perception of the woman which had been adopted as unofficial government policy a couple of years earlier and was ratified by the silence of the radio station and ZBC while millions listened, was still a reality thirty - one years later when Mugabe said Kalangas were uneducated criminals.

In response, what with the Gukurahundi Brigade butchering their kind, the surving Matabele were cowed into alien silence. The feeling of not belonging, of being lesser beings and second class citizens was compounded by a muffled helplessness and anger among the Matabele. On the other hand, some of the Shona found the radio incident very comical while some were simply nonchalant and some were probably disgusted but none said a word of disapproval.

There is an adage that says, 'give *a lie twenty four hours start, and you will never overtake it'*. When the government, allowed the lie about Ndebeles being dissidents in 1984 to go uncorrected, they indirectly perpetuated it for posterity. It was critical for the media, government and officialdom in Zimbabwe to do what American loosing presidential candidate John McCain did in 2008. When McCain was on a campaign trail, an elderly lady, clad in the Republican colours with McCain's face on her t - shirt stated that she did not like and would not vote for Barack Obama because *"he is an Arab"*. McCain promptly took the microphone from her and corrected her misstatement. He stated that Barack Obama was not an Arab. He also said that Obama was a decent family man with whom he (McCain) happened to disagree politically. Without implying that Arabs were not decent family men, he managed to factually correct her, instead of allowing a distortion of facts to persist as what happened in the above stated *muNdewere/* dissident saga. The radio presenter must have corrected that dangerous lie about dissidents on the spot.

According to Dr Davies (documentary film by Zenzele Ndebele), a German medical doctor at St Luke's hospital in Lupane, some 120 km from Bulawayo, *"Gukurahundi referred to their victims as dissidents"*. That meant that they would kill their victims and then ascribe the tag of dissident to them. That was in accord with the government's understanding of a dissident, a Ndebele.

Doran (2015), stated that Eddison Zvobgo, the all time ZANU lawyer who crafted the constitutional amendments that transformed Mugabe from Prime Minister to executive president, mentioned a *"decision of the Central Committee that there had to be a 'massacre' of the Ndebeles"*. That revelation by Zvobgo sent a chill down the spine as it betrayed the dearth of pathos by ZANU. There was no ambiguity on who was targeted for extermination. The Ndebele. The Ndebele and not dissidents. Zvobgo implicated the entire ZANU Central Committee of complicity in the sentencing to death of between approximately 100 000 Matabele.

Dissident became an ellipsis for all Ndebeles. The Ndebele, like a wounded buffalo, felt disdained, stigmatized and targeted. On their part, due to their inferior numbers in Matabeleland in the 1980s, some of the Shona learnt to live with the silent satisfaction of the contemptuous and victorious minority. On the national stage, most Ndebele people were cowed into frustrated acceptance of a doomed fate, while most of the Shona people were exhuberant and uninhibited in celebrating their dominence. Zimbabwe became the example of a country at loggerheads with itself due to colonial bungling, erroneous nationalist optimism and post independence leadership crisis.

The CCJP and LRF (1997) stated that when in 1983, Joshua Nkomo protested the murder of civilians by the Gukurahundi brigade, the Minister of Defence, Mr. Sidney Sekeramayi, singing Mugabe's shriek and eerie song, replied that it was acceptable for civilians to be murdered because not even Nkomo could distinguish between *"a dissident, a dissident supporter and an innocent civilian"*. To say that that was a lame argument and yet cruel response is an understatement. If it was indeed hard to distinguish between a dissident and a non dissident, one would assume that the security personnel should have been under instructions to arrest suspects pending trial and not kill on sight. The army and the police must have been given instructions to arrest suspects so that the courts of law would prosecute. The courts of law would decide who was a dissident and pass appropriate verdicts. But no, the minister was not interested in justice, he was simply being vindictive and brutish. He sounded very keen to kill innocent civilians.

It was such pugnacious arrogance that informed the behavior of the army when they treated the people of Matabeleland like stray dogs. It was not surprising that shortly after Sekeramayi's response, a pregnant woman in Matabeleland was accosted by a Gukurahundi soldier who frivolously yet tragically accused her of carrying a gun in her stomach. When the woman said she did not understand

Shona, the language used by the soldier, she was pushed to the ground and kicked thoroughly with booted feet (CCJP and LRF 1997). That treatment according to Sekeramayi's reasoning was acceptable because she could easily have been hiding a gun in her womb since she was a 'dissident'.

By decreeing that they were going to eradicate those that fed dissidents, Mugabe indicated his intent, to butcher civilian law abiding citizens of Matabeleland and Midlands. He knew from the experience of his ZANLA army during the war, that one could not deny food to men with guns. Still, this time around he was ready to kill women who provided food to men with guns. If indeed there were dissidents, who in their right mind would deny them the food that they demanded for? The rural people were almost always poor anyway. So poor they would never donate food even to their neighbors, let alone to dissidents.

It could not be in doubt that educated Mugabe knew that by referring to ZAPU as a cobra that had to be destroyed, under the prevailing environment, he meant that all ZAPU supporters had to be killed. Tragically almost the entire Matabeleland and half of Midlands and many in Mashonaland, Manicaland and Masvongo were members of ZAPU. Fortunately for all the other ZAPU members in Mashonaland, Masvingo, Manicaland and the Shona speaking half of the Midlands, the 5th Brigade had explicit orders not to harm them and was not deployed there because they were not Ndebele.

What was most despicable and scary about the perception of the people of Matabeleland, Nkomo, ZAPU and ZPRA as cockroaches (by Emmerson Mnangagwa), germs (by Edger Tekere) and snakes (by Mugabe), was that it was not the preserve of Mugabe and ZANU's murderous imagination alone. It was common belief in government corridors of power and among some segments of the population that dissidents were Ndebele (true) and Ndebeles were dissidents (false). By extension, it could be maintained that Tekere wanted to disinfect them with iodine while Mnangagwa wanted to poison and exterminate dissidents who were in the eyes of ZANU, the security apparatus and some people in the government, synonymous with Ndebele. Mugabe on the other hand wanted to re – educate / re - orient and eradicate the same Ndebele people. It was therefore the Matabele institution as a whole that was beleaguered and under siege.

According to Prof. Gatsheni - Ndlovu (2003) the security apparatus *"lumped together PF ZAPU as an opposition party, PF ZAPU leadership, PF ZAPU supporters, the demobilized ex - ZPRA combatants and all Ndebele speaking people as dissidents and as a security threat"*. That perception of dissident was unimaginably diabolic and sinister in that it revealed that what Mnangagwa and Mugabe wanted to poison and eradicate was the entire Matabeleland population.

Irrefutably, within Mugabe's cabinet, the ZANU Central Committee and Politburo, there was no doubt that all Ndebeles, save for the few in ZANU, were dissidents. Strangely, that idea was echoed by none other than Enos Nkala, a Ndebele and Minister of National Supplies. The Chronicle of 15 February 1984 reported that Nkala talking about Joshua Nkomo had declared, *"I am as much a Ndebele as he is. The issue of Ndebele is also a concern to me, but he incites the Ndebele to rebel against the government. I will cut this man to size. He is grown too big for himself, he has grown too big for this nation, he has grown too big for the Ndebeles".* Nkala was responding to a report tabled by Nkomo in parliament on 14 February 1984 to the effect that the government army was killing people in Matabeleland. Of note was Nkala's inference that the Ndebele people were rebelling against the government. If they were rebelling, then they were rebels and therefore the dissidents. Nkala's government did not physically cut Nkomo, although not without trying, but they did cut the Ndebeles to size. While Mugabe and Mnangagwa were propelled by raw tribalism, hate for the Ndebele establishment and tribal superiority, Nkala on the other hand was driven by an intense personal dislike of Nkomo.

When in April 1983 Mugabe stated that they do not differentiate between dissident and non dissident and they would eradicate both groups, he unwittingly gave currency to the view that Mnangagwa's DDT was meant for Ndebeles because the two were singing from the same hymn book of Shona nationalism and the one party state ideology. That explained why in hunting down some less than 400 dissidents, a 100 000 civilian Ndebeles, Kalangas, Xhosas, Sothos, Tongas etc were killed. A handful photos of decomposed bodies of men labeled as dissidents were published in the government press. It was also undeniable that the *"cockroaches"* that were eventually fumigated were the thousands of mostly defenceless villagers.

Therefore, Mnangagwa's statement that there was need to fumigate Matabeleland and the Midlands of cockroaches, meant that there was need to wipe out the Ndebele by killing them. Hence a black majority independent government deployed a seven thousand strong military battalion code named Gukurahundi, to kill the Ndebele. A feat that even the minority white regime had never even contemplated.

The Ndebele, like other genocidal victims that preceded and those that followed them still survive, not for revenge but for conciliatory, restorative and retributive justice.

Heroes, since time immemorial have always been revered by their followers who hang on their every word, even those words mentioned in passing and in jest. The orders of a commander of an army are treated with utmost obedience and are almost sanctified by the soldiers. Such was the case with Mugabe. When Mugabe was describing ZAPU and Nkomo as a snake that had to be destroyed, he knew that his army, police, prisons, secret police, youth militia and general supporters would treat ZAPU the way they treated a snake. ZAPU was made up of supporters, structures, administration, assets and former ZPRA personnel. For all intents and purposes, ZAPU was de facto the Matabeleland region and Bulawayo was its very soul. The 1980 and 1985 elections proved beyond any shadow of doubt that Matabeleland supported ZAPU only. Still, ZAPU was very popular in many parts of Mashonaland but the cobra slayer was not directed to the Shona speaking provinces.

True to diabolic instinct and instruction, primary school student dissidents, infant dissidents, dissident teachers, dissident pregnant women, dissident embryos, dissident traditional chiefs, dissident old men and women and dissident reverends were summerily 'eradicated' with a ruthlessness never matched in Africa before 1994 Rwanda. Mugabe went on to butcher about one hundred thousand civilians in the absence of any proof that they had fed dissidents. Not even one of them was ever arrested and charged with feeding dissidents. They were simply wiped off the face of the earth while the world celebrated Mugabe's victory, silver tongue, 'reconciliation' and seeming statesmanship.

That eradication mantra was incomprehensible in the background of earlier reconciliatory statements towards the white community. Such thick and almost palpable hate defied all positive psychological theories about mankind. That was the hate that Nkomo lamented about, at the funeral of Lookout Masuku on 12 April 1986, *"We are enveloped in the politics of hate. The amount of hate that is being preached today in this country is frightful. What Zimbabwe fought for was peace, progress, love, respect, justice, equality, not the opposite"*.

The hate was symbolized by ZANU's "pasi" (down with) slogan which Nkomo criticized as the apex of divisionist politics when he went on to say, *"no country can live by slogans, pasi this and pasi that. When you are ruling, you should never say pasi to anyone"*. Nkomo disapproved of that hateful slogan so much that even after the Unity Accord, till the day he died he never uttered the *pasi* slogan.

When Mugabe announced his eradication of the Ndebele, it was exactly two years after he had stood at the gallery to showcase his immense desire to reconcile with the former white Rhodesians. To his former torturers he had declared allyhood, love and forgivenss and to his former nationalists he now pronounced eradication.

Despite having attained no type of military training during the liberation war, Mugabe's ideas were heavily and chokingly laced and permeated through and through, with the violent, toxic and venomous voice and character of war. He never recovered from the war mode and when he got into state house he evoked violent strategies (Gukurahundi and the 1978 Shona Grand Plan) on real and imagined enemies, especially the Ndebele and ZAPU. He failed the demilitarization test which was demanded by the time and remained fixated with conflict. He set himself on a piteous trajectory and dragged the whole country down with him into an abyss of hate, violence, intolerance, intimidation, domination, marginalization, tribalism and death.

Winning the 1980 elections was never enough victory for Mugabe. Probably he wanted to satiate his hunger for a complete victory which he thought had been denied him by the Lancaster House conference and the subsequent cease fire agreement. He was always spoiling for war. His speeches were punctuated by references to *"victors and the vanquished"*. In that same mode was his long time colleague, prison cell mate and ZANU secretary general, Edgar Tekere. Just before the first battle of Entumbane, Tekere had threatened, *"Nkomo and his guerillas are germs in the country's wounds and they will have to be cleaned up with iodine"* (Meredith 2007). Still Tekere's sentiments were mild. Emmerson Munangagwa was to escalate the assessment, vigorously a couple of years later.

On 5 March 1983, the Chronicle newspaper reported that, *"likening the dissidents to cockroaches, the minister said the bandit menace had reached such epidemic proportions that the government had to bring in DDT (Gukurahundi) to get rid of the bandits"*. That was said by the Minister of State Security Emmerson Mnangagwa who was famously known as *'ngwena'*, which was Shona for crocodile. Mnangagwa went on to threaten that the government would be *"burning down all the villages infected with dissidents"*. Magnifying the dissident's problem to *"epidemic proportions"* was murderous tomfoolery on the part of the minister but it was in sync with the on - going agenda of painting Matabeleland with dirt. Despite giving the dissidents so much hype and threats, the government failed to apprehend the dissidents.

Instead of apprehending the rebels, the very next day after Mnangagwa's speech, the 5th Brigade killed fifty - five civilian villagers in Lupane. Once more it was made very clear that the minister was talking of civilians when he had referred to dissidents. The government was irrevocably committed to burning down all Ndebele villages with the people inside. They did just that.

DDT was a nerve poisoning chemical that was first isolated in Germany in 1874. It was used in chemical warfare in World War II. It was later processed into an insecticide. Once applied, its lethal effect caused the insect to dehydrate and collapsed its central nervous system. The insect died an excruciatingly gruesome, painful and lingering death. DDT was developed to eradicate pests. From 1981 to 1987, Mnangagwa's DDT was applied ruthlessly across the face of Matabeleland and parts of Midlands and tens of thousands of innocent people died.

That characteristic hard – line stance as exhibited by Mugabe, Tekere and Mnangagwa, resulted in the government and ZANU's failure to embrace the ideal of democracy. They therefore failed to establish democratic institutions throughout their tenure. By the 2000s, Mugabe would display his affinity for war by appointing retired army generals as ambassodors to other countries and CEOs of state enterprises eg NRZ, Tel 1, Air Zimbabwe, Net One, and GMB. He imagined himself as, and indeed he became the pilot of a massive political juggernaut that could *"crush"* all opposition and all dissent within his party and the country to powder. He was gripped by the bush war mentality and was ever hunting for dissidents and sellouts round him, in government and in the party. That naivety costed many their freedom, peace of mind and lives.

There are varying schools of thought about the types of dissidents that roamed the rich forests of Matabeleland and Midlands in the early 1980s. Three types of dissidents have been identified. There were the ZNA defectors that were former ZPRA soldiers, constructed dissidents and very few ordinary criminals who saw an opportunity to plunder and went about identifying themselves as dissidents.

What Gatsheni - Ndlovu called *"constructed dissidents"* were South African government sponsored agents and saboteurs calling themselves Super Zapu as well as the Zimbabwe government agents. Super Zapu saboteurs were created by apartheid South Africa on the southern border of Zimbabwe so as to keep her northern neighbour busy with an internal insurrection and not meddle in her affairs. They were infiltrated into the country for sabotage missions and conveniently withdrew to South Africa for supplies and instructions. They identified themselves as ZAPU / ZPRA, wore ZPRA combat uniforms and even t – shorts with Joshua Nkomo's face. Super Zapu made sure that ZAPU / ZPRA and by extension the ANC / Umkhonto Wesizwe remained Mugabe's enemies. That way the ANC would be emaciated and would not have a base from which to operate in Zimbabwe. When Mugabe declared on BBC that his country was not a Front Line State, he meant that the ANC would not be supported by his government in their struggle against apartheid the way his ZANU party had been supported by the Front Line States.

According to Dr. Obert Mpofu (ZANU PF Secretary for Administration), writing in the Sunday News of 14 July 2019, Super Zapu was created by South Africa and was code named *"Operation Drama"*. He stated that Super Zapu was under the directorship of Col Moeller and col Breytenbach.

Constructed dissidents also included Zimbabwe government security details that posed as law enforcement agents during the day and dissidents during the night. Those government agents would impersonate dissidents and ask villagers for food today and return with absolute and mean vengeance as the ZNA tomorrow, accusing the same villagers of giving food to rebels. They would torture or kill the elderly women that would have provided them with food the previous day. Obviously there were not enough dissidents to warrant the Gukurahundi excesses and the government had to upscale the numbers so as to legitimize their murderous operation. They too presented themselves as ZPRA soldiers, disgruntled with the new government.

The dissidents that killed Mr. Luke Khumalo, the headmaster of Thekwane High School in Plumtree and his wife in 1985, were suspected of being government agents. The students, some of whom at that time soon after independence, were former ZAPU refugees, attested to that possibility.

The kidnapping of the six tourists in Insuza, 76 km from Bulawayo, on the Bulawayo - Victroia Falls road in July 1982, which was officially blamed on dissidents was not consistent with dissidentry. The six were two Americans, two Australians, a Briton and a New Zealander. Mugabe's claims that, *"operating from instructions from ZAPU leaders....their actions are centrally motivated and are being carried out in order to bring about destabilization of our country, leading to a possible change of government"*, were empty rhetoric, devoid of truth and sincerety. The statement was designed to portray Nkomo as the 'dissident father' and it worked.

Soon afterwards, diplomats from various western countries, besieged Nkomo's residence in Bulawayo begging him to release the abducted six. Mugabe's statement implicating Nkomo was, many years later in 2018 proved to be a lie by his own nephew Patrick Zhuwao (MP) who claimed that the then Minister of State Security Emmerson Mnangagwa and 1 Brigade commander Constantine

Chiwenga had master minded the kidnapping (NewZimbabwe.com 29 January 2018).

Indications by then had pointed to either a government sting operation or a South African Super ZAPU project. The government appointed Col Lionel Dyke of the former Rhodesian Defence Forces, to command a 2000 strong battalion to hunt for the abductors and the tourists. Colonel Dyke later commented that, *"(y)ou often have to be cruel to be kind. Had an operation like (the 5th Brigade's) not taken place, the battle could have gone on for years and years as a festering sore. And I believe the Matabele understand that sort of harsh treatment far better than the treatment I myself was giving them, when we would just hunt and kill a man if he was armed.....if you were a dissident sympathiser you died"* (CCJP and LRF 1997). The racist and triumphalist innuendo pregnant in Dyke's avowal will be discussed some other day, but suffice it to say he was not qualified to lead soldiers into the Matabeleland population considering his unmistakeable prejudice. Col. Dyke also put it beyond doubt that the mission of his battalion was to mate out illiberal punishment to the Matabele.

Col. Dyke's crowing helped highlight the perplexity facing the Matabele at the time. They found themselves in a vicious circle whereby they were damned if they did and were damned if they did not. Many had to sympathise with the former ZPRA dissidents because they had been fighting a war against Col. Dyke only yesterday. It was difficult for rural people to support Col Dyke against their own kith and kin today. Some people knew that the rebels were being persecuted because they were Ndebele and therefore could not help but sympathise with them. They simply had many reasons for sympathizing with the rebels and non for supporting the government. Besides as Mugabe had admitted, the security forces were without the will to distinguish between dissident and dissident sympathizer. Therefore, to be Ndebele meant that one was walking around with a death sentence over their head.

By killing the tourists who literally disappeared until their remains were found not far from the kidnap site in 1985, whoever did it, won international acclaim for Mugabe and animosity for ZAPU and the Ndebele for being bandits and Matabeleland for being 'home' to the bandits. That was precisely what the Mugabe regime wanted to accomplish.

The killing of the tourists was immediately used as a pretext by the government to enact the Emergency Powers (Security Forces Indemnity) Regulations. That law was designed to protect security personnel from prosecution for atrocities including murder, if committed during the exercise of ensuring security for the country. From then on, security details from the CIO, Gukurahundi, ZNA, Supoort Unit, Paratropers, PISI, ZRP and even youth brigades could commit heinous crimes wantonly and get away with it. The innocent tourists were killed to justify the unleashing of the reign of terror that followed their disappearance.

Since ZAPU / ZPRA had historical and cultural links with the ANC / Umkhonto Wesizwe, it was convinient for the former to be blamed for insurgency in Zimbabwe so she could not offer any form of support to the latter in South Africa. To that end South Africa did not only create Super Zapu but according to Alexander et al (2000) South Africa in pursuit of the policy of destructive engagement towards the Frontline States sabotaged the Inkomo Barracks in August 1981 and bombed. almost destroying the Zimbabwe Air Force headquarters at Thornhill in Gweru in 1982. The intention was to have those terror events ascribed to ZAPU just like the attack on Mugabe's residence in Harare in June 1982.

The Catholic Commission for Justice and Peace and the Legal Resources Foundation, in the only report on the genocide available today, some thirty - nine years later, also asserted that apartheid South Africa was engaged in consistent and systematic misinformation to the Mugabe regime as well as espionage activities including bombings of infrastructure.

According to South African department of Foreign Affairs files for 1983, ZANU and ZNA officials negotiated with apartheid South African Defense Forces in 1983 to synchronise and co - ordinate their efforts to suppress ZAPU and ANC operations in Zimbabwe. Emmerson Mnangagwa was involved in the negotiations. (Scarnecchia 2011). Why would the two countries need a mid – night pact against their respective opposition political parties? That question brings to the fore the view that the ZANU government condemned apartheid South Africa during the day and yet they became cozy bedfellows with them, wining and dinning them during the night. That implied that ZANU was knowingly or unwittingly involved in the formation of Super Zapu by apartheid South Africa. If the South African Foreign Affairs files are anything to go by, it can be presumed that the Zimbabwe government was exchanging notes with the SADF, which notes the SADF went on to use in their repressive policy and practice towards the black majority in South Africa especially the ANC and their representatives in Zimbabwe in the 1980s.

Dabengwa (interview, 17 March 2017) corroborated the complicity of the South African and the UK governments. He stated that the United Kingdom was party to the massacres because they, *"..paid the North Koreans to train Gukurahundi. It was their making. South Africa knew ZAPU was an ANC and MK ally and did not mind the killings. They believed that to destroy ZAPU was to destroy MK"*.

According to Zvakanaka (2007), Douglas Moyo a former ZPRA, former ZNA and a victim of the Gukurahundi Brigade, said Britain orchestrated the slaughter in Matabeleland by manipulating apartheid South Africa. Yet most analysts said that South Africa was acting independently. She wanted to conjur up civil war in independent Zimbabwe so that regional and international attention would not focus on the quest for the independence of her black masses. The aparthedists were doing in Zimbabwe what they were doing in Mozambique and Angola at the time. Moyo said, *"Britain relinquished power without a fight in Zambia, Malawi and Botswana because the people there were fighting more for political independence. The issue was different in Zimbabwe. People were fighting for the equitable distribution of the country's wealth. Their struggle was centred on land.* According to Moyo, Britain wanted Zimbabwe to have a protracted internecine tribal war between the Ndebele and the Shona so that the government would not resolve the land question even after the elapse of the constitutional ten years before which land was not to be redistributed.

That meant that Britain's involvement and their softly softly stance towards Mugabe was motivated by a desire to delay the land redistribution programme which had been agreed upon at Lancaster. The British government was buying as much time for their nationals in the Zimbabwean farms as possible. That policy worked, and they got an extra ten years in addition to the constitutional ten years. Mugabe was prepared to continue being grateful to the British government for the favours done at Lancaster as long as his political skin was not scratched. Unfortunately for the British, twenty years after independence Mugabe could not continue being indepted to them. The Zimbabwe war veterans tied his hands behind his back and chained him to a post of history. He could not escape. He had no choice but to ditch the British and the white Zimbabwean farmers.

To corroborate the Britian / Mugabe conspiracy theory, was the fact that despite exterminating about 100 000 people outside a war situation, the Mugabe regime was never censured. The former colonial master did not lift a finger in condemnation of that wretched deed. Instead a Briton journalist, Donald Trelford working for the Observer newspaper in the UK who first published the Gukurahundi genocide, was fired from his job for doing so.

Britain, just like the Smith regime, realizing that the tide against colonialism was rising, was prepared to relinquish political clout but not economic power. Almost synonymous with economic power was land ownership. He who owned land, wielded immense power. Joshua Nkomo had been more vocal on the land question than Mugabe and it cost him the votes in 1980 and almost his life. Although too little too late, it subsequently became crystal clear through his approach and conduct; the policy of purchasing properties including many farms for former ZPRA soldiers and through his speeches, that Nkomo was not for land seizures and expropriation of property as undertaken by Mugabe and ZANU PF after Nkomo's death in 1999.

One did not need to be a rocket scientist to appreciate the fact that the killing of 100 000 Matabeles posed no economic threat to Britain. They simply had nothing to lose by the death of a hostile tribes people who had ninety years back killed many of their kith and kin in defense of their sovereignty against colonialism. The British had not forgotten that in 1893 the Shangani patrol led by Allan Wilson had been wiped out by King Lobhengula's body guard regiment. They also recalled that in 1896, six hundred white civilians were killed by the Ndebele *impis* (Berlyn 1978). Therefore, the security of the Ndebele people was absent from the British government's priority list .

The fact that the British did not care much for the Ndebele due to historical umbrage, was confirmed by Stuart Doran when he argued that the world looked the other way and left the Ndebele people's fate in Mugabe's sole hands due to, *"political objectives and ethnopolitical animosity"* (The Zimbabwe Independent, 6 – 12 April 2018). On the other hand, the British had more to lose by ruffling Mugabe's fresh feathers. As long as the white commercial farmers kept their land in Zimbabwe and many Anglo companies continued merchandising, Mugabe could kill as many Matabele as he liked.

Mzila – Ndlovu at the gukurahundi genocide commemoration in January 2011 addressed the question of why so much lack of concern for the Ndebele by Britain. He submitted that the Ndebele were the first to resist British imperialism and the latter were humiliated by *"people in loin skins"* and were compelled to use what Austin (1975) called rare *"undisguised conquest"* to subdue them. Furthermore, the largely Ndebele party ZAPU was funded by the Soviet Union with its military wing ZPRA being Soviet trained and armed. As a result, ZAPU and ZPRA were Soviet communist oriented in ideology. In a way the minister reminded the audience of Joshua Nkomo who once said, *"the real difference between Western interests in Africa and those of the Soviet Union is that when asked to leave, the Soviet Union has always left"*. Evidently such sentiments did not endear Nkomo and his followers and the Matabele people in general to the British government.

The British did not want Mugabe during the Cold War to ally with the Eastern Bloc communist countries especially Russia, in addition to a need to protect the vast economic interests of their nationals in Zimbabwe. However, when Mugabe for political gain in 1999, let loose the War Veterans under, first, the hardliner

Chenjerai Hunzvi then the joker Joseph Chinotimba, upon the white farmers, he provoked their infinite ire. The war veterans forced the white farmers, many of them British by descent, from their land, maimed some and killed eleven of them. The farmers were not compensated for the land and many were physically abused. The war veterans became the heroes for the second time in two decades, especially in rural areas where people lived on unproductive land. Mugabe won the votes but he transformed to a sworn enemy of the USA foreign policy under George Bush and the UK under first, Prime Minister Tony Blair, then Gordon Brown and David Cameron after him.

Now that their darling epiphany had suddenly turned devil incarnate, the USA and Britain awoke from a nineteen year long deep slumber. In 2001 roiled by Mugabe's betrayal, the US Congress enacted the Zimbabwe Democracy Economic and Recovery Act (ZIDERA). The act essentially denied Zimbabwe any form of assistance from institutions where the USA had an interest. Consequently, the IMF and World Bank withdrew 193 million US dollars funding earmarked for Zimbabwe. That did not knock sense into his head as Mugabe continued to show his middle finger to the West and the USA. The West publicly declared their hate, imposed sanctions on him and his coterie in the gravy train and announced they were funding regime change efforts to unseat Mugabe. They took that stance because Mugabe repossessed land from whites and redistributed it to blacks and was brazenly threatening their heavily invested economic interests in the country and was abusing their kith and kin while at it.

Frightfully, the USA ZIDERA only affected Mugabe and his crew very indirectly and superficially. Mugabe did not personally need the funding from the IMF and the World Bank but the poor people did. They felt the pinch. It was easy for Mugabe to convincingly tell the people that they were suffering because they were under USA and UK sanctions. If the Act had been part of the regime change agenda, it actually back fired because Mugabe turned it around so that he appeared to the poor rural people, especially in Mashonaland, as a victim of neo colonialism. However, the people were suffering because Mugabe and his former handlers had run out of the glue that had been binding them together for twenty years. It had nada to do with the rule of law as claimed by the USA and UK nor did it have anything to do with asserting Zimbabwe's sovereignty as claimed by Mugabe. It was all personal. The people suffered because Mugabe wanted to rule all the way to the grave. The people suffered because the West and the USA wanted to protect the Zimbabwe farms owned by their white citizens.

The nobility behind the disapproval of the British and USA governments could not be questioned. Politically it was not wrong that the British government condemned and ostracized Mugabe. While the land question had to be addressed and the land redistribution was justified, Mugabe and ZANU PF's motive and the method were far from humane and fair. Britain and USA correctly condemned Mugabe. However, they were standing on thin ice, lacking the moral high ground that would give their argument a trumpet tongue to reach and appeal to all. In their disapproval of Mugabe, the British sounded racist, selfish and myopic because they had failed to banish him seventeen years earlier for the blood bath in Matabeleland. In castigating Mugabe for the murder of eleven white people after having egged him on in butchering 100 000 blacks, their hypocrisy was laid bare.

The British found themselves in an ethical quandary. Their expostulation, seemingly smacked of raw racism and was devoid of any sincerity. None knew that better than Mugabe. Mugabe sensed the morally compromised and shacky ground on which his Western detractors stood and loudly screamed *"neo colonialism"*. Who in their proper frame of mind would take seriously the remonstrations of a country over the murder of eleven people when the same country had failed to condemn the massacre of between thirty and one hundred thousand people? The British merely handed Mugabe the cannon fodder he so much needed. He retorted that he was being *"demonized"* for correcting a racist and historical wrong and for economically empowering the majority blacks. The British lost a strong *locus standi* and were mostly tongue tied even as Mugabe railed at them during the United Nations General Assembly and at SADC meetings.

What had begun as hate for the Ndebele, became hatred for the whole country and all the people, including his former benefactors the British and their local kith and kin and even his own tribe. Some of the Shona were included in the hate list for their betrayal when they embraced the Movement for Democratic Change (MDC) in 1999 / 2000. The Mugabe whom the British, white Zimbabweans, Mashonaland and the opposition MDC experienced from 1999 was the Mugabe Matabeleland had experienced since 1980. If only the British, the Zimbabwean whites and the majority had not been too cozy under Mugabe's temporary patronage roof and too subjective to listen, they too could have sensed disaster earlier when Harare, Pretoria and London, in varying degrees of complicity, created dissidents. They could have averted the suffering that ensued when the winds of change came and blew away the fake roof and left them exposed to Mugabe's vulture policies.

Whatever purpose the dissidents were meant to achieve, the long and short of it was that all were unwittingly playing to Mugabe and the ZANU tune. Mugabe was dreaming of establishing a one party state and anyone who dared differ from him within or without ZANU, courted ruin. He was prepared to go to any lengths to achieve a one party and a one Shona nation state but Nkomo, ZAPU / ZPRA, Rev.

Sithole and his ZANU Ndonga and many others including many Shona people resisted him at great risk.

Nkomo (1983) in a letter to Mugabe exposed the latter's motivation when he remarked, "*it is now very clear to me that you were very unhappy with the extent of my cooperation and that of ZAPU because you did not want peace and tranquility, progress and development, because such conditions would not give you the turmoil and instability you required for political - military action to liquidate those you chose to, and thereby impose your one - ZANU Party State*".

Matikiti (2008) agreed that Mugabe endevoured to establish a one party state but his covert overtures were resisted by Sithole and ZANU Ndonga. He stated that in the absence of Rev. Sithole and ZANU Ndonga in 1985 Mugabe and ZANU would have ushered into Zimbabwe a one party state.

With the British handling the leash around his neck to ensure he did not upset white interests, Mugabe had attempted to follow in the footsteps of the long list of African dictators like Houphouet of Cote d' Ivoire, Kamuzu Banda of Malawi, Keita of Mali, Senghor of Senegal, Sekou Toure of Guinea, Jomo Kenyatta of Kenya, Kwame Nkrumah of Ghana, Milton Obote of Uganda, Mobutu Sese Seko of Zaire and such countries as Niger, Dahomey, Togo, Mauritania, CAR and Burkina Faso who had with assorted levels of failure implemented the one party state system.

An avid reader, follower and acolyte of Tanzania's Julius Nyerere, Mugabe restlessly endeavoured to emulate him. Nyerere an eloquent proponent of the one - party state system was greatly admired by Mugabe since the days of the ZAPU / ZANU split when he had supported Mugabe against Nkomo. Nyerere championed the one - party system by castigating multipartyism as suitable for Europe where society was stratified into socio - economic classes and needed different parties to represent the interests of those classes. He said African society was classless and therefore needed one strong party to unite the nation towards development (Meredith 2005). From Nyerere, Mugabe developed admiration bordering on obsession with the one party state.

Resonant with his mentor, Nyerere, Mugabe, despite having five bachelors' degrees and one masters degree at independence, failed to understand the basics of sociology and equated diversity to division and unity to uniformity. He feared and hated ZAPU, Nkomo and the Ndebele because they were different. To him their mere existence was divisive, therefore they had to be exterminated. They were an immediate threat to his dream of a one party state within a Shona state.

He therefore unleashed Gukurahundi in order to crush diversity and achieve uniformity. The Matabele had to be pounded into unity with the Shona by being uniform in ideology, language, culture and practice with them.

The sum total of the Nyerere's and Tanzanian influence on Mugabe was open to conjencture, although according to the Catholic Commission for Justice and Peace, some of the victims of Gukurahundi Brigade said that there probably were Tanzanians and Mozambicans in the battalion. What was established was that the 5th Brigade was trained by North Korea and indeed there was an acidic North Korean input in Mugabe's planning.

Due to the ZANU longing for a Shona - nation – one - party - state, Zimbabwe at independence quickly transmogrified into a monophonic political entity where the victorious unilaterally defined the history of the liberation struggle, claimed all the credit for the victory, distributed the fruits of the victory and theorised the vision for the future. The vanquished (ZAPU, Matabeleland and parts of Midlands) had only to play a single role; to acquiesce. It was a majoritarian set - up with no accommodation for the minority Matabeleland tribes.

That sorry predicarment was echoed so loud by the ZANU prime ideologist, Eddson Zvobgo in the Chronicle of 5 April 1983 when he equated the majority to God by stating, *"we worship the majority as much as Christians worship God"*. Inevitably, the minority tribes of Matabeleland became sacrificial lambs at the alter of majoritarianism. The country, from independence day in 1980, descended into tyranny by the majority. Matabeleland was suffering and dying under the burden of majority rule because it was home to the minority.

Mashingaidze (2005), argued, with specific reference to post independence Zimbabwe that, *"liberation movements, under whose banner independence was attained, fought for plurality of the political space, but upon assuming the portals of power, sought to obliterate difference. Zimbabwe's civil war of 1982 to 1987 was an outcome of the homogenous conceptualization and practice of nation - building in Africa"*.

Mashingaidze might have stirred controversy by describing the genocide as a civil war, because there never was a war, but he provided an insightful explanation of why Zvobgo, Mugabe and ZANU were so peremptory and obsessed with majoritarianism and a Shona – nation - one - party state. To them a country had to have one nation as a rule. That nation had to be their Shona and all the others had to be liquidated. Probably they envied and took literally Kenneth Kaunda's mantra of *"One Zambia, One Nation"*, an aphorism which never went beyond being a maxim fostering inter ethnic respect and cohesion among Zambia's numerous tribes. They did not respect the fact that Kaunda did not attempt to dercimate and domineer the Lozi, Bemba, Tonga, Lubale etc. in the name of the Nyanja.

That smoldering desire for a Shona - nation – one – party - state transformed and malformed them into the dragons they sought to slay during colonialism. They thus became a mirror image of the oppressive system, many of their comrades had died trying to abolish.

Like all dragons, in order to self perpetuate, Mugabe had to spit fire. He therefore went on to ensure the existence of dissidents (Progress Review of the 1979 Grand Plan 2000) so that his actions; declaring a curfew in Matabeleland, deployment of armed forces, genocide, arbitrary arrests, torture, prolonged detention without trial, expropriation of ZAPU land, confiscation of property including all ZAPU buildings and documents and records dating from the late fifties to the 1980s, could be justified.

According to Runyararo Mahomva (2013), Mugabe at independence anticipated a one party state which was engendered by *"early political insecurities"* and fears of a repeat of what happened to Nkwame Nkrumah in Ghana who was eliminated in a *"CIA coup"* soon after he had helped liberate his country from colonialism.

With such fears running amok in his head, while the independence euphoria was still thick in the air, in August 1980, Prime Minister Robert Mugabe maintained that there was a need to deal with domestic insurrection in Matabeleland. In pursuit of that endeavor, he in October 1980 signed an unholy pact with Kim II Sung the North Korean leader. Before the pact was signed, according to the Herald newspaper, in July 1980, Kim II Sung had told the world that under Mugabe's leadership, the people of Zimbabwe were *"unfolding a dynamic struggle to consolidate their independence"*. That was an astounding revelation and an indictment on Mugabe and ZANU. The statement was made soon after freedom day, before the emergence of the dissidents who were used as the pretext for deploying the Gukurahndi Brigade on Matabeleland and parts of Midlands. Clearly, consolidating independence meant having the North Koreans train the 5th Brigade so it would massacre the Ndebele and ZAPU who were a real threat to Mugabe's Shona – nation – one - party state.

The Kim II Sung concord provided for the training of a Zimbabwean army brigade by the Koreans. To that end, on 01 August 1981 a crack team of one hundred and six instructors from North Korea landed at Harare airport. They consisted of experts in armed combat, unarmed combat, special weapons and techniques, interrogation techniques (including torture), communications, reconnaissance, politics and close quarter battle tactics (Zim Defense Forces magazine Vol 7). It mystified the imagination and defied all conventional reason why Mugabe would be forming a battalion of fellow tribesmen allegiant to a singular political party in defiance of the rules of integration while talking reconciliation.

The British Military Advisory and Training Team (BMATT) under the command of General Sir Edward Jones (1983 – 1985), was in the country training the ZNA as part of their agreed obligations as former colonial masters. The British could not directly be party to Mugabe's plans of a massacre for obvious reasons. Chief among the reasons was the crime of colonialism including the blazing slaughter from Gadade to Bulawayo in 1893 and conniving with Mugabe to rig the previous elections on his behalf. They could not directly be party to yet another humanirarian crisis in their departure from colonialism. ZANU needed a cruel team of experts devoid of any relationship whatsoever with Matabeleland. The North Koreans were very suitable.

Some four thousand ex ZANLA combatants (Gama 2009) were recruited from the Tongogara Assembly point in Mutare to be trained by the North Koreans in Nyanga. It was alleged that some Tanzanians and Mozambicans were probably included. That could be true since Tanzania had a history of friendship with ZANU, ZANLA and Mugabe. Their understanding had been strengthened in the 1960s after the then Tanzanian President Julius Nyerere expelled ZAPU from the east and central African country. Nkomo (1984) did admit that Nyerere had a distinctive dislike of him. Whoever was comprised in the new brigade, the purpose of their training was singular: to kill Ndebeles and Kalangas. If there had existed any shred of doubt before independence, it became crystal, clear post independence, that ZANU policy towards all the tribes of Matabeleland in general and the Ndebele in particular was drenched, washed, rinsed, dried and ironed in vile tribal terrorism.

In typical conspiring fashion, ZANLA had not surrendered all their personnel and arms from Mozambique at the time of the cease fire agreement. They had retained arms of war and thousands of guerrillas beyond the eastern border in anticipation of the genocide. Those were kept as a secret weapon by Mugabe who then did not know that the UK and North Korea would support his plans. A train load of their arms and soldiers had disappeared en route from Mozambique and did not show up at their destination. Those became part of the reserved resources. Some of those were soon moved to Nyanga to join the 4 : 5 and 4 : 7 battalions to be trained by the North Koreans.

The brigade was trained for twelve months during which they were kept in isolation and shut out from the rest of the world. They were not allowed visitors and no news went into their camp and non left the camp. They were instructed in the art of mass killing without question or remorse. They excelled in imperviousness to human suffering and developed deafness to pleas for mercy. They were turned into deaf, blind and remorseless mass killers.

When the minister of defence Mr. Sydney Sekeramayi announced that the training was complete on 09 September 1982, the 5th brigade was placed under the command of former ZANLA commander Perence Shiri. Shiri later became air marshal and commander of the air force under Mugabe and was appointed a cabinet minister by Mnangagwa. Their headquarters were in Guinea Fowl barracks in Gweru, a town some 160km northwest of Bulawayo. Some of the troops were warehoused in Zvishabane, some in Gokwe and some in Ntabazinduna, some 40 km out of Bulawayo. The brigade was stationed in Matabeleland and Midlands so that they could be within easy reach of their victims.

With pride, the 5th brigade was accorded by Mugabe the acronym *"Gukurahundi"*, a term which still strikes a cord of terror in the hearts and minds of most people in Matabeleland and Midlands. It was a Shona term meaning the rain that washes away the chaff before the rains of spring. Wash away the 'Matebele chaff' in an ethnic cleansing orgy is what the Gukurahundi brigade specialized in in the five years that followed. The force was to be above the law and not subject to any code of disciplinary conduct. They were trained to be the law unto themselves.

Within a very brief period of time, the term Gukurahundi had assumed a meaning beyond a simple acronym for an army brigade. In Matabeleland and the Midlands, it grew to become many phenomena. The people used it to mean a genocide, soldiers, a period of tribulation or death.

Sithole and Makumbe (1997) espoused that ZANU's revolutionary policy was informed by Gukurahundi ideology when they stated that, *"Gukurahundi is a colloquial expression, which in Shona means "the storm that destroys everything". The peasants, from whom the expression or concept comes, use it with awe because gukurahundi is an early storm that "destroys everything", crops and weeds, huts and forests, the good and the bad, including people and beasts. After gukurahundi, usually nature ushers in a new ecological order. Such were the intended consequences of ZANU (PF)'s revolutionary policy as it evolved in the 1970s (ironically) from the countryside"*

Noteworthy in the Sithole and Makumbe observation was the ushering in of a new order after Gukurahundi. Indeed, after Mugabe's Gukurahundi storm had torn Matabeleland and Midlands to shreds, with tens of thousands dead, hundreds of thousands maimed and traumatized, thousands of homes burnt to ashes and uncounted many displaced and exiled in Zambia, Botswana, South Africa and Europe, ZANU set about establishing a new order. Until today ZANU PF is consumed by a passion to colonise Matabeleland in all ways imaginable.

Soon after the Gukurahundi genocide, Shona people were settled in Matabeleland and given jobs in every sector, given loans to start businesses and given houses. During the initial years many were given Matabele names, birth certificates and national registration (identity) cards so that they could blend in. The practice of giving Shonas Ndebele names and then deploying them to Matabeleland was later discarded as Mugabe's government gathered confidence and blatantly and arrogantly pushed the Shona into Matabeleland by beastly force. That recolonisation of Matabeleland to satiate tyranny by the majority gaves credence to the notion by Dr. Mhlanga (2009) that Mugabe perpetrated Gukurahundi on behalf of the Shona people in their generality.

No one, free from the influence of hallucinogens would wish such a marauding and pillaging phenomenon as the gukurahundi storm on any people. Yet Mugabe and his crew created it and let it loose on the Ndebele. Meredith (2005) revealed that the Gukurahundi pogrom was planned well in advance, was implemented by a political army and an exlusive regiment of Shonas that was instructed to kill the Ndebele and Kalanga tribes when he posited that, *"Determined to achieve a one party state, Mugabe provoked a war against ZAPU (the official political opposition party dominated by the Ndebele people) and its Ndebele and Kalanga supporters, preparing for it well in advance by establishing his own political army, recruited exclusively from Shona supporters and trained by North Korea for special combat duties"*

While others alleged that the 5th Brigade was exclusively Shona, Joice Mujuru, Mugabe's deputy for ten years and a member of his cabinet for twenty - four years begged to differ. After she was fired from ZANU PF and the government, she had nothing to lose in spilling the beans by telling on her former colleagues. She was quoted in the press saying that the battalion was a *"crack Zezurus only"* regiment. She also told a 'women in the diaspora' meeting in March 2017 that a colonel, Beta Guveya had been ordered by Mugabe to *"recruit a Zezurus – only brigade from Zvimba"*. Zvimba was Mugabe's home district. When she was challenged by Stephen Sucker of the BBC on why she did not oppose or protest against the Gukurahundi genocide in Matabeleland, she said the operation was an executive decision by an executive person (Mugabe) and therefore could not be opposed (Newsday Zimbabwe 14 March 2017).

The involvement of the ZANU Central Committee in the decision to exterminate the Ndebele was confirmed by Dabengwa during an interview with the author on 17 March 2017 in Bulawayo. When asked who the architects of the Gukurahundi massacres were, Dabengwa asserted that, *"..all cabinet knew. The central committee knew but of course the security ministers were the main players, i.e. Mugabe, Sekeramai and Mnangagwa".* The revelations that the central committee and cabinet were in the know poured cold water on protestations by Joice Mujuru on BBC's Hardtalk program in March 2017 where she dreadfully and barefacedly professed innocence about the Gukurahundi killings. Mujuru was a minister in Mugabe's cabinet for two years prior and for twenty - two years post the genocide and was vice president for an additional ten years. Like everybody else in ZANU PF and the government, she never spoke officially in criticism of the genocide until she was dismissed by Mugabe.

Joshua Nkomo tried in vain to downplay the fact that Gukurahundi was a tribal brigade designed to wipe the Matabele away, but the facts about its compostion and operation told a different story. Nkomo failed to be lucid on BBC's panorama as he said, *"probably it was a tribal army, but not a Shona tribal army".* Within the context of the Matabeleland and Midlands killings, that statement sounded timidly incoherent and betrayed Nkomo's failure to accept that he and all Matabeleland and parts of Midlands were victims of tribalism. He failed to realize that peace did not entail denying and hiding the truth. However, that vague statement could only make sense if Nkomo meant that the 5th brigade was a Zezurus only affair and not a Shona (Zezuru, Karanga, Manyika and Korekore) tribal army, in which case he should have elucidated his point because Zezurus are Shonas.

On the other hand, Nkomo's deputy, Mr. Josiah Chinamano, a Shona, did not mince his words about the tribal nature of the Gukurahundi masacres. He did admit that there was rationale in concluding that Gukurahundi was a tribal brigade pushing an anti - Ndebele crusade. Chinamano said *"people are bound"* to believe that it was a Shona against Ndebele military campaign since they were being terrorized by a Shona army (BBC Panorama).

In concurrence with Chinmano, was another of Nkomo's lieutenants, a Shona, Mufuka (2019), who clearly wrote that, *"in October 1980, investigative reporters revealed that Mugabe had been in negotiations with the North Koreans. A purely tribal army, whose only aim was to crush the Ndebele and ZAPU, was in the offing".*

On 6 June 1983 however, Joshua Nkomo was less circumspect when he authored a letter now referred to as an 'Informative Letter to Prime Minister Robert Mugabe'. In the letter he complained that, *"it is obvious to me why you decided to form the Fifth Brigade outside the structure and command of the National Army, so that you may use it as a party and Tribal Brigade for eliminating and liquidating, as you have many times said, those you chose to destroy. As a matter of fact, when I questioned the formation of the Fifth Brigade outside the Zimbabwe National Army without consultation, you angrily replied and said, "Who are you to be consulted? This Brigade", you said, "has been formed to crush those who try to subvert my government, and if you attempt that, they will crush you too"*.

Nkomo, ever the diplomat and peace seeker, on that occasion made one of the most accurate statements he ever made about Gukurahundi, by calling it what it really was, a *"tribal brigade"*. He was always at pains not to alienate the already polarized Ndebele and Shona by publicly calling a spade a spade. Perhaps he could afford to blame Mugabe of tribalism because that was supposed to be confidential correspondence between the two of them. Nkomo's logic was that although the 5th brigade was composed of Shonas, it was not representing the wishes of the Shona as a people but the caprices of the Shona elite. It is indisputable that in all governments, the elite coin policies and assign duties to the executive who in turn appoint generals who deploy the army. The people cannot be held responsible for the decay in both the policies of the beauraucrats and the practices of the army generals.

The formation and composition of Gukurahundi gave credence to Chinamano's observation, while throwing out the window any pretences to the contrary. The policy of integration into the army was that every new battalion had to comprise 50% ZPRA and 50% ZANLA. Initially that was the practice in all new battalions. However, battalions 4 : 5 and 4 : 7 (which were used to make the Gukurahundi brigade) were comprised along a portentously evocative trend. They were former ZANLA (Washington Post 26/2/1983) and from the Shona tribe. As covertly as they were formed, the two battalions were stealthily whisked away to the banks of the Nyangombe river in Nyanga in Manicaland province.

Many former ZANLA guerrillas who got wind of that furtive operation deserted the ZNA and volunteered to join the two battalions at Nyanga. Their desertion was not readily detectable due to the demobilization exercise which was also intended to wean the ZNA of the ZPRA influence and presence. Many a former ZPRA in the ZNA attested that when some of those ZANLA 'deserters' disappeared, they were privates but when they resurfaced a few months later, they had puzzlingly acquired additional ranks, two or three notches above private and were part of a new brigade that would soon shake the very foundations and pillars of the Ndebele and Kalanga establishment.

The Defense Minister, Sekeramayi was quizzed by BBC Panorama in 1983 on why the Gukurahundi Brigade was exclusively Shona and ZANLA. He in triumphant confidence unwittingly let the proverbial cat out of the bag by proferrig that the ZPRA army in the ZNA deserted during operations and joined ranks with the dissidents hence they had to send the Gukurahundi Brigade because *"they are loyal and wouldn't desert"*. One then asked, what was it with Gukurahundi that would render the Shona soldiers 100% loyal therefore immune to the desire to desert? The clear assertion in Sekeramayi's pregnant statement was that the brigade was made up of Shona ZANLA soldiers whose loyalty to tribal nationalism and ethnic cleansing was guaranteed. He put it beyond doubt that one had to be Shona to qualify into the 5th Brigade. He also implied that all Ndebeles in the army supported dissidents while all Shonas could not be dissidents. He therefore betrayed the tribal nature of the conflict.

Yet the government went all out to attempt to convince the world that the genocide was not tribal slaughter. On 28 August 2010 the Chronicle newspaper headlines stated that *"Government bans 1980s disturbances paintings / films"*. Surprisingly the article which was the main news of the day was covered in two very short paragraphs. It did not go beyond telling that in terms of sections 12 (1) and (2), 13 (1) and (2) and 14 (3) of the Censorship and Entertainment Act, the ministry of Home Affairs had banned the paintings and films by a Bulawayo based artist Mr. Owen Maseko who had been arrested in March of the same year for expressing his thoughts through paintings. The reason for the ban was summarily stated as that the paintings and films portrayed the *"Gukurahundi era"* as tribal and biased. That meant that the government, thirty years on, still denied the tribal nature and bias of the genocide.

What could not be missed in the story was the evident trivialisation of the Gukurahundi genocide. How on earth the Harare Bureau could scornfully pigeonhole the spiteful slaughter of a hundred thousand men, women and children by the country's security forces, as mere disturbances that were non tribal and non biased, pervaded all logic and drove a tiny, sharp and long spear through the hearts of many victims and survivors.

The tribal agenda of painting all Matabeleland with the big brush of dissident was exposed vivdly when on 6 February 1982, arms caches planted by the CIO double agent Matt Calloway on behalf of the apartheid South African intelligence were discovered by the government on two farms owned by a company called

Nitram. The government was tipped off by South African intelligence, whose spy Calloway worked for Mugabe. Nitram was owned by a group of former ZPRA soldiers.

Following the arms caches, on 8 February 1982, the government issued a statement blaming *"Matabeleland"* for caching enough weapons of war to equip an army of five thousand. Nkomo queried why it was twisted around from a Hampton Farm and Ascot Farm, to a Matabeleland crime. Matabeleland was not caching arms. It was a premeditated and calculated distortion.

Because of the arms caches, a few days later, the government confiscated all properties (eithteen farms and business enterprises) owned by Nitram, ZAPU, ZAPU members, former ZPRA soldiers, Nkomo and the Nkomo family members. That reaction exposed the twisted logic of the government, that a problem with one individual or institution from Matabeleland was the fault of all Matabeleland. That was the rationale in their behavior which said that if there was one dissident in Matabeleland then all Matabeles were dissidents.

According to Mugabe, the Ndebele people needed to be *"re – educated"* (Doran 2015). He said that in 1984, during an interview with Donald Trelford of the Observer (UK) had said, *"the solution is a military one. Their grievances are unfounded. The verdict of the voters was cast in 1980. They should have accepted defeat then…. The situation in Matabeleland is one that requires a change. The people must be reoriented"*. Mugabe also advertently failed to distinguish between the dissidents and the people of Matabeleland. Instead of going after the so called dissidents, he targeted *"the people"*. Mugabe also expressed his preference of a military solution over a political solution (Mhlanga 2009), while blaming all Matabeleland for the dissidents he himself had created.

By implying that the people of Matabelelend and ZAPU had not accepted defeat in 1980, Mugabe was pandering to his own propaganda. Many within his hierarchy had always feared that if ZAPU lost the elections they would continue the war as they themselves had planned on doing and had even said they would do in the event of ZANU losing. They thought the Matabele would declare a breakaway state and probably get the support from the Soviet Union just like the Katanga in Zaire had done and gotten backing from the Americans. However, either Mugabe and his mandarins were poor judges of character or they were purely mischievious killers, because after working with and observing Nkomo for so long, they should have known that he was very desperate for peace and that as he had stated too often, nationalism had won and he was content with that. As long as Nkomo was their leader, the Matabele were never going to declare their independence. Some of his critics said that he was too much of a nationalist.

Notwithstanding, for ZANU at that stage and always, the problem was neither ZAPU nor dissidents, but the Ndebele nation. The process of re – educating the Ndebele was therefore not mandated to academics in the classrooms as was the norm. From 1980 to 2019, the 5th Brigade, ZNA, the CIO, CID, ZRP, PISI, ZANU PF, the civil service and other institutions at the disposal of the state, jointly and severally in both covert and overt ways, were employed in re – educating the Ndebele.

The 5th Brigade was composed of 3500 details after some screening of the original four thousand recruited soldiers. Dropped out were those that had failed the training and those that were suspected to be Matabele or were judged to be having reasons for being sympathetic to the Matabele. At pass out, the three thousand five hundred were the most blood thirsty and zealous former ZANLA soldiers.

What remained secret to most, even to some in the military was that another 3500 soldiers from the Presidential Guard combined with the 5th Brigade to form what was commonly known as Gukurahundi. What the people saw in starched new army uniforms, red berets with AK 47s to which were affixed shiny and sharp bayonets, were 3500 5th Brigade soldiers and 3500 crack troopers from the Presidential Guard. Both those made up what became known to the public as the Gukurahundi battalion.

As the 5th Brigade exited Nyanga, in went the Presidential Guard for their own training stint. Their pass-out parade was in December 1982. After training by the North Korean instructors they were merged with the 5th Brigade before the seven thousand - strong combined battalion was secretly moved from Nyanga to Empress Nickel Mine on the Kadoma - Gokwe road. From there they were moved again to Ntabazinduna, Gokwe and Zvishabane to be a bullet away from their Matabele targets in the Midlands and Matabeleland.

The then ceremonial President, Rev. Canaan Sodindo Banana Ncube of Ndebele origin, attended the pass - out parade of the 5th Brigade. Most probably in stark darkness and ignorant of his Prime Minister's plans and less likely out of blind and grateful loyalty, Rev. Banana graced the unholy occassion. Unlike Enos Nkala the then Minister of National Supplies, also a Ndebele, Banana was not a zealous helper against his own people. While Banana listened, Mugabe's official instruction to the Gukurahundi battalion was to *"plough"* and *"reconstruct"*. Obviously in Banana's absence the Gukurahundi commanders were given completely different orders and rules of engagement, to wipe out his people from the face of the country.

The 5th Brigade was unleashed into Matabeleland North in February 1983, while the Presidential Guard joined them in February 1984. In March 1984 the 5th Brigade turned their murderous attention and blood dripping bayonets to Matabeleland South, then the Midlands. In Matabeleland South they established the most horrifying murder concentration camp and sadistic torture site after Nazi Auswitz; Bhalagwe. Bhalagwe was where women were gang raped before sharpened logs were pushed up their private parts, wombs slit open, foetuses dashed against the walls. Men were castrated by having their testicles smashed repeatedly with blunt objects then thrown down a mine shaft while still alive. Women in their monthly periods were forced to sit naked with their legs apart and some male victims forced to clean the women's private parts with their tongues at Bhalagwe. At Bhalagwe siblings were forced to have sexual intercourse and mothers forced to be intimate with their sons in full view of a boisterous and cheering army. Bhalagwe the site, a stone's throw away from where in 2017 Robert Mugabe had his lavish 93rd birthday celebrations amidst protests from the local Matobo community.

What happened on the ground was worlds apart from Mugabe's official command, unless to him and the battalion, ploughing and reconstruction meant to kill, maim, loot and plunder. What unraveled in the ensuing years was not a chapter of accidents nor was it a bolt from the blue. ZANU rolled out a meticulous plan, born of intellectual and scientific thinking processes, implemented tenaciously with rare and fiendish panache.

A seven thousand - strong battalion, trained to kill remorselessly, was officially deployed to contain some four hundred wily and elusive dissidents. On the ground they found themselves face to face with a civilian population with a lot in common with their prey. During training it had been inculcated into their minds that the prey was Ndebele and that the Ndebele were the prey. As Ndebele and dissident got entangled and intertwined, the former were mauled like wheat gobbled by a combine harvester machine.

While the 5th Brigade was frenziedly enthusiastic, ferocious and fierce, the Presidential Guard was tougher, methodical yet more ruthless and wretched. They both killed wantonly. Like the lioness and the lion, the 5th Brigade was the hunter and the Presidential Guard brought up the rear with systemic and nerve-jangling might. According to Shari Eppel (2001 interview with Kreiser) the 5th Brigade was *"Mugabe's hit squad....deployed to terrorise the local population"*.

Through torture, detention, rape, beatings, burning etc, Mugabe's private political and tribal army did his bidding.

The Support unit followed behind Gukurahundi as a mop - up and policing operation. They too committed atrocities, although they were a far cry from the Gukurahundi Brigade in terms of numbers of victims and intensity of cases.

The 5th Brigade was under the harsh command of Perence Shiri, at times referred to as black Jesus and later appointed Air Marshall, then Minister of Lands in 2018, under President Mnangagwa. Major Shallwin Muzite was the 5th Brigade Director of Operations. The Presidential Guard was commanded by Colonel Paradzai Zimondi who later became one of the trusted securocrats as Director of Prisons. Ironically the colonel's name and surname literally translated to 'Destroyer Murderer'. Col. Zimondi's Director of Operations was Douglas Nyikayaramba. Nyikayaramba two decades later led the chorus of sightless devotion to Mugabe by the army top brass as they took turns to declare that they would never allow anyone who did not go to the war of liberation to rule the country.

Perence Shiri also relied very much on consultations with Dominic Chinenge, who was in charge of 1 Brigade in Bulawayo. Chinenge's brigade provided the Gukurahundi Brigade with logistical support and a base from which to unleash terror when they were in Bulawayo. Shiri and Chinenge, like the fangs of a serpant spewing venom, *"were intimately involved in an apparent attempt to obliterate the Ndebele from the face of the earth"* (Doran 2015). Chinenge was to later operate *mutato nomine* as Constantine Chiwenga and was appointed ZDF Commander General by Mugabe. Years later in 2017, he and Mnangagwa were to force Mugabe to resign at gunpoint after which he became Vice President.

Like a marauding and manic buffalo bull, the 5th Brigade traversed Matabeleland, ferociously dragging behind them a harrowing scythe that cut through the population hideously. The population scampered and scattered. Hot on the heals of the 5th Brigade, the Presidential Guard crisscrossed their trail, slaughtering hundreds of innocents for every single 'dissident' they suspected, glimpsed, apprehended or killed. Between them they pillaged, plundered, blazed and murdered all in their sight. They desolated, widowed, crippled, and orphaned Lupane, Jotsholo, Tsholotsho, Nyamandlovu, Gwanda, Silobela, Gokwe, Vungu, Filabusi, Plumtree, Kezi, Matopo, Nkayi, Inyathi and all the other lands of Kings Mzilikazi and Lobhengula.

True to its name, the Gukurahundi Brigade was like a vigorous and angry whirlwind that lifted, twisted and swept away everything in its wake. The soldiers, police, militia and youths did not discriminate between men, women and children. They shot men, bayoneted women and bludgeoned infants and ripped out foetuses from the wombs of pregnant women without even twitching an eyelid. There was no doubting that the battalion was deployed on a civilian, mass murdering mission. Livestock and property were dealt with with equal reckless abandon and viciousness. Like a selective plague, they ravished through the two provinces. In their wake they left nothing but wretchedness, agony, desolation and death.

Their official primary target were dissidents, but in practice they were under instruction to wipe out all ex ZPRA soldiers, be they demobilized or intergrated into the ZNA. All former members of the ZPRA army were to be shot on sight if they were lucky, otherwise once apprehended they were gruesomely tortured by use of any satanic method imaginable, pummeled to a pulp till dead and dumped in the wild animal infested forests or into the nearest pit whose depth or lack of it was inconsequential. The ex – ZPRA that had been intergrated into the ZNA were most vulnerable when found off duty because they were conveniently accused of deserting the army and therefore dissidents. They were also shot by their colleagues in the army during operations because they were considered as informers for the rebels or they were would - be deserters. When on a few days vacation, they were picked up by hit squads on their way home from their base or on their way from home, never to be seen again.

Next in the line of fire were ZAPU activists, supporters, then all the people of Matabeleland in general and the Ndebele and Kalanga in particular and finally the Ndebele in the Midlands province. Those were marked for annihilation irrespective of age, sex or physical condition. People living with physical or mental disabilities were not spared either. Life in Matabeleland and Midlands became such a cheap commodity whose value for both ex ZPRA and all civilians of all ages was at the discretion of the Gukurahundi Brigade soldiers on the ground.

A malefic era of searches, threats, beatings, burnings and killings descended on the cobra as per Mugabe's description of Nkomo and ZAPU. The government army was on a crusade to *"eradicate"* the snake by dismembering its body.

On 8 March 1983 Joshua Nkomo, after walking and driving the dirt roads of Plumtree at night, crossed the Shashi river into friendly Botswana, fleeing from an erstwhile comrade. Disgraced and discredited, Joshua Nkomo was in flight from fellow nationalists and from a revolutionary fire he had played no small role in tending. For the sake of his life, he had to hastily turn his back and bolt away from the result of a revolution he himself had started and concluded.

When the six tourists were abducted near Insuza in July 1982, a harsh curfew regimen was declared in the entire Matabeleland North province. Ergo, the Gukurahundi Brigade intensified their activities. In the same month of July 1982 the Air Force of Zimbabwe's Thornhill Air Base in Gweru was almost razed to the ground in a clear case of sabotage. The damage was massive but no curfew was declared in Gweru and Gukurahundi Brigade was not deployed there to handle the *"malcontents"* and their supporting *"infrastructure"*.

Earlier, when an assassination attempt had been made on Mugabe's life in December 1981 in Harare, a stringent curfew schedule was not imposed on Harare and the Gukurahundi Brigade was not deployed there. Yet most bizarrely, Operation Octopus was rolled out in Bulawayo. A curfew was declared in Bulawayo for an attempt on Mugabe's life in Harare. How on earth a curfew in Bulawayo was going to help arrest the perpetrators of the crime that had happened some five hundred kilometers away, was earth shutteringly boggling to the mind. It became clear that according to the ZANU government, the only people in the world that could attempt to kill Mugabe were in Bulawayo, home of the Ndebele. Due to Operation Octopus which was executed in Bulawayo for a crime committed in Harare, many Bulawayo residents suffered and many more died.

The government's proclivity for underhandedness and double standards, was again exposed when twenty - two people were brutally murdered by dissidents in August 1985 in Mwenezi in Masvingo province. A curfew was not declared there and the Gukurahundi Brigade was not dispatched there to hunt for the dissidents and kill their supporters and those giving them food. Of course the government realized that deploying Gukurahundi to Harare, Gweru and Mwenezi would expose the Shona people in those areas to their murderous routine. Clearly, the Gukurahundi Brigade had been tailor – made for Matabeleland. Hence the claim that the brigade was meant to combat dissidents and malcontents was as mystical as it was false, unless if it was taken literally as Mugabe had put it. Mugabe had stated that the brigade was meant to combat malcontents in *"Matabeleland"*. If that was the idea, then the government should have trained three more brigades to kill the people in Masvingo, Gweru and Harare as well. Whichever way one looked at it, they zeroed in on one verdict only: the government had a murderous agenda towards the peoples of Matabeleland.

It could not therefore be denied that Gukurahundi was never meant to combat dissidentry and lawlessness. It was meant to annihilate the Matabele, especially the Ndebeles and Kalangas in Matabeleland and Midlands. The brigade was meant to torture, maim and kill Matabeles until they voted for ZANU and until they spoke the Shona language, thereby ushering in Mugabe's one party state. Just as he had declared before the 1980 elections, voting for anything but ZANU, was a call for war. They had not voted for ZANU and he was giving them war.

According to New Zimbabwe, March 11, 2006, Nathan Shamuyarira the information minister once said the, *"actions of the North Korea-trained Five Brigade that massacred thousands of civilians in the Matabeleland and Midlands provinces during political disturbances in the 1980s were not regrettable as [the Five Brigade was] doing a job to protect the people. It was because the dissidents were killing people, that Gukurahundi went to correct the situation and protect the people. We killed vana Gwesela (the Gweselas) in my own province in Mashonaland West, in Sanyati. We killed him because he played havoc. In Matabeleland, they killed the Shona-speaking teachers; it's not true to say the Ndebeles were the only victims. Europeans in Mat South fled their farms and went to hide in the city."*

Shamuyarira's reference to Shona teachers that were killed by dissidents implied that because Shonas were killed, Ndebeles were to pay and therefore the 5th brigade was deployed on a pound of flesh for pound of flesh basis. However, history showed the government getting recompense for the flesh of less than ten teachers from 100 000 dead Matabeles. It was quite puzzling and disconcerting that, although, as per Shamuyarira's claim, there were dissidents in Mashonaland West, the 5th Brigade was never deployed there. Why was Gukurahundi not deployed to Mashonaland West to *"protect the people"*? The answer was simple. There were no Ndebeles there for them to butcher. Yet there were formidable ZAPU structures there. Or simply, the 5th Brigade was not deployed to Sanyati in Mashonaland West province because it was not home to the dissident Ndebele people. Minister Shamuyarira was merely justifying the genocide.

The impunity and arrogance in Shamuyarira's statement was perturbing but expected as it was the general attitude among ZANU stalwarts and some people in Mashonaland then. It was most horrifying that Gukurahundi was deployed to Matabeleland purportedly to protect the people from about 200 to 400 dissidents but ended up killing a 100 000 of the people they were supposedly protecting. It was never established how many dissidents they killed or apprehended because they labelled everyone they killed a rebel. Only 122 (one hundred and twenty - two) dissidents surrendered their arms in response to the 1988 amnesty that was declared after the unity accord of 1987. However, the unavailable data on how many civilians were killed by the government army revealed how eccentric and scandalous the whole dissidents saga was. The statistics, the facts and the accounts by the people in the Midlands and Matabeleland showed that the government army was in actual fact hunting down and killing the civilian population.

Undeniably, some Shona teachers were killed in Matabeleland because the conflict was idiosyncratically tribal. Denying the loss of Shona lives would be an unforgivable insult to the relatives of the victims and that cannot be done without running the risk of sounding naively triumphalistic and tribal like Shamuyarira. There was no justification for the murder of Shona teachers in Matabeleland by dissidents (whoever they were), Equally horrifying was the massacre of 100 000 Matabeles by the government in an act of sheer hateful lunacy. The government of Robert Mugabe and its sequel, that of Emmerson Mnangagwa owed the relatives of the deceased teachers the truth, an explanation, an apology, a confession, justice and reparations.

Paradoxically, the same white farmers that Shamuyarira was claiming to protect, were the same that his party ZANU PF was plundering and killing during the farm invasions beginning in the year 2000. The farmers had to seek refuge in towns. A Gukurahundi genocide justifier, Shamuyarira was like one that denied the Germany holocaust, a criminal liable for prosecution.

According to Todd (2000), there was no debate on the presence of dissidents in Mashonaland. Those dissidents were not only former ZPRA but they were former ZANLA as well. Judith Todd, the daughter of former Rhodesian Prime Minister Garfield Todd, cited extensively a letter written to Robert Mugabe in 1980 by ZPRA commanders Lt. Gen. Lookout Masuku and Dumiso Dabengwa. The pair clearly stated their stance against ex – ZPRA dissidents, some of whom ZPRA had apprehended and had been subsequently incarcerated at Khami maximum security prison. They went on to cite a number of events proving the existence of ZANLA dissidents in Mashonaland as they argued that, *"on 22 June 1980 ZANLA dissidents at Marenga Business Centre fired two bullets, destroying the fuel tank of the vehicle driven by Sgt. Gava of Zvimba Police post in Sinoia... ZANLA shootings at Kachuta TTL on 17 June 1980..shooting at Murambinda 18 June 1980....ZANLA has been harassing and in some cases burning villages of the civilian population around Golf and Hotel Assembly points for their refusal to provide them with food...the above few examples involving ZANLA units exclude other wide ranging cases of murder, shooting, kidnapping, abductions and kangaroo courts by ZANLA or ZANU cadres which are never mentioned"*.

The question that kept loudly and rudely begging for an answer was, why did the government not send the 5th brigade and all the murderous formations of the security apparatus and ZANLA brigades, to the areas mentioned by Masuku and Dabengwa. Equally sturbbon was the persistent answer that, those areas were in Mashonaland and were not inhabited by the Ndebele people and could not afford to have the Gukurahundi killers deployed there because they had been trained to kill the Ndebele and not necessarily dissidents.

The ideological gap between Shamuyarira and the late ZPRA commander Lieutenant General Lookout Masuku was strikingly vivid. If Shamuyarira's statement was compared with that of Masuku, made in January 1980 in an interview with Time Magazine when he stated that, *"Only if you treat the population with respect do you find it easier to fight the enemy. We are fighting for the liberation of these people. If we kill them, whom are we going to rule?"*, the philosophical disparity left the reader confused as to who was the soldier and who was the cabinet minister. While Shamuyarira sounded like the supercilious, triumphalist and vindictive war monger that he was, Masuku the soon – to - be political prisoner, sounded like the all - embracing nationalist father figure and statesman that he was not allowed to become. Masuku was espousing the ZPRA ideology of respecting the citizens which was inculcated into the recruits before they were fit for deployment to the war front. Shamuyarira on the other hand was positing the ZANLA Gukurahundist doctrine of hammering dissent in order to gain compliance by monster force.

When the online Zimbabwe Independent newspaper of May 2014 revealed that Nathan Shamuyarira was critically ill and admitted at the intensive care unit of a private clinic in Harare, the report sparked conflicting public emotions. That was the same Shamuyarira who had in 1983 dismissed evidence of the Gukurahundi Brigade killings from the Catholic Church bishops as *"irresponsible, contrived, propaganda"* (Nkomo 1984). The correspondent reminded the reader that in October 2006, at a national reconciliation conference in Vumba, Shamuyarira had disapproved of Mugabe and Edison Zvobgo's *"apology"* over Gukurahundi. He said they should not have apologized (it is not known what apology he was referring to, because Mugabe was not known to have apologized). It was again revealed by the same publication that when asked if he regretted the genocide by the government, Shamuyarira had retorted *"no, I don't regret"*.

What was most shocking and disheartening about Shamuyarira's finale episode, besides the fact that the former ZANU PF chief propagandist was on the verge of accounting for his deeds before God but was still intransigent, was the revelation of how apathetic the Zimbabwean society was, to the plight and suffering of others. It was patent that the article about his critical condition was meant to inform the public about the health of a public figure, lay bare the historical facts around him and get the reader to interrogate Shamuyarira's values, morals and ethics before doing some soul searching.

However, those members of the public that commented on the internet beneath the article, displayed that they did not really care about Shamuyarira's role in perpetrating the Gukurahundi genocide. One comment from a Paul Masuku (probably Ndebele) said *"just go now"* and did not give their reason for so much revulsion (lamentably Shamuyarira died six days later on 05 June 2014). Another one called Goredema (probably Shona) said that Shamuyarira was not very evil. Another one calling themselves Goredema again said *"Dzino is my hero"* referring to Shamuyarira. Another commentator hailed Shamuyarira as a hero and wished him well. Another thought he was a *"sellout"* for having formed FROLIZ a political party before independence in 1978.

It was extremely interesting that forming a political party in 1978, which was everyone's right the world over, could earn one the abasing title of *"sellout"* even on their death bed, yet the murder of a 100 000 people, including women and children was not remembered by the commentator. None commented on Shamuyarira's expressed lack of regret for the Gukurahundi genocide. None mentioned Shamuyarira's role as a Gukurahundi propagandist since before 1979 through 1980 when he was appointed minister of information. None remembered his authorship of the 1979 Shona Grand Plan.

Common belief and practice for centuries globally was always that, as Shakespeare's Mark Antony put it, *"the evil that man do lives after them, but the good is oft interred with their bones...."*. That was nonetheless not the case with Shamuyarira? Mark Antony's observation was that, an hour of satanism by one was always remembered long after they had died, than a lifetime of sainthood. A moment of weakness could effortlessly become one's permanent character and overshadow decades of piety. It would appear that that moral law applied everywhere else but in Zimbabwe, where the massacre of tens of thousands, the physical and psychological injury of millions and the consequent displacement of hundreds of thousands, failed to discredit heroism. In Zimbabwe mass murderers had their praises sung during their funerals and were interred at the North Korean funded and built monument called the National Heroes Acre. Shamuyarira like many of his genocidal Gukurahundists was declared by ZANU PF, a national hero and was therefore entombed at the National Heroes Acre. That made him a hero of the Matabele as well, the people he had butchered.

In other countries, social misdeamors like a president having an extra marital affair or committing adultery, was enough to shut the doors to the hall of fame, yet in Zimbabwe a genocide could not detract from one's effort on the heroism continuum.

When Emmerson Mnangagwa took over power through a coup from Mugabe in November 2017, he, during his first months enjoyed more sympathy and support domestically and internationally than he would ever do in his entire future. No one was asking him to be in sack cloths and ashes, yet if he had apologized for the Gukurahundi genocide or at the least, acknowledged that the pogrom was an evil visitation by the government on innocent civillians, he probably could have earned some amount of respect even from the victims. Instead, during an interview on the sidelines of the World Economic Forum in Davos in January 2018, he squandered that opportunity. Sounding very much unnuanced, on four occasions during the interview, when asked if he would ever *"say I'm sorry"* for the genocide, Mnangagwa, both inarticulate and unintelligible in response, blew his chance away. What was cogent in his responses was that he neither regreted the genocide nor would he apologise. He failed dismayingly to convince the world that he was different from Mugabe.

Referring to the genocide as merely *"a bad patch"*, he seemed to think that the fact that he had recently signed into law the National Peace and Reconciliation Commission (NPRC) Bill, would have some talismanic cleansing effect on his barbarous past. However, the truth, as Jonathan Moyo put it on SABC was that, when Mnangagwa, cannoned into Mugabe's office, the bill was on the desk waiting for a signature. Moyo further informed the world that it was Mnangagwa and Patrick Chinamasa who had faught indefatigably and campaigned doggedly to have the truth component excluded from the bill after having failed to remove it from the 2013 consitution. Moyo further revealed that when the then Vice President Phelekezela Mpoko had presented the bill in parliament he had been fiercely resisted by Mnangagwa and his hangers on. Therefore, Mnangagwa's signing the bill was mandatory and his bragging about it was opportunistic. Without emboding the truth component, the bill which he signed was a pale shadow of what the people of Matabeleland expected.

Not content with claiming to be the hero who had promulgated the NPRC bill, Mnangagwa in Davos went on to belittle the genocide by claiming that the number of the dead had been exaggerated. He said the twenty thousand figure proffered by the Catholic Commission for Justice and Peace (CCJP) was *"not the correct figure"*. That impugnment, coming from the man that had equated the people of Matabeleland to *"coachroaches"*, the man who had vowed to *"shorten"* their stay on earth and the man who had administered *"DDT"* on them, was the most chilling and slanderous disparagement ever. It was denial. He wanted to kill the memory of Gukurahundi as argued by Iris Chang (1997) that, *"Denial is an integral part of atrocity, and it's a natural part after a society has committed genocide. First you kill, and then the memory of killing is killed"*.

Mnangagwa probably wanted to convince the world but ran out of guts, that he believed the Gukurahundi Brigade butchers had only slaughtered about one thousand five hundred civilians and dissidents. That, because the Chihambakwe Commission of inquiry of 1983 which was set up when he was the Minister of National Security, was mandated to investigate the deaths of some 1500 people. That figure could have come from or had been endorsed by his ministry since he was the gatherer of government intelligence. That was the number of casualties that the Mugabe government in a way admitted were probably killed during the time of the genocide.

At least Mngagwa, unlike Joice Mujuru then, albeit fleetingly, had the brainpower not to try and completely exonerate himself of the genocide. Nor did he at Davos attempt to blame it entirely on Mugabe like she did, because that way he would have waded deeper into the waters of absurdity. Be that as it was, Mugabe for his part did not hesitate to highlight Mnangagwa's guilt. A few weeks after the Davos interview, Mugabe, revealed that it was Mnangagwa and then CIO boss Danny Stannard that had bombed Dumiso Dabengwa's car during the early 1980s.

Despite that vital revelation, Mugabe went on to try and cleanse himself of responsibility for the genocide by blaming it on the Ndebele and ZAPU. Inspite of the fact that Dabengwa, Masuku and others had been acquitted at the high court, of charges of treason by caching arms, Mugbe came up with very fresh allegations that ZAPU was caching arms in the Hwange area. He even implicated former Zambian president, Dr. Kenneth Kaunda of complicity by conveying two train loads of military hardware to ZAPU after independence. He did not clarify on how the Ndebele (the victims) were guilty of the genocide. One would say that Mugabe's loyalty to the grave was amazing. After failing to rule to the grave, at 94, he was still resolute in denying the genocide all the way to the grave.

The little resolve and spine that had sustained Mnangagwa at Davos, was to fly from him and exposed him for the poor liar that he was, just like Mugabe and Rejoice Mujuru. Speaking in Harare in May 2018, Mnangagwa uttered the most poorly fabricated concoction of his life when he claimed that contrary to popular belief he was never on the same side with Mugabe, that he was perpetually in opposition to Mugabe and worse still that he saved dissidents and Ndebeles from extinction by the Gukurahundi army. In a dismaying portrayal of the gullibility and hypocricy of Zimbabwean politics, the audience was reported to have cheered and applauded such raw and uncalibrated lies. No one in the audience was unaware of Mnangagwa's past and none had an iota of belief in his falsehood, yet many applaused his insult to the dead victims of his tribal hate and previous allegiance to Mugabe.

The only minister from Mugabe to Mnangagwa's government on record of having expressed regret for the Gukurahundi genocide was Mr. Moven Mahachi, who later died in a mysterious car accident. In the Sunday Mail of 6 September 1992 Mahachi said, *"events during that period are regretted and should not be repeated by anybody, any group of people or any institution.."* (CCJP and LRF 1997). It was very courageous and honest of him to admit that and it was hoped that that did not in any way contribute to his untimely death.

When Bulawayo was besieged, the army went to Joshua Nkomo's house in Phelandaba township on a manhunt for him. When they could not find him, they gunned down his driver and two others. They ransacked the house, vandalised household property and damaged the windows and upholstery of three cars. The three casualties left behind at the house were some of the first recognised *"cochroaches"* to be given *"DDT"* poison in the *"re – education"* program for the Ndebele people.

On 5 March 1983, the same day Mnangagwa likened dissidents to cockroaches, the police, the army and the Gurkurahundi Brigade, in murderous cohorts cordoned off Bulawayo, the capital of the Ndebele nation. They besieged the city, abducting, beating up, maiming, raping, detaining and killing hundreds of civilians including wives of *"cochroaches"* and children of *"dissidents"*. Under the tribally polarised environment prevailing then, that was a malignant act of war against a particular ethnic civilian population. Moreso after Mugabe, the 'hero' at the time and commander in chief of the ZDF had propagated that Nkomo and ZAPU were like a cobra in the house and that *"the only way to deal with a snake is to strike and destroy its head"*.

When the 5th brigade and the Presidential Guard took turns to further Mugabe's mandate of re -educating the Ndebele and destroying the snake, a 100 000 civilians died. Re - education assumed a very strange design that ranged from down right murder to denial of education. By 2016 the ordinary villagers in Plumtree and Lupane were still fighting for the rights of their primary school children to be taught by teachers who could speak the local language. Re - education meant they had to be literally beaten and killed out of supporting ZAPU, while they were denied the right to education. They had to be sorry and apologetic for being Ndebele.

To an embarrassing extent, the people of Matabeleland were so painstakingly 're – educated', they consciously and subconsciously shied away from any Matabele initiatives. They were so thoroughly 're-educated' that most of the Matabeleland population understood the Shona language, yet the Shona civil servants and even shop attendents in Matabeleland, after working and living among locals for decades were proud to tell the members of the public that they did not understand the local languages. They learnt the lesson so much that by 1990, hundreds of them were queuing overnight to buy ZANU PF party cards.

By 2005 they would prove their 're – education' by voting for Morgan Tsvangirai instead of Welshman Ncube at a time when the former was violating every democratic principle in the book. They learnt quickly that voting for a Ndebele for president was an act of dissidentry and treason punishable by Gukurahundi genocide. Even as far ahead as 2018, many MDCT supporters from Matabeleland opted for Nelson Chamisa (Shona), an appointed party vice president, to be president ahead of Thokozani Khuphe (Ndebele) who had been elected at a party congress as vice president. They would not repeat their fatal mistake of 1980 and 1985 again. They had subconsciously accepted their fate as second fiddle while the Shona were first class citizens. They had come to thoroughly know that their salvation came from Mashonaland.

At village and ward level, the people of Matabeleland were loathe to elect into office a structure without Shonas. To have a Shona among Ndebeles in any institution guaranteed protection and cooperation by state agents and institutions for the whole structure. Principally and lamentably, that implied that the Shonas were integral to the survival or success of Matabeleland. Shona company or presence became the all enabling visa to success for the Matabele. Therefore, re – education meant loss of identity, conformity or even death to the Ndebele. Those that resisted re – education were *"crushed and crushed completely"*, (to use Mugabe's terminology).

Mhlanga (2009) described the 're – education' of the Matabele as a *"social death"* where the *"psychology of oppression, then, becomes a phenomenon derived from the state, where the oppressed, given their existential experience, adopt the attitude of 'adhesion' to the oppressor.....the oppressed rationalize and internalize their suffering. Their state of mental warping makes them appear as walking symbols of conformity. Such conformity makes them reject their enlightened brethren whom they tend to perceive as 'trouble makers'"*. The psychology of oppression was the reason why such political leaders as Dr. Dumiso Dabengwa, Prof. Welshman Ncube, Moses Mzila – Ndlovu, Thokozani Khuphe, Paul Siwela, Mqondisi Moyo, General Nandinandi, among others that represented dissension against zanuism, especially the idea of Mashonaland as perennial governor of Matabeleland, found it very hard to convince their own people to support them. The people had been subjected to violent and intolerant oppression, so much they were afraid of standing up, separate and distinct without a Shona person close by, because they would become easy targets.

Due to the DDT regimen and the re - education program, between 1980 and 22 December 1987 men, women and children fled into neighboring Botswana, Zambia, South Africa and Europe. Many sought refuge in the wild life infested forests of Matabeleland. Many were mauled by lions and crocodiles or trampled to death by elephants, as they attempted to cross the boundaries into Botswana, Zambia and South Africa on foot or by swimming across the Limpopo and Zambezi rivers. Thousands died on the run due to diseases such as malaria. Exposure to the harsh elements accounted for many more, especially the children. Some, tired of running and walking, hungry, confused and terrified got lost in the jungles and wondered themselves into exhaustion, delirium and died of fatigue and despair. Some women surrendered their bodies to and were gang raped by the Gukurahundi soldiers in order to survive.

In Matabeleland South, food was used as a weapon of the DDT and re - education war. There was a harsh food embargo as food deliveries were cut out including food aid by donor agencies. Shops were closed and there was a strict curfew for four months. The army stripped the land bare of all food. They shot and stole cattle from the villagers while claiming that the cattle had been captured as war booty in the 19th century by kings Mzilikazi and Lobhengula from their Shona ancestors. The people were deliberately starved as food supplies were cut off. The army told the people that they *"would first have to eat your chickens, then your goats, then your cattle, then your donkeys. Then you will eat your children and finally you will eat your dissidents."* (Johnson and Clark 1984, Meredith 2007). Hundreds died of starvation. None fought back. Hundreds of thousands carry the physical and psychological scars to this day, due to Mnangagwa's DDT and Mugabe's re – education regimen.

Former minister of peace and reconciliation, Moses Mzila – Ndlovu ruefully decried his and his ZPRA colleagues' betrayal of the people of Matabeleland and Midlands during the Gukurahundi genocide. He lamented, *"...my greatest regret is this. I will admit that as ZPRA we abdicated our responsibility to our erstwhile supporters. We failed to defend the people from the Gukurahundi onslaught. ZPRA must take responsibility for the genocide. How could we fail to defend the people like that?"* (interview with Mzila – Ndlovu, 02 February 2017, Bulawayo).

In response to the question, why ZPRA had not fought back and defended the Matabeleland and Midlands people against the government army, Dabengwa (interview 17 March 2017, Bulawayo) said that, *"it happened while we were detained. We could not defend our people*". Probably one of the reasons why ZPRA senior commanders were either detained or hounded out of the country, was to eliminate the possibility of organized military resistance against Mugabe's army. The government wanted a disjointed and poorly co - ordinated rebel group that would be an excuse for high handedness and extra judicial killings.

The people were butchered in their defenselessness. They were crushed so that they would never rise again. Many asked if they were not entitled to be defended especially by ZAPU and ZPRA? Many wondered why ZAPU and ZPRA were so desperate for peace, so much that they were prepared to sacrifice the lives of the Matabele so that ZANU could be at peace? Many, on the other hand celebrated Joshua Nkomo's refusal to order his ZPRA army back into the bush to be rebels against the ZANU regime, when he could have easily done that. They said a more devastating blood bath would have ensued and Mugabe would have used that as an excuse to justify his actions. As it turned out, the ZANU government were as guilty as sin and they have no defense to this day.

Still, the genocide did not achieve any peace for ZANU, as new side effects of Mugabe's nefarious and Mnangagwa's toxicant prescriptions are being discovered long after the coup of 2017. What Mnangagwa failed to realize was that, cockroaches were as old as mankind. He should have appreciated that that particular insect had been a household nemesis from pre-historic times, through the stone age to nuclear and computer technology cons. Attempts ranging from poisoning them with DDT, sterilizing male cockroaches with pheromones to puncturing their protective cuticles with diatomaceous earth, had failed to rid the earth of cockroaches.

Cockroaches could not be gotten rid of by any poisoning but by simple hygiene and cleanliness. Mugabe, Mnangagwa, Sekeramayi, Shiri and all ZANU, failed to maintain a politically clean home environment. Consequently, the 'cockroaches' are still there and are demanding justice. The only remedy, Mnangagwa should have suggested to his linchpin and party was political hygiene. Fair and equitable treatment of Matabele and Shona, ZPRA and ZANLA. That was all the hygiene required to rid the countryside of the handful of dissidents and not the cantankerous Gukurahundi battalion. Gukurahundi could only kill, cripple and cow but could never break the hearts of the Matabele.

In April 1983, Sekeramayi, like the blowhard line – shooter that his role in orchestrating the Gukurahundi genocide had made of him, vaunted that *"the army will stay a long, long time...the majority of people now realize they have been misled by PF ZAPU...."* and *"understand the national character of ZANU"*

(CCJP and LRF 1997). The character of ZANU that the people of Matabeleland now understood was that it was murderous, ruthless, vindictive, mean, tribal, domineering, contemptuous and loathsome. There was nothing national in the character of ZANU except that it thrived on the policy of rank coercion, marginalization and ruling to the grave. The people of Matabeleland and parts of Midlands were terrified of and did not understand ZANU. There was nothing for Sekeramayi to be proud of about his party's achievements in Matabeleland but they had a lot to be ashamed of.

When George Orwell remarked that *"a people that elect corrupt politicians, imposters, thieves and traitors are not victims but accomplices"*, he must have had the Zimbabwean case in mind. The majority kept electing into office the same policy makers who in turn went on to appoint the same butcher generals but failed to interrogate their policies and practices. Thousands of the same voters went on to be captured on BBC Panorama video in 1983 denouncing Nkomo in song, dance and slogans. In snapshot interviews, several of the ZANU supporters, claimed Nkomo *"must be arrested...because he is silly and mischievous.....must be hanged because he is disturbing the country....must die in exile because he is an enemy of the people because he is not in our party,... we will tell Mugabe to declare a one party state...".* The demonstrators had banners one of which read, *"...pamberi ne 5th brigade* (forward with the 5th brigade) *long live 5th brigade".* (BBC Panorama 1983).

It became certain that the reprobate policies and villainous practices of the elite were a reflection of the will of the electorate or at lease a portion of them. Such behavior could only mean that some of the ordinary many people and supporters of ZANU were proud of the Gukurahundi Brigade massacres of the Ndebele. That argument was corroborated by Sithole in Mabhena (2014) when he concluded that some of the ethnic Shona ZANU supporters endorsed the ruthless tactics of Mugabe's army in Matabeleland and the Midlands.

Indeed, that was a classic case of rule by a tribal majority and not rule by democracy.

What must be interesting today as it should have been scary in 1980, was Mugabe's angry retort to Nkomo's query on why he was forming the 5th brigade. Mugabe had said the brigade was meant to *"crush"* those that tried to *"subvert"* his government. His combination of the terms *"crush"* and *"subvert"* was most diabolic. Mugabe declared that people would be crushed. The Prime minister was threatening citizens by vowing that they were going to demolished, squashed, vanquished, jammed and broken down, for subverting, which included any offence like undermining, challenging, weakening, threatening and destabilizing his regime. All those offences remain part and parcel of political organizations as they relate towards each other, the world over. Forming a crack brigade to wipe out an entire tribe in order to counter an opposition political party was grossly making a mountain out of a molehill. Such a draconian and fascistic an approach was a display of saturated contempt, too condensed and blown – out to have matured within a few months of Mugabe's initial term as Prime Minister. It obviously was not a result of a threat to his government but a culmination of years of waiting for vengeance.

A vengeance that boiled over publicly after the 1985 elections when Mugabe ordered ZANU supporters in the Shona language to, *"go and uproot the weeds from your gardens"* (CCJP and LRF 1997). Following the Prime Minister's decree, retributive hordes of ZANU women's league members went on a rampage, destroying houses of ZAPU supporters. Wielding and brandishing axes and matchets, they chopped to death a ZAPU candidate, two pregnant women and dozens others. On the third day of the killings, the government halted the ruthless slaughter (CCJP & LRF 1997). How else could the Shona public view and treat the Ndebele, if the Prime Minister and his ministers described them as weeds, germs, snakes and cockroaches?

While in 1983 Nkomo could not admit in public that Mugabe and his tomahawk men in ZANU were anti – Ndebele tribalists to the core, that revelation did escape his lips for the second time, under the burden of grief when he was distraught by Lookout Masuku's untimely death after years of harrowing torture by the CIO in 1986. He stated that, *"(t)here is confusion and corruption and, let us be clear about it, we are seeing racism in reverse under a false mirror of correcting imbalances from the past".* Less than clinical scrutiny of that assertion revealed that it was made in 1986 when Mugabe was still tipsy tavy with the whites, therefore racism against whites was not what Nkomo was referring to. *"Racism in reverse"* could only mean tribalism or discrimination of black by black because normally racism was black versus white or one ace against another race. Once the setup was black versus black then it was racism in reverse. Besides, if Masuku, being black was a victim of racism in reverse and it was known that the black government had killed him, then racism in reverse could only meam black on black discrimination. Nkomo was accusing the ZANU administration of discriminating against the Matabele.

Further analysis revealed the reasons for the hate and prejudice that Joshua Nkomo was reffering to. He said that the anti – Matabele crusade was perpetuated in the name of *"correcting imbalances from the past".* A past grotesquely presented by white historians with a mischivious agenda of misinformation. A history of

Ndebele *impis* marauding, rampaging, vanquishing, looting, killing and capturing Shonas. A history written by colonialists with a divide and rule theme meant to keep the Ndebele and the Shona at loggerheads. A history record that has worked dangerously well to this day. A history that made Mugabe seek twisted justice for Mashonaland at the expense of Matabeleland.

A history clearly articulated on behalf of an unnamed Shona senior intelligence officer by Mr. Roger Martin, British Deputy High Commissioner to Zimbabwe from 1983 to 1986. Martin said the officer said, *"you must understand our history. Until 1890 when Rhodes blew the whistle and stopped play, the Matabele treated us Shona like cattle. Now seventy years later the whites have gone away again and they still believe that they are the same Matabele and we are the same Shona. In fact they have the rights and responsibilities of a 20% ethnic minority within a majority Shona modern state and we have to teach them their position in life and the way to do that is to beat them until they realize we are not the same Shona they used to terrorize in the past".* That was the historical inequity that Mugabe and his party were busy correcting by brutally practicing racism in reverse.

The idea of ruthlessly pounding the Ndebele into submission was a passion among many vengeful elite Shonas, marshaled by Mugabe himself. When addressing a rally in Mashonaland, Mugabe had declared, *"the time has come for us to show the people of Matabeleland that we can bark and bite. We surely shall bite".* (Mhlanga 2009). If anyone thought Mugabe was talking about dissidents then they clearly needed intense psychological scrutiny of the most thorough order. He simply had a meatless bone to chew with the general Matabeleland population. Indeed, Mugabe did prove that his bite was as good as his bark by deploying the Gukurahundi Brigade to tear the Matabeleland body to smithereens. None within his coterie of praise – singer leaders cautioned him and the majority electorate voted for him enmasse in the next elections in 1985.

The Matabeleland civilian population was therefore butchered, maimed and killed due to Mugabe's inscrutable instructions. Most ordinary Shona people could not further Mugabe's order to kill ZAPU supporters, but the quantum of that brazen command, to weed their gardens, was the development of contempt, arrogance, suspicion and hate for everything that was Ndebele, especially the people and their language. Most Shona civil servants downright refused to speak the Ndebele language even after working and living in Matabeleland for decades yet when they went to South Africa job hunting, they spoke isiZulu which was the same as isiNdebele, before they even get the job.

✓ ✓ ✓ ✓

There are episodes and memories that men and women from time to time remember, yet there are experiences they just will never forget. Events that are seared into the walls of human imaginations with a scorching hot branding iron, marked to be unforgotten for eternity. Those memories always haunt victims with unimaginable vividness and blistering frequency. The Gukurahundi genocide is one such experience that must not only be recorded in the annals of history as the most ineradicably sordid and barbaric act by Mugabe and ZANU but must be inerasably marked as an act of utmost savagery and odium of man by man in contemporary times.

At St. Paul's Mission, some thirty kilometers from Lupane, scores of villagers were rounded up in march 1983. They were force marched into thatched huts and the dry grass was torched by the 5th brigade soldiers. Mr. Smile Ndlovu, his two wives, and five children including a five - year old, were the victims. Their crime was that Ndlovu's brother was ex ZPRA and Ndlovu did not know his whereabouts. As the red flames with streaks of blue and black thick smoke fervently licked into the sky, the solemn voices begging for mercy fast turned to panicky screams of alarm and distress. Then they started coughing and choking pitifully. They were wailing as human flesh was eaten up by the raging fire. The victims choked and burned rapidly. Within a few minutes, only an occasional heart rending howl, sounding less and less hominoid could be heard. The thick smoke permeated the air with an overpowering whiff of sweltering human flesh. The screaming, the wailing, the howling and the odour still resonated with chilling frequency and vividness in the mind of the elderly MaNcube, a neighbor who was one of those forced to witness what the government did to dissidents. She, with tears of sorrow and regret rued that she lived to tell the tale.

Former Victoria Falls Municipality Town Clerk (1994 – 2012), Mr. Godfrey S. Maphosa (questionnaire and interview, 25 July 2011) was the District Administrator (DA) for Nkayi district in Matabeleland North during the 1985 general elections. He was a former ZPRA soldier and had been trained in Ethiopia and Zambia. In 1985 there was no established election management authority and all DAs were responsible for managing and organizing the conduct of elections in their districts.

The elections were held at a time when any attempt at reification of ZANU in Matabeleland was an exercise in futility, equivalent to attempting to cook a stone by boiling it. That was because, in addition to it being almost natural anathema locally, ZANU was the ruling party and was responsible for the Gukurahundi genocide. In the first polls in 1980, the entire Matabeleland region had not voted for ZANU because they preferred ZAPU and cared less about the rest, but by

1985 they hated ZANU and the government, for what they had done and were continuing to do to the people of the region.

Still, the contest was mainly between ZAPU and ZANU. In all districts ZANU was using government structures, personnel and equipment, in a bid to convince the local electorate to vote for them. The procedure was that voters congregated and showed their preferred candidate by a show of hands or by secret ballot. The ZANU elections coordinator in Nkayi, a Mr. Mkhwananzi, in stark and brute violation of electoral procedure, imposed that voters should queue behind their preferred candidate. That procedure was employed extensively in Mashonaland and only the suicidal dared to be brave enough to queue behind an opposition candidate. The fact that the queuing system rendered the whole voting exercise a farce, unfair, not free and undemocratic did not occur to ZANU, the government or the election observers nationally. The DAs were expected to acquiesce, since they were civil servants and ZANU was synonymous with the government and the state.

The then DA for Nkayi Mr. Godfrey Maphosa refused to have elections conducted in violation of electoral laws. He insisted that the elections were to be conducted by secret ballot which was one of the two legal options. An argument ensued. The DA asked to be furnished with written instructions, if he was to vary the voting procedure. There were none. ZANU's Mkhwananzi stuck to his guns. There was no voting on that day.

By defying ZANU, the DA committed a crime punishable by any assortment of crude and sadistic measures. At some point during the fracas, Mkhwananzi hissed to the DA, "*sizabonana nxa ufuna sibonane*", (I will get you if that's what you want). True to his threat, he indeed did get him the next day.

Calistus Ndlovu a government minister arrived in Nkayi the next day. He was accompanied by Mr. Jacob Mudenda, the then Provincial Administrator (PA) for Matabeleland North province. Mudenda was later appointed Governor of Matabeleland North. He was also elected ZANU PF Speaker of Parliament in 2013. Mudenda was in the DA's office when the latter received a phone call that the Gukurahundi Brigade and ZANU youths that had been bused to Nkayi from Kwekwe were assaulting villagers indiscriminately. The DA then relayed that information to Mr. Mudenda who assured him that the police would monitor the situation.

Despite the police 'monitoring' the situation, a few minutes later a report came to the DA that the youths were on their way to his office and were still assaulting people en route. Since the Provincial Administrator was present, the District

Administrator found no cause for panic, assuming he was safe under the wings of his immediate superior. When the ZANU youths – cum - militia and the Gukurahundi soldiers arrived at the administrator's offices in a frenzy of singing, dancing, sloganeering and denouncing ZAPU, the PA addressed them for a short while with the DA standing next him.

While the DA listened to Mudenda he was suddenly violently grabbed and yanked from behind. He was apprehended, his pistol taken away, dragged to the open and thrown to the ground where he lay protecting his face as a torrent of booted feet rained all over his body. They pounded him to a pulp and only stopped when they had had enough. when the youths stopped clobbering him, a young girl of about sixteen, using a tree branch for a whip took over. As she whipped the beleaguered Maphosa repeatedly, the girl as if reciting some kind of outré yet queerly comical incantation, was saying *"andina kumbomurova ini!!!, ayiwa mhani, andina"*, over and over, which was Shona for *"I didn't beat him up, oh no I didn't"*. Maphosa was so thoroughly assaulted he was blind for a week afterwards.

All the while the PA who was the chief civil servant in the whole Matabeleland North province and was a staunch ZANU stalwart, was watching and did not rein the assailants in. Maphosa whose eyes glazed with tears as he recounted the incident with the girl and the tree branch, was convinced that among the youths were soldiers in civilian dress as a disguise.

The DA was later taken to Inyathi hospital some seventy kilometers out of Bulawayo, then he was transferred to Mpilo hospital in Bulawayo. Mpilo was less secure and Mr. Maphosa was convinced that they were going to kill him there and blame it on the hospital or his injuries at the hands of the 'youths'. He requested and was transferred to Bulawayo Central hospital against the desires of Mudenda and company. He was admitted there for two weeks. He never went back to Nkayi again.

✁ ✁ ✁ ✁

Dr. Brilliant Mhlanga, a Zimbabwean academic working in the UK was a young lad in Tsholotsho during the Gukurahundi genocide which left an *"indelible mark"* on his memory and probably his character. He has written extensively on the genocide and below is a brief extract from his written experience.

"Soldiers had gathered us at our usual venue – a bus stop. We were getting used to these gatherings that would turn into overnight vigils. Do not ask me what the vigils were aimed at or who we were waiting for. Possibly, the answer would be that we were each waiting to be killed, or for God or something like that! The

callousness and horror of these gatherings will live to be told by everyone who became a victim – especially by women and girls; our sisters and mothers. They were picked one after the other, like chickens on sale; this time, to be raped and returned when bleeding. That also happened to my closest cousin – sister who was about seven months pregnant. She was repeatedly raped.

While the soldiers were being adventurous with the young women and girls, we were forced to sing and dance beside a bonfire. Suddenly, one very old and sick man was brought before us to be tried in a kangaroo court on the other side. This kangaroo court was known for its nefarious failure to be lenient. This man's sin was failure to attend the gathering. He was found preparing porridge by the soldiers while patrolling, and forced to pour it all in his pocket, hot as it was, before being forced to attend the meeting. He was genuinely suffering from malaria. He was quickly sentenced to death and tied to a big log, readying him for the usual human roasting process. On what later happened to this man, your guess is as good as mine.

The escapade with the young women and girls continued unabated until morning. Mid – morning, as usual, a call for general accusations was made. This time my pregnant cousin - sister who had been raped the previous night was arraigned before the 'kangaroo court'. Her husband we all knew was labeled a dissident; since he worked in town and was not present, she had to pay for his sins. This time a betting game was hastily arranged. Two soldiers moved the motion that the foetus in her womb was male, while the other two argued that it was a girl. This argument continued for about five minutes. They each produced ten cents and gave it to the adjudicator who then ordered that her womb be ripped open to prove which group was right. Eventually she died of excessive bleeding and pain. The foetus too". (Mhlanga 2009)

✒ ✒ ✒ ✒

Nyamandlovu is some fifty kilometers northwest of Bulawayo. It was established by King Mzilikazi kaMatshobana in the 19th Century as a garrison for the Nyamayendlovu Regiment under the command of Chief Mkhokheli Masuku. Nyamandlovu is now an administrative district in Matabeleland North. Nsezi is a settlement some twenty kilometers away from Nyamandlovu to the west. On the banks of the Nsezi river from which the settlement derived its name, is a village called Zimdabule.

Mr. George Ncube had his homestead of four huts at Zimdabule village, two wives and five children between one and sixteen years of age. Four of the children went to the local pole, mud and thatch classrooms of Zimdabule Primary School. The school comprised three rectangular classrooms and four tiny pole, mud and thatch huts for the teachers. All constructed by the villagers in 1982.

On the 17th February 1983 a platoon of the Gukurahundi Battalion camped at the school overnight. The following day in the afternoon they arrived at George Ncube's homestead where they found about fifteen men that were congregated and drinking home brewed opaque beer called *isgodokhaya*. Ncube, a man of the cloth in the Zion Apostolic Church, who needed the money his wives made from the once in a while sale of beer, always enjoyed keeping the patrons company and discussed issues ranging from politics, religion, agriculture etc. On that fateful day the men were talking about the infamous Gukurahundi Brigade in hushed tones when suddenly army trucks pulled up at the gate.

One of the men, an ex ZPRA guerrilla, bolted and ran into the bush as the two army trucks pulled up at the gate. The red bereted soldiers shot at the fleeing man and missed him. The soldiers did not bother chasing after the running man but they took out their anger at Ncube, his family and the visiting men. They beat up the men including Ncube with thick logs, as his family watched in fear from the kitchen hut. Mr. Ncube was severely assaulted for speaking the Shona language, the language of the soldiers. They harangued and interrogated Ncube's wives and children about the whereabouts of dissidents. They accused the two eldest boys who were sixteen and thirteen years old of being dissidents. They made them march around, stand at attention and at ease to see if they had received any military training. The assessor's judgment was that the boys were indeed dissidents. He ordered them to lie down. Usually after ordering their victims to lie down, the soldiers would either shoot them behind the back or would beat them up.

As the boys lay on the ground, oblivious of their proximity to death, one of the soldiers who spoke Ndebele intervened and explained that the boys were school students who were taught the marching etc. at school as was standard practice during Physical Education (PE) lessons. The soldier saved the boys' lives.

The older men and Ncube were not so lucky as the soldiers beat them thouroughly before they left. An ominous silence descended on the entire village that day. The villagers were somewhat relieved that the army had not killed anyone but were scared stiff. After three days of staying in the bush with his family, George Ncube would not take any risk. He, that night walked his children in the company of a neighbor, Mrs Moyo, ten kilometers to Igusi where they boarded the train early in the morning to the town of Bulawayo where the situation was less dangerous. In Bulawayo Mrs Moyo took the children to Njube township to the house of Paul Ndlovu a Catholic priest and a nephew to Ncube.

According to Mrs Elizabeth Ncube (interview with George Ncube's wife, Elizabeth Ncube on 04 November 2019 at Deli, Nyamandlovu), the 5th brigade returned days later early in the morning and took Ncube away but not before beating him up and breaking his back. This time they accused him of being a ZAPU secretary. One of the soldiers went into the Ncube bedroom, forced Elizabeth Ncube out of bed and to dress up while he watched. He also stole George Ncube's wrist watch and $7.00 which were on a table. Elizabeth Ncube was beaten thoroughly after they had accused her of being a ZAPU organizer. She suffered a broken arm.

They went from homestead to homestead arresting those men that they found after some had fled into the forest. They accused them of being dissidents, harboring or feeding dissidents, withholding information about dissidents or supporting ZAPU.

According to Mr Bheki Sibanda during an interview in 2011 at Zimdabule, after torturing the men, nine in number, they took them to Nyamandlovu where they had a torture and death camp. There, the men joined a larger group of about thirty other men arrested from other areas including Gwayi, Sawmills, Igusi, Majindane, Redbank and Nyamandlovu. The nine were detained there for five days and tortured through beatings, water treatment and denial of food. By the fourth day the beatings had taken their toll on Ncube who in his fifties was the oldest of the nine detainees and had taken most of the torture because a 'dissident' had run from his homestead when the army arrived the other day.

On the fifth day, the nine men were told they were going home. They boarded an army truck into which Ncube had to be lifted by his colleagues because his back and one leg were broken by the beatings. His body was swollen and he was bleeding from the nose.

When the truck left the police station, it headed towards Nsezi but it later took a north westerly direction away from their homes. The men soon realized which home they were being taken to. Night was fast approaching and it was beginning to rain as the truck forded and bumped along the dirty and dusty road towards Bhumane river some kilometers away from George Ncube's home. By the time the truck came to a halt on the banks of the Bhumane river, it was night dark and the rain was drizzling. The truck head lights were left on to supplement the lighting from the soldiers' search lights.

The men were disembarked from the truck and given a shovel each and ordered to each dig their own grave. The ground was rocky and the earth was the hard dark clay, difficult to dig even with a pickaxe, especially when wet.

George Ncube was lying down on the ground in the rain, maimed and physically disabled. He was complaining of numbness in his lower body and said he could not feel his legs. He was discernibly praying for death because he did not want to live and be paralyzed. He loudly prayed for his children too. His colleagues were ordered to dig him a grave since he could not even sit up, let alone stand up and dig. A most shallow hole in the ground was dug for him by two of the tired, tortured, injured and terrified men. One of the soldiers kicked George Ncube a number of times on the ribs while pushing him with his boot into the shallow grave. Some men were ordered to throw sand over him with the shovels. They complied. The grave was too shallow and the sand too little to cover Ncube who kept begging the soldiers to kill him first and not bury him alive.

The soldiers probably got impatient with the slow progress of grave digging, the cold, the darkness and the rain, therefore they decided to end it before the graves were even half a metre deep. The doomed men were ordered to turn around and stand in a line, each above his grave. The idea was to shoot them from behind.

The Gukurahundi soldiers were known to shoot their victims from behind. They would ask the doomed persons to turn around before a salvo of bullets tore onto their backs. For days the tortured men had been praying for that half chance. They knew some of them would be shot, but each one of them hoped he would survive. When they were ordered to turn around, they turned and ran into the night and the safety of the darkness and the forest. The soldiers were caught off guard. Some of them were still reaching for their guns as the men fled. By the time they realized that the men were fleeing and started firing at them, they were mere shadows and the firing was wild and aimless. One of the villagers Bheki Sibanda, was however shot on the right thigh and fell into the river some twenty meters away from the soldiers. He held on to a rock in the flowing river and kept quiet in the dark and listened.

The soldiers were very casual and did not bother chasing after the men. They retrieved their tools and were leaving when George Ncube begged them to kill him. He told them he was dying due to the injuries and the bleeding. He said they should not leave him for the wild animals to maul him alive. He was afraid of a slow and painful death from his injuries. He was literally begging his tormentors to be kind enough to give him his death. The soldiers did not give it to him. They got into the car and drove away. They left him to face a painstaking and lingering death.

Despite the rain and the flowing Bhumane river waters, Mr. Sibanda, the man clinging on to a rock in the water, said there was absolute silence when the army truck pulled away. Mr Ncube went quiet, probably he had accepted his fate or he had gone into shock. Mr. Sibanda did not remember how much longer he stayed in the water. He only remembered himself running, walking and limping deliriously into the night, heedless of the bullet and the pain in his thigh. He was found unconscious the next day in the forest by some young men looking for stray cattle.

George Ncube died on the banks of the Bhumane river on 7 March 1983. He was never buried. His remains were left there, in a very shallow grave for the wild animals and scavenging birds and the elements to inter in their wild and varied fashions. Fear gripped the Nsezi area. It was only a year later, after the Gukurahundi Brigade had left the area, that a relative Mr Banda cycled to Bhumane in search for his remains. He got to the banks of the Bhumane river and found some bones scattered around the area. He contemplated gathering the bones up, but it was too harrowing and ghastly for only one man. He was not even sure if the bones belonged to Ncube or a human for that matter. According to his culture it was taboo to handle human bones and worse if they were of a stranger or non relative without undertaking the cleansing rituals first. Too scared and full of doubt, Banda witnessed and went away without collecting the remains for proper burial. (that incident bears close similarity with the Zimdabule Resettlement Villages 3 and 4 Nyamandlovu report incident on page 110 of the CCJP & LRF report)

Mr. Banda only went back to the scene in 2011 with Ncube's two sons who had left their home that fateful night in February 1983. The sons were coming back to Nsezi for the first time since 1983 in the company of Mr J.J Moyo from Grace to Heal in Bulawayo. Grace to Heal was a humanitarian organization that among other services was offering free counselling to victims of the Gukurahundi genocide.

On arrival in Nsezi, the two sons discovered that the site of their home was now a bush and so were the tens of other homesteads that were in a liner arrangement along the dirt road that ran along the Nsezi river. The homesteads and the primary school had been burnt to the ground back in 1983. The neighbor Mr. Bheki Sibanda that had fallen into the river accompanied them together with the relative Mr. Banda who had cycled to the Bhumane river site. They showed the two sons the spot where their father had died 28 years earlier. There was nothing there but desolation and fresh tears. The wounds inflicted by the Gukurahundi genocide in their hearts were still fresh as they battled for answers. Answers which will, since Mugabe died without providing them and judging from the fortitude of Mnangagwa, Sekeramyi and Shiri as well as from the resolve of their accomplices and the lack of interest by the United Nations, African Union, SADC and the UK, probably never come during their life time.

Although now adults and aware of the country's socio – political background and present ethnic dynamics which were informed by a violent and intolerant past, the sons still wanted answers. Answers that only their father's killers could provide. What they knew was that their father was Ndebele, a man of the cloth and a supporter of ZAPU, although not an activist. Most probably not a saint and definitely not a dissident, but a man of peace, who respected and accommodated all men so much he at times sat and dialogued with beer drinking villagers in his own home while he did not drink alcohol. His sons asked themselves, which one of their father's characteristics, attributes or identities was a crime for which he deserved to die. Only Mugabe, Mnangagwa, Sekeramayi and Shiri had the answer.

On 22 January 201,1 a commemoration of the Gukurahundi genocide was organized and hosted by Ibhetshu LikaZulu, a Bulawayo based civic organization, at the Bulawayo Baptist Church. The guest speaker was Moses Mzila-Ndlovu, one of the three co-Ministers of National Healing, Reconciliation and Integration.

The Minister in his speech stated that in August 2010, his mother had died after surviving 28 years of torture complications. His mother had been a victim of the Gukurahundi Brigade. He related his mother's ordeal at the hands of the 5th Brigade.

He said that in 1983, Enos Nkala the Minister of National Supplies at the time and later Home Affairs minister in the company of minister Callistus Ndlovu, came to his home area in Plumtree in Matabeleland South to address a rally. Mzila – Ndlovu's mother, a victim of polio did not attend the rally since she would have to walk a long distance to get there. The soldiers, as was their habit came to the villages, forcing everyone to attend the rally and found her at home. After assaulting her with gun buts, booted feet and bare hands, one of them dragged her by the handicapped leg for some forty metres from the front of her hut to the road, whereupon they force - marched her and the other victims to the venue of the meeting.

Mzila - Ndlovu's mother was wearing a skirt and the male soldier was looking into her skirts as he pulled her by one leg. The humiliation she suffered, said the minister hurt her and him more than her physical pain. The minister mentioned that his son a former ZPRA just like him was killed by the Gukurahundi brigade.

At the same commemoration, a former Zimbabwe National Army (ZNA) senior officer, Col. Buster Magwizi (former ZPRA) of Shona descent proffered a chilling testimony of his experience at the hands of the brigade. Col. Magwizi was in charge of a platoon in Chiredzi, Mashonaland West, when in September 1983, one of his man whose rural home was in Tshongogwe, Lupane Matabeleland North died. As per ZNA requirement and Ndebele custom, his body was to be taken home for burial. When advised by fellow ZNA staffers that Lupane was a no-go zone due to the Gukurahundi battalion, Col. Magwizi defied them. His argument was that he was ZNA. He was informed that Gukurahundi was not a ZNA battalion and would not obey his authority. Still, he and his thirteen men proceeded to rural Lupane.

When he and his escort arrived at the Lupane police station, some seventy kilometers from their destination, the Officer in Charge (OIC) advised him against proceeding to Tshongogwe. He was told he risked not only his life but the lives of his men too. When the OIC realized that Col. Magwizi was not backing off, he offered to escort them in his police Nissan Patrol vehicle. Some thirty kilometers from Lupane at Jotsholo they came upon a 5th Brigade camp.

They drove into the camp to report their presence in the area. Before they alighted from the Nissan Patrol a warrant officer (a junior to Col. Magwizi) walked up to them and snatched the car keys from the police officer before speeding away in the Nissan Patrol without the courtesy of an explanation. There was a group of villagers near the entrance of the camp comprising obviously hungry, disheveled and brutalized old women and children. One member of the 5th brigade walked away from the group as he swore *"ava vachamama ava"*, which was Shona for *"these will be damned"*. Literally translated it meant *"these ones will be shit themselves"*.

Col. Magwizi whose ZPRA training was both guerilla and conventional and focused on protecting members of the public, could not believe his ears. He asked the rogue soldier what he meant and the soldier retorted *"asi newe urimuchuwachuwa"*? (so you are ZPRA?). *Muchuwachuwa* was a derogatory term used by Gukurahundi soldiers to refer to former ZPRA guerrillas. When he was about to respond, Col. Magwizi was restrained by the OIC of police from Lupane who told him earnestly that he risked death if he engaged Gukurahundi soldiers in a verbal duel. At that warning, his conscience laden with guilt and remorse Col. Magwizi turned away from the pleading old women and children.

Shortly the commandeered Nissan Patrol came back in a thick cloud of dust. From the vehicle was pushed, tumbled to the ground and fell on his knees, a man whom

Col. Magwizi instantly recognized as Abraham Mlilo. Mlilo had served together with Col. Magwizi in ZPRA during the war of liberation. After the war he had been demobilized and had joined the nursing profession. He was currently a nurse at the Jotsholo clinic. He was handcuffed. They had cut out his ears and blood was still gushing from his buttered mouth as well. His white nurse's uniform was scarlet red at the front and the sleeves. Col. Magwizi was astounded and tongue - tied in shock. He could only stare at the sorry sight of a man who had done his fair part in liberating the country.

Mlilo was disoriented and confused as he looked around wildly in search of a savior. He found him. He found him in Col. Buster Magwizi, his former comrade in arms. His voice was guttural and eerie as he called out *"Buster, Buster!"*. His call was muffled at the second attempt as an AK 47 gun but was rammed into his mouth, instantly breaking his jaw and smashing his teeth. He tumbled backward to the ground but amazingly managed to struggle to seat up. He tried to call out to Col. Magwizi again but this time only an unnerving and haunting sound came from deep down his throat and escaped through his mouth, punctuated by spouts of crimson blood.

Col. Magwizi wanted to rush to his Puma armored truck for his gun but the police officer sensing his anger held him fast by the hand. With a debilitating feeling of hopelessness and uselessness, he witnessed the most callous and fiendish act of hate. The warrant officer who had driven away in the Nissan patrol drew his pistol and shot Mlilo through the left ear at point blank range. *"I can still hear his cries today and I will take them to the grave with me"*, said Col. Magwizi obviously tormented by his memories.

Col Magwizi concluded by postulating that the Gukurahundi genocide was *"structural violence"* intended to wipe ZPRA and ZAPU supporters off the face of the country irrespective of tribe. His call for the prosecution of the perpetrators of the genocide was as impassioned as his pain was evident.

In probably the only instance when pretence at justice was ever attempted, an inquest was set up after a group of four Gukurahundi soldiers had murdered an off duty ZNA soldier, his wife and two others. The inquest magistrate noted that the murder was *"exceedingly cruel"*. He further lamented that the victims were *"repeatedly stabbed with bayonets, much as a hunter slaughtering a wounded animal with a spear"*. The magistrate was echoing the manner in which thousands of Matabeles met their deaths at the hands of the government army. The four murderers were then handed over to their colleagues the 5th Brigade and not sent to jail. They were eventually tried at the High Court and sentenced to death in 1986. The four soldiers were however instantly granted a Presidential pardon by Mugabe (CCJP and LRF 1997). The pardon was such a peversion of justice, it reduced the bench and the bar into a guerilla theater.

When Mugabe was quizzed by a BBC panorama reporter Jeremy Paxman in 1983 about the 5th Brigade's trail of murderous escapades in Matabeleland, the former got irritated and professed ignorance. He challenged the reporter to avail evidence so that his government would investigate. Mugabe said, *"if you give me the facts... let's not just shout noises for the press...inform me. You are alleging excesses. Do bring evidence, concrete evidence....I have said again and again, if we are given concrete evidence we will investigate"*.

That was the lamest excuse for inaction by a head of state ever. Serious allegations of mass killings by agents of the state and other human rights abuses were directed at the army and the commander in chief of the army was asking for evidence from a British reporter. It was the role of the government to investigate and gather the so called concrete evidence. Mugabe had the facts at his finger tips. The Joint Operations Command gave him security briefings on a daily basis. The Gukurahundi commanders through Perence Shiri reported directly to him.

Besides according to Kevin Woods, Mugabe knew what was happening on the ground in Matabeleland and the Midlands, since Woods had been tasked by Mugabe with establishing what the 5th Brigade was doing and finding out where the bodies of their victims were disposed of. According to Woods (2007), Mugabe, *"obviously wanted to know exactly what 5th Brigade was doing – either to egg them on to greater effort or to try and wind them in – I just don`t know. There was certainly no evidence of 5th Brigade slackening off; rather, they simply became more circumspect with the disposal of their victims..."* In a verbal interview that was posted on twitter by journalist Zenzele Ndebele in 2019, Woods described Mugabe as, *"very pathological about loyalty to himself"*. He further asserted that about 18 800 people were killed by the 5th Brigade. He stated that when he sent written reports to Mugabe about the killings of civilians, he was told that it was not his war.

Wood's claims were corroborated by documents declassified by the Australian government in 2015. The files included diplomatic correspondence and intelligence data leaked from the Zimbabwe government spies. According to Doran (2015), the files indicated that at the time of the genocide, Sydney Sekeramayi confided to Cephas Msipa (later appointed governor and resident minister of the Midlands province) that, *"not only was Mugabe fully aware of what was going on. What the 5th Brigade was doing was under Mugabe's explicit orders"*. Msipa at the time relayed the information to the Australian High Commission. He was a long time friend and at one time a roommate with Mugabe and a member of ZAPU. Msipa is said to have told the Australians that Mugabe was *"right behind what was happening in Matabeleland"*.

The same Mugabe who was demanding evidence from the BBC reporter with one corner of the mouth, according to Woods was probably challenging the Gukurahundi Brigade to come up with ways to best conceal evidence by disposing of the bodies of the thousands dead Matabele in less conspicuous ways, with the other corner of the mouth. Mugabe did not only stop at professing ignorance to the BBC. In a classic display of hypocrisy that relegated Judas to a bungler, blaming it all on ZPRA, ZAPU, Nkomo, dissidents and apartheid South Africa. He chided, *"these elements who now see South Africa as their ally, have killed and maimed hundreds of innocent people, kidnapped innocent Zimbabweans and foreign visitors to our country, burned thousands of dollars worth of both government and private property.....we shall proceed with ever increasing vigour to crush them....our consciences are very clear...my government has full moral...political and constitutional authority to wipe out the scourge..."*

Mugabe discovered the expedient, persuasive and convincing art of scapegoating by blaming his failures and evils on his enemies. Everybody believed the allegations against South Africa and ZAPU. The allegations were in keeping with South African foreign policy which was known for destabilising missions in Angola and Mozambique at that time. His story found currency again in that ZAPU could be viewed as sore losers intent on getting through a coup d' etat what they had failed to get through the ballot box. Yet it was he Mugabe that was in league with the South African security apparatus that was cooperating with his CIO. Over the years he would use the blame gamesmanship to point a soiled finger at the West, neo-colonialism, the opposition and even the gay for his political inadequecies and economic fiascos. Meanwhile he would use his inferior (by comparison to Nkomo and many others) liberation struggle credentials to buy credibility from those influential enough to sway public and international opinion in his favour.

The most bizarre manifestation of hypocrisy and betrayal of his Janus - face, was in September 1983, when Robert Mugabe set up the Chihambakwe Commission of Inquiry which was presided over by a lawyer Mr. Simplicius Chihambakwe. The other members were Mr. John Ngara a member of the CIO and therefore directly or indirectly a perpetrator of the genocide he was commissioned to investigate. Mr. Prince Machaya (later appointed attorney general) and retired Major – General

Mike Shute, were the other members of the commission. The commission's terms of reference were to investigate the alleged killings of some one thousand five hundred civilians and dissidents in Matabeleland. The intention was to allay weak international criticism of his policy towards Matabeleland as well as assuage domestic concerns over the massacres. The commission investigated from January 1984 and after nine months they reported to Mugabe, by September 1984. More than twelve months later in November 1985, Mnangagwa announced that the commission findings would not be made public. In 2000 after Legal Resources Foundation had petitioned the Supreme court to compel the government to release the report, Mnangagwa responded by stating that the report, together with the Dumbutshena commission report had been lost.

It was indisputably evident that setting up the commission was a mere charade and a roguish hoax. How could any serious and self respecting prime minister set up a commission to investigate a crime that was ongoing. By September 1983, the Gukurahundi genocide was gathering momentum? In February 1984, the 5th Brigade was deployed into Matabeleland South and a food embargo was imposed there. Throughout the twelve months of the commission's tenure, Gukurahundi was wrecking havoc in Matabeleland. Mugabe was investigating a crime with the left hand while the right hand was committing the same crime. If he was genuinely concerned, Mugabe should have arrested Perence Shiri the commander of Gukurahundi Brigade and Sydney Sekeramayi the minister of defense whose army was butchering people in Matabeleland and Midlands, instead of setting up a commission that would report to the same killers. Obviously he could neither arrest them nor stop the killings because they were his talons, doing his biding. They were his hatchets, ever dangling from his hips. By stopping the 5th brigade, Mugabe would be handicapping his own invention. He was therefore playing to the gallery. He was once more wooing the world by portraying a veneer of concern.

When the ethnic and politically unbalanced and gender biased commission of five members, all male, one white and four Shonas, submitted their findings to Mugabe in 1984, he opted to shelve the report permanently. Over decades he steadfastly set on the lid to make sure that the report never saw the light of day. Some thought that Mugabe and his government opined that if put in the public domain, the report would ignite tribal violence. Despite the obvious political, ethnic and gender bias in the structure of the commission, it was probable, judging from the government's response, that the commission had reported in a manner not of the state's liking. Either the commissioners' report was damning on the part of the government (most unlikely) or it was so appallingly shallow and skin - deep due to deliberate lack of serious effort. Maybe the report was evidently too partisan such that it would embarrass even the shameless regime. Probably the commission did not compromise ZAPU enough.

It was very much unlikely that the commission report was incriminating to the government, considering the ethno politics of the time and Mugabe's well advertised hostility towards suggestions that his army was killing civilians. The presence of a member of the dreaded CIO and a former army general in the commission was designed to ensure that the report would not implicate Mugabe. Besides, it was no mistake that he had appointed a cast of fellow tribesmen to the commission. However, the state - sanctioned silence over the report was very deafening and worrisome. Mere mention of it, it appears always haunted the perpetrators of the genocide, especially over the years when the silence became more observable due to the rise of human rights activism by civic societies.

While his army was exterminating civilians in Matabeleland and Midlands and his State Security minister was coining strategies on how best to poison more Ndebele 'cochroaches' on one hand, on the other hand, Mugabe was running from pillar to post as an emerging paragon statesman and an icon of reconciliation. In September 1983, while being hosted by then USA president Ronald Reagan at the White House, Mugabe buoyed by American financial aid, displayed his brand of rare munificence again, albeit false. He stated that he was committed to a non - racial society where all "*isms*" would be a thing of the past (Scarnecchia 2013).

He went all out to, and indeed convinced the Americans that "*racism, tribalism and regionalism*" had no room in Zimbabwean society and politics. The fact that at that very moment his Gukurahundi army was butchering civilians in Matabeleland and the Midlands was expediently ignored by the Americans whose foreign policy and intelligence network knew of Mugabe's hypocrisy and murderous rage and therefore his forked tongue. Mugabe was fast developing a consanguineous relationship with double standards of which he would soon become a master.

The United States president, Ronald Reagan joined his United Kingdon counterpart Magaret Thatcher in choosing to look the other way. He also preffered dinning and wining the tyrant and killer of the Ndebele and showered him with praises. That rendered the USA government and President Reagan complicit in the massacre of innocent people in Matabeleland and Midlands because intelligence abounded in CIA files on what was happening in Zimbabwbe. President Reagan betrayed the people who looked upon his office as a mature democracy to curtail Mugabe's craving for their blood. Reagan instead said, Mugabe's "*wise leadership has been a crucial factor in healing the wounds of civil war and developing a new nation with new opportunities*".

One could not help but wonder what it was that the US president was talking about. He simply endorsed tyranny and indirectly affirmed to Mugabe that he could get away with any magnitude of abuse of human rights. To Mugabe, it was a case of, he that runs may read. Mugabe read the message loud and clear. He had gotten the blessings of the US government. Reagan made it crystal clear that Mugabe could bath in all the blood of the black people of his country as long as he was wise enough to spare the white Zimbabweans, thereby healing their wounds suffered during the liberation war.

In late 1983, the Mugabe regime detained three white Zimbabwean airforce pilots who had been acquitted by the high court because they had been tortured to confess. They were detained after the acquittal because they were viewed as threats to national security. Since the officers were British citizens, the UK threatened to withhold funding for Zimbabwe's land redistribution program unless the officers were released. Mugabe went on to rave and rant, but he was cornered. He made sure that the pilots were expeditiously released from detention.

It was appalling to observe that the arrest of three white soldiers was more important to the British government than the heartless and bestial murder of a hundred thousand people from Matabeleland and the Midlands. The crucial question was, why did the British not threaten to withhold land reform funding because of the Gukurahundi genocide? Such decisiveness would have forced Mugabe back to his senses. But the Thatcher administration did not care much. Some said that the answer was that they cared less about the fate and human rights of the Ndebele who had killed many British mercenaries of the Pioneer Column force and the B.S.A. Company in 1893 and 1896 in defence of their sovereignty. It was on historical record that the British imperial armies in Africa never encountered stiffer resistance and never suffered more casualties than at the battle of Isandlwana in Natal in 1878 and at the battle of Pupu in Matabeleland in 1893. On both occasions King Cetshwayo and King Lobhengula respectively, made sure that the settlers were killed to a man. Otherwise, how on earth could a venal tyrant commit genocide for five years without attracting international and regional censure?

To aggravate the guilt of the British government and justify that judgement on their race priorities, were a number of statements by high profile Britons during the atrocities and years later. When the then commander of the British Military Advisory and Training Team (BMATT) attached to the ZNA, General Sir Edward Jones was asked by a BBC reporter why they had not sounded the alarm on Mugabe's slaughter in Matabeleland, he said it would have been *"counter productive"*. Whatever it was that Sir Edward Jones and his government were producing in Zimbabwe that they did not want jeopardized, must have been very special if it warranted them to ignore a genocide for its sake.

When Lord Howe was asked why the British government had not withdrawn aid to Zimbabwe because of the genocide, he said they were afraid that such action would have elicited a *"negative reaction not only on Mugabe's performance but on the economic stability of the country"*. One was left puzzled as to how much more negative could Mugabe's performance get, for the British to accept it was already as negative as it coulg get. If taking the lives of one hundred thousand Matabeles was not negative enough, then no action could be regarded as negative in the whole of Africa. Lord Howe also explicitly claimed that the British were so concerned with economic stability, so much that they just did not bother about political and social balance. That was a lie because never at any time during the 1980s (or at any other time) was the UK government not concerned about the political and social security of its citizens in Zimbabwe.

Gen. Jones' surbodinate in Harare, Colonel Chuck Ivey (BMATT), in March 1983, in an obvious moomish cover – up, unabashedly stated that the *"problems of two years ago have diminished to almost nothing"*. Upon being probed further by the BBC reporter on *"the stories in Matabeleland"*, the Colonel let the cat of the British position out of the bag when he revealed that *"there are stories in Matabeleland, stories in Ireland. You wanna believe who writes what story"*. Mugabe himself used that same ambiguity in response to a question on the *"stories in Matabeleland"*. It was as if they were saying that, if it was happening in Ireland then it was okay for it to happen in Matabeleland. They also implied that the stories in Matabeleland were a creation of the press. Whatever that response meant, Colonel Ivey made it abundantly clear that the British government did not care about the genocide that Mugabe was dealing out in Matabeleland. Col Ivey was evidently covering up for Mugabe by lying that the problems of two years ago had almost gone away, because in March 1983, the government army was on the hunt, killing, rapping, torturing and displacing citizns like never before. The colonel could not make that false and deliberately misleading statement, if it was not British army and UK government position.

Roger Martin, the British Deputy High Commissioner (1983 – 1986) to Zimbabwe admitted that he had visited a farm in Matabeleland South and found Gukurahundi soldiers torturing civilian farm workers and he had done and said nothing. He said they were afraid that if they objected, Mugabe would have expelled white British citizens from his country. That implied that the possible expulsion of a couple of thousand whites was worse than the slaughter of the entire Ndebele and Kalanga tribes. He stated that as they went their way, they were certain that the farm workers would not be killed. How he could be so confident that the murderous soldiers that had already killed thousands before, would not kill again was a plain lie. The farm workers were most probably butchered to death within minutes of the British delegation's departure, and Martin knew that.

The most high profile indictment of Britain's chosen stance on Mugabe's Gukurahundi genocide came from nowhere but the British monarchy itself, the cradle of civilization and propriety. In March 1984, Prince Charles visited Zimbabwe during the height of the massacres. After gracing Harare, dinning, wining and patting Mugabe on the back for a job well done, the Prince left for London without giving the Gukurahundi genocide victims even a perfunctory glance. Upon arrival back home, the Prince invited Donald Trelford, the editor of the Observer; 1975 - 93 (UK) to dinner. During the dinner, the Prince when asked about the genocide said that the foreign office had said that it was all exaggerated. One would have thought that the Prince as the custodian of all decorum and champion of civility, liberty, justice and human rights had just been given a chance to see for himself the situation in Matabeleland and Midlands. Since he had not bothered to confirm the foreign office position, it meant that he had accepted their reports without question. The long and short of it was that the Prince chose to conveniently believe that the genocide in Matabeleland was mere media hyperbole. If Prince Charles could not even dispatch a small delegation to Matabeleland during his visit to Zimbabwe, then no one could help Matabeleland.

Trelford however, did not believe the Prince and the foreign office. On 15 April 1984 he published an article titled *"survivors tell of tribal slaughter"* in the Observer newspaper. The article argued that there was rampant slaughter of civilians in Matabeleland. Trelford was shortly fired from the Observer because of contradicting the Foreign office in his Gukurahundi expose'. The foreign office was guilty of a forked tongue and double standards as demonstrated below.

Perhaps the most damning admission of guilt by the British government came from Sir Martin Ewans, the High Commissioner (1983 – 1985) to Zimbabwe. He told BBC that *"to have protested to Mugabe would not have been helpful. Mugabe would have resented it acutely"*. When he was asked if he regretted personally not having protested to Mugabe he said, *"No. This business is rather being blown up……..Matabeleland was a side issue…..the real issues were much bigger and more positive "*. Where in the world could the slaying of one hundred thousand people be treated as a side issue. Even the most exuberant kind of optimist, would find nothing positive in ignoring such a carnage. That line of thinking, which woefully influenced western government policies towards Zimbabwe, was obnoxious to the core. Even with the benefit of hindsight, Sir Martin Ewans still thought the genocide was *"being blown up"* and never deserved his remonstrance. What could be bigger than one hundred thousand lives? What more positive role could an emissary of the Queen of England play than expostulate against a blood bath? What could be more positive in the service of mankind in general and serving the interests of the British government in particular, than stopping a genocide? What could be nobler for the British to do than stopping a tyrant?

The side issue slur was captured by Geoff Hill in Scarnecchia (2011) when he asserted that, the British High Commissioner (Ewans) to Zimbabwe during the genocide said that the official British policy position was that the Gukurahundi massacres were to be treated as a *"side issue"*. He also observed that the British supported Mugabe as his army went about killing indescriminately. That showed that the 'side issue' narrative was neither a personal indiscretion nor a poor choice of terms by Ewans. It was official British government foreign policy. The British government chose to support the killers and not the victims.

The High Commissioner further stated that the advice from London on how to handle Mugabe on the Matabeleland issue was, to steer clear of it, *"in the interest of doing our best positively to help Zimbabwe build itself up as a nation"*. That was the same foreign office that had convinced Prince Charles that Mugabe's ethnic cleansing in Matabeleland and Midlands was *"exaggerated"*. The kind of nation that the British were building with Mugabe must have been one hell of a kind. Mugabe was resolved to rule an entire population into their graves and the British government was egging him on. A nation of dead Ndebeles, Kalangas, Sothos, Xhosas etc was being built.

In their equivocation, the British foreign office at one time said they were looking for the facts. There undeniably was a lot in common between Mugabe and the British foreign office. Mugabe too, had asked for facts when he was confronted with news of the genocide. The pedestrian nature of that gormless and mischievous request for facts was noticed and criticized by Nicholas Winterton, a British conservative MP who lambasted the foreign office on BBC as he disputed their search for facts by saying, *"the facts were there, hundreds, thousands of innocent Matabele had been slaughtered. If they were looking for facts, they must have been living in another world"*.

The British government were not alone in endorsing Mugabe's slaughterhouse and butchery. According to Eddie Cross, a former opposition MDC T MP, four more western governments had failed to read the riot act to Mugabe and his entourage of over – loyal courtiers. Cross who was a general manager of Dairiboard (a milk packaging parastatal) in 1983, in 2019 wrote on his blog that, after being informed by the Catholic Mission in Lupane that the 5th Brigade was on the rampage, he had called Charles Utete the then Secretary to the Prime Minister and Cabinet, inviting him to fly with him to Lupane for first hand witnessing. Mr. Utete had told Cross that it had *"nothing to do with me, too sensitive and I should leave it alone"*. Not satisfied with that response, Cross took the report from the Catholic Mission with him on a business trip to Scandinavia, where he showed it to four Foreign Ministers and asked them to get their Prime Ministers to rein in Mugabe.

Upon returning to Zimbabwe, Cross was summoned to the office of the Minister of State Security where Mnangagwa showed him a transcript of his discussion with the Norwegian Foreign Minister. He was threteaned and told that if he did that again something would happen to him.

Clearly, the Norwagian government, instead of telling Mugabe to stop the genocide, decided to abet him by arming him with information on who was 'leaking' information about the massacres to the world. The other three governments did not act on the information they were provided by Cross either, because no government is known to have taken any action to get Mugabe to stop the killings.

What the UK, USA, Norway and other western states wanted, was Mugabe's commitment to non - racialism and protection of the white establishment in his country. They wanted assurances that the farms, businesses, properties and lives of their kith and kin would be the sacred cows under Mugabe's wings. They were desperate for that assurance at all costs. Once they got that assurance, they ignored his policy towards his fellow blacks. He could do as he wished with the minority Ndebele whose leader Joshua Nkomo was known for constantly calling for land redistribution from whites to blacks anyway.

The British government and their colleagues would rather live with the deaths of so many innocents weighing heavy in their consciences than risk irking Mugabe and incuring his resentment. They opted to be party to his murderous machinations than look their gift horse in the mouth. Mugabe's endorsement and approval seemed to be a very important commodity to the British government.

According to Mpofu (2013) the Mugabe regime could massacre the Ndebele at will and not suffer any form of punishment, as long as they secured Western business interests in Zimbabwe. He further argued that, *"such spectacles as the genocide of 1994 in Rwanda, the civil war of Sierra Leone in 1999 and the Gukurahundi genocide in Zimbabwe in 1982 to 1987 have their causalities in Western economic and political interests"*.

Mugabe could ride roughshod over non – tribalism, democracy, the rule of law and human rights, for all they cared. The bafflement that resulted from the hypocrisy on the part of the USA and the UK was justified and could only be placated by the explanation that to those governments what mattered most was the sanctity of white blood, protection of white economic investments and keeping at bay Soviet interests in Southern Africa. That could only be achieved by being chummy with Mugabe and by so doing they abeted the genocide in Matabeleland and the Midlands. Another explanation proffered by Scarnecchia (2013) was that *"Cold War relations between Zimbabwe and the United Kingdom helped to provide cover for the Zimbabwean National Army's Fifth Brigade's campaign of terror"*. Due to the Cold War, the genocide was swept under the carpet and was not told to the world.

Mugabe was groomed into a sacred cow by the British government whose aid to the Zimbabwe government amounted to 57 million British pounds during the genocide period. Mrs Thatcher's government, at the height of the genocide in 1984 invited Mugabe for honours in the United Kingdom. On arrival in London Mugabe was showered with praises and accolades before being knighted by Queen Elizabeth II in the Order of the Bath. Although he fell shot of using the title 'sir', Mugabe could use the postnominal letters KCB (Knight Commander of the Order of the Bath). That honour was supposed to be accorded on merit only to an individual who had accomplished a rare, special and commendable feat for the general good.

It would appear that dinning with and abetting despots was a habit of the Thatcher administration. As noted by Pilger (2002), Saddam Hussein was sumptuously entertaining Mrs Magaret Thatcher's secretary of trade in his palace, while at the same time his henchmen were gassing the Kurds in Halabja on his orders. A month later the British envoy was back in Iraq with a 340 million pound deal and weapons of war for Saddam. So much for fighting terrorism and promoting the human rights of minorities.

Speaking at the Gukurahundi genocide commemoration in January 2011, the then Governmet of National Unity, Minister of National Healing and Reconciliation, Moses Mzila – Ndlovu opined that the UK government could not be absolved of the heinous crime of the Gukurahundi genocide. He said that in 1983, Robert Mugabe was conferred an honorary degree by the Edinbrough University. On that day of conferrement, fifty victims of Gukurahundi were buried in a mass grave at St. Paul's Mission Lupane Primary School in Matabeleland North.

The numerous questions to which answers were urgent included, what merit or service was the British sovereign appreciating and honoring in Mugabe? What was estimable and eminent about him at a time when his army was butchering and raping Matabeleland? What message was the Queen conveying to him and other despots around the world? What were they pampering Mugabe for? Whatever it was, he went on, on a harebrained killing frenzy after which a hundred thousand civilians were dead in a period of 'peace'. By kneeling before the Queen and accepting the knighthood, Mugabe became a British knight and indirectly a subject of the Queen and the British crown. He was supposed to qualify to and to uphold the values and the code of the knighthood. He never did and he was never censured, at least for the crime of genocide.

In addition to numerous honorary degrees bestowed on him by American and British universities, Mugabe was decorated with the Africa Prize for Leadership for Sustainable End of Hunger and the Jawaharlal Nehru Award for International Understanding. He chaired the World Solar Summit, the Commonwealth for three years, the G15 and was even awarded the Olympic Order of Gold for his contribution to Olympic ethos. Mugabe kept blooming and blossoming while standing knee - deep in the blood of the Matabele. All that recognition could only mean that indeed the people of Matabeleland were 'cockroaches'. How else could the butchery of so many of them be so insignificant as to fail to tarnish Mugabe's image and stature.

The answer lay in the annals of history. In December 1894, Leander Starr Jameson, while the groaning, wailing and mourning of the women and children of Bulawayo were still ringing in his ears and their blood fresh on his hands *"was also given honours due to the conqueror of the Matabele. The Queen made him Commander of the Bath"* (Thomas 1996:282). It would appear that Mugabe had managed to break Jameson's 90-year-old record. Jameson had massacred more than 18 000 Matabele and had been knighted by Queen Victoria afterwards in 1894. In 1984 Mugabe was the new *"conqueror of the Matabele"*. After slaughtering 100 000 Matabeles, the Queen accorded him the same recognition and honour bestowed on Jameson. How else could one explain the knighting of an African Prime Minister during the heat of a genocide. He was wiping his bloody dagger of the blood of a people historically detested by the Her Majesty's government.

Ironically, Mugabe was to trash all the honours benevolently yet prematurely bequeathed upon him. By the turn of the century he had transformed into enemy number one of the British monarchy and the United Kingdom government for abdicating and usurping his duties as a knight, when he forfeited farms from British nationals in Zimbabwe. The astute and magnanimous leader, Common

Wealth chairman and Olympic champion, turned rogue in full view of his benefactors. Deservedly, they were left with egg on their faces for having failed to be consistent and discreet twenty years earlier.

As if to affirm Mzila-Ndlovu's contention about the collusion by UK and ZANU against the Matabele, the Newsday (Southern Edition) 21 March 2011 reported that justice Blake, president of the Upper Tribunal of the Immigration and Asylum Chamber of the United Kingdom, had ruled that asylum seekers from Matabeleland in Zimbabwe were not to be treated equally as their counterparts from Mashonaland because the former region was peaceful. The judge went on to state that deportees from Mashonaland could not be deported to the Matabeleland region since the Ndebele were a violent tribe and would descend on the deportees with machetes.

That judgment was the most contemptuous, vile, inhibitive, prejudicial and segregatory official / legal position ever taken about Matabeleland and the Ndebele after the Matabeleland Order in Council of 1894. It was more strange and sounded vengeful because it was common knowledge that Matabeleland was the stronghold of the MDC formations and had never been Mugabe's favorite since his advent into politics. The judgement smacked of a racist, tribal and colonial verdict engulfed in the undertones of gukurahundism's mission to assassinate the character of Matabeleland

The honourable British, judge a member of the world acclaimed impartial and learned bench, did not know, despite professing knowledge of the situation in Matabeleland, that that very same month of his judgment saw twenty-two woman members of WOZA (Women of Zimbabwe Arise) Magodonga Mahlangu and Jennifer Williams, in Bulawayo being arrested and tortured for peacefully demonstrating against violence against women. Furthermore, a couple of months earlier, Sengezo Tshabangu (MDCT Matabeleland North provincial chairperson) and fifteen councilors from Nkayi had been arrested for having a meeting without police clearance. A few days earlier Paul Siwela, John Gazi and Charles Thomas had been arrested and were still in custody for calling for the secession of the Mthwakazi State (Matabeleland) from Zimbabwe.

The Newsday newspaper of 12 June 2019 published a report titled, *"Zimbabwe ranked among the worst countries in protection of indeginous people's rights".* The report mentioned that white Zimbabweans and the Ndebele were facing rights violations. They were rated as PUT (people under threat). The country was ranked togather with such countries as Syria, Somalia, South Sudan, Pakistan, Afghanistan, Yemen, Libya and Ethiopia. Therefore, in a manner of thinking, one could conclude that by 2011, concerning the Matabeleland question, the British government was fighting from the ZANU PF corner by being averse to the idea of freedom for Matabeleland just as they were in 1893, 1894, 1896 and 1918. Justice Blake must have been informed that the Ndebele were a people under threat from the ZANU regime from day one after independence in 1980. The least the UK government could do was respect their rights as political and economic refugees along their Shona countrymen and women.

As if the Robert Mugabe KCB. debacle was not enough, the British government invited the commander of the Gukurahundi battalion, Perence Shiri, to London in January 1986. He was invited to the Royal College of Defense Studies as an honored guest, a dream to many a great military generals and presidents from all over the world. As he entered the doors to the prestigious display and personification of British military ingenuity, he passed beneath the insignia prescribed, *concordia artus roborat,* on which stood the majestic crown of the Queen. What a travesty to all in Matabeleland and Midlands, who expected Shiri to be marched, hands shackled and legs manacled, into a court of law, charged with genocide and crimes against humanity.

There evidently was no end in sight for the woes of Matabeleland, ZAPU and Nkomo, since during the Cold War Mugabe could play the British and Americans on one hand and the Soviets on the other. Besides, Zimbabwe was a young country with a great future which could not be jeopardized by 'insignificant' local tribal rivalries. ZAPU was dumbfounded and did not appeal to the Soviet Union for any help, military or otherwise. The people of Matabeleland suddenly found themselves without any friends as the Soviets too were persuaded to sever ties with ZAPU and terminate all material support while accepting a cordial arms length relationship with the ruling ZANU junto.

Between 1981 and 1983, Mugabe received US$1.95 billion dollars as aid from various countries, the United Nations and donor agencies. That, at a time when his Gukurahundi Brigade was marching scores of people into grass thatched huts in rural Matabeleland and setting the huts on fire after bolting the door from outside. It was not amiss for the victims to observe that the killer tyrant was being financially rewarded for a job 'well done'.

The long and short of it was that the countries and agencies including the UK, USA and unbelievably the UN, indirectly funded the genocide in Matabeleland by oiling the terror machine with the resources Mugabe needed. No amount of clarification or justification could help reconcile the conniving silence of the US and the UK governments over the genocide with their sonorous protests over the incarceration of three white soldiers. They were complicit in Mugabe's political emasculation of the Matabele people and the dematerialization of ZAPU and ZPRA.

Mugabe had a fervent and almost fiendish belief in Robert Greene' 15th law of power, to *"crush your enemy completely"*. He wanted to leave no trace of ZAPU, so much he went all out to physically dismantle it and even commissioned the authorship of a distorted history account, called patriotic history (Ranger 2004). According to Ranger (2010), *"there is a public history in Zimbabwe which is still insistently propagated on state – controlled television, radio and the state – controlled daily and Sunday press. This version of the country's past (now generally described as 'patriotic history') assumes the immanence of a Zimbabwean nation expressed through centuries of Shona resistance to external intrusion"*.

Patriotic history. A disfigured account that relegated ZAPU's liberation war role to insignificance, while portraying Mugabe as the unparalleled doyen of African nationalism. A false record that was dangerously silent about the gukurahundi genocide and many chapters that ZANU PF willed their historians to forget. For example, despite rising to prominence late in 1977 after a suspiciously tribal coup against Ndabaningi Sithole, ZANU penmen fraudulently but successfully portrayed Mugabe as an icon of the liberation struggle and a founder of nationalism.

Mugabe had been recruited into ZAPU, where like other nationalists, he played an important role, but he was a junior secretary for many years. Mugabe had been recruited into ZAPU by Jason Ziyaphapha Moyo, the ZAPU Vice President in 1960, when the latter visited Ghana to officiate at the pass out parade of the first ZPRA recruits who had gone there for military training in 1959. In Accra, J.Z. Moyo identified Mugabe who was teaching there and recruited him into ZAPU. Until he and others, led by Sithole rebelled against Nkomo and ZAPU, Mugabe served as a low - ranking secretary until 1964 when he was arrested before distinguishing himself in anyway to warrant any accolades. He was released in 1974 and assumed ZANU leadership in 1975 after the death of Chitepo. During the four years at the helm, until the cease fire was declared, Mugabe did not distinguish himself politically or militarily. His performance as leader was as opaque as the circumstances under which he assumed the ZANU presidency. It was said that after the assassination of Chitepo in 1975, Sithole resorted to his position of party president but encountered stiff resistance. The resistance culminated in the ZANLA leaders and guerillas pronouncing the Mgagao Declaration from Tanzania. They denounced Sithole and it is said that Mugabe then *"assumed"* the reins of leadership. He was never voted into office. He was actually installed by the military ZANLA, in the first coup de'etat of ZANU.

The most distinguished ZANU nationalist during the late 1970s was Josiah Tongogara, the ZANLA commander. However, Tongogara and his fellow ZANLA commanders did not realize that by using military power to dethrone Sithole and install Mugabe, they had set the future of the country in a roller - coaster trajectory from which the country and entire Southern African region would not recover in many decades thereafter. Until he won the 1980 elections, Mugabe was mostly unknown in most of the country. He was actually popularized by the violent 1980 campaign and ultimate win.

Nonetheless, the editorial of the Sunday News of 29 January to 04 February 2017 described Mugabe as *"one of the most decorated authors of the liberation struggle in the continent...he ranks among the respectable torch bearers of the liberation struggle"*. That was an unashamedly gross distortion which was proven by the absence of information on how Mugabe took over from Sithole. Years after the underhanded takeover, the coup remained a hole – and – corner affair. Obviously Mugabe and ZANU were never proud of that aspect of their history and they kept a heavy lid on it.

That part of their history, together with the Mgagao and Morogoro murders of ZPRA / Ndebele cadres made / make ZANU PF, Mugabe and Mnangagwa bow their heads in shame. As revealed by Macaphulana (2016), *"....it was not a war of liberation but a bloody ethnic genocide where ZANLA guerillas were commandeered to slaughter their ZPRA counterparts in Mgagao and Morogoro.... It is this legacy of ZANU that Moyo...and many others including First Lady Grace Mugabe are ashamed of"*. The only possibility of error in Macaphulana's analysis was on Moyo, because the only senior person in ZANU PF who seemed not to be mortified of that extract from history was Jonathan Moyo, who had to flee from the carnage in Tanzania to save his life.

According to the Standard newspaper (July 2017) Jonathan Moyo, in response to allegations by members of the Lacoste ZANU PF faction that he was a sellout who deserted the liberation war, corroborated Macaphulana's account. He was less circumspect as he countered that allegation. He said that he indeed had ran away from the ZANLA camp in Mgagao Tanzania in June 1976 on arrival, because the Shona combatants there were killing Ndebele combatants. He being Ndebele and unable to speak the Shona language had to flee for his life. Since he was already in the system, Moyo could not join ZAPU's ZPRA in Morogoro and had to go back to Zambia where he had to promptly learn the Shona language in order to survive within ZANU and ZANLA. That was the violence that was mentioned by Berlyn (1978).

Moyo's and Macaphulana's delineation could be affirmed within many government departments, especially within the uniformed forces and other security branches. Moreso during the war days. If one were a ZANLA cadre he/she had to basically reject his/her own identity and assume a different and acceptable identity. Many had to assume a Shona name and or surname in order to have comfort in ZANU and to rise through the ranks. Ndebeles had to project themselves as Shonas in order to be treated with some modicum of fairness. The killings by ZANU at Mgagao were evidence that gukurahundi, as a policy of physically killing the Ndebele people did not start at independence in 1980 but was already in practice in Tanzania in 1976. As a tool of gukurahundi, patriotic history was employed to portray ZANU / ZANLA as heroes of all times, gloss over ZAPU / ZPRA's contribution and bury the genocide by either referring to it as a mere disturbance, a civil war or making no mention of it at all.

Mugabe then sought to demolish ZAPU completely because that was the only potential source of a correct historical account as well as a source of dissent to his aspirations of ruling to the grave. He then knit a strategy to frustrate ZPRA personnel out of the ZNA and falsely accuse them of plotting to oust him from the throne thereby winning the sympathy of all and sundry before killing them.

Whether they were apartheid South Africa sponsored and recruited, disgruntled ZNA deserters, self-styled and motivated or government stage-managed pseudo dissidents, the dissidents served Mugabe's purpose and served it well. Thanks to them, Mugabe crushed the opposition and for two decades he enjoyed relative peace and unfettered political largess with no voice at variance with his. Due to dissidentry, ZAPU and the Matabele were physically beaten, psychologically emasculated and ideologically depleted. Due to that predicament, Joshua Nkomo, reminiscent of a shepherd traumatized at seeing his flock mauled by angry vengeful wolves and tired of running and ridicule, succumbed to the temptation to negotiate with his persecutors.

On their part, most white people, just like the black people, had a right to support ZANU but they had no right to endorse the genocide in Matabeleland and Midlands the way some of them did. Instead of singing the ZANU song with amazing gusto and zest while dancing to the tune with rare nimble footedness, the influencial majority blacks and the rich minority whites could have helped the Matabele by screaming 'murder!'. Probably Mrs. Thatcher, if not the world, would have listened. Most however, chose to hold their peace, some looked the other way while some overtly supplied the oil and fuel for the ZANU terror machine.

In 1983, Mr. Jim Sinclair (a white Zimbabwean) was the Zimbabwe Commercial Farmers Union (ZCFU) president. When he was interviewed by BBC panorama, Mr. Sinclair stated with a sense of great security and immunity, born of the confidence inspired by Mugabe's conciliatory approach to the white community, that the government was not losing control and was justified in deploying the Gukurahundi Brigade to Matabeleland and Midlands. He contended that the government had a right to apply draconian measures since there was a *"war situation"* in Matabeleland. What Sinclair refused to believe was that there was no war in Matabeleland. He did not realize that the only gunshots that were fired throughout the curfew period were when government agents were shooting at civilians. That could hardly be termed a war. He was pontificating blindly from a distant, uninformed and false ivory tower of his farm in Mashonaland, far from the horrific situation in Nyamandlovu, Kezi and Silobela where the Gukurahundi gunboat was mowing down Ndebeles like dry grass.

Mr. Jim Sinclair might as well have quoted the words of his 19th century kinsman, the hunter Frederick Courteney Selous, who after the defeat of the Ndebele kingdom by the British, gloated with great self-satisfaction that *"(n)o one knowing their abominable history can pity them or lament their downfall. They have been paid back in their own coin"* (Moorcraft 1979).

In Nyamandlovu, another white farmer Mr. James Wood was interviewed by BBC panorama in his cattle ranch. Buoyed by the government issue of guns to all white farmers in the district for protection against dissidents, was singing from the same hymn book as Sinclair and Selous. He stated that he was *"happy with the 5th brigade"* operations. When asked by a journalist, how the 5th brigade treated Africans in Matabeleland, Wood evasively said he *"would rather not answer"* that question. There was a loud and offensive contradiction in Wood's line of reasoning. He obviously had deep and dark reservations about the 5th brigade's treatment of Africans but on the other hand he was happy with the same brigade's operations because it gave him a sense of security. Woods had misgivings which he could not express, either because he did not care about blacks killing blacks or because he was afraid of losing the white privileges given by Mugabe.

The fact that the government opted to give firearms to white farmers only in Matabeleland and Midlands and not the Matabele, betrayed the regime's perception of the conflict they themselves had created. If not all Ndebeles were dissidents, then the government would have armed those of them that were not, so they could protect themselves from dissidents like James Wood and other white farmers. Why did the government not give Mr. Luke Khumalo of Thekwane High School a gun too? After his murder by 'dissidents', why did the government not give the Matabele school headmasters in Plumtree, guns too? Why did the government not give Matabeleland businessmen and women guns too?

The answer was painfully simple. The government had concluded that all Ndebeles were dissidents. None of them could be given arms since that would be tantamount to reinforcing the enemy. The painful conclusion was that white farmers were given guns by Mugabe to shoot Ndebeles alongside the Gukurahundi Brigade as long as they put tags of dissidents on the corpses. Had the white farmers wanted, they too could have shot their employees and claimed they were dissidents. They would have gotten away with it too. Fortunately, although some white people supported Mugabe, none of them chose to shoot the Matabele with the guns supplied by the government.

The white farmers actually let Mugabe down. By arming the farmers, he had wanted the situation to escalate to a conflict between the Matabele and the white farmers too. He had envisaged a blood bath whereby whites gunned down the Matabele and told the world they had killed trespassing and marauding dissidents. That way the dissidents would kill more white farmers, who were mostly isolated and therefore easy targets out there in rural Matabeleland and Midlands. Just like the abduction and eventual murder of the six tourists, the hoped for murder of the farmers would win Mugabe international support for his genocide. By accepting the arms and exercising restraint, the white farmers kept a leash on their complicity with Mugabe in the crimes against humanity.

Whether for a fleeting moment of ethnic madness or in perpetuation of the 1979 Shona Grand Plan, Robert Mugabe and his coterie of overzealous underlings, conveniently forgot that when God created mankind, He had made a calculated and deliberate strategy to have her diverse. Within mankind, He assigned skin colour and pigmentation. He gave mankind varied languages, cultures, and also races and tribes. Those dissimilar shades of mankind then from time to time, since time immemorial, with God's blessing chose deviating philosophies, ideologies and creeds. God's plan as the vineyard owner was to make Zimbabwe just like Zambia, India, South Africa and Nigeria, a botanical kaleidoscopic garden of ethnic groups whose beauty lay in the assorted colours of its different flower varieties. A garden with only one flower is a tedious ho – hum affair that can hardly be classified as an interesting scenery. In a garden the daisy fleabanes cannot say the red rose is too red and therefore should be weeded out.

ZANU attempted to destroy the beauty of the garden by cutting down every other flower in a bid to have only the Shona flower chain and in particular the Zezuru species blossom and flourish. There can never be justification for a system where one flower species uproots all the other flowers and calls them weeds. Flowers cannot and must not weed each other out. Only the vine keeper has that prerogative.

Despite the British and American governments choosing to sweep the genocide under the proverbial carpet, there were some in Zimbabwe, United Kingdom and elsewhere that sounded the alarm. On 16 March 1983 Catholic Church Bishop, Henry Karlem (a white bishop of Bulawayo and the first person to sound the alarm on the genocide) and Bishop Mutume (Shona) together with CCJP chairperson Mike Auret (white), had a meeting with Mugabe. They presented him with evidence of the atrocities his battalion was doing in Matabeleland, just as he had requested. However, their evidence was ignored.

Shortly after the meeting, on Easter Day the Zimbabwe Catholic Bishops' Conference (ZCBC), wrote and delivered a letter to Mugabe titled *"Reconciliation is still Possible"*. In the letter they condemned dissidentry in Matabeleland. They also observed that while purportedly on a mission to flush out the bandits, the 5th brigade had embarked on a crusade of mass slaughter.

For their effort of championing the values of peace, justice, fairness and Godliness, the church incurred the wrath of Mugabe, himself a catholic. The Catholic Church bishops were doing their Godly duty in line with the mandate of the ZCBC and the Bible (Ester chapter 4: 8 & 14). They were the only church that called the government to account on the issue of the Gukurahundi genocide. Mugabe instead unsparingly fulminated against the bishops. He described them as a *"band of Jeremiahs"* and *"sanctimonious prelates......mere megaphone agents of your external masters"*. That marked the onset of an almost four decades long love - hate relationship between Mugabe and by extension, ZANU and the government on one side and the church on the other. They appreciated those churches and false priests that graced and blessed their ill-gotten wealth, weddings, divorces, lavish ceremonies and prophesied positively about and prayed for their election prospects.

Mugabe and ZANU became averse to criticism and hostile to the few truth - telling priests. He got obsessed with denigrating those priests who dared criticize his leadership. That became a chronic psychological malady for Mugabe. Years later he exhibited animosity for the South African Anglican Archbishop emeritus Desmond Tutu and Catholic archbishop of Bulawayo diocese Pius Ncube. His hate and contempt for some clergy transmuted into an infectious pathological habit. It infected Nathan Shamuyarira, a Mugabe - die hard who in 2005 castigated Pius Ncube for daring to criticize the ZANU PF regime. He remarked that *"Pius Ncube, a mad inveterate liar.....fits into the scheme of the British and Americans, who are calling for regime change and are feeding him with these wild ideas"* (News Day 06 June 2014).

In stark contrast to Mugabe, Joshua Nkomo implored the church to assume an active role in guiding politics. On 12 April 1986, addressing mourners at the burial of former ZPRA army commander Lookout Masuku, Nkomo petitioned the clergy thus, *"even the preachers are fightened to speak freely and they have to hide behind the name of Jesus......We invite the clergy to be outspoken. Tell us when we go wrong"*. Yet Mugabe was erecting a stone wall around himself, so that occasionally a compliant priest with a blind fold could be allowed in through a narrow gate to pray on independence day or on his birthday. He openly told the clergy to stay away from politics, yet he would implore church congregants to vote for him during his electioneering.

In spite of all the censure, the Catholic bishops were not deterred, nor were they cowed into silence by Mugabe's furious diatribe like the rest of the local and international clergy. When in 1985, according to the Chronicle, dissidents killed twenty Shona civilians in Mwenezi (Masvingo) the ZCBC and CCJP wrote another report to Mugabe titled *"Peace, Unity and Freedom"*. The report implored the government to take action against politically inspired violence and arrest the defense forces' slaughter in Matabeleland. They went a step further by stating that, *"shouting slogans against fellow Zimbabweans, individuals or groups such as down with so and so...engenders feelings of hatred in the hearts of the people.... let us build not destroy, let us unite not divide"*.

The bishops were apparently referring to the ZANU predilection for chanting slogans such as *"pasi naNkomo, pasi neZAPU, pasi nemadizidenti"* (down with Nkomo, down with ZAPU, down with dissidents). Once more, the church's advice was taken as a travesty. The killings intensified and the sloganeering continued through the decades. After the year 2000, ZANU apparatchiks led the rank and file in *pasi "naMorgan, pasi naWelshman, pasi naDabengwa"* etc. as they persisted in their policy of antipathy and devastation.

According to the Chronicle of 15 February 1984, the Minister of Justice, Legal and Parliamentary Affairs and leader of parliament, Dr Edison Zvobgo also joined the chorus of denying reports of and belittling the Gukurahundi genocide. Joshua Nkomo had, the previous day reported in parliament that the the 5th Brigade had butchered six people in kezi and that children in the area were dying due to starvation resulting from the food embargo. Nkomo was derided by Zvobgo who accused him of *"trying to lower the morale of Gukurahundi soldiers while boosting that of dissidents...publicity secretary for dissidents...he wants to use this house so that dissidents can hear that he still speaks on their behalf...some day this government will say enough is enough regardless of the size of the man".* While making reference to Nkomo's physical size, which at six foot six and more than three hundred pounds, was obviously intimidating to him, Zvobgo made it very clear that he thought the people of Kezi and their children were dissidents because Nkomo was speaking on behalf of the communities who were dying and starving. Yet Zvobgo said he was speaking on behalf of dissidents. He also left no doubt in anyone's mind that he thought the Gukurahundi brigade was doing a 'good' job by killing people and starving children to death.

It could be inaccurate to say that the people in Mashonaland were not adversely affected by the Gukurahundi Brigade, because it is possible that indirectly they were. None however could have been impacted directly and deliberately, because the 5th brigade was never deployed to Mashonaland. The abuses and massacres were carried out in Matabeleland and in the Ndebele speaking parts of the Midlands province only. The Gukurahundi Brigade assignment was to destroy ZAPU strucures and exterminate the Ndebele. Some scribes like Mutizwa (2010) claimed that because ZANU was responsible for the death of *"headmasters"* accused of witchcraft and selling out in Mashonaland during the war, therefore that was Gukurahundi. That was true but that must not be confused with the Gukurahundi Brigade. The headmasters and many other victims in Mashonaland were killed by gukurahundism and not by the Gukurahundi brigade.

Gukurahundism as an ideology had always been practiced by ZANU from its formation in 1963, although the term Gukurahundi was adopted and used officially in 1979 by Mugabe. The Gukurahundi / 5th Brigade, the physical regiment was commissioned in 1982 and was never officially disbanded. Until it was withdrawn from the public eye, it never operated in any Mashonaland provinces during the genocide years. Implying that Shonas were directly victimized by the Gukurahundi Brigade was shallow philosophizing, a futile and and sleeveless attempt at sanitizing the tribalistic nature of the genocide. What remained common to Matabeleland and Mashonaland, albeit experienced in varied dosages, were gukurahundism, zanuism and mugabeism.

Another fact that was beyond contestation was that, while gukurahundism killed many, zanuism and mugabeism were responsible for the other forms of suffering of many more in Mashonaland, pre and post – independence, although the killings and other evil visitations on the people of Mashonaland were political executions and not ethnic cleansing.

After accomplishing their mission, both battalions, the 5th Brigade and the Presidential Guard, contrary to popular belief were not disbanded. By 2011, the 5th Brigade was still stationed at Battlefields barracks, the biggest military base in the country, located 30 km out of Kwekwe town. The Presidential Guard was camped at Dzivarasekwa in Harare. They were lurking at the back of the house like a prowling predator, waiting to be called into action whenever needed to fumigate the Matabele 'cockroaches' again. The fact that they were never disbanded, court marshalled or prosecuted by the courts of law, always paused a threat to Matabeleland and the Midlands. They could be called into action anytime.

While the Gukurahundi battalion was recalled to the barracks, the Gukurahundi policy or strategy was pursued dogmatically by the government. Despite Joshua Nkomo having signed the Unity Accord on 22 December 1987, Mugabe's administration did not relent on oppressing Matabeleland. The bloodletting ceased but it was replaced by a sequel which proved to be equally enervative and corrosive. Gukurahundism or the strategy of Gukurahundi (Gatsheni – Ndlovu 2011) or the policy of Gukurahundi (Sithole and Makumbe 1997) took centre stage and continued from where the 5th Brigade had left. Matabeleland had just lept from the rain into the sea.

On 22 December 1987 Joshua Nkomo appended his signature to the Unity Agreement. By the stroke of an acquiescing pen, the final nail on the coffin of multipartism was sunk and it became the death knell for all democratic opposition and debate for thirteen years. Zimbabwe became a de facto one party state. 22 December was declared a National Unity Day and a public holiday to commemorate Mugabe's victory. Whether the day had any symbolic meaning or whether there was a need to redefine the same in terms of the wounds and scars that those affected by the genocide preceding the accord continued to sustain and nurse, over the years proved to be of little consequence to the government. What was clear though was that Nkomo achieved one objective and that, only. The wanton and wretched killing of the people of Matabeleland and Midlands ceased. The beast that was feeding insatiably on his flock was recalled to its dungeon where it was chained away, albeit for a season. Mugabe and ZANU had finally arrived at their much wanted one party state. They could now focus on pursuing the extension; the Shona nation one party state.

By the date of signing the Unity Accord in December 1987, about 100 000 people from Matabeleland and the Ndebele speaking parts of the Midlands province had been killed. Hundreds of thousands had been injured, displaced, exiled and traumatized. No wonder the accord remained a paper pie long after the death of Nkomo in 1999 and Mugabe in 2019. A desultory glance into social media debates showed that Ndebele / Shona relations were fractured after mugabe's death more than ever. There was no evidence of unity between the two, whose relationship was that of horse and rider. The length and breadth of the relationship was summarized at the top leadership purpoted national political parties (ZANU PF and MDCT) where the president was always Shona and one of two or three deputies was Matabele.

What Zimbabwe attained after the 1980 elections, from the Matabeleland perspective was not democratic majority rule but tribal majority rule. There was no room enough in the new dispensation for the minority tribes of Matabeleland. There was room only for the majority tribe. ZANU's mandate was to make the tribal majority happy and the minority had to cede their space and forego their rights, values and norms. After the Gukurahundi massacres, Mugabe set about an agenda of grinding to powder what his army had crushed, albeit by pernicious, yet equally baneful means.

The complexity with the sadistic practice of discrimination, domination, segregation, marginalization and oppression is that when perpetrated by a ruling majority, it gets institutionalized with extremely natural subtlety, ease and guise. It permeates the system of governance and takes over policy formulation so much that it spreads officially and infectiously. It gets accepted as the norm and it becomes the silent partner to the legal framework, making it immune from detection and prosecution. Any attempt to detect and isolate it, exposes one to a barrage of criticism by the law of the majority and the court of public opinion. Consequently, the victims tend to acquiesce and bend over backwards to appease the perpetrator. As a subconscious coping strategy, the victims eventually find their oppression by the majority tolerable and almost palatable. They learn to live with it, teach their children not to complain about it but to submit, in order to survive. Some victims even become critical and violent towards those trying to emancipate them.

That is oppression by a tribal majority. It is increasingly dangerous because while insidiously corrosive, it can be conspicuous and even popular. The popularity of the majoritarian leadership nationally and at times internationally is usually extended like a curtain that overshadows their evil style of governance. Therefore, the government's failures on human rights are veiled in the fame. The abuses on the minority are hidden under the trampling feet of the majority. Any criticism of or protests against the majority is met with extremely intimidating and at times fatal consequences. The majority can use their sheer power of numbers, brute political force, mammoth influence, potent popularity and infinite state resources to disdainfully repel away any criticism or protests.

There is always one constant in discrimination, be it by the minority or by the majority. The benefactors propping up the system, the architects and mandarins providing the master brains, that scheme and connive, are very few. The elite. They are a handful of men and or women that are at times very knowledgeable. They attempt to convince themselves and everyone that they serve a just cause, hence the votes they always win. The primary beneficiaries may be the elite but at times the unconscious and innocent majority are wooed into deriving some material benefits. Once the ethnic majority realizes or tastes the 'sweet' fruits of discrimination, they accord the perpetrators hero status and even martyrdom. That is why ordinary people may unwittingly sacrifice life and limb in defense of tyranny by the majority.

At the initial stages of oppression by a tribal or ethnic majority, the ordinary people may be oblivious of the discomfort and plight of the minority. Nonetheless, when they subsequently comprehend or accept that the other groups are suffering prejudice, the majority often opt to make-believe that nothing is amiss for fear of forfeiting their accrued privileges. Since the beneficiaries are the majority, the scenario becomes very dire and detrimental to national cohesion because there is always the absence of popular and common will to redress. Any attempts at rectification are usually crushed under the weight of the will of 'the people' or the law of the land. For example, when the Matabele on numerous occasions and Shangani people of Chiredzi under Chief Tshovani in April 2019, complained against Shona primary school teachers who could not speak any local language or Shonas resettled on their land, the response was that the law allowed Zimbabweans to live and work anywhere in the country. The law rudely ignored the plight of the minorities while protecting the interests of the ruling majority.

White minority rule in Rhodesia was condemned the world over because it was demonstrably an odious instrument of discrimination, oppression and segregation pursued by the minority to the detriment of the majority. It needed no political scientist to prove that having 20% of the white population which was only 6.5% of the national population, occupying 80 percent of the national arable agricultural land, was an affront to fairness, democracy, good governance, human dignity, the equality of all mankind and common sanity. Minority rule was condemned because there was hard empirical evidence of injustice and inequality by way of the abounding pieces of draconian legislation as well.

In South Africa, apartheid was structured to jealously protect the myopic privileges of the white minority ruling class at the expense of the majority blacks. Just like the successive white regimes of Rhodesia, the citadel of apartheid, left hordes of evidence of racism and discrimination all over the landscape. Apartheid was justifiably, unsparingly attacked and ultimately dismantled with international approval. It was easy to single out discrimination and oppression when it was perpetrated by the minority against the majority. What most failed to detect was when it was the majority that discriminated and oppressed the minority. Discrimination by the majority is equally evil if not worse, due to its potential to eclipse the minority within a very short period of time.

What makes it even more difficult to condemn is that, discrimination by the majority does not need oppressive laws against minorities to sustain it. A tribal majority uses seemingly fair and reasonable legislation to oppress the minority by practicing such laws as health budgeting based on population density alone. For example the maxim that Zimbabweans are free to settle and work anywhere in the country, while sounding logical, has been used to colonize Matabeleland in what can be termed, internal colonization under domestic imperialism.

The discrimination against a black minority by a black majority was not a conceivable prospect at independence in Zimbabwe but that did not preclude it from occuring. When it unraveled as a fresh substitute of the condemned white minority oppression, no one condemned it at all. Probably it happened too soon after, even during the wild celebrations after the fall of oppression by the white minority.

Ian Douglas Smith and Robert Gabriel Mugabe in their respective tenures were consistent and resolute in discriminating against black people and the Ndebele respectively. From 1965 to 1987, one after the other, with nerve-jangling formidability and persistency, they would renew the State of Emergency law which had diabolic consequences to the targeted populace. The only difference between them was that while the white minority regime coined laws specifically for the subjugation of black people, the black ZANU majority government did not. Instead it retained the same repressive legislation but applied it preferentially and devilishly disseminated unwritten yet effectual and perverse policies that deprived the Matabele of their human dignity and rights.

When it dawned on some in Matabeleland that there was no equality between the Matabele and the Shona in such spheres as education, health, commerce and employment, it was many years after independence and by then the damage was contagiously deep, too deep even for some of the victims, especially the youthful who had not witnessed its conception and enactment by the Gukurahundi genocide, to believe it existed. Too deep particularly for some of the innocent beneficiaries to notice.

It was rather injudicious for some members of the minority white community and some of the majority Shona to look the other way when the Gukurahundi Brigade was genocidally sweeping across Matabeleland and Midlands. Whatever was their reason for ignoring the reports of mass murders of the Ndebele, they realized too late in 2000 that they had haboured and nurtured a monster that turned on them, albeit with reduced and controlled venom. They should have taken heed of the Ndebele adage that *"umlilo ucitshwa usesemafusini"* (put out the fire while it is in the forest) because it may be fatal folly to console oneself that it is the forest that is burning since one may soon realize the fire encroaching on their home.

If the Zimbabwean whites, Great Britain and the Zimbabwean majority had teamed up with the then victims, the Matabele, between 1981 and 1987 to dowse the Gukurahundi Brigade flames, their precious farms and human rights would not have been razed to the ground by Mugabe from 1999. Mugabe and ZANU PF would not have destroyed more lives, agriculture, farms, social cohesion and political stability. Mugabe would not have collapsed the economy in such dramatic fashion as he did from 1998. Mugabe's intransigence, impunity, arrogance and contempt for human lives was born during and post the gukurahundi genocide when he realized that the international community and the domestic majority were overawed and mesmerized by his speechfying. They allowed him and ZANU PF not to be accountable and to be a law unto himself and that returned to haunt them within twenty years.

Be that as it may, the surviving victims, the relatives of the dead and the affected were still nursing fresh wounds, almost four decades after the genocide. Prof. Jonathan Moyo in May 2006 was speaking for them when he declared that,".. *as victims we were prepared to forgive but never to forget the massacres..... we will not forget our personal tragedies and losses and that means we will never remain silent about them...... we will never ever allow anyone, no matter how powerful or stupid they are, to intimidate us into silence through the making of tribal innuendos"*.

Chapter V

GUKURAHUNDISM

> *"Gukurahundi was a policy of annihilation; annihilating the opposition (black and white). Accordingly, an "enemies list" was published in mid-1979 in which ranking personalities of the "internal settlement" parties were singled out for liquidation"*

Sithole and Makumbe, 1987

Muzondidya and Ndlovu - Gatsheni (2007:282) posited that nationalist leaders used ethnicity as a political resource as they contested for power during the 1960s and 1970s. They said that in ZANU, power struggles were mainly between the three Shona sub-ethnic groups namely the Manyika from the eastern districts, the Karanga from the south and the Zezuru from the north. They cited Masipula Sithole's argument in *"Struggles within a Struggle"*, that it was contestations by these groups which resulted in ethnic based factions within ZANU as well as in the assassination of Herbert Chitepo, the first chairman of ZANU, in March 1975.

On the ZAPU side they posited that ethnicity fragmented the party into Kalanga / Ndebele politicians on one side versus their Shona contemporaries on the other. They argued that the ZPRA commander Alfred Nikita Mangena, who was killed, allegedly by a Rhodesian landmine in Zambia in 1978 was a casualty of Ndebele/Kalanga versus Shona rivalry. They asserted that the nationalist leaders, *"condemned ethnicity during the day but used it by night as a political resource in their own battles for power.... Zimbabwe was thus born with a very bad ethnic birthmark that was to negatively affect its national integration efforts"*.

The exigencies of waging a guerilla war against a well trained and resourced government army, interacting with the negative personal attributes of some nationalists, did not just promote within the nationalist movement ethnic conflict but more attributes at odds to democracy such as bellicosity, regimentalism, big - manism, unilateralism, intransigency, male chauvinism, impunity and personality cultism. To that list, post independant ZANU was to add a host of other vices including personal aggrandizement, patronagism, rent seeking, corruption, marginalization, sexism, nepotism, tribalism as well as uncompromising intolerance to dissent.

ZANU hogged into statehouse with their war policies which were evidenced by an artificial and habitual disposition to fight. Dissenters were dealt with swiftly, summerily and heavy handedly to deter future 'rebels' as well as to secure the tenure of the incumbent leadership for eternity. The strategy of Gukurahundi (Ndlovu - Gatsheni 2011) was used as a foraging arm to *"annihilate"* dissenters, be they internal or external, thereby eliminating the threat of any insurrection or challenge. Ndlovu - Gatsheni said the strategy of Gukurahundi was concocted by the broader nationalist movement and later adopted by ZANU PF who adapted it into an all – weather tool.

Ndlovu – Gatsheni (2011) was concurring with Sithole and Makumbe (1997) who had espoused that, *"Gukurahundi was a policy of annihilation; annihilating the opposition (black and white). Accordingly, an "enemies list" was published in mid-1979 in which ranking personalities of the "internal settlement" parties were singled out for liquidation"*. The list had been compiled by ZANU's Edson Zvobgo, it is alleged. It had names of people that had to be killed because they were perceived as sellouts, threats to ZANU and or individuals therein or simply people that were unwanted by the system for one reason or another.

It was futile to attempt to reconcile ZANU the liberation movement and the Gukurahundist policies that the organization had always embraced and propagated. The term 'liberation' which the party demagogues used often, meant emancipation or 'freeing' from a negative. It implied embracing certain international practices and standards such as respect for human rights, protection of the sanctity of human life as well as observance of democratic values. Yet the infamous mantra *"zanu ndeyeropa"*, which was Shona for, 'ZANU is a killer' or literally translated meaning, 'ZANU is of blood', was one self – contradicting policy statement that will live in infamy through infinity. For a liberation movement to sloganeer and brag about its propensity and penchant for blood – letting, was equivalent to making a burlesque of all that was promising about the liberty of the oppressed.

It was that unashamed thirst for blood that led to the genocide of Ndebeles by the 5th Brigade, the Presidential Guard and other state security organs.

The blood mantra was always the small brother to the deadly "*pasi*" (down/ ground/earth) shibboleth which condemned many within and without ZANU to their perile. That perpetual slogan was from the inception of ZANU in 1963, the top dog, underpinning the policy making and practice therein. Once the ZANU leadership said "*pasi*" with someone, that person became the enemy and deserved punishment, ostracizing or even death. Gatsheni – Ndlovu (2002) must have had ZANU in particular in mind when he noted that, *"the operations of the nationalist movement on quasi – military lines were not amenable to democracy and human rights within the movement itself.... To have a different political allegiance was tantamount to committing suicide and treason... the prosecution of the armed struggle also introduced the tendency of accumulating arms of war as the only surety of safety, and these arms of war were used to eliminate political opponents even within the nationalist movement itself"*.

Evidence of ZANU's predisposition for violence, which was part of the strategy of Gukurahundi, to eliminate not only external threats but internal political opponents within the party was littered all over their trail from the 60s to the 90s, through the turn of the millennium. That strategy / policy was put to 'good' use in ensuring that by independence, the Zezuru were fast and unwaveringly ensconced at the apex of the party, sidelining threats from the Karanga led by Dr. Edison Zvobgo and Simon Muzenda as well as from the Manyika.

As soon as the Zezuru elite assumed the reigns of power, they relegated the other Shona dialects and accorded their language version the 'standard Shona' status. They shared amongst themselves all the influential positions in government and the army. The other Shona groups were given the left - overs but were appeased because they were made to feel that they were invited to the party. They shared the wine glasses, hence they became accomplices in creating the hideous and repugnant condition of Zezuru hegemony. The Manyika, Karanga and Korekore elite were hoodwinked into thinking they were setting up Shona hegemony at the expense of the Matabele. Years later they would realize that as far as the dynamics of power and influence in the party and in government were concerned, they were second fiddle to the Zezuru with the Matabele at the rear.

To Matabeleland was thrust the thick end of the stick. Raw gukurahundism was employed since 1980, to frog - march the Ndebele, Kalanga and other Matabeleland tribes as well as the Karanga, Manyika, Korekore, Ndau and Shangani into servile compliance. Gukurahundism ensured that Matabeleland, the home and birthplace of some of pre – colonial Africa's greatest warriors, men whose courage was matched only by their loyalty to their souls, king and nation building, was reduced to cinder and ashes.

Gukurahundism was the policy of annihilating the enemy, the opposition and the different.

Gukurahundism employed the strategies of, political disenfranchisement of the different, isolating the disobliging, economically emasculating and marginalizing the disliked and competitive others, socially bankrupting other ethnic groups while extending social and cultural dominance over them and physically eliminating potential and perceived threats by any means necessary, including the use of hit squads and engineered car accidents.

Gukurahundism was denoted by assassinations, disappearances, fatal car accidents, imprisonment without trial, or other violent eliminations of fellow comrades and opposition figures through the usage of secret hit squads, military and para military structures which had a vetoing influence over civil administration. It is gukurahundism that saw to the demise via a parcel bomb, of Herbert Chitepo, ZANU's first chairperson in 1975 and leader for ten years when Ndabaningi Sithole was in prison. He was the man earmarked to lead after Sithole. Gukurahundism also killed Josiah Tongogara, ZANLA commander, in a mysterious car accident in December 1979, Armstrong Gunda, commander of Mugabe's body guards (2007) in a myserious car accident and Solomon Mujuru, former commander of the Zimbabwe Defence Forces and husband to the vice president, in a mysterious inferno at his home in 2011.

Gukurahundism also accounted for Sydney Malunga, (ZAPU spokesperson and MP) and Lookout Masuku (former ZPRA commander) who was tortured and probably poisoned to death at Chikurubi maximum prison. Mthandazo Ndema Ngwenya, the renowned Ndebele novelist and champion of Ndebele identity, died in a mysterious car accident in 1992 and Themba Nkabinde, a scholar and a writer critic of the Mugabe administration also died in a mysterious car accident. Many died and many more disappeared including Rashiwe Guzha, Cain Nkala, Captain Nleya, Itai Dzamara, the list is ad infinitum. The list comprised victims within and outside ZANU PF. Both Matabele and Shona tribes were not spared. All the victims met their fate in mysterious circumstances. Where an inquest was conducted, the findings were either disputed, inconclusive or unconvincing.

Violence invoking and mocking statements, hate speech, slogans and songs chiding the other side were endemic in gukurahundism. Irrevocably vulgar and unstatesmanly terms like *"umgodoyi"*, (a hopeless dog), *"imbwasungata"*, (a dog on a leash), sellout, traitor, puppet and dissident, were used as a precursor to further psychological, emotional, verbal and physical abuse. Once one was subjected to that kind of ridicule they had better quit before a more dire fate befell them. Reproaching and bullying songs such as *"maruza imi"* (you, ie. Ndebeles, ZAPU and Nkomo have lost the election), *"huyayi muone zvaita Nkomo, arembera pamuchinjikwa"* (come and see Nkomo, hanging on a tree) were examples of the chiding, harassing and punitive nature of gukurahundism.

Under gukurahundism there was no room for opposition political parties in the governance domain. It subsumed that the benefits of independence should accrue solely to, first, the ZANU elite, secondly, the relatives, lackeys and friends of the ZANU elite, thirdly, the ZANU rank and file and lastly, nobody else. In practice, however, the benefits were real at the top two tiers, at the third it was all imaginary and always promised. Nobody else had a right to expect any pickings from the fruit tree of the liberation struggle. That attitude was aptly portrayed in the ZANU 1980 election manifesto which sought to impress on the electorate the misinformation that ZANU alone had achieved all the success thus far and therefore had a monopolic legitimate right to independence benefits. Part of the manifesto read,

"we have fought to achieve both military and political power, and because we have produced the Lancaster House agreement we must not allow the others and the reactionaries to reap the ripe peaches we have tended. ZANU PF planted and tended the peach tree. ZANU PF is, therefore, entitled to reap her peaches" (Sylvester 1990)

In all their years of economic botch ups and political bollocks, ZANU were never more selfish, vainglorious and ludicrous than at that point in 1980. In addition to being hopelessly vain, ZANU proved to be incredulously false by claiming sole ownership of the Lancaster House agreement, which years later turned into a source of great inconvenience to them, thereby compelling them to conviniently refer to it as a British imposition. Anybody who could read knew that the ZANU delegation had been dragged to Lancaster sqeaking and screaming in protest. Pretending to be the heroes of Lancaster was as preposterous as it was misleading. Such falsity towards historical facts developed into a trademark of the regime. That was the beginning of the tendency by the party to relentlessly disfigure memories of the past and distort historical facts by writing a deliberately inaccurate 'patriotic history'.

Unsurprisingly, it was Mugabe himself who laid the foundation stone to the caustic praxis of perverting historical facts by claiming that it was ZANU that planted the peach tree that yielded independence. The historiography of nationalism in general and the liberation struggle in particular, then became a falsehoods infested exercise that resulted in mockery of history. The country was fed a combination of distortions, omissions and fiction, which was smuggled into primary, secondary and tertiary education curricula as well as through the radio, television and newspapers.

Examples included their forgetting to mention how Mugabe ditched Nkomo at Lancaster after they had agreed to contest the 1980 elections as one party, the Patriotic Front (PF). Included also was the fallacy they paddled for three decades that former Vice President Joyce Mujuru had shot and downed a Rhodesian Defense Forces helicopter during the war. That supposedly great feat, became part of her unassailable resume, propelling her to greater heights in government and the party and to the pedestal of super war heroine. However, when she was dismissed from ZANU PF in 2014 the government press went all out to discredit and prove that the helicopter exploit was complete fabrication. The fact that the story had been allowed to stand and was even marketed by ZIANA the state media, before she was dismissed, betrayed the decrepit and rickety layers of faux bricks that made the ZANU PF house and its library of history. Anyone who took ZANU PF's version of any history seriously after their volte – face on the Mujuru / helicopter story would be doing so at their own great risk.

The 'us' and 'them' mentality in the manifesto informed Mugabe and ZANU to divide the country into what he termed "we", the patriots, the comrades, the heroes and "others" the dogs, the sellouts, the puppets and the dissidents. That selfish and egotistical inclination to paddock and regimentalize citizens into 'us' and 'others' was exposed by Ndlovu - Gatsheni and Willems (2010) as they argued that, *"(b)ecause of PF-ZAPU's loss in the elections and its refusal to disband and be swallowed by ZANU-PF, Nkomo, his party, his supporters and ex-ZPRA members were 'othered' as enemies of the new republic.* Once they were 'othered' they automatically relinquished their rights to enjoy the fruits, not only of independence and their labour, but of being humans too.

Either one was ZANU or they were persona non grata, a dog and a puppet that did not belong to Zimbabwe. Witness how the military was ushered in to preside over civil matters. In a normal set up, an election derives its legitimacy and political sanctity in it's being a civil and politic process. The militarization of an election could only result in a chaotic dictatorship. From as early as the first elections, the ZANU party used their military numbers and militia weight to suppress the will of the masses and therefore submerged democratic ethos in militarism and ultimately gukurahundism.

By erroneously claiming that the struggle was about achieving military power, ZANU confused the priorities matrix, hence gukurahundism took centre stage. The struggle was never about military power, but as always, about civilian authority with which comes economic, social, political and military responsibilities. The war of liberation and the Lancaster negotiations should have been used to attain political power which in turn had to be used to set up an economic and social institution of government with all its surbodinate departments including the military. By equating military and political power, Mugabe created a de facto military dictatorship or junta, instead of a civilian government with authority over the military.

The military power which ZANU claimed they fought to achieve would become a thorn in their flesh in a couple of decades when the army literally called the shots within government to the chagrin of many. In 2008 the military allegedly forced Mugabe not to handover power after losing the elections to Tsvangirai, who was former ZANU himself. Old, buttered, illusioned and sick, Mugabe was forced to soldier on by his 'military power'. A decade later Mugabe was to lament his military power serpent when it was used to bite him out of political power. He tried in vain to convince even himself that the military should not meddle in politics and civil administration but no one listened because even SADC, AU and UN knew that he had tripped over his own snare.

Like most war mongers infatuated with an insatiable lust for power, Mugabe was oblivious of the fact that with more power comes more responsibility. He failed the litmus test of a nation builder. His self - admitted political creator Enos Nkala, in an interview with VOA radio, many years too late, disqualified Mugabe from the list of nation builders like Kings Shaka and Mzilikazi. Nkala said Mugabe was devoid of the basic make – up requisite in a nation builder; *"isineke"* (Ndebele for good natured tolerance of and rehabilitation of ordinary human weaknesses in others).

A comparison of Mugabe's peach tree statement with what Nkomo and Lookout Masuku espoused, seemed to reduce him to a warlord with an extremely pedestrian conception and appreciation of the ideals of African nationalism. While he claimed that the liberation war was meant to achieve *"both military and political power"* for his party, Nkomo told him in a letter that, *"we fought for liberty, freedom and the rule of law"*. Masuku a soldier through and through sounded more noble and prime ministerly than the Prime Minister when he said that the people fought for the right to *"express their will"* and *"to vote and to be able to choose our own destiny"*. Such magnanimity even after electoral defeat in clearly unfair circumstances, seemed to diminish Mugabe to a liberation and nationalist minion. Even if for a micro moment it was assumed that ZANU alone had tended the peach tree, would it not be African, humane, nationalist, Christian (he claimed to be catholic) and sober to invite all and sundry, ZANU and non ZANU to the celebrations? Clearly Mugabe in his reconciliation speech towards the whites had been blowing hot air in a hifalutin, hoity – toity stance for the media.

However, no matter how cruel one judged Mugabe, rating him as a pedestrian on African nationalism would be grossly miscalculating him. When it came to his policy towards the Matabele, Mugabe sounded like a junta strong man because he wanted his audience to understand him. He simply made the all too human error of expressing exactly the contents of his heart. That usually happens when one speaks off the cuff. His true ideas escaped though his mouth and luckily for him no one analysed and exposed his faulty logic. He was a mean, planning – all – the - way and calculating, book genius. His over confidence, popularity among his vociferous supporters, foreign and donor financial support gave him a buoyancy that periodically made him betray the troubled contents of his trully dark and troubled soul.

That dark soul promptly turned the fruits of independence into the sole preserve of ZANU and not for the *"others"*. 'Others', refered primarily to ZAPU and to a lesser extent ZANU Ndonga, UANC, UNFP and other political formations that contested the 1980 elections. Since ZAPU to ZANU meant Ndebele and by extension Matabeleland, then all the people of Matabeleland fell prey to ZANU triumphalism which did not recognize them as equals with Mashonaland. Matabeleland was in wholesale fashion denied the fruits of independence by a policy of fellow black people intent on tribal domination.

Gukurahundism therefore endevoured to vanquish all 'others', including political parties by establishing a one party state system, although ZANU claimed they wanted to attain it through agreement. Gukurahundism dictated that when coercive negotiation failed, the ruling party must crush by brute force or swallow the opposition by buying them into silence or merge with them in a setup where the opposition gradually disappeared and the ruling party remained intact. That opposition that would not yield to those manuvres got demonized and criminalized so thoroughly it would not attract serious funding or support by the electorate and therefore would be rendered enduringly innocuous.

Speaking at the Gukurahundi genocide commemorations of January 2011, then Minister of National Healing and Reconciliation, Moses Mzila – Ndlovu (MP) opined that the objective of the Gukurahundi genocide was not only to physically exterminate the people of Matabeleland but to instil perennial and acidic fear on the minds of the survivors and generations after them. Accordingly, they instilled an omnifarious fear of Shona people, ZANU PF and Mugabe. That, the minister said was done on behalf of all Shona people. The fact that outside election campaign programs, there were too few voices from Mashonaland condemning the Gukurahundi genocide as an odious feat of hate and dissociating themselves from it, emphatically and unequivocally implied that many were either complicit or they just did not care. They were complicit because they were benefitting from the marginalisation of Matabeleland. On the other hand, by being compliant, out of fear or willingly, Matabeleland squizzed herself into the system, thereby zanufying herself in order to survive. By conforming, Matabeleland was initiated into Mugabe's personality cult, was helping preserve regime security as well as entrench ZANU PF longevity and Zezuru hegemony.

He espoused that the Gukurahundi genocide was not limited to soldiers in red berets, but included many civilians like lecturers from the University of Zimbabwe who were today in the rank and file of anti-Mugabe critics. Civilians had abetted the system, they were armed by the state, they denied the genocide was real, they called Ndebeles dissidents, they came to Matabeleland to take up jobs at the expense of the Matabele, they spied for the sinister CIO and they pointed out ZAPU supporters to the security forces, he stated. He noted that the 'icing' of the Gukurahundi genocide 'cake' was evidenced by some of the Shona people that were still benefitting in land distribution, education, employment and business as a result of the brigade's activities, yet the land of *"Bulilima, Beitbridge, Binga and Murehwa"* should belong to the respective local peoples. Mzila-Ndlovu's other sentiments were that many Shonas were complicit in that they were silent as they witnessed and benefited. He was in sync with Martin Luther King Jr's philosophy that *"he who passively accepts evil is as much involved in it as he who helps to perpetrate it"*.

Mzila-Ndlovu further asserted that there were people even in the collective opposition movement that believed that the police and the army were proper until the year 2000. That was due to the fact that some current opposition elements were former ZANU PF and former Gukurahundi soldiers as confirmed by Gabriel Chaibva MP, who admitted in parliament and was recorded in the HANSAD, that he and other youths were deployed to public bus termini in Harare to beat up wantonly any people that spoke Ndebele in the 1980s.

Despite Mzila – Ndlovu's sentiments on the complicity of some of the Shona which were echoed daily throughout Matabeleland, there were exceptions. Some scholars and scribes of Shona ancestory had written in criticism of the genocide. On 02 June 2011 the Daily News reported that the MDCT spokesperson Douglas Mwonzora MP, had called for the establishment of a commission on Gukurahundi. He said *"Gukurahundi was clear violence directed at people of a certain ethnic grouping and where you direct violence against people of a certain ethnic grouping it is genocide"*. Outside a rally environment that was one of the strongest public condemnations of the massacre, coming from Mashonaland.

In reaction to Mwonzora's speech Rugare Gumbo, the ZANU PF spokesman, true to his party's cantankerous attitude and rancorous demeanor towards the independent press, accused the media of *"resuscitating the Gukurahundi issue to whip up emotions"*. Strange how the perpetrators of the genocide presumed the world, the witnesses and the victims were in a huryy to forget their anguish. Why Gumbo and his paymaster believed the issue was no longer emotive beat reason to the hills. What they feared and wished forgotten was always coming up to haunt them, for they had buried their sins under a dark cumbrous cloud that kept shifting and dissipating and collecting only to disperse again, thereby mischievously exposing their horrid deed now and again. The Gukurahundi issue did not need rescusitating, it was alive and livid almost three decades later.

Mzila-Ndlovu concluded by stating that Gukurahundi was not over, since the brains and talons of it were still in power, very influential and still pursuing their agenda, albeit in a subtle but most seditious manner. He implored the Shona as the majority ethnic grouping to speak louder and condemn the Gukurahundi genocide and policy. His valediction note was *"the perpetrators of Gukurahundi must not subsume the roll of self forgiving"*.

That last statement by the minister was informed by the frequent declaration by the ZANU PF and government officials who in desperation for legitimacy preached forgiveness for ills of the past. The statement was also a reaction to former ZANU PF and now opposition political party functionaries with a penchant for sweeping generalizations, that rushed to promise amnesty for all crimes once their party took over the pedals of the state machine. Both ZANU PF and MDCT kept forgeting that it was the sole prerogative of the victims to forgive and not the perpetrator to self pardon.

The assertion by the minister that Gukurahundi was ongoing but in a subtle and secreted form or as soft genocide or as gukurahundism was corroborated by events such as the following.

Uluntu-Ciisi Trust (UCT) a non – partisan, local minority groups human rights organization based in the Hwange District of Matabeleland North in concert with the Victoria Falls Combined Residents Association (VIFACORA) in May 2009 decided to intervene in a tribally motivated labour dispute at a prominent hotel in Victoria Falls. The facts of the matter were captured in the extract of a report from UCT, sent to various stakeholders and quoted extensively below;

"From the information they gave us, the verbal accounts of numerous employees, the written records we have since accessed and the observations during the meeting we had with the hotel General Manager on 16 July 2009, we can attest to the following;

The hotel employees started complaining about certain managers (in particular the Human Resources and the Food and Beverage managers) practicing tribalism since May 2009. The staff General Meeting minutes of May 2009 will reveal this. The executive meeting of management and workers representatives of the same month in which management promised to address the issue as well as the Food and Beverage department meeting of 25 May 2009 bear witness to this assertion. At the Works Council meeting of June 2009 the same sentiments were raised by the representatives of the workers. Management did not institute an investigation nor were the alleged perpetrators of tribalism ever questioned or cautioned despite the fact that the workers did authenticate their claims.

Sometime in June 2009 an anonymous letter was left at the office of the hotel General Manager. We are not privy to the contents of the letter but we are informed that the writer(s) were demanding that the Human Resources Manager should leave the establishment. The letter went on to threaten the wellbeing of the General Manager and his family should he fail to remove the HR manager from the hotel. This letter was taken to the police and subsequently fourteen employee representatives upon a written recommendation by the HR manager were taken into police custody as suspects. Two of the representatives were severely tortured by a C.I.D operative (name supplied) on 20 June 2009.

The torture of the representatives did not go down well with the general staff who felt that their leaders were being intimidated into silence. Sensing that the existence of the workers committee was under threat and that management was ignoring their complaint about tribal discrimination, the workers on 01 July 2009 signed a petition calling among other things for the removal of the HR manager. The workers went on to indicate that should their grievance be ignored they were willing to invoke section 104 subsection 4(b) of the Labour Relations Act. This section provides for employees to go on a job action without giving fourteen days notice if they have reasons to believe the existence of the workers committee is under threat. The petition was ignored.

On 07 July 2009 one hundred and sixty one employees went on a sit-in until the 08th July 2009. During the sit-in which was characterized by absolute peace as evidenced by lack of violence (the police were never called in to monitor or restore law and order) the employees expected to be addressed by the employer whom they hoped would listen to them this time around. Instead the hotel Deputy General Manager addressed them and declared the job action illegal and instructed them to return to their work stations. The workers did not heed the call.

On 08 July 2009 all the 161 employees were issued by the General Manager letters of suspension. On 16 July 2009 a delegation of three Residents Association members and three Uluntu-Ciisi Trust members had a meeting with the hotel General Manager, the HR and Loss Control managers. After reading two letters from the two organizations the General Manager promised to deal with the issue responsibly since the dismissal of all these personnel would have a "nock-on effect on the community". The delegation called for the removal of the tribally discriminative managers and the unconditional reinstatement of all the suspended employees.

Disciplinary hearings have since ensued from 17 July and are ongoing. To date more than sixty employees have been dismissed.....

.... We are gravely concerned that there are people who still prefer to work with their tribesmen only and endeavor to oppress the locals. This hotel is the only African Sun Ltd property that has a noticeable number of local employees.....................

The actions of the hotel management and headquarters indicate their contempt of the local community. They want the local people to wallow in poverty and lack. The overall effects of their actions are enormous. It will result in social tension between locals and people of Shona descent. Education will be adversely affected as many children will be pulled out of school. Most of the dismissed stay in company accommodation. They will be replaced by new employees from Mashonaland (as is the trend) who will occupy the vacated houses. The town infrastructure can barely cope with the influx . Social disorders and ills that attend on unemployment, like crime, domestic violence and other vices will escalate. Finally this conduct by African Sun Ltd is an affront on Article VII (Promotion of Equality, National Healing, Cohesion and Unity) of the Global Political Agreement....."

UCT and VIFACORA appealed to the Zimbabwe Lawyers for Human Rights to provide legal counsel and representation to the workers. The lawyers responded by saying the issue was a labour dispute and not a human rights violation therefore outside their jurisdiction. The lawyers had a branch in Bulawayo but their head office was in Harare where decisions on whether to take up a case or not were made. The lawyers would not represent the abused workers because they were Matabele whom the employer was marginalizing in line with gukurahundism. By 2019 the case of the tribally dismissed employees was still pending at the high court and many of the workers had died, disillusioned and poor. They were victims of gukurahundism and evidence that Gukurahundi was continuing in a devious yet dangerous format.

Secondly in March 2011 Mr. Paul Siwela (former president of ZAPU), Mr. John Gazi (former ZPRA) and Charles Thomas, all members of uMthwakazi Liberation Front (MLF), an organization calling for the separation of the Ndebele state (uMthwakazi) and the Shona state (Zimbabwe) along pre-colonial boundaries, were arrested and detained at the notorious Khami maximum security prison. They were charged with planning to topple the government,*"Egyptian and Tunisian style"* (after the Arab revolution of the time) by distributing maps of the Mthwakazi Kingdom and flyers urging people to revolt. The trio denied possessing and distributing the flyers.

When approached for assistance, the Zimbabwe Lawyers for Human Rights refused to represent the trio who were ultimately represented by Sindiso Mazibisa, Matshobana Ncube and Robert Ndlovu attorneys at law. Once more, when the state employed gukurahundism to marginalize and intimidate people from Matabeleland, the Harare based lawyers were not available.

Save for Bulawayo, the rest of Zimbabwe was disturbingly dead silent on the arrest of Siwela, Gazi and Charles Thomas. Their case was at the high court for years. Instead, a lot of criticism against the government was raised for the arrest of MDCT members, namely the Minister of Energy, Elton Mangoma charged with corruption, Copac Chairperson Douglas Mwonzora charged with inciting violence and former MDC MP Mr Munyaradzi Gwisai accused of planning to topple the government like the Bulawayo trio. The last three were among those arrested in Harare round about the same time with the Bulawayo trio and all were of Shona extraction. The lawyers, civic organizations, churches, the independent press and analysts rallied all their combative rhetoric and resources in defense of the Harare trio. In picturesque idioms, they condemned the Mugabe regime police for taking in the Mashonaland trio for questioning.

By failing to represent the sixty - nine Victoria Falls Hotel dismissed employees, Siwela, Gazi and Thomas, the Zimbabwe Lawyers for Human Rights made a candid statement for all Matabeleland activists to take notice of. They were saying, as long as the Matabele had human rights grievances against the Shona they would not represent the Matabele. If sixty - nine Matabele were dismissed from work after complaining against tribal discrimination by Shona managers, then the Matabele could go hang before the lawyers represented them. If the MLF trio were arrested for peacefully (distributing maps) advocating for the cessation of Matabeleland from Zimbabwe, then they might as well be convicted of treason and languish in jail before the human rights lawyers could represent them. The lawyers were implying that there were no human rights violations by the ZANU PF security apparatus as long as they were clamping down threats to Shona hegemony. The lawyers would not defend any Matabele arrested for resisting Shona economic and cultural dominance. By preserving sectarian interests, the lawyers sacrificed human economic and social security as well as legal ethos at the alter of ethnic Shona nationalism.

When the Bulawayo lawyers took note of the unwillingness by Zimbwabwe Lawyers for Human Rights to provide legal counsel to Siwela and others, they formed their own legal society called Abameli Lawyers Network. Siwela, Gazi and Thomas's case finally awakened and confirmed a long reluctantly observed fact, that even human rights were parceled out discriminatively by the so called lawyers for human rights. The Matabele people were not equal to their Shona counterparts even before human rights lawyers.

Many Chief Executive Officers, General Managers, Operation Managers, Human Resources practitioners, departmental managers, supervisors, lawyers, civil servants and even civic organizations that marginalized and ostracized the people of Matabeleland like the hotel managers above, proved to be surrogates and advocates of gukurahundism. The merchandise of their diabolic actions was the subterranean fortification of generations into dismal poverty, destitution, homelessness, ill health, illiteracy, innumeracy, crime, hunger and ultimately spiritual, psychological and physical death.

As a result, generations of Matabele had to involuntarily forgo economic wellbeing, personal peace, political liberty, cultural identity and even religious freedom and embrace servitude to dominance by the majority. If the Matabele could not hero worship Mugabe, Mnangagwa, Mujuru then it had to be Tsvangiarai, Biti, Chamisa or any other Shona or else they were labeled separatist, divisionist, tribalist and treasonous. Supporting Dumiso Dabengwa, Welshman Ncube, Mqondisi Moyo or Thokozani Khuphe or any other Matabele was labelled as tribal, secessionist and villagising the national political discourse.

If they complained peacefully against dominance and discrimination by Shonas, the Matabele got arrested and dismissed from work. If they could not speak Shona, then they would not be employed and would not be attended to promptly or at all, in many a government offices including police offices. If they protested against non - Ndebele speaking Shona teachers teaching their primary school children, they got arrested and their children would not receive any education. The list of abuses was ad infinitum. Such was the yoke of gukurahundism.

Giving an account of his experiences with the Gukurahundi brigade, Mr. John Gazi, at the 2011 Gukurahundi commemoration, charged that the crafters and implementers of Gukurahundi were still alive and working to fullfil their annihilistic vision. He said that members of the 5th brigade were being imperialistically and surreptitiously filtered from their camp in Kwekwe into the Matabeleland population and were being allocated land under the fast track government resettlement program. He went on to dispute the often cited figure of 30 000 as victims of Gukurahundi as a malevolent ploy to downplay the devastation and desolation of Matabeleland. He put the figure instead, at half a million dead.

What the Gukurahundi forces could not crush brutishly like the 100 000, they subjugated by gukurahundism and re - oriented so thoroughly only a resilient few could dare identify with their proud Ndebele past. For example, many former ZAPU members that joined ZANU PF due to the Unity agreement of 1987 got so intoxicated with their new party they embraced with gusto those malpractices they had previously loathed. In dread of being perceived as not being ZANU PF enough, they got so exhilarated with their new identity so much, they too, derided and denounced as sellouts their former colleagues in ZAPU that did not convert to ZANU PF or that later left the new party like Dabengwa and Thenjiwe Lesabe.

It was the character of gukurahundism to shamelessly use unfounded, blatant tribalist labeling or a torrent of constant tribal overtones and anecdotes to deal with those that were no longer liked, needed or loyal, so as to discredit them. Almost always, the one branded a tribalist was one attempting to stand against tribal discrimination like former Matabeleland North governor Welshman Mabhena, top legislator Sydney Malunga and former Bulawayo mayor Joshua Malinga. ZANU PF was accommodative to and comfortable only with those Matabele that were content with playing bigotry and being well paid and well fed slaves. Once labeled a tribalist, many would rather gravitate away from their policy path in frustration than suffer the consequence. If they opted to be obdurate then a violent campaign to remove them from the system ensued. Witness how Mr. Welshman Mabhena was discharged by Mugabe from the office of Governor of Matabeleland North, for demanding an end to the marginalization of his people.

One's ethnic identity, in gukurahundism became the basis for either their empowerment if they were Shona or marginalization if they were Matabele. The nepotism of gukurahundism was not evidenced only between Ndebele and Shona but it pitted one sub - Shona group against another, with the Zezuru destined for the fattest worm. Access to employment, appointment, loans, scholarship and tenders became a clandestine affair determined by whom you were, whom you knew, and where you came from and absolutely nothing to do with meritocracy.

Ndzimu - Unami (2012) classified gukurahundism as the *"Shonalization"* of Matabeleland because of its insistence that the Shona language be spoken by everyone everywhere, while the Shona people adamantly refused to speak the languages of Matabeleland. That was designed to kill and make extinct all other languages and cultures so that only the Shona language remained as the means of communication in Zimbabwe. The agents of Shonalisation included churches, especially Pentecostal churches founded in Harare, government departments, private companies, banks etc, that had made it a policy to man every office in Matabeleland with Shonas as well as radio and television stations that spoke in Shona and played Shona songs from sun up to sun down, thereby compelling listeners to learn the Shona language, he opined.

The marginalization of Matabeleland was subtle gukurahundism, which involved a furtive and inconspicuous systematic pulling down of the structures, practices and institutions that make a people themself. That was the more insidious and sadistic manifestation of gukurahundism, more so because it was silent and salient, therefore capable of prolonged poisonous infliction. It was simple to identify, understand and prove, yet it was vehemently disputed, denied and ignored. Its negative impact was therefore more profound and deep seated. That brand was most effective like the long acting poison that it was. It had a capacity to elude, like an odorless killer vapor that is released into space, unseen, unheard, unfelt and untouched. For a moment it is all around, it becomes one's environment and one becomes part of it. It is extremely annihilative. It becomes one's life before it becomes their death. People merely collapse and drop dead without choking or talking. That is how a language and a people are rendered extinct, by ignoring and excluding them from the mainstream while engaging everybody else. By pulling down their institutions and practices, for example ridiculing the need for a Ndebele monarch and delegalizing the coronation of King Bulelani Lobhengula Khumalo in March 2018 by the Mnangagwa regime.

That brand of gukurahundism in Matabeleland was epitomized by the 1979 Shona Grand Plan and its review of 2005. Thus far, the provisions of the plan had been applied with Swiss efficiency and clinical accuracy. The aim being, to terminate the human development of all the tribes of Matabeleland by forcing them to retreat into political invisibility, cultural oblivion, economic stupor, ethnic dubiety and social death in the face of triumphant majoritarian nationalism. Awestruck by the domineering spirit of gukurahundism exuding from the Shona aristocracy, the Ndebele euphemistically referred to Harare as *"bambazonke"* or the one that grabs gluttonously, all opportunities be they social, economic or political.

That aristocratic hegemonic immorality subscribed to the Centre / Core - Periphery theory. The centre - periphery theory as propagated by Friedman in Raagmaa (2003:3) espoused that *"the periphery is totally subordinated to the centre of political and economic dominance. The industries producing the highest extra-value are located in the core area"*. In Zimbabwe the centre was Harare, Mashonaland (Central, West and East), ZANU PF and Mugabe / Mnangagwa. According to the centre - periphery theory, development is always concentrated at the centre. Harare was the centre that housed parliament, cabinet, the judiciary and foreign embassies. Due to that focus on the centre, the capital benefited from development bias, as better jobs, improved housing, superior health care and education, lower prices of commodities as well as economic opportunities abounded in Mashonaland and ZANU PF for the benefit of the majority tribe. On the other hand the outlying regions and towns, or the periphery which was Bulawayo, Matabeleland, the Ndebele and other areas such as the Midlands, Masvingo and Manicaland lost out on development opportunities as there was inferior infrastructural development, poor government service provision, capital flight, brain drain, unemployment, higher cost of living et cetera.

While the centre – periphery phenomenon was not unique to Zimbabwe, what made the Zimbabwe case tragic was the *Bambazonke* syndrome. Not satisfied with the opportunities that abounded at the centre, the government dispensed their tribemen including school leavers and school drop outs from the centre, to voraciously and garrulously grab all jobs, land, contracts, tenders, college / university places, loans etc at the periphery. They even relocated industries, businesses and head offices of big and small companies from Bulawayo to Harare and in the process they crippled the economy.

Thoko Mkhwananzi of Nissan North America Inc, summed it all up when she espoused that there were a number of strategies employed by the enemies of Matabeleland including, *"Isolating and marginalizing the group: (pushing it out of the mainstreams of society), firing or laying off of Mthwakazi people from all government jobs and removing them from all civil service positions. Nazi Germany did the same towards the Jews, the Communists did the same thing in Russia, the Eastern bloc countries, China and Cuba. In Nazi Germany the Jews were denied positions in banks and most businesses. Those holding such positions were terminated. In Russia, China and other communist countries, the marginalized groups were denied higher education, all but menial jobs were precluded and all civil service except the military was prohibited. Mthwakazi has been denied all positions of influence in public life, government, meetings, legislatures, or anything that promotes the cause of Mthwakazi....*

Vilification, slandering and trashing of the group: the group is portrayed as evil, villainous, anti-social, dangerous miscreants who represent a very danger for the entire society. Years of this propaganda makes other tribes indifferent to the treatment and the plight of Mthwakazi. The people of Mthwakazi who are being vilified by anti-Semitic propaganda as having stolen cattle and women from the other tribe, are now labeled as subversive. The media now portrays the people of Mthwakazi as ignorant, unscientific, superstitious, absurd, crackpots, irrational, poor and we have fallen for that lie.

The period following the appending of the signatures to the Unity Accord witnessed the hiring of employees from Mashonaland in all levels and structures of employment and the neglect and dismissal of the Matabeleland tribes. It was ensured that managers were of Shona origin so that they would recruit their kith and kin and fellow tribesmen. They would come in hordes by all modes of transport, arriving in the morning, get the job in the afternoon and after work, search for lodgings. Meanwhile the locals would be queuing for those same jobs and would not get them. Soon it became an accepted norm that all employees and employers in both the public and private sectors were Shonas.

Not content with importing only those skills considered as rare, the system brought from Mashonaland, receptionists, cashiers, shop attendants, bank tellers, teachers, security guards, waiters, ice cream vendors, traffic cops, public area cleaners, delivery van drivers etc. To add insult to injury, the bused in workers were almost always incapable of and unwilling to speak Ndebele or any other Matabeleland language. It became the standard that a service provider would unashamedly state that he/she did not understand the local language and demand that the customer addresses them in Shona. It fast became taboo and a punishable offence in one way or the other for anyone even in rural Matabeleland to say they did not understand Shona, especially at the workplace or in the presence of the police, the army and prison officers.

The work setting simply became a Shona domain so much that some Shonas even had the audacity to complain to management if a shop attendant addressed them in Ndebele in Matabeleland. The 'offending' employee would be given a tongue lashing by management if they were lucky. If out of luck they would be demoted or dismissed.

Due to their superior numbers, economic muscle and political clout, to the ordinary Shona it was not beyond the borders of reason that they found their tribesmen permeating all sectors of socio - political, economic, religious and cultural life of Matabeleland. To them it was a blessing and business as usual when they found Shonas occupying all the jobs, owning the houses, occupying the political leadership roles, filling the church pews and singing their songs at all funerals in a region far from theirs. That, they thought was enterprising and a display of their inherent all – round acumen. Little did they realize the dismay and disapproval of some of the various tribes of Matabeleland that felt they were being gradually displaced and crowded out of their homes, land, jobs, culture and even lives.

Although they did not realize that they were beneficiaries of grabbed or even stolen loot, some of them must have noticed or sensed how unfair and encumbering Harare's all – grabbing culture was to Matabeleland, especially after some Matabeles had protested, as many did over the years.

The concept of domineering and intolerant Shona nationalism was argued by Mlambo (2013) when he argued that, *"The more extreme Shona nationalists were even denouncing Ndebeles who were critical of ZANU-PF policies as recent newcomers to the country who had no stake in it and should go back to Zululand where they originally came from. Increasingly, therefore, nationalism or national identity became little more than a narrow Shona chauvinistic particularism inspired by rising xenophobic tendencies"*.

It was the antiquated ideology of the 'holier than thou', that influenced the birth of the 'more Zimbabwean than thou' mentality, which in turn informed the 1979 Shona Grand Plan. The plan that placed the Ndebele in the league of settlers together with whites. The whites were effectively dealt with in 1980 and the Ndebele were works in progress, it was said. As opined by an elderly Bulawayo resident in 2010 during the Constitutional Parliamentary Committee (COPAC) outreach exercise, the Ndebele during the liberation struggle in the 1960s and

1970s had had a dangerous memory lapse. They chose to forget that they too were an ethnic minority like the whites. They also forgot that according to some Shona elite, they too, like the whites, were settlers, since a 150 years back they had settled in Matabeleland from Zululand. Had they not forgotten that, probably the Ndebele would not have been caught unawares by the Gukurahundi Brigade whirwind and gukurahundism.

The quest for total monopoly and uncontested ownership of all territorial dimensions, national identity, national history and the political space could and would eventually culminate in friction with the ZANU government on one hand and the Ndebele and the other ethnic groups domiciled in Matabeleland on the other. The only respite was a desperate belief in the possible correlation between nationalism and ethnicism as urgued by Msindo (2007). According to Msindo (2007), nationalism and ethnicity could co - exist in a complementary and correlated setup.

Nation building was supposed to be based on inclusivity and equity of all tribes under an umbrella of a Zimbabwe country, free from dominance and impositions by one group, just as God intended it to be. Probably the Zimbabwe nation project would work under such an accommodative arrangement. Witch hunting Mugabe and ZANU PF disqualified themselves very early from the class of nation builders when they either authored or implemented the 1979 Shona Grand Plan or both.

The Gukurahundists failed to remember that, God the Almighty in his immense and unbounded wisdom fashioned mankind. Then in a prelude that men has since failed to fathom, God made men diverse, distinct and matchless. God cherishes diversity but men loathes diversity and countless times has exploited it, selfishly resulting in dominance, hate, revulsion, conflict and death. God diversified mankind into races, tribes, clans, families and individuals that came with assorted colours, cultures, languages and dialects. He did not create stereotypes and copycats but gave mankind the power to make choices. Mankind oftentimes opts to usurp and maltreat this power by attempting to generalize and make everyone *homologos*. Those that resist pressure to conform are crudely beaten into submission and are ultimately twisted out of their original variety to subsist in an adulterated continuation, far from God's plan for them to be distinct and unique.

Those that insisted on maintaining their identity and creed were branded sell-outs, turncoats and treasonous by gukurahundism. If not their lives, then their characters were assassinated with the usual yet convincing (to the majority) presidential diatribe. They were rejected by the system and condemned, more so, if they attempted to speak out against what they perceived as injustice and prejudice. The consequences of that labeling ranged from mere exclusion to murder and even genocide. Like most mankind when under siege, some bent over backwards to be accommodated into the domineering majority's identity for certain gains and in the process lost their God given exclusivity, uniqueness and individuality. That act of self colonization or surrender often resulted in acceptance and rewards such as power, office and money. Power and or money being the most portent forces to impel mankind, then caused the beneficiaries to be agents of that colonization and they thus perpetuated the new master's agenda within their own kind with mindboggling fervour and overzealousness.

Due to such undue pressure from the dominant, it was prevalent, especially in Africa, for a people to be aggrieved on tribal grounds. When it was the minority (as it often was) that felt discriminated against and inclined to protest, they easily got dismissed as petty and pusillanimous cry babies. Any demands for fairness, justice and equality earned them the wrath of the majority who were often the ruling class and therefore had the law in their whims and the security instruments at their disposal. The minority tribes in most of Africa found themselves pursued by the army, charged by the police and tortured by the secret police if they were lucky to escape murder by the militia.

The label of tribalist is the nemesis of many an Ndebele in Zimbabwe. It is the ultimate tragedy of being Matabele in a country governed by a tribal majority. The leaders of the Matabele including Joshua Nkomo, Chief Khayisa Ndiweni the Ndebele paramount chief from Ntabazinduna, Chief Nhlanhlayamangwe Ndiweni from Ntabazinduna, Archbishop Pius Ncube of the Roman Catholic Church and winner of Scotland's Robert Burns Humanitarian Award, Welshman Mabhena former governor of Matabeleland North, Joshua Malinga former Mayor of Bulawayo, Dr. Dumiso Dabengwa, former ZPRA Chief of Intelligence in the National Security Organ (NSO), Sydney Malunga former MP for Makokoba, and Professor Welshman Ncube constitutional law expert and leader the Movement for Democratic Change, had three things in common. First they were Ndebele. Second, at one time or another they stood up for the rights of the people of Matabeleland or led organizations which were mostly favoured by people from Matabeleland. Lastly they were accused by the state media and by government agents of being tribalists because they dared to challenge the rule / leadership by a tribal majority.

Tribalism is negative differential treatment of someone or a group of people due to their tribe. That treatment could be denial of privileges that are enjoyed by other tribes or persons of another tribe. It could also be marginalization based on one's ethnic identity. Tribalism encompasses hate and undermining speech, exclusion and omissions prompted by ethnicism.

It is most strange that while all the Matabeleland luminaries and many more were being branded tribalists, none of their Mashonaland contemporaries were ever accused in the press of tribalism. Instead, arch - tribalists and Gukurahundists were always being paraded as angels. With ample evidence of their shameless tribal tendencies in politics, culture, religion, social and economic spheres littered all over the national floor, they seemed to be 'incapable' of tribalism.

On 22 December 1987 Joshua Nkomo on behalf of PF ZAPU and Robert Mugabe standing in for ZANU PF signed a historic concord referred to as the Unity Accord. The manuscript was very elementary and brief in content but exceedingly rich in intrinsic worth, symbolism and significance. In the pact, the feuding parties agreed to form a government of national unity whose president would be Mugabe, the first vice president would be Simon Muzenda, the former's long time colleague (rumoured to be Mugabe's traditional diviner) with Joshua Nkomo coming in as second vice president. There was also unwritten, an understanding that the position of party chairperson would be the preserve of PF ZAPU. It is also rumoured that it was verbally agreed that the next president would be Nkomo or someone from PF ZAPU.

The first unwritten understanding was honored, with the first chairperson being Joseph Msika, then John Nkomo and Simon Khaya Moyo were to follow over the years. After Khaya – Moyo, the position of ZANU PF chairperson was surreptitiously scrapped after the 2013 elections, thereby depriving PF ZAPU of some clout and influence. The provision for a chairperson was most probably scrapped from the party constitution because senior ZANU PF politicians from Mashonaland like Dydmus Mutasa were, after the 2013 elections vying for the position. Their argument was that the unity agreement did not expressly reserve the position of party chairperson for PF ZAPU. While the Mutasas in ZANU PF failed to win the chairpersonship, the former ZAPU lost the same but were probably mollified by the fact that they did not directly lose it to Mutasa and his ilk, without realizing how much power had been withdrawn from their wings.

Over and above those provisions, the document was distressingly mum on everything that would ordinarily concern other negotiators in similar circumstances. For example, the ZANU constitution and name were retained as the supreme law and identity of the new party. The ZANU tradition as reflected by slogans, symbols, songs, regalia and rhetoric were maintained. The accord could easily pass for the most exiguous pact ever put on paper. Its arrogance towards detail was as appalling as was its dearth in common logic. According to critics, it was tantamount to a compromise document, or worse, a surrender certificate. It had so much binding effect, particularly on ZAPU, yet its lack of requisite boardroom and negotiating nomenclature rendered it prone to abuses as was evidenced years later, especially after the death of Nkomo when it was used to warehouse and justify many a political injustice and gimmick. The accord failed to speak to the issues at the heart of the country's turbulent political landscape as far as the contemporary challenges of the time were concerned.

For all intents and purposes the biggest benefactor of the entente was Mugabe and ZANU PF. They could now relax in the knowledge that their headache of twenty - four years had been eventually exorcised and they could embark on the long desired one party state agenda. Now that the leader of the Matabele people had succumbed to the pressure of blood – letting, Mugabe could sweep the Matabeleland problem under the convenient proverbial political carpet. He told himself that he had by the stroke of a pen 'cleansed' himself of the blood of the Matabele and became the uncontested leader of the country in the absence of any formidable opposition, thereby attaining some all – round legitimacy and acceptance, albeit concocted and contrived.

ZANU PF and Mugabe once more fooled Matabeleland in the name of unity. They were not called upon to account for their sins. There was no mention of the Gukurahundi killings, reconciliation, truth telling and reparations. The negotiators missed the proverbial magic bullet. The past was simply ignored by men enlightened enough to know that the future is informed by the past and that history has an eldritch inclination to recur. ZANU PF assumed that by sharing a bit of power with Nkomo, they could appease the living genocide victims and the affected. Far from it. The living were livid, although too traumatized and powerless to even protest. The souls of the dead were restless. How could the dead rest in peace in shallow graves, mine shafts and make - shift mass graves? How could they, when their remains and ashes had been eaten by termites and blown by the winds, never to be found by their relatives?

For Nkomo and ZAPU, the security of the people was the most valued outcome. They were prepared to pay the ultimate price for it. Critics of the Unity Accord fell short of blaming Nkomo for agreeing to the most shallow concord in the history of political party mergers but between the lines the disapproval is detectable. Probably it is easy to be a critic because one is away from the responsibility and immediacy of the circumstances. Dabengwa explained why Nkomo and ZAPU accepted the defective Unity Accord. During the interview on 17 March 2017 he said, *"I agree with the critics. I was released towards signing. I was very angry with the whole thing. I was frustrated so much I stayed away. Nkomo called me and told me people were disgruntled at the absence of ZPRA commanders. I told him I would not be party to it and the agreement was a mistake. He explained that he too did not like it but people were dying and the only solution was the agreement... his words were, 'I signed in real desperation in order to end the continued massacre of the people'. He said he had been told to accept three things: that Mugabe was going to be president, there would be two vice presidents and that the party name was going to be ZANU PF. He was told to accept that or Robert Mugabe would never talk to him until he signed".*

According to the former Bulawayo executive mayor, Japhet Ndabeni Ncube (interview 12 February 2017, Bulawayo), the Unity Accord was a *"sellout for the Ndebeles. The saddest moment. Nkomo missed it at Lancaster and by signing the Unity Accord. Those are his two greatest errors".*

Ndabeni Ncube argued that, after Mugabe had proposed negotiations, Nkomo assigned Sydney Malunga to identify and supervise people to draft the ZAPU proposal of the agreement. Malunga had proceeded to identify Ndabeni Ncube, Agrippa Madlela, John Nkomo and others. The team met many times at Churchill hotel in Bulawayo and eventually produced a detailed dossier that covered various facets of the agreement. He said they had proposed five names for the party and had detailed a set up of equal representation of both ZAPU and ZANU in cabinet as well as equitable balance in the civil service, parastatals etc. they had done a thorough exercise in addressing future relations between the two parties and had crossed all the *t*s and dotted all the *i*s. They had paid meticulous attention to the requisite detail.

Ndabeni Ncube revealed that he and his colleagues were awaiting feedback from their negotiators in Harare when they heard on television that the Unity Accord had been sealed. He said that he and Madlela did not accept the Unity Accord and quit ZAPU on that day, shocked at the shallow contents of the agreement which had not taken even one proposal from the ZAPU side.

Professor Welshman Ncube (interview 29 March 2017, Bulawayo) agreed and differed with the critics as he contended that, *"Textually, pedagogically it's an extremely shallow document. It could not be otherwise, because basic terms were dictated..... There was no negotiation.... It was take it or leave it. From a regulatory point of view, it's rudimentary. In terms of impact and what it did to save lives, it is historically a very important document. It gave people under martial law and systematic genocide.... a measure of sanity. It was certainly not a surrender document, which is when there are two warring parties. Here only one side was armed….. At the end of it all there were about a hundred something dissidents emerging but you put a country on lock down mode. You kill so many people in a supposed war against hundred dissidents. For all practical purposes this was a war, military operation against civilians. I would never call it a surrender document. It was as an act of recognition that something needed to be done, however politically unpalatable, to stop brazen killing of civilians, Nkomo was not fighting back, he controlled no army. ZAPU was not fighting back, they controlled nobody. They were just being killed just like flies…. Nkomo decided that the best thing is to save lives. That is why the agreement is important. It stopped a genocide".*

As pointed out by Ncube above, there was undoubtedly one gain for Matabeleland and the Midlands. Nkomo's aspiration was attained. The horrific illegalities, the systemic and ruthless killings, kidnappings and disappearances of ZAPU supporters and the general Matabele population, ceased. Against the advice and feelings of some of his lieutenants, Nkomo chose to become a half wit who acceded to a defective entente so that the Matabele could live.

Be that as it may, the Zezuru buccaneers' hegemonic aspirations were triumphantly on the march for the second time in eight years. Another gain for ethno nationalism was the fact that Mugabe could abuse the technicality that the accord provided for a vice president from ZAPU and not necessarily from Matabeleland. As seen after the death of Nkomo, Mugabe appointed Joseph Msika (a Zezuru) from ZAPU to be the country vice president. That was a travesty and Mugabe knew Msika would pander to regional interests, while making believe that he represented Matabeleland. As Jonathan Moyo fittingly observed, there existed "...*a clique in Zanu PF that unashamedly believes in the domination of national politics by one ethnic group under the cover of some self-serving language of revolutionary nationalism and the Unity Accord of 1987. For example, under the Unity Accord, the ruling clique in Zanu PF has taken the view that former Zapu leaders are entitled to one of the positions of vice-president and that whoever occupies that position, even if they do not come from Matabeleland as is the case with Joseph Msika, necessarily represents Matabeleland as if ZAPU and Matabeleland mean one and the same thing. ZAPU is no more, while Matabeleland lives with political interests that must be addressed along with the interests of other regions in the country…… Such a view is neither revolutionary nor national — it is tribal, reactionary and wholly unacceptable*". Moyo was in agreement with Msindo (2004:265) who had suggested that ZANU PF's idea of unity was among other creeds defined by "*Shona tribal dominance as opposed to nationalism*".

The spirit behind the provision for a second vice president was for the people of Matabeleland to be represented in a presidency that reflected respect for ethnic diversity and regional balance. Instead Mugabe opted not to be circumspect around the concept of ethnic and reginal equity and circumvented the concord which had been signed in good faith by Nkomo. Consequently, and due to other reasons, soon after the death of Nkomo, a new party called ZAPU 2000, a reincarnation of ZAPU was formed. Shortly afterwards Dumiso Dabengwa and other ZAPU stalwarts withdrew ZAPU from ZANU PF amid a lot of allegations of tribalism from Mugabe and his associates.

It is hard to say if the multitude of losses resulting from the unity accord outweighed the single gain for Matabeleland. One of the losses was that the settlement opened the floodgates for the migration of the various Mashonaland sub - tribes into Matabeleland. Having previously viewed the region as hostile to ZANU and therefore by extension to Shonas, Matabeleland had not experienced serious immigration, save for civil servants and quasi public servants. The signing of the Unity Accord symbolized the lowering of the guards as there was a cessation of open hostilities between the two major regions. The state exploited the opportunity for internal colonialism by moving people from Mashonaland into Matabeleland in droves. With political clout and economic leverage on arrival, they seized every conceivable occupation from public area cleaner to Chief Executive while the locals were jobless. Daringly, a few years later the new comers assumed elected offices to represent the people of Matabelcland in local councils, municipalities and in the two houses of parliament, in a bizzare replication of colonial Belgian policy of *"we will dominate you to serve you"* (Sithole 1959).

Much to the dismay of Matabeleland, the new arrivals pursued a visible yet myopic agenda of marginalizing the Matabeleland tribes whom they excluded from employment and denied other economic empowerment opportunities. In a way, the accord became a continuation of the genocide by stopping it with the left hand yet commissioning it with the right hand. Before the Unity Accord, the Matabele were dying a political and physical death in a brazen genocide executed by the army, after the Unity Accord, they were dying a social, economic, cultural and spiritual death in a soft genocide perpetrated via civillians.

Over a period of almost three decades after the Gukurahundi genocide and the pacifying Unity Accord, the two main ethnic groups of Zimbabwe, the Shona making up 80% of the population and the Ndebele who were 18%, had never been further apart. The political arrangement that merged ZAPU and ZANU fell way below the target of reconciling the masses. The Unity Accord was perceived by many as a power sharing pact between the leaders only, more so when the anxiously awaited fruits of independence and unity still remained the proverbial pie in the sky for Matabeleland. Worse still the accord made assurance double sure that truth and reconciliation became sacrificial lambs for political peace which never translated into sustainable social and economic development.

The most sadistic and satanic treatment and certain way to annihilate a people is to deny them water. The Unity Accord failed to provide water to Bulawayo and her industries. A basic requirement and a right. According to Mr. Arnold Payne (The Weekly Agenda), the government deliberately failed to supply water to Bulawayo and Matabeleland. In a position paper, Payne revealed that in 1992 the Bulawayo City Council had collected from its residents and business community twenty million dollars for the construction of the Gwayi / Shangani dam which experts said would solve permanently the water crisis in the region. The government vetoed the plan and decreed that dam construction was the prerogative and duty of the government.

The government preferred the construction of a pipeline from the Zambezi river stretching through Matabeleland North to Bulawayo. The twenty million dollars was confiscated by the state and allegedly deposited into the government created Matabeleland Zambezi Water Trust (MZWT) Intermarket Bank account. The money was never recovered. The Zambezi river pipeline project was a luminous idea, if it could be coupled with the political will and financial commitment by the government. The idea was first conceived in 1912 but successive governments failed to allocate it a budget for one hundred plus years. After independence in 1980 the idea suffered multiple still births every five years after elections. According to Payne the artificial thirst imposed on Matabeleland was a means of punishing the region for not supporting ZANU PF.

The Unity Accord failed to generate equitable economic prospects for the Matabeleland entrepreneur as evidenced by the grim none emergence of a renowned economic entrepreneur from the region in almost four decades. While Mashonaland produced business moguls and economic magnets in the mould of Robert Mugabe, Mutumwa Mawere, Philip Chiyangwa, Peter Pamire, Roger Boka, Nigel Chanakira, Strive Masiyiwa, Shingi Munyeza, Ignatius Chombo, Solomon Mujuru, Emmerson Mnangagwa, Kudakwashe Tagwirei, Supa Mandiwanzira, Wicknel Chivayo, Aaron Chinhara to mention but a few, Matabeleland could not even produce enough primary school teachers for her few schools. Mashonaland became home to powerful and rich economic and or political tycoons and barons, all products of ZANU PF, independence and the Unity Accord. Each one of them was richer than the entire minority Smith cabinet in 1980. Black empowerment became a preserve for Mashonaland business giants. The system, for the Mashonaland elite, yielded a powerful and portentous ZANU PF and Shona bourgeoisie, more intent on self aggrandizement, self preservation, Shona dominance and regime security than on peace, equality and equity. For the Matabele, including those in ZANU, the system was encumbering and impoverishing.

The only figure from Matabeleland who amassed some sizeable wealth was Obert Mpofu, the Member of Parliament for Umguza near Bulawayo. During his tenure as Minister of Mines Mpofu appointed some Matabele into the board of directors of the Hwange Colliery Company which mined coal in Hwange, Matabeleland North as well as into the board of Clay Products in Bulawayo. The previous Shona ministers had always appointed Shonas into the board as was the norm in most ministries. As soon as Mpofu was reshuffled from the Mines Ministry, the next minister of Shona descent fired the board and appointed his kinsmen.

Mpofu also acquired assets and opened up businesses in transport, tourism, banking, cattle ranching, wild life and, retail. He had many business interests in Bulawayo, Victoria Falls and Hwange town where he employed many local people. For daring to challenge Zezuru monopoly and probably for investing in Matabeleland, his home area, Mpofu earned the wrath of the law, the press and therefore the gullible masses even from Matabeleland. Despite being a financial minnow by comparison to his Mashonaland counterparts, and a recent entrent into the list of the rich, Mpofu became the face of corruption. He was judged by the court of public opinion and found guilty. He was hauled to the courts of law charged with corruption.

Mpofu, like Jonathan Moyo, in business and in academia respectively were perceived to be attempting to outshine the Zezuru. By so doing they violated the golden rule of Zimbabwean tribal relations. They were promptly re – oriented and instructed on Robert Greene's (1998) first law of power, to *"never outshine the master"*. Between them, they were threatening to outdo the Shona hegemonic pinnacle of wealth and intellectual luster respectively. They failed to make the master more brilliant than the master actually was and therefore had to be reigned in. Bad publicity and court action proved to be the panacea for the master. Mpofu and Moyo became some of the most negatively talked about politicians even in Matabeleland especially within the opposition, yet by comparison with their Mashonaland contemporaries they were nanus.

The 1987 Unity Accord and the nationalism narrative hastily transmuted into a modern day Rudd Concession, a political colonising charter. A usurp instrument, deliberately made shallow in content yet bearing colossal repercursions. It opened wide the floodgates for the recolonisation of Matabeleland, this time by blacks. It helped ZANU PF sustain an iron grip of socio - political dominance around the neck of Matabeleland. Under the giant lock and key of economic marginalization, Matabeleland was groaning and dying as the isolationist and exclusionist policy of gukurahundism took its inevitable toll.

After the death of Joshua Nkomo in 1999, the Unity Accord became a celebration of his political demise and defeat, and that of, ZAPU and the Matabele. That idea was noted by The Weekly Agenda, a Bulawayo produced weekly newspaper published by Bulawayo Agenda a non - governmental organisation in its edition of 31 July to 06 August 20**. In the editor's column, it was observed that, *"... It is alarming that despite the fact that we have a government of National Unity, many members of society still remain sidelined. We feel that the connotation of the name Karigamombe is an insult to the late Dr. Joshua Mqabuko Nkomo, his family, the people of Matabeleland and Zimbabwe. It is a clear indication that this is a strategy to belittle Dr. Nkomo's contribution to the liberation struggle and undermine his significance to the development of Zimbabwe. The name is a ridicule of the PF ZAPU election symbol and is an indication that Dr. Nkomo was defeated.....The placing of his statue at the Karigamombe centre is a stark reminder of the gukurahundi era where PF ZAPU and its supporters were subjected to a crackdown of violence and ridicule. We concur with the Nkomo family and like - minded Zimbabweans that this is a reminder of the marginalisation that the Matabeleland region has suffered since independence".*

The name Karigamombe was Shona and it meant to fell the bull/cow. The ZAPU party symbol was a black charging bull. There was a school of thought which espoused that the name Karigamombe alluded to Joshua Nkomo himself because his surname meant 'cattle'. That protest, like thousands other remonstrations against injustice fell on deaf ears. The Karigamombe structure retained its name and the government did not even bother responding to the concern as was the norm. The building remained, to be a bitter reminder of a disageeable past to all the Matabele who were at grips with their history. They bowed their heads in shame every time they could not help but walk past the structure, as all the unpleasantries of political, cultural, social and economic subjugation rushed through their minds. Yet for many a Shona, it was just another structure with a good local name and deserving little fuss. To the elite Gukurahundists it was an edifice of past and present and promising future glory. In a permanent attitude of elated triumph, the ZANU PF political nabobs mockingly moralized about unity to the most ethnically divided land in Africa south of the equator.

Mlambo (2012) argued that at face value, the Unity Accord was deemed to have resolved inter - tribal conflict, yet the Gukurahundi massacres had militated deep resentment among some Ndebele people, not only towards the government and ZANU PF but also towards the Shona people in general. He cited the formation of the secessionist Mthwakazi Liberation Front (MLF) which was advocating for the creation of a separate state of the Matabeleland region called uMthwakazi. By 2016 more separatist political parties had been formed in Matabeleland and in the diaspora by people resolved on self determination and driven by the desire to distance the region from Mashonaland as far as possible.

On 11 January 2014 the Mthwakazi Republic Party (MRP) was launched in Bulawayo. In an interview on 25 March 2017, Mqondisi Moyo the party president explained his party position as: *"(t)he party came into existence after realizing that the merging of Mashonaland with Mthwakazi was undertaken in bad faith. This is substantiated by the 1979 Grand Plan which is the satanic framework crafted by some Shona people under the leadership of Robert Mugabe to dominate and eliminate the Mthwakazi nation. This saw programs like Gukurahundi being implemented.... Apart from killing our people, the ZANU PF government after Gukurahundi came up with indirect programs to intensify their domination.....our children are taught by Shona teachers.....all influencial positions are controlled by Shona people. MRP serves to destroy the satanic marriage that was forcefully imposed by the British.... We are fighting for the restoration agenda".*

Mashingaidze (2005) concurred that the Unity Accord fell short of international expectations and standards for such a concord by stating that, *"(t)he 1987 Unity Accord ended the war but did not bring peace and reconciliation. It was elitist and embodied a top – down approach to governance. Nkomo and Mugabe signed the Accord and then sold it to the people. The grassroots were never consulted in the peace – making process and no reconciliation efforts were made".* Indeed, some of the people of Matabeleland bought the unity accord out of respect for Nkomo. After Nkomo's death in 1999 they condemned it for the sham and defective product that it was and sought to return it to the manufacturer, Mugabe by reviving ZAPU. Mugabe however would have none of that. He held on in intense despair and defiance to the mast of unity like a rug in the wind, more out of selfish political mercenary self - interest and a twisted sense of a gone by tribal idealism than out of sober realism.

After the unity agreement and more so after the death of Joshua Nkomo, the term 'unity' became the most convoluted and enunciated term in politburo meetings, cabinet meetings, national executive meetings, rallies, caucuses and parliament. It then follows that it thereby became the most abused, therefore dangerously inhibitive term for Matabeleland. In the name and shelter of unity, the worst tribalistic injustices were committed by the government and political parties to the detriment of Matabeleland. Matabeleland was handcuffed to a stationery train of unity. They were not going anywhere.

The damage inflicted by the Mugabe regime in its first six years on Matabeleland during peace times relegated the damage inflicted by the Smith regime on Southern Rhodesia in fifteen years of open hostilities and war. The further damage inflicted on the body of Matabeleland by the same regime after the Unity Accord was as equally economically bankrupting and socially encumbering as was the gukurahundi genocide.

The abuse of the term unity by Mugabe and ZANU PF was aptly captured by Prof. Sabelo Gatsheni – Ndlovu (2002) when he argued that ZANU PF believed in *"monolithic unity"* which ignored diversity and pluralism but pursued the swallowing or embalming of all. He contended that that was proven in 1980 when ZANU PF embraced PF ZAPU in a unity government only for the latter to be hunted and haunted out of the government for pursuing a separate identity as a distinct political party. That all - encompassing and subsuming ideology of ZANU PF was further laid bare seven years later, when after signing the unity accord with ZAPU, the new name for the new party was still ZANU PF.

Contrary to the common belief, there is everything in a name. The name is the identity of the holder. It is the face of the individual or institution. To it is attached the reputation, beliefs and practices. When ZANU PF refused to change their name after the unity agreement, Nkomo must have realized the peril ahead. ZANU PF was not prepared to change in any way, like a duck that jumps into the water and emerges dry. There was not going to be any alterations by way of policy or practice. Consequently, ZANU PF emerged from the negotiating table unchanged, unrefined, unaffected and above all unrepentant. ZANU PF did not merely maintain her name but everything attached to it was hanging dangerously from her haunches like a bloody dagger. Her culture and practice of witch hunting, disenfranchisement, character assassination, impunity, ridicule, violence, murder etc, were intact if not stronger, while ZAPU vaporized into thin air. ZAPU was only accommodated as a parasitic partner.

The quantum of social, political, cultural and economic damage inflicted on Matabeleland by the Mugabe regime after the 1987 concord was colossal and confounding. The number of casualties of gukurahundism kept rising. The crimes of social domination and discrimination as well as economic marginalization were disguised or explained away in the name of unity. If anyone dared invoke attention to the vices by government and even by the private sector institutions they were quickly branded as divisive, sectarian, tribal, regional and anti the spirit of unity. The government conveniently forgot that the much trumpeted unity was between ZAPU and ZANU only. It was not between Matabeleland and Mashonaland. There were many people in the two regions that did not subscribe to the notion of unity between the two, while there were many who were neither ZAPU nor ZANU.

The argument was always that there was no difference between Ndebele and Shona since both were Zimbabwean, hence the former could not complain if a company in Matabeleland engaged only the Shona as employees. The people of Matabeleland were not supposed to protest if the government expropriated farms from white farmers in the region and allocated them to Shona farmers. Such a change of ownership did not in any way improve the livelihoods of the local people but when they protested they were dismissed as tribalist and divisive. There was something incredibly awry in the system that condemned the ownership of the bulk of the best agricultural land in the country by a few white people, yet it condoned the ownership of most and the best farms, hunting concessions, jobs and businesses in Matabeleland by Shona people. If that was not the climax of degeneracy and depravity, then God help us.

At times the advice proffered to Matabeleland job seekers was that the world had become a global village and her youth had to market themselves for global jobs competition. While that was wise counsel, ignoring marginalization at home and expecting to be empowered in foreign countries was tantamount to helping forge the chains that bound and gagged Matabeleland. Only a severe and rare poverty of thought could condemn the Matabele for demanding their economic, political, cultural, social and religious space taken away by the majoritarian regime.

While ZANU PF embarked on a trail - blazing orgy of self - deceit and en masse brain washing, using the name of Joshua Nkomo and the concept of unity as a training manual to achieve blind allegiance, Matabeleland was bleeding and remained largely alienated. As ZANU PF attempted to use unity as a talismanic mantra and panacea for all challenges, most of which they themselves were inventing along the way, the people of Matabeleland were quietly and bitterly calling for justice for crimes committed against them. They longed for the day when they would be treated fairly and equally with their Mashonaland counterparts, as a sign of reconciliation and ultimate peace. That day however was nowhere in sight.

Their calls were never answered as nationalism and unity deteriorated into a dual curse. Under Mugabe, nationalism became a euphemism for Shona hegemony and subtle annexation. That was evidenced by their occupation in both Mashonaland

and Matabeleland of all jobs from managers, priests, shop attendants, civil servants, bank tellers, security guards, drivers (of everything on wheels), hawkers, politicians and vendors. The list was endless. They took over land under the various government resettlement schemes, houses, political office, social roles and rigidly imposed their culture in churches and even in funeral proceedings.

The metamorphosis from Zimbabwe nationalism which was the dream of every nationalist during the war of liberation across the political and ethnic divide, to sectarian ZANU PF nationalism and eventually Shona nationalism was conceived during the liberation struggle soon after the birth of ZANU in 1963 and precipitated by Mugabe's original sin of Gukurahundi and its sequel gukurahundism. By Gukurahundi he initiated, escalated and perfected a sleazy legacy of tribal discrimination between his Shona tribe and the Matabele. ZANU PF bequeathed on the country, a sordid legacy that traumatizingly hovered over the country like a cloud of devouring locusts. Their typology of nationalism, if unchecked could only result in chaos, contestation, conflict and even more bloodshed in future years.

Due to their tribal nationalism, the Shona elite became powerful autocrats whose word was the law. No one could challenge the word decreed by ZANU PF barons like Sydney Sekeramayi, Emmerson Mnangagwa, Solomon Mujuru, Edison Zvobgo, Simon Muzenda, Dydmus Mutasa, Nathan Shamuyarira and in later years, Saviour Kasukuwere, Ignatious Chombo, and Grace Mugabe etc. Some of them were happy for an opportunity to brag about their ill gotten wealth and power even on national television. Vice President Simon Muzenda was broadcast on ZBC television bragging that, *"kana Mugabe asipo ndotonga ini....Ukangofambafamba wayenda iwe"* (if Mugabe is away, I am the ruler... if you move around you die). That was how reckless the power and the money had driven the ruling class. The country groaned under the leadership by a tribal cabal and ethnic cronies assisted by a coterie of boot lickers handpicked for their blind loyalty and economic desperation from Matabeleland.

The hired Matabele peons became a sorry lot of uninfluential and powerless hangers-on, ranging from as high as second vice president to as low as party district chairperson. It did not matter what prestigious office one occupied in government, ZANU PF, MDC T or civic society organization, if one was Matabele they were merely a figurehead without the authority that usually came with the office.

A case in point was when a relatively unknown Masunda from Mashonaland by descent hauled Vice President John Nkomo to court over a hunting concession in

Gwayi, Matabeleland North, a stone's throw from Nkomo's birth place. Nkomo lost the case. While it was celebrated as an indication of the independence of the judiciary, it was however an undisputed exhibition of the bias and selectivity of gukurahundism. Nkomo smashed the record of being the first Vice President and first member of the ZANU PF presidium to be dragged to court by a virtually unknown citizen and go on to lose the case in a judiciary system that was partisan. The message was there, on the wall, salient and smelly. Nkomo was Ndebele and Masunda was Shona and the system protected its own. No youth from Matabeleland not even one drunk with the most potent of herbs or chemicals could ever dream of taking Muzenda, Mujuru, Mnangagwa or Chiwenga to court in dispute over land ownership in Dotito, or anywhere in Mashonaland for that matter. Masunda's confidence was in his Shona identity which had to be protected at all costs.

The Nkomo – Masunda debacle showed beyond doubt that it did not matter how high in the structures of government and ZANU PF a Matabele was, he/ she was less influencial than any Shona from the streets. Many of the people of Matabeleland did not have the means and power of Jonathan Moyo's sharp tongue and quick pen, both of which he employed to diffuse gukurahundism's attempts to disenfranchise and marginalize him. They therefore were forced to learn the Shona language in order to subsist on their own land, get employed, survive employment dismissal or other labour malpractice. They had to be seen to be embarrassed by their own languages and speak Shona or suffer abuse by public servants and private sector personnel as they sought to access bank loans or to even get past a police road block.

Mugabe's brand mutated into a tribalism form of nationalism where all the ethnic groups had to kneel at the altar of self denial, unremittingly singing Shona songs at church, listening to Shona music in public buses, watching Shona drama on national television, having Shona clergy sermonize in Shona at church. That regimen which was prescribed since 18 April 1980 was demonstrated by the daily deliberate practice of having Shona news broadcast first on national radio and television then followed by Ndebele news.

Even the so called independent radio station, Voice of America (VOA)'s studio 7 broadcasting from the citadel of democracy, *egalite* and *fratenite,* Washington DC in the United States was complicit in that practice of Shona superiority. VOA broadcasted news daily from 7 pm to 8:30 pm first in Shona, English and lastly in Ndebele. Due to Mugabe's bantustan policies that forced the people of Matabeleland to learn Shona or sink, by the time the news was broadcast in Ndebele they would have heard them in Shona and in English and it was pointless for anyone to be listening. Most people that understood either Shona or English or both usually switched off the radio or television or changed the station instead of listening to the same news bulletin for the second or third time. Ultimately the Ndebele version of the news was destined to be irrelevant in line with the thrust of gukurahundism. The Ndebele language will be relegated just like the rest of the Matabeleland languages, i.e., Tonga, Nambya, Venda, Sotho, Kalanga, Xhosa etc, languages that were vanquished by gukurahundism at the birth of the so called Zimbabwe nation.

It was most woeful that through a weird combination of patronage and violence, ZANU PF managed to win such Matabeleland characters as has dotted their leadership list from time to time, while the rest of the population remained antagonized to the system of gukurahundism. At independence many in Matabeleland were indifferent towards ZANU PF and Mugabe. Soon afterwards they learnt to detest both. Over the years, the detestation matured into full - blown loathing. After the Unity Accord of 1987 the Matabele that joined ZANU PF did so out of respect and admiration for Joshua Nkomo their leader who had signed the concord and for no other reason. That is why after the death of Nkomo in 1999 ZANU PF started to crack at the seam especially in Matabeleland. By that time, the people of Matabeleland had realized that the Unity Accord was a poisoned chalice. The majority wanted political change. Anything other than Mugabe and ZANU PF would do. For that reason and less out of social approbation or conviction, many a Matabele was quick to support the MDC upon its formation in 1999.

Notwithstanding, despite its glaring shortcomings, the Unity Accord became the sole bridge between Matabeleland and Mashonaland. Tragically, before the ink was even dry on the paper on which it was signed, the accord transformed into a convenient alternating one - way bridge. It was abused by the government to convey a new colonialism with all its attendant evils from Mashonaland to Matabeleland. It was also abused to convey resources and revenue from Matabeleland to Harare. The concord made sure that despite her world class raw materials and abundant natural resources, Matabeleland became a modern day African Tantalus. Tantalus in Greek mythology was punished by the gods who made him to stand neck deep in water with a branch of berries dangling above his head. Whenever he attempted to drink the water, it receded only to rise up again when he quit. Each time he attempted to pluck the berries, the branch was blown away by the wind, then settled above his head again when he stopped trying. Consequently, Tantalus was in a state of perennial hunger and thirst. That was the curse of Matabeleland under gukurahundism.

Matabeleland, was endowed with so much riches, but was cursed by ZANU PF so that she had to subsist in perpetual deprivation and poverty. By attaining independence in 1980, Matabeleland transgressed from foreign to domestic colonialism. Under internal colonialism hardwood timber was harvested from Lupane, Tsholotsho, Hwange and Nkayi, yet the school pupils in Matabeleland had to sit on the floors of doorless classrooms. Coal was mined from Hwange, yet the few tarred roads in the district had multiple pot holes. The rest of the roads just like in neighboring Binga district, were terribly unnavigable dirt passageways. Revenue from the sale of wild life and trophies, gold and tourism was whisked away to the consolidated revenue fund, never to return back for the development of the region.

Gukurahundism was manifestly expressed in no other format than the cacographic satanic verses, allegedly written in 1979 by Nathan Shamuyarira's and ZANU PF's special committee of 26 Zezurus. Some analysts referred to the manuscript as the Shona Quran. The manuscript was popularly known as the 1979 Shona Grand Plan (*https://allafrica.com*). While Mugabe, Mnangagwa and Sekeramayi were training Gukurahundi, a devilish document was circulated among the "*elite*" of the Shona. From the expressive style, content and language, it was the artistic *magnum opus* of a skilled wordsmith who knew what he/she was preaching. The alleged author was Dr Nathan Shamuyarira, according to the Progress Review of the 1979 Grand Plan. Dr Shamuyarira who was ZANU PF's secretary for information and after indepence became the Minister of Information, knew only too well that the manuscript would spew out tribalistic venom and deep reaching ethnic divisions. Even the most moderate and liberal of readers would find the 1979 Grand Plan (as it was roguishly referred to) to be in the most sour taste, to say the least.

The timing of the document was of paramount significance and devastating effect. Coined some one year before independence, it was clear that the writer was as futuristic as he was articulate and equally tenacious. The ZANU leaders were already aware by then of the potential political currency that lay in churning out tribal politics and hatred. They set themselves to putting it to 'good' use. The plan showed that the marginalization of Matabeleland was not resultant from some accidental stroke of fate, but that it was premeditated and meticulously schemed way in advance. The document, just like the genocide, came out at a time when the Matabele least expected trouble from their fellow black countrymen and were thus caught napping.

The document was not well known until 1985 when first, snippets of it, then the full text hit the streets of Bulawayo. Since it was for the restricted distribution among the cream of the crop of the Shona, it was evident that the leadership were aware of it and they indeed kept it secret for almost six years. If they had not condoned it or authored it, it would have been exposed a lot earlier. Worse still, the government ignored it when it became public domain material and there was a public outcry in Bulawayo. No investigation was done to prove whether it was phony or genuine. The public media and government structures pretended that the document did not exist.

A fiendish sequel to the manuscript, titled Review of the 1979 Grand Plan was published and was discovered after the dawn of the 21ˢᵗ century. It was accorded by the powers that be the same sanctity and secrecy given to the original manuscript. No formal or informal discussion or even mention of the manuscript was ever made by the government. Instead, when individuals from Matabeleland mentioned and condemned it, they were arrested for inciting violence. Mr. George Mkhwananzi and Mr. Jethro Mpofu of Imbovane Yamahlabezulu (a Ndebele rights organization) were arrested and charged with treason after addressing a public meeting where they told delegates not to take their marginalization and the 1979 Shona Grand Plan lying down.

Those Shonas that read the 1979 Shona Grand Plan, absorbed in a life of privilege and advantage, ignored it as of no consequence. Most of them never read the document which was principally designed for their benefit. A document, all Shonas leaving or working in Matabeleland may have read and condemned, had they chosen to be fair and God fearing. A manuscript whose dogma had landed them in Matabeleland, bound by an invisible and unbreakable tribal thread of kinship and brotherhood. A document of bottomless contempt and limitless condescension for the Ndebele. Unwittingly and in many cases unconsciously, most Shonas benefited from a system that had a socio – economically genocidic and impoverishing impact on their countrymen in Matabeleland.

There was very little rationale in dismissing the 1979 Shona Grand Plan and its sequel, a fourteen page manuscript released in 2005 as either a work of fiction or a sour joke as some wanted to believe. The temerity with which the plans were crafted and the tenacity with which they were implemented disqualified them from the epistles of a lunatic or the effort of a sheer accidental scribe. According to Dr. Dumisani Maqeda Ngwenya (2018: 11), *"...there is no denying the correlation (by design or coincidentally) that exists between the objectives and plans set out in the so – called Grand plan of 1979 and what is happening. What has been playing out particularly in Matabeleland since 1980 to the present, bears a frighteningly similar pattern, right down to the t, to this document..."* The two manuscripts were authentic. They were meant for restricted circulation among the elite of the Shona but they were inevitably leaked out by honest and God fearing Shona persons that could not accept the influence of evil. Both documents were soon copied and became common material in the public domain. Still, officialdom ignored them, even when they became a subject of heated debate on social media platfoms such as facebook and whatapp.

On 26 October 2002, Matthew Parris published a report in The Times Online, titled *"the bloody catastrophe that awaits Zimbabwe"*. The fourteen - page Review of the 1979 Shona Gran Plan was published online under the title *"Zimbabwe: Blueprint for a Massacre"* together with Parris's report which argued that the Shona in pursuit of the Review document could forcibly expropriate land from the Ndebele. Parris was afraid of a violent invasion like the one that was unleashed on the white farmers. He did not realize that there already was a covert and underground land invasion under the secret auspices of subtle gukurahundi.

The Grand Plan and its Review became the epicenter, fomenting impregnable hatred, contempt, marginalization, discrimination, domination and abhorrence towards not only the Ndebele but all the non-Shona tribes of Matabeleland. The plan explained the praxis that had seen the heavy permeation of every aspect of life in Matabeleland by Shona influence and culture of doing things. By the 2000s Shona primary school teachers who could not communicate in any Matabeleland languages were deployed to schools in the region where elementary instruction was better aided by the combination of the child's mother language and English which was the language of record and instruction throughout the country. The childrens' education was deliberately designed to crumble at the foundation stage by that deployment.

Registry officers that issued birth and death certificates were Shona. Misspellings of vernacular or even English names was an all too common 'mishap' that at times was never corrected by the registry officer on the spot. Clearly the registry officers had very rudimentary education and training not beyond Ordinary Level. Shona civil servants were found manning government offices thoughout both rural and urban Matabeleland, as per the dictates of the grand plan and its review document.

Land in resettlement areas was allocated to many Shonas especially civil servants so that they had homes in Matabeleland. The main theme was to heavily populate Matabeleland with people of Shona origin so that they could 'reclaim' it and take charge of the day to day life of the region. Eventually ZANU PF would have increased its membership and ultimately the political leaders like councilors and MPs as well as the traditional leaders would be Shona.

All infrastructural development projects that were brought by the Harare administration to Matabeleland came with a full compliment of Shona workers. After completion of construction projects most of which took too many years eg the National University of Science and Technology, the Lupane State University, the Joshua Mqabuko Nkomo airport, the Victoria Falls Airport, the Shona labourers did not go back to their homes in Mashonaland. The projects were such that ultimately they would benefit people from Mashonaland more than those from Matabeleland. The above four examples were a case in point. The universities enrolled more than 80% students from Mashonaland and the lecturers were almost entirely Shona. The two airports employees during and after construction were almost all Shonas.

The gukurahundism in the Shona grand plans did not spare the church. Church goers in Matabeleland would not respond to non Shona songs at church services with equal verve as they did Shona songs. In actual fact they resorted to the defined habit of translating Ndebele songs into Shona. Those churches with head offices in Harare, in conformity with the grand plans, deployed (knowingly or not) Shona clergy to Matabeleland. On arrival the pastors conducted services in their own language, thereby compelling the Matabele to learn and speak Shona. Once more, the people of Matabeleland were being colonized under the cunning guise and the pretext of religion. It is very rare for converts to question even the most blatant malpractices as long as they are committed under the authority of the dais. Religion, just like in European colonialism, was used to opiate local communities into unquestioning and compliant followers of tribal nationalism just like it was used in the colonization of Africa.

Moyo Ndzimu - Unami (2012) criticized the church in Matabeleland for complicity in perpetuating gukurahundism by being, *"outposts of Shona imperialism and tyranny just like our universities, police stations and government offices"*. He questioned why the Shona should be *"Jew to the Gentile and Gentile to the Jew?"*. His question was motivated by the tendency of most Shona people in Matabeleland who did not want to speak isiNdebele, TjiKalanga, TjiNambya etc, yet St. Paul said he blended into those communities where he went and became like them so as to win them to Christ. By being Jew to the Jew and gentile to the gentile, St. Paul's message appealed to all races and he did not only win souls to Christ but helped the converts maintain their identities as per God's plan.

Ndzimu - Unami went on to single out such Christian denominations as Pentecostal Assemblies of God Zimbabwe (POAZ), Family of God (FOG), Zimbabwe Assemblies of God Africa (ZAOGA) and Apostolic Faith Mission (AFM) as the chief advocates of gukurahundism / Shonalization of Matabeleland who had discarded the gospel of justice, fairness and equality. He said the activities of the church seemed to promote *"linguistic and cultural domination, tribal hegemony, discrimination, inequality and imperial rule"*.

He further said that that tendency by the church was divisive, sinful and enmity to a united Zimbabwe and could only result in a time bomb whose explosion could have atomic repercussions. What prompted that fundamental yet accurate depiction of the church was that some churches conducted what was supposed to be God's business like they were excited appendages of ZANU PF, on a mission not only to collect money and send it to Harare, but to get the congregants to speak, sing, dance and think in Shona.

It was near impossible for the liberally disposed Shona and definitely for the victims of gukurahundism, to not believe the complicity of the Shona church in the domination, marginalization and oppression of Matabeleland. More so with the revelation by Shari Eppel (2001 interview with Kreiser), a researcher for the report, Breaking the Silence; Building True Peace by CCJP and LRF, that the report antagonized not just the government but the *"Catholic Church, because the Catholic Church in Zimbabwe is very divided. Many of the Shona bishops (Mugabe is Shona and Zanu is basically a Shona party) wanted to suppress the reports, and other bishops wanted them to come out. So this report actually threatened to divide the Catholic Church. And, in fact, it does. This report was released in 1997, and to date, it's never been officially acknowledged and released by the Catholic bishops. It was in the end released unilaterally by the Legal Resources Foundation"*. Either the previously fair and justice minded Shona bishops panicked and baulked or were overruled by their kinsmen when they eventually came face to face with the evils of their fellow tribesmen in cabinet and allowed their nature and base instinct to prevail over their calling, by attempting to gag the report.

The vice – like grip of the talons of gukurahundism did not intimidate the Shona bishops in the Catholic church only. It squeezed all the Shadreckan bravado out of the non - Shona clergy, who resorted to conducting services in Matabeleland in Shona so as to be accepted by the system. It ostensibly sounded more absurd than Godly for the Matabele clergy to be preaching to a Matabeleland flock in the Shona language yet Matabeleland was home to so many other languages. Either the priests were unsuspecting pawns in an imperialistic endeavor, with little understanding of their calling, or they were merely preaching for supper since their churches were founded and headquartered in Mashonaland. Those pastors that failed to succumb to Shona imperialism found themselves unofficially ostracized by both their head offices and their flocks. The ramifications of the ostracism varied from being posted to remote parishes in rural districts where one was allocated a very meagre allowance.

Some of the said churches down rightly refused to integrate into Matabele society. The too common and daily practice of interpreting sermons and songs conducted and sung in Ndebele to Shona was evidence of that refusal. It was almost a rule that when one addressed the church in Ndebele in Matabeleland, another would interprate into Shona so the Shona congregants could hear. That was done automatically, no matter how few the Shonas were in the church and regardless of the years they had spent in Matabeleland. That policy had completely nothing to do with understanding procedings. It was a cocksure and brash statement of defiance, proclaiming the existence of an uncompromising and unrepentant Shona society in the Matabeleland church. If not so, why was the interpreting not done in the Matabeleland languages like Venda, Tonga, Kalanga etc since the churches had members who spoke those languages? Instead, many a Shona speaker would take to the pulpit and dismiss the interpreter when who would be interpreting a sermon from Shona to Ndebele by insolently declaring, *"pane asinganzwe Shona"* (is there anyone who does not understand Shona).

That statement was supposed to be a question which on a normal day in Mashonaland would have sounded courteous in expressing a desire to ensure those that did not understand the Shona language, were not left out of the communication. However, when it was repeatedly posed in Matabeleland to a gathering comprising many non Shona attendants, it became a shameless and Godless imposition of the Shona language and culture to the church. That question / statement / declaration was never supposed to be said in the Matabeleland church unless the church was for the Shona people only. Imagine how absurd it would sound for a priest in a London church demanding in German if there was anyone who did not understand German because he wanted to preach in German. Would the Londoners be wrong if they told the priest to take his German god back to Berlin with him?

The Shona Grand Plans refered to both Ndebeles and Europeans as unwelcome settlers who should track back to KwaZulu and Britain respectively. There was no worse cock and bull story than that. History has it that Mzilikazi left Zululand in 1822 with about two hundred warriors. According to Thomas (1996) he left Zululand with three hundred followers. By the time he settled in Bulawayo seventeen years later in 1839, some of those warriors had died in the wars that characterized his trail blazing march while some had died of natural causes. At the same time people from other tribes in Transvaal, Limpompo, Barotseland, Bechuanaland and present day Zimbabwe had been assimilated to make a large nation by the time Mzilikazi died in 1868.

Speaking in cahoots with the Shona Grand Plan, Mr. Energy Mutoti, the Deputy Minister of Information in President Mnangagwa's government, in September 2019 shocked many when he stated that,"....*just about 1836 we accommodated thousands of South Africans who came into Zimbabwe fleeing from Tshaka and they were being led by Mzilikazi. They settled on the western part of the country, in Matabeleland and as I'm speaking right now, at least three million Zimbabweans have South African origin...*" While condemning xenophobic killings of foreighners in South Africa by some members of the public, Mutoti went out to prove how hospitable Zimbabweans were for accommodating Ndebeles who had run away from King Shaka in South Africa in the 19th century, yet in recompense the South Africans were now killing refugee Zimbabweans in their country. What was patent in Mutoti's tweeter display of his profound ignorance of historical facts, was not only his recorded hatred for the Ndebele people which he first publicized in 2015 when he claimed that Ndebeles had abducted buses carrying Shona people to South Africa, but a brazen threat to the Ndebele. Considering the response by some in Nigeria to the 2019 South African xenophobia, Mutoti was implying that Zimbabweans (Shonas) could also choose to attack the South Africans (Ndebeles) in Zimbabwe but had not done so. That coming from a member of cabinet, was the most vile and dangerous assertion since the cockroaches insult by Mnangagwa in 1983.

Mutoti's video recording of his message, which was widely circulated on social media, to the South Africans, was made from his government office, with the portrait of President Mnangagwa hanging on the wall behind him and the Zimbabwean flag clearly visible above his right shoulder. All the insignia, seriousness and clout of official ministerial authority were there. He was communicating in his official capacity as Minister of Information. He was representing the state. There was no doubt that in the mindset of senior government officials, by 2019, a hundred and eighty years since their arrival in Matabeleland, the Ndebele people were considered foreigners by people who had arrived in the area earlier. That revelation explained the according of second class citizens status to the Matabele by the government.

The Mthwakazi state as posited by Maphenduka (2015) was already in existence as composed of a loose coalition of Kalanga, Sotho, Venda, Tonga, Nambya and

Karanga chieftainships when Mzilikazi arrived in the area which was dominated by the San (abaThwa) people. Mzilikazi settled into the Mthwakazi state. The view of the Ndebele state as heterogeneous was corroborated by Muzondidya (2009) when he contended that, *"the Ndebele state was a heterogeneous collection of communities and groups, cultures and languages whose collective cultural and linguistic input all went into the making of modern Ndebele identity"*.

The queen of the San was called Muthwa. The Ngunis, probably under Zwangendaba and Nyamazana had earlier on called the place Muthwakazi / Mthwakazi after the queen. Due to his military prowess and ingenuity, Mzilikazi eventually became the de facto leader of the Mthwakazi state, which became more politically and socially coherent, compact and structured as well as militarily formidable. Therefore, the few Ngunis that left Zululand with Mzilikazi made up a very small portion of present day Mthwakazi.

Nonetheless if the migrants debate was to be entertained for the benefit of those with a taste for conflict and controversy born of the idea of Ndebeles going back to Zululand, then the Shona themselves were indeed settlers since they migrated from the great lakes region, Malawi, Tanzania and Mozambique. The only principal distinguishing factor was the period of the three (European, Ndebele and Shona) 'settler' groups' advent into present day Zimbabwe. That fact, according to the 'migrants going back theory', disqualified all the groups from laying any claims to wholesale and singular title to the land. History however has recorded that the original (oldest) inhabitants of present day Zimbabwe are the Khoisan / San. The Kalanga, Venda, Nambya and Tonga settled in the area way before the Shona groups started to arrive in present day Zimbabwe. If that socially warped theory could be observed, only the San would remain in the country.

The Grand Plan authors stooped as low as to instruct Shona men to wantonly impregnate Ndebele women and abandon them to a life of suffering while raising a Shona child who would eventually perpetuate the same plan that led to his/her conception. That section earned the owners of the plan a place in the antithesis of the Guinness Book of records. Credit must be given to the authors of the plan for being the most dastardly and malevolent schemers in pre and post colonial Zimbabwe.

Further scrutiny of the document revealed it for what it was, a xenophobic, tribal, imperialistic, discriminatory, elitist, supremacist, aparthedist and genocidic communiqué, spewing vile contempt for the Ndebele. The document propagated for the elevation of the Shona language to be the *"lingua franca"* of Zimbabwe, to be used in every sphere of government, business and society. That was the situation prevailing on the ground from the late 1980s, as most Shona office holders in Matabeleland (police, immigration, customs, army, registry, politicians, bankers, receptionists, clerks, nurses, name them) would not speak any of the local languages. The Review document celebrated the achievement of the original document in that *"95%"* of government jobs in Matabeleland and *"100%"* in Mashonaland were held by Shonas. While the accuracy of those statistics were never confirmed nor denied, it was easy to believe that claim due to the stubborn facts on the ground. One needed to walk into any bank, hotel, shop, police station, post office, port of entry / exit etc, in Matabeleland to prove that indeed the Shona people had all the jobs, were not apologetic about that and were loving it. The only place in Matabeleland where one was guaranteed to find more Matabeles than Shonas was inside a police holding cell or prison.

The two documents which were arguably the prototypes for gukurahundism went on to prescribe that colleges, polytechnics and universities should enroll Shona students only. That was the situation obtaining throughout the years, even in those institutions in Matabeleland e.g. National University of Science and Technology (NUST), Lupane State University (LSU), Hillside Teachers' College, Joshua Mqabuko Nkomo Polytechnic, Gwanda University of Technology, United College of Education, and Bulawayo Polytechnic. Students from Mashonaland were bused in with recommendation letters from senior ministers. In one incident in the 1980s a bus load of students from Masvingo province arrived at Hillside Teachers' College with instructions from deputy president Simon Muzenda for the principal to enroll them. Fearing for his job and personal security, the principal could only comply.

The *"rampant tribalism"*, according to Bulawayo24.com of 20 March 2018, at Hillside Teachers' College was evident in the enrolment of students, sporting teams and in lecturers delivering lectures in the Shona language. According to a student, one lecturer *"always delivers his lectures in Shona and when we ask him to speak in English he insults us and says Zimbabwe is a Shona country. How are we expected to pass when we can't hear what the lecturer is saying. Most of us don't attend his lectures anymore"*. The Hillside story was a tip of the iceberg but it was proof enough that the government of Zimbabwe, in perpetuation of gukurahundism's 1979 Grand Plan endeavored to and had done exceedingly 'well' to keep Matabeleland in educational Cimmerian darkness. Indeed, the few tertiary education institutions in Matabeleland had more Shona students and lecturers than Matabele students. The Shona teachers instructed in Shona even at elementary levels. According to one social media commentator, by 2017 there were more Shona Primary school teachers who spoke the Shona language with pupils in Matabeleland than there were pupils with good passes at grade seven annually. Nathan Shamuyarira was cited in the revised edition as having decreed that Ndebeles should be denied education as a way of guaranteeing their perennial domination by the Shona.

The nursing schools in Matabeleland were recruiting student nurses based on tribe as well. Mpilo Hospital in Bulawayo, United Bulawayo Hospitals (UBH) in Bulawayo, St. Lukes Hospital in Lupane, St. Anne's Hospital in Mangwe, Tsholotsho Hospital in Tsholotsho, Gwanda Hospital in Gwanda and Wankie Colliery Hospital in Hwange were some of the culprits. In 2019, The Chronicle newspaper of 06 October 2019 revealed that the interviews and selection of student nurses were conducted in Harare. The report showed that only two student nurses from Matabeleland North and South had been recruited by UBH, while ten were from Harare. St. Anne's had no students from Matabeleland at all, all were from Mashonaland. Gwanda and St. Lukes hospitals had zero students from Matabeleland, all were from Mashonaland. The director of Mpilo Hospital and also in charge of the school of nursing, Dr. Solwayo Ngwenya told The Chronicle that all the twenty four recruits enrolled in October 2019 were recommended by the Ministry of Health and Child Welfare in Harare.

If what was happening at the nursing schools in Matabeleland was not subtle genocide or gukurahundism, then the devil resided in paradise.

Matabeleland found herself in a state sponsored pervasive darkness that anchored her in one spot in the middle of a stormy economic ocean. The Matabeleland ship was full of, unemployment, hunger, disease, medical supplies shortages, poverty and death. Both Mugabe and Mnangagwa could not dare claim lack of knowledge about the backward state of affairs in Matabeleland. Nevertheless, according to Johnson and Clark (1984), Mugabe claimed on independence day celebrations in 1984 that, *"We have built more roads, schools, clinics and boreholes in that area than we have anywhere else in the country,"*. He was defending the socially porous ZANU government's policies in Matabeleland. One wondered what he was talking about when, for example Victoria Falls where the ZANU PF government still made hundreds of thousands United States dollars per month from entrance fees into the rainforest, entrance fees into the national parks, hotel revenue taxes, customs and excise duties and tax at the port of entry and exit, immigration charges, hunting revenues, sale of wildlife and wildlife trophies, licenses etc, his claims were downright false. The government had not built a single school in thirty - seven years by the time he was elbowed out through a coup in the resort town. The only two government primary schools in existence by 2019, Chinotimba and Baobab schools, were an inheritance from the Smith regime.

The only and noxiously oversubscribed secondary school was built by the poor residents under the supervision of the then Town Council in 1984.

By the turn of the millennium, the residents of the town had to seek medical treatment in Zambia's Livingstone town where there were drugs, equipment, nurses and doctors (some of them economic refugees from Zimbabwe) in the government hospital. The drugs in the Zambian pharmacies were affordable compared to the hardly available drugs in Zimbabwe. Many deaths e,g from malaria, in the resort town which was visited by very rich tourists who spent a lot of foreign currency in various activities, were due to lack of medical facilities. Those that could not afford to seek treatment in Livingstone died on the hospital beds daily of curable diseases.

The major roads in Matabeleland were an embarrassment to any government anywhere in the world and could only be useful as examples of a failed road network. The Bulawayo – Nkayi road, the Bulawayo – Kezi road, the Bulawayo – Tsholotsho road, the Binga road, the Lupane Tsholotsho road, the Bulawayo – Beitbridge road and even the Bulawayo – Victoria Falls road, all constructed by the Smith government were a sorry sight and by 2019 nothing had been done to repair or upgrade them. Mentioning the minor roads would be an insult to the users who did not even view them as roads in the first place. By South African standards the major roads including the Bulawayo – Harare road, were deplorable, and collecting road tax on them was criminal. Clearly Mugabe was just defending the gukurahundism in the 1979 Shona Grand Plan and had deviated from the truth when he made that claim.

Sadly, the evil schemata of the Shona Grand Plans was perpetuated even in the house of God. The plan went on to instruct churches in Matabeleland to conduct services in Shona. A visit to any of the churches founded in Harare e.g. FOG, AFM, ZAOGA and a litany of new denominations led by the young so called prosperity prophets and miracle workers from Harare left one confused if they were not witnessing a Shona language study group of some sort or a money mongering social club in action. Not surprisingly after the document had said that the days were numbered for those priests that were resisting the Shonalization of the pulpit and alter, Catholic archbishop Pius Ncube who had instructed his parishes in Bulawayo to use the Ndebele language and not Shona, was ensnared by the state in a display of an amorous relationship with some woman.

Like many men, the archbishop was not the Admirable Crichton but the prompt coverage of the scandal by the state press was further proof that the plan was hatched by powerful offices in the government. Many asked where the press had been when Mugabe himself had eaten the forbidden fruit and fathered two Children (Chatunga and Bona) with his married secretary Grace Marufu while his wife Sally was suffering on her hospital death bed (Bridgland 2008).

The display of photographs and videos of Ncube in a compromising state with a woman by the state print media and television broadcaster was proof enough of what was at stake. The gloves were off and Mugabe who had previously threatened Ncube with unspecified action was evidently going for the jugular. It was personal. The savage attack on his privacy by the CIO, the deputy sheriff accompanied by ten state journalists (Sokwanele 2007) spoke volumes on the interest of the government in the civil case. Ncube was observably being taken to the cleaners so that the court of public opinion could hang him. Hang he did indeed, but not for adultery. For daring Mugabe and his murderous cretins, the archbishop was damned. According to Bridgland (2008) archbishop Ncube was felled also because he was a Ndebele that was widely tipped to win the Nobel Peace Prize, a feat which ZANU PF's gukurahundism could not allow a Ndebele to achieve.

The archbishop was crashed out of his office within the Catholic church and divested of his archbishop privileges by being removed from the powerful socio – political pedestal to which he had been elevated as the voice of the dominated and oppressed in Matabeleland and the Midlands. His removal from his position by the Vatican and his disgrace did not embarrass his flock and Matabeleland as much as his ignominy and moral divestiture deprived the victims of ZANU PF's misrule, of an influential, leather - tough and consistent all - weather ally.

Inopportunely, unlike the archbishop, the Matabeleland tribes succumbed to the Shona cultural invasion onslaught, in servitude to the Grand Plans. For example, in the Ndebele culture, handshaking and dancing, depict a happy occasion, hence those rites are not performed at funerals or throughout the mourning period. However, during funerals and the mourning period, the Shona shake hands and their women dance and ululate as if in celebration. The celebratory funerals culture was silently brought into Matabeleland through the churches in furtherance of the Shona Grand Plans as if it was a Christian practice. That uncultural practice, according to Ndebele culture, took root in Matabeleland. That practice was the epitome of cultural imperialism and an abomination among the Matabeleland cultures, yet it become the order in most funerals.

The Shona Grand Plan review vaingloriously gloated that in his *"brilliance"*, Mugabe created dissidents as a pretext to unleash the Gukurahundi brigade on the Ndebele so as to crush the Ndebele spirit and the ZAPU structures. Indeed,

ZAPU structures were decimated so thoroughly any attempts to resuscitate them by former party gurus like Dabengwa met with an anxious combination of stiff resistance and reluctance by erstwhile colleagues from the party. As for the Ndebele spirit, the script reads differently. It was beaten by the Gukurahundi genocide and it was tormented and suffered all imaginable abuses under gukurahundism. Hitherto it survives. The Ndebele spirit could not be broken or decimated.

The Ndebele spirit just like that of the Shona or any other people was a free gift from God and could not be crushed by any mortal. Bigotry by Mugabe and his tribal lieutenants could only vary the conditions under which the spirit of the Ndebele subsisted, thereby causing it a lot of discomfort and dismay, but they could never destroy it. Only God can destroy a people's spirit. Any misplaced attempts to do so by anyone was trying to play God.

The most disparaging, impairing and dehumanizing aspects of the Grand Plans was that its advocated canons were not just historical facts but were daily experiences in Zimbabwe. Presumably the bulk of Shona people never read or heard of the Grand Plan documents. Probably the vast majority of those of them that read the plans, rejected the extremism endemic in the xenophobic proposal. Most did not have the platform to challenge their dogma while many more lacked the political will to entangle themselves in such mucky business. Still, what was equally irrefutable was that the majority of them were beneficiaries of the plan, albeit unknowingly.

There was an unsettling comparison that analysts were either downright blind to, or were unwilling to make, probably due to the reluctance of gazing at the naked probable truth thereunder. In Rwanda just prior to the 1994 genocide, some among the majority Hutu elite alleged that the minority Tutsi were not indigenous to Rwanda and had migrated from Ethiopia in the north. They argued that when colonialism was defeated in Rwanda, the Tutsis replaced the whites as settlers. The Tutsi were therefore marked for death. The Hutus assumed the status of natives who had the duty to rid Rwanda of foreigners (Mpofu 2013).

Similarly, some among the majority Shona (migrants theorists) had similar misgivings about the Ndebele whom they said were pre - colonial invaders from Zululand in South Africa. They said Zimbabwe was a Shona country.

The Hutu propaganda machinery advocating Hutu Power by use of the state media, termed Tutsis *"inyezi"* (cockroaches). The Hutu moderates who were accommodative of Tutsis were referred to as *"ibyitso"* (accomplices). To be either *"inyezi"* or *"ibyitso"* was punishable by death. Emmerson Mnangagwa the then minister of state security in Zimbabwe and later appointed Vice President, before barrelling Mugabe out of the presidency, referred to dissidents as cockroaches and went on to administer *"DDT"* on the entire Matabele population in Matabeleland and Midlands provinces.

The Rwandan weekly newspaper Kangura of 6 December 1990 published what was called the Hutu Ten Commandments which bore strikingly common traits with the Review of the 1979 Grand Plan document of the 2000s. It was very probable that the Hutu Ten Commandments were probably inspired by the ZANU 1979 Shona Grand Plan. Another possibility could be that the Progress Review of the 1979 Grand Plan (PRGP) was enthused by the Hutu Ten Commandments.

The resemblance of the two manuscripts was further made prominent in various ways. Those included the commonality between Hutu Commandment number 5 and the PRGP paragraph titled 'jobs'. Hutu commandment number 5 decreed that, *"all strategic positions, political, administrative, economic, military and security should be entrusted only to Hutu"*. The PRGP paragraph titled jobs stated that *"positions that matter as well as low grade jobs"* in government departments as well as in the private sector should be a preserve for Shonas. It was a cruel and bitter pill to swallow, to note that employment trends in Zimbabwe since April 1980 religiously complied to that creed with religious steadfastness. One needed to randomly pick any hotel in Victoria Falls or government office complex in Plumtree or anywhere in Matabeleland and ask a public area cleaner in Ndebele/Nambya/Tonga/Kalanga/Xhosa/Sotho/Shangani for assistance. The certainty was that the employee would respond in Shona saying they did not understand the language.

Hutu commandment number 1 displayed intense contempt for Tutsi women who were potrayed as lesser beings, dishonest and less beautiful by comparison with their Hutu counterparts and therefore could not be taken in marriage by Hutu men. The Progress Review of the 1979 Grand Plan displayed similar loathe and insolence towards Ndebele women. Ndebele women were presented as loose prostitutes and adulterers, suitable only for sexual gratification and production of illegitimate children with Shona men so that the Shona population could keep getting larger.

The Rwandan army was ordered to be exclusively Hutu, by commandment number 7. That is why four years after the publication of the aggressive ordinance the almost Hutu only army had the mettle and chutzpah to execute wholesale murder of Tutsis. Under the languages and jobs paragraphs, the PRGP, advocated for a Shona only army and police force. That was a reality in Zimbabwe and one needed to go into a police station or police road block in Matabeleland (at the risk of being detained for hours or days on the charge of disorderly conduct) and insist on speaking in any indigenous language other than Shona to prove that. The police, customs, immigration, registry, you name it were almost entirely Shona. Those members that were not Shona had learnt to adapt and be Shona in language and conduct so as to survive on the job. The army periodically recruited the Matabele just in case there was need to deploy soldiers to a war. For example, many Matabele soldiers died in the DRC war of 1999 as well as in the Mozambique war of the 1980s. They recruited the Matabele because they did not want to find themselves having to send to war a Shonas only army.

The education sector was not given any reprieve either as Hutu Commandment number 6 stated that school *"pupils, students and teachers"* should be from the *"majority Hutu"* tribe. The PRGP also provided for the *"majority indigenous Shona"* students enjoying the impartation of skills by tertiary training institutions, while students enrolment in colleges and universities should reflect a Shona *"dominant"* enrolment. It went without saying that that was an apprehensive and perturbing character of Zimbabwe's education system since 18 April 1980 as has been previously argued. Zimbabwe became a country where priviledge (being Shona) was bankable than one's effort, honesty and hard work in all sectors, including in education.

That ghastly spectre of inequality was appositely echoed by one, Raisdon Pasipanodya (a shona) when he argued on social media, borrowing from the term 'Brexit' that, *"Ndexit (Mthwakazi) is more than justified"*. As if transcribing a summery of the PRGP effects, Pasipanodya observed that, *"..we as a nation in general and as Shona people in particular have allowed things to drift to the ugly picture it is today...the history of this country is that of suppression and marginalization on the part of the Ndebele people, tribal privilege on the part of the majority of Shona people and blatant denial on the part of government.. just by being called with a Shona name, speaking the language was enough to get you a job, get one a college place, ease one's way at a roadblock, give one unwarranted marks at college, the list is endless..the inequalities economically, infrastracturally and educationally have been done intentionally. None of those in power can say they did not see this. The reality cannot be argued against when all the border posts are manned by our people right up to the toilet cleaners, our police stations even right in the depth of Matabeleland are manned by Shona officers, same applies to colleges and universities, same applies to hospitals and clinics, same applies to the judiciary and prison services. No one can argue that this happened naturally.."* It was a consolation to note that many Shona people disapproved of the effects of the PRGP.

Probably the most acrimonious of Hutu commandments was the eighth, which encouraged the majority Hutus to treat Tutsis with utmost mercilessness. It was that diabolic mandate which instigated the importation of some 15 000 machetes into Rwanda for the hacking to death of hundreds of thousands minority Tutsis. The Gukurahundi brigade did not need machetes. On their rifles were affixed bayonets which were used to split open the wombs of pregnant women in Matabeleland and the Midlands. Just as the Gukurahundi brigade was merciless to the Ndebele, the Interahamwe was unremitting to the Tutsi.

It was crystal and poignantly clear that as much as the Hutu Ten Commandments were designed to stimulate and foment ethnic conflict, the PRGP was fermenting the so called '4th Chimurenga' which would guarantee 'Shona nationhood', Shona supremacy and the vanquishment of Matabeleland by a combination of subtle maneuvers and animal brutality.

Despite the stain on Rwanda, born of being home to the Hutu Ten Commandments that contributed in precipitating a genocide, there was respite in that the Rwandese managed to rise above the dark horizons of hate and tribalism. They confronted the truth. The truth was told, painful secrets were made public, perpetrators apologized, criminals were taken to account in the courts of law and justice was served. They eventually reconciled. On the other hand, Zimbabwe was still embroiled in the politics of hate, tribalism and evasion until Mugabe was ousted, almost four decades after the genocide. The crime of genocide was still a curse on the land. A grey cloud of secrecy and conniving sponsored by the drivers of the genocide hovered over the potential of truth telling and reconciliation. The Hutu ten commandments may have been exorcised in Rwanda but their evil twin, the PRGP was very much alive and active in Zimbabwe when Mugabe's co perpetrators took over from him in 2017.

If the 1979 Shona Grand Plan was a prank as some Mugabe apologists in the employ of ZANU PF averred, was the PRGP also a hoax? If so, is it not too strange a coincidence that the provisions of the two policy documents were *in toto,* the undeniable reality on the ground? Matabeleland was without new schools, clinics, roads, houses and industry, yet her resources were being plundered daily with amazing nerve, tempo and obstinacy. She was stinking poor and her students were less conversant with science, geography, mathematics, history and culture than their Mashonaland counterparts. Her young women are heavy with child and were doomed to single motherhood too soon. The young men were jobless and angry while the elderly were disillusioned and disoriented. Those challenges were crafted for, but were not unique to Matabeleland especially after 2000, since the collapsed economy extended the suffering to Mashonaland as well.

Those Zimbabweans across the tribal divide, that were inclined to honesty, agreed that the gukurahundism that was paddled by the grand plans and pervaded the country, was an unofficial government policy. Otherwise the government would have implemented measures to counter the provisions therein in order to ensure the equality of all its citizens, moreso after the 1987 Unity Accord.

After going through both the Hutu ten commandments and the Review of the 1979 Shona Grand Plan, one did not wonder why the Interahamwe of Rwanda and the Zimbabwe Defense Forces (ZDF) were to conjure up an unhallowed genocidal entente in the DRC from August 1998 to July 2003. The two armies had been involved in genocide in their respective countries. The ZDF which butchered civilians in an ethnic cleansing and political orgy of mass slaughter in Matabeleland and Midlands was deployed by Robert Mugabe to repel marauding Congolese rebels who were bearing down on Kinshasa and President Laurent Kabila in 1998.

In the DRC, the ZDF became a legionnaire force in cohorts with the interahamwe from Rwanda, helping to prop up the President Laurent Kabila who was under siege from Tutsi rebels who were backed by Uganda and Rwanda from the eastern DRC. According to Meredith (2005), Kabila had in 1998 recruited the Interahamwe to avert a coup plot against him. He also asserted that the ZDF were training the Hutu rebels in Katanga so they could raid Tutsi Burundi. The ZDF - Interahamwe league was no common *omnium gatherum,* but it was a vicious collusion of pogrom masters with a contemporary history of consummate sadism and a dangerously murderous aptitude.

Probably it was inaccurate and madcap generalisation to assert that Mugabe, his hotchpotch of cronies and loyalists, ZANU PF, the ZDF and the Gukurahundi brigade influenced the carnage and butchering of the Tutsi during the Rwandan genocide, but it was not unfair for history to judge the government harshly for failing to veto Mugabe's dispatching to DRC of the Zimbabwean National Army. Mugabe deployed the ZDF into DRC unilaterally and out of greed as well as to spruce up his dying image as a Pan Africanist. The injudicious deployment was at a time when Kabila was, through the state radio, encouraging the use of *"a machete, a spear, an arrow, a hoe, spades, rakes, nails, truncheons, electric irons, barbed wire"* to kill the Rwandan Tutsi (Meredith 2005). The Zimbabwean army was imparting skills to and reinforcing a tribal militia and warlord that was using the above - mentioned hodgepodge of primordial weapons against fellow humans whose crime was that they, like Mugabe's genocide victims, the Ndebele, were different, supported a different political party, had a different history, culture and language and were an ethnic minority, therefore perceived as a threat and a nuisance to the establishment.

That was the kind of man and regime that the Zimbabwean army was defending in DRC. The personnel they trained went on to use their acquired skills on an atrocious undertaking. Hundreds of Zimbabwean soldiers died defending tyranny and the wealth of Zimbabwean military barons feathering their nests on blood minerals in the Congo.

The DRC war was also known as the 'Coltan War'. Coltan was a *"valuable black mineral combining niobite and tantalite; used in cell phones and computer chips"* (WordBook XL Dictionary). Coltan and diamonds were some of the priceless magnets that lured many into the internal conflict in the DRC and not the need to bolster the rule of law by a constitutional government.

Coltan and diamonds were probably why Zimbabwe dispatched thousands of soldiers and more than forty AFZ aircrafts into the war. According to WikiLeaks cables, John Bredenkamp and Billy Rautenbach, the rich British / Zimbabwean business magnets had diamond and cobalt mines in the DRC. The rebels were threatening their businesses there. They influenced the decision to deploy the ZDF in the DRC. The ZDF was deployed to prop up the DRC government of Laurent Kabila while on the other hand Zimbabwe was selling weapons of war in exchange for diamonds with the DRC rebels. That means that possibly the thousands of ZDF soldiers that died in that war were killed by arms supplied by their own commanders. According to Yamamoto (2019), financial benefits from, *"rampant racketeering, illegal mafia – style smuggling, double - crossing, double dealing as well as illegal arms peddling"*, then accrued to Mugabe, Mnangagwa, *"General Vitalis Musungwa Gava (now late), Perence Shri, Constantine Chiwenga, then Brigadier General Sibusiso Moyo...Air Commodore Mike Karakadzai...Colonel Simpson Sikhulile Nyathi and Charles Dauramanzi"*. The Zimbabwean strongmen provided an environment whereby both the DRC government and the rebels could sustain the war, so that they could continue looting Congolese minerals, supplying arms to both sides and supplying goods and services to the Zimbabwen army in that country.

That was most likely why in November 1998 the Zimbabwe government acquired a US$54 million shipment of helicopters, fighters and spotter aircraft to be part of the Coltan War. With the benefit of hind sight, it became very difficult to justify Zimbabwe's role in the DRC war. Was it worth the AFZs razing to the ground a five -kilometer long armoured convoy of rebels that were barrelling down towards Kinshasa on 26 August 1998? (BBC news). Was it worth the AFZs bombing and sinking six ferries on Lake Tanganyika and sinking them with their 600 Burundi and Rwandan troops on 22 November 1998?

The DRC war cost was overpaid, overpaid in human blood. The blood of thousands of Zimbabweans, Angolans, Rwandese, Burundians, Ugandans and Congolese. Four million Congolese died between 1998 and 2003. Many of those were civilians who died of disease and starvation born of the war. In addition, the war cost Zimbabwe almost US$ 1 million a day (US$ 27 million per month, Yamamoto 2019). The ZDF played an unholy part in that acerbic and virulent slaughter of millions. Why? Probably to satiate and caress Mugabe's ego. So that Mugabe could outplay Nelson Mandela and spruce his emergence as a regional power broker and king maker. So he could placate the greed of his hangers - on for Congolese coltan and diamonds while rekindling and honing the genocidal nerves of his gukurahundist ministers and generals of war.

Mugabe was obviously Kabila's mentor and confidante. There existed between the two a camaradarie and mutualism that blossomed into complete trust. If Mugabe's blood – letting had been nipped in the bud in 1982 he would have had better counsel for Laurent Kabila by 1998. But he was allowed a free rein and he got away with too many murders. His 'success' with Gukurahundi implored him to order his troops to help butcher four million people in the DRC. Beleagured Kabila was not so lucky though. He was assassinated by his own body guard, who in turn like Duncan's aides in Shakespeare's 'Macbeth', was immedistely killed, probably to hide the identity of the real killers. The truth behind the genocide in DRC and the role played by the ZNA, just like the truth behind Gukurahundi is yet to be told in full.

Gukurahundism was used widely in character assassinations in order to crush completely and eliminate those individuals posing a threat to ZANU PF or Mugabe and his ruling tribesmen. If they could not kill one physically, they would cripple their reputation and career. There were too many victims of that form of gukurahundism, including some that helped set it up or had applied it on others at a time when they were trusted by Mugabe. Once persons like Joyce Mujuru, Emmerson Mnangagwa, Constantine Chiwenga, Didymus Mutasa, Rugare Gumbo, Edgar Tekere, Jabulani Sibanda, Morgan Tsvangirai etc had outlived their usefulness, they fell prey to a system they had meticulously perfected. They became its victims. They were called all sorts of bad names in the book in a bid to have them rejected by the electorate and even imprisoned. They quickly found themselves having to hastily put out the flames of the terror they had helped to assemble.

Those from outside ZANU PF were given the thicker end of the stick. Chief Khayisa Ndiweni (1913 – 2010) from the 1970s until his death at an advanced age of 97, was convinced that the Ndebele / Shona question had two possible answers. Federalism or secession. He on 16 November 1978 formed the United National Federal Party (UNFP), a political party which advocated for non – domination of one people by another and equal representation of Matabeleland and Mashonaland. The notion of equal representation of the two was based on the fact that the two were previously two separate and sovereign states (Mthwakazi and Mashonaland). He firmly believed in an autonomous state of Matabeleland with an arms length relationship with the state of Mashonaland. That philosophy made him most unpopular with, first, Chief Chirau who labelled him a tribalist and then with Robert Mugabe and ZANU who dreamt of a one party state within a unitary system of government. Paramount Chief Ndiweni's credo that Matabeleland should be a sovereign state called Mthwakazi bordering the territories of King Mzilikazi's 19th century kingdom endeared him to some of the Ndebele people while some who preferred nationalism disagreed with him. He was censured by the ZANU PF regime.

The chief was definitely a reliable repository of history. His ideology which was informed by the history of the Ndebele and Shona kingdoms, was not misplaced although unpopular for a number of reasons especially among nationalist leaders at a time when nationalism in Africa was the in thing. Nationalism was misconstrued by many to be at odds with Federalism. At the 1979 elections his party won nine seats, only in Matabeleland. In the 1980 elections with his character assassinated, his party fell prey to nationalism and lost all the nine seats to ZAPU. For demanding self actualisation, self regulation, self determination and independence, he earned the socio-politically debasing tag of tribalist and divisionist which became an albatross around his neck for thirty years until he died a victim of gukurahundism in 2010.

Of all the clergy, it was only the Roman Catholic Archbishop of Bulawayo, Rev. Pius Ncube who tackled Mugabe head on. He had the mental fortitude, moral fiber, backbone and spiritual calling to understand and apply the lesson from the history of the Jews exiled in Persia under the emperor Xerxes. The archbishop was not blind to the verse; *"Do not think in thy soul to be delivered in the house of the king, more than all the Jews, but if thou keep entirely silent at this time, respite and deliverance remaineth to the Jews from another place, and thou and the house of thy fathers are destroyed; and who knoweth whether for a time like this thou hast come to the kingdom?"* (Ester 4: 13 – 14). The Archbishop was standing in protection of his people in accord with his religion.

Archbishop Pius Ncube was a most audacious yet humble man of the cloth, in the mould of South African Anglican Archbishop Desmond Tutu. He was nonetheless shackled with the fetters of the tag of tribalist until he succumbed. For daring to carry out his Christian duty of telling the president that: *"number, God has numbered the days of your kingdom; weight, you have been weighed on the scales and found to be too light; divisions; your kingdom is divided up and given to the Medes and Persians"*, the archbishop was chewed up by Robert Mugabe and dressed down mercilessly by the President's tagalongs in ZANU PF and the government. He had been threatened by Mugabe and warned not to meddle in politics but to instead confine himself to prayer and fasting. The archbishop had risen to prominence for using his influence on the pulpit, the press and various international forums to condemn the Mugabe regime for crimes against humanity including the Gukurahundi genocide. He also accused Mugabe of human rights violations, crisis of governance, rigging elections, abusing food aid and refusal to relinquish power. He once proclaimed during a sermon that he was praying for God to take Mugabe's soul. The archbishop's confession was as surprising as his prayer was unorthodox, but it was not unbiblical considering Psalms 109: 3 - 9. In terms of precedent Archbishop Pius Ncube was well within his biblical limits.

Robert Mugabe resorted to persistent vitriolic attacks, ever punctuated by rancorous name-calling and threats of unspecified action against the archbishop and everyone and anyone whom he perceived to be a threat. Mugabe went all out and out against all criticism of the government and took personnally any disapproval of his actions as president. Contrary to international practice that a president's actions and pronouncements were a reflection of collective executive and cabinet policy, therefore criticism of such policies was not an attack on the person of the president, Mugabe took it very personally. His conduct proved that he was not prepared to be the whipping boy for his team because he alone was the team. His voice and his voice alone had reason, logic and wisdom. By the turn of the millennium it was a case of *vox Mugabe vox Dei,* not *vox populi vox Dei* (the voice of the people is the voice of God), as indeed his pronouncements became so compelling and his voice became that of a demi god. Standing up against him was as vacuous as rushing headlong into a stationery steam locomotive.

In May 2004 he described archbishop Ncube as *"an unholy man, a replica of South African Anglican archbishop Desmond Tutu"*. Archbishop emeritus Tutu an anti apartheid icon and Nobel Peace Prize winner, had previously been slighted by Mugabe as *"an angry, evil and embittered little bishop"* (BBC 25 May 2004). Mugabe further ascribed to archbishop Ncube such allegations as *"gay, HIV positive, and sexual molestor"* who was under British colonial influence. Those claims were extremely preposterous and childish, more so because they would constitute a breach of confidentiality ethics, if true. By berating and demonising such renowned men of the cloth, Mugabe exhibited unprecedented amounts of venomous contempt and infrequent apostasy, since he at one time like the archbishop had been under Jesuit tutelage.

However, Archbishop Ncube was never deterred. He, Mordekai – like, condemned the massacre of and stood up for his people against a government that was hell - bent on consigning them to the doldrums of deprivation and fourth class citizenship. For preaching gallantly against the evils of the regime and raising international awareness to its flaws which he said included subjecting the poor to hunger and starvation, Archbishop Ncube earned the dreaded title of tribalist. Very few, if any, within the swelling ranks of the opposition and civic society came to his defence because, for demanding equality for the Matabele he was perceived to be anti – Shona.

For acknowledging his responsibility not only to his flock but to his folk too, the bishop torched a storm. A Gukurahundist storm that swept him off the pulpit and forced the Vatican to instruct him to shy away from politics. Mugabe was then left to his business, free to prance around without any priest warning him against villainous and satanic conduct. The archbishop revealed (interview on 7 March 2015 at Marist Brothers Secondary School, Dete), that after his disgrace he was offered by the church to stay in Italy. Other bishops offered him sanctuary in South Africa and Botswana but he had declined all the offers of kindness. He said that he could not accept *"living in comfort and foreign peace while my countrymen were languishing in poverty and abuse by the government".*

Archbishop Ncube further stated that the government, before crudely cutting the ground under his feet had attempted to buy his 'silence'. He stated that, *"I have no respect for this government because of what they did to innocent people in Matabeleland. They offered me a farm. MaFuyana, former Vice President Joshua Nkomo's widow was sent to offer me the farm but I declined. It was going to compromise my position on the evils of the government. It was going to shut me up".* For turning down the farm, Ncube sealed his own fate. The government realized that he was not susceptible to perverted diplomatic persuasion and trammeled him in an amatory affair.

Throughout his arduous tenure as governor of Matabeleland North, Welshman Mabhena never lost an opportunity to demand fair distribution of resources between Matabeleland and Mashonaland. Befitting his office, he spoke and behaved like a leader of Matabeleland and not a leader of the whole Zimbabwe as his detractors would have wanted him to do. Mabhena understood that leading

Zimbabwe was primarily Mugabe's job while his mandate was to help Mugabe lead that portion of Zimbabwe called Matabeleland North. Calling for the elevation of his province to the stratum of Mashonaland provinces earned him the ticket into the dungeon of divisionists and tribalists which stuck on his forehead like the mark of Cain until he died, poor and isolated but with his honour intact in 2010.

Years before his death Mr. Mabhena had been terminated by Mugabe from the office of Governor of Matabeleland North. He was handed the letter of dismissal signed by the President by an employee of the state in the corridors of parliament, he said. He accepted that disgrace with honor and principle and with his head held high. His successors and most ZANU PF leaders from Matabeleland, learnt the lesson hard and fast. None ever spoken as loudly and unapologetically for the region. None dared demand equity for Matabeleland. They accepted the bondage of patronage and opted to be politically correct in order to live lush lifestyles under Harare's indulgence.

According to Dr. Dumiso Dabengwa (interview, 17 Mrach 2017, Bulawayo) at a politburo (the supreme policy making organ of ZANU PF) meeting in 2007 he had moved a motion that the oncoming ZANU PF December 2007 conference should be an elective process whereby the party would decide on who would be the party presidential candidate in the 2008 elections. Joseph Msika the then Vice President then endorsed the recommendation as a pointer to a democratic process. The motion implied that Mugabe who had been at the apex of the party and government for twenty - seven years, would have to step down and not be the party's presidential candidate in the impending harmonised plebiscite. The motion was discussed further as members wanted to know how that would be done. Dabengwa suggested that there could be nominations and if more than one nomination was proposed and seconded then there would be elections by secret ballot. Suddenly a coterie of Mugabe die hards started agitating, and as Dabengwa put it in Ndebele *"basihoza"* (mocked boisterously and chided us).

After Dabengwa had been called on the carpet by a mob – style dressing down, Mugabe who was chairing, guided the meeting to the next item for discussion and left Dabengwa's recommendation hanging. Thus the motion to have Mugabe replaced before the 2008 elections was defeated.

According to Mufuka (2019), Dabengwa was betrayed because he had previously agreed with some politburo members that they would push for Mugabe's stepping down. The most prominent among Dabengwa's colleagues was Solomon Mujuru the Zimbabwe Defence Forces commander. It had been agreed that Dabengwa would move the motion, while Mujuru would second it. Unbeknown to Dabengwa, prior to the fateful politburo meeting, Mujuru *"was called and his alleged corrupt activities read to him"* (Mufuka 2019). That meant that Mujuru was blackmailed into backing down from the arrangement with Dabengwa. That was how he *"failed in the hour of most need"*.

Consequently, weeks before the 2007 conference, a statement was issued by the party to the effect that the conference would merely endorse Mugabe as the party presidential candidate in 2008 because he had been elected to party president at a congress and that would not change before the next congress. Dabengwa did not attend the conference in December 2007 because, as he stated, he could not endorse Mugabe's candidature.

Moving the motion implying Mugabe's replacement was as very onerous a task as it was fateful. Dabengwa had displayed infrequent nerve and determination, considering the character of Mugabe and ZANU PF. For his troubles Dabengwa was isolated psychologically during the meeting and socio – politically ostracized afterwards. The silent treatment made him realize that Mugabe thought he had abused his freedom of thought and speech in the politburo meeting. He also felt grossly let down by his colleagues in the politburo who had failed to stand up with him.

Such a betrayal of democratic ethos must have felt like a physical dagger sticking out on his back. Suddenly there was no breathing space for him in ZANU PF and he subsequently resigned from the party. He revived ZAPU shortly afterwards but was dismissed by the press and government officials as an obdurate and sour tribalist. Mugabe led the chorus of intolerance by calling him *"tribalist Dabengwa"*, in keeping with the dictates of gukurahundism.

Defiant Mujuru however, did not quit ZANU PF, but rumours from his party grapevine that he had helped form the opposition MDC intensified. He died mysteriously three years later, probably a victim of gukurahundism which he had had no small hand in setting up.

In 1999 Professor Welshman Ncube, a commanding intellectual of unparalleled intelligence, a genius of boardroom politics and a constitutional law expert, played a pivotal role in the formation of the Movement for Democratic Change. He helped elevate Morgan Tsvangirai from the scrapes of the trade union movement into the limelight. There, Tsvangirai became a politician of immense guts and charisma thereby propelling him to the presidency of the party in 2000.

When five years later Ncube differed with Tsvangirai, the party split. The state controlled press as well as some pro Tsvangirai journalists in the independent press preferred to downplay the real reasons for the split. Instead they blamed Ncube for breaking ranks with Tsvangirai by calling him ambitious and tribal. Within the MDC he was accused of being a sellout and a CIO spy on a mission to destroy the opposition movement. Despite the fact that the accusations were pedestrian and were never substantiated, they served the purpose of gukurahundism. Ncube and his faction were politically emasculated and socially sequestrated.

The apple of discord was raw tribalism and impunity on the part of Tsvangirai, who during his days as a ZANU PF youth had been nurtured to believe in Shona supremacy and in the infallibility of the leader. There was no justification for Tsvangirai's peremptory assertion before the split that *'ndini ndinema key"* (I have the keys). He was claiming to be the omnipotent and omniscient leader. He tried to convince the party faithfulls and the world that he and he alone had the silver bullet to the economic woes bedeviling the country. Sounding very much like an ordinary braggart and an empty vaunter, he had claimed that nothing could be done by the party outside his wishes and consent. That was tantamount to saying he was the man and everybody else had to bow down to his caprices. Clearly he gave an early warning sign that once elected into the country presidency, precious little, if anything at all would impede him from aping the French Louis XIV declaration, *"L 'etat, c'est moi"* (I am the state).

In that superior state of mind, Tsvangirai in October 2005 vetoed an MDC National Executive Council (NEC) resolution to participate in the recently introduced senate elections. During the decisive NEC meeting and subsequently through the media, Tsvangirai frog marched constitutionalism, democracy and consensus out of the MDC and covertly ushered in unilateral decision making and cultism. By so doing, he substituted himself for the people and in the process scoffed at the rule of law within the party. Everyone could see, save for those blinded by tribal bias or by a strong need for the material benefits or rank, that came from Tsvangirai's patronage, that they were face to face with a younger and surprisingly widely accepted Mugabe, at a time when the real Mugabe was vilified and condemned at home and by the international community for dictatorship. Despite his popularity, Tsvangirai, just before the split exhibited too much a similarity with Mugabe. Zimbabwe was at the risk of replacing a strongman with another strongman and would remain a very exposed institution and a weak democracy in all respects. If anyone, especially in marginalized Matabeleland, believed that the MDC and Tsvangirai represented real change, they needed to exit from the garden path along which they were being walked.

There was a wide belief and a justified hope that Tsvangirai was going to dethrone Mugabe. Notwithstanding, some like Ncube noticed, probably too late after making him, that Tsvangirai, like Mugabe, was perverted with a rare kind of palatial sense of egomania that would make most despots look boyish. He converted the party, with the blessing of the majority party members and sympathizers, into a personal fiefdom where he was judge and jury, thereby pausing a direct threat to the fundamentals of democracy and accountability. That became a tacit blending and conforming into the ZANU PF despotism that the MDC was supposed to be fighting.

Ncube and most of the Ndebeles as well as many liberally minded Shonas in senior positions stomached the abusive tribalism, but when eventually feuds and even violence erupted, they could not go further. The centre could not hold anymore and the party split. The president Mr. Morgan Tsvangirai led a faction, later called MDCT which outshone (as reflected by the general elections of 29 March 2008) the other faction which retained the name MDC. In a bid to retain the so – called 'national' character of the party by dispelling the perceptions that their faction was a Ndebele party, the MDC elected a robust and high sounding United States based Prof. Arthur Mutambara of Shona pedigree, to lead the party.

It is probable that Ncube, whose detractors in the party had accused of tribalism and of habouring ambitions to form his own party, wanted to prove them wrong. He and his team therefore identified a Shona to lead the party. That decision backfired and the Prof. Ncube and Prof. Mutambara led MDC lost seats in both the House of Assembly and the Senate in the 2008 elections.

Noteworthy is that Tsvangirai's faction emerged from the split with a world record dangling like an albatross medal around its neck. Its name was changed to Movement for Democratic Change Tsvangirai (MDCT). A first in the history of politics the world over, that a political party should bear the name of a person who was the incumbent leader. Under normal circumstances, voters, civic society, pundits, analysts and donors would have questioned the seeming personalization of the party as it was an antecedent or substantiation of an already existsing personality cult or fiefdom. Many, within and outside the party were content with the party capture into Tsvangirai's personal property, probably because they were already victims of the same regimen in the hands of ZANU PF's gukurahundism which hero worshipped and did not question the leader's unilateral decisions.

The disturbing factor about the split of the MDC was that Ncube was personally blamed for the split and earned himself the permeated and soiled mantle of tribalist. He was also labelled as a CIO spy, a member of ZANU PF, divisive and ambitious by senior party leaders. For daring to face up to a popular Shona, he was damned. The international community, in their desperation to see Mugabe's regime collapse, were clutching at straws. They committed the same blunder they had done in endorsing Mugabe in 1980. Tsvangirai, with an unusual penchant for gaffes, was prematurely conscripted by the local independent press, western media houses and the international donor community into the pantheon of heroes. They once more got entrapped in a web of populism as opposed to justice and fairness and blindly endorsed a man with a roughshod approach to policy and practice alike. Ironically Tsvangirai's dictatorship did not only split the party in its early days in 2005, but he split it again in 2014. Tsvangirai's unilateralism was to haunt the party posthumously in a confounding manner as he once more managed to split the party after his death in 2018, as shall be revealed later. Strangely, on all the three occasions, someone else but him the leader, was blamed for the split.

The West and many Zimbabweans forgot that it took more than popularity to become a country's president, especially in Africa. Tsvangirai had the numbers behind him. According to David Coltart, a Bulawayo lawyer and member of parliament, in a letter to Geoff Nyarota the former editor of the Chronicle newspaper soon after the split, "*Morgan undoubtedly has majority support of party members but virtually all the leadership talent, acumen and integrity lies in the other side*" (The Standard, 15 – 21 April). The West endorsed and the majority party supporters opted to be led by a popular figure who was without personal frugality, public rectitude, intellectual acuity and institutional discipline, just because he was popular.

That endorsement cost dearly the aspirations of all progressive forces internally. It weighed down the drive and momentum for political change as well as the West's own agenda of regime change. What quickly became indesputable within a very short period after all the splits but especially the 2005 one, was that whatever successes and challenges were encountered by both MDC formations, by splitting, they successfully caught the shadow yet lost the substance, thereby triggering wild and boisterous celebrations from ZANU PF who were generously handed a new lease of life by that indiscretion of the opposition.

Despite the obvious agenda of the MDC to assume political power and form a government, they kept turning their own guns at their own heads at every election. It was probably that endorsement that made Tsvangirai over confident and started taking matters for granted. He individually committed too many politically costly mistakes. In 2008 the people that matter most, the voting masses, tried one more time to invest their trust and confidence in Mogarn Tsvangirai as an alternative to Mugabe but he proved to be bigoted and exhibited rare naivety by claiming victory and then flying away from the country. He flew away from the people that had voted for him due to a suspected threat to his life. He also flew away from a losing and desperate Mugabe, till the aged tyrant located his scattered wits and refused to vacate the office.

By 2013 while Mugabe was still floating on the borrowed wings of victory by abrogated laws, Tsvangirai had hit rock bottom but surprised many by emulating Mugabe by refusing to allow fresh legs to take over from him. Worse still, against informed advice from SADC, South African president Jacob Zuma, Zuma's international advisor, Mrs. Lindiwe Zulu and his own lieutenants, that the elections could not be held in the absence of compliance to an electoral road map and requisite security sector, media and legislative reforms, Tsvangirai single handedly and single mindedly chose to contest. He lost the election to Mugabe again. That time around he managed to legitimize and sanitize Mugabe who emerged not only confident in victory with a rejuvinated spring to his usually languid gait, but more acceptable even to the European Union (UE) who started lifting targeted sanctions on his government executives.

By recklessly endorsing Tsvangirai and vilifying Ncube, after ignoring the facts, the west and the local independent media perpetuated gukurahundism. By accepting at face value the misinformation by Tsvangirai and the MDCT propaganda mandarins, they irreparably damaged Ncube's chances of convincing the electorate that a systems change in Zimbabwe was not dependent on individuals but on democratic institutions. They further entrenched Tsvangirai's dictatorship and personality cult, thereby costing him, Tsvangirai, the subsequent elections. By endorsing his veto power, they showed approval of his unilateral decision making and they confirmed his misinformed claim that he was indeed 'the' man without whom the party was doomed.

Perplexingly some of the so called Ndebele 'tribalists', throughout their illustrious careers sacrificed their resources and even lives for the good of the nation at large, yet were ascribed that disparaging status. Welshman Ncube set up Morgan Tsvangirai for the presidency of the MDC instead of Gibson Sibanda a fellow Ndebele, at its formation. After the split he propped up Professor Arthur Mutambara for the presidency of the splinter group. Both Tsvangirai and Mutambara were Shonas. So much trust and good faith from a tribalist.

According to Prof Ncube, the *raison deitre* of conflict and eventual split of the MDC in 2005, was raw tribalism designed to push the Ndebeles out of positions of influence. It was a strategy to compel the Matabele into conformity with the dictates of Shona nationalism. He attested that the issue of the senate was merely a convenient excuse which was projected as the official reason for the split. According to Ncube even after crisscrossing the dusty rural roads of the Matabeleland region and condemning the Gukurahundi massacres and decrying the lack of infrastructural development in the provinces, back in their Harvest House offices in Harare, his Shona colleagues would complain that there were too many Ndebeles at Harvest House, the party headquarters.

Consequently, in 2004 at a National Executive meeting held at Wild Geese in Harare, Lucia Mativenga, a powerful voice of the Women's Assembly and a formidably potent ally to Morgan Tsvangirai, uttered the most bizarre profanation in the history of unorthodoxy and the MDC itself. Mativenga unashamedly declared that the recruitment and employment of personnel at Harvest House was skewed in favour of one region, Matabeleland. It needed no deviner to fathom that she was alleging that there were more Ndebeles within the workforce than Shonas or that there were too many Ndebeles than needed. Trudy Stevenson, a white Member of Parliament for Harare North, condemned Mativenga's statement as pregnant with tribal allusion (Stevenson was, a few months later beaten to a pulp by MDC party youths for unknown reasons).

The then Deputy General Secretary Mr. Tendai Biti (MP) pointed out that Mativenga had made a complaint that was quantitative in nature and therefore could be proved or disproved. Therefore, a head count of the secretariat was done. It was discovered that there were only three Ndebeles as compared to twenty - two Shonas within the party secretariat. What was most frivolous about that case was neither the underlying mischief and inaccuracy of the allegation nor the contempt for the Ndebele that was exhibited by Mativenga, but the innate tolerance of intolerance by the party. Mativenga was not chastised for fanning tribalism despite Trudy Stevenson's recommendation. The profundity of psycho - social depravation in the complaint about Ndebeles was unheard of, yet it was accorded the treatment of a genuine concern.

In sync with Mativenga, Isaac Matongo the first National Chairperson of the MDC was known to publicly declare, within the corridors of Harvest House that *"maNdeere awandisa"* (there are too many Ndebeles in the party). He was neither apologetic nor secretive in his belief. Matongo wanted the party senior echelons to be devoid of Ndebeles, particularly Gibson Sibanda, Welshman Ncube, Esap Mdlongwa, Paul - Themba Nyathi and Fletcher - Dulini Ncube.

Gukurahundism was therefore employed to arrest the 'runaway' numbers of Ndebeles in the MDC secretariat which at 12% was deemed to be too much. It must be noted that the gukurahundi genocide by Mugabe and ZANU had been unleashed to arrest the numbers of the Ndebele and the Kalanga in the country. It was disturbing in the extreme, to hear such sentiments from within the senior opposition ranks.

In 2002 Elias Mudzuri won the MDC party primary elections for the candidature of the mayor of Harare. The procedure was that if one won a primary election, they would then be assessed and vetted by the National Executive Committee for final approval. Mudzuri's supporters, chanting slogans and praising him, demanded that he be instantly declared the candidate. The supporters included many vociferous youths with a mob mentality. In blatant breach of protocol, the presiding officer Mr. Fidelis Mhashu was arm twisted into proclaiming Mudzuri as the party's candidate for mayor of Harare.

Thereafter, Mr. Paul - Themba Nyathi (interview, March 2010, Harare) the then Director of Elections in the MDC, received numerous complaints from party members alleging that Mudzuri had employed violence to influence the outcome. There were further complaints from Mudzuri's former workmates in the municipality, accusing him of corruption during his previous tenure as Director of Engineering. Mr. Nyathi then went into Tsvangirai's office to urge him to ensure that Mudzuri's candidature was on the agenda of the National Executive meeting which was due, for final approval. As they were discussing the issue, the party chairperson Mr. Isaac Matongo walked into the office and was briefed by Tsvangirai about the issue. Matongo retorted *"kudi kwacho?"*, meaning, what about it? Nyathi then remineded Matongo of the party procedure and informed him of the allegations against Mudzuri, but to his surprise Matongo went on to question him, *"pamakasarudza mayor wenyu kuBuruwayo isu takapindira here"?* (when you elected your mayor in Bulawayo did we interfere?). Nyathi was out of words as the ground was crudely cut from under his feet in the presence of Tsvangirai. Not surprisingly, the proposed item was not included in the NEC agenda and the 'us and them' mentality triumphed.

The lesson conveyed by the MDC chairperson and sanctioned by Tsvangirai was that Ndebeles were to have no say in the selection of candidates for elections in Harare or Mashonaland. The selection was a Shona affair which the Ndebele had to shy away from and leave the Zezuru, Karanga, Manyika and Korekore, bound by a common language, culture and geography to grapple with even if a Ndebele was the party director of elections.

Nyathi was oblivious of the intra Shona squabbles and therefore was not aware that Mudzuri's ascent to mayorship was a victory by the Karanga over the Zezuru. In that frame of mind, he was viewed as a Ndebele first and not the director of elections. Yet he was merely carrying out his mandate as National Director of Elections, and not as a regional leader of the Ndebele. Once more, the brazen trashing and defiance of party policy, protocol, values and norms meant to hold, not only the party but the country together was not corrected by the party and by the president.

University of Zimbabwe lecturer Prof. Eldred Masunungure at the time of the split asserted that, ... *"(b)oth Ncube and [deputy president Gibson] Sibanda must have realised... that in Zimbabwe politics, and given the grip of ethnic consciousness, a Ndebele would have a very faint chance of making it to State House," (ZimOnline website).*

That statement portrayed Ncube and Sibanda as willing participants in a drama of what was conveniently termed *"ethnic consciousness"*, yet they were victims of raw and rabid institutionalized tribalism. Masunungure was right, Ncube and Sibanda put Shonas as party presidents ahead of themselves because they knew most Shonas would not vote for a Ndebele, not after Mugabe's 1980 victory and the Gukurahundi genocide. A Ndebele would not make it to state house in Zimbabwe because the ruling Zezuru hegemonists had decreed to most Shonas, high and low, that Ndebeles should not be allowed anywhere near any form of power, be it social, political or economic. Many Shona people had been indoctrinated and socialized into believing that power was their collective monopoly, while in actual fact Mugabe was labourng tooth and nail to guarantee that it remained a Zezuru preseve.

Masunungure's view was proved in February 2011 when in accordance with the party constitution, the splinter MDC led by Prof Mutambara held its first five yearly elective congress in Harare. All the party's thirteen provinces were represented. The congress was attended by approximately five thousand delegates but twelve senior party leaders boycotted as they protested Ncube's party presidency ambitions. They termed the congress a farce and illegal. The party president Professor Arthur Mutambara was present and before the congress had declared that he was not seeking election for that office. All the thirteen provinces nominated Professor Welshman Ncube for the party's president. He was appointed unopposed. The outgoing president accepted the results and gave a magnanimous speech which was hailed by all and sundry as a mark of rare political aptitude. Analysts accoladed Mutambara for being the unselfish astute athlete who did not run into the woods with the relay button stick, Mugabe - style.

Soon after the congress, the MDC National Executive Committee convened and resolved to re-deploy its officials in the inclusive Government of National Unity.

The Government of National Unity (GNU) had been created on 15 September 2008 by MDC, MDC Tsvangirai and ZANU PF, after the two disputed elections of March and June 2008 had resulted in an impasse. The parties had signed a Global Political Agreement (GPA) to share government power. Prof. Mutambara by virtue of being president of the MDC had signed the agreement. The agreement was crystal clear that Mugabe would be State President and Tsvangirai would be Prime Minister. It also provided for two deputy prime ministers, one from MDC and one from MDC Tsvangirai. The three senior members of the GNU were to be three principals, namely the president, prime minister and the deputy prime minister from the Mutambara led MDC.

The prerogative to deploy and re-deploy officers to the GNU, save for Mugabe and Tsvangirai who were mentioned by name, was vested on the respective political parties by the GPA. That was one of the injustices of the agreement. If it was to usher in a government of national unity, it had to have a national outlook at the top. There was no way, not even by the most generous stretch of the imagination, Mugabe, Tsvangirai and Mutambara could claim to represent the people of Matabeleland. Their record as representatives of Matabele interests was atrocious to say the least. (two of them were personally involved in the 1980s genocide in Matabeleland and how could they when among the three of them they could not speak any of the thirteen languages of Matabeleland?) There was supposed to be a regional and tribal balancing mechanism embedded within the agreement. It had to provide for someone from the three million citizens of Matabeleland to be one of the three principals. Otherwise what happened proved that the struggle in Zimbabwe was about personal power. The quest for personal glory was why Mutambara argued that he had to be one of the three principals because he had signed the GPA with Mugabe and Tsvangirai. He got deliberately oblivious to the fact that he had done so as an instrument of an institution, and that technically the signatory was the institution.

The Global Political Agreement should have provided for a president, a prime minister and a deputy prime minister. The offices of the two vice presidents were supposed to be abolished, while that of the second deputy prime minister should not have been created, for economic austerity. Therefore, it would have made both administrative and political logic that Mugabe be the president with Tsvangirai as prime minister while Ncube was deputy prime minister. The GPA was supposed to specify that, before going on to provide that a percentage of cabinet positions were to be allocated to Matabeleland. That was one way of guaranteeing that the government was indeed national.

Two examples will be used to prove the logic in the above criticism of the GPA. As observed by Mnangagwa on 28 June 2019 during a meeting with Matabeleland and Midlands traditional chiefs in Bulawayo, the Ndebele could not claim to represent the Shona and obviously the reverse was true. The meeting had been requested by the Matabele chiefs. They had invited all the Matabeleland chiefs as well as the chiefs from the Ndebele speaking parts of the Midlands. That irked the president so much he had to violate protocol and demanded to speak before his time in the program. Mnangagwa complained that the invitation and attendance was based on tribe and he did not like the fact that the Shona chiefs from Midlands province had not been invited to the meeting. He also complained because the chiefs had indicated that Chief Charumbira, the president of the council of chiefs, was not welcome to the meeting. Chief charumbira was Shona but his tribe was probably not the basis for his exclusion. What Mnangagwa was saying was quite comprehensible. The meeting agenda aside, the Ndebele speaking chiefs from the Midlands could not claim to represent the Shona speaking chiefs and their people. Whether or not the Shona speaking chiefs were relevant to the agenda of the meeting was immaterial to him. He wanted the Shona to be represented by the Shona because the Ndebele could not represent them or represent them enough

Secondly, the analogy between Mnangagwa's complaint and the story told by Rev. Ndabaningi Sithole in his book, 'African Nationalism', was very compelling. Sithole cited Kenya's Jomo Kenyata who had told the story before the Mau Mau revolt of 1952. He had said that a man had allowed an elephant to partially shelter in his hut away from a thunderstorm. Shortly the elephant moved wholly into the hut and evicted the man. The man complained to the King, the lion. The lion set up a commission comprising the rhino, the buffalo, the alligator, the fox and the leopard. Upon requesting that "*one of his kind*" be part of the commission, the man was assured that justice would be served by the appointees who were chosen by God, besides his "kind" were not educated enough to understand the law of the jungle. The commission conducted hearings and passed a verdict giving the elephant ownership of the hut.

The man went on to built another hut but the rhino came and occupied it. A commission was appointed without the man's "*kind*". Once more the man lost his hut, this time to the rhino. The man built another hut and another, but kept losing them in similar fashion. The man eventually decided to trap the animals and killed them all (Sithole 1959).

The lesson that Mnangagwa seemed to understand very clearly in line with Kenyata's story was that, one needed to be represented by their 'kind'. That is why the GPA of 2008 was inadequate. It did not have a Matabeleland representative at the principals' level.

It made political logic but not social and administrative justice that the most senior member of the MDC party, Mutambara was deployed as Deputy Prime Minister to the GNU. Ms Thokozani Khuphe the second most senior party member was sworn in as the second Deputy Prime Minister by her party, the MDCT, while ZANU PF retained the two vice presidents. Khuphe from Matabeleland was a ceremonial appointee and was not one of the principals who made the decisions that turned the wheels of the state. It was the most extravagant power sharing deal and the most top heavy structure in the history of developing countries.

After the congress the MDC resolved to re-deploy Prof. Welshman Ncube, the party new president as the new principal to the GNU and therefore as new Deputy Prime Minister, taking over from Mutambara. Deputy Prime Minister Prof. Mutambara was assigned the less glamorous Ministry of Regional Integration and Cooperation portfolio. That resolution proved to be yet another dagger on the mutilated back of Ncube's resume. He was immediately assailed from left, right and centre like Shakespeare's *"deer stricken by many princes"*. Mutambara made a sudden and shocking *vaulte farce*. He denounced Ncube and stopped recognising him as party president.

Mutambara refused to step down as Deputy Prime Minister on the grounds that he was the signatory to the GPA and as such could not be replaced. In his refusal to step down, strangely to all democracy builders and monitors, Mutambara got support from Mugabe. Mugabe who uncharacteristically spoke in Ndebele dismissing Ncube's overtures and MDC official communication requesting him to appoint Ncube as Deputy Prime Minister, emphatically said "…..*angifuni*" (i don't want). Despite working as a teacher in Matabeleland for many years and working under Joshua Nkomo and with many Matabeles in ZAPU, Mugabe was not known for speaking any of the Matabeleland languages, let alone Ndebele. Instead he always addressed rallies in Matabeleland in Shona and English, yet all Matabeleland politicians addressed rallies in Mashonaland in Shona. However, this time around he wanted to make sure that Ncube and all the Ndebele heard him loud and clear.

Mugabe's response was a personal diatribe. It indicated that he personally did not want to appoint Ncube, a Ndebele and legally dethrone Mutambara a Shona. Mugabe further stated that he was working well with Tsvangirai and Mutambara. That affirmation was neither questioned nor disputed by Tsvangirai or his party's vocal spin machinery which was always trigger happy when it came to firing disagreement and criticism at Mugabe. That was a very dubious confession by Mugabe since the media was ever awash with contestations between their respective parties especially with regards to electoral and media reforms.

Morgan Tsvangirai refused to help Ncube to deal with Mutambara when he absolved himself of any responsibility by declaring that the issue was an intra party matter that did not warrant his intervention. Strange that Tsvangirai and Mugabe, perceived protagonists that had always seized every opportunity to criminalise and scandalise each other, were serene and contented in consensus. That episode proved that Mugabe and Tsvangirai could differ on politics, ideology, methodology, the land issue etc but not on Shona nationalism which called upon them to close ranks, prop - up and back their own tribesman. When it came to issues between Ndebele and Shona, they discarded all pretence on the political stage and became each other's pillar of support. From their superior tribal pedestal, they could never sacrifice Mutambara, a fellow Shona for Ncube, a Ndebele who wanted to encroach on their private ethnic picnic santuary.

At a time when seemingly Mugabe was impervious to Ncube's demands for equality, while Tsvangirai thought he was exempt from the use of opposition party political logic and Mutambara was grateful to both fellow tribesmen for preserving their ethnic 'holy' ground from Ndebele enchroachment, the elite terzetto got support from a most unlikely source. Dr. Lovemore Madhuku, a constitutional lawyer and Chairman of the National Constitutional Assembly (NCA) condemned Ncube too. When it came to Shona nationalism, even the experts threw professional ethics out of the window. The learned doctor was supposed to be less impartial and know better, at least enough to be capable of interpreting the provisions of the GPA more accurately.

Numerous other political commentators condemned Ncube as power hungry and devisive. He was labelled a tribalist once more, despite the fact that only four of the thirteen provinces that had nominated him at the party congress were from the Matabeleland and Midlands regions. The rest were from Mashonaland. A vicious onslaught of bombardment after barrage was sustained in the media against Ncube for exercising his democratic right. For daring to dethrone a Shona as party president and therefore aspiring to be the country president, Ncube attracted the abandoned wrath of gukurahundism. He was assailed and decampaigned so mercilessly even the American embassy weighed in by describing him as *"devisive"*. It was such a torrent of disapproval, criticism and labelling, only the blind and deaf would vote for him. Even in his home region, Matabeleland and Midlands few voted for him in the 2013 elections because they were made to believe that the Matabele were too few to beat the Shona in an election. The election results reflected a tacit admission that in Zimbabwe, elections were a tribal process or merely an ethnic census as had been revealed by Professor Masunungure.

It became apparent to the politically objective, that Ncube was guilty of one crime and one crime mainly. He was a Ndebele who dared to challenge Shona power and went on to win at party level. At that political juncture it became demonstrable that ZANU PF and MDCT politics uncomfortably suggested that the Ndebele and the Shona simply could not work together in an equal partnership or where the former was the leader. The Ndiweni / Chirau precedent, the Nkomo / Mugabe set - up, the Sibanda / Tsvangirai affair, the Ncube / Mutambara debacle, all put paid to the notion that in Zimbabwe a Matabele simply could not be president. No matter how better endowed or qualified they were as leaders, the Matabele were not supposed to lead in Zimbabwe.

During an interview (29 March 2017, Bulawayo) Ncube explained why Muatambara who had initially accepted the party congress resolution later made a sudden u – turn. He stated, "… *I know that he had a conversation with Mugabe and Mugabe said to him, but why would you accept that? We must all finish our terms. Why should you establish a precedent like that. Stay, we will back you. He then, being a peacock, he preferred being in power rather than the principle, he allowed himself to be used for personal gain rather than for advancement of the things that we said we stood for. Mugabe said as much to me. He said, where in Africa have you seen a leader of a party just removed like that? Why should we cooperate with you? We were in his office just across the table. It was plain that he didn't accept the notion that a political organization can remove its leader*"

Prof. Mutambara's refusal to accept redeployment by the party reflected failure to abide by the principle of serving the people as opposed to personal grandeur. The principle of service dictated that the customer is always right. In politics the customer is the people. It never matters how wrong one may feel the people are, if they disagree with him / her, he /she had better comply and never impose on them. Adherence to the principle of service was remarkably displayed by South African president Thabo Mbeki in September 2008 as well as Jacob Zuma in 2018. Both Zuma and Mbeki were recalled from the office of the president of the republic by the African National Congress (ANC), a body which had not elected them into that office. They had been elected into office by the South African Parliament. Both constitutionally and technically speaking, they could have refused to vacate office until they were recalled by parliament. Getting parliament to recall Mbeki was going to be an uphill task for the ANC, given party dynamics and the composition of parliament at the time.

According to Chikane (2012:23), just before he was informed by the ANC delegation and prior to accepting the decision of the party's National Executive to recall him, Thabo Mbeki had said that, *"if his organization asked him to leave office he would comply, since he saw his role as that of 'service to the people' rather than 'a position' that he needed 'to fight for'..... He re – emphasized his commitment to ensuring that the country was not destabilized by his problems with the ANC. No one should pay a price for the negative politics of the party"*. After he had been told that the ANC had summoned him back, although he knew that that was the constitutional role of parliament, Thabo Mbeki in a farewell message referred to a code of conduct and a revolutionary value system to which he swore unselfish allegience. He declared that that value system, *"..has told me that I must always strive to serve the people....never to betray those who are my comdrades – in – arms, committed to achieve agreed common objectives....never to dishonor the revolutionary democratic cause, by allowing my personal desires to assume precedence over the interests of the masses of the people"* (Chikane 2012).

In similar fashion Mutambara must have overruled his personal desires and respected the fact that while it was Mugabe that had sworn him into office and it was him alone that could legally dismiss him, it was the party / people that had appointed him by recommending him to the state. He and Mugabe could not refuse to accept the MDC's vedict to order him back and still make democratic sense. Hence when the party / people recommended another in his lieu, he should have accepted that decision based on the principle of service, if any other reasons were not appealing. By refusing to be re – deployed, Mutambara continued in the GNU but was engaging in self – embroidering, appeasing Mugabe and probably Tsvangirai while unleashing gukurahundism on Ncube.

Mbeki's nobility, level headed deportment and calm during the storm was nowhere near Zimbabwean politics where ZANU PF succession battles, Mugabe's refusal to accept electoral defeat and party calls for him to step down had literally collapsed the country into an economic refuse dump. On the other hand, the opposition's Tsvangirai's insistence on single handedly attempting to unseat Mugabe, leapfrogging from one electoral defeat to another, rigged or otherwise, left Zimbabweans politically disheveled and bereft of economic hope. It would appear as if there was a curse on the Zimbabawean voters because when Tsvangirai finally saw the sense of an alliance with other opposition parties, it was too little too late. He was cronically ill and died a few months before the elections. With his death, the hopes of many that were pinned on his Alliance with other opposition parties, died.

In January 2012, Ncube who was the minister of industry and commerce was interviewed by Ray Ndlovu of the Financial Gazette on his relationship with Mugabe and Tsvangirai in the GNU. When he was asked if the perception that Mugabe and Tsvangirai were sidelining him from the GNU because he was Ndebele and they were Shona was real, he responded thus: *"(w)hat is clear between President Mugabe and Tsvangirai is that they are in agreement to make sure that I will never assume the post of Deputy Prime Minister as is allowed by the due process of law. These are one of the few rare instances that President Mugabe and Tsvangirai are in agreement over something. Blocking my rise to the post of deputy premiership is something they can easily do as President Mugabe is the one that swears in people, and he could refuse to swear me in.*

The reasons and motivations as to why I am not being allowed to become the Deputy-Prime Minitser are known only to them. I have not bought into the ethnicity position waved in political circles as the main reason. I however, believe that the two men fear that the hegemonic contestation that has always involved just the two of them would be thoroughly threatened if I rise in the ranks of the inclusive government".

Reminiscent of Joshua Nkomo thirty years earlier, Ncube opted to be diplomatic and failed to call a spade a spade, although he did not rule out tribalism, probably due to a good contingent of senior Shonas in the party leadership. Just like Joshua Nkomo in the 1980s, he was wary of pinpointing an anti – Ndebele crusade by the two, based on ethnicity for fear of alienating members of his team. Ncube too, like Nkomo wanted the Mashonaland vote and could not afford a predicament that pitted him on one side and Shonas on the other. He probably saw prudence in describing the scenario as a Ncube versus Mugabe and Tsvangirai debacle and not a Ndebele versus Shona conspiracy for the sake of cohesion within his party. He already stood accused of tribalism. Meddling and wading deeper into the tribalism debate could easily cement him as a tribalist to his Mashonaland supporters. That was a risk he was not prepared to take and he let the sleeping dogs lie. Maybe Ncube did not realize it, but he was a victim of gukurahundism because he was a Ndebele encroaching onto the holy ground of a tribal triumvirate.

The ZANU PF / MDCT and the Mugabe / Tsvangirai nexus during the GNU exposed the mystique of the two sides of the same coin concept. Those institutions and personalities proved to be two sides of the same coin, bound together by a strong cultural inheritance, a single political background and a belief in tribal nationalism. Indeed, the coin may have two sides that never see the same view at the same time, therefore implying that they may never agree on what they see and perceive. Their relationship may be characterized by accusations and counter accusations of bias, misrepresentation, blindness, ignorance, incompetence, etc. Notwithstanding, the two faces will always be the coin, which is the life, blood and the basis for their existence. The faces have the same value and they are interdependent and one is irrevocably planted into the other. Similarly, to both ZANU PF and MDCT and the leaders therein, what mattered most was existence as advocates of many principles, chief among them being tribal nationalism more than whatever political beliefs and values they espoused for the gallery. They could easily close ranks whenever their nationalism was under threat. The Matabele and Shona rank and file in those parties were oblivious of the ties binding them together and the chasm casting them asunder.

Some four months after the MDC inaugural congress, in the Newsday daily newspaper of 31 May 2011, Dr Madhuku commented that *"the support that the Ncube faction gave to Moyo was because the MDC N did not have a candidate and had to support someone from Matabeleland"*. The erudite Dr Madhuku was evidently encouraging the Morgan Tsvangirai led MDCT to neither appreciate nor reciprocate the support extended to them by the Ncube led MDC during the election for Speaker of Parliament which Lovemore Moyo of the MDCT had won.

Dr. Madhuku might have had other reasons, which lie beyond the scope of this book, for downplaying the importance of cooperation between the two MDC formations but what could hardly be ignored was the tribal connotation and patronizing innuendo, heavy and thick in his contention. Madhuku betrayed a feeling all too familiar and common in Zimbabwe, a raw and unjustified contempt for any Ndebele led institution, notwithstanding how noble its motivations and sincere its practices. While pedestrian pontification on parliamentary procedure could be forgiven coming from a layman, there were no excuses for it spewing forth from the desk of a doctor of law.

What was fallacious and advertently disingenuous in Dr. Madhuku's avowal was, first, the claim that the MDC did not have a candidate. He obviously was not privy to the intricate dynamics within the MDC or he simply opted to ignore facts. It is well known that just like the MDCT, the MDC party had no dearth of parliamentary experience, skill and enlightenment. If anything, they could have fielded former MP, Paul Themba Nyathi who had lost the speaker of parliament election in 2008 in a process that was condemned by the supreme court and a re - election ordered. It would be absurd for any political party in the world to fail to present a candidate for an office of Speaker of Parliament whose only qualification was to be a citizen of that country.

Secondly the humdrum yet dangerous projection that the MDC voted for Lovemore Moyo, because he was from Matabeleland was way too elementary and not marketable by any stretch of the imagination. The eventual Speaker, Lovemore Moyo was contesting against ZANU PF's Simon Khaya Moyo. The two Moyos hailed from Matabeleland. It can therefore be concluded that the MDC voted for one Moyo and not the other Moyo for some and any other reasons but definitely not because one Moyo came from Matabeleland because both came from Matabeleland. Apperantly the MDC opted for Lovemore Moyo because he was MDCT and not Simon Moyo because he was ZANU PF. Madhuku's, was an attempt to tribalise and regionalise the MDC's voting for Lovemore Moyo probably in a clear betrayel of deep seated derision for the Ndebele led MDC. Such arguments coming from a renowned, informed and influential personality like Madhuku could easily and in all probability did estrange Ncube and his MDC from the Shona electorate.

Gukurahundism was for many years used to discredit the image of many, both in Matabeleland and Mashonaland. It was responsible for tarnishing reputations of and portraying Ndebeles as a backward, austere, bloodthirsty, illiterate and inumerate mob. Most politicians, clergy, civic activists, community leaders, business leaders, civil servants etc from Matabeleland spent their tenure scampering away from the corrosive and insidious cloak of tribalist, which was tossed at them at the first hint of them being aggrieved with the agenda of internal Shona colonial expansion or whenever they were perceived as a threat to the provisions of the 1979 Grand Plan and its review document.

In a bid to evade that dreaded title of tribalist, the Matabele ran incessantly and far, they ended up accomplishing virtually nothing while in office due to the fright and fatigue. Most that stood up to be counted for Matabeleland were instantaneously and surreptitiously straitjacketed in that hideous cloak. They were hastily condemned, dismissed and therefore forgotten even by their own people. Matabeleland was between the proverbial devil and the deep blue sea. It was on a stage of the classic theatre of stand up and be damned.

There was inalienable evidence that the people of Matabeleland were mass slaughtered because they were tribally different, were still by 2019 denied equal opportunities in leadership, infrastructural development, education, health, housing, employment, land, access to capital finance etc due to ethnic differentiation. When the men and women of Matabeleland pointed out the injustice of the system they are castigated and accused of propagating ethnic disharmony and at times were arrested for insulting / provoking Shona people.

Mugabe was the all - time champion when it came to disparaging and undoing Matabeleland. He was the piloting culprit in that conspiracy as evidenced by his 2015 unstatesman, undiplomatic and bigoted claim that Kalangas were uneducated and were involved in petty crimes in South Africa. Mugabe who had done everything possible to keep Kalangas uneducated, unemployed and unemployable in his country, had the nerve to open his mouth in such a dogmatic and pompous manner. That utterance, coming from a president that was presiding over the worst social and economic implosion in recent human memory, a catastrophe that forced three million Zimbabweans including Kalangas to seek economic respite and risk xenophobic attacks in South Africa, was the most basic and contrived tribal tirade any responsible head of state could make.

Generally, the government's attitude towards that challenge was anything between mediocrity and propagative, depending on the conditions prevalent at any given moment. If the government was not actively perpetrating tribalism through such departments as the police, customs, justice, immigration, registry, education, health and all uniformed forces, it was passively but consciously ignoring the protests and discomfort of the victims. Tribalism against the Ndebele became such an everyday occurrence it became normal practice. Antipathy, discrimination and marginalisation became so common a conduct that its materialization went by unobserved, uncorrected, unchecked and unmentioned. The people of Matabeleland ultimately accepted that jobs, houses, cars and even respect were a preserve for Shona people.

In the mid 1990s a popular and prominent Shona musician composed and released a song which was played dreadfully often on national radio and tevelvision. The song had a lyric which stated that a donkey cried in its Ndebele fashion. The song was never banned or censured. Despite complaints by ordinary people from Matabeleland, there was never an official condemnation of the song and every once in a while some cantankerous disc jockey would play it for the fun of rubbing the message in. Very few, if any people in the world have been called donkey on an official broadcaster, let alone a whole nation. The naivety of the inference that Ndebeles were donkeys was so obvious it could not be missed even by primary school children.

The singer presented gukurahundism in its most vulgar form. A type of gukurahundism that dictated that, the Matabele were supposed to accept that they were aliens, uneducated, unemployable and incapable of leadership. They had to be ashamed of themselves, run away from their shadows like a donkey, shade off their colours and find a hole in the ground and hide. If one did that they were a good Ndebele and would benefit from the patronage of the majority who would stuff and decorate the hole and make it comfortable. Those that did not comply were labelled rebels and tribalists, fit for exclusion from the mainstream economic activity and politics. For his courage and fortitude in insulting Ndebeles, the musician was accorded by his admirers, the epithet *Dhongi* which was Shona for donkey. The nickname was an honorary title, reminding all and sundry, that 'here is the man who called the once mighty Ndebeles, donkeys'.

Universally, all cultures abhor insults and all cultures take strong and unequivocal exception to likening humans with such animals as donkeys and dogs. Calling a donkey Ndebele was tantamount to calling all Ndebeles donkeys. A country's leadership cannot let slip of the reigns of leadership as to allow such denigration of a section of its populace regardless of how few or petite the section is. The playing of the song by the Zimbabwe Broadcasting Corporation (ZBC) perplexed listeners and left analysts nonplussed. The silence by the authorities was so conspiratorial it spoke volumes into the thin façade of national unity. It was the crowning point of gukurahundism.

The gukurahundism narrative was that those Ndebeles that had survived the genocide had to be crushed one way or the other, hounded out of the country or have their identity and culture distorted or changed. They had to be reduced in numbers or dignity in all insitutions. Those that could not be somehow removed had to be sledge hammered to submit to tribal nationalism.

Addressing a Food, Agriculture and Natural Resource Policy Analysis Network (FANRPAN) 2009 annual regional policy dialogue meeting in Maputo, Mozambique, the senior minister responsible for National Healing, in the Inclusive Government, Mrs Sekai Holland (MDCT) reportedly delivered a calculated insult at the Ndebele people. She claimed that King Mzilikazi, the founder of the Ndebele nation and his 'band' of warriors were cattle thieves and murderers. Despite repeated complaints and demands for retraction and an apology by Matabeleland civic society, ordinary people and the Khumalo clan, neither the government nor her political party took heed. Such raw and callous disregard for tribal relations, deplorable for its calculated inaccuracy and deficiency of conventional wisdom and diplomacy, coming from a senior member of the cabinet whose task was attending to the gangrene infested wounds of tribalism and racism, was most reprehensible to say the least. By their silence and lame mediocrity, the MDCT and the government implied complicity and sanction of her demeanour that was designed to debase and abate the character and attributes of the Ndebele monarchy.

The Herald newspaper of 22 July 2010 on page 2 published a report on a high profile meeting of the ZANU PF politburo, the MDC national executive committee and the MDCT national executive committee. The meeting was called under the theme of peace and reconciliation. The article stated that the three political parties had agreed to convey the message of peace to all people at grass roots levels. The reporter however somehow forgot to mention that speaker after speaker had stated that Zimbabwe had known peace and tranquillity until, according to one of them, "thirteen years ago", referring to the late 1990s and afterwards. That was the period that saw the formation of the Movement for Democratic Change party, farm invasions, the deployment of the Zimbabwe National Army to the Democratic Republic of Congo, the resurfacing of election violence, an unpopular and violent operation to remove illegal settlements in towns, code named 'Operation Clean-up' or *Murambatswina* and the collapse of the economy.

Between 1998 and 2008 a number of people had died as a result of political violence during electioneering, covert security operations and farm invasions. Hundreds of whites were displaced from their farms and a number were severely beaten up. The bulk of those disturbances occurred in Mashonaland provinces. The blame was put squarely on the door step of the Robert Mugabe government. Therefore, at that meeting of 22 July 2010, the speakers, rightly, did not mince their words in condemning those political excesses. One speaker Mr. Joshua Mhambi (MDC) however, was the lone voice as he drew attention to the point that the people of Matabeleland expected the process of peace and reconciliation to deal with the national challenges from 1980 including the Gukurahundi genocide to date. He implored the meeting not to assume that the country only knew political violence when Mashonaland experienced the wrath of ZANU PF after 1998 as the preceding speakers had implied. Mr Mhambi was lambasted by ZANU PF stalwarts including David Karimanzira and Dr Sikhanyiso Ndlovu for attempting to grate old wounds (interview with Joshua Mhambi, 12 August 2010, Bulawayo).

The fear of grating old wounds or the reluctance to rock the boat was greatly misplaced when it came to reference or debate about an act of genocide which was never investigated and interrogated. The fear became an illegitimate excuse, more so if it was paddled by the perpetrator, ZANU PF and the government. In attempting to shield Mugabe and other Gukurahundists from scrutiny and interrogation Dr. Ndlovu, Karimanzira and their ilk, sounded like they were attempting to deny that the Gukurahundi genocide ever happened. They should have known that the wounds of Gukurahundi had not healed because they were never nursed in the first place. The wounds were ignored in the bigoted illusion that they would heal miraculously by themselves.

Paradoxically and in stark contrast with the claims in 2010 and earlier, that the genocide was an old wound that did not need to be awakened, in 2019 the traditional chiefs from Matabeleland and parts of Midlands told President Mnangagwa at a meeting in Bulawayo that, *"For too long this matter has been neglected and as a consequence victims and survivors are hurting. For many victims and survivors, the physical and emotional injuries are still fresh. They are looking for answers, justice and closure".* (Paper presented by the Matabeleland and Midlands chiefs to President Mnangagwa on 28 June 2019 in Bulawayo)

In the Sunday Mail of 11 May 1997, Mugabe was reported to also have sought refuge for crimes against humanity in fantasy and by historicising his crimes and playing the victim. He claimed that, *"if we dig up history, then we wreck the nation……. and we tear our people apart into factions, into tribes and villagism will prevail over our nationalism and over the spirit of our sacrifices. If we go by the past, would Ian Smith be alive today?.. perhaps I would be the first man to go and cut his throat and open his belly…….we have sworn not to go by the past excerpt as a record or register. The record or register will remind us what never to do. If that was wrong, if that went against the sacred tenets of humanity, we must never repeat, we must never oppress men".*

Hypocrisy is the mark of every dictator. Mugabe was conjuring historically justified emotions selectively for his convenience in order to divert focus from his regime's murderous conduct. Mugabe proved to be a true despot who shied away from interrogation by bringing up other people's out of context and irrelevant crimes. Instead of admitting that he committed terrible crimes in the past, he was quick to profess innocence and feign victimhood by tacitly reminding the world that he had been wrongly treated by Ian Smith and his regime during the war years. He shamelessly refused to acknowledge that his barbaric murders over five years in Matabeleland and Midlands were a part of history that was ever laid bare and did not require to be dug up because they were never properly laid to rest. He nonchalantly assumed a state of perpetual denial that his brand of nationalism had failed and that he had divided the country into two rival villages. That the Ndebele and the Shona were worlds apart was as distinct as day was from night. (one visit to a soccer match between Highlanders and Dynamos football clubs revealed that, as much the employees register of the biggest hotel in Victoria Falls exposed the lie in the nationalism fetish).

Mugabe's polarization of Matabeleland and Mashonaland via his plan of nationalism was aptly described by Prof. Jonathan Moyo. Moyo was one of very few political heavy weights from Matabeleland who acquired prime farming land in Mashonaland. By so doing he incurred the wrath of Mugabe for this violation of Shona nationalism which provided for the acquisition of land in Matabeleland by people from Mashonaland and not vice versa. In 2008 Mugabe's spokesperson George Charamba insinuated that Jonathan Moyo, coming from Matabeleland had no right to criticize Mugabe's disastrous policies since he owned a farm in Mashonaland. Moyo whose tongue was known for being as sharp as his pen was swift, succinctly retaliated by describing Mugabe in an article in The Zimbabwe Independent newspaper as, *"an ethnic bigot masquerading as a nationalist"* and Mugabe's brand as *"tribal bigotry....tribal nationalism or ethno nationalism....bantustan ideology.....tribal hallucinations ...that bred the Gukurahundi atrocities".*

Nationalism, among various constructs, was abused as a phylactery to hypnotise into zombies, dissenters in general and the victims of the Gukurahundi genocide in particular. Under the guise of nationalism, the liberation struggle, patriotic history, unity, peace and reconciliation were usurped to ensure that fresh wounds and heinous crimes were committed then swept under the carpet. A horrific precident was set for future leaders.

On the same page of the Herald of 22 July 2010, was an article titled *"Matabeleland leaders take Tsvangirai to task"*. The gist of the story was that the regional leaders of Matabeleland were unhappy with having too few representatives from their region appointed by the Prime Minister's party to the GNU cabinet. Moreso since the region was the traditional stronghold of the party even after the populous Mashonaland provinces had finally embraced the party after years of rebuffs. Tsvangirai failed to pacify and satisfy the Matabeleland leaders. Like Mugabe he hid behind the banner of nationalism.

Victoria Falls town, located on the northwest of Zimbabwe was the furthest geographic location from Mashonaland in the country. Being one of the wonders of the world, the tourism capital of Zimbabwe and a compelling international destination, the town offerred a lot of job and economic opportunities. On 14 November 2010 the town witnessed a continuation of the most ludicrous yet calculated labour recruitment practices ever. A restaurant chain, Food Express was opening a branch in the resort town. The company through the Group Human Resources Manager transported into town by bus, thirty employees from Gweru, a town some six hundred kilometres away. Of the thirty, twenty nine were of Shona extraction.

A resident witnessed the thirty disembark from the bus and alerted the Residents Association Chairperson, Mr. Morgan Dube who in turn alerted other civic society activists. A marathon of meetings were held with residents demanding that the thirty waiters, chefs, cashiers and general hands return to their homes in Gweru. They also demanded that the restaurant chain employ locals instead. The company acceded to popular pressure and all thirty went back to Gweru. The residents celebrated winning a minor battle in a war they were losing everyday. People from Mashonaland were arriving by bus, train, private cars and even by plane to take up jobs everywhere in Matabeleland and neither education nor qualification had anything to do with it. Most of the beneficiaries were made to sincerely believe that the people of Matabeleland were either unqualified or were too lazy to work, yet some were willing actors in a sadistic plot of domestic colonialism.

The cruel rejection of the local from the circle of the employed was portrayed by an innocent beneficiary of gukurahundism at one of the churches that Ndzimu – Unami called outposts of Shonalization of Matabeleland. In 2018 at a church service in Victoria Falls, an excited young man took to the pulpit in testimony. He thanked God because when his fate had been sealed to a life of heading goats in rural Mashonaland, God had had mercy on him, he said. After going only as far as grade seven at primary school, he had had no hope of a life far from heading the neighbor's goats. Suddenly a relative of his had gotten a job at a Victoria Falls hotel. The relative then organised a job for him as a kitchen porter at the hotel, away from the goats. Today he was a successful chef with skills enough to have him travel from country to country training hotel chefs. The local youths with university degrees, Advanced and Ordinary level certificates were left wondering how he had goten the 'favour' ahead of them when he did not possess the requisite five passes at Ordinary level. Clearly there was no Godly intervention involved in the story. It was Shona chauvinism through and through. The name of God was being dragged into the mud by sectarianism and flag – waving tribalists who imposed job entry requirements with one hand and violated them with the other.

What made it all the more cruel and inhuman was that that acrimonious praxis was not only rampant but it was official. It may not have been written down as policy, but it was the *sine qua non* in the civil service. It then was a given that every job from CEO to genitor was a preserve for people of Shona origin. The net and intended effect of that tendency was that the non - Shona tribes of Matabeleland became perennially underemployed, unemployed and unemployable. As a consequence many of the Matabele became unemployable in South Africa and elsewhere but not in their own country. That insidious practice rendered all talk of unity and nationhood nothing but convenient window dressing at public meetings. In reality, Zimbabwe as a united nation was but all smoke and mirrors. Unity and equality for Matabeleland remained as elusive as the mirage, very visible and seemingly tangible from a distance but once you get to the ground it never was.

The examples above were a tip of the iceberg. There were too many symptoms indicating that the people of Matabeleland had had enough of gukurahundism. The telltale signs were glaring the government in the face, yet they looked the other way. Bulawayo residents in Emganwini demonstrating against ZETDC for importing labourers from Mashonaland. A demonstration against a road construction company resurfacing the Bulawayo - Plumtree highway. The arrest of seven members of the uMthwakazi Joint Youth Resolution (MJYR) and villagers from Mangwe district for evicting a Shona headmistress who was deputised by a Shona and whose Shona husband was a teacher at the school. (the Chronicle 31 July 2014). The arrest in 2016 of villagers in Lupane for demonstrating against a Shona headmistress at Mlamuli Primary school, who could not speak isiNdebele. The violent fights in January 2017 at the Inyathi gold panning mines between Ndebeles and Shonas with the former claiming the latter were invading their lands in droves to take away economic opportunities.

It was gukurahundism that in 2016 saw Harare residents take to the streets demonstrating against vice president Phelekezela Mphoko's *"long stay"* at a government owned hotel. The demonstrators claimed that Mphoko was abusing tax payer's money. They went on to plunder and loot groceries and other staff from Mphoko's Choppies supermarkets. While the demonstration sounded like a justified call by tax payers, one wondered why now since that was standard government procedure that had too many precedents to site. One wondered where were those demonstrators when fifteen billion United States dollars (US $15 000 000 000) from the Marange diamonds simply disappeared from the government coffers in Harare. Where were they when Mugabe was globetrotting like a modern day Vasco da Gama and sending his daughter at tax payers' expense to give birth at a Singapore private hospital? Where were they when ZANU PF and Shona barons were buying lavish and flushy properties around the world using tax payers' money. Where were they when Mnangagwa, Chombo, Mujuru, Kasukuwere and other super rich Shonas were feathering their nests while in government and in ZANU PF? The answer was right under their noses, Mphoko was Ndebele. It was a crime for a Ndebele to trade leather for leather with Shonas. Mpoko was not supposed to spend public funds like Shonas or to be a successful business person like them.

It was Shona hegemony that saw the deputy speaker of parliament ordering Obert Mpofu, the MP for Umguza and Minister of Transport to be *"orderly"* and speak in Shona after Mpofu had responded to a question in Ndebele. The question had been put to the house in Shona. Mpofu refused to speak in Shona and answered in Ndebele (New Zimbabwe 24 July 2014). Witness, Proffessor Jonathan Moyo lamenting in October 2016 that *"so traditional leaders in Matabeleland are just ordinary people and empowering them and the region is fraud, corruption and abuse of office"*. That was after Moyo had used his mandate as Minister of Higher and Tertiary Education to bail out the Tsholotsho Rural District Council by using ZIMDEF funds. That expenditure caused a lot of discomfort and complaints from all and sundry in government, ZANU PF, MDCT and civic society.

Under siege Moyo questioned why he was being arrested and harangued for buying bicycles for chiefs in Matabeleland while others (referring to vice president Emmerson Munangagwa) had not been subjected to similar treatment for using *"ZINARA funds to build tarred roads to their village farms.."* The answer to Moyo's question was crystal clear. He was Ndebele and had developed a reputation of spending some of the money in his ministerial budgets for the good of Matabeleland while Mnangagwa was Shona and therefore did not have to account to anyone including civic society and the opposition. The tendency of straining at a gnat and swallowing a camel, where the gnat was Shona and the camel Ndebele was rampant in all spheres from the farms, schools, banks, uniformed service, the church and obviously cabinet.

While the 5th Brigade was strictly made up of Shona soldiers, gukurahundism utilized many civilian people who may or may not have been aware that they were pawns in an evil chess game of internal colonialism. Some paid and at times some downright gullible and pliable personalities from both sides of the ethnic divide, were used to propagate gukurahundism against both Shonas and Matabeles.

All the Matabeleland tribes and even those Shonas that had been localised in the region became hewers of wood and drawers of water. The Shonas owned the land, houses, cars and the means of production. The young men and women of Matabeleland found themselves with three unenviable options; to join the great trek to Johannesburg in neighboring South Africa, go rural and be the peasant farmer or cattle header. The third choice was to accept the burden of a happy slave who spoke Shona even in his own home as well as effect the demeanor and aptitude of a Shona in public so as to have a job.

The third option had the 'blessing' of earning one the B class citizen status. One would get the coveted job, the fat bank loan, the connections in the right places and the financial deals and the immunity that came with them. Lamentably the third lure proved too onerous for many a Ndebele. Some rose in the ranks of ZANU PF and government to become ministers of state or some junior civil servant. Some became moderately rich, but so very poor the only thing they had was money. They got despised and rejected by their own, having lost the two most important things in life. People and conscience.

In their Gukurahundist frame of mind, ZANU PF failed to treat Matabeleland as equals with Mashonaland. They could have read the labour matters column of the Chronicle newspaper of 25 November 2010 where Davies Ndumiso Sibanda commented thus as he proposed the promulgation of laws protecting locals, *"its irresponsible for us as a nation to label locals who complain and chase away non locals as tribalists or regionalists. We need to look deeper than that and address the problem at its root"*. That was an indictment of ZANU PF's gukurahundism at a time when very few noticed and even fewer dared write in a national newspaper that the doors to opportunity in Zimbabwe were not open equally to all. Consonant with subtle marginalization, the powers that be never disagreed with such views publicly and officially. They actually allowed such articles to be published once in a while to portray a modicum of democracy yet it was merely a veneer. They would go on to ignore such pleas and went on to trash them by importing all forms of human labour from Mashonaland into Matabeleland.

ZANU PF should have taken heed of the Zimbabwe Independent newspaper (19 – 25 February, 2016) editorial which read, *"as long as we avoid confronting the issue of ethnicity and fail to develop mechanisms of managing diversity and ensuring equal opportunity for all within a sustainable framework, unity, peace and stability will continue to elude us. Zimbabwe can no longer afford Mugabe's failed ethnic model and its toxic identity politics"*.

Instead of adopting a policy paradigm that elevated all citizens to the same level, ZANU PF attempted to ethnically sanitize Mugabe so that he could be acceptable to the Matabele as was exposed by the News Day (southern edition), of 27 November 2010. The independent publication had the headlines, *"Mugabe - Matabeleland ties dismissed"*. In the article it was reported that the minister of higher and tertiary education, Stan Mudenge (one of the ZANU PF historians) had informed delegates to the graduation ceremony at Lupane State University in Matabeleland North province that Mugabe had close links with Matabeleland. He said that in the 19th century, Mugabe's grandfather (name not supplied) had served under King Lobengula as a powerful subject in a vassalage arrangement common at the time.

The minister also confirmed what had always previously been whispered as an heretic rumour that Mugabe's father, Gabriel had migrated to Bulawayo where he married a Ndebele woman and begot some of Mugabe's siblings. He did not state explicitly that Mugabe was not an offspring of that woman but it was implicit. The minister went on to mention that Mugabe, a teacher by profession had taught at Empandeni and Hope Fountain Mission Schools in Matabeleland before joining politics. The minister also forgot to mention that Mugabe's father was Gabriel

Matibili, supposedly of Malawian origion and that the name 'Mugabe' was adopted from some benevolent missionery servant at Kutama, where Mugabe and his mother sought refuge after his father deserted them for the Matabeleland woman.

The conspicuous attempt to establish some sort of a positive relationship between Mugabe and Matebeleland met with bitter and justified rebuttal from civic organisations and the generality of Matabeleland. They expressed unreserved repugnance and revulsion at what they considered to be *"intellectual terrorism"* as described by Effie Ncube a civic activist. Mr Rodrick Fayayo the spokesperson for the Matabeleland Civic Society Consortium stated that *"we are all aware of Mugabe's disdain for Matabeleland. If at all he has such close ties with us, he should then explain to us why Gukurahundi took place and why the people of Matabeleland are marginalized"*.

When all had been said and done, the claim of being related to Matabeleland was dismissed as a cheap, malicious and mischevious political gimmick to woo voters to his much reviled ZANU PF party in the impending 2013 plebiscite. What the people of Matabeleland needed was to be treated equally before the state, law, employer and social and economic institutions as the people of Mashonaland, not a high profile hallucinatory historical relationship.

From 1980 to 2019, job creation nose - dived nationally, yet the few jobs that were there remained a preserve for Shona people. The unemployment rate among the Matabeleland tribes was drearily appalling. If anyone had bothered to conduct an ethnic groups specific unemployment survey, they would be have been shocked at the injustice. Nationalisn, the Unity Accord of 1987 and the GNU of 2008 all failed to correct historical imbalances not only in the distribution of wealth but in infrastructural development. Those roads, schools, hospitals and dip tanks built by the minority Smith regime before 1980, still stood albeit dilapidated and run down as a reminder that development was possible. The attempt at providing modern infrastructure by the Mugabe and Mnangagwa governments proved precariously inept and casual due to lack of political will.

The political dispensation of the GNU of 2008 which was ushered in by the old and untrusted government and the new hopefuls led by the MDCT and MDC, merely served to perpetuate and exacerbate the suffering in the region. The MDCT proved to be a chip off the old block when thay caused a furore in September 2008. When required to contribute 12 ministers and 15 deputy ministers towards the formation of the inclusive government, Morgan Tsvangirai opted to subscribe to the 1979 Grand Plan instruction about jobs. Despite having its very blood arteries running from, through and around Matabeleland, the MDCT accomplished what even seclusionist ZANU PF had failed to do as far as disregard of regional balance in the allocation of cabinet portfolios was concerned. Only one person from Matabeleland, Mr. Joel Gabuza, an MP from Binga was appointed as minister of Water. One out of twenty - seven (3.7%) was a dismal performance by any standard in the world.

If the MDCT lacked the requisite policy and intellectual sophistication to derive a fair and suitable formula, they could have used any one of the following common rationale in distributing cabinet power between Matabeleland and Mashonaland. By using the number of provinces, Matabeleland should have been allocated 30% of the cabinet posts. By using the population density, Matabeleland would have been allocated 25% of the posts. By using support and loyalty statistics, Matabeleland should have obtained more than 70% of the MDCT cabinet posts. However, the MDCT did not lack the intellect to derive a fair formula but they were simply devoid of the political will to share the cabinet seats equitably. They gave way to the avarice and egocentric character of ZANU PF before they even assumed office. Allocating a single ministry to Matabeleland did not only betray Tsvangirai's deep and dark Mugabe – style resentment for the region, but indicated clearly, that should he have found himself forming a government, he would have pursued ZANU PF's policies of marginalization and dominance of Matabeleland, probably with more vigor.

Tsvangirai's party's lowly opinion of Matabeleland was again laid bare at a Matabeleland North provincial council meeting of the MDCT held in Hwange on Saturday the 31 July 2010. The Secretary General of the party and the Finance Minister of the country struck a handicapping blow to the Matabeleland aspirations. The meeting occurred against the backdrop of the much publicised and anticipated COPAC constitution making process. It was no secret that all Matabeleland was pushing and craving for the devolved state as a system of government. At the meeting Tendai Biti in all his honesty, unwittingly let the cat out of the sack by categorically and unambiguously declaring that the MDCT was not in support of devolution of power. The delegates were utterly dumpfounded by the rude face of derision for their aspirations, since they knew the official party position was to advocate for devolution of power. No one dared question the leadership on that fateful occasion, but it became plain as the nose on one's face that party policy was not only determined by the elite but could be deceptively autocratic under the guise of democracy. Just like ZANU PF, the MDCT wanted Matabeleland to perennially remain a vassal of Mashonaland in a unitary system of government.

The fact still remained, resolute, and defiant, sticking out like a sore thumb on the Zimbabwe body politic. To those objective enough to shade off politically misted-up glasses and unprepared to sacrifice the soul of the region on the alter of political expediency, the writing was on the wall. Neither ZANU PF nor MDCT had the survival and sustenance, let alone the development of Matabeleland on their agenda. When it came to tribal and regional politics, the leadership of both parties closed ranks, sang the same song and closed the sole hymn book then contentedly withdrew to pursue their conveniently divergent programmes.

Matabeleland still remained the rich hunting ground where the kill occured. Nevertheless, all she had to show for it were the signs of the struggle and blood stains on the grass and the sand. The money, meat, skin and the trophy were whisked away, leaving Matabeleland scarred and scared. The idea of the libeation struggle by ZANU PF was to propagate tribal nationalism which in the name of majority rule conveniently replaced the much abhorred British imperialism. Matabeleland and Mashonaland, the Ndebele and the Shona were still worlds apart as they were in November 1893.

The ordinary Shona was merely an innocent beneficiary of gukurahundism, oblivious of his status, in a vengeful and hardnosed game of political murder, economic dispossession and social condemnation. Conversely, many ordinary people from Matabeleland, even during the Gukurahundi genocide, while feeling the load of marginalization, did not realise they were victims of an intricate and meticulous plan, intended to overrun their languages, identities, cultures, beliefs, norms and values. Little did they appreciate that the ultimate consequence of being jobless, having no property in towns, no schools and colleges, no university graduates, no clinics and hospitals, no good roads into the rural areas and no political leaders from the region in positions of influence, was as evil as apartheid itself. They did not recognize the axe of gukurahundism swinging and cutting their children, husbands, wives and parents, down by the dozen on a daily basis.

It is often said that the minority will have their say and the majority their way. A number of civic organisations attempted to raise national and international awareness to the sorry plight of the region of Matabeleland in the late 1990s and early 2000s. Such organisations as Imbovane Yamahlabezulu, Uluntu-Ciisi Trust, Bulawayo Agenda, Ibhetshu LikaZulu, Bulawayo Dialogue, Habakuk Trust, Umhlahlo WeSizwe SikaMthwakazi, Matabeleland Constitutional Reform Agenda, Matabeleland Collective etc, all attempted to elevate the people of Matabeleland to a level pedestal with the rest of the country. However much to the vexation of many activists, their efforts always hit a solid stone wall as they were arrested and charged with one crime or another.

When Uluntu-Ciisi Trust was advocating for the reinstatement to work of seventy - nine employees dismissed from work by the famous Victoria Falls Hotel after they had complained of tribal discrimination in the workplace in 2009, they were crudely reminded that 'it is only the dog that bucks, not the lion'. The implication was that the Matabele could always complain all they wanted but the government would never take heed. Despite the support of cabinet ministers from the region that Uluntu – Ciisi Trust got, the seventy - nine, who included the Ndebele, Nambya, Tonga, Nyanja, Lozi, Lubale, Kalanga and a couple of sacrificial Shonas, were never reinstated. Contrary to demands by the employees, the tribally inclined human resources manager was accorded the worker of the year accolade. The strategy therefore, was to allow the people of Matabeleland to clamour and wail, huff and puff as much as they wanted, until they inevitably gave up and the status quo prevailed. That strategy worked wholesomely for the ZANU PF administration and to the triumph of their tribal nationalism. By 2019, ten years after their unfair dismissal, some of the seventy - nine employees had died of various causes, including stress related complications, while their case was still pending in the labour courts.

One of the corrosive effects of gukurahundism which over a period of almost four decades had been compounded, wass the demonization and criminalization of everything Ndebele, from the Ndebele language, Ndebele cultural practices, Ndebele names, Ndebele - led institutions including the Ndebele monarchy. In 1998 a political movement which was eventually registered as a political party was formed. It was called ZAPU 2000, was head quartered in Bulawayo and its leadership comprised Cont Mhlanga a brilliant theatre artist, producer, dramatist and writer of amazing luster and courage, Paul Siwela, Goden Moyo who later became a minister in the inclusive government of 2008, Joshua Mhambi and others. The manifesto of ZAPU 2000, a reincarnation of the original Joshua Nkomo's party, and its constitution were typical in content, of any political organisation. ZAPU 2000 was immediately condemned by the government controlled press and ZANU PF as a tribalist and a Ndebeles - only party. That label had an obvious handicapping effect on the organization. It was tantamount to being branded a dissident at a ZNA army barracks in 1983. The Ndebeles - only label had become a dangerously slippery and treacherously proscribed status, attended to by all manner of misfortunes ranging from unsupported to unfunded. The populace, save for the few with stubborn hearts shunned ZAPU 2000 because Gukurahundi was still fresh in their minds. Instead, most people influenced by the independent press, civic society and the white community flocked to swell the ranks of the MDC which was formed a year later and was led by a Shona with headquarters in Harare

There is an adage that says, 'the most dangerous weapon in the hand of the oppressor is the mind of the oppressed'. Gukurahundism as an act of annihilation and as a policy of seclusion, exclusion, dominance and marginalization, cowed the minds of the tribes of Matabeleland so much they failed to identify legitimacy and appeal in any institution or activity that was not led by a Shona or was unpopular among Shonas. The anti – Matabele politics of ZANU PF pervaded the socio – political discourse so thoroughly, there existed a compelling loathe of Ndebele leadership. Therefore, idea of a Ndebele president was fertilized as taboo and loathsome to some and as far fetched ambition to many.

While the ruling elite perpertuated gukurahundism by invoking the 1979 Grand Plan to the benefit of Mashonaland, the Matabele acceded to the inclination to cope by compliance. To the triumph of Shona hegemony, Mugabe and his acolytes, the people of Matabeleland and some some parts of the Midlands succumbed to the subtle demonization of all Matabele institutions, be they social, cultural or political. The systematic dismantling and rape of their land, resources, cultural identity and language was so much of an every day experience, it had become normal practice to them. They witnessed year in and year out, their youths being denied education and employment in their own towns and villages. To them the 1948 Universal Declaration of Human Rights and the 1992 United Nations Declaration on rights of persons belonging to national, or ethnic, religious and linguistic minorities were meaningless since they had been physically brutalized, socially domineered, politically disenfranchised and economically marginalized by a state that was a signatory to the United Nations Charter, while the United Nations was watching.

R. G Mugabe

- en.wikipedia.org › wiki › Robert_Mugabe
- www.bbc.com › news › world-africa-49604152

Joshua Nkomo

- foursquare.com › joshua-mqabuko-nkomo-international-airport-buq

R. G Mugabe

- en.wikipedia.org › wiki › Robert_Mugabe
- www.biography.com › political-figure › robert-mugabe
- www.burundi-forum.org › afrique

Joshua Nkomo

- www.postermywall.com › index.php › posters › gallery
- en.wikipedia.org › wiki › Poster

Left; Solomon Mujuru, ZANLA Army Commander
Right; Dumiso Dabengwa, ZIPRA Intelligence Supreme, 1979

- en.wikipedia.org › wiki › Lookout_Masuku

Akim Ndlovu, 1st ZIPRA Army commander

- en.wikipedia.org › wiki › Akim Ndlovu

Lookout Masuku, 3rd ZIPRA Army Commander

- en.wikipedia.org › wiki Uganda_National_Liberation_Front
- africacenter.org › spotlight › troubled-democratic-transitions-african
- www.globalsecurity.org › military › world › para › unla
- www.southerneye.co.zw › tag › zimbabwe-national-liberation-war-vet

**George Ncube, killed by the Gukurahundi Brigade
on 7 March 1983 in Nyamandlovu**

- en.wikipedia.org › wiki › George Ncube

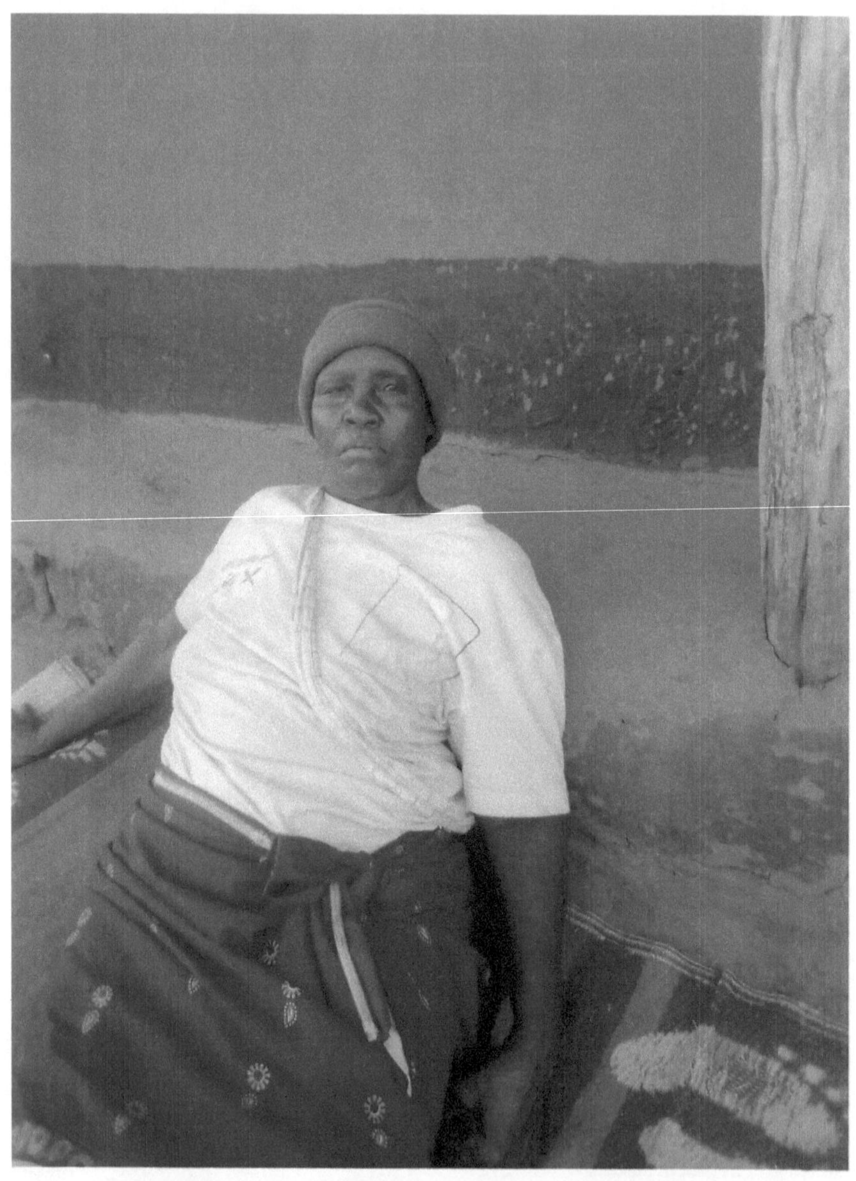

**Elizabeth Ncube (2019) George Ncube's widow, tortured
by the government army and suffered a broken arm**

- en.wikipedia.org › wiki › Elizabeth Ncube

Proffessor Welshman Ncube, opposition leader and founder of MDC

- www.zimeye.net › Homepage – Big Slide
- www.zimeye.net › Homepage – Newspaper
- www.povonews.com › world › africa › zimbabwe › video-candidate

Hope for the future

- https://lh3.googleusercontent.com/T1kWOst6bwlIhFU1VAPzzT4GJaNsvLJ3Br
oFSj1f99s-apOdTGmDRPdi6_I6H3P_YcAIuyI=s85

**Tendai Biti; served diligently as MDC Finance Minister
during the government of national unity**

- www.mafaro.co.uk › 2019/04 › mdc-tense-times
- nehandaradio.com › News

Map of Zimbabwe

- bulawayo24.com › index-id-opinion-sc-columnist-byo-139355
- thenewexaminer.com › hail-the-king

Esau_Ncube

- en.wikipedia.org › wiki › Esau_Ncube

Chapter VI

ZANUISM

"This is not government, it is the abuse of government, an abuse which transforms the rule of law into the law of rule....... oppression, division, violence and poverty will shadow all our hopes, and make a mockery of the freedom struggle..."

Joshua Nkomo 1983 (Informative letter to the Prime Minister, Robert Mugabe)

Ndlovu - Gatsheni (2011) theorized the Chimurenga Ideology and the Strategy of Gukurahundi. He said that the Chimurenga ideology compelled and rail - roaded everyone to acquiesce to the ideas and practices of the ZANU party. Failure or unwillingness to conform implied that one was anti - establishment. He said that that was the ideology and strategy that reared its ugly face within the nationalist parties in the 1960s and 70s. It gave birth to the sellouts, puppets and patriots narrative. That means that if one decided to think alternately and behave differently they automatically relinquished any trust previously bestowed on them and they became part and parcel of the foe. They became a puppet and a sellout.

He argued that the Chimurenga ideology was developed by the broader nationalist movement as early as the 1960s when every black African was expected to support the nationalist movement or else they were on the side of the enemy of the revolution. It was the manifestation of the 'either you are with us or you are against us' approach. It was that cast of mind that informed the intolerance of diversity which proved to be primordial and principal in the hearts and minds of the victors after the February 1980 Zimbabwe general elections.

During the liberation struggle ZAPU had prepared for the eventuality of forming a government should they win the first majority elections. The preparations involved setting up what they termed, a government in exile. That involved replicating every vital government department and organ. It entailed sending personnel for training in civil service and public administration with friendly countries like Libya, the Soviet Union, Algeria, Yugoslavia, Botswana, Zambia, Cuba and others. Through the programme many ZPRA recruites were trained as civil servants, diplomats, medical doctors, nurses, pilots, teachers, engineers, immigration and customs officers etc. That showed that ZAPU did not intend to have the military run the government as they wanted a civilian administration by proffessionals.

On the other hand, ZANU did not have such a strategic plan nor its equivalent. The government in exile was not part of their precautionary and contingency planning. Their plan was simply to take power, then hazard their way by the rule of thumb until they got the feel and hang of it. Consequently, when they assumed power in 1980, ZANU was in pitch darkness about running a government. They had no training and experience whatsoever of professional civilian administration. They were ill advised and semi prepared for the rigorous routine of state - craft. Therefore, it was not surprising that they committed iretreiveable, unforgetable and unforgiveable political and economic errors on day one in the office.

They attempted to put out the fires of doubt and inexperience by roping into government elements from the Smith regime. That wise remedy failed to yield the desired results because both the executive and the civil service were seemingly possessed by the victors mentality. They would not be dictated to by the losers, some of them said. The white and black former Rhodesians could neither manage nor train them on the job. They even coined the denial phrase in Shona, *"saka unoda kundidzidzisa basa?"* (so you want to teach me how to do my job?). That statement over the years became a defiance mortif that was overused widely within the public service to resist suggestions, instructions and constructive criticism.

Mugabe and his assemblage therefore brought with them the asperity of the liberation struggle and ZANLA zeal and abrasiveness into statehouse, cabinet, parliament, and the judiciary. Hence the new government inherited the wartime machinations of both ZANU and ZANLA. War mongering schematics, conquest ideologies, sloganeering, patronaising, plotting, conniving, contestations and assassinations. All those vices and more that were to be manifest in the very short term, became part of the new government's DNA. Corruption, nepotism, economic incompetence and political bungling ensued and set in like a plague thereafter.

All the ills were born in April 1980 and matured like old wine through the years. By failing to plan ahead, ZANU had planned to fail. Instead of formulating a holistic and sustainable economic strategic plan during the first days in office, they expended a lot of energy on the 1979 Grand Plan. To make up for their administrative deficiances the ZANU government found a scapegoat and a red herring in ZAPU.

ZANU was tormented by the awareness of their own economic and administrative shortcomings during the day, while consciousnesses of ZAPU's strengths summoned the demons in their nightmares during the night. They could not rest as long as ZAPU lived. That became ZANU's nemesis and they decided to atone for their inadequacies in the most tragically farcical of ways. ZANU PF's administrative fears coupled with their wartime experiences and a naive fear of a possible coup by ZPRA, compelled them to do what they claimed they knew best. To fight. Fight even though there was nothing and no one to fight. They invented a series of 'chimurengas'. That is how zanuism came onto the stage; troubled, conflicted and ever screaming, *"chimurenga"* and *"pasi"* with him, *"pasi"* with so and so!'.

Although they were too conceited to admit it, they soon realized that there was more than wartime ideologies, slogans, firebrand speeches and hate, needed to run a country.

Zanuism was a covert ideology that propagated a set of political attitudes and practices to the effect that only one particular individual could, and only one particular ethnic group should lead.

Zanuism manifested through collapsing, then conflating the three arms of the state into the party machinery. A party machinery which was presided by tribal and loyalist or paid academics under the radar of vigilante securocrats, who at the expense of human, economic, social, cultural and political security, engaged a range of vices including, patronage, coercion, rent seeking and negotiation to create a personality cult and hero worshipping of the leader whose word transmuted into gospel truth, in order to guarantee personal and regime security, political longevity and tribal hegemony.

Zanuism had massive economic, political, cultural and social ramifications while ostensibly presenting a veneer of unity, but in essence practicing divide and rule. Manipulating and banking on ethnic and other cleavages, merely as a strategy of self preservation and maintaining power, zanuism was characterized by a number of distinctive features including but not confined to: firstly the notorious use of the red herrings to deflect attention from the real national challenges caused by and vexing the state. The Democratic Republic of Congo war of 1999 was such a decoy. The war was meant to divert attention away from domestic challenges due to poor economic policies onto the situation in the DRC. Operation Clean Up (Murambatswina) of 2005 was another. The exercise was designed to destabilize the politically agitated urban voters who were apperantly anti ZANU PF, so that they could focus on bread and butter issues and not on the politics of Mugabe's much anticipated exit. Those two decoys however saved a short-lived purpose as they attracted a lot of national, regional and international criticism for the government, in addition to drainig the fiscus as dry as hay, especially the DRC war.

Secondly, an infinite appetite for power, self preservation and perpetuation at whatever cost and by whatever means necessary, through the employment of draconian legislation, was a prominent feature of zanuism. Legislation like AIPPA (2002), POSA (2002), Broadcasting Services Act (2001), LOMA (1960), Indemnity Act, the Unlawful Organisations Act and the Emergency Powers Act (1960) were used to curtail the activities of, and muzzle the freedom of the press, the opposition, civil society, Non Governmental Organizations and the general public. In order to maintain power, the system aspired to conflate every institution and individual into ZANU PF.

In 1983, Joshua Nkomo protested compassionately to Mugabe for the latter's retention of the above last four pieces of legislation as well as some of the Rhodesian security personnel which were part of the evil balance brought down from the Smith regime. Nkomo presumed that those shackling legal instruments were kept intact for use on all Zimbabweans, but he was proved wrong. He did not realize the new order had retained the Smith laws and personnel not for use against the people of Zimbabwe but for the first twenty years they were used mainly against Matabeleland, the Matabele, ZAPU and ZPRA. The usage of the draconian statutory instruments was extended to the rest of the country especially urban Mashonaland around the turn of the century when they rebelled againt ZANU PF and the government due to economic incompetence. The essence of zanuism was that the state and dissenters in general, including ZAPU, ZPRA, the Matabele, and later the opposition MDCs and other political parties and civic society needed to be converted to ZANU PF.

Parliament, taking advantage of the Westminster – style whipping system was always the hunting ground for ZANU PF and a breeding bed for its warped and wretched pieces of draconian, partisan and even vindictive legislation. Ever enjoying the majority in parliament, ZANU PF assumed the arrogance of a sated beast, from the onset in 1980. Motions would be adopted at a glance and bills would sail through minus any kind of serious debate. Nevertheless, that Russian Duma – like demeanor of the legislature evaporated at the start of the new millennium with the advent of the MDC. Arrogant inertia was substituted by chaotic engagement characterized by mudslinging and even inter – party insults and fist fights by members of parliament.

Despite the advent of a vibrant and at times rambustious opposition, ZANU PF did not mend their ways, instead they took advantage of the new arrivals' inexperience and perennial excitement, to entrench further their tenderloin policies and to dig - in deep their self preservation apparatus.

Thirdly, disputed electoral results with strong suspicions of usage of a complex rigging system as well as voter trafficking, buying and intimidation while using state resources including the army for campaign programs as well as to implement gukurahundism to win elections and achieve personal and organizational goals, were the other invidious marks of zanuism. The 2008 harmonised elections were a classic example of zanuism in action. After killing some, beating many and threatening many more and using every dirty tactic in the book and still being out – polled by Tsvangirai, ZANU PF and Mugabe bluntly refused to hand over power. Instead, they withheld the results for an entire month until it became obvious that their securocrats and intellectuals were on over – drive, cooking a sour dish for the expectant electorate. When they eventually emerged with the results, it was announced that Tsvingirai had not garnered enough votes to form a government despite out – polling Mugabe. A re – run was ordered as per the constitution and Mugabe claimed victory.

Fourthly, zanuism was typified by a demented belief in the *aut Ceaser aut nullus* ideology with the scorched earth policy and the divide and rule strategy in proximate attendance. Zanuism believed that it had to be ZANU PF, the ZANU PF candidate, the ZANU PF policy, the ZANU PF history, truth, way etc, or no other. They believed that it was either ZANU PF or nothing. They would have it or no one else would. Parliament, the executive and the judiciary had to pander to ZANU PF interests and not those of the people. Anyone who wanted to have it any other way would have blood. As a result, they coined the fiendish phrase "ZANU *ndeyeropa*" (ZANU is bloody or is made of blood or is about blood). They repeatedly, at all levels of administration, leadership and activism evoked that jingle with much gusto and pride to galvanize support for any given cause.

True to the blood mantra, it was always the ZANU PF way or the bloody way. Given the historical paroxysm of violence binding ZANU PF to blood - letting, the majority terrified Zimbabweans opted to support them. That was misinterpreted for popularity and even those that were coerced into the unfair choice (ZANU PF or blood) ended up believing ZANU PF was indeed a popular people's party.

During the war ZANU PF had used the *pungwe* all night vigils to drill the people of Mashonaland into supporting them without deviation and question. People were frog marched to attend the *pungwes*, forced to sing liberation songs, dancing and chanting slogans all the way. The drilling was mostly tolerable because it was perpetuated in the name of ending colonialism and oppression by whites. During the vigils the people were fed with political propaganda denouncing not only the minority white regime but fellow liberation war fighters ZAPU and ZPRA as well as Bishop Abel Muzorewa, Ndabaningi Sithole etc. That way they drove a wedge between ZAPU and ZANU, a block which soon became poisonously divisive between the ordinary Ndebele and Shona peoples. A wedge that commanded party supporters to be forever loyal to ZANU and to never support any other until death.

For twenty solid years ZANU PF's infallibility and zanuism's divide and rule policy relentlessly pushed Matabeleland to the periphery and to the brink of economic neglect and utter poverty. Notwithstanding, as nature would have it, the hour which Mugabe could not go beyond without faultering and slackening his death hold on popularity, even in his darling Mashonaland was at hand. It had to take Mugabe's terrible economic bungling, for the majority to disentangle themselves from the belief in the *aut Mugabe aut nullus* syndrome as illustrated hereunder.

By the late 1990s the rest of the country was fast coming to terms with what had long been an everyday lived reality in Bulawayo and Matabeleland since day one after Independence Day. Safe and elated in the comfort of belonging to the ruling class, ruling party, ruling tribe and to some, the ruling elite, Harare, Mashonaland and parts of the Midlands provinces had refused to accept that the government had neglected parts of the country, especially Bulawayo and Matabeleland in terms of social, economic and infrastructural development. They had refused to believe that human rights were in jeopardy in Matabeleland and Midlands. Prior, the majority tribe, as evidenced by their voting trends and statements by their leaders, was very happy with Mugabe and ZANU PF, to say the least.

Still, not all the Mashonaland provinces (Mashonaland Central, West and East, Masvingo, Manicaland) benefited equally from the government's development initiatives. There was preferential treatment among the ruling party / tribe provinces. Some like Mashonaland Central and Mashonaland West, Mugabe's homeland benefited more than others. However, most people were grateful and content with the idea of being independent and in charge. Judging by their silence, they gave a deaf ear to the complaints about genocide, political killings of opposition supporters, torture, imprisonment without due process, underdevelopment, unemployment, domination, underfunding of government projects and general marginalization in Matabeleland. Some judged the people of Matabeleland as rebellious and lazy perennial cry babies. Their heads were still cool, buried in the sand, ostrich – like, until Mugabe managed to collapse the economy in a spectacular fashion that no other world leader had done in the history of economics, outside a war situation.

Finally, around 2000 the economic plane was switched to auto pilot and was on the verge of crushing. With Mugabe and lavish Grace parachuting out and whisking the national cake to Malaysia, Singapore, the UK etc, for lunch and shopping sprees, Harare and Mashonaland finally admitted, the man was an economical fiasco and ZANU PF a scourge on the land. The general economic environment fast degenerated to a milieu where the three basic meals a day became a priviledge only a few could afford. Wanderlust - struck Mugabe and his young wife did not care. He and his ministers and senior civil servants went on one foreign trip after another, shopping expensively, dinning and drinking uncontrollably in the process. Mashonaland started to reject Mugabe from 2000 onwards because he failed their expectations and crushed their aspirations economically. Economics and economics alone is what made the majority reject Mugabe and ZANU PF. Zanuism's damning mantra, that it was Mugabe and Mugabe alone, suddenly was an unbankable philosophy devoid of buyers.

If Mugabe had not managed to crush the economy in such wonderboy fashion, he would still be a hero to many in Mashonaland even after 2018 as proved by Morgan Tsvangirai's sentiments in 2010. According to Macaphulana (2010) Tsvangirai told South African journalist David Smith that *"Mugabe is my hero"*. Tsvangirai was purpoted to have continued to state that he only differed with *"the violence that Mugabe started in the past ten years"*. That implied that to Tsvangirai, Mugabe had been a paragon of good governance until the year 2000. The Gukurahundi genocide, gukurahundism and zanuism prior to the year 2000 were not an issue to Tsvangirai who is alleged to have been a ZANU PF youth leader during the Gukurahundi era. As noted by Macaphulana, Tsvangirai did not find fault with *"Mugabe's capital crime against humanity and his worst offence on record. We know of course that Tsvangirai started finding fault with Mugabe well after he had packed in his guns in Matabeleland"*.

When Tsvangirai declared his current (2010) and historical admiration of the killer of the Matabele, it was at the height of his popularity and he was of course speaking for many in his party whom he had convinced Mugabe's worst sin was collapsing the economy. The fact that no one in the MDCT questioned the wisedom, or lack of it, in hero worshipping Mugabe, was proof enough that he was elucidating his party position. Hypocritically, at rallies in Matabeleland, Tsvangirai would not spare Mugabe for deploying the 5th Brigade. Lamentably his theatrics were bought by the Matabeleland voters who did not see through the grand masquerade.

As if Tsvangirai's betrayal of the trust bestowed on him by many in Matabeleland was not enough, his party secretary general and Minister of Finance, Tendai Biti left the same faithful and more, wondering what it was that opposition political heavyweights at times imbibed, inhaled or chewed in their ivory towers, that made them sound so much like Mugabe's spokespersons. Biti confessed that, *"we find counsel and wisdom in him (Mugabe)…when he is gone, that is when you will see that this man was Zimbabwe. Some of us who came from different parties have had a lot to learn from the man. He is a fountain of experience, a fountan of knowledge and, most importantly a fountan of stability"* (Sunday Mail 2/7/12). The stability that the young and obviously excited - with –power Biti was talking about, was and remained mythological to many.

Mugabe's experience that Biti was talking about, which was dominated by the genocide and other murders at his door step, was mostly Mugabe's false front, punctuated by superfluous rhetoric that disguised economic and political ineptiness. As for the knowledge, the whole world could bear witness that Mugabe knew absolutely nix about how to manage an economy and bountifully everything about how to collapse it. All other experience and knowledge he had, got reduced to absolute nix and insignificance by his infamous reduction of a 'bread busket to a busket case'.

When Mugabe eventually died at a Singapore hospital in September 2019, Biti was at it again. He told BBC that, *"Robert Mugabe was a product of a certain era, an era that confronted the colonial regime powder for powder, blow for blow, so violence came naturally to him…His legacy shouldn't be detracted by the fact that there were atrocities….today we must …thank him for leading the battle against colonialism…I don't feel bitterness, I feel indeptedness, I feel gratitude to the work he did in liberating our country.."*

The fiction, excitement and falsehood that made Biti blame colonialism for Mugabe's propensity for violence and murder as well as to claim that Mugabe who only led ZANU for less than four years before independence, actually iconically led the liberation struggle aside, such high sounding praise for a known despot whose infamy for vindicative cruelty, genocide, theft by himself, family and cronies as well as world class economic failures was no secret, was uncharacteristic of leaders of a so called 'main opposition' party. Mugabe had not only destroyed the lives of millions in Matabeleland but had wrecked the livelihoods of millions more in Mashonaland. The people of Matabeleland had nothing to be grateful to Mugabe for and had no business being thankful to a tyrant.

If Mugabe was so 'good', what business were Tsvangirai and Biti and their hordes of unquestioning followers doing in the opposition ranks. They were campaigning for and praising Mugabe in broad daylight, not only within Zimbabwe's borders but internationally. No wonder Julius Malema and his Economic Freedom Front (EFF) in South Africa, in hasty excitement held a memorial service for Mugabe. They were behaving like an opportunistic spurious opposition whose major thrust was siphoning USA, British and European funding through the ostensive legitimacy of the 'Mugabe must go' incantation. They were fighting ZANU PF because they merely wanted an opportunity to rule. Theirs was nothing but a power game. After playing the game during the day, they went back home where they paid homage to common goals with Mugabe, Mnangagwa, Sekeramayi, Shiri etc, during the night. They undoubtedly were using the MDC as a vehicle to power and not as an institution for political, social and economic reformation and transformation.

Had it not been for the economic meltdown precipitated by Mugabe's *"sunset policies"* as noted by some political analysts, Mugabe would still be revered as a hero, and indeed to many, a saint and even a tribal god, long after 2017 the year of the coup that dethroned him and after his death almost two years later.

The economic implosion and not the Gukurahundi genocide, not tribalism not human rights violations prior to 2000 and not the mysterious deaths of his opponents, alienated him from a vital section of his power base. ZANU PF, despite all their pontificating in public rallies, planning during the five yearly party congresses, myth making during their annual conferences, threatening in the media, fantasizing during the 21st February celebrations and caucusing in cabinet, could not wave the economic magic wand. Resuscitating the dead economy simply proved to be beyond their colourful and deceptive rhetoric.

The flagging economy forced a group of former liberation war fighters under their umbrella organization called the Zimbabwe National Liberation War Veterans Association (ZNLWVA) under the leadership of a former ZPRA and Polish trained doctor, Chenjerai Hunzvi, to match on Mugabe with their demands. They disturbed his Heroes Day speech in August 1997 and demanded his audience.

They delivered an ultimatum to Mugabe demanding mainly two things. A monetary monthly gratuity for each surviving ex war veteran or the widow of such and land that had to be expropriated from white commercial farmers. They premised their demands on the fact that they had 'fought and died for this country', as was popularly cited by their critics. Therefore, they had to be paid. They said the essence of the struggle against colonialism had been to repossess land from the minority whites who had a hundred years back forcefully displaced the majority black people from the land. They demanded land redistribution to the majority blacks as a precursor for their economic empowerment.

Despite the leader of the war veterans being former ZPRA, the association violated a ZAPU ethic and practice. Upon independence, ZAPU had adopted a policy of acquiring land for the economic empowerment of its struggle veterans by buying a total of 38 properties all of which were however later seized by the government between 1981 and 1987. The funds ZAPU used to purchase the farms were partly contributions from the beneficiaries and partly provided by ZAPU. ZAPU believed in sourcing funding and buying land for the resettlement of landless blacks. The forceful expropriation of land was in line with ZANU ideology which they managed to conceal from their British allies at Lancaster in 1979 and soon after independence. An ideology which ZANU PF conveniently discarded for twenty years but to which they hastily resorted when they were frantic for votes after 2000.

Mugabe promptly found himself in an unprecedented catch - 22 scenario. He capitulated by acceding to the demands of the war veterans after initially attempting to resist them. He had previously banked on the veterans for support and manpower during elections and they were threatening to withdraw their future votes at a time when a new and popular political party had recently been formed. The new party was founded against the backdrop of the economic woes that were beginning to take a bite on ordinary citizens. He was not about to throw away his trump card in the face of such an electoral threat.

The veterans had managed to sqeeze him between the proverbial rock and a hard place. Scared of being crushed, he buckled. Mugabe was compelled to commit one of his many mammoth economic botch - ups. Without consulting the Reserve Bank of Zimbabwe, economists, and parliament, Mugabe issued a decree that the approximately fifty thousand war veterans or their widows should be paid by treasury an allowance of ZW$50 000.00. The bill was a staggering ZW$3.5 billion which Finance Minister Herbert Murerwa paid out reluctantly. The war veterans celebrated, but the country cringed in consternation as bankruptcy set in.. The order was unsustainable, but the die was cast.

In another unilateral decision around the same time, Mugabe committed the ZNA to defend DRC's Laurent Kabila against internal rebels in 1998. The initial daily cost of the war was astronomic and grew exponentially to approximately US$1 million a day. Coupled with the war veterans' monthly pay outs, it became an unbearable burden on the fiscus. The free falling spree of the economy was thus commissioned.

Robert Mugabe became the great escapist by successfully blaming it all on whites, the west, sanctions, colonialism, the opposition and the hand of God (drought) but never on his failed policies. His impulsive reaction to challenges of all sorts was to shoot from the hip and at times in the dark because he was a unilateralist. When his policies failed, his quick finger always pointed in the direction of the West and their "puppets" in Zimbabwe. He blamed European governments in general, Great Britain, the USA, *Rhodesians* (a derogation by him), gays, the opposition, puppets, sellouts and the independent media. In a bankrupt tirade that became all too familiar at state functions, high profile funeral speeches, independence day commemorations, Heroes Day celebrations and even at international and regional forums like the United Nations general assembly and SADC meetings, he took to the stage like a prefect of Africa, verbally lambasting his more - imagined – than - real enemies and declaring *"Zimbabwe will never be a colony again"*. An entertaining yet senseless assertion devoid of any political or economic worth. He became obsessed with deriding western hypocrisy at even the most unlikely and inappropriate of occasions as he attempted to be some kind of super Pan Africanist.

Many applauded his futile and gaga rhetoric about USA and European colonialism, despite the point that the last vestiges of colonialism had been wiped off the face of Africa in 1996 when apartheid was dismantled in South Africa. No radical stretch of the imagination could envisage any country re – inventing European imperialism in the 21st century. Moreso after the previous six decades had been expended condemning and fighting imperialism in Africa at great cost to the whole wide world. Still, his blame game and sophistry worked for him because many Zimbabweans sung his song and voted for his ZANU PF party despite the economic mayhem in the elections of 2000, 2002, 2005, 2008, 2013 and 2018. By opting to believe his own false creations and focusing on trivial external factors, yet ignoring the vital internal inter relating dynamics, Mugabe set his own tail on fire. Ruefully the ordinary Zimbabwean caught fire too. Yet tragically, some of the hemmed - in, in an orgy of infatuated partisanship, were celebrating all the way to the furnace where their already crushed – to - powder livelihoods and carcuses were burnt to ashes. Zanuism made sure that everything, including the opposition was ZANU PF in character and practice so that party, regime and tribal hegemony could be maintained.

Fifthly, zanuism thrived on the creation and sustenance of an obligatory and myopic personality cult so as to create and sustain party, regime and tribal hegemony. Once the leader Mugabe became the iconic subject of worship, then his wife, children and kinsmen also mutated into the stuff of legends. It became a given that the next leader would come from among them. When anyone indicated intentions of wanting a different leader from Mugabe, his wife, children and kinsmen, they courted Mugabe's wrath. Vice president Phelekezela Mpoko in 2016 tasted that wrath when he was rebuked by Mugabe and told to be *"responsible and avoid making statements which encourage tribalism"* (Zimbabwe Independent 19 – 25 February 2016). Mpoko had incurred Mugabe's censure for having said that after Mugabe, it did not follow that a Karanga (Mnangagwa) would be the next president. There was nothing tribalistic in Mpoko's sentiment that Mugabe could have found unpalatable except that he had implied that anyone else including himself a Ndebele, was eligible for president after Mugabe. Mpoko was proved wrong almost a year later when a Karanga and indeed Mnangagwa became the next president after removing Mugabe through a strange softly softly coup d' etat.

Mugabe from independence used the powers invested in the office of Prime Minister, and after 1987 in the executive President, to tuck himself away as the political patriarch who was beholden and even worshipped by all cabinet members. He used the powers bestowed on him by both the Lancaster House (1979) and the COPAC (2013) constitutions, to parcel out cabinet posts to party members, at times based on no known or even perceivable merit. Mostly, the appointees would be so grateful for the appointments they would stampede to hail him as a Godsend. As a result, cabinet always consisted of cronies, tribesmen, henchmen, praise singers and loyalists. Expecting any kind of service delivery in any form, shape or magnitude from that caliber of executives was foolhardy. No wonder within two decades in power the government had miraculously collapsed virtually all industries in the industrial capital, Bulawayo.

All had to kneel and worship at the altar of the 'President and first secretary of the party, commander in chief of all armed forces and chancellor of all universities'. Mugabe. Mugabe like a sufferer of multiple role psychosis, a disfigured personality complex resulting from having multiple role models and probably resulting from battling against too many imagined enemies, chiseled himself into an all – time Caeser on the Zimbabwe stone monument. Some say he probably wanted to live up to the venerated Nkwame Nkrumah of Ghana who was known for his preference of North Korean propaganda movies. Like Nkrumah he also seemed to revere the

North Koreans. Like Nkrumah he declared his birthday a public holiday, the 21st February Movement, a day characterized by lavish public shows, extravaganza and heavy spending sustained by the public budget and mandatory donations. Framed portraits of his face garlanded every central and local government office, banks and even hotel receptions countrywide as a reminder to every villager, worker, executive, diplomat and tourist of the omni presence and omni potency of Mugabe and ZANU PF.

Although he eventually failed to usher in a one party state in Zimbabwe reminiscent of the system, politics of patronage took root from the onset and became his *modus vivendi* for almost four decades as jobs, appointment to cabinet, appointment to directorship of boards of parastatals, awarding of contracts, tenders and loans by state corporations and even private banks, was done to conform with cult membership, tribal ideation and party affiliation. Tribe and party membership became proxies for acceptance. Opposition political parties were permitted by the constitution but belonging to one was an onerous mistake punishable by imprisonment on trumped up charges, denial of food aid, unemployment, exclusion, deprivation, torture or death.

He set himself up to be the all - powerful supremo of Zimbabwean politics. After witnessing the collapse of his one party state dream, he resorted to the belief in Cote d Ivoire's Houphouet, who championed that *"democracy is a system of government for virtuous people, in young countries such as our own we need a chief who is all powerful"*. He preached the will of the people as sacrosanct in rallies, yet he in practice brazenly rode roughshod over democratic ethos, so treasured by both ZAPU and ZANU during the struggle for independence.

Those in ZANU PF and in government who acquiesced and knelt to worship at Mugabe's feet, benefited immeasurably from his largess. Cabinet ministers were known to literally kneel while clapping their hands in greeting him. Some cabinet ministers stampeded in competition to adore him. For example, minister Obert Mpofu was reported in the media as being fond of signing off all correspondence to Mugabe as *"your loyal son"*. Such grovelling at Mugabe's feet guaranteed one a permanent seat his cabinet, parliament and the ZANU PF politburo or central committee. He was literally worshipped and showered with praises like a god. Such idolization and blandishments seemed to caress his vanity, sense of entitlement and godliness which exuded immense benefits for the worshiper. He would spare no expense or other form of reward. The worshippers benefited materially but the chief victor was Shona hegemony, as all, including many in Matabeleland ended up believing that no one could lead any political party and the country except a Shona. They accepted as normal the fact that all job vacancies even in Matabeleland and all leadership roles in political parties had to be filled in by people of Shona lineage.

Zanuism's dictum of preserving Shona hegemony through creating a personality cult, was not the exclusive mandate of ZANU PF, as the opposition MDCT party soon followed suit. On 11 September 1999 a new opposition political party, the Movement for Democratic Change (MDC) had been formed by a consortium of civic organizations that included the Zimbabwe Congress of Trade Unions (ZCTU), National Constitutional Assembly (NCA) and the Zimbabwe Students Union (ZINASU). The leadership comprised, Gibson Sibanda (President) Isaac Matongo (Deputy President) and Morgan Tsvangirai (Secretary General). On 20 January 2000 at its inaugural congress, a new leadership was elected and the President became Morgan Tsvangirai and the Vice President was Gibson Sibanda. The party national chairperson was Isaac Matongo and the secretary general was Welshman Ncube who was deputised by Gift Chimanikire while the treasurer general was Fletcher Dulini Ncube.

A cursory analysis of the first six office holders exposed a deliberate attempt to balance the Ndebele / Shona mix, with three leaders coming from Matabeleland and the other three hailing from Mashonaland. That fifty / fifty set-up was not sustainable as far as zanuism was concerned. It did not guarantee Shona hegemony and did not reflect the majoritarian character of Zimbabwe politics. Given the potential potency of the MDC, which ZANU PF could not help but acknowledge, there was a real 'danger' of a near - future Ndebele president and it had to be averted.

According to Tsvangirai and Bango (2011), a deliberate ploy was undertaken to ensure that he being of Shona stock took over the leadership of the MDC at the inaugural congress. He admited that Gibson Sibanda was more endowed with leadership qualities and more experienced than him. Bwititi (2011) contended that *"Tsvangirai benefited from tribalism"* and Gibson Sibanda was *"sidelined because strategists felt his Ndebele origins made him an unsaleable brand"*. One was persuaded to assume that the Matabele in the party were also convinced of that, otherwise there would have been an outcry when Tsvangirai became party president ahead of Sibanda. Obviously the intoxication of the 'Mugabe must go' agenda was so concentrated in the minds of the so called strategists, it deprived them of the root of sobriety and reduced their logic to tribal oriented beer hall quality. Otherwise how else could one explain the insult in saying a Ndebele was *"unsaleable"*, simply because he was Ndebele.

Japhet Ndabeni Ncube (interview, 12 February 2017, Bulawayo) revealed that Tsvangirai's rise to the presidency of the MDC in January 2000 was not a product of consensus by the so called strategists. It was cauterized and tribal blackmail. According to Ncube, way before the inaugural 2000 congress, some of the Shona contingent in the new party had argued that the party had to be led by a Shona because a Shona would attract more votes than a Ndebele. When the Matabele did not buy that and insisted that Gibson Sibanda remain the party leader, those Shonas started mobilizing to form another party to be led by Tsvangirai. The maneuvers to form a parallel party were at an advanced stage when the Matabele realized that the Shonas were adamant and the party would split so soon after formation. The Matabele relented, including Gibson Sibanda and Tsvangirai took over at the congress while Sibanda became his deputy.

Welshman Ncube's (interview, 29 March 2017, Bulawayo) account differed with Japhet Ndabeni – Ncube's version in that he did not mention the plans by Tsvangirai's contingent to form a parallel party, prior to the inaugural congress. According to Welshman Ncube, a handful of people bore responsibility, in terms of the decision to prevail on Gibson Sibanda who was the interim president, not to contest for the position of president. They persuaded Mr. Sibanda, by opining that if he was the party president and automatically the presidential candidate at the next elections the new party would not win *"given the ethnic politics of the country"*. Ncube admitted to being one of those people together with Fletcher Dulini Ncube, Esaph Mdlongwa, Paul Themba Nyathi, Tendai Biti, Grace Kwinje, Yvonne Mahlunge, Sekai Holland and two others. That group of the then MDC core leadership met at Avondale in Harare a few weeks before the MDC inaugural congress.

At that Avondale meeting, it was clear that there was going to be a contested congress. Gibson Sibanda was available to stand as a candidate for party president. It was clear that there were a lot of people that were prepared to support his bid since a number of provinces were ready to nominate him as a candidate. Had that been allowed to happen, Ncube said, that would obviously have weakened and divided the MDC from day one because there would have been a contest on the flow of congress and the fallout from that contest could not be predicted by anyone.

Ncube observed that given what later transpired in the life of the MDC, one could see the possibility of a split on day one if they had not persuaded Gibson Sibanda to stand down because it was beyond question that *"Morgan was going for it. He wanted to lead and there was nothing that anyone could do to stop him from doing so. If it had come to a contest he would have gone to a contest. On that there was no doubt".*

There also was no doubt that Tsvangirai was very popular within the young movement. Ncube credited Tsvangirai's popularity to the fact that during the formative stages of the structures of the MDC, which were formed around the structures of the Zimbabwe Congress of Trade Unions (ZCTU) which was by far the largest of civil society organizations which were at the working people's convention which led to the birth of the party, Tsvangirai had doubled up as secretary general of MDC and ZCTU. That placed Tsvangirai in the lucrative position of point - man, in touch with the nationwide ZCTU structures. He was able to convert the ZCTU structures into MDC structures. During the process, he as an individual also got the loyalty of the people who were going to vote at the inaugural congress. Clearly during the process of formulating the structures, the message that the people must vote for Tsvangirai was passed along. By the time of going to congress it was plain that a large number of people understood that Tsvangirai, being the ground person who had been moving around, would contest for the position of president and they owed him their votes. Notewithstanding that, there were a lot of people within the ZCTU who respected Sibanda and thought he was a better unifier.

Fielding both men would divide the ZCTU where Sibanda was president. The Avondale group observed that people would be more supportive of Morgan's presidency than of Sibanda's presidency, moreso because of the ethnic balance. Mashonaland had seven of the party provinces which would most likely vote for Tsvangirai while Midlands had two and Matabeleland had three.

Ncube went on to state that the group then deliberated and asked themselves if they wanted to take the direction of a divisive contested inaugural congress. They asked themselves if they wanted a contested congress and their answer was a 'no'. They also debated that, given the ethnic politics of the country, were their chances of winning nationally in the 2000 elections better fielding a person from Matabeleland as opposed to fielding one from Mashonaland? The kingmakers did not believe that, given the dominant politics of ethnicity which had been nurtured by ZANU PF since 1980. They aware also aware that the ZANU PF base was still relatively strong at the time, if they fielded another *"muNdeere"* (Ndebele) who would conjur the images of Joshua Nkomo and all the fears of *"maNdeere apanduka"* (the Ndebele are dissidents), they would not win. They were in agreement with Bwititi (2011), that Sibanda's Ndebele origins rendered him *"unsaleable"* to the majority Shona members of the new party.

Ncube revealed that their focus was to try and consolidate everybody, since they thought it would be easier for the people of Matabeleland to support the MDC as a national project, than for the people in Mashonaland to be convinced that they could remove Mugabe, a Shona and replace him with Sibanda, a Ndebele. They also tried to avoid sowing the seeds of disunity and a split by having a contested inaugural congress. It cannot be denied that the considerations that played in the minds of those men and women in Avondale, although they may not have said it, tacitly, they agreed that no matter how much economic ruin the Shona people had suffered under Mugabe, the majority voters would still vote for him because he was Shona, instead of voting for Sibanda a Ndebele, if Sibanda had gone on to be the president of the MDC.

While the reasons projected for having Sibanda stand down in favour of Tsvangirai were comprehensible, the reality stood out like a sore thumb. Without noticing, the Avondale group were jiving to the tune of zanuism which dictated that a Shona must lead at all times in order to propagate and guarantee Shona hegemony. The MDC project could only be accepteable to the majority in Mashonaland as a substitute for ZANU PF, only if it promised the ascension of another Shona.

The only delegate, as pointed out by Ncube, who remained unpersuaded that Sibanda should step down was Sekai Holland (a Shona) who lamented that, *"you are making a mistake. The person who can lead us democratically and who can deliver victory is Gibson.....however I have to go by the consensus of the majority but in my heart I am not persuaded"*.

When the idea was given to Gibson Sibanda, he graciously acceded to the proposal for him to stand down. According to Ncube, it was also agreed that *"the Morgan people"* would be approached to inform them that Sibanda would stand down in favour of Tsvangirai. Sibanda would be the deputy president and Welshman Ncube would be the secretary general. The three offices would not be contested.

Morgan Tsvangirai and his supporters agreed to the arrangement *in toto*. Ironically at the inaugural congress while the Sibanda camp did not contest the position of president, they felt that the Tsvangirai grouping had betrayed the concessions and understanding that had been made, by fieldeding Gift Chimanikire to contest the position of secretary general against Ncube.

Those machinations, leading to, and during the inaugural congress, revealed that the dark side (tribalism, majoritarianism, violence and non - democracy) of the history of nationalist politics was haunting the MDC kingmakers as they went to the congress. Among the leaders of the party were former members of ZAPU

/ ZPRA and ZANU / ZANLA. They were former ideological and revolutionary adversaries brought into a marriage of convenience, not by common ideological and policy perception, but by a need to terminate what they perceived as a two - decades old regime that had precipitated in economic collapse, political mayhem and social disharmony.

The Matabeleland contingent was mostly former ZAPU / ZPRA. On the other hand, until very recently the Mashonaland delegation had mostly been ZANU and former ZANLA, including Tsvangirai and Roy Bennet. Roy Bennet who according to Macaphulana (2010) had been a fundraiser and an aspiring ZANU PF house of assembly candidate by 1999 just before the MDC was formed, defected to the new party because he felt cheated at the ZANU PF primary elections of that year and not out of ideological variance with the ruling party. No wonder why ZANU PF grew to loathe Bennet so much, he had taken his funding abilities and funders to the MDC with him. The historical orientation of both former ZAPU and former ZANU was fundamentally at odds, as they had been nurtured and acculturated differently. Besides, ZAPU and ZANU had been socialized to view the other as the enemy.

The concoction of ZAPU / ZANU and ZPRA / ZANLA in the MDC was bound to be a time bomb, a self-consuming poison, primarily because Tsvangirai and others were recent ZANU PF dropouts who had studied at the Mugabe school of empty rhetoric, despotism, unilateralism, character assassination, tribal superiority, self aggrandizement, electoral fraud, nepotism and violence.

That view of the MDC as a mismatch was corroborated by Muleya (2014) when he asserted that, *"while the MDC's vision was good, there were problems with the assemblage of constituent groups, quality of leaders and the ideological base".*

Concomitantly, the new politics of opposition by the MDC fell prey to the politics of non democracy, ethnic tension and contestation and the violence that characterized pre and post - colonial Zimbabwe. That ignoble state of the MDC was exacerbated by the fact that Tsvangirai, like Mugabe, had been inaugurated into the notion that only he, could win the elections and definitely not a Ndebele. He promptly evolved into a cult god and expected everyone to worship at his feet. It was merely a question of when, the party would be mauled and undermined by those dark forces, and not a matter of 'if'.

While all and sundry were excited at the formation of what was credited as the most formidable and all-encompassing opposition political party since independence in

1980, a few realized that it was born of two institutions with historical animosities so deep that the MDC was already cracking at the seam when it was formed.

The MDC was to triple and fall at the ethnic factor which split ZAPU in 1963 into ZAPU and ZANU. The ethnic factor which split ZANU in 1976 into ZANU and ZANU Ndonga, split ZANU again into ZANU and FROLOZI in 1978 and saw ZANU surreptitiously sneak out of the Patriotic Front in 1979. Therefore, the MDC castle was built on a shaky foundation, characterized by a long history of tribalism, conquest, violence, non-democracy and subjugation. That is why it fell apart soon after its fifth birth day.

As a matter of course, in 2005 the MDC split into two acrimonious factions. The reasons for the split can be summed up in three terms, non - democracy, violence and ethnicism. At leadership level, it split into very distinct groups conforming to former ZAPU and former ZANU membership.

Before the split, the Zimbabwean parliament had recently gazetted a law allowing for the establishment of a bi - cameral legislature, by introducing an upper house, the senate. The MDC found themselves in a dilemma, whether to participate in the senatorial elections or not. A meeting of the party National Executive Committee (NEC) held on 12 October 2005 to deliberate on the matter voted 33 to 31 in favor of participation in the senate elections. Disparaged by the vote outcome, Tsvangirai who did not mince his words about his next course of action which he spelt out in his valediction of the day, said, *"well you have voted, and you have voted to participate, which as you know is against my own wish. In the circumstances I can no longer continue…… No I cannot let you participate in this senate election…. I am president of this party. I am therefore going out of this and will announce to the world that the MDC will not participate in this election. If the party breaks, so be it…"* That said, the party President walked out of the meeting.

What Tsvangirai almost said he was no longer prepared to continue doing was open to conjecture, but many believed the vestiges of democracy and respect for the popular will which he might have had, as well as the pressure of the moment, almost compelled him to step down from the presidency of the MDC. However, something sinister in him quickly triumphed over reason and he opted to "break" the party. What was indisputable though, was the fact that the art of losing gracefully was as enigmatic to Tsvangirai as it would prove to be equally barbellate to Mugabe three years later when he lost to, but could not cede power to, ironically, Tsvangirai. Both men proved to be sore losers and to be both sides of the recondite coin of Zimbabwe's tribalised politics.

Morgan Tsvangirai went on to effect his threat by informing a press conference that the party was not going to participate in the impending senatorial elections, thereby overriding the democratic voice of the party organ on policy. He misrepresented to the world that when it came to the vote on the senate issue there had been a tie and he had used his casting vote to decide against participation in the Senate elections. That was a deliberate lie and the minutes of the day's proceedings were proof of that. He somehow conveniently forgot to mention that during the pivotal meeting, he had admitted that the NEC had voted to participate in the Senate polls, before he walked out of the meeting in frustration.

The group which was in favour participation, under the leadership of Vice President Gibson Sibanda and the guidance of Prof. Welshman Ncube, could not stomach what they viewed as flagrant flouting of democratic processes. They moved for the suspension of the president, pending a disciplinary hearing and eventually dismissed him from the MDC.

While there was lack of consensus and disagreement on the senatorial issue, it was public knowledge that there already existed deep seated differences between the president and the secretary general of the MDC. Which differences were proven and compounded by the latter complaining about the use of violence to silence dissent by the former. There also existed allegations of tribalism against the secretary general. Ncube was accused of favouring those employees of the party that were of Ndebele origion. (MDC Commission of Inquiry Report 2004). There were also counter allegations that the president and other senior party leaders including the then national chairperson Mr. Isaac Matongo were anti – Ndebele crusaders.

Welshman Ncube (2014) detailed his side's grievances against Tsvangirai. He said they had demanded that Tsvangirai should, *"(a)bide by the MDC constitution and the decisions collectively made by the leadership under that constitution... Cease what had become his habit of unilaterally and alone reversing the decisions of the national council.... Disband his youth militia which was terrorizing party leaders and members...unequivocally committ to the non - use of violence as an instrument of political organization and settling internal debates and discussions...... He and his kitchen cabinet should refrain from deploying ethnicity as a weapon to silence those in leadership who had different views on issues of the day"*

Dogged and bedeviled by those challenges, the party split into two distinct entities with most members of parliament from Matabeleland supporting the Welshman Ncube faction while those from Mashonaland supported Morgan Tsvangirai. A good number of the Matabeleland MPs a few months later soon defected to the Tsvangirai faction after some alleged clandestine negotiations at a hotel in Botswana where money was said to have exchanged hands and promises of prominent positions were made.

There was a school of thought prevalent among political pundits and commentators that the senatorial debate merely provided the spark for the split and became the official cause for the split. However, the real reasons included Tsvangirai's use of violence against fellow party members who thought alternately, lack of democratic practice and raw ethnicism.

Herbert Moyo (2012) in the Zimbabwe Independent newspaper article titled "Deep Rooted Culture of Political Violence", corroborated that view. He said that in 2005 *"the party faced a split over violent internal power struggles with the dispute over senatorial elections as the catalyst"*.

Tsvangirai's employment of violence, a creed copied and pasted from ZANU PF, to resolve differences within the MDC, was confirmed by Coltart in his book, *The Struggle Continues: 50 Years of Tyranny in Zimbabw*. He stated that, *"in the same meeting when asked which faction I was likely to join, I said the outcome of the two congresses would determine my ultimate allegiance. If Tsvangirai dumped his kitchen cabinet (which I viewed as responsible for the violence), I said I might side with his faction. Tsvangirai's kitchen cabinet was a group of colleagues, not all of whom had an elected position in the party, whom he regularly seemed to turn to for advice. On occasion he had acted on their advice in conflict with the resolutions of the party, such as the re – employment of those expelled from the party for their involvement in the Harvest House violence"* (The Standard, 15 – 21 April 2018).

Years after the split in 2011, Tsvangirai in his book titled *'At the deep end'* accused the then South African president Thabo Mbeki of orchestrating the party split. He said Mbeki engineered the MDC split so that Ncube's faction could join forces with a ZANU PF splinter faction led by Emmerson Mnangagwa and push to oust Mugabe. He said Ncube's motive in joining forces with Mngangwa was to guarantee Ndebele interests. Tsvangirai's story was hard to buy, simply because both Mbeki and Ncube would need to be excessively presumptuous to split the MDC in the hope that Mnangagwa would in turn split ZANU PF. It was also extreme naiviety to believe that Mnangagwa, of all Gukurahundists, could be used to further Ndebele interests. Be that as it was, had he Tsvangirai refused to guarantee Ndebele interests? If so, why? Every group of people engages in any exercise in order to promote or protect their interests. Why did Tsvangirai's MDC fail to guarantee the interests of the Ndebele? And why did he make it sound like the Ndebele were not supposed to have their group interests?

What was however beyond contestation, because of abundant evidence was that there was violence and autocracy in the MDC.

When interviewed (29 March 2017), Welshman Ncube said that, although they were fairly united in standing up to Mugabe, factions existed within the party from day one, and those factions led to the split five years later. He said the senate issue was not a principal issue at all. Instead, after failing to dislodge Mugabe and ZANU PF in 2000 and in 2002, there arose internal contradictions within the party which played into external contradictions driven by others outside the MDC. He argued that some of the various foundations from across the world who had worked with the ZCTU and by then working with the MDC, persuaded themselves that the MDC was better off if it became not just a social democratic party as stated in its constitution, but a socialist party. In that regard, there were personnel who were working for the Frederick Ebert Stufftung Foundation who were convinced that the MDC needed to split. They were ready to fund and facilitate the split so as to get rid of what they called the liberal intellectuals. They wanted to remain with a pure core workers element, which they hoped would be shepherded into defining themselves as a socialist party. They somehow believed that the MDC would be stronger for that reason.

That external force then sponsored the split by funding MDC staff members and some people in the party structures, in order to cause the split deliberately, so as to create a purely socialist component of the MDC and let the so called intellectuals and liberals go their separate way, he said. Ironically that external force worked in cohorts with right wing foreign entities that were completely their opposite ideologically. Those foreign entities believed in the American model, that elections were won if there was an individual who was an undisputed leader. A face like Ronald Reagan or Bill Clinton and not so much as the Republican party. They believed that the MDC had failed to dethrone Mugabe that far because they were not projecting Tsvangirai as the alpha and omega of everything. They then focused their attacks on those within the party that insisted on collective leadership and the view that among the top six, Tsvangirai was number one among equals and he needed the others to buy – in, in order for him to have his way. By so doing, the donors with the cooperation of Tsvangirai and his kitchen cabinet, foisted zanuism upon the MDC.

Ncube's argument was corroborated by the observation that prior to the 2005 split the MDC did not have t – shirts, posters etc which emphasized the face of the person, but they accentuated the party symbol. That was because the opposition had wanted to drift away from the corrosive and manipulative strongman / single person politics of the nationalist era. They had endeavoured to build strong institutions as opposed to strong individuals. The right wingers did not believe in the collective and preferred to work with an individual. That explains why after the split, Tsvangirai's faction adopted the name Movement for Democratic Change Tsvangirai (MDCT). They were conforming to the injunction by funders and thereby officilized the personality cult.

By the 2008 elections, the MDCT was completely severed from the collective. It had become a one person show with such statements as 'Morgan is More', 'Save' (Tsvangirai's totem), Morgan the one, the man. A perfect cult. It was therefore a socialist force and a rabid right wing force, united by a common agenda to split the MDC, that historically carried that eventful day in 2005.

Nevertheless, the external forces would not have succeeded, according to Ncube, if there had not been internal contradictions within the MDC. Those contradictions somehow mirrored the American model, that whereas the rest believed they were a collective leadership, Tsvangirai increasingly felt that the buck stopped with him, such that even when he was in a minority of 1 : 5 in the top 6 or a minority of 1 : 66 in the NEC, it did not matter. If he did not agree, he felt he had a right to say, *"I am the leader, I will answer to congress".* Some of his colleagues like Ncube, disagreed, thereby setting themselves on a collision course with their leader.

Those internal contradictions played out in a number of ways. Ncube revealed that as the battle to defeat ZANU PF became harder, and as the principles and values of peaceful resistance and non violence became more and more difficult to justify in the face of concerted ZANU PF violence, some started to believe that the MDC had to fight fire with fire by using violence against ZANU PF in order to defeat them. That idea was rejected by the majority but was supported by Tsvangirai and the external forces.

Those that believed in giving ZANU PF a taste of their own medicine, then, behind the back of their colleagues started recruiting youths for training in mass action and violence in Yugoslavia. That was not detected until the youths returned from training and took over the MDC Harvest House head office and seized party vehicles. The young men that later participated in the MDC's final push programme and burnt buses in Epworth in Harare were part of that programme.

Some twenty - four youths were trained, according to Ncube. They included *"the Khawuzani brothers, the Ndira brothers, Beta, Chokuruma and others"* and were all regrettably later killed to a man by ZANU PF in the 2008 election re – run. One of the Khawuzani brothers was the only survivor after they were deployed to meet the ZANU PF violence machine, head - on in rural Mashonaland. Within the party, MDC youths were attacking each other as some were tasked to recover the vehicles from the other youths.

Towards the final stages of unity in the MDC, the Yugoslavia trained youths were expelled from the party. They were expelled by a resolution of the NEC and not by the disciplinary committee, which showed how grave their case was. To the dismay of many, within a week of the expulsion, Tsvangirai reversed the decision and reinstated the youths unilaterally. Before any decision could be made on how to reinforce the decision of the NEC, the senate debate came up. Once more Tsvangirai decided that he was not going to accept the decision of the NEC and reversed it.

Soon after the 2005 split, the MDCT rebranded itself into a personality cult in the mould of ZANU PF. While the American Republicans and Democrats believed in a powerful leader that they sold to the electorate, they had an entrenced and seasoned democratic ethos that provided for checks and balances guarding against a dictatorship. Soon after winning the elections the candidate was accountable to the party, congress and senate. However, after losing the 2005 elections Tsvangirai became the god of his party and that of all opposition politics. He became so individually portent that even the neighboring country presidents recognized him, unlike any other opposition politicians in the region. Within the MDCT, one had to cow tow to his whims in order to stay in a respectable position within the party structures.

It was clearly indisputable that by sending youths for training in Yogoslavia, outside the sanction of the party NEC, Tsvangirai and his kitchen cabinet practiced gukurahundism and zanuism. There also was no guessing as to where the penchant for violence which inclined them to want to destroy both their internal and external adversaries originated from. Some of the very senior founding members of the MDC had brought with them from ZANU PF, their modus operandi and paraphernalia.

Previously in 2004, the MDC party, rocked by incidents of intermittent violence within its headquarters at Harvest House had resolved to set up the Mudzingwa Commission of inquiry. Three commissioners were appointed with Dr. Tichaona Mudzingwa as chairperson. Members of parliament, Moses Mzila - Ndlovu and Giles Mutsekwa were the members. The three - member commission was mandated to investigate and report on *"disturbances at party headquarters"*.

Note how the term 'disturbance', had become a too commonly abused euphemism for illiberal physical violence and even murder within the broader Zimbawean political discourse since the Gukurahundi genocide.

The commissioners conducted the inquiry and interviewed 15 party employees ranging from directors of departments to messengers. They submitted their findings to the party secretary general on 14 December 2004.

According to Peter Guhu, the then national director of security for the MDC who had been assaulted within the party headquarters building on 28 September 2004 by a vigilante group of twenty - five, tribalism was rife within the institution. In his testimony, he revealed that the vigilante group was operating within the party at Harvest House with the endorsement of some senior party leaders. He further testified that the militant youths were paid for their services, yet they were outside the party national security structure. Peter went on to elaborate how Mr. Isaac Matongo, the then party national chairperson, Mrs Lucia Matibenga (women's national chairperson), Ian Makone (elections committee chairperson) and Dr. Tichaona Mudzingwa (national executive committee secretary for security and chairperson of the commission of inquiry) among others had established themselves into a tribal clique that was anti - Ndebele and anti-Welshman Ncube. Seemingly what had brought them together was an insidious trepidation of a Ndebele / Welshman take - over of the party.

The report further stated that Isaac Matongo, consonant with the 1979 Grand Plan was known for publicly declaring within the party headquarters that the office of the party president must never be occupied by a Ndebele. He had boldly made that pronouncement at a time when Tsvangirai was being tried for treason at the high court and the party had to come to terms with the likelihood of a conviction. Matongo and his tribesmen wanted to make double assuarance that neither Ncube, Sibanda nor any other Ndebele or any Shona sympathetic to them, would become the president of the party. In a classic scenario of going for a hunt with salt in one's pockets in readiness for the braai, they went on to anticipate Tsvangirai's incarceration and distributed the power to an all - Shona cast as follows, Issac Matongo president, Gandi Mudzingwa, vice president, Lucia Matibenga national chairperson, Dennis Murira secretary general and Ian Makone, treasurer. They had also recruited and trained a 100 youths to attack Welshman Ncube and Renson Gasela and take over the party headquarters at an appropriate time. Peter also revealed that he was convinced the conspirators were working in cohorts with the government's Central Intelligence Organization (CIO). He also stated that he had been accused by Matibenga of *"selling the party to the Ndebele"*.

Another witness, Khazamula Chirilele informed the commissioners that, *"... tribalism is rife in the MDC and one person I would not hesitate to mention as a champion of this is Dr. Mudzingwa who hates the secretary general (Ncube) with a passion. He has a bad attitude towards Ndebeles and he can't hide it [the national chairman (Matongo) is of the same view]"*. Khazamula also stated that Mr. Isaac Matongo was fond of stating that *"the party was dominated by Ndebeles"*, an unfortunate setup which he thought needed to be rectified.

Another witness, Zwakele Sayi revealed that she thought the secretary general, Welshman Ncube's management style was a *"stumbling block to riches and political clout"* for the conspirators which partly explained their hatred of him. She also noted that *"there is a strong enemy (ZANU PF) hand and tribalism at play in this case because to these people selling out does not mean to ZANU PF but to the Ndebele. The likes of Dennis have declared war on the Ndebele"*. The invidious fear of Ndebele dominance or influence meant that Tsvangirai, Matongo and others saw in Welshman Ncube, a Ndebele first and not a human or an equal colleague. It implied that influential and capable Ndebeles were not desirable, but the docile, malleable and compliant ones were preferred. Nothing could fit the definition of tribalism and blend into the framework of zanuism more than that frame of mind.

The commission findings noted, inter alia, that there was a vigilante group stationed at party headquarters operating outside party structures but on party payroll. Staff members that were deemed to be aligned to the secretary general lived in perpetual fear of attack by the group. The commission report also noted that there was, *"a strong anti - Ndebele sentiment that has been propagated, orchestrated and instilled in the innocent party members' minds by a senior party leader under the guise of sheer hatred for the secretary general"*. They also argued that it was difficult to make the distinction between the vigilante and their handlers and the ZANU PF agenda to destabilize the MDC. They also noted that the next party national congress was meant by the conspirators to see the Ndebeles removed from senior leadership roles since the treason trial had acquitted Tsvangirai and denied them the opportunity to remove them by brute violence. The report clearly stated that there were senior leaders who were behaving like warlords by having militia - style groups of youths loyal only to them.

A compendious summery of the report stated that the group led by national chairperson Isaac Matongo was aggrieved because Welshman Ncube occupied the office of secretary general and they wanted it occupied by one of Shona stemma. They also thought he was parsimonious and miserly (he was known for refusing to sanction unauthorized expenditure and flouting financial procedures) with money in order to frustrate the Shona. They also thought Ncube wanted to depose Tsvangirai or launch a new party. However, interviewed witnesses had exposed the group as being driven by three factors; avarice, hate and tribalism.

It was manifestly clear from the report that by October 2004, there was within the MDC, operating with tacit and subtle official approval, a replica of a miniature Gukurahundi brigade, intending to cleanse the party of Ndebleles. Tsvangirai knew of the plans by the conspirators and of the activities of the vigilante group as indicated by the interviewees. Indeed as observed by some analysts, "….. *realities show the difference between Zanu PF and MDC-T to be similar to that of Castle Lager from Castle Lite …. different levels of fermentation and alcoholic concentration, but the same ingredients and flavor"* (Macaphulana 2011).

In view of the findings, the commission made several recommendations, which included disciplinary action against Dennis Murira who had outright refused to appear before the commission. Disciplinary action against the named perpetrators for, first, the attempted murder of Peter Guhu, secondly, the attempted stabbing of Aaron Mthombeni at Tsvangirai's residence, thirdly, tribalism and regionalism, fourthly, use of terror and torture during investigations, among other offenses. They also recommended that the party management committee should engage senior politicians fingured as behind the conspiracy and the violence.

However, the Chairperson of the commission Dr. Mudzingwa who had been singled out as one of the perpetrators of violence at Harvest House by witnesses to the commission, disputed some of the commission findings in an apparent bid to discredit the whole process and claimed that there was no concensus. ZANU PF - style, the MDC shelved the report, ignored the findings and wasted an opportunity to nip the problem in the bud. Hence the differences between the president and the secretary general grew to chasmic proportions.

Less than ten months later the party split into two, due to the deep seated issues of greed, corruption, violence, impunity and tribalism. Strangely, in a bizarre twist of facts, despite overwhelming empirical evidence gathered by the Mudzingwa commission and another commission that was set up in 2005, the split was blamed on the doorstep of Prof. Welshman Ncube who was labeled an arch - tribalist. The domestic and international press even at the time of the split was quick to call Ncube the leader of the "smaller" faction of the MDC, despite the fact that his faction had one more member of parliament than Tsvangirai's faction. Media houses, civic society and and the press in general failed to condemn Tsvangirai's blatant intransigence as displayed by his overruling the majority decisions of the NEC and the subsequent lie about the senate debate and vote outcome.

The US embassador, Christopher Dell, as revealed by the the wikileaks cables had no kind words for Ncube either. He wrote that Ncube was a, *"genius"* but went on to say, *"Welshman Ncube has proven to be a deeply divisive and destructive player in the opposition ranks and the sooner he is pushed off the stage, the better"*. (Wikileaks: Dell - Zimbabwe report, 29/11/2010). That inclination to condemn a person with utter disregard to objectivity and facts while devoid completely of any evidence yet baselessly vilifying his contemporary, by the international and local community was not novel to Zimbabwean politics. Just like they had done with Mugabe in 1980, they had discovered an ally in Tsvangirai and they therefore ignored his dark side, in a stampede to prop him up.

Despite admitting that Tsvangirai was far from presidential material, as revealed in the Wikileaks cables, the US government and the west continued their financial support for him and his party and did not fund Ncube a *"genius"*. Pushing Ncube *"off the stage"* was obviously USA diplomatic lingo for assassinating him or politically crippling him or both. For daring to challenge Tsvangirai, thereby upsetting the plans by the West to effect regime change, in a travesty of all political logic, Ncube courted the ire of the US government so much he became to them worse than Mugabe whom they had never wanted to *"push off the stage"*.

In responding to allegations of tribalism against him, Ncube (interview, 29 March 2017), observed that that was a pretext. He argued that if indeed the issues were in reality and substance to do with tribalism, Tsvangirai would not have lost the NEC vote on that fateful day in October 2005 because more than three quarters of the membership of the NEC were Shona like him. He lost the vote because Ncube and his pro - senate faction were not considered motivated by tribal interests.

Notwithstanding, in the run - up to the split and when the split occurred, in order to delegitimize a particular argument, many ideas were categorized as an argument *"yemaNdeere"* (of Ndebeles). He explained that in order to lobby for support at head office, some would say *"maNdeere awandisa apa"* (there are too many Ndebeles here). Consequently when the split occurred, instead of the real disagreements being projected as the causes, the issue was turned around to *"maNdeere apanduka"* (the Ndebeles have become dissidents). In order to consolidate the support of the party strauctures in Mashonaland, some would delegitimize the disagreements by saying there was really no disagreement but the Ndebeles had rebelled and had been paid money by ZANU PF to cause trouble for Tsvangirai. Ncube was alluding to an all too familiar tendency within Zimbabwean politics, where within the opposition, if one could not win an argument on its own merit, they delegitimized it by accusing another of being CIO, pushing a ZANU PF agenda or of being a tribalist.

Ncube cited the example of former MDC national chairman, Mr. Isaac Matongo who when he wanted money for the weekend, would come up with a budget and claim to be going to Manicaland for some party meeting during the weekend. Ncube as secretary general would sign the paperwork and release the money. The following weekend he would come up with another budget for a meeting in Masvingo. That practice went on for four weekends until the secretary general, realized that the purpoted meetings never took place. He then refused to release the money and required the chairperson to refund the money since he had not travelled to the said places. The chairman then claimed that they refused to give him the money because *"barikudya bega"* (the Ndeblele are eating alone) in Matabeleland.

The chairman complained to the president and Ncube was called to Tsvangirai's office, whereupon he was admonished for being too rigid and required to release the money to Matongo. Despite Ncube's protests that the money was for Matongo's personal use and that that was a bad habit and precedent that would manifest, once the MDC was in government, Tsvangirai ordered the money to be released. However, by the time time the issue came out, it was an ethnic remonstration.

That ferociously disconcerting predilection of negatively labeling, name calling and even getting rid of fellow party members who held a different view, was used by some of the nationalists during the days of African nationalism. It was adopted as official strategy by ZANU PF in 1980 and perfected by the same from 2013 when it was used to deal with some of its conceivers like Joice Mujuru and Emmerson Mnangagwa. It was employed when the MDC split. Welshman Ncube was branded a CIO operative, a ZANU PF mole, a tribalist, among other labels, all of which were never substantiated but were believed by many, including voters, unfortunately for him. Zanuism was triumphing.

Prior to the Mudzingwa Commission there had been the Advocate Zhou Commission. It had been established to investigate the violence that broke out when Trudy Stevenson, MP for Harare North was in clobbered by MDC party vigilante youths for irreverence towards Tsvangirai during the senate issue debates. She was resoundingly mobbed, so much she was hospitalized. Another commission which also turned out to be a mockery of justice was set up in 2005 to investigate allegations of violence within the MDCT. The commission came up with more or less similar findings as the Mudzingwa commission. This time a couple of youths and junior employees were dismissed from the party. Two of the dismissed, namely Mr. Nhamo Musekiwa and Mr. Washinton Gaga were unilaterally reinstated by Tsvangirai within a few weeks.

The dismissal of the youths only was a shock to many who still haboured the doomed illusion that the MDC as it was then constituted, would some day be a conduit for democratic governance, including the party legal secretary Mr. David Coltart, who conveyed his distress thus, *"I cannot believe that the youths involved in these despicable acts acted independently. It is common cause that they were unemployed…they had access to substantial funding. The money must have come from people with access to resources. The instruction to act must have come from people within the party. In expelling the youths…we have only dealt with the symptoms of the problem, not its root cause".* Indeed, the root cause happened to be in the offices of the party president and that that of party chairperson. The root cause saw to violence erupting again shortly and this time the secretary general Welshman Ncube was smitten hip and thigh by the youth militia.

Another commission headed by Roy Bennett was mandated in 2009 to investigate the violence against the party Director General Mr Tonderai Shone. The Phulu/Seyiso Commission. Hot on its heals was the Khuphe Commission.

Before and after the elective MDCT 2011 Congress in Bulawayo, violence once again rocked the party in Bulawayo, Chitungwiza, Masvingo, Midlands North and Mashonaland West, MDCT provinces. The Trust Manda Commission was set up and its findings were that violence was used as an arbiter in party affairs, factionalism was high and money was used to buy votes. Some of the recommendations were that perpetrators of violence were to be desciplined and constitutionalism had to be promoted.

All the commission reports were gaged.

Such a litany of commissions on violence meted out on party members by the same youths was most worrisome and enigmatical. The situation was rendrered more bizarre by the failure of the standing committee to act on the recommendations. Those reports that saw the light of day only went as far as the standing committee and the recommendations were never implemented. At times, as in the Mudzingwa commission, some of the commissioners were the perpetrators of the violence they were investigating. Hence, the schemers and executors were never brought to book. At times one or two youths were dismissed from the party in a bid to lenify the aggrieved and violated, only for them to be reinstated and even promoted shortly after.

However, true to the Ndebele saying *"inglube ayiluphoxi udaka"*. Literally translated the meaning is "the pig will never quarrel with the muddy waters", but appropriately put, it means old habits die hard and so it did with Tsvangirai. Nine years after he had presided over the party split and succeeded in blaming it on Ncube, he was at it again in February 2014. Tsvangirai split the major opposition party once more, and this time Welshman Ncube must have been vindicated by a seeming confirmation of the Mudzingwa Commission findings.

The original fault lines were there. Abiding religiously by the first split script, Tsvangirai reproduced it and dramatized it for the world stage. In a manner reminiscent of the violence that preceded and precipitated in the 2005 party split, on 15 February 2014 party Deputy Treasurer General and acting Treasurer Mr. Elton Mangoma and Secretary General Tendai Biti were beaten up by party youths in the presence of Tsvangirai at party headquarters.

Many concluded that the violence in the MDC T was not a bolt from the blue, but a nurtured serpent which was ever preying, silent and lying low from the onset. Like Macbeth's *"worm . . . that in time will venom breed"*. To many, the news that Secretary General, Tendai Biti, Deputy Treasurer, Elton Mangona and National Youth Secretary Promise Mkhwananzi had been pummeled by party youths at Harvest House in the presence of Tsvangirai on 15 February 2014, came as no surprise. By then it was a rude and bald – faced revelation that violence flowed in the veins of the party. Clearly the party senior leaders were pacifiers by day and warlords by night. It was crystal clear that Mangoma was thumped up and was eventually suspended for the impiety in writing a letter to Tsvangirai suggesting that the latter should stand down from the position of party president. Some of Mangoma's reasons were that Tsvangirai had lost the presidential elections to Mugabe too many times (thrice). He also said that Tsvangirai's personal conduct had fast deteriorated into an opprobrious public spectacle due to one amorous and adulterous scandal after another. Such criticism of the leader flew in the face of zanuism in the MDCT. Its was inexplicably sacrilegious. It did not portray Tsvangirai in the best light and did not augur well for marketing the party brand. Therefore, the authors of the letter had to be punished.

Prior to Mangoma's call for Tsvangirai to step down, Roy Bennet, the Treasurer General based in South Africa, Mr. Ian Kay former Marondera East MP and Mr. Elias Mudzuri former Harare mayor, had made the same plea and should have considered themselves lucky to have escaped without being beaten up by the militia party youths. Biti and Mkhwananzi were battered because they were in cohorts with Mangoma.

After the trio was beaten all hollow, the MDCT spin machinery and mandarins, poorly marshaled by spokeperson Douglas Mwonzora, told the press that ZANU PF youths had done the bashing. They also claimed that Welshman Ncube was the mastermind behind Mangoma's actions. That was a blatant falsehood and display of political profligacy and hypocrisy. Instead of looking inward in self - introspection the MDCT chose to search for non - existent scapegoats and missed an opportunity to self audit and reform. Even ZANU PF could afford to laugh at them for such a poor and clumsy attempt at imitating them

Biti, Mangoma and Mkhwananzi were not the only victims of the contemporary violence as Sengezo Tshabangu, the vocal Matabeleland North provincial chaiperson, his secretary Gift Mabhena, Julius Magarangoma, the Manicaland provincial chairperson and his secretary, were also suspended and summarily replaced without due process for supporting Mangoma's calls for leadership renewal in the party.

Tragically, the character of violence that had dogged Tsvangirai's administration in life, was to follow him to the grave. After succumbing to colon cancer, Tsvangirai was buried on 20 February 2018 at his rural home in Buhera. When Thokozani Khuphe, his deputy president arrived at Tsvangirai's home for the funeral, she was welcomed by a hailstorm of stones, bottles and verbal vulgarities from fellow party members suspected to be Nelson Chamisa's vigilantes and supporters. Baying for her blood, the approximately 150 raging youths, pelted and pursued Khuphe, Douglas Mwonzora the party Secretary General, Abednico Bhebhe, the Organising Secretary and others, until villagers gave them refuge in a grass thatched hut at a neighboring village. Unrelenting, chanting Chamisa's praises and uttering obscenities, the youths went to set the hut on fire but luckily, the grass could not catch fire because it was wet due to the rains.

There was no doubt the incensed crowd wanted to kill Khuphe and her entourage. In their infuriated state, they betrayed the known, pertubing, yet always denied, ugly character of Zimbabwean politics. Gukurahundism and zanuism. They shouted in the Shona language, *"Khuphe go back to Matabeleland. We will not be led by a Ndebele woman".*

Reminiscent of the language of ZANU during the Gukurahundi genocide of 1982 – 1987, they called Khuphe and her mainly Matabeleland delegation *"dissidents".* During the genocide, Ndebeles had been referred to as dissidents and therefore deserved to be killed by the army. ZAPU's spokeperson Mr. Iphuthile Maphosa vouched that, *"it's a cancer that Mugabe and ZANU PF infected our society with and MDC T just like any other offspring, is taking after the father. They are simple tribalists"* (Southern Eye 22 February 2018). A few days after she was almost killed at Tsvangirai's funeral, Khuphe and her colleagues were beaten up by hooligans at the party offices in Bulawayo. The thugs wanted Khuphe to give up the fight for the party presidency and make way for Nelson Chamisa. It was crude and unbridled tribalism at play and Khuphe was a victim of tyranny and oppression by the majority.

Chamisa's supporters at the funeral were not the first to tell a Ndebele leader to go back to Matabeleland. In 1980 Robert Mugabe told Joshua Nkomo to go and campaign in *"your country"* Matabeleland while he campaigned in his *"country"* Mashonaland (The Zimbabwe independent 23 February 2018). Clearly Mugabe was referring to the pre – colonial setup whereby the two had been two separate states of Mthwakazi and Mashonaland. However, Mugabe had alluded to that only because it suited his tribal agenda. Otherwise he never wanted to secede. Nkomo was also told by Eddison Zvobgo the ZANU secretary for legal affairs after his Mercedes benz had been short at in Masvingo to *"go back to Matabeleland"* or else the people would kill him.

In both Nkomo and Khuphe's cases, the supporters of Mugabe and Chamisa respectively, were tightening the fetters of zanuism around their victims who were Ndebele, for wanting to be the president of the country, since zanuism abhorred and condemned Ndebele leadership. Khuphe wanted to succeed Tsvangirai in keeping with the party constitution. Paradoxically, it was at about the time when the coup vultures were hovering over Mugabe's carcass, that Nelson Chamisa was staging his own palace coup within the MDCT, thereby stopping Khuphe dead in her tracks.

There was no doubt that Khuphe was violently and unconstitutionally elbowed out because she was Ndebele and was a woman. In the same manner that the majority had accepted the coup against Mugabe a few months earlier, the majority accepted the coup against Khuphe, albeit for varied reasons. Chamisa benefited from the politics of tribalism and not from the law, a phenomenon not at all alien in the Zimbabwean political arena.

The malady within the MDCT was a carbon copy of the ZANU PF syndrome, a quadruple trap with intertwining tentacles, namely, a belief in what Sabelo Gatsheni - Ndlovu (2011) termed the Chimurenga ideology and the strategy of Gukurahundi, development of a personality cult, failure to learn from other people's experiences due to obduracy and finally, the hypocrisy of donor aid.

Since the Chimurenga ideology and strategy of Gukurahundi were ZANU PF creatures, it would appear that being ex – ZANU PF, Tsvangirai, and later Chamisa, simply perfected the artistry of ZANU PF. Secondly the MDCT had irrevocably degenerated into a personality cult where there was asinine hero worshipping, hapless praise singing and unblushing bootlicking. In such situations, the actors were rewarded by an amorphous web of patronage, funded by donors, unwitende.

There is a belief that the chameleon does not change its colour to blend with the environment, but it is the environment that changes the chameleon. By climbing the ZANU PF tree, the MDCT like a chameleon was changed without them making a conscious choice to change. By the end of four years (GNU) they were irreparably intrigued and irrevocably spellbound, so much they fast degenerated into a miniature ZANU PF. The MDCT, as Muleya (2014) put it in The Zimbabwe Independent weekly newspaper, was a chip off the old block. He contended that, *"embracing repression, personality cult and overstaying in charge, began Zanufication of the MDC..........the party abandoned its founding values. Hostility to dissent, intolerance and violence crept in. The use of violence now structural and systematic in the party, and impunity, had become a preferred political instrument"*.

After fourteen years, they were at par with the demon they were promising the voters they would exorcise. They elevated Tsvangirai to deity status just like ZANU PF had done to Mugabe. For example, Tsvangirai on 02 March 2014 at a rally in Harare, conscious of his superiority, equated himself to a father figure or somekind of super human to Welshman Ncube and Job Sikhala as he implored them to rejoin his party or they risked to *"die of hunger and be a destitute"*. No reward for guessing how re – joining him would bring food on Ncube's and Sikhala's tables. At a rally in Harare on 03 March 2014 Nelson Chamisa, the MDCT organizing secretary (and later appointed vice president by Tsvangirai before he self – appointed himsrlf party president in 2018) declared that Tsvangirai could not be replaced from the helm of the party because he was chosen by God to lead the party. It was such honeyed words that endeared worshippers to the subject of worship in a personality cult and it yielded dividends for Chamisa.

Chamisa's, was an all too familiar and common declaration in ZANU PF circles and rallies. Examples included Tony Gara, a ZANU PF member of parliament who elevated Mugabe to the *"second son of god"*. The apotheosis of Mugabe was further declared by party political commissar and Minister for Local Government Mr. Saviour Kasukuwere, bantering to the gallery that, *"there is only one ZANU PF and it is the one led by our god, President Robert Mugabe"*, (Mhlanga 2015). Obviously ZANU PF apparatchiks were scaling new heights and venturing into *terra incognita* in a bid to please the leadership. That was more than reverse anthropomorphism, it was heresy. Like all evil habits, heresy proved to be infectious. It reared its ugly head in Masvingo when the Governor and Resident Minister, Josiah Hungwe at a celebration party in December 2014 called Vice President Emmerson Mnangagwa the *"son of God"* (Moyo 2016). Everybody including Rev Andrew Wutawunashe of the Family of God (FOG) church who blessed the occasion, knew all too well that 'the Son of God' was a title reserved for Jesus Christ, who according to the trinity theory is part of the God - head. How Mnangagwa, a mere mortal qualified into that holy trinity could only be explained by Hungwe himself.

The stampede of overzealous bootlickers tripping and falling over each other to please and placate tyranny and personality cultism, marked a striking similarity between Mugabe and Tsvangirai and between ZANU PF and MDCT. Upon being ensconced as a demigod, Tsvangirai like Mugabe, became inviolate and could no longer be accountable to the system that had created him. Instead his pronouncements and casual comments assumed a rare resonance and became decrees within the party. None could dare oppose him.

The official opposition leader's office was designed for Tsvangirai whose mission was to remove Mugabe even if took two decades while the party constitution gave him as the president only two five year terms. Just like Mugabe in ZANU PF, Tsvangirai became the strongman and godfather of the MDC, all had to bow before him and many were prepared to die for him. Anyone who became a real or perceived threat to Tsvangirai's presidency of the MDCT quickly became the enemy and had to be railroaded out of the party.

The zanuism that many had fled from ZANU PF by forming or joining the MDCT, caught up with them too soon. The MDCT leadership and general membership failed to learn from their own experiences and those of others before them. They wanted and waited to experience or re – experience the same negative experiences themselves. Tendai Biti the MDCT secretary general, Elton Mangoma and Promise Mkhwananzi did not have to wait to be clobbered by Tsvangirai's militia to know he had gangstar tendences. They should have been kicking themselves while Tsvangirai's goons were hammering at them, for not agreeing with Welshman Ncube back in 2005 when he accused Tsvangirai of hosting a kitchen cabinet, sponsoring a youth militia, unilateralism, flagrant violation of constitutional provisions, promoting violence and drifting away from the founding principles of the party. When Ncube after 2005 repeatedly warned that Tsvangirai internalized and acculturated violence like ZANU PF, they had accused him of smear campaigning the latter.

Neither did Thokozani Khuphe have to wait to be almost burnt to death in a grass hut in Buhera by a mob chanting *"Chamisa chete"* (Chamisa only) and to be battered by the party mafia in her Bulawayo offices, to admit that violence was the instrument of choice to the MDCT leadership. By the time she complained that Chamisa had sought power through violence and fraud, not even the High Court judgement by Justice Edith Mushore in her favour in May 2019 could help her cause.

Sadly, despite his world class political blundering and theatrics with women which suggested that he, despite being in his late 50s was still having his salad days, the MDCT rank and file still thronged the stadia to listen to Tsvangirai's monosyllabic demands for Mugabe's departure. Credit though must be given to Tsvangirai for knowing what the masses wanted. Many of the voting public wanted to witness first hand, Mugabe's unceremonious exit from statehouse. Tsvangirai brought no other tidings to his rallies for eighteen years, but news about Mugabe's impending departure. He promised the people Mugabe's back and they loved the prospect. Attendance at his rallies swelled, unfortunately for the people, so did his ego. The numbers at the rallies dupped him into thinking that he was infallible and popular enough to dethrone Mugabe alone.

The cult worshipping made him think his critics were jealous of his success and were exaggerating his flaws. Realizing his vanity, the state CIO machinery was used to give Tsvangirai false buoyancy and haughtiness by posting praises of him on comments in the internet and social media while belittling and even denigrating his colleagues in the opposition. Such praises of Tsvangirai and demonization of Ncube by the media further drove deeper the wedge separating them. Regrettably the champions of democracy in the USA and Europe had a very big share in contributing to the mess in and failure of the MDCT by continued financial propping up of an opposition despot simply because he sounded like an anti - Mugabe crusader and sang the anti - ZANU PF song loudest. They were prepared to fund for the sculp of Mugabe even if legality, constitutionalism, democracy, accountability and human rights were sacrificed at the alter of regime change. They refused to rethink a strategy or quit, even when it was obvious that they for almost two decades had put their money into a bottomless pit by betting for a lone horse who kept losing to Mugabe, not because he did not have the support of the masses but because he kept shooting himself in the foot in preparation for the race.

While his ZANU PF - style youth militia were pommeling Tendai Biti, Elton Mangoma, Promise Mkhwananzi and company senseless, Tsvangirai went on a whirlwind tour of the country, holding rallies and comically inviting those that had been bludgeoned out of the party, allegedly on his orders by the same militia earlier to return to the party. Crowds grew at his rallies and that incensed him into dismissing those that were calling for leadership renewal.

On 29 April 2014 the MDCT National Executive Council met and dismissed from the party, Secretary General, Tendai Biti, deputy Treasurer General, Elton Mangoma, Lobhengula MP, Samuel Siphepha Nkomo, and others. These had earlier on met and suspended Tsvangirai, his deputy Thokozani Khuphe, chairperson Lovemore Moyo, deputy chairperson Morgan Komichi, Spokeperson, Douglas Mwonzora, national Organizing Secretary Nelson Chamisa and his deputy Abednico Bhebhe. There now were two MDCT factions.

A battle for the soul of the party unfolded in parliament where the fight for the party assets became a dog eat dog affair. Both factions maintained the name MDCT. The Biti faction said their acronym MDCT denoted Movement for Democratic Change Team, while Tsvangirai's faction maintained the name Movement for Democratic Change Tsvangirai. Although both factions were skeptical about losing the votes attached to the name MDCT, the Biti formation subsequently braved it out and adopted a new name, PDP (People's Democratic Party) with former finance minister Tendai Biti as president.

For all intents and purposes the party split in 2014 in part for the same reasons it split in 2005. The use of violence to resolve differences, failure by senior members to respect the cult god, unilateralism and the big man mentality that among a host of complexes would not countenance criticism. That proved to be an indictment of both the leadership and the supporters because any self - respecting living organism should learn from its history and avoid tumbling into the same pitfalls over and over again.

Judging by the reaction of pundits and political analysts in the aftermath of both the 2005 and 2014 splits, Zimbabweans once more missed an opportunity to read the situation and bail themselves out of the feeble and counterproductive influence of the one - step forward and two - steps back approach characteristic of the MDCT. They failed cataclysmically to see Tsvangirai for what he was, a ZANU PF caricature, infiltrated into the labour union movement in the 1980s, eventually propeled into prominence by a bizarre combination of policy failure, leadership crisis on the part of ZANU PF, tribalism and accident. Morgan Tsvangirai simply lacked the strategic vision, knowledge of party craft, let alone statecraft and potential to run a government.

Many Zimbabweans refused despite copious evidence, to accept that Tsvangirai was immoral, paranoid, indecisive and as Jonathan Moyo put it, stricken with *"serious delusions of grandeur"*. He became a classic act in policy and ideological contradiction, but just like Mugabe, many a voter were still routing for him as he incessantly pulled down the very building blocks of a potentially democratic opposition movement he was attempting to build. He turned out to be a man whose only attractive attributes were guts and charisma, yet one has to admit that a great deal more than that is required to run a country.

As for the Matabele, they were ever at variance, at a cross roads, torn between two giant wheels of crushing dilemma. A self inflicted dilemma between two similar choices. As Effie Ncube, director of Matabeleland Constitutional Reform Agenda (MACRA), remarked in 2010, the tragedy of Matabeleland was that its people were ever wrangling over Shonas, with one Matabele claiming *"my Shona candidate is better than your Shona candidate"*. His point was classically proven in the 2013 harmonised elections which were contested by Prof. Welshman Ncube (Ndebele), Mr. Morgen Tsvangirai (Shona) and Mr. Robert Mugabe (Shona). Both Mugabe and Tsvangirai outpolled Ncube by a vast margin in Ncube's region, despite Mugabe having failed the same region for thirty three years including butchering one hundred thousand of them, and Tsvangirai having failed to win against Mugabe in three previous successive elections and having displayed character weaknesses and personality deficiencies beyond tolerance in any leader anywhere in the world.

It was also clear that while Mugabe was not so much interested in the alleviation of hunger and poverty in Matabeleland as in self - preservation, Tsvangirai himself was not so much interested in the democratic process, the rule of law and economic restoration as in the chance to occupy State House for its own sake. In all those ambitions, Matabeleland was important solely as a vehicle for attainment of that political power. Ncube who could have been a clear choice for the country, given that he had no skeletons in his cabinet like Mugabe and no chain of amorous scandals soiling his name like Tsvangirai, was probably too clean to be elected. Mugabe had proved beyond reasonable doubt, over thirty - three years that he had no idea about administering an economyy. Tsvangirai had proved over twelve years that he could not dislodge Mugabe and that he did not possess the requisite intellect, fortitude, morals and general sophistication of a head of state. Yet the electorate seemed to find those very two candidates most attractive. Probably Professor Lumumba was right that, *"Africans' affinity for people without ideas is amazing..."*. Maybe it is true that when oppressed for too long, people develop a strange and quixotic fondness for the fetters that bind them.

Zanuism's major creed has always been the fixation with a Shona leader. That was the reason ZANU was formed in 1963. They wanted the leader of the nationalist movement to be Shona so that the eventual leader of the country, come independence was Shona. The former ZANU members in the MDCT lived by that imperative and imperious dogma. It was zanuism that informed Tsvangirai's decision in 2016 to appoint two more deputy presidents to his party. When he was diagnosed with cancer of the colon, which was to later claim his life on 14 February 2018, the MDCT president hastily appointed Harare Kuwadzana MP Nelson Chamisa and former Harare mayor Elias Mudzuri, both of Shona discent, as vice presidents in addition to Ms. Thokozani Khuphe, a Ndebele. Despite the fact that Khuphe had been elected by congress and the other two were Tsvangirai's appointees, they automatically assumed seniority over her. The move was designed to ensure that a Shona presidency would be maintained in the likely event of Tsvangirai's death. The rationale in appointing two Shonas instead of one, was a guise. If he had appointed just one and later on that one became party president under whatever circumstances, it could turn out to be a Ndebele versus Shona debacle. However, if there were two Shonas and one of them became president, there would be no allegations of tribal bias since a Shona would have lost the race as well as a Ndebele.

When Tsvangirai took that fateful medical trip to South Africa in January 2018 amid rumours that he had died, he appointed Chamisa as acting president before he left so that in the event of his death, Chamisa would have an advantage over Khuphe and the decoy Mudzuri. Indeed, when he died and before he was buried, Chamisa called a National Council meeting which was not attended by many members including Khuphe, Mudzuri and National Party Chairman Lovemore Moyo. The meeting endorsed him as acting party president for twelve months, guaranteeing him the presidential candidacy in the 2018 polls. Mudzuri lost the race because there never was meant to be a race between him and Chamisa anyway. He had been from the beginning, a red herring. Khuphe lost it because she was primarily Ndebele and secondly a woman. Whether or not Chamisa's contested ascent to the presidency was in accordance with the party constitution, it did not take away the indubitable fact that zanuism and the strategy of gukurahundi had triumphed over democracy, fairness and common sense.

In May 2019 High Court Judge, Justice Edith Mushore resolved the obvious impasse by ruling that Morgan Tsvangirai had acted unconstitutionally when he appointed Chamisa and Mudzuri as core Vice Presidents of the MDCT with Khuphe. Khuphe was vindicated, although in practice the judgement proved to be a dead rubber for her.

Tsvangirai displayed zanuism's self serving nature on countless occasions but when he attempted to win the support of the military chiefs so they could facilitate his ascent to state house, he betrayed uncanny desperation and his subscription to zanuism's usurping of the military. As Prime Minister in the inclusive government (2008 - 2013), Tsvangirai had been commoved by the conduct of security service chiefs including Zimbabwe Defense Forces Commander General, Constantine Chiwenga and Police Commissioner General Augustine Chihuri. The military strongmen were in sync with the jingle started by the then Zimbabwe Defense Forces Commander, Lt. General Vitalis Zvinavashe in 2002. Zvinavashe had threatened that the army would not accept anyone without liberation war credentials to be the president of Zimbabwe even if that person had won the elections.

Zvinavashe's constitutionally treasonous threat had offset a chain reaction by a coterie of other senior uniformed forces commanders, namely, Paradzai Zimondi, Happyton Bonyongwe, Douglas Nyikayaramba, Trust Mugoba and Martin Chedondo. They had fallen over each other in a stampede to vow never to salute anyone who would win a presidential election if he / she were not a former liberation war veteran. Clearly by war veteran they meant former ZANLA. The service chiefs had also shamelessly declared that they would fight tooth and nail for the preservation of Mugabe and ZANU PF in government.

Augustine Chihuri, the Commissioner General of the Zimbabwe Republic Police had shocked the world foundations of professional policing in 2001. Chihuri was quoted by the Zimbabwe Independent newspaper of 15 June confessing that, *"many people say I am ZANU PF. Today I would like to make it public that I support ZANU PF, because it is the ruling party. If any other party comes to power, I will resign.."* No wonder why the ZRP had thoroughly cultivated an inglorious reputation for suppressing the freedoms of assembly, expression, movement and association of citizens and was arresting opposition and civic society activists like never before.

That bungling by, and ineptitude of the military which was well documented in the public domain, was the climax of uniformed forces unprofessionalism. Condemned by SADC, a concern to the AU and an embarrassment to every sober reasoning Zimbabwean, that dearth in discipline by a force that should have been apolitical and non - partisan was most alarming even by the most modest of judgements.

There was no doubt that the statements by the military were directed at all Zimbabweans, but more so at Tsvangirai, who at the time was at the fore of the Mugabe must go crusade. In a frantic attempt to win the support of the securocrats yet unwittingly and nocuously subscribing to zanuism, the Prime Minister Tsvangirai in April 2013 went on a charm offensive. Media reports said the Prime Minister had either met or had attempted to meet service chiefs in a bid to get them to accept the will of the people in the next plebiscite or to facilitate a smooth transition from Mugabe to himself, should he emerge victorious in the elections scheduled for June of the same year. It was also reported that Giles Mutsekwa of the MDCT was having secret meetings with the army chiefs. Neither Tsvangirai nor his party refuted the reports.

The reports were however scoffed at by Chiwenga the commander of the ZDF who stated that he would never have a meeting with Tsvangirai, a *"psychiatric patient and a sellout"*. That brazen insult was in tandem with the sentiments by Chihuri who had also intimated something to the effect that Tsvangirai was a malcontent, as he also dismissed the reports that he had met the Prime Minister.

Piqued by such blatant lack of professionalism by the military, Tsvangirai hit back, alleging that the military had staged a *"silent coup"* and were in charge of the state and not the octogenarian Mugabe. His party lieutenants weighed in by averring that some securocats behaved like they were part of the ZANU PF commissariat. However, none in the MDCT disputed the reports of meeting or attempting to meet the military chiefs.

The allegations of bribing or softening the securocrats towards the prime minister could have been true, considering the report in The Zimbabwe Independent newspaper in September 2013. It was reported that the WikiLeaks confidential cables had revealed that the MDCT had asked the USA to contribute to a *"trust fund"* to *"buy – off the loyalty of Zimbabwe's top army and police commanders"*. The then Power and Energy minister, MDCT's Elton Mangoma had made the request in 2009 through a cable which was signed by one Katherine Dhanani, a US diplomat.

A surface examination of the media reports revealed nothing amiss, apart from the below the belt insults which were outside the borders of normal political discourse. However further Socratic analysis exposed the vicissitudes of the Prime Minister's logic. While the barefaced disregard for professionalism and protocol by the service chiefs could never be excused and was condemned hammer and tongs by civic organizations and the opposition, it was equally and patently clear that Tsvangirai had decided to emulate their bungling. Zimbabwe needed a professional uniformed forces that would protect the sovereignty of the country while safeguarding the personal security, rights and integrity of each individual, be they popular or infamous with anyone including the president or the military. At the same time the country needed a leadership not famous for blundering and equivocating. A leadership that was all over in terms of policy, strategy and practice and a partisan security sector were a cold cast – iron cauldron for calamitous governance.

It was bothersome to observe that it was not just the securocrats who needed to reform so that they could be trusted with securing the nation, including opposition political party leaders. Basic appreciation of Zimbabwe's recent history revealed that those same securocratic strongmen had been in command of the butchering 5th Brigade and had presided over the Gukurahundi genocide. That they reported to and accounted to Emmerson Mnangagwa (Minister of Defense in 2013 and Minister of State Security in 1983) and Sydney Sekeramayi (Minister of State Security in 2013 and Minister of Defence in 1983), the architects and defenders of the genocide, was both a historical and a contemporary fact. Furthermore, a deeper examination into the history of the liberation struggle revealed that ZANLA had a prominent influence over ZANU and unlike in ZPRA and ZAPU, there was no distinctive line between political administration and military operations in ZANU/ZANLA. Those two observations should have piqued Tsvangirai.

He should have been better informed than to even consider negotiating with or accosting the stereotypical generals who swore political and military allegiance to their two gods, Mugabe principally and ZANU PF secondly. It was also manifest that the generals had amassed great wealth, courtesy of the system of patronage which was endemic to zanuism. Those factors precipitated against any attempt by any individual to talk of shifting their allegiance and changing their monophonic conduct. Negotiating with them was as futile as negotiating with Mugabe while Mngangagwa recorded the proceedings and Sekeramayi stood guard. They simply had a lot to protect in terms of information, secrets, friendship and wealth by being dogmatically loyal to Mugabe. They personally had nothing to lose by rebuffing him and more to gain by insulting him the way they did.

The question that clummered for an answer was, whether Tsvangirai's attempts to personally and privately reform and woo the securocrats was in pursuance of the GPA and whether he was going to appeal to them to accept Welsman Ncube or Dumiso Dabengwa as president, in the event of any one of them winning the presidential elections. Anyone who followed Zimbabwean politics could tell Tsvangirai's was a very personal mission. Probably Tsvangirai and his advisors did not fully comprehend the implications of his actions. It was also apparent that that individual or one party attempt to meet the security chiefs was a distressed and unwitting bid to swing their loyalty from Mugabe / ZANU PF to Tsvangirai

/ MDCT. He wanted to court and assuage the military into being an MDCT commissariat as opposed to being a ZANU PF tool.

Those machinations by the Prime Minister were a tacit recognition of and a de facto appreciation of the role of king maker being then played by the military, which role he wanted to benefit him and his party. He wanted to rise to the presidency through the assistance of the military, thereby making the service chiefs political supervisors under his presidency just as they were under Mugabe. It implied that once / if he assumed the presidency he was going to recognize and facilitate the supremacy of the military over the ballot box and civil administration, further entrenching gukurahundism and zanuism. The Prime Minister and the MDCT disapproved of the stance of the service chiefs as long as it was detrimental to their interests not because it was in violation of constitutional provisions, their oath of office and code of conduct, democracy, ethics and professionalism. By attempting to recruit the securocrats to his side Tsvangirai displayed a dangerously desperate, wretched and negligent attitude towards constitutionalism. That he could not be trusted with chief custody of the country's supreme law was no longer in doubt.

Tsvangirai's escapade with the military top brass further proved his cadetship and adherence to zanuism. ZANU PF had always been beholden to and vetoed by it's military. Their militia and the armed wing called the shots since the time of the liberation war. Unlike in ZAPU and the ANC, where ZPRA and Umkhonto Wesizwe respectively, were subservient and accountable to civil administration. Wishing that awry arrangement to persist under him, was thoroughly improvident of Tsvangirai.

Instead of meeting or attempting to meet the service chiefs and negotiating or desiring to negotiate a smooth transfer of power from Mugabe to himself, Tsvangirai could have used superior numbers of opposition members in the House of Assembly to summon the generals to appear and answer to parliament for their unconstitutional conduct. He could have taken Mugabe to task by getting him to explain to the nation the meaning of the statements by his commanders. Alas, he felt his office as Prime Minister was more powerful than parliament and the courts of law, thereby betraying his lack of principle, depthlessness on constitutional nomenclature, desperation for the imperial crown and his adherence to zanuism's usage of the military to win elections.

Besides, both the Lancaster House (1979) and the COPAC (2013) constitutions had precise provisions for transitional mechanisms which did not involve the military. His importunity and respect for peripheral and even extraneous structures on the subject of power transfer, was dangerous in that it perpetuated the interference of

---

the military in the administration of the state. It was ironic that he condemned the involvement of the ZNA, Air Force, PISI, CIO, prisons and the police in political matters, especially during elections, yet he wanted to involve them in ensuring his ascent to state house.

Assuming they had aided him into office, would they not continue sustaining his stay there? How far would they go in exerting their influence? Tsvangirai wanted to continue from where Mugabe would leave it. He desired to continue with Mugabe's much feared military junta. A military junta that was notorious for abductions, unlawfull arrests and detentions, torture and mass murder and therefore most dreaded in both Matabeleland and Mashonaland.

The sixth character of zanuism was its employment of a nefarious patronage system which was unbelievably lavish and generous, even at a time when the economy was bleeding. That stalwart feature of zanuism engendered boundless levels of graft that brought the country to her knees economically. Some ZANU PF party members of all ages and both sexes, benefited limitlessly and luxuriously at the largess of zanuism's patronage. The elite got stinking rich, so much that education and hard work lost their value and appeal to a youthful population that was held hostage to an average of 95% unemployment rates from the start of the 21st Century and for decades later. Zimbabwe degenerated into the dishonorable league of the very few countries on earth where education was substituted by party membership as the social escalator.

Ownership of immovable property, posh cars, business asserts, mines, farms, hard cash and bank loans (which were usually never paid back) were the benefits of sloganeering and singing Mugabe's and Mnangagwa's praises loudest. It was the ZANU PF provincial chairperson, cabinet minister, politburo member, youth league president, women's league boss, mayor, councilor etc that had the best and lucrative deal, the best car, the well funded business and the biggest house with eighteen bedrooms. Strangely the ZANU PF members in Matabeleland did not enjoy that patronage as much as their Mashonaland counterparts did. They were always mesmerized and awestruck by the posh and shinny youth leaders and the confident and balmy ministers from Mashonaland, yet, probably in the narrow and pathetic hope of 'making it' some day, they raised a feeble fist and chanted the *'pasi'* slogan.

Zanuism's patronage tendency became so infectious that the opposition became severely susceptible and emulated it and replicated it in their own parties. Patronage encouraged party aparatchiks to exhibit blind loyalty to, unthinking trust of and unquestioning respect for the leadership. That predisposition became the undoing of Zimbabwe's political parties in both the pre and post independence eons.

The patronage assumed two forms. There was the usual type whereby one was showered with rewards for being loyal and obedient to the leader. The reward could be a cash bonus, mere recognition, friendship, a promotion, an appointment, a material gift eg a car or a house, the list is endless. The other genre was whereby one was allowed to get away with corruption without being stopped or arrested because they were protected by the leader. That was the system that enabled ZANU PF heavies to loot and plunder state resources unprecedentedly. That was the system that qualified the MDCT councilors to commission their own gravy trains in local authorities like Harare, Bulawayo, Gweru, Victoria Falls, without fear of party reprisal.

It was that element of zanuism, so strong in the opposition MDCT that silenced the voice of effective leadership by Matabeleland leaders. It was acutely lamentable that ZANU PF and MDCT over the years used patronage to recruit both somehow sabotaged foot soldiers for hire and some ostensibly honourable men and women from Matabeleland who were economically desperate enough to trade their birthright for a bowl of nutricious soup from Harare. In the early 1980s, ZANU patronage adorned Enos Nkala with the ill-fitting clocks of Minister of Finance, Minister of National Supplies and Minister of Home Affairs. Those potfolios and their attendant benefits probably went straight into his head. Being one of the very few Ndebeles in ZANU, he must have felt unbelievably special. He scorned his own people and regarded them with rare disdain. To date his statement uttered at Jahunda stadium in Gwanda in 1986, to the effect that if it was possible for him to wash away his Ndebelehood and lineage, he would gladly take the bath, ranked him as a recherche and classless turncoat.

The worst sin one can ever commit is one against his / her own people, clan or family. No matter how hard Nkala tried to endear himself to his Ndebele people after the Gukurahundi genocide, his efforts at self sanitization proved to be as hopeless as they were futile. At times the people sounded like they were angrier with him than with the actual architects and drivers of the Gukurahundi genocide, Mugabe, Mngangagwa, Sekeramayi, Mujuru and Shiri.

In June 2011, some three decades after the genocide, Nkala disowned the Jahunda stadium statement as an intrigue of persons bent on tarnishing his name. He volubly denied ever saying that, but he did not explain why he had allowed such a demeaning falsehood to take root and only attempt to rectify it some twenty - five years later. Nkala however admitted to repeatedly saying in the

1980s "*ngizalifakela insingizi*" (I will let loose the bugs on you). He even claimed that he actually saved Joshua Nkomo's life on 5 March 1983 when three people including Nkomo's driver were killed by the Gukurahundi army in Nkomo's house in Pelandaba, Bulawayo. According to Nkala, he was part of an investigating committee of three set up by the regime to probe the genocide. He claimed that they recommended the withdrawal of the marauding battalion.

In 2009, during an interview with the Zimbabwe Times, Nkala challenged Mugabe, Mnangagwa and Sekeramayi to face him before a Truth and Reconciliation Commission presided over by a panel of foreign judges, to talk about ZANU PF's Gukurahundi attrocities. During a Voice of America (VOA) radio program, *'liphuma lendaba litshone lendaba'* hosted by journalist Ntungamili Nkomo, Nkala did not mince his words as he declared that ZANU PF was captive to a clique of "*turncoats, mercenaries*" and "*Zezurus*". While confirming the existence of the ruling committee of 26 Zezurus, Nkala absolved himself of involvement in the Gukurahundi genocide. He intimated that the architects were Mugabe, Mnangagwa and Sekeramayi. He said his role was tipping ZAPU leaders of what ZANU PF was planning. Nkala went as far as proposing the arrest by the International Criminal Court (ICC) of Mugabe, Mnangagwa and Sekeramayi. Referring to Mugabe and his lieutenants as cutthroats, he also stated that Mugabe was all eloquence yet as empty and hollow as a can, on nation building attributes. He rated Mugabe far below the league of nation builders like King Mzilikazi of the Ndebele and King Shaka of the Zulu.

Probably Nkala's protestations and claims of innocence came too little too late, as most people in Matabeleland had already painted him as a Gukurahundist par excellence. Some said it could be in doubt how deep his involvement was in the planning and execution of the Gukurahundi massacres, but it was as clear as day that at that time, Nkala was working *pari passu* with the masterminds of the onslaught.

On his deathbed in August 2013 at Harare's Avenues clinic, Nkala recommended to Mugabe, Emmerson Mnangagwa, the minister of defence as the only one who could "*fit...Mugabe's shoes well*". (Nehanda Radio 28 Aug 2013). Probably the recommendation could be described as a case of 'from one one Gukurahundist, through another, onto another'. Interestingly, five years later, Nkala's recommendation was respected, albeit in an unothordox manner.

Still, according to the Independent of 6 September 2013, Nkala had earlier in the year, during an interview with Foster Dongozi stated his preference for Rejoice Mujuru as Mugabe's successor. With those two conflicting reports, probably reflecting the grey shadow of equivocation that defined Nkala's political life, it will never be known for certain whom he preferred as Mugabe's successor between Mnangagwa and Mujuru. What can be known however is that he preferred a Gukurahundist as president. He himself named Mnangagwa as a Gukurahundist fit for the dock at the ICC. He also knew that Mujuru was one of two permanent members of Mugabe's cabinet from 1980 and was by then Vice President. Mujuru's husband, General Solomon Mujuru was the commander of all the armed forces during the Gukurahundi genocide which was perpetrated by a section of the army. Rejoice Mujuru's resume put her at a heavily compromised position vis a vis her involvement and complicity in the Gukurahundi genocide, more so since she had never in thirty four years, until after she was fired in 2014, condemned the slaughter in Matabeleland and the Midlands. Therefore, whoever was Enos Nkala's preference between Mujuru and Mnangagwa, it could be deduced that despite his vehement denials, he had a heart and a soft spot for Gukurahundists. That element ensured that he benefited from ZANU PF's porous web of patronage even in death. Nkala was the only person from Matabeleland to have deserted ZANU PF and yet be accorded the national hero status and be buried at the Heroes Arce shrine in Harare.

Straight from the side of Nkala's hospital death bed, Mugabe went on to pronounce him a national hero during his inauguration speech (after the August 2013 elections) despite the fact that he had long left ZANU PF and had gone on to be its bitter critic. That was probably some form of *post - obitum* gratitude to one of the men who had founded and in whose house ZANU had been formed in 1963. A good number of nationalists that had turned against ZANU PF and behaved less confrontationally, had been denied the national hero status.

It was zanuism's patronage policy that caused some Matabeleland politicians, especially those that participated in successive governments under the ruling ZANU PF party, including the GNU of 2008 to 2013, to get entangled in the trappings of power. Most failed to address pertinent issues and betrayed their constituencies by seemingly representing Harare in Matabeleland and not representing Matabeleland in government. It is said that, he who lies with dogs will rise with fleas. That is why some Matabeleland politicians after bedding ZANU PF, shamelessly defended and sheepishly attempted to exonerate Mugabe of the crime of genocide. A crime Mugabe himself admitted committing, although he said he had been insane. For the sake of some rich pickings from underneath the Harare dining table, some Matabeles including some former ZPRA soldiers who had survived the genocide by a whisker, shamelessly attempted to exonerate Mugabe and his killer cabal.

Not every leader from Matabeleland was guilty of soliciting and benefiting via zanuism. Despite, at some time or the other, subscribing to some ZANU PF and MDC ideology for one reason or another, or after holding some esteemed office in government, Matabeleland politicians like Dr. Dumiso Dabengwa, Mr. Welshman Mabhena, Professor Jonathan Moyo, Professor Welshman Ncube, Mr. Moses Mzila – Ndlovu, Mr. Goden Moyo, Ms Thokozani Khuphe, Mrs. Thenjiwe Lesabe and Senator David Coltart among others, were not on record for having stooped so low as to engage in the heretical abomination of glossing over and trivializing Gukurahundi. Otherwise history would judge them harshly for exchanging their birthright for a bowl of the not so nutritious soup.

Nevertheless, the script read differently for other Matabeleland politicians. Soon after the split of the MDC in 2005, buoyed by the seemingly infinite prospects of power and influence resulting from vacancies left behind by the departure of men and women that had previously dwarfed him, Lovemore Moyo then an MP (later elected Speaker of the House of Assembly) sang out of tune in an awkward endeavour to belong. Addressing a rally, Moyo asserted that Mugabe should be forgiven for unleashing the Gukurahundi brigade on Matabeleland and the Midlands in order for the country to "*move forward*". Moyo just could not get it. That the future was irrevocably tied to its past and that a coountry could not just soldier forward by ignoring its critical past like a genocide, was Latin rocket science to him. The then Archbishop of Bulawayo, Pius Ncube rebuked Moyo's overzealouness and questioned if the latter had lost any relative during the genocide. Still, Moyo did not have to have had a relative killed for him to know better than call for Mugabe's pardon.

The contradictory positions espoused by his leader Morgan Tsvangirai did not help Moyo much. Tsvangirai, in his characteristic fashion was blowing both hot and cold in the same breath on restorative and retributive justice. During campaign rallies he would call for the prosecution of Mugabe for crimes against humanity and then at the next meeting he would promise amnesty for the same. He at one time said demanding Mugabe's arrest for crimes against humanity was unnecessary retribution. He claimed that Mugabe's challenge was to salvage "*his legacy*" before he died so that his image remained in good standing. Salvaging his legacy was a euphemism for stepping down so that Tsvangirai could take over. All that Tsvangirai and his funders wanted was for Mugabe to step down as president so the MDCT leader could be president. Then Mugabe's multitudinous sins including genocide would be as white as snow. Yet it is true that no amount of detergent, scrubbing, polishing, shinning can sanitize cow dung. Tsvangirai should have known that Mugabe's crimes would never escape probity in court. What Matabeleland wanted was Mugabe's legacy of bloodletting and poverty to be exposed and interrogated by a court of law like the ICC as proposed by Enos Nkala.

However, history gave a streak of some rationality to Tsvangirai's flip flopping, if one recalled that he had been a ZANU PF youth during the Gukurahundi genocide. He had also joined the ZCTU at the instigation of the ZANU government. The ZCTU had been formed by the Zimbabwe government's Ministry of Labour under Mr. Kumbirai Kangai in the early 1980s to police and control workers. It is said that Tsvangirai was trained thereupon, probably so he could dilute the strong Matabele dominance of the labour movement then, as well as to be the eyes and ears of the state. According to Mugabe, years after the formation of the MDC, Tsvangirai still had a ZANU PF membership card. While no serious judge could take Mugabe's allegation to mean that Tsvangirai was a ZANU PF member after 2000, it could not be disputed that Mugabe meant that Tsvangirai had at one time been ZANU PF. As leader of the MDCT, he was always torn between the demand to be a genuine opposition leader and the old yet elastic loyalty ties that kept dragging him back to Mugabe's stable. That common history with Mugabe compromised Tsvangirai enough to make him want the former pardoned for the genocide.

If anyone doubted Mugabe's insinuation that Tsvangirai had been a member of ZANU PF, then they had to believe Vice President Phelekezela Mpoko, when he revealed in detail the MDCT leader's earlier flirtation with ZANU PF. According to Mpoko, as reported by MLO's Israel Dube writing in *umthwakazireview.com* on 23 March 2017, in addition to being ZANU PF Mashonaland Central Province Political Commissar, during the Gukurahundi genocide era, Tsvangirai had been a member of a secret hit squad that was terrorizing people in Matabeleland. His squad's accomplishments included shooting at Joshua Nkomo's motorcade in Masvingo and bombing a police station in Tsholotsho. Both Mugabe and Mpoko's allegations were never denied by Tsvangirai who had always kept a heavy lid on the book about his role when he was a ZANU PF activist.

By trashing the wishes of his Matabeleland power base and preferring to be Mugabe's leniency- pleading advocate, Tsvangirai showed that despite being the leader of the opposition, he still haboured sympathy for the perpetrator of the Gukurahundi genocide. Tsvangirai was at it again when he was excited by the prospect of power born of the hope and sense of victory which later on turned false. After the 2008 polls, Morgan Tsvangirai elected himself outside any consensus, the guarantor, assurer and spokesman for all Zimbabweans in general and Matabeleland in particular. He saw it incumbent to guarantee and assure the country that once in power, he would pardon Mugabe of all crimes against humanity including the Gukurahindi genocide. Tsvangirai was quoted by The Guardian on 07 April 2008 saying that, *"we have assured Mugabe that the new government will not pursue him legally through government offices. The work ahead is monumental and we need no further self - made distractions. Recrimination is not on the new government's job list"* (Sabelo Gatsheni Ndlovu 2008)

Tsvangirai had, by saying that, surrendered himself to the servitude of assumptions that were inherent in his statement. He assumed he was on the verge of and was going to form a government. In his *"delusions of grandeur"*, he assumed he could think, decide and speak for the entire population. His announcement was an unequivocal indication that his ascent to the presidency was much more important than the rights of the victims of political abuse who had suffered untold hurting at Mugabe's behest. He forgot that forgiving or persecuting Mugabe for historical and contemporary crimes against humanity was the prerogative of the victims and the affected. That legal entitlement could be exercised by individuals or organizations in their private capacities, through a court of law or by the state through a truth and reconciliation commission. Any political leader worth the support of the people of Matabeleland should have known that the official way forward on the Gukurahundi genocide was not subject to individual discretion.

Tsvangirai, like Mugabe always did, made a wholesale unilateral arrogation of the people's right to decide for themselves what to do with the wounds inflicted on them by a government and political party which he Tsvangirai supported and was active in at the time. What was clear to many as a consequence of such statements, was that Tsvangirai too, would have risen to a god – president, had he managed to form a government in 2008 or at any other time for that matter.

Probably by sharing state power which included a lot of teas and biscuits and social talk in between lengthy one – on - one meetings with Mugabe from 2008 to 2013, Tsvangiarai, despite occasional rally rhetoric castigating the former, rekindled his affection for Mugabe. Besides, the public media had records proving that limitless patronage was extended to Tsvangirai by Mugabe during those years. Tsvangirai simply could not help himself and had to be indebted and beholden to Mugabe for past and contemporary largesse.

There is an old adage that says, *"one must not stare at the abyss, because there is at the bottom, an inexpressible charm that attracts us"*. Maybe Tsvangirai gazed at Mugabe for too long. Maybe he observed in his erstwhile master, traits that he had always believed in. He then re - admired abyssal Mugabe. Therefore, having a soft spot for Mugabe on the Gukurahundi genocide was only natural.

However, when on 9 March 2017 Tsvangiari said, *"there will neither be vengeance nor retribution against anyone. There is certainly nothing to fear. In fact, there will be a pension for those who are afraid...*, he crossed the Rubicorn. By promising payment to Gukurahundi killers living in dread of the law, he declared immutable commitment to the endorsement of human rights abuses. In other words, he was promising to tax the people of Matabeleland and Midlands so that their torturers and killers of their fathers could be given a golden handshake as a retirement package. By so saying Morgan Tsvangirai maneuvered himself into what Jonathan Moyo said of him, *"one who approaches issues of national interest with an open mouth and a shut mind"*.

Probably there was more to Tsvangirai's spontaneity and unilateralism than succumbing to zanuism's patronage, intoxication with possible state power and gazing at the devil for too long. Those revelations by Phelekezela Mpoko that Tsvangirai had been a member of a Gukurahundist hit squad that butchered people in Matabeleland in the 1980s, suggested that the latter had a very personal reason for amnestising the genocidaires. Disguised in the internationally supported cloak of opposition politics, a former Gukurahundist could not only call for a pardon for mass murderers and Gukurahundists and get away with it, but could even get the international community to fund a gratuity pension for the butchers. One could even hypothesise that that could have been the driving force behind having the MDC split in 2005; so there could be a powerful opposition party, not only championing Shona supremacism but amnesty for crimes against humanity which was going to be impossible for Tsvangirai to do in the company of Welshman Ncube, Gibson Sibanda, Fletcher Dulini Ncube, Paul Themba Nyathi, Renson Gasela etc.

Tsvangirai was not the only opposition leader who desired to forgive Mugabe. Not surprisingly, Joyce Mujuru a former ZANU PF and Zimbabwe Vice President for ten years and a cabinet minister since 1980 until she was appointed Vice President and wife of Rex Nhongo (Solomon Mujuru) the first commander of the ZNA, also promised to forgive Mugabe for his various crimes including Gukurahundi. In 2017 after she had formed her own political party (Zimbabwe People First), she told SABC and the Sunday News (29/01/17 – 4/02/17) that, should she win the 2018 elections, she would forgive Mugabe. She did not have any moral right to speak about forgiving the Gukurahundi genocide perpetrator since she had been a cabinet minister at the time. Her husband had wanted to demobilize all ZPRA soldiers from the ZNA and was one of Mugabe's military right handmen during the genocide. As a member of the cabinet and MP, she had never expressed regret about the genocide for more than three decades. She, just like Tsvangirai had been silent about the macabre pogrom until she had left ZANU PF. She was guilty, if not directly, then by association. Mujuru had no right to self exonerate by seeking forgiveness for a fellow accomplice.

When she was quizzed by the BBC Hardtalk journalist on why she did not walk away and that Zimbabweans would have to judge her for her failure to dissociate herself from the genocide, Joice Mujuru also sought refuge in being spokeperson for the victims. She replied that, *"Zimbabweans will not forget what they have gone through but what they are looking forward to now is a good future. They are now futuristic"* (BBC Hardtalk March 2017). Mujuru must have known that her claim was nothing but a train load of supercilious conjencture, born of desperation for votes and an artificial and tardy need to cleanse herself of the blood of the Matabele. She should have been informed that resolution of past injustices was very much a part of the aspirations of the people of Matabeleland and the Midlands, as was praying for future justice.

While there was nothing perceptibly wrong in admiring Mugabe and hero worshipping him, there was a great deal of wrong in pronouncing wholesale amnesty for him for crimes committed against the people of Zimbabwe. A man, his military echelon and political camarilla, encumbered with every perceivable malady from corruption, voter trafficking, ballot staffing, vote buying, economic incompetence, crimes against humanity, tribalism to assassinations and genocide, Robert Mugabe and ZANU PF, were not figures to be granted amnesty by a megaphone politician, playing to the gallery a thousand kilometers from the Gukurahundi crime scene.

Many observers querried what other sweeping and impromptu modifications and off the cuff decisions with far reaching consequences would Tsvangirai or Mujuru make if voted into the presidency? By 2005, many within the policy making elite grouping around Tsvangirai were taking an exception to his penchant for his Mugabe style patronagising, unilateral decision making and kitchen cabinet making. By the time of the Mangoma / Biti beatings in 2014, it had mutated into a very bad involuntary habit.

On the other hand, Lovemore Moyo's desire to pardon Mugabe could only betray his desire to present himself as a 'good' Matabele to the ruling class, which included his bosses in the MDCT. A 'good' Matabele was a candidate for generous patronage. He was trying to please his master who in turn still believed in the justification of the Gukurahundi genocide. By throwing his deeper convictions to the wind and paying homage to the cult god, Moyo could keep his lucrative party position. It was tragic that the prime targets of the Gukurahundi genocide like Lovemore Moyo and Simon Khaya Moyo (both former ZPRA) were tripping over each other in a stampede to forgive Mugabe for the massacres as much as it was sardonic and fiendish that the Gukurahundists and their hangers – on were claiming to speak for their victims.

It was strange for ZANU PF surrogates in Matabeleland like Naison Ndlovu who on 04 July 2011 called upon the Ndebele to *"forget"* the Gukurahundi genocide and send their children to school, to engage in the self delusion of believing their own propaganda. That was a dangerously short sighted piece of thought, probably inspired by a pathetic Lazarusiosis: a slothful spirit of begging, which sent one under the dining tables of the ruling class, in search of bread crumbs. An attitude that most philosophers and even the clergy the world over would condemn. Sins and crimes did not necessarily have to be forgotten, but could be forgiven. Those that attempted and pretended to forget became hypocrites and lost the vital lessons from the evil they themselves or others had committed. They provided a fertile ground for the commitment of similar or worse crimes in the future.

It was rather ironic that it was the leadership of Matabeleland that over the years displayed a strange impetuosity towards forgiving and forgetting the atrocities. It was bizarre to find the supposed representatives of the victims too keen to forgive the villain that blatantly and arrogantly stated that they had no regrets and would say anything but apologize for the Gukurahundi genocide. After Mugabe, Mnangagwa, Sekeramayi, Shamuyarira, Shiri and others' almost four decades long hubris, insolence and impunity over the massacre of 100 000 civilians, it bordered on timidity and cowardice for anyone claiming to speak for the victims, to implore the same victims to forget their pain and suffering.

Instead of doing what civilised humanity the world over had done, like what the Australians did with the aborigines, the perpetrators of genocide and marginalisation of Matabeleland opted to co-opt surrogate leaders from the region with a shameful need for financial back-up, to wash their soiled laundry. Attempting to patronize the people of Matabeleland as well as trivializing and excusing the genocide and its three attendant evils, was the lowest any Matabele could stoop. According to Paul Themba Nyathi (interview 10 May 2010), the act by some leaders from Matabeleland to periodically take turns to absolve the perpetrators of the Gukurahundi genocide, gukurahundism, zanuism and mugabeism, deprived the affected of the power to speak with one voice against the injustice done to them. Any leader from Matabeleland who attempted to excuse and justify the Gukurahundi genocide and marginalisation including blaming Matabeleland people for those tribal evils, deserved the worst punishment nature could ever give.

In the Sunday News of 19 - 25 June 2011, Simon Khaya - Moyo, former Minister of State in the President's Office, former ambassador to South Africa and then ZANU PF national chairman added his voice to the list of marionettes. During an interview with a journalist, Khaya - Moyo said that the much touted marginalization of Matabeleland was, like Brutus' sword, nothing but a *'figment of the mind, a false creation'*.

He said marginalization was a product of *"retrogressive individuals"* sitting on their *"laurels"*. Khaya - Moyo's conscience could not permit him to deny marginalization downright and he admitted that there *"could be marginalization of the region to some extent"* but *"real marginalization was in the minds of some people in the region"*. What difference there was between marginalization and real marginalization, one would ask. What the Matabeleland people knew was that, to borrow from Khaya - Moyo's vocabulary, it was only a *"mind made of tissues"* that denied that the marginalization of Matabeleland was real and that it was an issue of grave concern. Khaya - Moyo was definitely beside himself with excitement at being under Mugabe's cozy armpit of patronage. He therefore resigned himself to the dictates of absurdity and lack of common sense. If he had alighted from his ZANU PF high horse, the situation on the ground would have looked very different to him.

That was the disturbed mentality of many a well fed Matabele, who frowned upon his/her tribesmen that were not party to the ZANU PF feeding frenzy. He viewed them as lazy and stupid.

As if competing with Khaya – Moyo for some accolade to be awarded by Harare to a Matabele who denigrated his people the most, on 23 June 2011, John Landa Nkomo the then Vice President, made News Day (Southern Edition) headlines by saying *"Matabeleland people are lazy"*. On a tour of the Joshua Mqabuko Nkomo International Airport, the vice president chose to be politically correct with his Harare captain, by blinding himself to the reality obtaining of the ground. He said the people of Matabeleland were lazy and were blaming their woes on marginalization. If only he had read Chinua Achebe's *'Things Fall Apart'*, he would have known that the Igbo say *"those whose palm kernels were broken for them by a benevolent spirit should not forget to be humble"*.

If John Nkomo had had the energy to be awake during the Minister of Transport, Nicholas Goche's speech on the same tour, or if he had the interest to read the newspaper report of the tour the next day, he would have learnt that the project was budgeted for and kick-started in 2002 and intended for completion in eight months but nine years later it was still facing funding challenges.

It sounded like the Vice President in his wisdom or lack of it, expected the largely unemployed people of Matabeleland to contribute money from their meagre earnings for the construction of the airport. He undoubtedly had his bearings on the functions of government terribly and grotesquely twisted and mixed up. If he was telling Harare that the citizens of Matabeleland should arm themselves with axe, pick, shovel, and trowel to construct an airport that would create jobs for people from Mashonaland or dig a 500 km long pipeline from the Zambezi river to supply the arid region and Bulawayo with water, then he really needed to be schooled on the art and science of governance and statecraft. Nowhere in the world have common citizens funded the construction of an airport let alone one that would save very little of their economic needs while being a vibrant and nourishing source of livelihood to people from other provinces.

Without taking anything from the hardworking generality of Mashonaland people, the funding for the construction of the Harare International Airport and the National Sports stadium in Harare, the Tokwe – Mukosi Dam etc came from the national fiscus and not from their hard earned private earnings. Instead of funding those projects and numerous other infrastracture projects dotting the Harare metropolitan skyline and landscape, the citizens were employed during and after construction and paid by the state.

Khaya – Moyo and John Nkomo's vocalizations were the most foul *"hogwash"*, if one was to borrow from the former's rich vocabulary dictionary again, to ever proceed from the mouth of a Vice President and from a strong aspirant for that same office, considering that the best positioned person in Matabeleland to ensure there was budgetary provision for the airport, was the astute Vice President himself and not the "lazy" people of Matabeleland.

Laziness could not be a manifestation of regional or tribal conduct, identity or culture. For Nkomo to ascribe laziness as a characteristic of the tribes of Matabeleland, was the most weird and wacky case of reverse tribalism. The same could be said about Khaya – Moyo's denial of marginalization. Reverse tribalism was whereby one discriminated against his / her own people. If a Shona had uttered those statements there was going to be social pandemonium. There was going to be an outcry, with all and sundry from civic activists to opposition politicians even from Mashonaland demanding retraction, albeit for diverse reasons. However, since that was conveniently uttered through an 'appropriate' mouthpiece, marginalization was dismissed as a non - existent phenomenon, found only in the minds of the lazy people of Matabeleland. The drivers of zanuism had realized that the best way to sweep marginalization under the carpet in order to extensively perpetuate it, was to get the very same people who were marginalized to deny its existence.

It was a fact that Nkomo's and Khaya – Moyo's utterances were instructed by common belief within government circles. They were singing parrot - fashion, a popular refrain. It was such false bravado that endeared a Matabele to tribalists in ZANU PF, MDCT and government, as evidenced on 6 April 2013. The challenge in Matabeleland was that those of their leaders who got access to the power of the ruling party always failed to represent their interests in the face of a senior party leadership that was anti - Matabele. Save for an exceptional few like Professor Jonathan Moyo, they lacked political power and clout within the corridors of government. The people of Matabeleland could not, by any stretch of a fertile imagination be regarded as lazy. A blanket generalisation like John Nkomo's, that the Ndebele, Tonga, Kalanga, Nambya, Sotho, San, Shangani, Dombe, Xhosa, Venda, Lozi, Lubale and Nyanja were lazy, was tantamount to sweeping with a very wide broom in the dark. For one to say all those people were lazy, was taking his liberty too far and the people for granted. Within a tribe like the Ndebele, there were many lazy people and many hard working individuals, as much as there were many good and hardworking people of Shona origin who also had their opposites within the tribe.

At a public meeting on peace and tolerance held at Edmund Davis Hall in Hwange town, three speakers were invited to speak for ZANU PF, MDC and MDCT. The minister of mines Obert Mpofu represented (ZANU PF) and Dr. Qhubani Moyo represented (MDC). Reacting to sentiments by Moyo, condemning zanuism and the Gukurahundi genocide, Mpofu said there was no need to talk about history and that, *"besides history does not start in 1980"*. He went on to say crimes were committed prior to 1980 and those should be part of the discussion as well if the meeting was to talk history.

It was clear that Mpofu was implying that Ndebeles could not demand justice for the Gukurahundi genocide, unless they wanted to account for the Mfecane (pre-colonial movement and conquest by the Nguni peoples including the Ndebele from Zululand to present day Zimbabwe which was characterised by conquest, subjugation, negotiation and assimilation) period and the years upto 1893. Mpofu like many other Matabele (Kembo Mohadi, Jacob Mudenda, Cain Mathema, Abednico Ncube, Eunice Sandi etc) in ZANU PF had the dilemma of either rocking the Gukurahundi genocide boat and irk the ruling Zezuru elite, or tread softly softly and keep their ministerial offices and pay cheques. What he did not realize was that his view was narrowed, his tune eerie and his melody offensive to many in Matabeleland, especially those that had or those whose relatives had experienced persecution by his regime.

The flaw in Mpofu's thought processes lay in the fact that the Mfecane wars had been, for a period of more than eighty years, subjected to both fair and prejudiced interrogation, analysis and recording. Every question, conjecture and criticism of the Mfecane period was in the public domain. There was nothing secretive about the Mfecance wars, unlike the Gukurahundi genocide. Zimbabweans from all walks of life, had the right to resort to whatever legal course of action they deemed necessary, to come to terms with the Mfecane period or the events therein. If Mpofu was implying that the Ndebele should apologize for the Mfecane period conquest over the Shona, he was misinformed. While the Shona more specifically the Rozvi deserved an apology, the Ndebele were not in a capacity to issue an official apology because they had no sovereign state anymore. They could not apologize as individuals. If anyone wanted them to apologize they had to restore their sovereignty or their monarchy so they could speak for themselves authoritatively. Otherwise the government of Robert Mugabe was supposed to apologize to the Shona for crimes allegedly committed by the Ndebele.

Moyo, at Edmund Davies Hall, represented a section of the population that merely wanted the Gukurahundi genocide to be accorded proper scrutiny, and not to be forever hidden under a secretive veil of political and tribal intimation and threats. What was however not hidden to many was that, Mpofu was inanely doing his best to curry favour with his pay cheque signatory in Harare and was prepared to sacrifice the bitter memories of his people.

Joshua Malinga a former mayor of Bulawayo and a ZANU PF politburo member, speaking on VOA radio station, Sudio 7, broadcasting from the USA, on 04 July 2011 stated that the people of Matabeleland were not lazy but were being let down by the leaders from the region. He said regardless of political persuasion and association, the leaders from Matabeleland were supposed be meeting to share notes and ideas on regional developmental issues. That was quite an accurate observation, but as always ZANU PF was completely deaf and impervious to logic and advice. Zanuism made sure that the who is who of Matabeleland could not meet under the same roof. On those rare occasions they did meet, it was not in the absence of state security agents. Strangely, for defending the people of Matabeleland against such demeaning and divisive insults like those by John Nkomo, Simon Khaya – Moyo and Sekai Holland, Joshua Malinga was on numerous occasions in the press labeled an obdurate tribalist.

When he was asked to comment on the views of some Matabeleland politicians in ZANU PF who kept saying there was no marginalization, Welshman Ncube (interview, 29 March 2017) said that, that was what people say in order to ingratiate themselves to ZANU PF. He stated that many Matabeleland politicians made the grade in ZANU PF by going through a beauty contest titled *"muNdeere akanaka ndewuphi wacho"* (who is the beautiful Ndebele) on the basis of who was perceived as not threatening to the interests of the people in the *"northern provinces"*. The polititians then scrambled to present themselves as the good ones while the others were the bad ones. He noted that in most political parties, the prettiest Ndebele was one that acquiesced to the hegemony of Mashonaland over the country.

That was the context under which Khaya – Moyo, John Nkomo, Obert Mpofu and others, denied that Matabeleland was being marginalized by Mugabe's and Mnangagwa's ZANU PF governments. They were behaving like zanuism slaves, in a do – or - die rush to win the coveted title of a 'beautiful Ndebele'.

Ncube explained that the deployment of Shona speaking people in all state institutions across the length and breadth of Matabeleland was happenning because there was marginalization. He further argued that there had been the military version of Gukurahundi until 1987, yet it continued by economic means post 1987. He said that, one needed to be *"stupid or deliberately daft to say there is no marginalization. You see it, its on your face everywhere, in every facet of life everywhere. That's not the debate, the debate is why, and how do we reverse it. You can't debate whether there is marginalization. Its just plain silly to do so".*

At the heart of the root of the Ndebele / Shona crisis in general and marginalization in particular, was a century old historiography which had been designed to mislead the world for imperialist gains. The British version of history that maliciously distorted the past in a way that pronounced a harsh judgement on the future relations of the two tribal groupings. A version of history that was accepted as gospel truth and unwittingly perpertuated by some Ndebeles such as Mpofu and some Shonas, to the detriment of peace and harmony.

Mpofu and his ilk were captives of a biased European version of history. Upon setting foot in Africa, the Europeans had claimed to be on a civilizing mission. They claimed to be ministering to and saving the lives of hordes of savages and their victims. In present day Zimbabwe, the Ndebele, because of their militarised history, which was a critical survival attribute for any state at the time, fit perfectly into the British profile of a savage people. Moreso because they had gallantly fought the British and killed many of their colonizing army. On the other hand, the agriculturalist Shona, some of whom were paying tribute to the Ndebele, also fit well into the profile of victims that needed a savior. Moreso because they had been colonized without lifting a finger of resistance. Therefore, the Europeans had to paint a picture of themselves intervening to save the 'captive' Shona from the 'marauding' Ndebele. They portrayed a scenario of Shonas (without specifications as to identity, area, dates, numbers etc) being slaughtered and butchered by Ndebele 'savages' *en masse* (Thomas 1996), women being raped and entire villages burnt to ashes. That became an agonizing and enduring depiction of Ndebele brutality against the Shonas. A depiction that has over the years influenced not just social interactions but seemingly, government policy as well.

However, the 'savagery' of the Ndebele was at one time a ruse to justify European conquest of both King Lobhengula's kingdom and Mashonaland. That was made more accurate by the fact that the last Rozvi Mambo (king) was killed by Zwangendaba, a few years before the Ndebele arrived in what was to become Matabeleland. The Ndebele found the Rozvi empire already weakened to the extent that they were incapable of military resistance. Secondly, when the B.S.A. Company occupied all Mashonaland including the areas of the Munhu Mutapa empire in 1890, there was no armed resistance. That could mean that the Shona were not prepared or capable to militarily resist any foreign occupation of their land from the time of Zwangendaba, through the arrival of the Ndebele to the occupation by the B.S.A. Company. What then would be the point for the Ndebele in massacring a cooperative people?

Mzilikazi was engrossed in a nation building endeavour. He needed people more than anything, in order to be king of a populous nation. Some Shonas were killed but many of the affected (Karanga) were assimilated. Their lives were disturbed and they lost their identities and property but Mzilikazi needed them more alive than dead. Hence the Ndebele state was, and modern day Ndebele people are a sum total of assimilated Kalanga, Tonga, Venda, Sotho, Birwa, Nyubi, Nambya, San, Shangani, Tswana, Lozwi, Xhosa, Karanga etc, peoples and very few of the between two hundred and four hundred Zulus that left Natal with King Mzilikazi. Even some of those that bear the royal Khumalo clan name were assimilated peoples who were assigned a Ndebele name upon acculturation as was the norm.

There was a curious absence of known specific events of Ndebele brutality against the Shona, except from accounts by white hunters and missionaries whose motive was to justify the B.S.A. Company takeover of Matabeleland to Britain, as well as to antagonize the Ndebele and the Shona in order to rule them. For example, it was a historical record that in about 1830 Zwangendaba attacked the Rozvi and killed their king who turned out to be the last of the *Mambos*. It is also known that the B.S.A. Company executed Mbuya Nehanda and her brother Kagubi. How about the Ndebele, who in specific terms did they slaughter? That information gap points to a probable gross exaggeration by European writers. Those were the same writers who made reference to 'slaves' within Ndebele society yet slavery was a very foreign phenomenon. They, with an attitude of malicious mischief deliberately mis – equated for slave the term *amahole* which was a reference to those Matabele who had been assimilated in the territory between the Zambezi and the Limpopo rivers. The term was in no way demeaning until European writers lept on to it, neither did it have anything to do with slavery as evidenced by the fact that some amahole were *izinduna* (army general and therefore chief) in charge of the king's regiments.

If the Ndebele were indeed that cruel, why were they so brutal to the Shona alone? Mzilikazi migrated through Transvaal, Barotseland and Bechuanaland before ultimately settling in Matabeleland. There were reports of wars, some of which he lost but no tales of mass slaughter. Most intriguingly, the Ndebele did not massacre the Kalanga, Venda, Tonga, San and others that they found settled in modern day Matabeleland. Why would they massacre the Rozvi / Karanga? As for the Munhu Mutapa empire, it was too far for the Ndebele impis to raid. By the time the warriors got to modern day Harare and Mutare they would have died of exhaustion and hunger, thereby becoming candidates for massacre themselves.

Without dismissing claims of Ndebele massacres as downright fiction by spiteful European writers, it is critical to accept that there was an urgent need to re - look at the settler's account of Ndebele / Shona relations before the advent of the colonialists. Otherwise it was most probable that the relations were those of a conquering militaristic power, neighboring a weakened confederacy that was forced by the former to pay periodic tribute, in the absence of any massacres. Admittedly, conquering the Shona meant that many were killed, displaced, captured, assimilated and died of other causes. They were definitely wronged, but allegations of massacres are yet to be substantiated.

The Europeans merely wanted to drive a wedge between the Ndebele and the Shona. They actually accomplished that with astonishing nerve and to permanent damage. By so doing they planted a drought resistant and all – weather seed of mistrust and hate between Ndebeles and Shonas. The tension and even socio – economic and political conflict between the two was informed by that all time misinformation.

That wedge of anger, mistrust and mutual hate was evidenced by a ZANU PF MP Lawrence Katsiru who in March 2017 during public consultations for the National

Peace and Reconciliation Commission (NPRC) Bill in Marondera stated that the Ndebele would never be compensated for the Gukurahundi atrocities unless they paid restitution for their violating Mashonaland in the 19th century.

After the May 2008 wave of xenophobia in South Africa that unleashed violence against Zimbabweans, Malawians and Mozambicans, first in Alexandra before spreading to Durban, Cape Town and parts of Mpumalanga, North West and Free State provinces, sixty - two people lay dead. The Human Sciences Research Council of South Africa (HSRCSA) identified four causes of the xenophobia. The very first was *"relative deprivation, specifically intense competition for jobs, commodities and housing..."*

The HSRCSA seemed to be echoing the situation in Matabeleland since 1980. The Zimbabwean government was intent on ignoring the situation in the country and was intent on allowing it to deteriorate to that extent of anarchy. Instead of addressing the injustice and inequality, the Mugabe and Mnangagwa governments buried their heads in the sand and willed Matabeleland to heed the bankrupt theories from the Nkalas, Mpofus, Khaya – Moyos and John Nkomos.

Condemning and banishing one's own kind has always been the inalienable mark of misplaced loyalty to a cause, since time immemorial. That action consistently and inevitably attracted rewards. It also caused the oppressor to be more ruthless in their undertaking to exploit, since they would be having a voice among the oppressed. However, such a mixture of chauvinism and discrimination undermined a people's trust in the system, retarded social progress towards tribal tolerance, threatened civilisation and bred xenophobia.

Enos Nkala, Simon Khaya-Moyo and John Nkomo violated the cardinal rule of brotherhood which dictated that 'blood is thicker than water'. While their people did not expect them to discriminate between Ndebele and Shona, they expected them to propagate their elevation to the same level as Mashonaland. They did not expect them to verbally tarnish their image and crush their ego and confidence. The people expected the leaders to be positive about them and the region and to market them as a good product and not demean them and call them names. Strangely, all three, during their time held the acclaimed office of party national chairman in their respective political parties. They failed dismally to influence party policy for the upliftment of their region but spent valuable time coining Mugabe's and Tsvangirai's praises. It would seem that cult worshipping was endemic to the office of ZANU PF and MDCT chairperson. Probably puppetry or intellectual pedestrianism were requirements for that office during their time. They, in their glory failed to acknowledge that the people of Matabeleland were inherently similar to any people in the world. That they craved for success, just like their compatriots in Mashonaland and reacted with no less haste and passion to same stimuli.

Nkala was a powerbroker in ZANU PF in 1979. He was present at the Lancaster House talks and could have put all his energy to the Patriotic Front project which would have seen a merger of ZAPU and ZANU. In 2008 and with more conviction and vigour in 2013, Lovemore Moyo the speaker of parliament supported, Thokozani Khuphe who swore that only over her dead body would her MDCT coalesce with Prof. Welshman Ncube's MDC. Both misgivings against ZAPU and MDC by the powerful party leaders from the region cost the people of Zimbabwe and moreso, Matabeleland dearly.

The seventh trait of zanuism was that it exploited and abused soldiers, women and youth structures by turning them into the horns of the ZANU PF campaigning and electioneering stratagems. Women and youths made the party visible as they doned the party regalia with the face of Mugabe and the ZANU PF logo emblazoned on t - shirts, caps, shirts, bandanas and dresses. They sung and danced at airports and on the side roads as Mugabe's motorcade sped past. Women and youth wings became party functionaries and apparatus to advance individual and corporate agendas. Some of them benefited lavishly from generous patronage while some youths and an occassional adult, got given opaque beer to stay sober enough to chant slogans and rough up opposition supporters, yet drunk enough not to worry about their personal wellbeing and future.

The list of ever gleeful women, ready to be the talons of zanuism, stretched from as high as cabinet ministers to as low as party cell group members. They at various times were fronted by the likes of, Shuvai Mahofa, Oppah Muchinguri, Olivia Muchena, Joice Mujuru (for 34 years untill her unceremonious fall from graces in December 2014), Grace Mugabe and Thokozile Mathuthu. Under their influence and organization, ordinary women would dare and defy the devil in defense of Mugabe and ZANU PF.

Zanuism used state military personnel and equipment, government machinery and budget, as if they were part and parcel of the party structures. At times the army worked in cahoots with the militia and youth wing, providing them with the means, sway and audacity to unleash violence on the opposition while guaranteeing them immunity from arrest. The military were pivotal in the ZANU PF electoral fraud in 1980. Yet no one but a few ZAPU luminaries and the victims of violence in the country's eastern districts noticed, principally because Mugabe was by then lovey dovey with the British, who were prefecting the elections. After the unity accord of 1987 there was no formidable opposition politics. The army was confined to the barracks.

When he frawned on his benefactors, twenty years after the first plebiscite, his electoral fortunes were wanning thus Mugabe resorted to using the military establishment once more. The senior security personnel took to threatening the opposition and electorate in order to cow them into submission and into voting for ZANU PF. Junior officers criss – crossed the districts in plain clothes campaigning for ZANU PF along the women and youths.

From inception, the ZANU PF government had always been dictated to by the partisan military establishment that was instrumental in Mugabe winning the 1980 elections. However it was not until 2000 that it became clear that the country was what Mandaza (2016) termed a securocrat state where, *"the backdrop of a bloody armed struggle in which a number of its survivors still constitute a significant, if not a central, factor in the securocrat state, and the (ideological) rhetoric that has accompanied and sought to pervade the entire post – independence period to this day, contribute towards the attempt to sustain and justify the twin pillars of contemporary securocracy in Zimbabwe: violence (or the threat of it) and entitlement and/or patronage…"*

It was the same military establishment that Ndlovu – Gatsheni (2011) described as a *"military junta"* that worked hand in glove with ZANU PF sticklers to curtail progress towards the attainment of a non Shona nation – state in Zimbabwe. That argument went all the way in proving zanuism's propensity for tribal Shona hegemony which was always wary of and against the establishment of a non Shona nation – state.

The securocrat state was oiled by such ZANU PF and military pedants like Brigadier General Douglas Nyikayaramba who in 2008 was temporarily retired and appointed ZANU PF's Director of Elections. He was re-engaged after the bloody and disputed elections where Morgan Tsvangirai outpolled Mugabe, but the latter would not relinquish power. In May 2011, in sync with the other loyalists and die hard ZANU PF service chiefs, namely Director of Prisons, Paradzai Zimondi, Defence Forces Commander General, Constantine Chiwengwa, Commissioner General of Police, Augustine Chihuri and Director of the CIO Happyton Bonyongwe, Nyikayaramba recited the eleven - year old despotic mantra, that the military would never salute any other president but Mugabe. Those that had worked closely with the echelon of the Gukurahundi genocide, would attest that, as operations director of the Presidential Guard, just like Shallwin Muzite his counterpart in the 5th Brigade, Nyikayaramba was a mono – minded and blood hardened Mugabe loyalist who outshone his commander in vices, callousness and brutality. His sentiments therefore had to be taken seriously.

Nyikayaramba was singing an old and established refrain started in 2002 when the then ZDF commander, General Vitalis Zvinavashe had officiously declared that, *"the highest office in the land is a straitjacket whose occupant is expected to observe the objectives of the liberation struggle.. we will not accept, let alone support or salute anyone with a different agenda".*

The securocrat state reared its ugly head again on 02 September 2015, when Brigadier – General of the Presidential Guard, Anselem Sanyatwe, addressing five hundred army officers, stated that, *"professionalism is over... I do not want you to hear through the grapevine...the animal called ZANU PF shall rule forever and that is the reason I am saying forward with ZANU PF! Forward with President Robert Mugabe! Down with Joice Mujuru.....what I want you to know today is that another sun does not rise before another one sets"* (meaning no one can rule when Mugabe was alive) (Mambo 2015).

That trenchant disdain for military professionalism and integrity was directed at the opposition in general, and in particular at former Vice President, Mrs Joice Mujuru who, not regrettably, was getting a sip from a sour decoction she had helped brew. It was crystal clear that zanuism's forced and artificial loyalty to Mugabe's life presidency, ZANU PF longevity and Shona hegemony were the theme of Sanyatwe's diatribe.

The army was perversely indoctrinated into thinking that no other party had legitimate claim to forming a government, and that no other person among the 13 million plus citizens, could be president as long as Mugabe, who at 92 years, seemed to be defying death, still breathed. Joice Mujuru who had recently launched a political party should have understood that language better than anyone else, having refined it herself for thirty - four years of a long and illustrious career in ZANU PF.

As it turned out during the suppressed Mugabe succession dabates in the seventeen years after 2000, everybody who thought differently, including those within ZANU PF's rank and file, had *"a different agenda"* that was hostile to ZANU PF and Mugabe's presidency. The essence of the general's proclamations was that, the army would stage a military coup if anybody other than Mugabe won the 2018 elections and that for one to be eligible for the office of president of Zimbabwe they had to be ZANU PF, ZANLA and Mugabe. The army was saying no one but Mugabe was eligible to be president. Not even Mugabe's age old acolytes and close associates like Mnangagwa, Mujuru, Sekeramayi and Mutasa, as later events proved, were qualified to have ambitions of president.

In June 2013, Mugabe justified the earlier errant conduct and injudicious utterances by the generals at a SADC meeting in Maputo, Mozambique, as a mere liberation war complex. He said the generals had to be treated with *"sensitivity"*. Still, he himself on countless occasions in collusion with the generals would tell the world that there was no vacancy in the office of president. That was in stark opposition to democratic ethos, which accorded every Zimbabwean the right to campaign for the office of president at any time of day or night.

In mature democracies, the office of president was magnetic to and elicited aspirations and applications from any citizen, year in and year out. Yet not in Zimbabwe under zanuism. The chair of president could never be vacant because there was supposed to be a president on it all the time, but there was always a vacancy for the job and Mugabe and his generals knew that. Any citizen, including the not so bright ones could mobilise support for them to occupy that office, come next elections.

Just as the army, war veterans, women's league, youth league, senior policy bureaucrats and hundreds of thousands general party members who on numerous occasions took to the streets on a *"million men march"* in a display of support for Mugabe, said loud and clear, that the position of party and country president was created for Mugabe and hin alone, events in the opposition MDCT proved to be similarly worrisome. Once ensconced as party president and recognized by the international community as the man to remove 'intransigent' Mugabe from power, Tsvangirai the person and not MDCT the institution became the opposition. He gathered around himself an equivalent of Mugabe's tribal generals in the form of combative senior tribal mandarins, a belligerent youth militia, a vociferous coterie of woman praise singers, all vowing that no one could lead the party but Tsvangirai.

The eighth distinguishing feature of zanuism was the party politburo's omnipotency. The most supreme and elite organ in the party structures whose membership bestowed on one, more influence and clout than being a member of parliament, the source of administrative policies between five yearly congresses, the politburo became the defacto parliament, executive and judiciary of the country. That amalgamation and crowding of the three arms of the state into the party usually accorded one institution immense political power, clout, unrivalled administrative authority and biased judicial privilege. (Hunter et al 2001). What the politburo wished became a command and the three arms of the state merely rubber stamped its decisions in a set up where the lines between civil, government, political and militarily formations were always crisscrossing in a web of manufactured encroachment. Due to the deliberate distortion of the principle of separation of powers, ZANU PF, ZANLA, the Zimbabwe National Army and the government got entangled in a giant overlapping affair of aggregated corruption, incompetence, violence, riches, poverty, assassinations, plots, arrests, betrayal, you name it.

The politburo which always met at party headquarters in Harare, never met in Mugabe's absence just like the cabinet. The politburo met and decided on issues of government policy despite being a party organ. Then cabinet, usually comprising members of the politburo would meet to adopt and implement politburo resolutions. Appointments to government senior positions, parastatals, boards, judiciary, commissions etc, were made and concluded at the politburo. In the event of those crucial policy matters which somehow originated from and were concluded by ministers, turning out to be unpopular within the politburo, the politburo's will prevailed. It was a supreme party organ with powers of veto.

Zanuism proved its formidability and adamantine capacity to manipulate and conflate cabinet especially from 2008 to 2013 during the tenure of the Government of National Unity. Even the most prolific of opposition MPs that were appointed into the cabinet flattered to deceive as they either spent all the five years chasing the shadows of their ZANU PF counterparts or the approving signature of the president or a fellow line minister. Some exhausted the years wallowing in the trappings of power and achieved precious little, if any results at all. Some of the opposition ministers were so impressed with the packages and benefits of their offices they took to praising their erstwhile antagonist, Mugabe himself. By the end of the day, Mugabe and the politburo were running the country solo.

By the year 2000, Mugabe was the banal darling of controversy and failed social, political and economic policies. Thousands of university graduates were laughing stock as the economy could not create jobs for them and they were vending in the streets of Bulawayo and Harare. It was hardly believable that the president had so many earned and honorary degrees because his administration had no respect for university and college certificates. Millions of Zimbabweans in towns could hardly afford the basic three meals per day. Food aid for the millions of hungry rural folk was used as a vote buying tool by ZANU PF.

Mugabe was unceremoniously expelled from the Commonwealth group for errant conduct. Despite possessing a master's degree in economics, Mugabe's management of the economy provided ample and concrete evidence to the conclusion that the previous honours conferred on him were either uninformed tomfoolery and products of immature exhilaration, or an exercise in executive manipulation gone wrong. The man was a disaster. Without much effort he simply and crudely severed the economic fruit tree that Ian Smith had tended so well.

Mugabe's modus operandi was such that no cabinet decisions could be made without him, since cabinet could not meet in his absence. During his annual vacation he made sure that not even his deputies could convene cabinet meetings. Ministers in charge of key ministries like finance, had to report to him and take instructions from him even on issues they had mastered and on which he was a layman. Many a minister was hamstrung by his operational policies but most preferred to take it lying down than stand their ground and lose the pay cheque. That style of governance ensured lack of individual responsibility and accountability by line ministers who fast assumed the role of ceremonial ministers who were in cabinet for the gravy while policy implementation and service delivery suffered.

As appointment to cabinet was Mugabe's prerogative, and since he did not have to justify his decisions to anyone, his approval became the most saught after commodity within his party. As many as thirty plus ministers and their deputies as well as twenty non constituency members of parliament, numerous commissioners and judges were appointed at his personal whim, based on loyalty, tribe, nepotism and party affiliation. Such appointees could not be held accountable. As a result, corruption, the most caustic and pervasive malady ever to beset Zimbabwe politics, set in hard, thick and fast like a plague. That morbid habit depriving officers of the moral obligation and legal responsibility to provide a service without deriving personal benefit, infected all the public service. Corruption in Zimbabwe became like a cancer whose minute yet deadly tentacles spread thoughout the body, infesting every cell, from vital organ to the hair. Corruption was gnawing at the decomposing Zimbabwean body like moths devouring a forgotten hide under a bush, on day one after independence. By the time Mugabe was couped out by Mnangagwa, corruption was full blown and was common practice.

Many party activists and hangers - on that could not even interpret any section of the national constitution, found their way into cabinet, parliament, commissions and boards of state enterprises. The fate of the economy was placed squrely at their disposal. The ministers in turn appointed into key posts within their line ministries, boards and parastatals, their cousins, half brothers and sisters, friends, in – laws, sons and daughters, girl friends and even church mates. They deliberately twisted the Shona tradition of *"chawawana idya nehama"* (eat what you catch/find with relatives). That socially upright saying, meant to engender domestic responsibility and the spirit of sharing, was abused to entrench nepotism, tribalism and greed of an appalling kind.

The most carnival and prehensible atmosphere developed within the governing boards of ministries and parastatals as money and asserts inherited from the Smith regime were avariciously converted to personal usage. State enterprises were run aground within a very short period. National economic giants that produced for export like the Cold Storage Commission (CSC), the Dairy Marketing Board (DMB), the Grain Marketing Board (GMB), ZISCO Steel, Wankie Colliery Company (WCC), Posts and Telecommunications (PTC) and Air Zimbabwe were stripped bare of their capacity, reputation and asserts in the most barbaric orgy of looting.

Within twenty years, zanuism had reduced what the whitemen had built over eighty years, to a sorry, derelict, dilapidated and obsolete shell. Within another ten more years, Mugabe who according to the American ambassador Christopher Dell in secret communication with Washington DC, knew virtually zilch about the economy, despite possessing a degree in economics, had collapsed the economy to scrap, in spectacular fashion. One classic example of ZANU PF's miraculous failures was national airline (Air Zimbabwe). When Mugabe and his gang took over in 1980 the airline boasted a fleet af eighteen squeaky clean and efficient air planes. By 2017, after Mugabe had appointed his son in law, Simba Chikore as CEO, the airline had no planes to its name and was insolvent.

Ian Smith must have been vindicated from the grave when Mugabe smashed the economic jewel he had inherited. Smith's dooming prophecy was that, *"if blacks are to rule themselves, people in towns will walk on sewage until they believe its normal. All the gains from colonization will varnish. Infrastructure will collapse, roads will be impassable, trains will kill people until they are abandoned as an unsafe mode of transport".* The ZANU PF government seemed to be in a hurry to fullfil that prophecy completely.

Zimbabwe managed to defy the book makers on corruption, by spewing forth the most eccentric and grossly unconventional cases of degeneracy. From the time of the Willowvale car scandal in the early 1980s where ministers abused their priviledge to buy cars at a local assembling plant in Harare for a song and then sold them lucratively to third parties, to the theft of a steam locomotive engine by one, Haruperi, in a country where there were no private trains and the government owned the rail tracks. Then in 2016 the disappearance without trace of fifteen billion United States dollars (US$15 000 000 000) made from diamond revenues at a time when the country was failing to honour a US$ 1.8 billion debt to the

IMF and World Bank and was applying for a US$2 billion dollar funding from the African Development Bank. Then there was the traffic cop who swallowed a ten United States dollar (US$10) bill in a mad bid to conceal evidence of a bribe he had just solicited from a motorist. It was just a strange mosaic of comical and tragic fiascos, all dragging the country down the proverbial drain.

They say fish start rotting from the head. Mugabe and his acolytes set themselves on a mission of swagging and ransacking, self - aggrandizement and nest - feathering in 1980. By 2017 they were still at it relentlessly. When Mnangagwa's coup government took over in 2018, they simply continued from where they had left with Mugabe. They got filthy rich. The ZANU PF sponsored gravy train was more jucy in Zimbabwe, a third world and below - developing country with inflation at one time above 1000%, than it was in the developed world. The moral pervasion and seeming impairment of all virtues was novel but common place as evidenced by the lack of interest by the state, political parties, parliament, attorney general's office, civil society, churches, the media and the public, in the theft of the US$15 billion in 2016. The fraud was mentioned in the press and in passing by one or two politicians, otherwise it was business as usual and the feeding frenzy continued unabeted. Just like the Command Agriculture allocation of US$3 billion which disappeared from under the noses of the President Mnangagwa, the Chief Secreatary to the President and Cabinet Dr. Misheck Sibanda and Perence Shiri the Agriculture Minister in July 2019, it generated a lot of social media interest but no legal action. Parliament did ask a few questions about the cases but nothing concrete happened.

Zimbabwe was the only country in the world where US$15 billion simply vanished into thin air and nobody appeared in court to account. Silence was the government's primary weapon to deal with social media complaints against such corruption. Commenting on the US$3 billion, the MDC Treasurer General, Mr David Coltart said, *"it is common cause that Mnangagwa was the lead actor in Command Agriculture, which is where this money disappeared. This is a scandal of unfathomable proportions. But all we get is silence from the regime"*.

By 2013 as the country was abuzz with the excitement of the new constitution and imminent elections. The whole country from Victoria Falls in the north west to Mutare in the east, was gripped by a feeding whirl. ZANU PF institutionalized patronage had never been more visible and accessible. Media reports in June revealed ZANU PF extravagance at its best. During a rally in Mashonaland West, Phillip Chiyangwa the ZANU PF candidate, reputedly went to the venue of an MDCT rally, parked his car outside while the rally was ongoing and started issuing hundred dollar bills (US) to all that walked out the gate. As a result, all people walked out and abandoned the rally and got US$100 each.

In Matabeleland, where ZANU PF had a dearth of young, educated and capable cadres, they gave money to some youths and re-capitalised some small businesses in a bid to win votes. In towns and in rural growth points there were long and winding queues where hungry people jostled for foodstuff that was distributed for free.

Mugabe, a protege of former Ethiopian president Mengistu Haile Mariam, a clandestine yet permanent visitor to Harare who had escaped justice in his own country, had acquired from the later, the inhuman strategy of abusing humanitarian relief, in particular food, as a weapon of enforcing political compliance. During the 1984 famine in Ethiopia, Mengistu had used food aid to foster political support and conformity, especially in the Wollo and Tigray regions. Mengistu's foreign minister even admitted that, *"food is a major element in our struggle against the secessionists"*. Mengistu's ministers and senior party executives were the main beneficiaries as they got very rich and their largess benefited the party.

The same scenario prevailed in Zimbabwe. The ministers, MPs, and select few, got immeasurably rich and they periodically donated part of their ill gotten wealth to ZANU PF. For example, it was habitual and expected for party members to donate towards the party's five year national congress or towards Mugabe's annual birthday. Ministers would endeavour to outdo each other as they donated as many a sixty head of cattle and hundreds of thousands US dollars towards the events. While to some ZANU PF had become an impregnable edifice of marginalization and exclusion, to some it was a capacious vessel for self – aggrandizement, while to some it was a treacherous and slippery feeding trough where voracious men stabbed others on the back and cut each other's underbellies and throats. A blessing to the peverted and a curse to the virtuous.

Therefore, zanuism initially facilitated, created and permitted corruption in cabinet, parliament, judiciary and in the public service in order to foster loyalty, gratitude, obedience and conformity to ZANU PF and Mugabe. The situation however spiraled out of control and like a spooked horse, it galloped away from the handlers. There was no going back and they all became slaves to corruption and the country continued to decay.

Lastly zanuism abused the courts of law to prosecute, stampede and suffocate the opposition, civic society, out of favour fellow party members and targeted ordinary citizens on real and or invented charges. At times the state would allow one's crimes to accrue in secret, only to dig them up and reveal or threaten to reveal them when they needed to destroy or rein in the perpetrator.

There was no rule of law under zanuism. Court judgements and orders were defied by the state, individuals in power and the party. There clearly was no equality before the law. On their part, the bench and the prosecution on countless occasions since 1980 were pursuaded to become keen natural prolongations of, or were at times coerced into being reluctant appurtenances of ZANU PF. Prosecuting with a Mephistophelian vendetta today and a languid compliance tomorrow, the prosecution and the judiciary were on many occasions churning out cases and decisions based on the whims and shenanigans of the ruling elite.

The courts of law were used to silence opponents in and outside ZANU PF, to gag civil servants and to intimidate critics of the party and the government. Via an intricate loyalty sifting and vetting system, many, both Matabele and Shona, were crushed under the weight of zanuism. Former Finance Minister Mr. Christopher Kuruneri, business man Mr James Makamba, MDC MP Roy Bennet, Pius Ncube, Morgan Tsvangirai, Welshman Ncube, Renson Gasela, Paul Siwela, John Gazi, Dumiso Dabengwa, Lookout Masuku and Ndabaningi Sithole were at different tmes plagued by zanuism in the courts on concocted charges. It was always nothing but hot air, meant to keep them off balance and off focus. Hence none of them was found guilty of the charges preferred against them.

For years, some of the accused severally appeared at the Supreme Court with the specter of the maximum death sentence hanging over them like the proverbial sword of *Damocles*. Some languished in remand prison for years. At times the charges were clearly so frivolous they had to be dismissed outright but due to pressure from the state, the judges would simply put the accused on remand for indefinite periods. Inevitably all cases would be eventually dropped, but after years of harrowing torture for some like Dabengwa, Siwela, Gazi and Kuruneri. Masuku died in prison due to torture complications.

On 12 April 1986 addressing mourners at the burial of Masuku, Nkomo lamented, *"why should men like Lookout Masuku and Dumiso, after being found innocent of any wrongdoing by the highest court in the land remain detained? When we ask, we get the same answer from the Minister as we used to get from the Smith regime.... We can not blame colonialism and imperialism for this tragedy. We who fought against these things now practice them. We are enveloped in the politics of hate.... Our country cannot progress on fear and false accusations which are founded simply on the love of power".* The country had sunk into the chocking arms of zanuism where state power and the law were used to secure individual and party convictions.

Ndebele paramount chief of Ntabazinduna, Nhlanhlayamangwe Ndiweni was dragged to court in August 2019, charged with criminal conduct after he and a group of villagers had enforced a verdict of the traditional court he was constitutionally empowered to preside over. Everyone knew that Ndiweni was sentenced to six months in prison by a magistrate in Bulawayo, not for a criminal offence but for working towards the resuscitation of the Ndebele monarchy under King Bulelani Lobhengula. Nor was Chief Ndiweni being persecuted for attending an MDCT congress. The MDCT was not a serious source of discomfort for the Mnangagwa government but the restoration of the Ndebele Kingdom was a nightmare to the gukurahundists. The Ndebele monarchy represented a reversal of the achievements of the genocide, gukurahundism and zanuism in Matabeleland since 1980. They did not want the Ndebele to regroup and be a powerful and proud people once again.

Indeed, from the onset, democracy, good governance, human rights and all other liberation war ethos took a stern knock from zanuism. That, as Joshua Nkomo put it, made *"a mockery of the freedom struggle"*. The country tumbled in a tart cocktail of corruption, patronage, coercion and personality cultism. Mugabe and Mnangagwa after him, instead of respecting the rule of law, used the law as a blunt instrument of force, to rule. Many, both in Matabeleland and Mashonaland bore the brunt of their excesses. There was, even after searching very hard, no distinction between the party and the state.

Chapter VII

Mugabeism

"The current political and economic problems facing Zimbabwe are due to the fact that the country is being ruled by a hopelessly clueless, tired and terrified undemocratic clique which desperately wants to cling to power by fair means or foul at the clear expense of national interest.......those behind the project of ethnic domination call themselves nationalist and anti-colonialists when their deeds tell a different story".

Prof. Jonathan Nathaniel Moyo

Icons and legends have straddled over the history of mankind from the days of Moses, Shakespeare, Pluto, Sun Tsu, Mozart, DA Vinci, Pythagorus, Washington, King Shaka, King Mzilikazi, Haille Selasie, Martin Luther King to the eon of Mother Theresa, Nelson Mandela and Barack Obama. Those great individuals shaped the destiny of countless many. Their contribution to civilization was recorded indelibly in the annals of history. They graced and bestowed court rooms, board rooms. parliaments, palaces, museums, theaters and history books with legacies and virtues, unique and unprecedented. They were roll models par excellence, exuding affection, honour and respect, so much they influenced the world in their own different ways.

It is said that, for every promising silver cloud, there is a dark ominous one, so it was with each breed of humans. The likes of Charles Taylor, Obiang Nguema, Oma Bongo, Kamuzu Banda, Mobuto Sese Seko, Idi Amin and Robert Mugabe. Each of these men too left behind them an ugly mark on the Afican face. A mark reminiscent of the stain of Cain. Scary, villainous and dreaded by many. That genus of leaders left nothing in their wake but desolation, sedition and pain for many innocents in their respective countries. Many wanted to meet them not out of admiration but awe, awe that such evil was capable of two feet, two eyes and a human countenance. In their trail they left their own type of twisted legacy.

Like very few of his predecessors and contemporaries in Africa, Mugabe laid a trail of doom and gloom that whirled across the geography of Southern Africa like a poisonous gas as his countrymen and women scampered and scattered all over, as economic and political refugees and squatters.

By 2010, his 30th year at the apex of not only national politics but African leadership as well, Mugabe had long become dementedly obsessed with the mantle of dominion and rulership. He convinced all and sundry that it was designed for his shoulders and them only. Anyone who attempted to wrestle it from him, was, to use his words from various of his vitriolic rhetoric, a puppet, a dreamer, a dog on a leash, a fool, an ignoramus, a counter revolutionary, unpatriotic, a heretic, a sell-out, ugly and gay (he developed a rather strange, personal, passionate and inherent hatred for gay people).

He would brook no dissent or opposition to his views. Taking a position parallel or at odds to his was according to him, hostility to freedom, the revolution, the armed struggle and national security. Opposing him on any issue earned many a barrage of presidential unprintables. At one time, frustrated with Archbishop Pius Ncube, Prof. Welshman Ncube, Trevor Ncube (owner of various independent newspapers) and Fletcher Dulini Ncube (treasurer of the MDC), all gallant fighters against gukurahundism and zanuism, Mugabe blurted out that those brave and astute men had, "*turned the Ncube clan name into an acronym for turn-coats...., bent on reversing the gains of the revolution*". He just could not accept that people could oppose him and still be right and still be true to the values of peace, progress and national security. Opposing, critising, disagreeing with and challenging him and his party in an election was tantamount to a reversal of the gains of the revolution.

Mugabe amassed all power and authority and concentrated it around him so intensely he became a hammer - wielding behemoth, smashing and crashing all in his wake. He grew into a Thor of the Scandinavian mythology, a god of thunder who wielded a hammer emblematic of the thunderbolt. All - powerful and arrogant. His spin doctors at one time insinuated him as a potential and suitable for the South African presidency (Herald 24 April 2004). Many an astute analyst, even in the opposition despaired and would begrudgingly admit that only God could unseat him because he had defied all odds, foreign and domestic, including age and death itself.

In 2006, Jonathan Moyo, estranged with ZANU PF, philosophized thus; *"perennial wisdom from divine revelation and human experience dictates that all earthly things, great or small, beautiful or ugly, good or bad, sad or happy, foolish or wise must finally come to an end. It is from this sobering reality that the end of executive rule has finally come for Robert Mugabe who has had his better days after a quarter of a century in power"*. Many a Zimbabwean hoped that prophecy would be fulfilled before the end of that year but eleven years later he was still president for life and was still digging in. Many, even wished he would die, but Mugabe who had the proverbial nine lives of a cat proved them all wrong. It appeared as if he simply refused to die and nothing would compel Mugabe to stand down. Not even a personal scandal of a romance with his married typist, severe illness including prostate cancer, old age and rheumatism, the ghosts of the Gukurahundi genocide, political upheavals or economic ruin and catastrophe, would force him to resign.

After twenty years at the apex, Mugabe had somehow transfigured into the armed struggle itself. Only he could define such concepts as revolutionary war, sovereignty, history, patriotism and unity. Only his view mattered. Questioning his legal and moral right to be in office elicited his trademark response, resort to a detail of his role in the struggle, his dedication, his losses, his incarceration and torture while those questioning him were, according to him deliberately absent from the war, fearful cowards or born - frees. His role in the struggle seemingly bestowed on him an open license to say and do whatever he deemed fit and disqualified everyone he detested, from being a true liberator or genuine nationalist.

Mugabe, a former teacher became a refined speaker of the English language, a skill he used to fool, convince, coerce, confuse, cajole and mesmerize many, with equal measure, including the British and Americans whom he hypnotized from 1979 to 1999. Thereafter his charm offensive was running thin. The West awoke from their twenty - year long trance and turned hostile to him. Thereupon he conveniently gravitated into the willing embrace of Chinese economic imperialism. Arguably, the only attributes he had above most African leaders, was his articulate command of the English language, Dutch courage, a rather blunt tongue (when he needed one) and nothing requisite in statecraft.

Tragically for Zimbabwe, it turned out that running a country, especially a sound economy required more than vocal charisma, charm and bravado. Enos Nkala, Mugabe's former national supplies, home affairs and finance minister and one of the founders of ZANU, during an interview said of Mugabe, *"he is eloquent, very eloquent, but beyond the eloquence there is nothing"*. Nkala admitted that when he and his colleagues robbed Ndabaningi Sithole of the leadership of ZANU, it was to make way for Mugabe whose eloquence in articulating issues impressed them into wrongly assuming there was substance in him. He said in Mugabe, was absent the nation building attributes requisite in a leader of a country.

The summation of Mugabe's legacy, which accomplished precious little to improve the livelihoods of his countryfolk and everything to collapse human confidence and trust in mankind, was mugabeism. He bequeathed his fellow citizens with the fiendish fetish and sulphurous relic of mugabeism.

Mugabeism was the mastery of commanding, eloquent, compelling, entertaining and populist rhetoric to attain and to sustain a de facto life presidency.

Mugabeism stemmed from a fixation with the popular past, to portray an appearance of statesmanship, yet disguising a serpentine deception, a megalomaniac craving for own adulation, tribal hate and fervent personal ambition for greatness. While enforcing unilateralism and high sounding but contentless socio – economic government policies, mugabeism never accepted responsibility, but played the blame game for the failure of the same policies.

The trademarks of mugabeism included surrounding one's self with a motley cocktail of both handpicked, incompetent and competent executives. Some were identified for their undying loyalty, born out of years of friendship, some for their tribal lineage and some for their expertise. Gratitude for the lavish benefits proffered by the patriarchal octogenarian was always the bonding factor that kept them all under one roof and swearing allegiance, not to the national constitution but first to Mugabe himself and then to ZANU PF next.

Among Mugabe's priviledged desciples were, former first Vice President Simon Vengesai Muzenda, the zealot suspected to have been Mugabe's traditional doctor and a *sangoma* who decreed that his master would rule *"kusvikira madhongi amire nyanga"*, (until donkeys developed horns). Also in the long list was former Vice President Joice Mujuru and her husband, the late general Solomon Mujuru. Notwithstanding, Solomon Mujuru who was rumoured to be one of the richest Zimbabweans by the time of his mysterious death in an inferno at his home, was rumoured to have eroded his commitment to Mugabe long before his demise.

The list included almost all securocrats and a long chain of ministers and party activists and affiliates. Some, like Dr. Nkosana Moyo and Prof. Jonathan Moyo despite their known revulsion and declared aversion to ZANU PF were handpicked for their rare skills and expertise. Some, like Dr. Simba Makoni were appointed for their administrative ability and party membership. However, once within his inner circle, one was expected to be a parrot singer, aping Mugabe's praises even for his worst and embarrasing stunts. Failure to conform to that expectation resulted in summary withdrawal of priviledges, untold humiliation, overt and covert threats of unspecified action, imprisonment and various forms of psychological torture.

Such professionals like Jonathan Moyo were instrumental in rebranding, redifning and refining the legislative apparatus, party policies, campaign materials and stratagems and positions of propaganda that the regime from time to time needed in order to survive at the helm of oppression. They provided the oil for the rusty and cricky regime spin machinery. For example, when the ninety - two years old President Mugabe fell embarrassingly at the Harare international airport in full view of the world press in 2015, Moyo was called upon to downplay and humanize the obviously old age induced infirmity. Moyo assumed the unenviable and insuperable task of convincing the country that it was commonplace for humans to stumble and tumble. Yet the world knew, Mugabe was no common pedestrian, but a president of a country at war with itself and he needed corporal and mental fortitude to literally and figuratively stand up to the economic, social and political paralysis mortifying the country.

Many, even within ZANU PF were asking why Mugabe had to endure such a rigorous schedule of running a country and attending international conferences at that unproductive age. What with roumours of arthritis eating away at his legs and prostrate cancer gnawing edaciously at his insides. What with cruel jokes about his one almost blind eye which needed constant surgery in Singapore. Moreso, each passing birthday made him appear more and more like a rugged political fossil, recently unearthed by amateur archeologists. What with severe memory lapses and failure of concentration causing him to ignominiously slumber at UN, AU and SADC summits. Especially at international conferences, Mugabe proved to be a constant victim of Hypnos, the Greek god of sleep. Apperantly, sitting upright and keeping awake was like burning the candle at both ends for him, yet he insisted that he was as fit as a fiddle. It was the unenviable duty of his over worked propaganda machinery to paint a brighter and more positive picture of the ailing president, so as to preserve his so called legacy.

It was concentration regression that resulted in Mugabe reading a wrong speech from start to finish in parliament in 2016. It was obvious dementia that caused him to, after reading the openning speech, take his seat at the official opening ceremony of the Victoria Falls airport without declaring the airport officially open in 2017. He then admitted that he had forgotten to declare the airport officially open, after being reminded by an embarrassed Vice President Mnangagwa. How

***

about admissions of being under the thumb of a wife young enough to be his grand daughter, at a ZANU PF congress attended by more than 5000 delegates including invited members of foreign embassies. The inane admission that the grey mare was the better horse at the Mugabes, left all and sundry in no doubt as to who was running the country. For all intents and purposes, Mugabe was lamentably, an overripe pawpaw fruit waiting to fall.

Perceptibly, despite Moyo's well worded doctrinaire excuses for Mugabe, there was nothing normal in an individual so thoroughly and mercilessly afflicted by disease, old age and other maladies of a physical, physiological, psychological and cognitive nature, hanging on to power so desperately. Even Moyo himself knew, without having to dig deep into his heart, that his story was bereft of both logic and hope and would find no buyers. No one was unaware of the same Moyo's opinion given in the Zimbabwe Independent nine years earlier in 2006 that, *"..the most compelling reasons for Mugabe to resign now have to do with his own fallen standing.......Mugabe now lacks the vision, stature and energy to run the country, let alone his party. He is without compassion, maybe because he is now too old, too tired and not in the best of health..."*

Assigning one holding such an opinion to rationalize Mugabe's fall and launder his soiled past was an indication of Moyo's ideological superfluidity and ZANU PF's policy inconsistances and contradictions which were responsible for the wholesale paralysis gripping the country. Clearly Moyo had to tow the line so as to justify his relevance to a system that was ever closely sifting and monitoring him for any deviations. For Moyo to mislead the population against the national interest and against his own convictions by glossing over and sanitising such politically decayed and decadent theatrics by a man bent on his life pursuit of governing till the graveyard, was worse than perjury bordering on treason against the poor and starving population.

Very few ever gravitated away from mugabeism's manipulative embrace like Dr. Nkosana Moyo. Dr. Moyo resigned from the office of minister of finance when Mugabe tried to get him to adopt economically obsolete and archaic policies. Dr. Moyo had deluded himself by presuming that as finance minister, it was his responsibility to advise government on financially sound monetary and economic policies, yet Mugabe had other ideas. He wanted a figurehead minister, one that was malleable and unquestioning. When Dr. Moyo realized that Mugabe was not content with the presidency and wanted to be the finance minister as well, he bolted out of the ZANU PF government stable. Probably for dear life, he left the country and faxed his letter of resignation to Mugabe. Mugabe bitterly lambasted and castigated him and called him spineless and not man enough.

Even when her husband died under suspicious and mysterious circumstances in an inferno at his Beatrice farm in Harare, Vice President Joice Mujuru was always mesmerized by mugabeism. Worse still, she would not cease kneeling at Mugabe's alter even when she was being given the bell, book and candle treatment by Mugabe's wife Grace, towards the ZANU PF elective congress of December 2014. Even when Mujuru was literally and unceremoniously booted out of ZANU PF by the johnny - come – latelys after 34 years in Mugabe's cabinet, 10 of which she was Vice President, she kept begging him to protect her. Mugabe would have none of that, as his response to her pleas made it obvious that he preferred her room to her company. Even as she left ZANU PF to form her party, she blamed Mugabe's gang and not him. She evidently had been one of mugabeism's primal embodiments for too long. So potent was mugabeism, only a handful of senior government and party personnel, ever managed to disentangle themselves from its corruptive and erosive embrace.

Disillusioned with ZANU PF's unending economic blunders, a one - man dictatorship and domination by Zezurus, Dr Simba Makoni, a Manyika also jumped ship. Dr Makoni quit ZANU PF and joined leagues with Dr Dumiso Dabengwa to campaign as an independent candidate in the 2008 presidential elections. Dr Dumiso Dabengwa had himself quit ZANU PF earlier after he had proposed to Mugabe at a politburo meeting that Mugabe should step down at the next party congress in 2007.

Prof. Jonathan Moyo defied Mugabe and ran for a parliamentary election as an independent candidate for Tsholotsho North in 2008 and was fired from the party for his noncompliance. Moyo contested as an independent candidate because his constituency had been designated for a ZANU PF female candidate in an obvious bid to politically ostracise him. The female candidate turned out to be the wife of Cain Mathema, a ZANU PF stalwart who later became Resident Minister of Matabeleland North. Moyo had no kind words for the poor Mrs Mathema whom he promptly reminded that she had been Mathema's domestic maid before he dumped his wife for her. She lost the election to Moyo and he was latter admitted back into ZANU PF, only to be described by Mugabe as using his *"knowledge and intellectual ideas"* to destroy ZANU PF on 06 June 2014 when he was Minister of Information.

Prof. Moyo developed and sustained the only known record of defying Mugabe, embracing Mugabe, defying Mugabe and embracing Mugabe at will and on each occasion getting away with it, thereby beating and being beaten by mugabeism. Many said Mugabe did not like Prof. Moyo but could not help but admire his work ethic. Described by some as a workerholic and by Macaphulana (2010) as one that *"does hammer and chisel words into such a shape that delivers old ideas as if they were novel discoveries of today. Words obey him, and he is a champion of politispeak. Any political party will be happy to have him"*. A strategist par excellence, Moyo proved to be what the doctor had prescribed for ailing Mugabe and fast failing ZANU PF. Yet to the opposition he proved to be very infernal.

Mugabeism depended on astute and articulate lieutenants like Jonathan Moyo to be permanently scheming and rebranding the resume of Mugabe and the facade of the party so that it regained its appeal to a disenfranchised and disillusioned electorate. While Mugabe was seemingly committed to be steadfast in consistently coming up with chaotic policies and pronouncements, Moyo proved to be proficient at cleaning up after him. Prof Moyo became the grand master with the penchant to rebrand and resuscitate ZANU PF from the throes of decay and collapse. He pulled a masterstroke in the 2005 elections when all, even within ZANU PF had admitted that their party was done and out. Phoenix – like, ZANU PF rose from the ashes of a rejected constitution writing exercise, courtesy of Moyo. From that time he became Mugabe's savior, single - handedly hoisting him, till 2017.

He repeated his polished grand scheming again in the watershed elections of 2013 and the geriatric leader would be forever grateful to him. Due to Mugabe's intransigence, the spirited attempts of professionals to make something with a semblance of democracy and sound economic policies out of the ZANU PF government, always ended up in smoke. All such attempts became a charade and a showmanship of maintaining and polishing the outside walls while the original structure, theme and character remained defyingly intact and dirty as ever. ZANU PF remained the biblical sepulcher of skeletons which looked clean outside yet decomposed inside or the shinning general's boot that housed a fowl stinking sock inside. The few that attempted to sanitize and democratize ZANU PF, soon realized after burning their fingers that the party was impervious to reform and hostile to new ideas, because the party had become Mugabe's project and nothing moved without his sanctioning rhetoric.

On 18 November 2004 at Dinyane Secondary School in Tsholotsho, was held a critical gathering of ZANU PF heavy weights, which later became known as the Tsholotsho Declaration. The architect of the event which irked Mugabe so much that his party suspended all six of the ten provincial chairpersons that were party to the meeting, among governors and ministers, was none other than Prof. Jonathan Moyo. Mugabe was so exasperated he accused Moyo of plotting a coup d' etat against him. One of the resolutions of the meeting which was meant to be moved and adopted at the next ZANU PF elective congress of 2004 was that the top four positions in ZANU PF, that of president, two vice presidents and national chairperson should be occupied by men and women democratically elected through a secret ballot with respect for *"regional diversity and ethnic balance".*

They agreed to influence the amendment of the party constitution so that what they termed the four major tribes of Zimbabwe being the Ndebele, Manyika, Zezuru and Karanga would always share the top four positions of the party. That thinking was precipitated by the fact, as revealed by Moyo (2007) that *"attempts at ethnic domination of the diversified nation by one group through foul means are not different from similar colonial and UDI attempts that sought to impose racial domination".* Moyo went on to decry that, *"the current situation in which three of the top four leaders in ZANU PF and the government, Mugabe, Mujuru and Msika, come from one ethnic grouping..",* was not tenable.

Moyo and his colleagues were trying to exorcise ZANU PF of its ever present ghost and shadow of mugabeism which chronicled Zezuru dominance and heralded Mugabe's life presidency. To that effect, the Tsholotsho declaration sought, *"to promote and maintain representative national cohesion, development, peace and stability while fostering a broad – based sense of national belonging and identity; that the top position of president and first secretary of the party should not be monopolized by one sub – tribe (or clan) but should reasonably rotate among the four major ethnic groupings"* (Moyo 2007). The idea of a rotational presidency, conducting elections at the ZANU PF congress by secret ballot and ethnic balancing, would have seen Mugabe using the exit door of State House, at most ten years after the date of the Dinyane meeting, i.e. by 2014. It also guaranteed the Matabele, Karanga and Manyika, a chance at the presidency, in the event of ZANU PF winning presidential elections.

However, by the time of the Tsholotsho declaration, gukurahundism, zanuism and mugabeism had matured like an unholy wine. They had grown beyond being traits of ZANU PF and had become, lock – stock and barrel, its very nature and life - blood. Without that satanic tripartite combination, ZANU PF would collapse into a scrap yard of ethnic conflict and regional disceptation. The party had grown into a giant crocodile whose teeth were held together delicately by the three diabolical *isms,* whose usage was supervised by Mugabe himself, assisted by several, including the ministers of defense, state security and police. Without the three, Mugabe and ZANU PF were just like a worm, tossing and writhing and breaking itself apart. While the three held ZANU PF together, they tore the social fabric apart and the very soul of the country went down the drain.

The intelligence apparatus relayed a conflated version of lies, half truths and allegations about the Dinyane meeting to Mugabe whose instinct for self – preservation and presidency to the grave pressed the panic batton. Realizing his life presidency project was in jeopardy, he lashed out at Jonathan Moyo. His obsession with Zezuru hegemony and Shona dominance propelled him at the 2004 ZANU PF national congress, to emotionally suspend Moyo while professing innocence from tribalism. He stated that he was not a tribalist as insinuated in the Tsholotsho declaration, but a revolutionary (as if it was impossible for one to be both). Spewing fire, venom and hailstorms, he suspended from the party, Jonathan Moyo and his team of advocates for regional and ethnic balance. Thus the only real threat within ZANU PF to his leadership since 1975 was diffused and ZANU PF simply refused to reform, thereby opting to cling on to mugabeism.

Strangely, Mugabe did not suspend Emmerson Mnangagwa (Karanga) who had been party to the planning and funding for the Dinyane meeting. Mnangagwa's keynote speech as guest of honour had been read at the event. Inn addition, Mnangagwa had been penciled to be the chief beneficiary of the declaration which sought to elevate him to the office of ZANU PF and country vice president at the oncoming ZANU PF national congress in 2004. Also saved from Mugabe's guillotine, was Patrick Chinamasa (Manyika), another party linchpin who attended the meeting and had been earmarked by the 'coup' plotters for the powerful position of party national chairman. Only Mugabe knew why the two were not punished, yet they were as guilty as Moyo, who had no known direct benefit from the meeting aims.

Mugabeism did not only manipulate the subordinates in government and the party, but fellow presidents and diplomats, regionally and internationally. Mugabe employed a very rare charm offensive, which included playing the humble and generous host, while his country was afflicted of hunger, unemployment, malnutrition, poverty and underdevelopment. Seeking, and even claiming non existent friendship ties with influential presidents and institutions, then playing them against his enemies was a mark of mugabeism. For example, by the turn of the millennium the Southern African Development Community (SADC) was divided on the nagging Zimbabwean question, with countries like Namibia, Angola, DRC and South Africa under Thabo Mbeki reportedly supporting Mugabe who was in a war of words with the European Union (EU), the United States and Australia. On the other hand, Botswana and Zambia under Ian Khama and Levy Mwanawasa respectively, were very critical of him and his failed economic policies and political melodramatics. Mugabe was very warm and cosy towards the regional heads of state that sympathized with him. Those that would not condemn him even if they did not support his shinanigans were also offered exaggerated respect. Still, he did not outright ridicule and antagonize those that were openly critical of his policies like Botswana's Khama. That way he managed to disarm many African leaders and win them to his side.

The absence of consensus within SADC helped sustain Mugabe's despotic hold on power. Never the one to hesitate or shy away from a self asserting opportunity, Mugabe would even blunder deliberately and act undiplomatically for the benefit of winning sympathy and friendship. That is what he did very blatantly in 2015 by visiting the winning Zambian presidential candidate and congratulating him even before the results had been announced. Stained and unusually infamous in Southern Africa as an unscrupulous politician and rigger of elections, Mugabe was welcome to very few Zambians. His excitedly hasty visit in the background of his elections chicanery irked some of the Zambian people so much they demonstrated in Lusaka waving 'Mugabe Must Go' posters. The candidate Edgar Lungu went on to win the elections and his first state visit was to Mugabe in Harare, obviously to express gratitude and probably to concretise mutual allegiance. Exhibiting the diplomacy of a buffalo bull in a China shop and smacking of archaic and feudal aristocracy, the 91 year old had just won himself the support of yet another head of state within SADC.

Attention seeking and hogging the limelight by making a grand entry and pontificating at regional and international conferences against world leaders like Britain's Tony Blair and USA's George Bush while sympathising with controversial leaders like Iraq's Saddam Hussein, typified mugabeism. Mugabe pretended to be ever at war against long - extinct British imperialism by shouting *"Zimbabwe will never be a colony again"*, a somewhat too banal, threadbare, obvious and self – evident fact. Speechifying and lambasting such power houses as the UK, could only draw attention and even attract a cheer or two, but that was always the full extent of Zimbabwe's achievements. A pat on the back of Mugabe by Venezuela's Hugo Chavez and Libya's Muammar Gaddafi and nothing else by way of concrete and lucrative trade agreements, investment protocols, balance of payments support etc. However so long as his ego was stroked by hitting the West and the USA below and above the belt, he became a hero to some in and outside Zimbabwe.

By politically grandstanding at SADC conferences, AU summits and United Nations General Assemblies, Mugabe always attempted to steal the thunder by denigrating his erstwhile friends, the British. He developed a policy of passing the buck for all his sins including hyperinflation, a demonitised currency, de - industrialization, zero foreign direct investments, mega debts to IMF and World Bank and other economic failures, on to the West. For lashing out at such commanding personalities as the USA President George Bush and British Prime Ministers Tony Blair and Gordon Brown, he always managed to score a point or two as some uninformed listener applauded.

Upon arriving home, he would be pumpered and showered with praises by the government controlled press, his henchmen and the ZANU PF women's and youth leagues. Nevertheless, for the common men and women, his trips and hot air speeches became mere adventurous outings and barren forays as he always came back home with a bit of kudos and a big empty begging bowl. For the voters it was always a struggle below the poverty datum line, raw sewer flowing around tiny high density houses, uncollected garbage, unaffordable bills for rarely available electricity and water, pot holes on all the few roads tarred by the Smith regime before they were ousted in 1980. The list of evidence of stark political, social and economic failure stretched *ad infinitum*. Yet for mugabeism, the only concern was how to win the next plebiscite by hook or by crook in order for Mugabe to remain president for life.

The truth was appositely illuminated by Mathuthu (2004) when he noted that, *"Mugabe who is supposed to occupy his true position as a puppet and tyrant in the annals of history now lays claim to heroism....because of the recorded insincerity of the West...people imagine that Mugabe is a true African leader. The truth is that once his friends in the West discarded him, Mugabe's mask fell and cleverly he picked it up and fled crying "imperialist".* Mathuthu's strikingly befitting observation duly pointed out that those that saw or knew about him for the first time at that time, thought Mugabe was a democrat being demonized relentlessly by Blair and Bush for defending his people's sovereignty. Yet he was engaging in delusional fulmination in an attempt to draw attention away from some one hundred thousand skeletons of genocide victims in his closet. Some, however were not duped. They knew he was guilty of human rights violations, abuse of the rule of law, state capture by himself and his tribal cabal, failure and crisis of governance, racism, tribalism and unprecedented economic ruination of his instigation.

When Tony Blair spoke of the scar on the conscience of the world, he must have had Mugabe in mind. Ironically Britain had been party to scarring the world with Mugabe. Blair must have regretted the then British government's role when they created Mugabe in 1979, refined him in the 1980s and perfected him in the early 1990s. By 1999 he was overmade so much that he started bitting the hand that had been feeding him for two decades. He left the British with no choice but to dismantle him but they were a shade too late. Pretending to be his own man and hollering sovereignty all the way, he made a *de facto* defection to his old time funders, the Chinese. Leaving 13 Downing St with hot air and egg on their faces, Mugabe told Blair to, *"keep your Britain and I will keep my Zimbabwe"*. He went on to vow that, *"…only God who appointed me will remove me. Zimbabwe is mine"* (BBC).

Contrary to what he wanted the world to believe, after the 1980 independence, Mugabe was never a victim of European imperialist interests and colonialism. Instead he became a champion of coloniality, which according to Mpofu (2013) could persist long after the end of colonialism. It was coloniality that saw him continue perpetuating the crimes of colonialism after the attainment of independence. Mugabe failed the de – colonization test and blamed his inadequacies on colonialism. The duplicity of the West, especially the British, in dealing with despots like Mugabe, Saddam Hussein and Muammar Gaddafi could not be misconstrued to portray their targets as victims or saints. For fording the artificial rivers of the blood of those they slew and then claiming to be heroes, they deserved to go down in history as venal tyrants having a taste of their own medicine.

Mugabeism thrived on populist policies and positions like nationalization of industries and mines owned by conglomerates or foreign investors, expropriation of farming land from minority rich white farmers and redistributing it to the majority poor black citizens. In the name of black empowerment and indigenization, the most incompetent policies were crafted to the detriment of the economy and the intended beneficiaries. In the case of land reform, the otherwise noble policy was undone by the implementation matrix, which proved to be catastrophic in its tribal, racist, partisan and corrupt nature.

The land reform programme, an otherwise most splendid concept, was one exercise that ZANU PF magically managed to aberrantly turn into one of the most callous and inhuman programs epitomizing mugabeism. ZANU PF implemented the program off the cuff from 1999 and contrary to common sense and the well articulated ideology espoused by the late Joshua Nkomo in 1980, Mugabe persecuted white farmers by hounding them off the farms and allocated the same to hangers – on, tribesmen, cronies, party linchpins etc. While mostly ZANU PF ordinary supporters were crowded into the Model A1 Resettlement Scheme farms, the elite ZANU PF and government officers got the lucrative and productive farms under the Model A2 Resettlement Scheme farms.

By 2016 when ZANU PF was riddled by factionalism with two major camps (G 40 purpotedly led by Mugabe's wife Grace and masterminded by Jonathan Moyo and team Lacoste allegedly led by Emmerson Mnangagwa) fighting a pitched battle for the successor to the ailing Mugabe, team Lacoste via social media released a list of who owned how many farms. Top of the list was Mugabe with 13 farms. All ministers, service chiefs, judges, senior civil servants and Mugabe's relatives had a farm, with many of them owning multiple farms.

While Joshua Nkomo had been an advocate of a brand of African nationalism conjoined to the land quest (a fact which did not help his already weakened standing before the British, to the benefit of Mugabe at Lancaster in 1979), Mugabe's 1999 impromptu variety of land reform was a corruption of the aspirations of the liberation struggle as envisaged by the former. Nkomo had a very clear plan on how to go about the land question, while his counterpart was a *tabula rasa* on the topic. In 1981 Nkomo wrote a book, *The New Zimbabwe,* which spelt out how he thought the country could go about with the *"reorganization of our country and people"* including guidelines on reorganization in rural areas, urban areas and mines.

He articulated methods that would not only enhance agricultural and industrial production, but models that would ensure sustainability of production and impact. Nkomo's (1981) guidelines on resettlement stated that, "*..big tracts of land must be acquired in present commercial farming areas for use by those in communal areas side by side with present commercial farmers. Government and all concerned must insist that such acquired areas be used in a manner that will not turn them into the current state obtaining in communal areas....if these acquired areas are to be viable they must be non – racial and non – political"*. Yet when for his political survival two decades later, Mugabe found himself starring the imperative land question in the face, he trashed, not for the first time, Nkomo's invaluable advice and superior logic.

The book and its detailed proposal, together with Nkomo's request that he be appointed minister responsible for land reform and agriculture, was contemptuously frowned upon. Instead Mugabe dismissed him from the government on trumped up charges of treason. How Nkomo intended to stage a coup from the office of minister of agriculture remained a mystery.

Mugabe by the year 2000 had a dilemma of two choices. First he could extensively engage stakeholders to identify the best strategies to swim along the turbulent waters of the land issue. Secondly, he could planlessly plunge and hazard into the deep and flooded river of the land question, flap across and sink. He opted for the latter, with dire consequencies. He violently evicted the white commercial farmers by promoting a racist aberration, racist slurs, racist attacks and even murders of those white farmers that resisted eviction. He went on to politicize the resettlement program. It became a party exercise in line with Mugabe's 1979 exhortation that only ZANU should harvest the peaches of independence. With very few exceptions, the resettlement program mostly benefitted ZANU PF members only. So much for Nkomo's non racist and non political reorganization.

Those non ZANU PF citizens that benefited were compelled by the war veterans and youth militia to exist with their political tails and colours between their hind legs. The opposition parties were circumscribed from campaigning in the resettled farms. By leaping headlong into the program, minus any form of planning, then attempting to improvise along the way, Mugabe was like an amateur skydiver ejecting himself ferociously from a plane without a parachute before trying to use his shirt as wings with which to fly. Consequently, he hit the rocky ground hard and shattered the agricultural industry to smithereens. The commercial farms became exactly what Nkomo had advised against; *"communal areas"*. Still, hounded by his imperviousness to counsel, his planning ineptitude and deficiencies, Mugabe blamed the chaos in the resettled areas on the whites, colonialism and targeted sanctions.

Mandaza (2000), writing an acknowledgement to an edition of Nkomo's book *The New Zimbabwe* stated that Nkomo said on ZBC in 1999, *"..government wants equity, government wants peace and prosperity, government wants to increase production to all people. What we are doing is not to bring down the white man. What we are doing is to lift up, together with the White man, the Black people to the same position as themselves in order to bring about stability..... We are going to acquire land for the good of everybody and this is why we are bringing white farmers and industrialists to be part of the changes that we are bringing about. The white people must know and understand that they are part of this country"*.

When Nkomo said that statement, it was at the twilight of his life, a few months before he died. He was haunted by the fact that he had failed to address the land dispute to his standard and satisfaction. He was echoing part of his speech made almost twenty years prior in 1980 at Jahunda stadium in Gwanda, Matabeleland South province. He had declared that he envisaged a farming model where Mr Jones (white), Mr. Chamunorwa (Shona) amd Mr. Ndlovu (Matabele) were farming side by side as equals with similar rights and priviledges. He had also stated that he and ZAPU did not want to chase the white people back to Europe as much as they did not want to evict them from the farms. Mugabe did the exact opposite. He made the whites feel they were not Zimbabwean and even told them publicly to trek back to England. He did not consult the various stakeholders and managed to bring down the whitemen.

By 2020, three years after Mnangagwa had taken over from Mugabe it still remained to be seen if production in the resettled farms would surpass the agricultural output before the resettlement exercise. The much talked about land audit which was hoped to rationalize the resettlement program by among other actions, addressing multiple ownership of farms was nothing but a theory.

The tragic truth about many despots including Mugabe, was that they derived their intransigency and contempt from ordinary people including some of their would – be victims. Sectors of the community unwittingly provided them with the dye for their wool so they became dyed in the wool tyrants. Mugabe got his dye from ordinary citizens who were excited by the idea of indepemdence, from some of the beneficiaries of his numerous public and private policies as well as from some black fundamentalist activists and from some traumatized victims of colonialism and white oppression in and out of Africa. After 2000 they gave him kudos and credit, yet he was doing the right thing wrong. In response, he, like the lunatic that dances moderately to an imaginery drum before suddenly jumping violently into the air at the sound of a real drum, horned his appetite for tyranny when he was applauded by people observing him from a distance. ZANU PF supporters coined and churned songs in his praise and many a speaker would intimate that the new farmers should be grateful to Mugabe for the land. Mugabe simply lost it. In his false glory he uttered irreversible obscenities against the West, white people, and the opposition. Meanwhile, due to poor planning or no planning at all, he succeeded in carelessly tossing the country's productive agricultural sector into the refuse can.

Many people did not realize Mugabe was getting undue credit for cleaning his own mess. In a pitiful simulacrum of Josua Nkomo's proposed land resettlement model, Robert Mugabe managed to cut the tree branch on which he was seating while many egged him on. Had the land reform program been embarked on in 1990, as per the Lancaster House agreement and constitution, it would have been implemented before it became the politically emotive, hasty and haphazard exercise it became in 2000. Instead, the government shily-shallied and dragged their feet while squandering the money donated by the UK and USA governments towards funding the land reform exercise. The donor governments were indifferent as their money was abused by Mugabe because it was to their advantage that the land was not repossessed from their nationals. Their money acted as a bribe to Mugabe so he could not repossess land from the white farmers.

Alas they only bribed Mugabe and not the masses. The people wanted the land so they could also own the means of production as per the socialist principles that had propelled them into the liberation struggle. Then without due consideration and consultation, the government bowed to pressure from the people that had gotten impatient with the state's procrastination and stalling. They then designed laws that enabled them to seize land from whites and not compensate them. The laws were abused so that anyone purpoting to be a war veteran could seize land, mafia - style for themself or redistribute it to others on the spot.

While no one from whatever political formation, in whatever frame of mind could dispute the need for land reform policies which should have been formulated and implemented ten years after independence, many were justified in criticizing the high - handed manner that characterized its implementation twenty years later. The haphazard, random, selective, corrupt, politically prejudiced, discriminative and indiscriminate style of enforcement of the land reform project qualified it for the most controversial and frowned upon way of achieving justice for land related historical wrongs ever. Many a nation in the region, took a leaf from the Zimbabwean experience and were informed on how not to redistribute land, while some got skeptical about the whole land reform concept and steered clear of it, much to the detriment of many landless blacks.

On 15 April 2015 Mr. Gwede Mantashe the Secreatry General of the African National Congress (ANC) of South Africa distanced the ANC from Mugabe's chaotic land reform exercise when he said, *"the ANC theorizes colonialism differently from ZANU PF"* and *"has no desire to drive white people into the sea".* (Bulawayo 24 news). A few loyal friends of the regime gave thin and at times oblique verbal support of the program publicly but discreetly and sternly admonished their technocrats and policy makers never to dare emulate the Zimbabwean experience.

The brutishly racist nature of the implementation of the land reform project was echoed by former Minister of Primary and Secondary Education (2008 – 2013) in the Government of National Unity, Mr. David Coltart. Coltart attacked Media and Information minister Prof. Jonathan Moyo, describing him as hypocritical. He said Moyo was cherry picking what *"types of xenophobia or racism"* to condemn. Moyo had condemned the events against foreigners including Zimbabweans, that had started in Durban, South Africa in 2008 as xenophobic and racist. The essence of Coltart's stance was that Moyo should have condemned attacks and racism by black people against black people in South Africa as much as he should have condemned the attacks and racism by black people against white people in Zimbabwe.

Some white farmers had been beaten, maimed and some killed by ZANU PF activists during the farm invasions. Some were force marched from their farms and all their immoveable property including some movable assets were expropriated and automatically became the property of the new farmers who were on numerous occasions escorted by armed state security personnel. That act of black on white racism should have been condemned by Moyo as xenophobic, with equal verve and concern as the xenophobic attacks in South Africa. That was Coltart's argument. The problem with the fast track land reform program was that it was used as a tool by mugabeism for the benefit of Mugabe and ZANU PF first and for the good of some of the people next while it was for the doom of the white farmers last. Otherwise the ideal of righting past wrongs could not be disputed.

As if committing more wrongs to right wrongs from the past was not enough, the allocation of the overtaken farms was based on partisan and caste criteria. The expropriated farms were allocated through a myriad of official bureaucracy which was mostly short circuited by the land officers, ministers, permanent secretaries, retired generals, the military, the police, the CIO and party heavy weights. The end product was a deliberately cacophonic process engineered by anyone from the above mentioned groups and more. The resettlement program was characterized by resultant and deliberate confusion with government offer letters and other correspondence flying around. Corruption was consequently rampant. The noble idea degenerated into a brazen cut – throat, dog eat dog political jamboree.

The racist nature of the exercise was so palpable, even the blind could see through it because only the land owned by whites was repossessed and redistributed, while all the beneficiaries were black. There were black people who owned more than one farm and those were not expropriated, while farms were repossessed from whites who owned just one farm. Some black people were allocated more than one farm.

Ironically what was not so obvious and conveniently so, was what was echoed by none other than the utility minister Prof. Jonathan Moyo, that the land reform process was fraught with tribalist practice, with the arch – tribalist being Mugabe himself. He accused Mugabe of tribal bigotry, tribal intimidation, ethnic hallucinations and a Bantustan ideology. Moyo (2006) protested that, *"Charamba's response to my artitle is to assert that I have no right to criticize or challenge Mugabe from the "anthills of Mazowe", where my family is doing agriculture on 627 hactares we are currently developing from previously derelict land, last used for grazing purposes, because I am from Matabeleland and thus belong to a clan 'whose lineage never dreamt of having land in the heartland of Mashonaland.."* George Charamba, Mugabe's personnal spokeperson had attempted through a weekly newspaper instalment, to strip Moyo of his farm in Mashonaland or black mail him into silence on the basis that the latter was Ndebele. By criticizing

Mugabe, Moyo had failed to be a good Ndebele and had to be reminded of the rare privilege of owning a farm in Mashonaland if one was Ndebele.

That the land reform exercise was embroiled in tribal politics, was again revealed on 21 June 2014 at a joint ZANU PF provincial council meeting for Matabeleland North, Matabeleland South and Bulawayo. At the meeting where the ZANU PF national chairman Simon Khaya Moyo uncharacteristically conceded to the delegates that Matabeleland was not benefiting from national projects, Chief Dingani Nelukoba of Hwange protested against the skewed allocation of wild life conservancies in Matabeleland North. He gave an example of a conservancy previously allocated to him but had been taken away and allocated to someone from Harare. That, once more was an exposure of brazen tribalism and regionalism.

For all intents and purposes, ZANU PF managed the unenviable feat of not only setting the black and white segments of the population on a collision course, but antagonized the international community as well. They chose to hide behind the very tapered and severely disfigured finger of national sovereignty. A finger they themselves mutilated through gukurahundism, zanuism and mugabeism. National sovereignty, a phenomenon that Sithole (2002) excoriated as, *"a dying concept in a world that has become a global village... What irony that we are busy destroying the little sovereignty we still have, through self inflicted injuries, both politically and economically...we are less sovereign today than we have ever been".*

In 2008 Mugabe's government gazetted a policy that would send business and potential investors scurrying for cover. The Indigenization and Economic Empowerment Act required all foreign owned companies to cede 51% of their shares to local people or face closure by the government. Once more, ZANU PF 'chefs' (lingo for moguls), their relatives, Mugabe's clansmen and relatives, security chiefs and the entire 'usual suspects' of already empowered cronies, got their oily noses into the feeding trough. The ordinary people, the job seekers, the informal sector labourers, the market place traders, the college and university graduates from Harare's poor townships of Mabvuku and Bulawayo's Nkulumane, could only bear witness.

Mugabe and his ministers sounded very much like Uganda's Idi Amin, when they were elucidating their land reform and indigenization policies. They knew that they were walking a precariously narrow path, already trodden by Africa's number one dictator who went on to catch fire and burnt his country's economy to the ground, but they kept walking anyway. According to Jan Jelmert Jorgensen (1981), in justification of his persecution of Asians and Europeans, Amin said, *"(we) are determined to make the ordinary Ugandan master of his own destiny and, above all, to see that he enjoys the wealth of his country. Our deliberate policy is to transfer the economic control of Uganda into the hands of Ugandans..."* If one ignored the word 'Uganda' in the above statement, it would read very much like what Mugabe was fond of saying during an all too often occurring combination of bouts of economic hysteria and nonchalant abandon. The results in both Uganda and Zimbabwe were economic mismanagement and a disastrous collapse of the economy. No company shares and wealth accumulated to the ordinary people, yet the 'chefs' got richer.

The indigenization policy precipitated capital flight and skepticism among potential foreign investors. Companies simply closed and the economy floundered even more precariously. The country became a no – go zone for serious business. Who in their proper frame of mind would invest seriously in a country that was so legislatively unreliable, they could wake up the next morning minus 50% of their investment. As a result, unemployment escalated exponentially with the few jobs created being taken by Mugabe's cronies or those connected to influential politicians.

All Mugabe's intervention policies were economically bankrupt yet popular among the influential in ZANU PF who stood to gain from them. Woefully the same barren policies were popular among many of the poor, jobless and landless who had been watching while others benefited and never lost hope in the chance of them benefiting as well. To sell those drossy policies to the masses, mugabeism utlilized cattch phrases and lingo that captivated the masses while depriving the very same populace of the same benefits the policies were meant to avail. Such terms as *jambanja* (disorder), fast track (hasty, impromptu, unplanned), *rambayi makashinga* (be resilient while you suffer) *kiyakiya* (make deals), s*isonke* (we are together), etc were coined and popularised to psych people into action or inaction whenever appropriate for the leadership. People were encouraged to be disorderly, to be resilient in their suffering and to be a nation of unscrupulous dealers.

Despite trying and failing with one socially mendacious and economically impugnable policy after another and even after hitting rock bottom, ZANU PF kept digging. Determined to make history, never learning from the experiences of other countries and therefore never reforming and definitely destined to collapse ruinously, due to mugabeism, ZANU PF technocrats kept reinventing the wheel, yet failed to get it right. Their eventide and knee - jerk policies were never researched thoroughly for instruments of such scale and always lacked national contribution. Therefore, the policies easily militated against social cohesion and wellbeing, resulting in economic mayhem and meltdown.

The deficiencies of Mugabe's extempore interventions should have been obvious to all in cabinet, parliament, industry and ZANU PF, especially since the policies were always analysed and practically criticized by the public in the media. Still, cabinet and government were leg ironed to the policies that somehow turned obsolete the very next day after initial implementation. Yet ZANU PF officials and supporters hung on Mugabe's every syllable. None among the influential could dare say a word of caution. Some were too busy satiating their gluttonous appetites while some were too full of consternation of mugabeism and strangely, some were hopeful. Those that had the potential to stand up for sanity to prevail were terrified of Mugabe and therefore sought the security in numbers and joined the hurum scurum in urging Mugabe and his band of failures on. By the 2000s, everything Mugabe and his minister troopers touched seemed to quickly wither and die. So did the economy.

Mugabeism cultivated a chronic detestation and morbid abhorrence for facts. Facts and reality were replaced by flowery and high sounding but false idealism, testaments, conjencture and sentiments. Mugabeism manifested itself in eloquent cosmetics, while glossing over the nuts and bolts of the issues at hand. Facts and requisite details were either given superficial attention or were twisted to suit the whims and caprices of the leader. The leader became allergic to the unpalatable truth and his lieutenants learnt to tell him only what they knew he wanted to hear.

Mugabe started off as a demagogue that made sense, although a lot of it was contrived and disguised falsehoods, hypocrisy and double talk. Gradually he became an oral words smith whose speeches were overflowing with entertainment and devoid of facts, political, economic and human development content. Words masonry, instead of the truth, became mugabeism's tool. He was a classic example of *vox et praetarea nihil*, merely a voice and nada above it. The delivery of his speeches was always better than the content. For all that, the country needed more than words and phonetics to grow its economy. He used a silver tongue to capitalize on a combination of half baked and ill conceived consensus, deliberately induced confusion, tribaly motivated cronyism, brute coercion and begrudging consent, to sustain an unrelenting iron and death grip on presidential power.

The eloquence, the promises of future success and the nationalist argot were used to keep the expectant public focused, so much they did not pay attention to historical facts which would have otherwise helped them to see through the self - serving plots. For example, one needs not be a good student of history to know that the land issue was never Mugabe's cup of tea. At Lancaster he was mum about it and that endeared him to the British ahead of Nkomo who was vocal about it. His administration squandered GB£40 000 000.00 donated by

Britain for the resettlement program and another US$40 000 000.00 donated by the USA in 1984. He delayed implementing the constitutional provision that enabled his administration to address the contentious issue after ten years, until when nineteen years after independence the war veterans came knocking rudely at his door. His hard and fast approach to the land issue was simply a reaction, an act and a charade to sustain his stranglehold on power.

Mugabeism dictated that only the leader could be a hero. No other person could carry the day and be in the limelight in the party, in the country and in Africa. That was the root of Mugabe's seeming insanity. It was the basis of his discomfort with South African president Nelson Mandela. He simply could not live with the fact that Mandela was a better person and abler president than he. His dream of being a Pan Africanist went up in smoke when Mandela came out of prison. The fact that Mandela instantly set ablaze the whole world with his stature, grandeur, character, charisma, credentials, popularity and diplomacy and still remained humble, miffed Mugabe. Mandela entered the stage from Robben Island and in 1996 walked away with everything that Mugabe treasured including fame and international respect. He hated the South African icon for that.

Back home, Mugabe who had always been dwarfed not only by Nkomo's domineering physical presence and graceful demeanor, but by his well known selfless nationalist ideals, had been chagrined by the SRANC, NDP, and ZAPU stalwart. Mugabe hated Nkomo and everything that he articulated, advocated for and simply everything that he thought Nkomo stood for. Hence Mugabe's reluctance to implement the land resettlement program stemmed from the fact that it was Nkomo's declared passion. Not only was Mugabe at odds with the resettlement policy, he was at a loss on how to go about it and probably that is why when he could not avoid it, he committed economic suicide thereby dragging the whole of Southern Africa into an economic refugee drama with Zimbabweans being the sorry main actors, ever begging for jobs from South Africa, Botswana, Zambia, Britain, USA, Canada, Australia etc.

Joshua Nkomo had prophetically advised Mugabe in 1981, eighteen years before Mugabe invented the best method of how not to conduct agrarian reforms and land redistribution. Nkomo in 1981 had reminded the then Prime Minister in a letter, of an earlier meeting where he had told Mugabe that, *"your Resettlement policy was a national disaster, and you agreed with me"*. Nkomo was referring to Mugabe's preference to the communist – style *"minda mirefu"* (long fields, in Shona).

However not content with armchair criticism, Nkomo offered his services as Minister of Lands and Resettlement but Mugabe refused. He said Nkomo who was 63 years old by then, was too old for that portfolio. Ironically Mugabe was to later botch up the land policy at 75 years of age. In an apparent show of being *non compos mentis*, Mugabe denied Nkomo's request at a time when he was struggling to identify a ministry for the latter, in a set up that he wanted to present as a government of national unity. However, the fact was that Mugabe was driven by a manic fear of Nkomo's influence. He just could not take advice from those he classified as his enemies. No wonder in 2000 he resorted to yet another resettlement policy whose execution would once more fit into what Nkomo termed, a *"national disaster"*.

Nkomo was not deterred by Mugabe's rebuff. He went on to plan and set up what he called, *"practical approach models, to both rural and peri-urban resettlement, that would embrace everybody and not just a few who are said to 'qualify'"*.

To set an example and lead the way, he established the Makwe Grand Settlement Scheme, comprising his family farm and the Makwe irrigation scheme in Gwanda. He approached the white farmers in the area for more land and they had promised to sell or donate land willingly. The scheme plans were given to the ministry of lands and resettlement. ZIMCORD had been approached for funding and the future of the project was very bright.

Nkomo and ZAPU purchased Kennellworth - Carisbrook farm in Harare, the Lingfield farm in Gweru and Mbalabala farm at Esigodini. The farms were to be handled as the Makwe Grand Resettlement Scheme. Nitram and Ascot farms in Bulawayo and Gweru respectively were bought for commercial use and settlement by more than 8000 former ZPRA combatants who had been demobilized from the ZNA. The pilot project was the Mguza Farm and Secretarial College near Bulawayo, which the then Minister of Finance Enos Nkala recommended as *"a model of its kind"*. Nkomo further displayed his unselfish, non - tribal and non – regionalist genius in development, by instituting the Nijo Project. The Nijo project was a \$1.2 million ZAPU Composite Agricultural Project in Harare. Mugabe was invited by Nkomo to visit that project which Nkomo was proposing as a practical model for resettlement but the Prime Minister refused (Informative letter to Mugabe 1983).

Nkomo's, was a mammoth resettlement and agrarian strategic plan and effort by all standards, given the short period within which it was planned and implemented and in view of the prevailing hostile political circumstances and the back – stabbing nationalist background. Yet all the meticulous planning, the resources and dedication were flushed down the drain when all the farm properties, companies and buildings owned by ZAPU in Bulawayo, Gweru and Harare as well as private properties owned by ZAPU members and asserts worth millions of dollars were banned and confiscated by the government. (Sunday mail, 07 February, 1982). Some of the confiscated properties were distributed among ZANU PF and government officials for their private use, some buildings were taken over by government departments, while some still lay derelict by the day Mugabe was kicked from office by Mnangagwa in 2017. The four thousand head of cattle at the Gweru farm were treated in similar manner. It was a looting carnival, reminiscent of the B.S.A. Company parceling out land to the white officers and sharing the 800 000 head of Ndebele cattle among the mercenary soldiers and their 652 Shona batmen in 1893 after they had defeated the Mthwakazi state and razed Bulawayo to the ground.

Mugabe on 13 February 1982 addressed a rally in Marondera where he informed the audience of largely ZANU PF supporters that ZAPU possessed twenty - five farms and thirty companies and properties all for the purpose of starting a civil war against his government. By so saying, he deliberatitely and mischievously twisted Nkomo's effort at setting up practical examples on how to reorganize and resettle the nation, into acts of treason. He knew because Nkomo had even written to him and informed him of the purpose of the purchased farms.

Faced with the behavior of a true hero, Mugabe baulked and changed it into the behavior of a sore loser and a coup plotter. Mugabe knew that Nkomo and ZAPU had accepted defeat regardless of their reservations on the polls being free and fair. He knew Nkomo had assured his supporters, ZAPU and ZPRA that they had fought for independence under a black majority government. That aspiration had been achieved and Nkomo had therefore urged all to settle down to the task of nation building. He did not just pay lip service to nation building and land resettlement, he led the way. However, in an eccentric twist of logic, it was the winners that were sore. The winners were the ones that were spoiling for war. ZANU PF and Mugabe were determined to have a civil war and if Nkomo and ZAPU were not going to start it for them, they were going to push them into a corner and kill them then blame them.

In order to start the civil war and to overshadow Nkomo's land and agricultural ingenuity and passion, Mugabe cut him down by ruthlessly discrediting and destroying all his projects. Matt Caloway the former Smith regime operative and an agent in Mugabe's CIO, planted arms caches in some of the farms owned by ex ZPRA soldiers before claiming to have discovered them. The state charged Nkomo and former ZPRA commanders with treason and set the whole Matabeleland country ablaze with the Gukurahundi brigade, a tribalist and party army.

Joshua Nkomo's resettlement models went up in a dark cloud of smoke and fire. The resettlement model projects were killed at inception by Mugabe who eighteen years later transformed into some kind of wacko heroic agrarian and land resettlement revolutionery. Still, how ever hard Mugabe tried to use the land resettlement program to present himself as a genuine revolutionery, his true colours stood out to betray him like the irrepressible sneeze of a thief in hiding. He shone for the complete racist and tribalist that he had always been. The land reform that he served the people on a fissured wooden dish was a far cry from what Nkomo had envisaged and what the masses (both black and white) deserved. It was a horrific product of mugabeism, designed to prolong his rule beyond his life. It was not an all embracing national project meant to foster equity, justice, national cohesion and enhance productivity.

For 37 years at the pinnacle, with the endorsement of the Chinese - style politburo and central committee of ZANU PF, Mugabe discharged a contagious influence. He spewed out a debilitating virus that affected both himself and the country. The leader thought, spoke and acted for the people and the led learnt to acquiesce and not question. Mugabeism's unilateral decision making, like a killer virus infected many including opposition politicians.

The 1979 Shona Grand Plan, the Re – Orientation thesis by Robert Mugabe, the DDT Regimen by Emmerson Munangagwa and the Gukurahundi genocide, were proof that Mugabe's and his Committee of twenty - six Zezurus' anger at the Ndebele knew no bounds. However, the purges within ZANU PF, the succession battles pitting Mugabe against Mnangagwa at one time, the elimination of some members of the committee of twenty - six and numerous other sinister machinations, firmly pointed at a Mugabe life presidency as his primary aspiration. From the Mgagao Declaration that dethroned Ndabaningi Sithole from, and ensconced Robert Mugabe at the apex of ZANU leadership, the ultimate agenda was his life presidency first and Zezuru supremacy second.

Almost everyone in ZANU PF was comfortable with Mugabe's arrangement of ruling to the grave, until his wife started a fire in the party board room. Aghast, Mnangagwa who had always wanted to carry on from wherever and whenever Mugabe would have left, decided to wrestle the crown, just before he caught fire, on that fateful day in November of 2017. But the odds were against Mnangagwa. The 2013 constitution provided for a miximum two presidential terms yet he wanted more like his mentor. The opposition was most threatening, with the MDC Alliance intact for the first time as a coalition of opposition parties under the leadership 0f a much younger candidate. Elections were due within eight months from the date of his inauguration after the coup. Most worryingly, the economy was in tatters with the country currentless. He was incapable of complete mugabeism since he obviously lacked the requisite magniloquence and oratory skills. His only respite was a resort to gukurahundism and zanuism at a time when he needed to convince the world, especially the skeptical USA, that he was not another Mugabe. It would appear that the coup which he thought was his life saver had suddenly become a poisonous brew in his throat even before he settled into the throne. He was hemmed in.

Chapter VIII

Mugabe: A Victim Of Gukurahundism

*"The coup was internally and externally popular. So you had
the irony of an illegal act which was extremely popular on the
ground. The popularity of the illegality disallowed any debate
about the unlawfulness of the act. Everyone wanted to see the
back of Mugabe"*

Prof. Welshman Ncube (Interview 18 January 2018)

On 24 November 2017, Zimbabwe's former Vice president Mr. Emmerson
Mnangagwa was sworn in by Chief Justice Luke Malaba as the second chief
executive of the country in almost four decades. On that day, Mnangagwa became
the longest serving member in successive governments since independence in
1980. He had out run his mentor Mugabe whom he had just overthrown in a
military coup d' etat on 15 November 2017.

Had it not been for his advanced age and the concomitant memory loss, Mugabe
would have remembered Joshua Nkomo's wise counsel many years back. In a
letter to Mugabe in 1983, Nkomo had told him that one can not teach young
men to disrespect human life and expect them to respect his own life. The army
generals who in 2000, 2011 and 2015 and on other occasions in between, had
clearly vowed that they would never salute (essentially meaning they would stage
a coup) anyone they perceived was working versus the objectives of the liberation
struggle, had now classified him as one working to reverse the gains of ZANU PF.
They told themselves that Mugabe had adopted *"a different agenda"* and could
not be saluted anymore. Paradoxically, he had nurtured and defended the coup

ideology in the generals on the assumption that he, ZANU PF and the liberation struggle were synonymous.

Mugabe had over the years put the generals on a coup default mode, ever ready to paratroop in, to impose themselves on the people on his behalf, should the need arise. He never imagined that he could be ranked as a counter revolutionary by his own army, until days after the coup when it eventually dawned on him that he did not possess monopoly over influence and that his generals were no longer solely his after all. On that ruinous day, he stopped believing in the age old African adage that had been recited in his fortification by many including Brigadier Sanyatwe in 2015 that, *"another sun does not rise before another one sets"* (Mambo 2015). Suddenly the power of that theory deserted him as it became as effective as a sieve in holding water. It became the most bankrupt philosophy of ideologoies for him. There was, high up in the eastern sky, a Manyika sun while the Zezuru sun was still visible in the west albeit teetering.

On that day Mugabe rued the day he could have listened to Nkomo in 1983. He realized that he should have disciplined the army when they took turns to declare that they would not salute a constitutionally elected president whenever they so wished. Instead he let them believe that that illegality was possible even in a constitutional democracy and now it had come back to haunt him. They bluntly refused to salute old Mugabe.

On 18 January 2018, Prof. Welshman Ncube a constitutional law expert and president of the Movement for Democratic Change (MDC), hosted an interview on what had transpired in ZANU PF and government in November 2017, culminating in the new political order. He argued, *"First let us recognize two contradictory, in a normal world mutually exclusive events. First is that these guys basically carried out a military coup. They overthrew a government technically which was the lawful government of Zimbabwe by unconstitutional means. That there can be no doubt about it. That you had a coup orchestrated by the command of the army. At the time it was not clear that they wanted power for themselves. It was as if they are overthrowing the leadership of ZANU PF to allow ZANU PF to select different civilian leaders. The events which transpired since then now make it clear that they were actually making a coup for themselves because they have since taken over the government and ZANU PF as well. In short you had ZANLA elements in collusion with ZPRA elements misusing the military in Zimbabwe, the armed forces, to basically fight their political battles as ZANLA in order to win a political battle they had lost at the battlefield of political ideas".*

More than ten years earlier at a time when Jonathan Moyo was sharpening his spear against Mugabe and ZANU PF in line with the character of his chequered relationship with his former master, he had written a newspaper article which he could not have fathomed would be succintly accurate years later than it was then. He had stated that Mugabe was trapped in a spider's web of his own making. If Mugabe had read that article then, it would have conjured memories of his own belligerency towards advice and warning.

On that fateful event of 15 November 2017 the country was awash with excitement for some and with consternation for others. One thing for certain, many were shocked at the events unfolding in Harare on that day. None could have predicted Mugabe's downfall. Africa's most commanding and adamant strongman had been crashed out of power by his right hand man and aide of forty years. Mugabe, the most unwavering and obdurate of despots ever concieved by an African womb, was rumoured to be on his knees begging for his life and that of his beautiful grand daughter trophy wife. The whole world was surprised because the suffering meted out on the Zimbabwean landscape by Mugabe and his acolytes and taken lying down by the population, had convinced all that no one in Zimbabwe was capable of such decisiveness. All forms of abuse in the book had been dished out to Zimbabweans by Mugabe and the man who was now cleansing his hands in Mugabe's political blood. They had been starved, butchered, flogged, impoverished, insulted, robbed and exposed to any vices imaginable and yet had survived, probably to witness Mugabe's downfall, if indeed it was a downfall. That day of witnessing had finally come.

Had Mugabe's dream of ruling to the grave just turned nightmarish? Had mugabeism just collapsed on his lap like a house of cards? Had the ghost of Gukurahundi finally exorcised itself like a candle that burns itself to a dead heap of wax? Was zanuism on its death bed? Had gukurahundism been overthrown with the demise of its chief architect? Had his fiendish legacy of gukurahundism triumphed over him as well? Had his endeavor of pulling the country's future down with him to the grave been foiled? Or was Mugabe and his quadrominium trap legacy living on in his protégé of many years? Or was this his escape plan?

As ninety – four year old Mugabe was disgraced and humiliated out of State House by his sparring partner and the men who in the last decade had employed the gun to prop him up, many people wondered what had become of his wife, the kantankerous Grace Mugabe. The woman many within ZANU PF dreaded and on whose sword many a political heavy weight had perished. A woman of numerous controversial exploits and one who just did not know when to stop, yet was well known for her mantra "*stop it*". Grace Mugabe had known nothing but victory since the day she stole Mugabe's heart, soul, mind and body while his first wife, Sally, was groaning on her sick bed. Elated by every previous victory, she had plundered her husband's comrades in ZANU PF as well as farms, companies, properties and the state coffers. She had gotten so dangerously intoxicated with her victories and got so overwhelmingly confident such that her speeches were overstuffed with the contempt and insolence of the super immune.

By the time of her husband's fall, Grace Mugabe had managed a feat no other woman in the world had done in living memory. She had dismissed two vice presidents and countless cabinet ministers and party heavy weights from the ruling party and government within three years. Despite all the success, Grace could not take heed of her own words. She kept overextending herself. Like Icarus from Greek mythology, she in her triumphant flight forgot that wax was used to attach her artificial wings on her and soared too close to the sun. Before long the wax melted and she plunged into the tumultous sea and drowned.

A week before the day she temporarily fled the country in November 2017, she had managed to convince even her most staunch critics that she was going to be the next vice president of the country in the next month. Many had also succumbed to the notion that she would become president when her husband vacated the office. Her mind was clouded by her success. The drums of her victory celebrations were pounding in her head as she was evidently gunning for the highest office in the land at a blind and break - neck pace. Despite the obvious barriers ahead of her, she was too excited and over confident to accept they were real threats until she hit the ground hard.

As Mugabe was hounded out of the president's office at the barrel of a gun, many could swear that his wife, young and high spending, had blundered too many times for him to remain in charge. Never in the history of the evolution of the female species had a first lady terrorized state institutions and functioneries and her husband's surbodinates in the manner Grace Mugabe had done before the fall. None had to wonder how powerful she was; it was written on her forehead and her bragging broadcast it to the world. Hers, became the classic example of a head into which power had gone in in full force.

In the months preceding, Mugabe, pepped up by thirty - seven years of immunity, arrogance, self confidence and truculance born of absolute power, had continued to entomb himself in the delusion of complete loyalty and fear by his lieutenants. Like a leviathan tortoise, secure in his shell despite repeated warnings from the G40 ZANU PF faction and Minister Jonathan Moyo, that his deputy Mr. Emmerson Mnangagwa was plotting a coup, he moved slowly and lacked decisiveness until the snake whose tail he cut, recoiled and bite him venomously. He made the mistake of assuming Mnangagwa would take his dismissal lying down like his predecessor Joyce Mujuru. That mistake nearly cost him his life and probably that of his young wife.

Had the conspirators not succumbed to the need for legitimacy for their government, had they failed to realise that Mugabe was a persona non grata domestically, regionally and internationally, they would have killed him. However, they did not do the radical coup because they noticed that they could get away with committing an illegal act as long as it was very popular on the ground. Indeed, no one came to Mugabe's rescue, not SADC, not the AU nor the UN, South Africa or DRC. All looked the other way and left antiquated Mugabe to his new fate.

Ironically Mugabe's woes had started in November 2017 when he dismissed one of his two deputies, Mr. Emmerson Mnangagwa from the office of vice president of the country and a few days later from ZANU PF. On 06 November 2017 Simon Khaya Moyo, the Minister of Information, Media and Broadcasting Services had informed the world that Mnangagwa had been relieved of his duties. The letter of dismissal which was widely circulated on social media, stated that in accordance with section 329 of the constitution, the President had relieved Mnangagwa of his duties because, *"it had become evident that his conduct in the discharge of his duties had become inconsistent with his official responsibilities. The Vice President has consistently and persistently exhibited traits of disloyalty, disrespect, deceitfulness and unreliability. He has also demonstrated little probity in the execution of his duties"*.

In the preceding years, Mnangagwa had been embroiled in an internecine life and death struggle against the young turks in ZANU PF, led by Prof. Jonathan Moyo and called Generation 40 (G40). The G40 faction's prominent members were Moyo, Grace Mugabe, cabinet minister Saviour Kasukuwere and Patrick Zhuwawo, Mugabe's nephew among others. The G40 assemblage dragooned the Vice President to retreat into a faction called Lacoste. The term lacoste was derived by pundits from Mngangwa's nickname 'crocodile'. The lacoste clique consisted of Mnangagwa, Defence Forces commander Constantine Chiwenga, Christopher Mutswangwa the former minister of War Veterans, Charles Charamba secretary to the cabinet and permanent secretary in the Ministry of information, among other powerful cabinet ministers and party cavaliers.

The Mugabe succession snafu had became a cut throat business, where the players were ever dicing with political peril on the treacherous ZANU PF precipice, as Mnangagwa discovered at a party politburo meeting on 19 July 2017 where

Jonathan Moyo relentlessly went for his jagular. With the aid of modern high tech equipment seen in the ZANU PF politburo for the first time, Moyo had played an hour long video recording, arguing that the Vice President was plotting a coup against Robert Mugabe. In the video Moyo had choreographed the capture of state operations and the defrauding of the state of millions of United States dollars. It was a no – holds barred presentation where Mnangagwa was essentially accused of treason in front of Mugabe. Moyo had sought to prove that Mnangagwa and some ZNA commanders had captured such state institutions like the Zimbabwe Anti - corruption Commission (ZACC), the National Prosecuting Authority (NPA) and the state controlled print media, Zimpapers. He accused Mnangagwa of doing all that in order to control the party commissariat and overthrow Mugabe at a planned ZANU PF special congress. That, it was alleged by Moyo, Mnangagwa was doing through the implemention of a strategy document code named *"Blue Ocean"* which aimed at him taking over the ZANU PF party.

Next, he accused the beleaguered and jolted Vice President of siphoning millions from the ZANU PF companies under his control by claiming that he had destroyed the institutions. Meanwhile he was allowing certain party officials to transfer money from the companies to their personal bank accounts. Mnangagwa's woes were not over as he was also inculpated of colluding with foreign companies to defraud the country of millions, eg. he mentioned the 2015 deal with an Indian company, African Chrome Fields, whereby Mnangagwa had allegedly misrepresented to Mugabe who went on to officiate at the launch of the project which later prejudiced the government of millions.

After Moyo's presentation Mnangagwa sought to defend himself but he could only do so much, because he had been caught napping and the blows were predatory, fierce, hard and fast. He tried to remind the meeting of his 40 - year old loyalty to Mugabe but Moyo fended him off by observing that the history of nationalist movements was littered with examples of long term allies, and not the *'mafikizolos'* (Johnny come late) betraying the founding fathers. Mnangagwa lamely claimed that Moyo was a CIA spy, in his poor and porous defence. Mugabe was livid with anger but his fury seemed to freeze him into inaction. He only berated and censured the army for meddling in politics. Obviously he had forgotten his own writing in 1979 when he had inspirited the ZANLA guns to go with the people's vote. The President also allowed Mnangagwa to prepare his defense for presentation at the next politburo meeting. What was as clear as the difference between north and south, at that stage was that Mnangagwa, who for more than forty years had been Mugabe's *vade mecum*, a constantly consulted handbook, was in serious trouble.

A couple of weeks later Mnangagwa had presented his defense to the party politburo in a case titled, 'The Anatomy of party capture'. His main defense was the tired story that Jonathan Moyo had infiltrated the party working for the CIA. His evidence, he alleged was that Moyo had on 03 August 2017 given the video recording of his earlier presentation attacking Mnangagwa to the US embassy and Western diplomats. He said the embassies had admitted as much and claimed that the US ambassador was prepared to affirm that he had indeed been given the recording by Moyo. He said Moyo's agenda was to destroy ZANU PF from within. He also claimed that the real successionists were Moyo, Vice President Phelekezela Mpoko and Minister of local government Saviour Kasukuwere who were holding clock and dagger meetings to discuss the succession issue in defiance of Mugabe's orders for everyone not to discuss the topic.

Clearly Mnangagwa was hemmed in, with the young turks tearing at his soft under belly skin like famished and covetous mongrels. His defense against Moyo's allegations was an old mundane, humdrum story and his evidence not convincing while the charges against him were more scathing, virulent and tangible. Ncube (Interview 18 January 2018) maintained that the G40 faction won *"hands down"*, the battle to get Mugabe on their side. *"Mnangagwa, Chiwenga and company lost. Having lost the political fight, they turned it into a military fight. They had the guns, so they used the guns to push out the Jonathans and Mugabe himself and effectively therefore carried out an illegal, blatantly illegal coup in terms of the constitution"*.

The crocodile had his back against the wall. Many thought he was torn by two giant horns of dilemma; to jump ship or to stay put and suffer the heat. He opted for the latter. By the time of his sacking, he had long been rendered redundant. He was unwanted and was waiting for the axe to land. Jonathan Moyo had hounded him out of his esteemed office. As the letter of his discharge was published, it was expected by everyone. Many analysts had anticipated his resignation from both the government and the party. What was unexpected, what hit many squarely on their faces, taking them off their feet, including Mugabe and Moyo, was his actual reaction.

Mnangagwa had not resigned because he had anticipated that at 94 and severely sick, antediluvian Mugabe would soon drop dead somehow. He was poised to grab power, should he fail to get ZANU PF to crown him president after the death of Mugabe. He was not prepared to grab power from Mugabe especially before the 2018 elections which he wanted Mugabe to win first before either dying in office (like many, considering his age, he was hopeful that Mugabe would not survive long after 2018) or being incapacitated by ill health and old age. Bidding his time, with that hope in mind, he braced himself for all the ridicule, derision and taunting that the G40 cabal could and would definitely hurl at him.

Whatever was the motivation of the coup plotters, an indubitable fact was that the coup d' etat was not in sympathy of the common people. It was not about liberating the oppressed citizens nor was it about rescuing the free falling economy or remedying the divested of social order. It was personal and probably idiosyncratic if the rumours that Mnangagwa had slapped Mugabe at a politburo meeting a couple of years back were true. It was about Mnangagwa and Chiwenga and not about the people and the country. Bitter at being fired by Mugabe, the pair accelerated their plans for a coup because they could no longer wait for Mugabe's demise since whenever that would occur, they would have been rendered irrelevant within ZANU PF and would not be eligible to take over the throne.

The coup was an ad hoc personal coping strategy precipitated by their laying off. It was far from being motivated by policy deviation or ideological contradiction with Mugabe. If it was for the people, Mnangagwa and his cavalrymen would not have waited for more than thirty - seven years to bail the country from Mugabe's punishing claws. Besides they had been Mugabe's talons, willing and enjoying the bloodletting and the accompanying wealth. It was now a power game. A dangerous power game they had lost within the ZANU PF political narrative and one they determined to win by the gun.

Constantine Chiwenga's statement as he flouted executive orders from the President relieving him of his duties, clearly portrayed a personal agenda. The commander of the Zimbabwe Defense Forces obstreperously defied his boss's order to vacate office, because he had all the guns. No one could arrest him. Instead he issued a statement on 14 November 2017 as reports of a coup started trickling in. In the statement, he lambasted the expulsion of senior party members who had participated in the liberation war against the Rhodesian government. He also criticized the take over of ZANU PF by what he termed counter revolutionaries. By discharging the old guarde and promoting the *mafikizolos,* Mugabe was said to be dismantling ZANU PF and defeating the objectives and reversing the gains of the liberation struggle.

Had Mugabe remained the convenient political fossil that he had become, he would have stayed a relevant burden on the securocrats. When he however according to them, transmutated into a dangerous counter revolutionary, they resovled paradoxically to salvage his *"legacy"* by defying him. They made the coup in the name of Mugabe by claiming that they were restoring his legacy. With the social media awash with statements from embattled Mnangagwa promising to soon return to the country and Chiwenga recalcitrant that he will not be fired by Mugabe, it became apparent that a coup was going on.

Therefore, Chiwenga defied Mugabe because he and Mngangagwa had been expelled from ZANU PF and government. The fact that both of them had been discharged immediately before orchestrating the coup, can only depict the putsch for what it was; a very personal project. Since they were not the first to be expelled in similar circumstances and they had not done a take over of government and ZANU PF when others had suffered the same fate, it can only mean that their insurgence was personal. Had they done it when Mujuru and others were expelled some few years back, maybe the world would have believed they were revolutionaries.

If the coup was not a personal project, they would have formed a transitional authority in the form of the Government of National Unity of 2009 – 2013, to administer the government in preparation for proper elections within a reasonable period of time. Instead they sent the opposition on a wild goose chase by raising their expectations for such an arrangement. Instead of genuine and sincere talks, the coup plotters kept sending informal emissaries to the opposition. The various emissaries were meant to pull the wool over the eyes of the opposition. They misled the MDC Alliance of mainly Welshman Ncube, Morgan Tsvangirai and Tendai Biti, into believing that the coup executors were willing to talk and were going to talk with them, right until Mngangagwa's inauguration day. Morgan Tsvangirai who had been expecting a telephone call on behalf of the Alliance, inviting them for talks was astonished to hear Mnangagwa declare that he was forming a ZANU PF government alone.

The ploy was to keep the opposition expecting something positive to happen, so that no one acted contrary to their plans. That strategy worked because no one in ZANU PF and outside of it, condemned the coup until it was too late to do so and still influemce the tragic trajectory the country was taking.

When he was asked for his opinion on the coup d'etat on 18 January 2018, Welshman Ncube, president of the MDC opined that, *"..those who overthrew Mugabe were not revolutionaries. They were from day one Mugabe's enforcers. Chiwenga was commander of 1 Brigade right here during Gukurahundi. Even though they were not doing the foot soldiering, they provided all the logistical transport support to 5th Brigade to do what they were doing. It was supported logistically by 1 Brigade, commanded by Chiwenga. Mnangagwa was the gatherer of all intelligence. In fact, as many people were killed by the CIO as were killed by the 5th Brigade. What is the significance of all this? The very people who had imposed Mugabe on us by subverting electoral processes, are the ones who then took him out in order to install themselves. So what fat chance do we have that they have any fundamental ideological differences with Mugabe on governance and economic issues? Zero".* A shocking surprise was awaiting many that thought Mnangagwa unlike Mugabe would deliver the country from socio – political and economic evil.

Many people thought that for the national interest, the best way forward that would turn around the economic fortunes of the country, after the coup, would have been a transitional authority made up of all the parties in parliament and prominent organisations and experts outside parliament. Despite coming from the painful loins of a coup, such a transitional government would gain domestic, regional and international traction and legitimacy faster and therefore better than the tokenism that rolled out when Mnangagwa did eventually form a government. Despite British optimism, the new regime would not address the unfinished business of the 2009 – 2013 GNU, namely issues to do with harmonized elections, the constitution (for example devolving power to provinces), the voters' roll and electoral laws among others. ZANU PF on their own in government would never address such issues because they thought that would be tantamount to reforming themselves out of power.

Mugabe on the other hand was a victim of his own old age and arrogance. If he had been different, Mnangagwa and Chiwenga were never ever going to get close to orchestrating the coup. Jonathan Moyo had been singing himself hoarse on the megaphone, telling everybody who could listen that Mnangagwa and Chiwenga were plotting a coup. The fact that the coup did eventuate vindicated Moyo. It means that Moyo had had evidence and had presented it to Mugabe, not only at the ZANU PF politburo meeting. Knowing Mugabe's ruthlessness, which was on record, his dilatory tactics elicited questions. Why did Mugabe not act long before firing Mnangagwa and allowing him to escape the country. If Mnangagwa could be fired, if he indeed attempted to and failed to drive through Forbes boarder post into Mozambique, it means he could be arrested. Why did Mugabe not arrest Mnangagwa and charge him with treason for plotting to overthrow him just as he had arrested many others before in the absence of any shred of evidence. Suddenly he forgot that coup plotters, the world over, are arrested and not merely discharged from office. Embalmed in old age, tribal loyalty and a bloated sense of both invincibility and infallibility, Mugabe ignored Moyo's advice.

How could Mugabe whose stay in office especially after 2000, was due to the loyalty of the securocrats fail to command a section of the army to come to his help. Not even a shoot out between those loyal to him and those loyal to Chiwenga and Mnangagwa occured. Yet Ignatius Chombo's bodyguards did resist and a shoot out ensued at the minister's residence resulting in the reported death of a foreign mercenary bodyguard. The answer was simple, or was it? Mugabe was unwanted at home, in the streets, in the party, in government, in parliament, in cabinet and in the barracks.

The only form of resistance was offered by Simon Khaya Moyo through a press statement on 17 November 2017 when it became common knowledge that a coup was underway. He appealed for adherence to constitutionalism and democracy. For the first time in the history of ZANU PF, they appealed for the observance of democracy and constitutionalism. It must have sounded very eerie and hollow even to Khaya - Moyo himself. One would expect Mugabe himself and not the party information secretariat to issue an authoritative statement ordering the army to stay in their barracks and await instructions from no one but himself. Khaya – Moyo's statement was very feeble and evoked pity and not compliance. It was clearly less than a half - hearted attempt at countering a coup. For the first time in the life of the Zvimba monster, he was solitary, deserted by those that had created him into the tribal chauvinist and male gorgon that he had become.

When the coup happened, it was merely an extension of ZANU PF factionalism. It had nada to do with the suffering masses. Upon realizing that zanuism had bestowed upon them one supreme god whose word was the law and a structure where one person decided who stayed and who did not, Mugabe's lieutenants took to factionalism. The G40 camarilla were quicker to figure out that they had created a party in respect of which only one office mattered. Therefore, the G40 and the Lacoste, like all their predecesor factions faught each other in a tussle that on occasions turned into mortal combat in order to win Mugabe to their side. They all always bolted into Mugabe's door in a rush to prove who was the more fervent and zealous worshipper of the ZANU PF cult god and his goddess wife. In the process they employed all the dirty tactics from hell and beyond aginst each other.

As observed by the Zimbabwe Independent newspaper of 13 November 2015, the two factions, just like other factions before them, were products of the Mugabe succession debate - cum - feud. The formations were a result of personality clashes. Individuals would then coalesce around their preferred potential successor to Mugabe. The factions never had policy or ideological contestations against each other. They were designed to propagate one's chances of succeeding Mugabe. Consequently, the potential successor would mobilise support within the party for their cause. The contestants and their hangers on would then compete and fall over each other in a bid to out do the other in pleasing Mugabe, while manipulating and massaging the party structures. It was said that by the time of her dismissal, former Vice President Joice Mujuru had won to her side, nine of the ten party provinces. Those structures were going to vote for her candidacy as party president at the next party congress.

The soft nature of the factions would in a normal democracy preclude them from possessing a propensity for violence. However, debarring them from violence, yet they were ZANU PF would be an oxymoron, because violence had always been structural and immanent to the party. There was nothing civilized in the succession battle. It was characterized by treachery and back stabbing, scheming, labelling, conniving and even murder. Allegations and counter allegations typified the mudslinging in the various ZANU PF meetings with Mugabe being the final court of appeal. He was the judge and jury. His approval was the most sought after product, like the proverbial hot cake.

Unlike Mujuru, Mnangagwa did not enjoy popular support. He however had the support of what mattered in ZANU PF. The support of the military and thier guns. Having been Mugabe's *aide de camp* during the liberation war and having held the Defence and National Security ministries for many years since independence, he had had ample time to recruit officers more loyal to him as a person than to any other individual, especially Mugabe. It was in the public domain long before the coup, that Mnangagwa's roots and power base were in the army and in particular in the office of the Commander of the Defense Forces, Constantine Chiwenga. Knowing Mugabe, how he allowed that scenario to subsist under his watch was incomprehensible.

While he had an iron grip on the military, his sway over the judiciary was dealt a heavy blow, although ultimately that proved to be of little consequence to his agenda. Being in control of the judiciary was important because under zanuism whoever commandeered the office of the Chief Justice was the law unto himself. That is why in January 2017 Vice President Mnangagwa retired the then Chief Justice Godfrey Chidyausiku a month before his retirement was due and appointed his own votary, George Chiweshe as acting Chief Justice ahead of Luke Malaba the deputy Chief Justice.

Ten months later in October of the same year, Mugabe handled the Chief Justice saga in a way that proved that indeed the Zimbabwean people and land were his private fiefdom. It was then that Mugabe came to know, by his own admission, after being informed by Chidyausiku that the latter was no longer Chief Justice and had not been for ten months. Chidyausiku was then ordered back to work by Mugabe and he reported for work the next day. (The Zimbabwe Independent) Mnangagwa's Chiweshe had to give way. The big question was, how could the president of the country spend ten months without knowing who was the Chief justice of the country, yet he was the appointing authority. The unpalatable and embarrassing answer was that he was not accountable to the electorate and therefore could afford to be shambolic. Mnangagwa lost the Chief Justice tussle, but the events which rolled out in November 2017 relegated the incident to a minor battle loss in a war he was determined to win.

The Chief Justice rigmarole, while proving the lack of probity and the deceitfulness allegation in the letter dismissing Mnangagwa, also proved beyond doubt that the unaccountable and slovenly Mugabe was too old and was no longer in charge, not just of the country but of his faculties as well. No one could be better aware of that foible in Mugabe than Mngangagwa. He realized that ZANU PF, and by extension the country, was being run by Mugabe's wife, Prof. Jonathan Moyo and the entire G40 ring. Mnangagwa could live with many horrors, including the Gukurahundi massacres, but not the spectre of Jonathan Moyo and Grace Mugabe calling the shots at State House. Therefore, he resorted to the guns of ZANLA.

One school of thought has it that the ZANLA conspirators had never wanted to seize power from their idol, but their hand was pushed by the woman who had suddenly mutated into the party goddess. Grace Mugabe under the tutelage of Jonathan Moyo. Driven by the terror and knowledge of her husband's mortality, Grace became predatory and even barbaric in her attack of members of first, the Gamatox (Joyce Mujuru faction), then the Lacoste faction, as she galloped preposterously towards her husband's throne. She had to be impetuous because her husband was the politically powerful, yet sick and frail old horse, meant to carry her to the presidency. While the looming menace of Grace Mugabe and her allies taking over from Mugabe spooked Mnangagwa, on her part, Grace was incensed out of her wits by her husband's physical infirmities. The 21st of February was declared a public holiday to celebrate Mugabe's birthday. Instead of bringing joy and contentment to her, with Mugabe succumbing to old age, the day must have reminded her of how late she was at getting to the throne. She was obviously gunning for the presidency despite her and Mugabe's initial denials. By 2017 she was brazenly hurtling and hotfooting for it through the front door. In the process, she committed the cardinal sin. She tossed all caution to the wind.

Because of Jonathan Moyo, Grace Mugabe and the entire G40 crew, whose mission was patently to elbow him out, Mnangagwa had become increasingly hostile to his mentor for accommodating his tormentors. In the Lacoste caucus, the conspirators observed a very alarming trend. Mugabe under influence had managed to isolate himself from the old and trusted conservative guarde. He had discharged from the party and government, his trusted band who had stood with him from the time they rebelled against ZAPU and Joshua Nkomo, through the war, independence, the Gukurahundi genocide and the turbulent economic disaster he and them had actuated. Mugabe had broken ties with such ZANU and ZANLA gurus like Dydimus Mutasa, Joram Gumbo, Rugare Gumbo, Joyce Mujuru, Emmerson Mnangagwa, Christopher Mutsvangwa, Constantine Chiwenga etc. Yet throughout the purging, no personality of substance from Matabeleland had been shown the exit door. By November 2017 the tribal alarm bells in ZANU PF were at their loudest, as fears of state capture by minority Ndebeles scaled fever pitch.

Robert Mugabe had unwittingly surrounded himself with the Matabele. The tribal supremacists cried foul because Jonathan Moyo was at the helm of the executive with Grace Mugabe as his proxy. Phelekezela Mpoko (a Ndebele) was the sole Vice President and was working hand in glove with Jonathan Moyo. The judiciary was superintended by Luke Malaba (a Matabele) the Chief Justice who was appointed ahead of George Chiweshe whom Mnangagwa had preferred. The legislature was presided over by Jacob Mudenda, (a Tonga) from Matabeleland while Philip Valerio Sibanda (a Ndebele), commander of the Zimbabwe National Army was most senior and qualified within the army to be the next commander of the Zimbabwe Defence Forces. The three arms of the state and the army were under the command of people from Matabeleland. That was taboo, a complete anti – thesis of the 1979 Shona Grand Plan. It had to be stopped.

While that scenario sent shivers up their spines, the elephant in the living room of the conspirators was Robert Mugabe's imminent death. If the old and sickly Mugabe were to die by fair or foul means while under the mastery of Matabeleland, they dreaded to think of who would take over from him. The formula and recipe before them pointed to a Ndebele president: a prospect that was anathema to the Gukurahundists. They feared that if Mugabe died with Mpoko and Grace Mugabe as Vice Presidents, there was a high likelihood of shrewd and sapient Jonathan Moyo employing his sharp canniness to prevail over his G40 groupies to elect Mpoko as president ahead of the inexperienced Grace Mugabe. They neither could ignore the scary bet that if Mugabe died under those circumstances, the army under Sibanda could be soft – soaped into using the gun to facilitate a Ndebele take – over. That could be the explanation why the two most wanted men during and after the coup were Jonathan Moyo and Phelekezela Mpoko in that order. Jonathan Moyo had to go into exile in an unknown country because he was afraid for his life.

That sense of foreboding was so live and real, it propelled Mnangagwa and Chiwenga into decisive ation. Their trepidation was not entirely unreasonable since they were haunted by the sins and crimes they had committed against the

Ndebele, post independence from Britain in 1980 until 1987. Jonathan Moyo's persistent reminders that they were tribalists and murderous Gukurahundists might have conjured in them the worst angst at the possibility of Ndebele revenge for the genocide. They baulked and decided to nip it in the bud.

Another school of thought had it that the coup d'etat was orchestrated by a cartel of powerful politicians, securocrats and business moguls. Mugabe who was naturally stubborn, had become a hindrance to the business interests of the cartel and old age had made him even more obstinate and sluggish and therefore a liability. Thus the cartel leaders wanted him out. It is alleged that the WikiLeaks cables revealed that Chiwenga, John Bredenkamp and Billy Reutenbach were the leaders of the cartel, with many powerful members drawn from government, the private sector and the army but fronted by Kudakwashe Tagwirei (Sakunda Holdings, holder of the sole fuel import licence). The cartel which had monopoly over gold, diamonds, fuel and grain production, distribution, import and export, had under its control and pay roll, government ministries, departments, the armed forces and parastatals such as the Reserve Bank of Zimbabwe (RBZ), Zimbabwe Electricty Supply Authority (ZESA), Mines Minerals Coporation of Zimbabwe (MMCZ), National Oil Company of Zimbabwe (NOCZIM), Zimbabwe Revenue Authority (ZIMRA) among many others.

The cartel had chosen Mnangagwa to take over from Mugabe. They had attempted to force Mugabe to hand over power to Mnangagwa, way before the coup but Mugabe had let them down especially when he attempted to have Chiwenga assassinated and fired Mnangagwa from ZANU PF and the government. It was clear to the cartel that Mugabe was not towing the line. He wanted to have Sydney Sekeramayi deputized by Grace Mugabe and Phelekezela Mpoko, take over from him. Sekeramayi and the G40 grouping which was closer to Mugabe would be a blow to the cartel. As a last resort, the cartel influenced the army, the general public, civic society and even opposition political party supporters to march against Mugabe. By so doing, the cartel gave a public outlook and popular face to a project that was as selfish as it was illegal.

As a result, the coup was very popular among many within the elite in Mashonaland because it averted a possible Ndebele coup or take – over and terminated the state capture by the same. It was welcomed because it was the bigger picture, beyond the person of Mugabe. While ensuring the protraction of Shona hegemony, it also sheltered and preserved the ZANU legacy and paradoxically protected and preserved Mugabe as a legend.

Therein lay the reason for their being loathe to expose Mugabe for what he was, a ruthless tyrant, a remorseless mass murderer, an inveterate megalomaniac, a congenital tribalist and an unabashed thief. They protected him from the scrutiny of the world at a time when the previously thick and impervious cloak of immunity had fallen off from his shoulders. They sheltered him from the prying and accussing questions from journalists and the so called long arm of the law. They gave him millions of US dollars as a retirement package instead of arresting him and forcing him and his family to return the billions they had syphoned from the state coffers.

They wanted to maintain and build on his status as an icon and paragon of Shona supremacy. They wanted his notch in history to remain intact. For that reason, they blamed everybody around Mugabe for his failures. They merely acknowledged his advanced age and consequent diminished capacity and decided to embrace a new hero who would continue from where Mugabe had left. When Mnangagwa therefore proffered himself, many bowed down at his feet. They accepted their new hero, who promptly retired their old hero and amnestised him from prosecution for all the crimes he had committed against humanity especially the sin of the Gukurahundi genocide.

For ZANU PF as a party, it was imperative that Mugabe had to exit from the political stage because the writing was on the wall. He was too old and sick to parsonally participate in the rigorous campaign for the 2018 elections. Voters were not going to vote for a dying candidate whom they would not see at rallies and who if glimpsed would inspire sympathy and regret than voter confidence. Going around the country as was his strategy at previous elections was going to be physically impossible for the doddering and teetering president. Besides, at 94, naturally Mugabe had become a favourite gathering spot for memory loss, poor eyesight, hard hearing, slurred speech, somnolence, and poor psychomotor coordination, all weaknesses not needed in a presidential candidate, especially in public meetings. Despite his desire to rule to the grave, he could not do it due to health and physical constraints. He had become a liability and by the time of the 2018 elections he would be as good as dead.

Many in ZANU PF did not want the party to die with him, yet not even his close advisors could convince him of that. There was all round consensus that Mugabe had long become a liability, but his succession was not easy to decide. He too was conscious of his ebbed capacity but he could not just pick a successor because that would divide the party which already had dangerous schismatic lines along tribal identities. Besides, picking a successor would not augur well for democracy even in undemocratic ZANU PF. He could not allow democractic processes to decide the seccession conundrum either, because he was scared of the possible outcome. In a democracy, anyone can win and he could easily find himself facing the gallores should a 'wrong' candidate win. Caught between the devil and the deep blue sea, Mugabe hatched a plan to stay put and declare a moratorium on the succession debate until he died. Probably that strategy would have worked if he had not listened to his wife and discharged Mnangagwa.

From a ZANU PF perspective, if Mugabe retired, resigned or lost the presidency through a democratic process, eg. intra party elections, his successor would inherit international and domestic censure. But if his own lieutenants rebelled against him, they would win the hearts of the much needed rich West, because like the West, they would have become Mugabe's enemies. Then the old and trusted dictum, 'my enemy's enemy is my friend' would apply. Hence the logic in the participation in the coup by the British who allegedly helped Mnangagwa. Hence the involvement of the civic society who were under the illusion that the length and breadth of their enemy and woes was Mugabe.

Civic society was hoodwinked into spending donor funds in marching to Mugabe's residence to dethrone him (the coup plotters actually coerced Mugabe into resigning by telling him that if he did not step down they would allow the marchers to deal with him the way the Libyans had dealt with Gaddafi).

Therefore, ZANU PF longevity would be assured if there was an internal revolt against Mugabe. ZANU PF would also have sanitized themselves of the curse of Mugabe to the international community and their government would win the lucrative favours and cooperation from international institutions and governments. ZANU PF would get a new lease of life since many in the opposition that had left the party due to dismissal or out of disapproval of party policies, procedures and personalities would easily bury the hatchet and return to the party, blaming all the past differencies on Mugabe. Disillusioned with the perennially losing MDCT, the West, in particular Britain would support a 'new' ZANU PF, now that their nemesis was gone. The coup was therefore a blessing in disguise for many in ZANU PF.

For the people of Matabeleland, the coup was popular for all the different reasons. Their enemy number one had fallen. The killer of their fathers, mothers, sons, daughters, brothers and sisters had finally met his match, or so they thought. They celebrated the coup the way a rape victim celebrates after the rapist has been killed, without realizing that her savior is an armed robber. They did not want to celebrate Mnangagwa's advent but they could not celebrate one without celebrating the other. On its own merit and in isolation, the rise of Mnangagwa they would never celebrate.

Many a Matabele thought that ZANU PF had collapsed. They thought the end of Mugabe was the end of gukurahunism, zanuism and mugabeism. The party of their woes, they believed had finally fragmented and come elections in a few months time, they would rout it out. Little did they know that Mugabe was just a fraction of their tribulations and misfortune in a giant quadrominium trap. They could have known that Mnangagwa had wrestled power from Mugabe with a gun in each hand. One for Mugabe and one for the ballot. He had captured ZANU PF and government for his own posterity and did not intend handing the reigns over to another, just because that person would have won an election. He would never risk limb and life so that the ballot would usher in someone from the opposition. The presidency and deputy presidency were his spoils of war. Little did they realise that ZANU PF, gukurahundism, zanuism and mugabeism were on the march.

Whether Ndebele, Shona or British the fact was that, standing in complete contrast to the illegality of the coup d' etat in terms of the constitution, was the fact that the act was extremely popular. The reason for the popularity of the illegal act was that Mugabe as president of the country had overstayed. Internationally everyone wanted Mugabe gone, while nationally everyone including ZANU PF people wanted him out. Therefore, the coup was internally and externally overdue, such that everyone was prepared to turn a blind eye to illegality and therefore prepared to give Mnangagwa a chance.

Almost everyone including the British, who Welshman Ncube (18 Janury 2018 interview) accused of complicity in the coup, wanted to give the new regime a chance. *"The British participated with Mnangagwa and Chiwenga to actually execute the coup",* he observed. That was not the first time the British had been identified as Mnangagwa's allies. The Zimbabwe Independent of 29 September 2016 had published an exchange of correspondence between journalist Dumisani Muleya and British envoy John Culley. Muleya's contention then, was that the British were in Mnangagwa's corner and the British envoy lost an opportunity to be coherent in disputing the allegation.

Immediately after the coup, the British were the only ones who seemed to be literally in love with the Mnangagwa regime and wanted to do business with Harare almost unconditionally. Their challenge was to convince the rest of Europe to embrace Mugabe's former hatchet man. Their challenge was to convince the United States who were hardline and saying there were no opportunities that could come from Mugabe's storm troopers who had removed him from power only to ensconce themselves.

The British were optimistic that if they hand held Mnangagwa, he would do the right thing. The right thing being principally, the unfinished business of the 2009 to 2013 Global Political Agreement, including electoral reforms. For all their enthusiasm and optimism, the British were bound to fail. Either they chose to be ahistorical or they were downright naïve. They should have known that it was in the ZANU PF DNA not to do the right thing. If Mngangagwa did the right thing, he would lose the looming elections. If the Mnangagwa regime did a proper election they would lose political power. Losing political power was not the reason they had staged the coup. If they lost the elections, they would resort to the 2008 methods and the British would be back in the *cul de sac* of the 1980s where they could not condemn their choice inspite of him having gone rogue.

The British once more found themselves in the same thankless predicament and corner they had manuevred themselves into in 1980. They put their money on the wrong horse and sooner rather than later they would regret it again. Despite his atrocious record, they embraced Mnangagwa. If anyone was as guilty of the Gukurahundi genocide as Mugabe, it was no doubt, Mnangagwa. If anyone was as guilty as Mugabe of decaying into a shell and a morass, the economic gem inherited from the Smith regime, it was none other than Mnangagwa. It was the same Mnangagwa that had chaired the Joint Operations Command (JOC) meetings which reversed the 2008 election results and made decisions to kill people during the ZANU PF engineered re – run electoral violence. Mnangagwa and the JOC, pre – emptively carried out a coup against Tsvangirai so that he could not assume office and installed Mugabe in 2008. In November 2017 they then removed their own puppet that they had installed and put themselves in power (Ncube interview 18 January 2018).

Somehow the British were then suffering from volitional amnesia. Probably like many people, the British never had had a problem with the Gukurahundi genocide, gukurahundism, zanuism and mugabeism, all of which Mnangagwa also personified as much as his predecessor. What was on white paper was that they had had a problem with Mugabe the person. Now that Mugabe had exited the stage, they went back to ZANU PF with a begging bowl and ditched the collective opposition movement, probably in the hope that the new regime would reverse the controversial land reform programme. What other logical foundation could one identify for the British's throwing into the wind such previously cherished values as political and economic reforms, the rule of law, human rights, democracy, constitutionalism and good governance by embracing an individual and a party known to be the converse of all those values?

How else could one reconcile the duplicity and gullibility of the West? Mnangagwa was cursorily invited to the World Economic Forum in Davos, Switzerland, in January 2018 before the echo of the guns of the coup had subsided. During an interview in Davos he disclosed that the British Prime Minister Teresa May, had sent him an envoy to pledge the willingness of the British government to *"cooperate"* with his government within an hour of his inauguration. The impetuosity of the British government was further betrayed by Mnangagwa's revelation that Prime Minister May had invited him to rejoin the Common Wealth from which Zimbabwe and not Mugabe had been expelled. The desire to admit Zimbabwe into the Common Wealth just because there was a new head of state showed that, either the initial dismissal or the desired readmission, or both were not based on principle, because Mnangagwa's less than two months old government had done nothing by way of reforms to warrant readmission.

Charles Charamba an integral member of the Mnangagwa cohort, in an interview with a local broadcaster also divulged that the Pope had sent a congratulatory message to Mnangagwa. If that claim was true, one found it unfathomable how such staunch crusaders and exponents of democracy and piety could billet such thuggery and sins. So much for Papal infallibility.

The West was very much aware of Mnangagwa's role in the Matabeleland genocide. They knew he had hung on Mugabe's hip like a hatchet for more than forty years without ever questioning his policies and practices. Not once did Mnangagwa differ with Mugabe. How could they not know that Mnangagwa was as guilty of collapsing the economy, rigging elections, electoral violence, human rights abuses, corruption including looting Congolese diamonds, abusing the military to loot Chiyadzwa diamonds etc. They also were alive to Mnangagwa's entry into State House via the back door.

The Pope, the Queen of England, the British Prime Minister, the UN, the AU and SADC suddenly forgot that that was the same Mnangagwa that had been fingered by a UN Security Council Investigation set up in 2001, as having been the central strategist in and being to party to, *"striping DRC resources"* The report indicated that Mnangagwa was key to a network that, *"derive financial benefit through a variety of criminal activities including theft, embezzlement and diversion of public funds, undervaluation of goods, smuggling, false invoicing, non – payment of taxes, kickbacks to public officials and bribery"* (Yamamoto 2019). The UN Panel of Experts revealed that the Zimbabwean barons led by Mnangagwa, Sekeramayi and company did not intend to wind up their operations in the DRC even when the ZDF which had been stationed in areas including the diamond hub of Mbuji Mayi, were pulling out. They were determined to continue looting by usage of joint ventures and off shore companies operating in DRC. Therefore, his sins in the DRC should have counted for something before the Pope and the British Queen and government endorsed Mnangagwa as Zimbabwe's President after the coup.

The people of Matabeleland shuddered at such skullduggery and underhandedness. Once more they found themselves betrayed by the British. They wondered how the British could fail to see that ZANU PF as a party was constructed philosophically on the marginalization of Matabeleland. The people knew that there was nothing that united ZANU PF politically more than the southern region accepting that she was the illegitmate daughter who could never be heir to the father's throne.

Mnangagwa's description at Davos, of the Gukurahundi genocide which he and Mugabe had orchestrated, as just *"a bad patch"* on the history of Zimbabwe and his argument that the numbers of the dead given by the CCJP were exaggerated, were an unambiguous communication of his view of the people of Matabeleland. If anyone had entertained thoughts of a better future for Matabeleland, they needed to rethink. Mnangagwa's administration was set to continue from where Mugabe had left. Gukurahundism, zanuism and mugabeism were anchored in the ZANU PF genes. Mnangagwa's military junto was set to perpetuate Shona hegemony, nationalism and supremacy. The only difference was that the new regime had ushered in the Karanga, a Shona sub – group, while replacing the Zezuru as the new taskmasters. There was no respite for Matabeleland. She had just experienced a giant leap to nowhere. She was destined to wallow in poverty and reel under the york of social exclusion, economic marginalization, cultural subjugation and political emasculation.

Chapter IX

Quo Vadis Matabeleland?

> *"Where lies and falsehoods are sown, there suspicion and division flourish. Corruption too and political or ideological manipulation, are essentially contrary to the truth: they attack the very foundations of social harmony and undermine the possibility of peaceful social relationships.... Forgiveness, far from precluding the search for truth, actually requires it.....another requisite for forgiveness and reconciliation is justice....forgiveness neither eliminates nor lessens the need for reparation which justice requires"*

Pope John Paul II, 26 January 1997.

The ZANU PF government has managed to set the Ndebeles and Shonas on a collision course. Abounding and incontestable evidence corroborating that assertion subsists in all social, political and economic spheres. Arguably the Shona majority are given aristocracy in education, employment, government, the economy, politics and in social development. A litany of vices, including genocide, subjugation, marginalization, isolation, unemployment and de – education, are being employed as tools of managing potential and perceived Matabele dissent, ascendency and political take – over.

The tribal conflict in Zimbabwe, or precisely the Ndebele - Shona acrimony will not miraculously go away overnight, nor will it be ignored ad infinitum into insignificance as is obviously the ZANU PF strategy. Piecemeal attempts and half baked measures like the setting up of a peace and reconciliation commission and ministry without mandating them to search for the truth behind the Gukurahundi genocide falls short of sincererity and seriousness.

The ZANU PF and the Mugabe and Mnangagwa prayer and hope has always been that the Matabele will someday soon capitulate and accept to be dominated forever. Officialdom pretends that there is no conflict, yet it long attained crisis status, like a time bomb ticking ever closer to the eleventh hour. As former revolutioneries they must know that people cannot bear the yoke of oppression forever.

The endeavour to make the Shona taskmasters over the Ndebele and other ethnic groups of Matabeleland is ongoing. The minority ethnic groups are not fairly or proportionately represented in all sectors of influence and decision making such as the civil service, the police, the army, commissions, management boards of quasi state institutions, cabinet etc. These domains and all others are sacred ground for Shonas, with an occasional dotting of those Ndebeles that have repudiated their Ndebeleness or those deliberately handpicked for window dressing purposes.

An example of the tribal nature of appointments was published by Bulawayo24 News whereby the Minister of Information, Publicity and Broadcasting Services, Monica Mutsvangwa appointed board members of the Broadcasting Authority of Zimbabwe, Transmedia and ZBC. The online publication observed that, *"(t) he board members are mostly drawn from Mashonaland, Manicaland, Midlands and masvingo provinces"*. Matabeleland was not represented in the boards. Sindiso Mazibisa, a lawyer, commenting on the same publication noted, *"the brazen violation of the constitution by the minister ....more specifically section 18 of the constitution which says there should be fair regional representation in board appointments"*. Mbuso Fuzwayo of Ibhetshu LikaZulu, a pressure group demanded that the boards be dissolved and new appointments with respect for regional balance be made. The complaints fell on deaf ears.

The ethnic arithmetic was twisted from independence day and remained so for decades. Tension, conflict, contestations and hate are fermenting. There is subtle ethnic cleansing to guarantee Shona supremacy in all sectors. After the genocide of 1982 to 1987, the ZANU PF government relentlessly and successfully sowed the seeds of devious tribal genocide on the Zimbabwean soil. Over the years, the subtlety has fallen away and the bold manifestation of the 1979 Shona Grand Plan is plain for all to see.

One does not need to be a specialist of any kind to appreciate that the magnitude of the Matabeleland question is of such nature that it requires urgent surgery, otherwise it will inevitably transmute into a cancerous tumor of catastrophic proportions.

The principal argument is that the people of Matabeleland are denied an opportunity to participate in the governance of Zimbabwe. They are unremittingly excluded from all government structures, economically disempowered and socially subdued. After surviving the dressing down diatribe of mugabeism, followed by zanuism's vicious attempts to conflate and flux them into ZANU PF, then penultimately annihilation maneuvers by gukurahundism and ultimately the Gukurahundi genocide, Matabeleland deserves and is due for a respite.

Grievances from Matabeleland by varied individuals and organizations including civic society, churches, pressure groups and political parties, validate calls for justice, equity and fairness as much as it puts on historical record for posterity that a great sin was and is being committed. As long as past horrors are not laid to rest and current evils are not rectified, the people of Zimbabwe in general and Matabeleland in particular will subsist with the pervading fear of another Gukurahundi genocide, under the bondage of gukurahundism, the manipulation of zanuism and the puppetry of mugabeism.

Invariably, the passage of time will render justice too expensive or even entirely elusive. Many survivors, orphans, widows and widowers of the crackdown in Matabeleland have since died, pregnant with the undying hope for justice. Many key drivers of genocide, gukurahundism, zanuism and mugabeism have managed and will manage to get away with murder by dying before the evidently not long enough arm of the law catches up with them. Notwithstanding, the elusive nature of justice does not preclude its protective character. There has to be an earnest and honest quest for future security against similar horrific government pogroms.

Washington DC based, Genocide Watch, in 2010 officially classified the Matabeleland atrocities as genocide and called for the prosecution of Mugabe and his cronies for genocide and crimes against humanity over the Gukurahundi massacres. Its president Gregory Stanton called for the establishment of a mixed UN - Zimbabwe Tribunal to try Robert Mugabe and his generals. Many Zimbabweans, especially the victims and survivors of victims, whose voice should be supreme on this matter agree with this notion. The International Criminal Court is an ideal institution with jurisdiction over such crimes and as Enos Nkala suggested, Mugabe (*post obitum*), Mnangagwa and Sekeramai should be top of the list of those to be indicted at the ICC for master - minding the Gukurahundi genocide.

Sadly, the wheels of justice seemed to be square and the long arm of the law rather too short when it comes to the genocide in Matabeleland. If that was not so, Mugabe, Mnangagwa, Sekeramayi, Shiri and their hatchet men would have been tried and probably convicted by a special tribunal or at The Hague, long before they too started dying. It is quite possible that Mnangagwa who ranks high in the list of evil killers and despots like Mugabe, Jean Bedel Bokassa of Central African Republic, Ferdinand Marcos of the Philipines, Papa Doc Duvalier of Haiti, Idi Amin Dada of Uganda, Gnassingbe Eyadema of Togo, Ne Win of Mynmar/Burma, Stalin of USSR, Adolf Hitler of Germany, Mobuto Sese Seko of Congo and Saddam Hussein of Iraq, may elude justice like most of these men. The Zimbabwean gang should be charged with various crimes including genocide, persecution, murder, abduction, torture, unlawful detention, forced transfer, failure to protect, corruption and rape.

On 17 May 2011 the United Nation's International Criminal Tribunal for Rwanda (ICTR) sentenced Major General Augustin Bizimungu to 30 years in prison for crimes committed during the Rwanda genocide of 1994. He had been the head of the Rwandan army and orchestrated the mass slaughter by compiling inexorable lists of Tutsis to be exterminated.

In September 2014, AFP reported that the UN – backed tribunal for Rwanda in Arusha had upheld life sentences for Matthieu Ngirumpatse and Edouard Karemera, the former head and deputy head of the National Revolutionery Movement for Development respectively, for genocide, crimes against humanity and for failure to prevent or denounce the crimes committed by Interahamwe. The conviction in a small way pacified the hearts and minds of the survivors of the atrocities but also is a lesson for posterity and a bold unequivocal statement by international justice to all current and future human rights criminals.

One can only wonder why post – Gukurahundi genocide Zimbabwe was not treated in similar manner, while Kenyan electoral violence of 2007 attracted international justice. The Rwandan genocide and the elections related violence in Kenya happened long after the remains of the last victims of the 5th Brigade had decayed. The question why the UN, AU and the International Criminal Court (ICC) did not intervene like they did elsewhere is howling for an answer. Their interventions would have exposed the evil by interrogating the Gukurahundi genocide into the public domain.

All those that were in positions of influence in Mugabe's cabinet and in ZANU (1980 – 1987) should know that they are liable for prosecution on the charge of genocide, failure to prevent or denounce the Gukurahundi genocide among other charges.

Lamentably, genocide case studies and precedents of justice prevailing over evil are too few, relative to the crime rate. Consequently, some African leaders either missed the lesson or were too engrossed and consumed with the trappings of power to be capable of learning. Witness how by November 2013, African Union member states were appealing to the International Criminal Court (ICC) not to prosecute Kenya's Uhuru Kenyatta and his deputy Ruto who were on trial for crimes against humanity for the 2007 inter tribal election violence that killed 1200 civilians. Whatever it was that the concerned AU leaders were exposed to, had taken their reason prisoner.

The people of Matabeleland and parts of Midlands, insist on justice taking its course, in the form of a truth and reconciliation commission, reburial of victims and observance of cultural rites, payment of reparations for victims and the families, accelerated development for the marginalized regions, mental health and intervention programs for the traumatized as well as the re – writing of history to eliminate the bias in the ZANU PF version of patriotic history, among numerous other interventions. These are some of the issues that insistently come out of consultations, debates and other engagements with the affected communities.

Numerous solutions to the genocide, tribalism, domination, discrimination, marginalization, tension, hate and distrust that characterize the missing rapport between Matabeleland and Mashonaland, as evidenced in the skewed social relations, politics, economics, employment, land resettlement, resources distribution, budget allocation, development disparities, to name but a few, have been proffered by scholars, analysts and pundits. The theorized solutions are each a summation of a logical attempt at healing and bridging potentially explosive gaps within a polarized country. It is pertinent to discuss some of them with the view that someday soon there will be the political will to adopt and implement some or one of them so that future generations may coexist in peace and so that present generations are not judged harshly by history as a people that laid the foundations and maintained the pinnacles of tyranny by the majority, dominance of one tribe by another and entrenched the desolation of oppression by the dominant. Zimbabwe must make a break with black apartheid.

Zimbabwe must admit that, *"since the colonial era, African states have frequently been hampered by instability, corruption and ethnic violence. Great instability has mainly been the result of marginalization of other ethnic groups"* (Cocodia

2008:14). There already is ethnic conflict in Zimbabwe and utmost care must be taken to avoid it mutating into ethnic violence as what happened during the Gukurahundi genocide eon.

There is a lot of research, investigation, documentation and concept interrogation that has been conducted around the phenomenon of crimes against humanity the world over. There is information ranging from reports by international and regional organisations like the United Nations (UN) and the African Union (AU) to precedents from the courts of law. There are fortresses of knowledge banks ranging from the United Nations library to university libraries of both developed and developing countries with data on crimes of war, genocides, and the holocaust. Horrific details on the gruesome murders of innumerable individuals are available in all magistrates' courts in the world including Zimbabwe. There is information in computerised information systems, books, newspapers, magazines, journals and organisational files on mass killings.

Yet it is disheartening to realize that there is precious little information on the Gukurahundi genocide in private archives and zero official data in the files of the Zimbabwe government, UN, AU and SADC. There is very little knowledge among the ordinary people about the operation, outside of Matabeleland. Even in Matabeleland, it is only the victims that know what happened and those memories are subject to natural erosion. There are very few available records on the killings even within civic society and churches apart from the Catholic church and Legal Resources Foundation. There is extreme reluctance due to fear of gukurahundism, among all people including the victims to discuss the topic. The government of Robert Mugabe kept a very heavy and tight lid on the topic for close to four decades. To his credit, President Emmerson Munangagwa lifted the lid and allowed free discussion of the genocide.

The inadequacy of the amount of work applied to, and the dire lack of political will towards investigating, evaluating and documenting the Gukurahundi genocide in Zimbabwe is appallingly distressing and a cause for serious concern. Invaluable efforts by the Catholic Commission for Justice and Peace in Zimbabwe and by Legal Resources Foundation, after researching on a small sample of the affected areas revealed evidence that suggested that about twenty thousand people were killed by government soldiers in Matabeleland and Midlands. As a result of the restricted work by independent bodies and zero effort by the government, the numbers of the dead were open to conjencture, with recognized estimates of between thirty thousand and one hundred thousand dead between 1982 and 1987. Some have said that as much as five hundred thousand people were killed while as many as a million were displaced. The range in the above estimates was testimony to the fact that zero official effort by the state, was ever made to arrive at the quantum damage of the genocide in human, material, social, cultural, political, religious and economic terms. That is why President Mnangagwa had the temerity to tell the world at Davos in 2018 that the CCJP and LRF 20 000 figure was exaggerated.

There also has been isolated individual efforts to expose the enigma code named Gukurahundi, but all have either been conveniently ignored, dismissed or have been trashed as desperate attempts to foment disharmony and despondency among Zimbabweans. Former President Robert Mugabe and his ZANU PF government's Gukurahundi project qualifies for the world's best kept public secret. Otherwise how else could the murder of one hundred thousand elude international attention. One cannot help but admit that justice has been omitted and ghastly sins committed in the names of nation building, national security, stability, unity and peace in Zimbabwe.

If the international community, through the UN and OAU had taken stern measures against Mugabe for the Gukurahundi genocide, probably Rwanda 1994 would not have happened. Without belittling efforts done by a few brave individuals, the silence on the Gukurahundi genocide is intriguing. A movie called '*Sometime in April*' *was* made and another, '*Hotel Rwanda*' was made, both on Rwanda, amid numerous other exposes. Idi Amin and Mobuto Seseseko, were captured on video documentaries exposing them for what and who they really were. All the above work was vital, not only for information and posterity but for both restorative and punitive justice. Exposing evil the way it has been done in Rwanda helped bring some form of closure and reconciliation between the Tutsis and the Hutus. After the extensive exposure and healing missions undertaken in Rwanda, it is impossible to imagine any future government going that horrific route again. That, however cannot be said about Zimbabwe.

Justice delayed is justice denied. Facts on the Gukurahundi genocide, like anything that stays covered for more than 39 years, have become sterile, barren, elusive and inconclusive since they are subject to human memory. There is need for a UN appointed tribunal to conduct a full scale investigation into the Gukurahundi genocide. The tribunal should, among various mandates, establish the full extent of the damage caused so that a more specific number of those killed can be arrived at. That process will also kick start the wheels of justice. It is said that one cannot hide the smoke of the fire they make, but to date Mugabe and his gang have defied that wisedom, while international justice is standing by.

Fully cognizant of and in part agreement with the CCJP and LRF's recommendations in the Breaking the Silence, Building True Peace report, on national acknowledgement, violators of human rights, legal amendments, identification and burial of human remains, health, communal reparations, constitutional safeguards and on the future, the following submission is made:

The Healing Process

For the sake of future peace, it is mandatory and a basic inalienable necessity that a process to foster healing be embarked upon. Healing encompasses coming face to face with the past, despite its horrors, accepting the facts about what transpired, in order to be able to cope with the effects of the events without sensations and feelings of hurt and anger. Healing precludes erasing memories and covering the scars. It merely renders them non traumatic and deprives them of their capacity to evoke and spawn pain and suffering. Healing is a critical step towards reconciliation.

According to Ngwenya (2018:6), the search for national healing cannot sideline the need for individual healing because a nation cannot heal when the individuals that make up the nation are hurting. He continued to envision healing as, *"processes or strategies that rehabilitate or reconstruct the psychological, social and economic wellbeing of the affected communities and individuals"*.

In order for healing to take part there must be **forgiveness**. In the absence of forgiveness, healing is impossible. It is however critical to accept that forgiveness is not forgetting. One does not need to forget in order to forgive. What is imperative according to Elshtain (2003:48) in Ngwenya (2018:6) is *"knowing forgetting"* which he described as *"a way to release present day agents from the burden of the past, in order that they may not be weighed down by it utterly"*.

Forgiveness is neither excusing/tolerating the wrong nor is it giving up the demands for justice. The perpertrators need to know that their crimes/sins were/ are not acceptable and never will be acceptable and that the victims have a right to demand punitive and restorative justice even if they have forgiven (Ngwenya 2018).

Therefore as propagated by Enright et al (1998:46 – 47) and Staub et al (2005:301) in Ngwenya (2018:7), forgiveness, *"is willingness to abandon one's right to resentment or letting go of the anger and desire for revenge"*.

It is a fact that exposed evil is exorcised evil. Unless the Gukurahundi genocide is thrown into the limelight for public scrutiny and interrogation, it will forever remain dangerous, lurking and threatening the peace of all in Zimbabwe and Matabeleland in particular. The secretive veil covering the atrocities should be lifted through the rescinding of decrees and provisions that make it illegal to publicly talk, exhibit pictures or paintings, write books and make video documentaries and movies on the genocide and through the release to the public of the Chihambakwe and Dumbutshena Commission of Inquiry reports.

It has always existed in Matabeleland and to some in Midlands and Mashonaland, that the 5th brigade genocide should be openly discussed, in order to rest the case in a manner acceptable to the affected communities. Despite Mnangagwa's decree that the genocide may be publicly discussed, the presence of plain clothes security details during all public meetings including those under the auspices of the National Peace and Reconciliation Commission, display insincerity on the part of the government.

The genocide cannot be swept under the carpet forever. The extermination of a population estimated at 100 000, should, in the first be immortalized by being accorded the serious treatment it deserves by the perpetrators and the sufferers through official debate and interrogation. Therefore, the Mugabe government's criminalization of all efforts to expose their grisly and gory operation was not just a violation of human rights and freedoms but a permanent injury to peace. The arrest of Mr. Owen Maseko an artist who painted and displayed his impressions of the Gukurahundi genocide memories was one such example of an affront to demystifying and exposing crimes against the common people of Matabeleland and Midlands by the powerful tribal ZANU PF elite.

The process of debate and engagement would expose the lingering and often denied questions of distrust and suspicion between the two major centres of ethnic and cultural identity in the country and will aid the healing process.

There is a dire need for the observance of cultural rites, by urgently setting in motion a process of official mourning for the dead and the missing persons, by the respective family units/relatives and communities in general. For four decades the state has disallowed and banned the grieving process. From 3 March 1997 when security forces stopped a ceremony planned to give victims of the 1982-1987 massacres a proper and decent burial in the first public commemoration of the victims of the genocide in Gandangula in Matabeleland North [Deutsche Presse Agentur (DPA)] to 2016 when the High Court in Bulawayo allowed Ibhetshu LikaZulu to commemorate the genocide after the police had censured the event, the government has made sure that the deaths of the victims remained unmourned and unrecognized.

Talking about a national day of commemorating the demise of a large chunk of the Ndebele nation remains a sensitive issue that has been avoided for a period of almost four decades. This could be a once off period, or better still, a day in each calender year, to remind the country, the region and the world that life is sacrosanct and must be protected always, instead of commemorating non – existent unity every 22 December.

The importance of the processes of mourning and proper burial is embedded in the socio-cultural values of the typical African communities, as a requirement for other cultural ceremonies to take place. According to Ndebele culture, the spirits of the dead will never find rest until they receive proper burial. Reburial is essential. Thousands of victims were never buried, some were tossed into shallow graves that were later plundered by hyenas, some were compacted in mass graves, while some were burnt to ashes and many more disappeared. After reburial such rites as *umbuyiso, ukuthethela, ukwethesa* and memorials can then be effected at clan level by those that want to. Until that is done, the dead souls will be restless, will torment in various ways, the killers and even the relatives of the dead who should ensure the government facilitates their proper burial. However for reburials to ensue, proper exhumations by experts so that evidence is not tempered with, should be made.

Psychological scars have remained an awful price and a lingering reminder for the victims, the affected and the perpetrators. These have not been explored, addressed and documented. Once recorded, the detail is for posterity. Generations must know not only what happened to their relatives, tribesmen and women and fellow countrymen, but they will be aware of the side effects of the events as well. That will go down as a lesson in history. Future leaders will draw from it inspiration on how not to acquire and sustain power. They will know how not to govern, due to the knowledge of what damage their rogue actions may cause.

It is the official burden of the state to provide documentation of the atrocities. That darkest aspect of Zimbabwe's history needs to be officially recorded, not ignored. It should be a volume in the history section of all university libraries. Critical evidence is being obliterated by time and memory failure. Such social phenomena as HIV/AIDS is exacerbating the situation as entire families and victims have passed on with sad yet vital memories and episodes locked in their hearts. That loss of data is working in favour of the perpetrators, both living and dead.

A comprehensive and empirical list of all victims including the dead, the maimed, the displaced, those that lost properties including livestock, the dispersed and others adversely affected, must be compiled so that individual and communal reparation procedures may ensue. The list will alleviate the effects of lack of documentation e.g. no death certificates were issued for the victims to acknowledge the deaths or disappearances. The effect of that lack of documentation is evident on children and other dependents who cannot access birth certificates and therefore cannot attend school, cannot procure identity registration, therefore cannot be employed, cannot get passports, and therefore cannot travel. A monument with the names of all the dead victims must be constructed at one or many major sites where people were murdered or tortured e.g. at Bhalagwe in Matabeleland South, at St. Paul's at Lupane in Matabeleland North, on Joshua Mqabuko Nkomo street in Bulawayo and at Silobela centre in the Midlands.

Hundreds of thousands of victims and relatives of victims are in need of mental health intervention programs such as counseling therapy and medication for various Post Traumatic Stress Disorders (PTSDs). The state, with the assistance of Aid agencies and NGOs must initiate the provision of psychosomatic therapy and other psychiatric intervention strategies to help the survivors still suffering from disorders such as sleeplessness, depression, anxiety, traumatic psychoses, stress, schizophrenia, paranoia, psychosomatic reactions, character disorders and other neuroses.

Reparations have to be paid by the government to the surviving victims and relatives of the dead with accelerated development for the four regions (Midlands, Matabeleland North, Matabeleland South and Bulawayo) as a means of community reparations. The longer the process of reparations takes, the more complex it will get to calculate the quantum of the atonement and the identities of the beneficiaries.

The government must commission the re writing of history so that it captures all material facts without being selective or biased. It is the duty and responsibility of every government to be loyal to historical facts and candid to the truth, or the system of government becomes a sham hinged on falsehoods. The Mugabe and Mnangagwa regimes have paddled misrepresentations, twisted accounts, intentional omissions, half truths and blatant lies under the guise of *"patriotic history"*. It is zanuism and mugabeism in general but gukurahundism in particular, that saw the emergence of patriotic history championed by ZANU PF historiologists. As noted by Mlambo (2013), in that parochial and bustardized *"version of history, the other liberation movement, ZAPU, has virtually been written out of Zimbabwe's history"*. Patriotic history lays to naught the input of arch nationalists Joshua Nkomo and Ndabaningi Sithole, the founding president of ZANU PF while perpetuating the dissimulation that Mugabe was the father and founder of African nationalism.

Brown (2003:256) observed that, "...*history is always written by the winners. When two cultures clash, the loser is obliterated, and the winner writes the history books – books which glorify their own cause and disparage the conquered foe.... By its very nature, history is always a one – sided account.* Such is the character of Zimbabwe's version of history, more of a victors' fictional construct than a factual historical record.

There is therefore an urgent need for a non - partisan history account to be written by academics, while the current patriotic history is set aside, because Zimbabwe does not need a partisan school curricula with such examination questions as quoted by the Zimbabwe Independent of 26 March 2004. The questions were, "*which political party in Zimbabwe represents the interests of imperialists and how must it be viewed by Zimbabweans?*" and "*African leaders who try to serve the interests of imperialists are called what and how do you view patriotism?*". Apparently the education ministry was on a mission to poison the minds of young scholars against the MDC and its leadership of Morgan Tsvangirai. What Zimbabwe needs is a modern history text, written by professional academics and not by advocates, surrogates and apologists of ZANU PF. A non partisan account that embodies everything and everyone and that will not rely on the 1965 text by L.H Gann (Ranger 2010).

Another very imperative step that must be taken towards healing, is the setting up of a Truth and Reconciliation Commission (TRC) in the mould of the South African Truth and Reconciliation Commission chaired by Anglican Archbishop Emeritus Desmond Tutu in 1996. The commission should have as its members, individuals assessed and endorsed by a regional or international body such as SADC, AU or UN. At least two of the members should be appointed from or be recommended by the UN. The mandate of the commission will include the investigation of the Gukurahundi genocide through the holding of hearings on the origins, operations and the conduct of the 5th brigade in orchestrating the killings. The TRC will have the authority to summon any Zimbabwean citizen or other, for interviewing as well as to recommend prosecution by a special tribunal or by the ICC.

The National Peace and Reconciliation Commission Bill signed by Mnangagwa in January 2018 was a far cry from the envisaged TRC. The commission deliberately shunned the truth component because the government was not interested in true healing. The 'heroes' of the genocide were concerned with maintaining their hides intact and polished and not in the truth which would definitely leave them scarred. The commission itself did not inspire reconciliation as it comprised all Shonas and one Matabele. Speaking through an interpreter, the commissioners were chased away by community members from the Bretheren In Christ Church (BICC) in Bulawayo on 20 February 2018 and in Lupane on 26 February 2018. The people argued that the government, by appointing an exclusively Shona panel to address a genocide that they, rightly or wrongly, perceived as having been a Shonas – killing - Ndebeles escapade, was being salacious and insensitive. Some alleged that the government had sent its agents, probably the same 5th Brigade soldiers to come and gloat over the death of their relatives. To them the Mnangagwa government was not serious about healing the wounds of the genocide.

At the 15th anniversary of Joshua Nkomo's death, on 1 July 2014, his son Sibangilizwe Nkomo said, *"the birth pains of this nation were too prolonged and we are all still bleeding, years after the birth of our country. We've been torn between black and white, both suffered untold pain and it is time to let true healing. We've fought brother against brother, region against region..let's promote self healing and calm... I'm personally in pain and hurting. I believe you could also be bleeding too. Kodwa yithina esingaqeda lokhu ukopha (It's us that can stem this bleeding). It's time we seriously heal ourselves"* (The Chronicle, 2 July 2014).

Such was the noble make - up of Joshua Nkomo, manifested in his son. Plausibly, three and a half decades of hurting and bleeding had failed to heal Nkomo Jnr. and millions of Matabeleland denizens. It is almost as certain as day follows night, that over the years, the victims had attempted in their own varied ways to heal themselves because that is innate in all earthly living organisms. Nonetheless, if the hurting people had failed to self - heal in thirty - four years, how could they succeed now? After thirty - four years a condition becomes permanent and so were the wounds of the genocide. Sibangilizwe Nkomo's entreatment was to the effect that since the government was resolute in its refusal to responsibly bring proper closure to the wounds it inflicted on the people, the people had to learn to live with that fact.

When the perpetrator won't apologize, the victim becomes desperate for healing and attempts to heal themself. However noble the idea of self healing may be, it does not always work, especially under the circumstances prevailing in Zimbabwe. The reason why self healing failed was that the damage was simply too extensive and it was deliberately inflicted by a government that should have been protecting the people but pretended nothing ever happened. Instead of being conciliate and placatory, the government was seemingly triumphalistic while continuously propagating other schemata to accentuate the original infringement. How could the people heal when they did not even know what hit them and why? How could they heal while habouring fears that the government could attack them again? How could they self - heal, with ample evidence that the government still treated them with political and social contempt as well as economic neglect? How could they?

There were just too many questions that impeded any attempts at self - healing. All the odds militated against the notion of self – healing. Besides how could the common people who were not benefiting from ZANU PF's patronage and were still victims of its social and economic bellicosity, dominance and marginalization, even contemplate self – healing? The Gukurahundi genocide was still haunting them night and day, while gukurahundism, zanuism and mugabeism were wrecking and raping their livelihoods unremittingly. Who would they forgive since no one was accepting responsibility. What guarantees would they get that there would be no repeat of that *"moment of madness"*?

The task ahead of all leaders in general and the political leaders in particular and the nation at large is of mammoth dimensions and no less daunting. Ndebele - Shona interaction started off on a bad note and the entire relations structure has been contaminated. The time and severity factors have rendered the challenge of healing intimidatory and to some, insurmountable. The temptation to ignore and wish the problem dies a silent natural death is strong, yet it is as hazardous as the coping strategy of denial is perilous.

Reconciliation

Reconciliation, in the Zimbabwe context, is the process of causing the Matabele in general, but the Ndebele in particular and the Shona to find common ground and build a future relationship, despite past conflict, in order for the parties to coexist in harmony. Reconciliation, after the genocide and marginalization is not about reestablishing friendship, because that state of affairs was never there. Friendly relations are possible without parties becoming friends. Unless one chooses to be ahistorical, they must acknowledge that Matabeleland and Mashonaland have always been two different entities, subsisting side by side and did not need to be friends. Reconciliation will ensure that the two, enjoy mutual respect and do not have to fight or marginalize each other. Friendly relations. Reconciliation entails a commitment by all parties, to bury the hatchet in all its manifestations, to the principle of never engaging violence as a political tool to resolve differences, to create and respect democratic institutions, to embrace equality, to respect of the rule of law and not to extend any form of dominance over other ethnic groups.

Reconciliation may follow the healing process. It comes after achieving mental and emotional equilibrium resulting from the exchange of apologies and from seeking and obtaining forgiveness and after charting a way forward in order to inform future relationships between the victim and the perpetrator. Reconciliation, just like healing, does not engender amnesia by erasing memories and miraculously taking away the scars. Memories may linger vividly and the scars may remain to be addressed by time and natural progression whose pace varies from one victim and perpetrator to another. At times the scars remain as permanent features, reminding all about the horrors of the past.

In the Ndebele tradition, the process of reconciliation was aptly summerised in a rite called *ukukhumisana umlotha*. When two or more parties were in a bitter dispute, an intermediary would be assigned to reconcile the warring persons. The antagonists were given an opportunity each, to present their cases to the community elders and honestly empty their chests of all reservations, bitterness and anger. After all measures for justice and fairness had been followed, i.e. the requisite apologies had been proffered and fines paid if warranted, then *ukukhumisana umlotha* would ensue. One of the elderly sages would go into the forest for the correct herbes. The herbes would be burnt to ashes and then mixed with other potions. The ashes would then be served on an *udengezi* (a special plate for burning medicines) and offered to the feuding persons. The parties in dispute would then take turns to dab their forefingers in the ash (*umlotha*) and then lick it with their tongues from the finger (*ukukhumisana*). Once the ash was finished, the elders would declare the dispute over, for eternity. The two would swear not to pursue the matter anymore and never to raise it up by way of revenge or retribution. The issue immediately became part of their history, valid only for the purposes of teaching future generations, like the common folk lore stories. Pursuing the matter after the rite would be tantamount to insolence, impunity and contempt for the very foundations of the community, an act frowned upon by the offender's ancestors and community leaders, punishable by sentences of varying intensity including excommunication and banishment from the community.

History, religion, science and nature are yet to conjure up a substitute for reconciliation as the only building block to lasting peace. Zimbabwe is nowhere close to that almost mythical discovery of all times. Instead of attempting to re-invent the wheel thereby pulling a rug over the challenge, the country must face it head-on, like the South Africans deed under the icon Nelson Rolihlahla Mandela, who commissioned the Desmond Tutu presided Truth and Reconciliation

Commission. Anything less will be preposterously insulting to all citizens, especially to the people of Matabeleland.

The *sine qua non* to reconciliation is the **truth**. There can be no reconciliation without truth telling. The truth, the whole truth and nothing but the truth, no matter how unpalatable, uncomfortable and bitter. It should be told. The truth about how, who, what, when and why the Gukurahundi genocide, must come out in order for sustainable and lasting healing, reconciliation and peace to be achieved. Hence the assertion that the National Peace and Reconciliation Comission (NPRC) of 2013 which deliberately excluded the truth component, was a farce and a pillow sham. The NPRC was just another half measure like the unity accord of 1987, the ineffective National Healing, Reconciliation and Integration Ministry which was co-led by then Vice President John Nkomo, minister Moses Mzila – Ndlovu and minister Sekai Holland (2009 – 2013) and the Human Rights Commission which was confined to crimes after 1999. Those purportedly democratic institutions were maliciously designed to be instruments for short circuiting the peace building process. The Mugabe and Mnangagwa governments wanted to go for broke in order to achieve 'unity' and peace at the expense of the truth. They did not care if the people of Matabeleland were still hurting and bitter, as long as they joined ZANU PF, attended their rallies and voted for them en masse.

In a Truth and Reconciliation Commission (TRC), the architects, the generals, the foot soldiers, youth brigades, ZANU PF party functioneries, security agents, former dissidents and the government executives of the genocide era, will have an opportunity to tell their true stories and get a chance to ask for forgiveness if need be as well as get a chance to forgive. Those who perpetrated brutalities may want to clear their consciences and meet the families of those they executed in order for them to have peace with themselves, men and God. The survivors, and the victims will also be accorded a chance to tell the world the grizzly details of their heart-rending encounters and experiences, to a victim friendly panel of commissioners. The length and breadth of reconciliation is embodied in the truth coming out.

Of critical value is the exercise whereby victims will come face to face with their violators. Some of the people that were tortured and or whose relatives were murdered will engage in a dialogue with the perpetrators of those acts and get to pour out their hurts, pain, grief, fears, tears, thoughts and feelings. That is an indispensable and incontrovertible step towards resolution, reconciliation and closure. That way there is something and someone to reconcile with. Peace, therefore becomes a natural by - product that an individual arrives at once attaining psychological equilibrium which in turn can only result from reconciliation. That kind of peace is not a political concoction or mantra. It is the genuine kind that will reflect in the day to day social discourse and even on social media which currently is characterized by the most vile hate language between Ndebele and Shona people.

Speaking at the funeral of Joshua Nkomo in July 1999, Mugabe begrudgingly branded Gukurahundi, *"a moment of madness"*. That harebrained explanation on the side of Nkomo's casket, was the closest Mugabe ever came to admitting his actions were wrong and apologizing for his Gukurahundi theatrics. Otherwise over the years Mugabe had always adeptly eschewed conviniently from the topic. Those in his inner circle in ZANU PF or in government always either skirted aloof around the subject or outrightly stated that they had no regrets about the genocide.

During a South African Broadcasting Corporation (SABC) interview with journalist Dali Tambo in 2013, Mugabe, when asked about Gukurahundi was visibly perturbed and stammered and bumbled a response;*"..it was very bad, we don't want to talk about that, but it is, it is a story which has not been told in full, how it started and so on, you know what was happening, its not a story that we should continue. You see, when wars do occur, it doesn't matter the forms of the war, it hurts, you know what soldiers do on the ground, even when they are under instructions, there is always the personal. Sometimes they go out of their way to commit acts which are outrageous, so those things happen, but also on the guerilla side, they committed atrocious atrocious things, cutting off people's noses and ears, but people emphasise what they allege are the acts of the soldiers but are silent completely on what the guerillas were doing".*

It was sad to note that at that twilight moment, at an age of nine decades, given what could easily turn out to be his last chance to cleanse his soul, Mugabe, who was still as sound as a bell was still prevaricating and would not accept responsibility for his actions. He was still shoveling blame around. Interestingly, no soldier had been court martialed in line with military rules for disobeying orders and killing civilians. That alone rendered his response as hollow as an old pipe. Noteworthy however, was his reference to *"guerillas"* and not dissidents or insurgents. Probably deep down his old heart, he knew that the so called dissidents were people fighting for a just cause and the *"dissidents"* were his own creation.

Mugabe's argument that individual soldiers committed atrocities on their own volition in violation of their orders was as spurious as was his tacit claim of insanity. The Matabeleland and Midlands chiefs on 28 June 2019 disagreed with Mugabe. They informed President Mnangagwa that the people who committed the wholesale murders did so on behalf of the state. In the presentation, the chiefs stated that, "…*the perpetrators were employees of the state, were paid and housed by the state, were funded by the state, were transported by the state, carried state – issued weapons and ammunition, flew the Zimbabwe flag in their bases and offices, were promoted after the atrocities, are earning retirement benefits from the state, and were not arrested or in any way punished by the state for the crimes they committed, and, most importantly, the state did not at the time and since that time, distance itself from the crimes…..the government of the day had the right, ability and duty to control the actions of those who committed Gukurahundi atrocities on the ground because they were acting in its name and were accountable to it. It chose not to exercise this power*".

The undiluted message by the chiefs to Mnangagwa was that, the world over, soldiers got promoted and were allowed to eventually earn a retirement benefit for obeying orders, for acts of valour and for ensuring the security of the citizens. Therefore, they were saying that the promotion of the Gukurahundi crew, especially the commanders who rose through the military ranks while some became cabinet ministers, ambassodors to foreign countries, CEOs and directors of state enterprises, was an appreciation of their obedience to orders and for doing a 'good' job. How did Mugabe promote Perence Shiri to commander of the Air force and how did Mnangagwa promote the same to cabinet minister after the 2017 coup, if the soldiers under his command had butchered 100 000 civilians in violation of their orders and the military rules of engagement? Clearly, the soldiers had carried out their orders to the latter. Hence, Mugabe's, was a hypocritical and malicious lie.

Nowhere in the world is a president or leader of a country allowed to be mad. It is against the constitution of all countries for a president to lose his / her sanity and still continue to occupy that office. Once that happens, the president is declared "*incapacitated*" and is replaced by another of a sober disposition and free from insanity. Whether his madness had been momentary from 1982 to 1987 or was permanent, Mugabe should have stepped down from the office of Prime Minister during that years - long moment of madness. It was also critical that Mugabe, Mngangagwa and their cohorts should have been informed that honour and reconciliation were more than a mere admission of madness, but both hinged precariously on a full confession preceding an apology.

The most imperative and requisite step towards resolution, reconciliation, justice, closure and probably forgiveness is an admission by the state that a gross wrong was done by the government against the people of Matabeleland and parts of Midlands. After the admission then an official apology by the state to the victims, the survivors, the region, the country and the whole world for committing genocide, war crimes and crimes against humanity.

Once the state has admitted its culpability and apologized officially, then the uninhibited confessions by the individual architects and the foot soldiers under the supervision of a properly constituted institution like a truth commission, as suggested below can follow.

Instead of being evasive, Mugabe and Mnangagwa as the successive heads of state should be resolute and follow the above steps or do better, without equivocation. Anything short of that will always be justifiably construed for cosmetic, window dressing, an insult to both the dead and their memory as well as scorn to the intelligence of the surviving victims of the Gukurahundi genocide.

At the Bulawayo State house meeting with President Mnangagwa, the Matabeleland and some of the Midlands chiefs on 28 June 2019 presented their position on the need for an apology for the genocide. They said, *"It is a fundamental principle of both domestic and international law that the obligations of an entity at law do not terminate or cease to exist in consequence of change of leadership. Just as much as Zimbabwe should benefit from the assets that accrued under the previous government, it should in the same manner take responsibility for the liabilities. Debts must be paid and obligations fulfilled because they were assumed in the name of the state. The same applies to Gukurahundi atrocities. The state committed the atrocities and therefore the state should assume responsibility for the atrocities and issue an official apology and in our constitutional architecture, the state is represented in the office of the Head of State".*

If Mugabe was indeed a catholic, he, for the good of his soul, could have disclosed his sinfulness before a priest in the sacrament of penance in the hope of absolution. Thereafter for the public good, he could author and sign a document acknowledging his crimes and petition the surviving victims and relatives of the dead to forgive him, even after he had been ousted from power. He could also admit his sins and crimes before a truth and reconciliation commission. His successor Mnangagwa, after inheriting Mugabe's legacy and being an architect of the genocide as well, could have seized the opportunity to rectify the issue on his advent. However, both missed that opportunity to date.

Omar Hassan, of the Kenya National Commission on Human Rights, on 21 December 2010 said *"peace and Justice are mutually supportive, there cannot be one without the other".* The people of Matabeleland and parts of the Midlands cry for justice. Peace without justice is like a windowless room but with an air extractor, it suffocates the breath out of the occupants. That has proved to be the litmus test for the Mugabe and Mnangagwa regimes. A temerity and propensity for shamelessly empty unity rhetoric, minus any attempt at justice is as hypocritical and misguided as it is Machiavellian. It is murderously oppressive.

The way Mugabe insisted on and pontificated about unity every time he opened his mouth to speak, betrayed its absence as much as he condemned himself for insincerity. It was false peace that was achieved at a deliberate exclusion and omission of truth and justice. False peace and unity are what was obtaining in Zimbabwe from Mugabe to Mnangagwa.

There can be no question as to the need for peace building and nation building, especially by the Ndebele and Shona. While people from both ethnic groups need not be sorry for who they are and need not despise the other, they both need as a matter of necessity and Godly decree to accept the other as dissimilar yet equal. That mental paradigm and attitude is indispensable to peace and reconciliation but is only feasible after the full course of admission, confession, apology and justice has been undertaken.

Prince Zwidekalanga Peter Khumalo, a direct descendent of King Lobengula wrote an article which was published in the Weekly Agenda of 2 - 8 May 2009, page 6, titled *National Healing: Ubuntu Perspective*. He argued that;

"The situation on the ground is such that due to some heinous acts by the outgoing government, such as a deliberate planned massacre of innocent and defenseless people in Matabeleland and the Midlands (through Gukurahundi).......there is immense anger among those who suffered the brunt of that cruelty. The intensity of the anger is so much that it represents absence of peace.... and remains a potentially explosive situation that may one day lead to serious retributive and vengeful action by the aggrieved...... It is for this reason that the issue of national healing and social reconstruction is necessary in this country.. The aggrieved and the perpetrators should be identifiable humans. The perpetrators should admit that they performed the acts and are apologetic..

...The understanding is that the Shona massacred the Ndebele people in cold blood.. There is need to research and create a correct bank of knowledge to prepare for a national healing process. The process should not be seen to give automatic amnesty. Some people who are not prepared to accept that they are guilty may have to go through the normal justice system".

Prince Zwidekalanga acknowledged that there had been no attempts to heal the gaping wounds inflicted by the 5th Brigade on the Matabele people in particular and the Zimbabwean landscape in general. The open wounds had been exposed for too long and had attracted a lot of irritation and infection in the form of tribal foreboding and suspicion which could culminate in vengeance missions in future. He pointed out the common misnomer in many circles, that the Gukurahundi massacres were deliberately conceived and orchestrated stratagems by the general Shona people to exterminate the Ndebele, yet the truth is that it was the machinations of the government elite.

The tragedy in locking away information is that the resultant dearth of knowledge on the subject, instead of helping arrest runaway flawed perceptions, actually perpetuates dangerous falsehoods. It is patently and painfully incontestable that the killings were well premeditated and executed. The cold, callous and sadistic ingenuity of the conceptualization is equally self evident, but can not be blamed on all the Shona people. Culpability cannot be generalized but can be arrived at through the full process of healing and reconciliation as outlined above.

Prince Zwidekalanga (2009) asserted that both the victims and the perpetrators should be identified so that there can be complete and frank face to face reconciliation. He stated that while in pursuit of healing and reconciliation, there should not be a blanket general amnesty for the perpetrators. That idea brings to the fore, the amnesty granted in 1980 at the stroke of freedom, by the British Governor Lord Soames to all that had committed war crimes during the liberation struggle for independence in Zimbabwe.

Some of the beneficiaries of the 1980 amnesty went on to commit similar and worse crimes during the Matabeleland genocide and were again amnestised by Robert Mugabe in June 1988. Through the 1988 amnesty Mugabe pardoned himself of genocide but did not cleanse his soul, as evidenced by the springing up of gukurahindism, zanuism and mugabeism from the ashes of the 5th Brigade, like the Arabian phoenix known for burning itself to death only to emerge from its ashes as a new and stronger phantom. The 1988 amnesty was criminal and those that derived refuge from it against indictment for crimes against humanity from the period of 1982 to 1987 should be liable for prosecution by a competent tribunal or by the International Criminal Court (ICC)

It is only after healing and reconciliation over the Gukurahundi genocide that the country may start talking about the possibility of a harmonious co – existence between Matabeleland and Mashonaland. Even at that juncture, 'unity', a rather Utopian concept under the circumstances, may still be out of the equation. Only after reconciliation can there be peace. It is noteworthy that unity is not synonymous with peace, neither is it a prerequisite to peace. What the Zimbabwean anatomy needs in bountiful measures, are generous dosages of peace and not the poisoned arrows of 'unity'. Mugabe, Mnangagwa and ZANU PF's much vaunted 'unity' only left the Matabeleland side of the body suffering with economic amputations and social perforations. It is in Matabeleland that the saying *'peace is not the absence of war'* holds true. It was in Matabeleland that the last gunshots of war were heard in 1978/9, yet the region has known less peace and worst turmoil than Southern Rhodesia during the war.

Another vehicle through which healing, reconciliation and peace can be achieved is by adopting the recommendation in the Washington Post of 26 February 1983. Rev Robert Mercer, the bishop of the Matabeleland Anglican church, in 1983 called for an independent investigation of the genocide by Amnesty International or the International Red Cross.

Since the recommendation by a white bishop was not adopted, maybe a more recent one by a traditional leader of the victims, Chief Vezi Maduna Mafu of Avoca in Filabusi in Matabeleland South will be. On 13 November 2018 Chief Maduna wrote a letter to the UN secretary general Mr. Antonio Guteres, after he had failed to get a response from President Emmerson Mnangagwa, requesting for a tribunal or commission to investigate the Gukurahundi genocide. According to the Standard Newspaper, Chief Maduna observed that, *"since the government of Zimbabwe is led by a Shona tribesman who was highly involved in the perpetration of this crime against humanity, he is seriously compromised to set up an effective and objective commission to look into these atrocities".* The elderly chief went on to recommend members for the investigative tribunal. He recommended King Goodwill Zwelithini of KwaZulu in South Africa, Chief Felix Nhlanhlayamangwe Ndiweni of Ntabazinduna, Chief Mathema, Chief Fuyane (all from Matabeleland), Advocate Thuli Madonsela (former South African Public Protector), Dr Godfrey Stanton (USA, Genocide Watch), Moses – Mzila Ndlovu (former Zimbabwe cabinet minister), Ms Conolezza Rice (former US Secretary of State), a male and female survivor of the Gukurahundi genocide, the UN Human Rights Chief, Prince Zeid Raad Al Husein, a CNN journalist, a member of the pathologist firm that investigated the Yugoslavia genocide, a member of the pathologist firm which investigated the German Jewish holocost, a sitting female judge from the ICC, a member from the Israel Actuary firm, the President of the UN office on Genocide Prevention and Responsibility to Protect, and lastly Mr. Nothiwani Dlodlo (Chief Maduna's secretary).

Once the Investigative Tribunal, as proposed by Chief Mafu and or the TRC exhausts its mandate, the onerous task and the final step in reconciliation will be deciding on the nature of existence and kind of relationship to be established or maintained between Matabeleland and Mashonaland. The best possible and ideal setup and relationship has been a headache and a source of tension and friction to many scholars, journalists, authors, pundits, parliamentarians, lawyers, ordinary people, Mugabe and Mnangagwa. A number of attempts and proposals on the nature, character and form of that setup and relationship have been explored. Hereunder are some of them.

Installation of the Ndebele King

The installation of the Ndebele King within the Zimbabwe constitutional framework and not necessarily restoring the Mthwakazi state, has been recommended by many as part solution to the Matabeleland question. Mr. George Mkhwananzi, a Ndebele historian and scholar, addressed some of the pertinent aspects on why, how, who and what, about the resuscitation of the Ndebele monarchy. Below is his presentation which was given soon after the government of Zimbabwe had denied the Matabeleland chiefs, the Khumalo clan and the general Matabeleland public, the right to install Prince Bulelani Lobhengula Khumalo, as King of the Ndebele on 03 March 2018. The Bulawayo High court had concurred with the government that the planned coronation was unconstitutional.

Mkhwananzi observed that, *"..we need the institution of the King to: reverse the cultural and linguistic erosion suffered by the multi – tribal Mthwakazi nation.. lead our people on a crusade to conserve our culture and language against all forms of threats...revive some of our ancient but relevant cultural heritage and ceremonies such as inxwala, umhlanga, umthontiso and ukusoka...spearhead efforts to recover our lost and stolen land and 800 000 heard of cattle...spearhead the development in the region through proper land administration, ukusisa system and isiphala seNkosi...make final adjudication on all referral cases from the chiefs.."*

when the colonization of our country occurred in 1893, the Ndebele nation lost.. their land which they have not recovered. People were evicted from within 150 km of Bulawayo to be resettled in the semi arid Gwayi Reserve (Tsholotsho, Nkayi and Lupane)..the new King will have to lead the rectification of this history of dislocation....They lost their cattle. Thomas Meikles and his brother presided over the Looting Committee which was set up to collect 800 000 cattle belonging to the Ndebele and distributed them among themselves and their African batsmen.

The government of Zimbabwe cannot champion that agenda. The King will lead the rectification of this history of dispossession in which the government of the United Kingdom has a case to answer.

They lost their monarch. The Ndebele people are the only people who lost their institution of the King to colonization...They lost their independence. Arguably this is the only thing which was achieved after the demise of colonialism but many still feel that Mthwakazi never regained her independence since 1893, her colony status was simply inherited by Zimbabwe".

Mkhwananzi went on to contend that, *"Being an old institution does not make it irrelevant. Royal families are symbols of national unity and sources of pride. Many countries including the English still have genuine affection for their monarchies. These include the Netherlands, Spain, Denmark, Belgium, Luxemburg, Norway and Monaco...South Africa, Swaziland, Lesotho, Zambia, Uganda, Nigeria, Morocco etc....As part of the strategy to deny the Ndebele people of any rallying point, Cecil John Rhodes and his cronies exiled most of the King's boy children in South Africa or England. These princes included Njube, Mphezeni and Nguboyenja. Njube was banished to the Cape colony and is the direct ancestor to Prince Bulelani Lobhengula Khumalo who has been identified as the successor to the throne".*

"In the 1950s, the advent of African nationalism caused a slump in the demand for the revival of the monarchy because the nationalists said it could wait until independence was won by Africans. When constitutional talks for independence came in 1979, the nationalists ducked the issue even when both Ian Smith and the British government raised it. Ndebele people were actually let down by the leaders of the Patriotic Front co – led by Joshua Nkomo and Robert Mugabe who selfishly marginalized the issue.

Mkhwananzi further pointed out that, *"…Free people do not beg their government for permission to practice their culture. They notify the government.....No Ndebele seed, let alone the cub of the Matabele Lion, is a foreigner in Mthwakazi, no matter how long they stayed in forced exile...the objective of exiling all the eligible princes to South Africa was to defeat the resolve of the Ndebele to revive their monarchy. By overlooking the foreign – based Ndebele princes, the elders will be double – punishing the royal descendants after an injustice first done to them by Cecil John Rhodes. By appointing Bulelani, the elders have reversed Cecil John Rhodes'125 year long temporary victory..."*

It is most lamentable that the government of Emmerson Mnangagwa elected to join the list of previous administrations that had denied the Ndebele people their right to practice their culture by restoring their monarchy. However, many a Ndebele were praying that it be only a matter of time before their cultural, biblical and Godly desire was fulfilled.

It was as plain as a pikestaff that the decision by both the government of Mnangagwa and the High court, to bar the coronation of the Ndebele King at Barbourfields stadium in Bulawayo on 03 March 2018 and the violent dispersal of throngs of people that had come to celebrate the momentus occasion, by anti – riot police was ill informed, malicious and tribal. Speaking to The Standard newspaper of 04 – 10 March 2018, chief Mathema, chairperson of the Crown Council that was organizing the event, did not mince his words in expressing displeasure at the government's ineptitude.

Chief Mathema ruefully observed that, *"..more than a 100 years after, we have a black led government that still has a mentality of the Pioneer Column that destroyed the Ndebele Kingdom...as black people, we are different, we have different traditions and cultures and government must just respect that. I think government is being paranoid to think we want to cause cession, no, far from it".*

The government which is run by a majority tyrannical elite, does not want the Ndebele people to have a rallying point, an institution that for thirty - one years since the demise of PF ZAPU would enjoy the 100% loyalty of all the Ndebele. Such a centre of power and source of inspiration, pride and guidance is perceived as a threat to the state. The Ndebele monarchy evokes not only their paranoid fears but their jealousies as well. The people in charge of government do not have dreams, let alone plans of having a king(s) according to their culture, probably because their pre – colonial political structure was somewhat fluid and not as disctinct, discernible and defined like the Ndebele Kingdom. It would be difficult if not impossible for Mashonaland to have a king. They therefore concluded that a king is not necessary within the Zimbabwe boundaries.

Chief Mathema went on to clarify that, *"..a lot of people now have a feeling that this is all about tribalism since a certain tribe is being stopped from wanting to enjoy and practice some of its traditional practices. People are being beaten up simply for wanting to respect their tradition....if that is not tribalism, what is?*

It was a striking irony that a black High Court judge, dressed in Western, strange and foreign regalia and a black cabinet minister, both whose offices were a product of colonialism, were barring the traditional coronation of King Bulelani

Lobhengula Khumalo in Bulawayo. If the minister was not a mouth piece of Cecil John Rhodes and the Pioneer Column, he should have cited the section of the Zimbabwe constitution that would be violated by the coronation of the Ndebele King. Furthermore, he should have caused a motion to be moved in parliament, that a legal instrument be quickly put in place to legalise the coronation. Instead of being facilitative and affirmative, which is the role of government, the minister opted to be inhibitive.

Besides, the Ndebele people did not expect the government to financially support the monarchy. The monarchy would not be a burden to the country tax payer per se. As opined by George Mkhwananzi, *"….. whatever budget for the sustenance of the institution of the King will be defrayed by the tourist revenues he is expected to rack in…. The King will live in his palaces which we expect to be constructed in the four provinces where the King's jurisdiction extends; that is Bulawayo, Matabeleland North and South as well as Midlands province"*.

A Rotational Presidency

A rotational presidency within a unitary state was proposed by ZANU PF reformists at the Tsholotsho declaration in 2004. What was most valuable in the Tsholotsho declaration (discussed above) resolution was, its accommodation for diversity which is integral to a democratic dispensation. The spirit in the resolution was that, in order to embrace ethnic harmony, regional fairness, equality as well as *"national cohesion, peace and stability"*, ZANU PF should have embraced a constitutional order that was reminiscent of the Tsholotsho Declaration resolution. That way all regions and tribes would get a chance to, from the office of president, influence policy and engender development. Not only would the state president and the two Vice Presidents come from different tribes at all times but those positions would rotate among the country's four major ethnic groupings of the Matabele (Matabeleland), Zezuru (Mashonaland), Karanga (Masvingo) and Manyika (Manicaland).

That formula was going to see the country, within a forty year period having a Matabele, Zezuru, Karanga and Manyika president for a maximum of two terms each, assuming ZANU PF remained in power that long. If such a policy had been adopted at independence in 1980 the country would be under the leadership of a fourth president by 2020. Zimbabwe would not have been under the monopoly of the Zezuru and Mugabe for thirty seven years under that arrangement. With such an ethnic groups accommodating constitution, probably ZANU PF would not have had to be coercing and buying people into their ranks and forcing and beating them into voting for the party.

Devolution of Power

"Devolution simply means a legal granting of powers from central government to lower levels of government such as provincial, district or municipal tiers. It is a political and financial issue as it involves election of local representatives by local people and giving those lower levels of government a budget that is normally administered by central government" (Moyo 2012)

The Zimbabwe constitution that became law in 2013 after a long period of public consultations, provided for devolution of power within a unitary state. The ZANU PF government which was vehemently anti devolution of power made double sure that the devolution provision remains a paper - only concept. Years after the constitution became law, the government is yet to put up the requisite policy and structural changes to facilitate full implementation as regards the devolution of power clause.

The reluctance of the government to embrace the new constitution in its fullness is not surprising, considering that the powers that be, did everything to convince the populace not to endorse the devolution of power proposed clause during the constitutional outreach program that culminated in a referendum. A lot of persuasion and convincing had to be made for the majority Zimbabweans to say yes to devolution of power during the constitutional consultative meetings, to the disenchantment of the centralist regime. Civic groups and opposition political parties were at the forefront of calls for devolution of power.

Some of the reasons projected in favour of devolving power were that it would result in the voices of the majority poor being better heard and in improved quality of and better access to public services by the poor (Jutting et al (2005). Kauzya (2007) argued that devolution of power strengthens accountability and transparency by leaders to the communities they serve. Some in Zimbabwe argued that that model of governance would result in spatial equity and in enhanced development as provinces would take charge of planning, implementing, monitoring and evaluating their budgets and capital projects. For example, Matabeleland North would manage her forestry, wild life and tourism, while Matabeleland South exploited the gold reserves she is endowed with. Manicaland would specialize in the exploitation and refining of diamonds while Midlands would bank on platinum revenues and the Mashonaland provinces would concentrate on agriculture.

The centralized system of governance was rejected by the majority of Zimbabweans because, *"highly centralised systems of governance, combined with bureaucratic top-down decision making systems tend to impose decisions on people at the grassroots level."* (Rukuni, 2003)

Advocating for a centralist unitary system of government and doing all they could to project devolution of power as evil, ZANU PF came up with all arguments against the policy and practice of devolution of power. Protecting their overtly fragile and fraudulent 'unity', they argued that the system would divide the people. In a bizarre scenario of a fish claiming fear of water, they claimed devolution of power would promote corruption. They even claimed the country was too small to devolve power.

It was due to arguments by many, including the one below by the then MDC National Executive Council member and policy secretary Dr. Qhubani Moyo in the Independent of 23 March 2012, that carried the day; *"It is quite clear, the current system of a highly-centralised state as we have in Zimbabwe has promoted autocracy, inefficiency, corruption and exclusion of people from full participation in how they are governed. Devolution can certainly help to address some of these problems.....claims by Mugabe and Chombo that devolution divides people are not just misleading but also false....... In fact, devolution, instead of dividing people, promotes equitable distribution of resources and above all national cohesion.*

The only reason why Mugabe wants to maintain the current system is that it enables him to control and run the country like his backyard. We have all seen what the results of that approach have been. So his argument is completely driven by self and not national interest....... The truth of the matter is, devolution in our context is mainly about social justice and equitable distribution of resources. Mugabe and the likes of Chombo are responsible for the current patterns of uneven development in the country and have presided over systematic impoverishment of some regions which are rich in natural resources but don't benefit because of the failures of central government"

Civic society organisations especially those under the banner of the Matabeleland Civic Society Consortium (MCSC), were very loud in calls for devolution of power. Dumisani Nkomo the CEO of Habbakuk Trust, a member of MCSC summed up the position of civic groups in an article in the Independent of 23 March 2012 when he posited that;

"Corruption and inefficiency can be curtailed through inbuilt mechanisms to ensure transparency and good governance. Basic standards can be set at a

national level while region-specific instruments can be put in place to address issues peculiar to geographic and ethnic communities.

Centralised governance has resulted in centralised corruption, but devolution of power....... will significantly increase public scrutiny thus ensuring sound stewardship of resources.......... The key here is a well-defined governance architecture with elected governors who have budgets and operate with an executive and provincial authority or government...... Devolution will lead to equitable distribution of resources throughout different regions and disadvantaged regions will benefit from equalisation mechanisms through central government fiscal instruments. National cohesion will actually be enhanced because Zimbabwe's various ethnic groups....... will be promoted through the efforts of accessible and empowered regional and local governments, which are able to craft policies which are relevant to local conditions and experiences..... Citizens will be able to influence and participate in decision-making thus building strong local democracies, which is the basis of a healthy national participatory democracy. Devolution is not a problem; it is a part of the solution".

The people listened and voted overwhelmingly for devolution of power in the referendum. The people ignored Mugabe and Chombo's criticisms of devolution of power which were clearly desperate efforts at maintaining ZANU PF and Zezuru hegemony. The people built so much hope in a new people - centred devolution of power model. Yet because they wielded political power and the national purse, ZANU PF, until Mugabe was ousted from power ignored the constitution and continued with the centralist system of government. According to media reports, Mugabe's self – appointed successor, Mnangagwa's administration, upon assuming office, were threatening to amend the constitution by scrapping off the devolution of power clauses, should they win a two thirds parliamentary majority in the 2018 elections. By 2019 that threat was still not substantiated but had been replaced by promises of implementing devolution of power.

Federalism

In post independence Africa, one of the challenges resulting from numerous colonial governments, was development bias in favour of towns whose development needs tended to subordinate those of the rural areas. That phenomenon was a result of a number of factors including a lack of planning foresight propagated by short term economic reasons. The Zimbabwe post - colonial eon saw the propagation of that Centre – Periphery theory (Raagmaa 2003), with Harare being the centre and hub of all development, while the rest of the country, especially Matabeleland became the underprivildged periphery.

Since independence day, Zimbabwe has been characterized by successive ZANU PF governments that have presided over what Mazrui (1980: 78) termed the *"sub - regional distortion"*. He noted that in many African countries, some regions are more developed than others, resulting in a *"burden of uneven development"*. He used the example of the Buganda sub - region of Uganda, which was more developed than its neighbours to the extent that it acquired not only extra economic, political and social leverage over other regions, but also incurred their jealousies and mistrust. He went on to state that the phenomenon of uneven development had contributed to chronic instability as a consequence of ethnic confrontations. Mazrui's account read very much like a summery of the Zimbabwe indictment. It lined up with the observation by Suberu (2003), that ethnic conflict was resultant from the disgruntlement of some ethnic groups with the dominance of other groups that were given preferential treatment by the government.

Zimbabwe is entangled in a self - made vicious *cul de sac* of uneven development, whereby local economic opportunities (jobs, loans, tenders, investments, land allocation etc) in Matabeleland have become an exclusive holy terrain and preserve for the Shona. While most meaningful development (dams, roads, schools, hospitals, colleges, universities, shopping malls etc) happens only in Harare and Mashonaland, the proceeds from Matabeleland natural and mineral resources are whisked away to the capital *in toto,* never to benefit the source. That disparity has engendered feelings and emotions of neglect, jealous and even enmity as the Matabele claim a piece of the developmental cake while the government treats them as second class citizens and lazy cry babies.

Tormented by that differential treatment, Matabeleland civil rights movements, politicians and community leaders have been leading a sustained demand for decentralizing government political, administrative and financial authority in a decentralised or federal setup. The first call for a federal governance system was made by the Ndebele paramount chief of Ntabazinduna, Khayisa Ndiweni, when he formed the United National Federal Party (UNFP) in 1978. One of the reasons for Ndiweni's call for federalism was historical. Matabeleland had existed as the Mthwakazi State beside Mashonaland before the two were bundled into one country by colonialists in 1923.

Federalism is a practice of governmence whereby states are created or agree to *"grant control of common affairs to a central authority but retain individual control over internal affairs"* (Collier's Standard dictionary). Moyo (2012) defined federalism as, *"the sharing of power to govern between the national and state or provincial governments as defined by the constitution".*

There was a very strong voice among some, that Zimbabwe must be a federal country in the mould of Nigeria, the USA, Germany etc. The root cause for recent demands for a federal system of governance are primarily the glaring contemporary inequalities between Matabeleland and Mashonaland in terms of economic and development opportunities. In addition to the economic disparities between the regions, the Gukurahundi genocide was projected as one event in history that indicated that each of these regions should manage its own affairs with minimum interference from the other. Due to the neglect of human, social, infrastructural and economic development in Matabeleland by the government for almost four decades, the locals felt they needed political and governmental autonomy so as to determine their own development trajectory.

They wanted a federal government whereby power would be split or shared between the central government in Harare and the constituent states (Matabeleland, Masvingo, Manicaland and Mashonaland). That would require a new constitution to allocate duties, rights, and privileges to each state. The constitution would define how power is shared between national government and the constituent states. The power to amend the constitution would be granted to the citizens or their governmental representatives (Kincaid, 2011). The individual states that make up a federal government would have their constitutions which would be subservient to the federal constitution.

It was envisaged that such a setup would allow a welcome degree of autonomy to Matabeleland, Masvingo and Manicaland provinces which play economic second fiddle to the three Mashonaland provinces. It was further assured that that type of self - government would bring about a diplomatic arms - length relationship among the provinces, thereby avoiding friction and conflict since each would be responsible for her own social and economic development.

Japhet Ndabeni Ncube, a Human Rights Commisioner, a former ZPRA scholar who studied economics at Lancaster, Wales and the USA before becoming mayor of Bulawayo in 2001 argued (interview 12 February 2017, Bulawayo) that federalism should have been adopted as a system of governance at independence in 1980. He stated that he was studying in UK by the time of the Lancaster House talks. At that time, other ZAPU students based in London authored a position paper on federalism as requested by the Ndebele paramount Chief Khayisa Ndiweni of Ntabazinduna in Matabeleland North. Before submitting to the conference, the proposal to restore the two states of Mthwakazi and Mashonaland to their original status of 1890 neighbors, the chief had sought to convince and obtain the support of the nationalist politicians. He presented his idea of a federation of Matabeleland and Mashonaland on the sidelines of the conference to Joshua Nkomo and other nationalists but it was shot down. Consequently, the notion of the restoration of the Mthwakazi state was swept away by the tide of nationalist politics. That is how the fate of the state of Mthwakazi was once more decided, without their requisite input or that of their traditional leaders.

Barber (2017) contended that pretending that Zimbabwe was one country, *"is a dangerous hallucination". The country has to be divided into two federal states of Mashonaland and Mthwakazi (Matabeleland). The issue of the statehood of mthwakazi should have been resolved at the pre – independence negotiations in 1979 and the error was a tragic constitutional omission on the part of the delegation led by Joshua Nkomo. It should not have been assumed that the Mthwakazians embraced the Zimbabwean identity. That assumption has never been put to test. This has to be achieved by negotiation under the auspices of an independent body of the United Nations".*

According to Dabengwa, Nkomo in a private engagement with Chief Ndiweni had expressed his precarious predicament in that, while he understood the latter's cause, he had been advocating and even fought a war in the framework of a nationalist republic of Zimbabwe with a unitary governance system. Turning around so late at Lancaster and demanding a federation of Matabeleland and Mashonaland would have portrayed him as one throwing spanners into the attainment of independence. That would have been a call to delay the negotiations or even thrown them into disarray. Besides, Nkomo would have needed to consult not only ZAPU leaders and structures but Zambia's Kenneth Kaunda and Botswana's Seretse Khama who were neighbors and sponsors of ZAPU / ZPRA.

What probably made it even more difficult for Nkomo to support the federation concept was the composition of his ZAPU team. Despite his right hand men such as Chinamano, Msika, Munodawafa, etc (all Shona) having proved that they regarded Ndebeles and Shonas as equals, there was no guarantee that they would continue respecting Nkomo's leadership once he embrassed federalism which has never been popular among the Shona people. Secondly, Nkomo had been unsparingly criticized by the likes of Leopold Takawira and the entire ZANU bench led by Ndabaningi Sithole, Herbet Chitepo, Enos Nkala and Robert Mugabe for initially acceding to the 1961 constitution. They had mercilessly castigated him and called him irresolute. Changing his position into supporting federalism was definitely going to convince many that his critics had been correct. Another factor was that Nkomo at Lancaster was almost assured of leadership of the Patriotic

Front which would catapult him into the Zimbabwean presidency. Therefore he would not have wanted to rock the boat.

Lastly, probably Nkomo had never been amenable to the concept of federalism as advocated for by the Ndebele paramount Chief, Khayisa Ndiweni. Chief Ndiweni, a son of former Chief Gundwane Ndiweni, King Lobhengula's maternal uncle and King Mzilikazi's trusted Induna, had been appointed Ndebele paramount chief by Queen Lozikeyi (King Lobhengula's wife) after the king's death. The Queen had appointed him to that role so that he could lead the resuscitation of the Mthwakazi / Ndebele state. Hence his creed of federalism, which the chief hoped would preserve what still existed of the Mthwakazi kingdom, which would in turn restore the monarchy. The traditional Khumalo monarchy of the Ndebele would bring about complications in its interactions with nationalist politics, some nationalists and probably Nkomo as well, thought so. Nkomo's dream had always been that of a united republic with invisible or even non – existent boundaries between Matabeleland and Mashonaland. Therefore, Nkomo and Ndiweni's ideologies were seemingly at odds. Nkomo wanted Zimbabwe while Ndiweni wanted Mthwakazi.

In his denial of federalism, Joshua Nkomo must have assumed that his stance was popular and was shared by most nationalists even from the ZANU / ZANLA stable. He could not have been more wrong. While Mugabe and his ZANU retinue favoured nationalist politics and the establishment of a Zimbabwe republic like Nkomo, they were fighting for a unitary Shona state which was also preferred by the British government. The British could not envisage a scenario where the Ndebele wielded any political power, because the latter could easily demand for redress for the crimes of colonialism such as the slaughter of about 12 000 civilians by the B.S.A. Company, the razing and burning to the ground of their capital Bulawayo, the looting of property including hundreds of thousands of cattle and the probable murder of their king, King Lobhengula Khumalo in 1893. A ZAPU / Ndebele government was not practicable to the British, because even if they would not make demands for redress for historical crimes, their cooperation was a far - fetched ideal because of those crimes. What the British needed at the decolonization stage was to install a very compliant and pliant administration.

Federalism at a time when the ill – fated Federation of Rhodesia and Nyasaland was still fresh in the minds of many, stood no chance. The idea of federalism of Matabeleland and Mashonaland therefore was still – born. However modern scholars of politics and economics are increasingly buying into the concept whose strengths are as compelling as its weaknesses are not insurmountable.

Federalism has proved to be what the doctor prescribed for many economies even in developed countries.

Secession

Due to the numerous reasons already discussed above and due to ZANU PF's intransigence in refusing to respect the Zimbabwe constitution by devolving power into a three tier authority set up of central, provincial and local governments, the calls for the recognition and the restoration of the two pre – colonial states that were amalgamated by the colonialists in 1923 intensified. The late Dr. Edwin Ndabezinhle Mkhwananzi, the founder of Mthwakazi People's Congress and Mthwakazi People's Convention was credited as one of the pioneers of the concept of the restoration of the Ndebele monarchy through a referendum in Matabeleland (Bulawayo 24 News). The restoration process, within the discourse dominated by a vocal heterogeneity of political and civic organizations within Zimbabwe and in the diaspora, has been referred to as secession or self determination, depending on the writer/speaker. Whatever political nomenclature one prefers to use, the idea is about having an independent or sovereign state of Matabeleland.

It has been stated above and elsewhere by various scholars and historians that Mashonaland as a region and a collection of numerous small polities, was colonized by the B.S.A. Company in 1890, in the most peaceful (without use of war) of processes. Matabeleland on the other hand was colonized by the B.S.A. Company in 1893 after the most inhuman and barbaric bloodbath in the region before the Gukurahundi genocide of a hundred years later. In March 1896 the Ndebele rebelled against colonial rule. The Shona also revolted against the company three months later in a war against imperialism and foreign domination whereby the company fought two separate wars simulteneously. Both the Ndebele state and the Shona, were defeated by superior weapons of war used by the British. The Matabeleland Order in Council of 1894 by the British, was used to legalise the subjugation and to rule the territory by conquest. The two nations faught their wars distinctly and separately. Even after they were defeated, they remained distinct and separate.

In 1914 the Matabele National Home Society (MNHS) was formed. Its thrust was to advocate for an autonomous Matabele homeland, free from B.S.A. Company rule. In the same year, Prince Nyamande Khumalo (King Lobhengula's son) and the MNHS organized a series of prolonged protests against white administration. Instead of giving Africans back their independence and land, the settler administration tightened the screws of domination by crowding Africans into native reserves.

In 1918 the Matabeleland Royal Council sent a delegation led by Prince Nyamande, to Britain to petition the Queen to grant Matabeleland her independence. Once more the call was dismissed.

It is a historically uncontested fact that for almost three decades the two territories had been governed separately by the B.S.A. Company until its charter power was terminated in September 1923 when the two territories were annexed as one British colony. In October 1923 the territory was granted 'responsible government', i.e. the status of a self governing British colony. The 'responsible' aspect of that government remained elusive as it proved to be extremely irresponsible towards Africans. That is how in 1923 Matabeleland and Mashonaland were irresponsibly and recklessly amalgamated into one country.

The colonialists under Cecil John Rhodes, clubbed together for their own economic, political and personal interests, with blind and arrogant disregard for local ethnic disparities and political dynamics, the two kingdoms plus other smaller entities, into what they selfishly called Southern Rhodesia. It is a combination of that tumultuous history characterized by a profusion of interactions of Western imperial force, coercion, collaboration, negotiation and dissent and numerous grievances centred around tribal domination, discrimination, marginalization and genocide by the ZANU PF regimes, that has seen the emergence of voices for the secession of Matabeleland from Zimbabwe. There is a strong sentiment with many advocates in Matabeleland and in the diaspora that Zimbabweans must reconcile and secede.

Secession according to Maru (2008) is an act of pulling away or disengaging from a union, a political or geographical entity and acquiring a sovereign or independent status. Examples of countries that have successfully seceded include South Sudan in 2010, Serbia and Montenegro in 2006, Slovenia, Somaliland, Eritrea, Kosovo, Herzegovina, Yugoslavia and Croatia. It is a right of the people of Matabeleland and Midlands and any other region for that matter, to aspire and campaign for secession. That is a right, despite of the Constitution of Zimbabwe amendment (No. 20) Act 2013 chapter 14 stating in the preamble that, *"whereas it is desirable to ensure: (a) the preservation of national unity in Zimbabwe and the prevention of all forms of disunity and secessionism....there must be devolution of power and responsibilities to lower tiers of government in Zimbabwe".* It would appear as if the ZANU PF government eventually relented to devolve power on condition the people would never demand for secession. The terms secessionism and secessionist were tarnished into becoming synonymous with disunity, tribalism and conflict, yet they too can represent a people's democratic ethos.

Notwithstanding, the demands for secession have grown in leaps and bounds. That is largely because the government showed reluctance to devolve administrative, political and fiscal (Work 2000) functions of the centralist government to provincial councils and local authorities. The Matabeleland region was hopeful that devolution of power would usher in equitable distribution of resources, infrastructural development, employment creation, local self determination among other expectations. Six years down the line, with devolution of power still as remote as it was before it became law in 2013, the people of Matabeleland and parts of Midlands are demanding their right to secede.

According to Moyo (2011), *"(t)heir (secessionists) demands are fortified by the fact that both the opposition and ZANU PF government do not seem to prioritize the need to endorse a non - biased historic record of the Gukurahundi genocide which might give closure to the Ndebele.......It is this legacy of impunity and state sanctioned amnesia which has bolstered this community's demands for internal and external self-determination. In an international legal system which applies equally to all, secession would be ideal since the group has a shared culture and is territorially based. In any event, a Ndebele monarchy which was divorced from the rest of the Shona territory existed before colonialism. Further, this community has fewer prospects of effectively participating in the country's governance"*

There are very compelling ideas for the secession of Matabeleland from Zimbabwe and not surprisingly, there are voices from Mashonaland in support of the idea of independence for Matabeleland. Although it is natural that the rider is more comfortable in a horse and rider relationship, it is vindicative to note that some modern generations of Mashonaland Zimbabweans appreciate the need for others to be free and enjoy their right to self determination.

Any views on the separation of Mthwakazi from Zimbabwe coming from the ruling ZANU PF have been anything but tolerant. According to Mugabe, *"Zimbabwe is one entity and shall never be separated into different entities. It's impossible. I am saying this because there are some people who are saying let's do what Lesotho did. There is no Lesotho here. There is one Zimbabwe and one Zimbabwe only.* (The Sunday Mail, 20 November 2005)

Of course, expecting Mugabe to have thought differently would be the same as expecting the sun to rise from the west. From before independence was attained in

Zimbabwe, Mugabe wanted to create a monolithic Shona nation state, ignoring the existence of the multitudinous languages, cultures, and pre colonial boundaries. Without proffering any reason beyond his personal feelings or stopping to listen to what the people of Matabeleland themselves had to say, he, like many of his supporters dismissed talk of an independent republic of Matabeleland or Mthwakazi as outright nonsensical. Mugabe's attitude towards the secession of Matabeleland was a summation of the feeling of many in ZANU PF.

How ironic and tragic that those people who radically demand their own freedom from oppression will deny others their freedom. They will go out of their way to fasten hard, the chains that oppress others. That is what the ruling elite of ZANU PF has been doing unremittingly to the people of Matabeleland.

The very vocal voices for a separate state of Mthwakazi include the pressure groups, Umhlahlo WeSizwe sikaMthwakazi, Ibhetshu LikaZulu, the 1893 Mthwakazi Restoration Movement, and the UK based Mthwakazi People's Congress and political formations like the Mthwakazi Liberation Front (MLF), the United Mthwakazi Republic (UMR), the Mthwakazi Liberation Organisation (MLO) and the Mthwakazi Republic Party (MRP). The view has gained a lot of currency with the advent of a facilitative social media where radical or revolutionary views can be exchanged rapidly without harassment by state security apparatus. All these organizations also articulate that the Mthwakazi State is not home to the Ndebele alone but to all the ethnic groups in the region represented by present day Matabeleland, parts of Midlands and parts of Masvingo. They all unanimously converge at the core of a non tribal and all embrasive Mthwakazi State, home to all ethnic groups within its pre – colonial boundaries.

One of the powerful proponents of secession was the late former ZAPU secretary general, former prisoner of the Smith Regime, former prisoner of the Mugabe regime and former Governor of Matabeleland North, Mr. Welshmen Mabhena.

Welshman Mabhena, in Gatsheni - Ndlovu (2008), in correspondence with the British embassy in 2007 contended that, *"(y)our excellence, you may be surprised to hear that I usually get lost when I come across people who mix up my country Matabeleland with Zimbabwe, because Zimbabwe is a former British Colony which was colonised in 1890 and granted independence on 18 April 1980. While my homeland Matabeleland is a territory which was an independent Kingdom until it was invaded by the British South Africa Company (BSA Co) on 4 November 1893, in defiance of the authority of Her Majesty Queen Victoria. Actually in terms of the Moffat Treaty of Peace and Unity of 11 February 1888 between Queen*

*Victoria and King Lobhengula, Britain and Matabeleland were allies, and due to
our respect to our late King we have not renounced this vow"*

Mabhena went on to file a court case demanding a review of the verdict of the
Judicial Committee of the Privy Council on the land case of Matabeleland on
the 19th of July 1918 by the British Government. In the application he argued as
follows;

*"I also submit that the Respondent went further to legalise the said contraband
contract through the proclamation of the Matabeleland Order-in-Council on 19th
of July 1894…The Respondent further ruled through the verdict of the Judicial
Committee of the Privy Council in 1918 that: 'The Ndebele Sovereignty had been
broken up and replaced by a new, better system as defined by the Matabeleland
Order-in-Council of 1894'……….*

*In 1980 again the Respondent went further to use the said order as the legal basis
of simultaneously decolonising Mashonaland with the status of an independent
Republic of Zimbabwe, to which it consequently transferred the mandate of ruling
us, in Matabeleland by conquest to black majority supremacy regime comprising
of Shona tribes through 'The Constitution Order 1980 (S.I. 1980 of the United
Kingdom) made 19th March 1980.' an act which has perpetuated tribal domination
for 27 years bringing the duration of repression in Matabeleland to a total 114
years.* (Ndlovu - Gatsheni 2008).

Those calling for the separation of Matabeleland from Zimbabwe argue that
the Mthwakazi State should be based on the pre – colonial boundaries. The
Mthwakazi boundary with the Boer Republic / South Africa to the south was
the Limpopo river as is today. The boundary with Barotseland / Zambia to the
north was be the Zambezi river as is today. The boundary with Bechuanaland
/ Botswana to the west was the Shashi river as is today. The boundary with
Mashonaland / Zimbabwe to the east was the Jameson line (Tokwe river and
Sanyati river) as it should be today.

UMhlahlo weSizwe sikaMthwakazi lobbied the British government through its
embassy in Harare to facilitate the process of secession, since they were legally,
politically and militarily involved in the subjugation, colonization and eventual
semi - decolonization of Matabeleland (Matabeleland was not entirely decolonized
because it was handed over to Mashonaland to dominate in the same way it was
dominated by the British before 1980). The British embassy washed their hands
of the case by claiming that it was not within their jurisdiction. UMhlahlo also
filed court cases in British courts with the view of having them revoke the legal

instrument, the Matabeleland Order in Council of 1894, but the wheels of justice do turn slowly and heavily. UMhlahlo also petitioned the United Nations whose universal declaration of human rights supports the self determination bid of minorities. Nothing has come of it yet.

During an interview on 29 March 2017 in Bulawayo, Welshman Ncube said that in order to restore the Mthwakazi state, there has to be done a secession. He then pointed out that woefully, there was no precedent of a secession ever done peacefully, even in the so called civilized world. The price of a secession, he observed, was that people had to take up arms and make war and some had to die. He argued that there could not be a secession by constitutional argument or by media debate. The only examples, he noted were where people went to war, faught to a stalemate, then negotiations ensued, resulting in secession. He posited that those that were genuinely and sincerely advocationg for secession should know that they could not talk the government into seceding but had the choice to go to war for it. He advised that people could choose to fight peacefully for equality, for recognition, to reverse marginalization, to vote in ways that will make it impossible for people to dominate others, or choose to go to war.

Welshman Ncube stated that his personal and his party position was that what was realistic and achieveable without going to war was devolution of power whose foundations were already in the national constitution. He said the challenge was finding ways of putting in power people who believed in it and who would allow devolution of power to take place. He said since it was impossible to secede lawfully without going to war, the only other option was federalism. However, seeing that it was difficult to secure the less threatening devolution of power, the federal state would even be more difficult to achieve. Therefore, according to Ncube, people had to demand for devolution of power. He said, *"there are things which are doable without treason, and devolution is doable without treason. The other option, you have to defeat the existing political and legal order and you cannot do that without going to war with it".*

On whether or not the Matabeleland Order in Coincil of 1894 could be used as a legal basis for restoration, Ncube said, *"the Mthwakazi state ceased to exist by conquest. It didn't cease to exist by the 1894 Order in Council. The 1894 Order in Council was legalizing a military victory which had taken place on the ground. The Mthwakazi state was not legislated out of existence. It's pointless to be legalistic....some people from Mashonaland want to pretend that there was always a country called Zimbabwe or there was one country. Historically there was Mashonaland and there was the Mthwakazi state. There were two countries, colonized on different dates. I don't think we should be debating whether or not there was a Mthwakazi state. It was there. It's a fact".*

Ncube argued that in 1980, when the British decolonized Rhodesia, they should have been asked to restore the boundaries which existed when they conquered the two. They were not asked to do that because *"all of us wanted to talk as umntanenhlabathi / mwana wevhu (son of the soil), one big fictional Zimbabwe. Zimbabwe is a colonial construct. It did not exist before colonialism. That is a fact, but its not a legalistic issue. If the British were to reverse it, they would say, we conquered you, we now restore you. Not because of the legal instrument which announced it but because of the military victory they scored on the ground. You go political not legal... The British gave power to Mugabe because we all then were seduced by the fiction of umntanenhlabathi and that all the nationalists were nationalists, believing these things about being equal. The reality is that now we have marginalization and subjugation of other people because the mntanenhlabathi / mwana wevhu mantra was simply a political fiction".*

It was easy, convinient and yet selfish for anyone like Mugabe to simply engage in a tirade of lambasting the notion of seceding the two regions, without addressing the chief reasons given for the desired separation. The position of being the ruling aristocratic majority, coupled with random access to the armoury and being life time beneficiaries of gukurahundi, gukurahundism, zanuism, and mugabeism has rendered the executive impervious to common logic when it comes to the demands from Matabeleland. Many even in the opposition and civil society get indisposed to objectivity on the secession debate. Besides, they have grown accustomed to subconsciously accept Matabeleland as their domain, political protectorate and economic hunting ground, so much they can not even contemplate letting her go. The political clout and rich economic pickings from Matabeleland and Midlands are simply too much to forego.

Lamentably some Matabeles have tasted the sweet crumbs that fall from Harare's sumptuous dinner table and are happy to be like the abused wife with access to the husband's visa card. The relationship between Matabeleland and Mashonaland vis a vis secession is typified by the analogy of the rodeo master and the performing gorilla. The master has ownership of the gorilla because he paid money for it or risked life and limb to capture it from the dark and dense jungles of the Congo. It is his source of livelihood. Occasionally he canes it or denies it food to instill discipline but he also provides it with shelter and other essentials. The offspring of the gorilla are born into captivity and the cage is all they know. Since the gorilla is ever in a cage and leash, he no longer recognizes them to be the shackles of a prison and symbols of abusive tyranny. The cage has been part of his life for so long he feels sound and secure in it.

From a distance the picture of the gorilla - in – the - cage is beautiful and audiences are captivated and entertained by its performance on stage. After the stage show they all retreat to the comfort of their homes and the gorilla to his confinement while the master counts his cash.

If the master was asked to release the gorilla, he would refuse and project all sorts of reasons including sound ones, as to why the gorilla should never be granted freedom. White colonialism projected 'good' reasons against independence for Africans. That was precisely what Ian Smith was saying and doing from 1963 to 1979. He was the master. From 1980 to 2017, Mugabe was the master, From 2018, Mnangagwa and tribal nationalism have been the masters and are counting their cash. They will not allow Mthwakazi to be free.

Some of the gorillas grow to like the cage and become extremely grateful to the master for the bananas. Even if it is left unlocked they will not step out and if left outside the cage, without the leash, they will not wander away because they feel vulnerable and incomplete outside the cage. They will voluntarily walk back into their prison and even attack those of their kind who want to leave the cage.

The danger with such a setup is double pronged. The gorilla is a wild animal with primate animal instincts which may be suppressed to extinction or which may awaken someday posing a danger to the gorilla, the master and the audience. The second danger is that the gorilla will die someday. Once deprived of his income, whom the master will cage next is anyone's guess. The quadrominium trap of Gukurahundi, gukurahundism, zanuism and mugabeism is capable of being perpetrated by anyone and can ensnare anyone in future, therefore it is prudent to help dismantle it today even if one thinks they are presently not a victim.

As in the gorilla analogy, attempts to liberate a people that have been oppressed for long and some of whom have been benefiting materially from the oppression, can be very dangerous to the liberator. Many a liberstor has met with vehement protests, insults, threats as well as violence at the hands of those they attempt to liberate. At times the oppressed kill or commit suicide out of fear of their own freedom.

Such is the mind of the oppressed. It is denoted by the mania that informs such supper scribes like one Michael Mhlanga (2017) to claim that Bulawayo has, *"a legion of political parties, all contesting against each other on who is more angrier than the other and who is more Ndebele than others...who can wail louder about Gukurahundi than the rest...* Obviously Mhlanga was making a mockery of MLF, MRP and all that have reservations, and grievances with the Gukurahundi genocide. The fact that he was accorded space in the Sunday News to write his lengthy polemic which was clearly a bid to endear himself to Harare and prove that he was a 'beautiful Matabele', shows that he was indeed a pitiful yet sated servant of the anti – Ndebele crusade.

A 'beautiful Matabele' is one that will roast his tribesmen over burning coals in a bid to delegitimize their victimhood in order to position him / herself on the right side of gukurahundism, zanuism and mugabeism.

Mr Siphosami Malunga, director of Open Society for Southern Africa and the son of the late ZAPU spokesperson Mr. Sydney Malunga, observed that, *"on Gukurahundi no efforts will succeed to delegitimize victims, including myself. I don't need anyone to validate me or my victimhood...I am a victim and there are thousands others"*(News Day 15 January 2018). Scribes like Mhlanga would want the people of Matabeleland and Midlands to be silent about their victimhood and make believe that they are at peace with the Mugabe, Mnangagwa and ZANU PF governments

✒ ✒ ✒ ✒

It is the right of the people of Matabeleland to decide their destiny and to not consent to be governed by the people of Mashonaland. Whether they want to be an independent state or to continue being a province of Zimbabwe is entirely theirs to decide. They must put their case forward for debate and consideration in the Zimbabwean parliament, SADC, AU and UN. They can pursue any course of action that is constitutional, to achieve their independence and freedom. Harare has no right to unilaterally say no to the restoration of the Mthwakazi state.

The Zimbabwe state may have a lot of reasonable sounding, yet selfish reasons to stifle debate and throw delaying spanners into the works. The fact will always stand out like a thorn on the Zimbabwean flesh. Matabeleland has a right to self – determination. The issue may be decided by a referendum where only the people of Matabeleland will participate. That is not without precedence. It happened elsewhere, including in Scotland, Kosovo and South Sudan.

The great question that only Matabeleland can answer is; **Quo vadis Matabeleland?** Will Matabeleland continue to subsist only for the sake of existence under the yoke of tribal dominance, subjugation and marginalisation or will she aspire to survive for the pursuit of independence, freedom and self-determination? Will she avow?

"when in the course of human events it becomes necessary for one people to dissolve the political bands which have connected them with another, and to assume among the powers of the earth, the separate and equal station to which the Laws of Nature and Nature's God entitle them, a decent respect to the opinions of mankind requires that they should declare the causes which impel them to the separation".

The Declaration of Independence, 1776

References

Alexander, N.J, McGregor, and Ranger, T. (2000<u>) Violence and Memory: 100 Years in the Dark Forests of Matabeleland.</u> London: James Currey.

Austion, R. (1975) <u>Racism and apartheid in Southern Africa Rhodesia.</u> Paris: The Unesco Press.

Barber, D.H. (2017) <u>Matabele Rising</u>. Footprint Press.

Beach, D.N. (1986) <u>War and Politics in Zimbabwe, 1840-1900</u>. Gweru: Mambo Press.

Berlyn, P. (1978) <u>The quiet man,</u> Salisbury: M. O. Collins (PVT) Ltd.

Bhebe, N and Ranger, T.O. (1995) <u>Soldiers in Zimbabwe's Liberation War</u>. Harare: University of Zimbabwe Publications.

Bhebe, N. (1999) <u>The ZAPU and ZANU Guerrila Warfare</u>. Gweru: Mambo Press.

Bridger, P. (1973) <u>Encyclopaedia Rhodesia</u>. Salisbury. The College Press Pvt. Ltd.

Bridgland, F. (2008) Pius Ncube – Silenced. Sunday Herald Scotland 22 March 2008. Available at <u>www.sundayherald.com</u>

Brown, D. (2003) <u>The Da Vinci Code.London</u>. Transworld Publishers

Bwititi, K. (2011) Tsvangirai benefited from tribalism. The Zimbabwe Independent Sunday, 23 October 2011 01:52 Local News

CCJP (Catholic Commission for Justice and Peace) and LRF (Legal Resources Foundation). (1997) <u>Breaking the Silence, Building True Peace: A report on the disturbances in Matabeleland and the Midlands, 1980 – 1989</u>. Harare: CCJP and LRF.

Chikane, F. (2012) <u>Eight days in September: The removal of Thabo Mbeki</u>. Johannesburg: Picador Africa.

Cocodia, J. (2008) Exhuming trends in ethnic conflict and cooperation in Africa: some selected states. African Journal on conflict resolution, Vol 8 Number 3. Accord

Coltart, D. (2016) <u>The Struggle Continues: 50 Years of Tyranny in Zimbabwe</u>

Dictionary of the English Language, Fourth Edition copyright ©2000 by Houghton Mifflin Company.Updated in 2009.

Doran, S. (2015) The Dialy Maverick

Gama, L. (2009) Gukurahundi Massacres: Lessons drenched in blood. Newzimbabwe.com

Hill, G. (2003) <u>The Battle for Zimbabwe: The Final Countdown.</u> Cape Town: Zebra Press

Hole, H.M. (1932) <u>The Passing of the Black Kings.</u> Bulawayo: Africana Book Society.

Hunter, G. Farren, L and Farren, A. (2001) <u>Voices of Zimbabwe: The pain, the courage, the hope.</u> Weltevredenpark: Covos Day.

Johnson, M and Clark, M. (1984). Zimbabwe: Terror in Matabeleland available at <u>http://www.time.com/time/magazine/article/0,9171,951050,00.html#ixzz1T QnqPbg0</u>

Jorgensen, J. J. (1981) <u>Uganda: A modern history</u>. London Croom Helm.

Jutting, J, Corsi, E and Stockmayer, A. (2005) <u>Decentralization and Poverty reduction: Policy insight No. 5</u>. Moulineaux: OECD

Kauzya, J.M. (2007) <u>Political decentralization in Africa: Experiences of Uganda, Rwanda and South Africa</u>, New York: United Nations.

Kincaid, J. (2011) <u>Federalism</u>. Thousand Oaks: Sage Publications Ltd.

Mabhena, C. (2014) Ethnicity, Development and the Dynamics of Political Domination in Southern Matabeleland. <u>IOSR Journal Of Humanities And Social Science</u> (IOSR-JHSS) Volume 19, Issue 4, Ver. III (Apr. 2014), PP 137-149 . www.iosrjournals.org www

Mabhena, W. (2007) Re: The Question of Matabeleland. Letter 30 May 2007

Macaphulana, D.N. (2010) Ncube: when the truth is not enough, The Zimbabwe Independent 07/12/2010

Macaphulana, D.N. (2011) Welshman Ncube: sins of the fathers, The Zimbabwe Independent 11/02/2011

Mahomva, R. R. (2013) Power Struggles in Zimbabwe: The Legitimization of Mugabeism and the future of Zimbabwe after the 2013 fate. Leaders for Africa Network.

Mambo, E. (2015) General Threatens to Combat Mujuru, the Zimbabwe Independent 02/10

Mandaza, I. (2016) The Political Economy of the State in Zimbabwe: the Rise and Fall of the Securocrat State. The Zimbabwe Independent 8 April

Mandela, N. (1994) <u>Long Walk to Freedom</u>. Randburg: Macdonal Purnell (Pvt) Ltd.

Maphenduka, J. (2015) <u>The battle for Mthwakazi, Rule by Conquest</u>. Bulawayo

Mashingaidze, T.M, (2005) The 1987 Zimbabwe National Unity Accord and its Aftermath: A Case of Peace without Reconciliation?

Mathuthu, M. (2004), Black murder, White murder. The story of Zimbabwe. Newzimbabwe.com

Matikiti, R. (2012). <u>Christian Theological Persepectives on Political Violence in Zimbabwe: the case of the United Church of Christ in Zimbabwe</u>. Harare: University of Zimbabwe.

Maru, MT. (2008). <u>Devolution of power and its role in strengthening Good Governance</u>. Presented to the Public Discussion Forum for Political Parties organized by African Initiatives for a Democratic World Order. Addis Ababa: United Nations Conference Center.

Mazrui, A.A. (1980) <u>The African Condition: The Reith Lectures</u>. Ibadan: London Heinemann.

Meredith, M. (2005) <u>The State of Africa: A History of Fifty years of Independence</u>. London: Free Press; Simon & Schuster

Meredith, M. (2007) <u>Mugabe: Power, Plunder and the struggle for Zimbabwe's future</u>. New York: Public Affairs

Mhlanga, B. (2015) Mugabe our god: Kasukuwere. The Zimbabwe Independent 24 February

Mhlanga, B. (2009) On the psychology of oppression; blame me on history. Critical arts, 23. <u>http://dx.doi.org/10.1080/02560040902738990</u>

Microsoft, (2005) Encarta Encyclopaedia.

Misihayirambwi – Mushonga, P. (2010) Ndebele President: The fear, The Zimbabwe Independent 09/12/2010

Mlambo, A.S. (2013) <u>Becoming Zimbabwe or Becoming Zimbabwean: identity, nationalism and state building in the historical context of Southern Africa</u>. Hamburg: GIGA. Available at <u>www.africa-spectrum.org</u>

Mpofu, W. (2013), Entanglements of tyranny, puppetry and Eurocentric knowledge, *The Thinker* Vol 56, pp 10 - 14

Moorcraft, P.L. (1979) <u>A Short Thousand Years: The end of Rhodesia's rebellion</u> Salisbury: Galaxie Press.

Moyo, H. (2012) Deep Rooted Culture of Political Violence. The Zimbabwe Independent, 30 November Harare

Moyo, H. (2016) 'Mugabe succession war: it's not yet over until it's over', the Zimbabwe Independent 19 – 25 February 2016

Moyo, K. (2011) Minorities in post colonial transitions. African Journal of Legal Studies Vol 1 (2011)pp 149–185, Martinus Nijhoff Publishers

Moyo Ndzimu – Unami, E. (2012) Lushanduko, The re - birth of Bukalanga

Moyo, J. (2006) Why Mugabe should go now. The Zimbabwe independent

Moyo, J. (2006) Mugabe, an Ethnic Bigot Masquarading as a Nationalist. The Zimbabwe Independent.nb.

Moyo, J. (2007) Tsholotsho saga: the untold story. The Zimbabwe independent

Moyo, Q. (2012) Devolution is the way to go. The Zimbabwe independent

Msindo, E. (2007) Ethnicity and nationalism in urban colonial Zimbabwe: Bulawayo, 1950 to 1963, Journal of African History, 48 pp. 267 - 90. United Kingdom: Cambridge University Press.

Msindo, E. (2004) Ethnicity in Matabeleland, Zimbabwe: a study of Kalanga-Ndebele relations, 1860s-1980s. Cambridge: University of Cambridge.

Mufuka, K. (2019) Dabengwa Story shows how our dreams were betrayed. https://nehandaradio.com/2019/06/09/ken-mufuka-dabengwa-story-shows-how-our-dreams-were-betrayed/

Muleya, D. (2014) Zanufication of the MDC T. The Zimbabwe Independent 14 March Harare

Mutizwa, R. (2010) Gukurahundi Ideology; Why Zimbabwe is in Crisis. Johannesburg: Novell Zwange

Muzondidya, J. (2009) Historicizing the Ndebele. Africa Review of Books / Revue Africaine des Livres Vol 6 No 1 – Mars 2010.

Muzondidya, J and Ndlovu – Gatsheni, S. (2007) 'Echoing Silences': Ethnicity in Postcolonial Zimbabwe, 1980–2007', African Journal on Conflict Resolution: Special Issue on Identity and Cultural Diversity in Conflict Resolution in Africa, 7 (2) (2007), p. 276.

Ndlovu –Gatsheni, S.J. (2011) <u>The Zimbabwean nation-state project. A historical diagnosis of identity and power-based conflicts in a postcolonial state</u>. Uppsala: Nordiska Afrikainstitutet.

Ndlovu - Gatsheni, S.J. (2008) Nation Building in Zimbabwe and the Challenges of Ndebele Particularism. <u>African Journal on Conflict Resolution</u> Volume 8, Number 3, 2008 African Centre for the Constructive Resolution of Conflicts (ACCORD)

Ndlovu – Gatsheni, S.J (2003) The post Colonial State and Matabeleland Regional Perception of Civil - Military Relations, 1980 - 2002

Ndlovu - Gatsheni, S. J. (2008) Reaping the Bitter Fruits of Stalinist Tendencies in Zimbabwe. African Concerned Scholars Bulletin: Special Issue on the 2008 Zimbabwe Elections, No. 79 (Spring 2008), pp. 21–31.

Ndlovu - Gatsheni, S. J. (2002) Dynamics of the Zimbabwe Crisis in the 21st Century, <u>Journal on Conflict Resolution</u>. Organization of Social Science Research in Eastern and Southern Africa (OSSREA),

Ndlovu-Gatsheni, S. J. and Willems, W. (2010) Reinvoking the past in the present: changing identities and appropriations of Joshua Nkomo in post-colonial Zimbabwe. <u>African identities</u>, 8 (3). pp. 191-208. ISSN 1472-584

Ndlovu – Gatsheni, S.J. (2011) The changing politics of Matabeleland since 1980

Ndlovu, T.M, Ndlovu D.N and Ncube B.S. (1995) <u>Imikhuba Lamasiko amaNdebele</u>. Gweru: Mambo Press.

Ngwenya D. (2018) <u>National Healing Perspectives from Matabeleland</u>. Paper presented at the Western Region Envisioning Collective at Cresta Churchill hotel, Bulawayo 22 – 23 February 2018.

Nkomo, J. (1984) <u>The Story of my Life</u>. Harare: SAPES

Nkomo, J. (1981) <u>The New Zimbabwe</u>, Second Edition 2001. Harare, SAPES Books.

Nyathi, P. (2005) <u>Zimbabwe's cultural heritage</u>. Bulawayo, amaBooks

Nyathi, P. (2017) JZ Moyo's death: Seeking the identity of interests behind the heinous act; The Sunday News 29 January – 4 February

Owens, D. (2018) Mugabe a deeply conflicted zealot. The Zimbabwe Independent, 6 – April 2018

Payne, A. (2005) The Water Politics in Matabeleland. Reflections on Focus Group Conversations. Socio - Economic and Political Hotspots. Bulawayo Agenda. Bulawayo.

Payne, R. (1965) The Rise and Fall of Stalin. London: Pan Book Ltd.

Pilger, J. (2002) The New Rulers of the world. London: Varso Publishers.

Raagmaa, G. (2003) Centre - Periphery model explaining the regional development of the informational and transitional society. Paper presented at the ERSA 43rd Congress, Jyval Skylal.

Ranger, T. (2004) Nationalist historiography, patriotic history and the history of the nation: the struggle over the past in Zimbabwe. Journal of Southern African Studies, 30 (2), 215-234.

Ranger, T. (2010) Review of Becoming Zimbabwe – construction of Zimbabwe

Robert, W. Fyn. (1993) The Lost Bone. Harare: College Press Publishers (Pvt) Ltd.

Rukuni, M. (2003) Why Land tenure Security in Africa is Central to Land Reform and Community Based Governance, Economic and Social Progress. Centurion Pretoria. August 2003.

Sagay, J.O and Wilson, D.A. (1978) Africa: A modern History (1800 – 1975). London. Evans Brothers Ltd.

Scarnecchia, T. (2013) Gukurahundi, Mugabe's Cold War Cover. The Zimbabwe Independent Newspaper sept 2013

Scarnecchia, T (2013) How Zimbabwe assisted apartheid SA 5/9/13 Zimbabwe Independent

Scarnecchia, T. (2011) Rationalising Gukurahundi: Cold War and South African Foreign relations with Zimbabwe, 1981 – 1983. Cape Town: Kronos (37).

Shaw, W. H.(1986) Towards the one-party state in Zimbabwe: a study in African political thought. <u>Journal of Modern African Studies</u>, Vol. 24 pp (3), 373-294.

Sibanda, M. (1981) <u>UMbiko KaMadlenya</u>. Gweru: Longmen Press

Sithole, M and Makumbe, J. (1997) Elections in Zimbabwe: The ZANUNPF Hegemony and its Incipient Decline. <u>African Journal of Political Science</u> Vol 2, No 1, 122 - 139.

Sithole, M. (2002) National sovereignty is a dying concept. Paper for presentation at MPOI serminor. Selbourne hotel, Bulawayo 28 June 2002

Sithole, N. (1959) <u>African Nationalism.</u> Cape Town: Oxford University Press.

Suberu, R. (2003) Ethnic minority conflicts and governance in Nigeria. Lagos: Spectrum Books Ltd.

Sylvester, C. (1990) Unities and Disunities in Zimbabwe's 1990 Election. <u>The Journal of Modern African Studies</u> Vol. 28, (3), pp 375 – 400.

Tindall, P.E.N. (1968) <u>A history of Central Africa</u>. London: Longman Group Limited

The Zimbabwe Independent, 23 March 2012. Harare

Thomas, A. (1996) <u>Rhodes: The race for Africa</u>. Harare: African Publishing House.

Todd, J. (2007) Through the Darkness: A Life in Zimbabwe: Cape Town: Struik Publishers

Tsvangirai, M. and Bango, T.W. (2011<u>) At the deep End</u>: New York: Penguin Random House

Vambe, L. (1972) <u>An ill-fated people: Zimbabwe before and after Rhodes</u>. London: Heineman.

Wohlers, J. (2010) <u>People of Skies</u>. Xlibris Corporation

Woods, K. (2007) <u>In the shadow of Mugabe's gallows.</u> Johannesburg: 30 Degrees South Publishers.

Wook, R. (2000) The role of participation and partnership in decentralised governance: A brief synthesis of policy lessons and recommendations of the nine country case studies on service delivery for the poor. New York: UNDP.

Yamamoto, K. (2019) http://bit.ly/1RqSLME

Zvakanaka (2007) http://www.opednews.com/articles/genera_charles__070528_britain_behind_gukur

www.ingramcontent.com/pod-product-compliance
Lightning Source LLC
Chambersburg PA
CBHW051431250726
48655CB00001B/6